Rwanda
with Eastern Congo

the Bradt Travel Guide

Philip Briggs
Contributing author Janice Booth
Updated by Sean Connolly

edition
7

www.bradtguides.com

Bradt Travel Guides Ltd, UK
The Globe Pequot Press Inc, USA

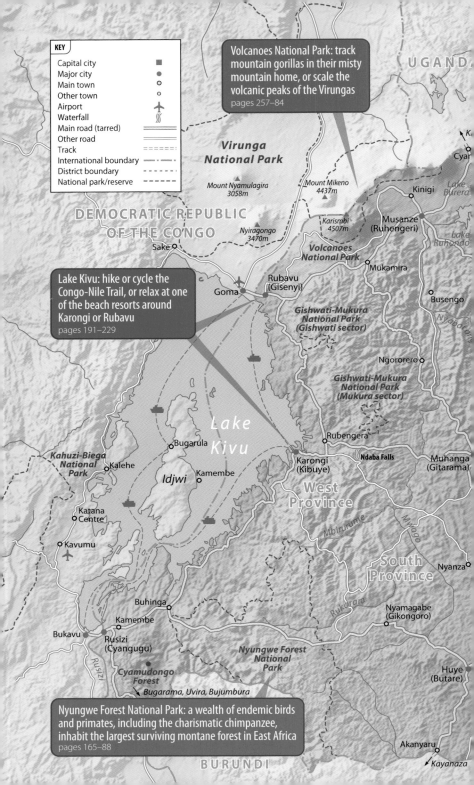

KEY

Capital city	■
Major city	●
Main town	◎
Other town	○
Airport	✈
Waterfall	♒
Main road (tarred)	═══
Other road	───
Track	═════
International boundary	─·─·─
District boundary	─────
National park/reserve	────

Volcanoes National Park: track mountain gorillas in their misty mountain home, or scale the volcanic peaks of the Virungas
pages 257–84

UGANDA

Virunga National Park

Mount Nyamulagira 3058m

Mount Mikeno 4437m

DEMOCRATIC REPUBLIC OF THE CONGO

Nyiragongo 3470m

Karismbi 4507m

Sake

Lake Kivu: hike or cycle the Congo-Nile Trail, or relax at one of the beach resorts around Karongi or Rubavu
pages 191–229

Goma

Rubavu (Gisenyi)

Kinigi

Lake Burera

Musanze (Ruhengeri)

Lake Ruhondo

Volcanoes National Park

Mukamira

Busengo

Gishwati-Mukura National Park (Gishwati sector)

Ngororero

Gishwati-Mukura National Park (Mukura sector)

Lake Kivu

Bugarula

Idjwi

Kamembe

Kahuzi-Biega National Park

Kalehe

Rubengera

Karongi (Kibuye)

Ndaba Falls

Muhanga (Gitarama)

West Province

Mbirurume

Katana Centre

Kavumu

Buhinga

Kamembe

Bukavu

Rusizi (Cyangugu)

Cyamudongo Forest

↘ *Bugarama, Uvira, Bujumbura*

Rusizi

Rukarara

Nyungwe Forest National Park

South Province

Nyanza

Nyamagabe (Gikongoro)

Huye (Butare)

Nyungwe Forest National Park: a wealth of endemic birds and primates, including the charismatic chimpanzee, inhabit the largest surviving montane forest in East Africa
pages 165–88

Akanyaru

↘ *Kayanaza*

BURUNDI

Kagitumba → *Ntungamo*

Kigali Genocide Memorial: this sobering museum and memorial marks the site of one of the largest massacres that took place during the 1994 genocide
pages 117–18

Akagera National Park: Rwanda's only savannah reserve, where the reintroduction of black rhino means it's once again home to all of the Big Five
pages 305–23

Nyagatare

TANZANIA

Kabale ↑
Gatuna

Ngarama   Gabiro

Gicumbi
(Byumba)

North Province   Rukumo

East Province

Akagera National Park

Gakenke

Lake Muhazi   Kayonza   *Lake Ihema*

Kigali

KIGALI   Rwamagana   Kabarondo

Ngoma
(Kibungo)   Cyasemakamba

Nyamata

East Province

Nyakarambi

Nemba

Lake Rweru   Rusumo

Kirundo   *Nyakanazi*

Nyanza: the hilltop Rukari Palace Museum marks the site of the old Mwami's (King's) palace
pages 141–7

TANZANIA

National Museum of Rwanda: the top cultural site in Rwanda's second city, Huye, provides a rich insight into traditional cultures
page 158

N

Bradt

0   25km
0   20 miles

Rwanda
Don't
miss...

Intore dancing
Dance is as instinctive as music in Rwanda and its roots stretch back through the centuries. Performances are infectiously energetic, no matter the time of day (AZ) page 31

Gorilla tracking
Tracking mountain gorillas in the Virungas is a peerless wildlife experience, and one of Africa's indisputable travel highlights (AZ) pages 267–75

Hiking on dormant volcanoes
Hike through atmospheric hagenia woodland to reach the summit of Mount Bisoke, where you will be rewarded with stunning views of the crater lake
(AZ) pages 280–2

Arts and handicrafts
Weaving is one of the specialities of Rwanda — baskets, mats, pots and bowls are crafted in a variety of colours and traditional patterns
(AZ) pages 31–2

Forest and savannah wildlife
Reintroduced in 2017 after a decade-long absence, 19 rhinos now call Akagera National Park home (SS/AMC)
pages 309–10

Rwanda in colour

above left Tracking golden monkeys, which are more or less endemic to the Virungas, is a popular activity in Volcanoes National Park (AZ) pages 275–6

middle left The red-throated alethe is one of several elusive Albertine Rift Endemics associated with forests in Rwanda (AZ) page 175

middle right Common and widespread in Rwanda, chameleons are arguably the most intriguing of African reptiles. Pictured, a rudis chameleon (EB/MC) pages 176–7

below Consisting of six extinct and three active volcanoes, Volcanoes National Park is home to over half of the world's population of mountain gorilla (AZ) pages 257–84

above   The hike up to the mountain gorillas' preferred habitat involves a combination of steep slopes, dense vegetation and high altitude (AZ) pages 267–75

right   Set at just under 3,000m in altitude between mounts Karisimbi and Bisoke, the grave of famed researcher Dian Fossey and the surrounding gorilla cemetery are today a popular destination for day hikes in Volcanoes National Park (AZ) pages 278–80

below   With habituated groups ranging from 15 to 30 individuals or more, the strikingly varied personalities of each gorilla can quickly become apparent over the course of your hour-long visit (AZ) pages 267–75

"NYIRAMACHABELLI"
DIAN FOSSEY
1932 – 1985
NO ONE LOVED GORILLAS MORE
REST IN PEACE, DEAR FRIEND
ETERNALLY PROTECTED
IN THIS SACRED GROUND
FOR YOU ARE HOME
WHERE YOU BELONG

AUTHOR

Philip Briggs (**e** *phil@philipbriggs.com*) is one of the world's most experienced and knowledgeable guidebook writers, having been researching and writing guides for Bradt and other well-known publishers for almost 30 years. He undertook his first major backpacking trip in 1986, when he spent several months travelling overland from Nairobi to Cape Town. In 1991, he wrote the *Bradt Guide to South Africa*, the first such guidebook to be published internationally after the release of Nelson Mandela. Over the rest of the 1990s, Philip wrote a series of pioneering Bradt travel guides to destinations

that were then – and in some cases still are – otherwise practically uncharted by the travel publishing industry. These included the first dedicated guidebooks to Tanzania, Uganda, Ethiopia, Malawi, Mozambique, Ghana and Rwanda, new editions of which have been published regularly ever since. More recently, he authored the first dedicated English-language guidebook to Somaliland, as well as a new guide to The Gambia, both published by Bradt. Philip spends at least four months on the road every year, usually accompanied by his wife, travel photographer Ariadne Van Zandbergen, and spends the rest of his time battering away at a keyboard in the sleepy coastal village of Wilderness in South Africa's Western Cape.

CONTRIBUTING AUTHOR

Janice Booth's career has ranged from professional stage management and archaeology to compiling puzzle magazines, while fitting in travel whenever possible. Recently she has co-written Bradt guides to south and east Devon, the English county where she lives within sound of the sea. Seventeen years after co-writing the first edition of this guide, she's still lecturing and writing enthusiastically about Rwanda. In this edition, she is responsible for the history sections, from ancient legends to the present day, and talks more about her involvement with Rwanda on page vi.

CONTRIBUTING AUTHOR AND UPDATER

Sean Connolly (**w** *seanconnolly.me*) first worked with Bradt in 2011, and has since updated the Bradt guides to Malawi, Mozambique, Ghana, Uruguay, Sierra Leone, and two editions of Rwanda. He is also the author of the first edition of Bradt's *Senegal*. When he's not updating guides or discussing the many merits of camel meat, you may find him hitching a lift on a grain truck, sampling questionable local delicacies, or seeking out a country's funkiest records. Raised in Chicago, Sean stays on the move whenever possible,

though lately you'll find him most often in Berlin. For this edition, Sean has substantially expanded the Virunga National Park and Eastern DRC chapter.

Seventh edition published September 2018
First published 2001

Bradt Travel Guides Ltd
IDC House, The Vale, Chalfont St Peter, Bucks SL9 9RZ, England
www.bradtguides.com
Print edition published in the USA by The Globe Pequot Press Inc,
PO Box 480, Guilford, Connecticut 06437-0480

Text copyright © 2018 Philip Briggs
Maps copyright © 2018 Bradt Travel Guides Ltd Includes map data © OpenStreetMap contributors
Photographs copyright © 2018 Individual photographers (see below)
Project Managers: Anna Moores and Carys Homer
Cover research: Pepi Bluck, Perfect Picture

ISBN: 978 1 78477 096 9 (print)
e-ISBN: 978 1 78477 551 3 (e-pub)
e-ISBN: 978 1 78477 452 3 (mobi)

British Library Cataloguing in Publication Data
A catalogue record for this book is available from the British Library

Photographs
Akagera Management Company: Horst Klemm (HK/AMC), James Hogg (JH/AMC), Jes Gruner (JG/AMC), Morgan Trimble (MT/AMC), Sarah Hall (SH/AMC), Stuart Slabbard (SS/AMC); Ariadne Van Zandbergen (AZ); Elspeth Beidas & Matthew Coates (EB/MC); Eric Lafforgue (EL); Flpa-images.co.uk: Frans Lanting (FL/FLPA), Pete Oxford/Minden Pictures (PO/MP/FLPA); Michael J. Renner (MJR); Shutterstock.com: Black Sheep Media (BSM/S), LMIMAGES (L/S), LMspencer (LM/S), Tetyana Dotsenko (TD/S), Willem Tims (WT/S); Steve Venton, Kingfisher Journeys (SV/KJ); Superstock.com (SS)
Front cover Baby mountain gorilla (AZ)
Back cover Lake Kivu (TD/S)
Title page Tea plantation (AZ); Intore dancer (AZ); Great blue turaco (PO/MP/FLPA)

Maps David McCutcheon FBCart.S. Colour map relief base by Nick Rowland FRGS.

Typeset by Ian Spick, Bradt Travel Guides Ltd
Production managed by Jellyfish Print Solutions; printed in India
Digital conversion by www.dataworks.co.in

Acknowledgements

As always, my thanks go to Philip Briggs for once again giving me the opportunity to explore such an enthralling country and contribute to such a superlative guide, as well as the whole team at Bradt, including Janice Booth, Anna Moores, Carys Homer, and Rachel Fielding.

For her invaluable insight, advice, and companionship in the researching and writing of this guide, my warmest thanks are due to my partner Imke Rueben; your keen eye and thoughtful perspective contributed immeasurably to the success of our trip and of this guide.

In Rwanda and the DRC, dozens of people helped us along the way, and this update wouldn't have been possible without the gracious assistance of Sarah Tjeenk Willink (Inspired Journeys); Christian Uwizeye, Geoffrey Bungeri and Sam Boarer (Discover Rwanda); Julie Williams, Kevin Siri and Vianney Harakandi (Virunga National Park); Emmanuel Rufubya (Okapi Tours); Luc Henkinbrant and Espérance Mawanzo (Agence Espérance); Eugene Rutagarama (Emeraude Kivu); Nsengi Barakabuye (Nyungwe Top View); Patrick Ngeli (Yambi); Alberto Benvenuti (La Locanda); Harjot Brar and Ankur Chaturvedi (Gisovu); Sarah Hall (Akagera National Park); Alissa Ruxin (Heaven); Florence Uwimana (Tea House); Hanna Moges (Radisson); Vanessa Delgado (Marriott); Claire Umubyeyi (Volcanoes Safaris); Gisele Bahati (Five Volcanoes); Paul Ndayishimye (Home St Jean); Dennis Rwiliriza (Rwandair); Lara Good (PC Agency); Charlotte Launder and Janelle Drummond (Grifco PR); Claire Roadley (Ethos); Danny Bizimana (Bizidanny); Chris Munyao, Robert Gakimbiri Impano, and Eric Manirakiza (Primate Safaris); Gloria Mwenge Bitomwa (Kahuzi-Biega National Park); Steve Venton (Kingfisher Journeys); and especially Jean-Pierre Ngabonziza, for so generously sharing a bit of his life with us on the road.

Contents

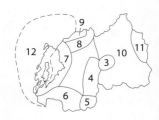

Forty years ago a young Rwandan wrote to me from Uganda; he was studying there, despite the tough nature of life as a refugee, because Tutsis (like him) had a hard deal in Rwanda at the time. Copying my address from the back of a letter I'd written to someone else, he announced that we were going to be friends.

Cynically I expected a follow-up request for money, but I was wrong. Aged just 20 (half my age at the time), he kept his promise, and once or twice a year would write with scraps of news. Life was clearly a struggle, but he didn't complain.

After qualifying in electrical engineering he went home to Rwanda, writing delightedly 'Janice, I have a *family* again!' He got work, and set about paying his younger siblings' school fees. Proud of his country, he sent me a postcard of Akagera that I still have. I felt I had become a kind of honorary aunt.

He carefully didn't mention politics, but I knew things weren't good. In October 1990 he was (with other Tutsis) thrown into prison for around three months, and wrote afterwards: 'So many died, of the hunger and the beatings'. Much later I learned that these included his partner, with whom he had a baby daughter.

One of his sisters was completing secondary school and I wrote wishing her luck in her final exams; she replied in good French. Later he sent a photo of her at her graduation in 1992, with him, two brothers and a teenaged sister. Bit by bit I was meeting the family.

In the summer of 1993, he wrote that he planned to get married, asking 'How do you see that, Janice?', and I replied that it was great news. His bride, in a fuzzy wedding snap he sent, was beautiful. We exchanged letters as usual that Christmas, while the country's condition worsened. Then, on 6 April 1994, it exploded into genocide. No more letters came, and eventually I assumed he hadn't survived.

As the years passed, I tried – but failed – to get news of his family. Finally, in 2000, I booked a flight to Kigali: my first visit to Rwanda, portrayed by the disaster-loving media as still damaged, violent and volatile.

In fact Kigali when I arrived seemed calm and safe; while the countryside, as I rattled around it in local minibuses, stunned me with its beauty and laid the foundation for this guidebook. And people helped, checking leads for me until news finally emerged.

My friend had indeed died, as had his wife, their newborn baby, the sister I'd written to and other relatives. But I met survivors too, including his ten-year-old daughter, two brothers, and the young sister from the graduation photo. I paid her university fees and later went proudly to her wedding. We're still regularly in touch and she, her husband and their three lively daughters are a delight to visit. My friend's daughter is now a beautiful young woman, whose smile – I'm told – is very much like his. Their story, with its tragedy and subsequent success, mirrors that of Rwanda itself.

Neither I nor the young student of forty years ago could have imagined the outcome of the friendship he proposed; but I still feel so very lucky that he wrote that first letter, and welcomed me into his life.

LIST OF MAPS

KEY TO SYMBOLS

—·—·—	International boundary
········	Province boundary
	Paved roads (town plans)
	Unpaved roads (town plans)
|||||||||||	Steps (town plans)
············	Featured footpath
⟨5.5km⟩	Road distance pins (in km between pins)
✈ ✈	Airport (international/domestic)
✛	Airstrip
⛽	Filling station/garage
🚌	Bus station/taxi park
ℹ	Tourist information
⊖	Embassy/high commission
☗	Museum/art gallery
🎦	Theatre/cinema
▦	Important/historic building
⚑	Statue/monument
$	Bank/bureau de change
⊠	Post office
⊞	Hospital/clinic etc
✚	Pharmacy/dentist
⌂	Hotel/inn etc

Å	Campsite
✗	Restaurant
♀	Bar
⊐	Café
☆	Nightclub/casino
@	Internet
✝	Church/cathedral
☾	Mosque
►	Golf course
⤢	Beach
⌒	Cave/grotto
⑊	Waterfall
○	Hot spring
⤙	Fishing
●	Other attraction
▲	Summit (height in metres)
	Dry lake/river bank
⊛	Stadium
	Contours
	Marsh
	Urban park
	Market
	National park/reserve

Introduction

Is there any other wildlife encounter to match tracking mountain gorillas through the thin moist air of Rwanda's Virunga Mountains? Ascending first through fertile volcanic slopes dense with cultivation, one crosses the boundary into Volcanoes National Park, to follow a narrow footpath into a hushed montane forest composed of impenetrable bamboo skyscrapers, broadleaved herbaceous shrubs and fragrant hagenia stands. This is nature in the raw: the muddy forest floor scattered with elephant and buffalo spoor while birds and monkeys chatter overhead and spiteful nettles lie waiting in the margins.

Deep in the misty forest, you finally come upon your quarry. It might be a young female attempting to climb a liana, soft black coat comically fluffed-up as it demonstrates the arboreal incompetence of this most sedentary of apes. Or perhaps a barrel-headed silverback, no taller than an average human, but thrice as bulky, delicately shredding a succulent stick of bamboo as it sits peaceably on the forest floor. Or a curious mother, taking two paces forward then raising its head in your direction to stare questioningly into your eyes, as if seeking a connection. Or maybe a young male putting on a chest-beating display for your benefit, safe in the knowledge that this naked ape won't challenge its dominance. No two gorilla encounters can be exactly the same but, as anybody who has looked into the liquid brown eyes of a wild mountain gorilla will confirm, it is always an awesome experience – inspirational, emotional, and profoundly satisfying.

Rwanda is the world's premier gorilla-tracking destination. It was here, on the southern slopes of the Virungas, that the late Dian Fossey studied gorilla behaviour for almost 20 years, and on these very same bamboo-covered slopes that the acclaimed movie *Gorillas in the Mist* was shot in 1988. At that time, Rwanda was entrenched as *the* place to see mountain gorillas, and tourism had become its third main source of foreign revenue. All else being equal, that should have been the start of Rwanda's emergence as a truly great ecotourism destination. Instead, the country was destabilised by a protracted civil war that started in 1990 and four years later reached its horrific climax: the 1994 genocide that claimed the lives of one-eighth of its population, and forced almost twice as many to flee into wretched makeshift refugee camps in Tanzania, Uganda or the Congo.

In the restless eyes of the international mass media, the likes of Rwanda are deemed newsworthy only when disaster strikes. The moment things calm down, cameras and correspondents shift their attention to the next breaking crisis. And so it was that, once the genocide had been quelled by the Rwanda Patriotic Front after barely 100 days, interest faded and the world largely ignored the country as it embarked on its long and arduous road to normalisation – miraculously, a path from which it has barely deviated in more than 20 years. For a long while, like Uganda after Idi Amin or Ethiopia after the 1985 famine, it remained known to most outsiders only for the genocide. Today, with its energetic programmes of recovery and reconstruction, it is widely considered to be among the most economically buoyant and politically enlightened African countries.

Few could travel through Rwanda and not be cognisant of the terrible events of 1994. Indeed, almost every town and village houses a genocide memorial paying respect to the massacred, while also highlighting the survivors' determination that such atrocities should be neither forgotten nor repeated. However, for potential visitors it is more important to dwell on the future and the capacity of tourism to stimulate economic growth and nurture political stability.

Some figures. In 1999, when Volcanoes National Park reopened for gorilla tracking, it attracted fewer than 2,000 visitors, most of them backpacking or on overland trucks making a pit-stop visit from Uganda. By contrast, in 2015 an estimated 987,000 tourists visited Rwanda and tourism is now the country's largest source of foreign revenue, contributing more than US$300 million to the annual GDP and providing direct or indirect employment to over 350,000 people.

So if you've ever dreamed of tracking gorillas on the same misty slopes once trodden by Dian Fossey or Sigourney Weaver, go to Rwanda. And while you're about it, don't forget that there is much to see there besides gorillas. The mountain-ringed inland sea that is Lake Kivu; the immense Nyungwe Forest National Park with its chimpanzees, monkeys and rare birds; the wild savannah of Akagera National Park – and, perhaps above all, the endless succession of steep cultivated mountains that have justifiably earned Rwanda the soubriquets 'Land of a Thousand Hills' and 'The Switzerland of Africa'. It's a wonderful place to visit.

HOW TO USE THIS GUIDE

AUTHOR'S FAVOURITES Finding genuinely characterful accommodation or that unmissable off-the-beaten-track café can be difficult, so the author has chosen a few of his favourite places throughout the country to point you in the right direction. These 'author's favourites' are marked with a ✳.

MAPS
Keys and symbols Maps include alphabetical keys covering the locations of those places to stay, eat or drink that are featured in the book. Note that regional maps may not show all hotels and restaurants in the area: other establishments may be located in towns shown on the map. On occasion, hotels or restaurants that are not listed in the guide (but which might serve as alternative options if required or serve as useful landmarks to aid navigation) are also included on the maps; these are marked with accommodation (⌂) or restaurant (✖) symbols.

Grids and grid references Several maps use gridlines to allow easy location of sites. Map grid references are listed in square brackets after the name of the place or site of interest in the text, with page number followed by grid number, eg: [103 C3].

WEBSITES Although all third-party websites were working at the time of going to print, some may cease to function during this edition's lifetime. If a website doesn't work, you might want to check back at another time as they often function intermittently. Alternatively, you can let us know of any website issues by emailing e info@bradtguides.com.

Part One

GENERAL INFORMATION

THE REPUBLIC OF RWANDA AT A GLANCE

GEOGRAPHY
Land area 26,340km² (less than half that of Scotland)
Location 120km south of the Equator
Capital Kigali
Rainfall Annual average 900–1,600mm; rainy seasons March–May and October–December
Average temperature 24.6–27.6°C; hottest August and September
Altitude From 1,000 to 4,500m above sea level; highest point is Mt Karisimbi (4,507m)
Terrain Mostly grassy uplands and hills; relief is mountainous with altitude declining from west to east
Vegetation Ranges from dense equatorial forest in the northwest to tropical savannah in the east
Land use 47% cropland, 22% forest, 18% pasture, 13% other
Natural resources Some tin, gold and natural gas
Main exports Coffee and tea
National parks Volcanoes (northwest); Nyungwe (southwest); Akagera (east); Gishwati-Mukura (west)

HUMAN STATISTICS
Population 11.9 million (2017 estimate)
Life expectancy At birth 64 years
Religion Roman Catholic (majority), Protestant, Muslim, traditional
Official languages Kinyarwanda, English, French. Swahili is widely spoken.
Education Primary, secondary, technical/vocational, higher/university
GDP per capita US$2,000 (2016 estimate)

POLITICS/ADMINISTRATION
Government Multi-party democracy dominated by the RPF, which won 99% of the vote in the 2017 presidential election and 76% in the 2013 parliamentary election
Ruling Party Rwanda Patriotic Front (RPF)
President Paul Kagame
Prime Minister Edouard Ngirente
National flag Blue, yellow and green, with a sun in the top right-hand corner
Administrative divisions 4 *intara* (provinces) plus Kigali City, subdivided into 30 *uturere* (districts; singular *akarere*) and 416 *imirenge* (sectors, singular *umurenge*)

PRACTICAL DETAILS
Time GMT + 2 hours
Currency Rwandan franc
Rate of exchange £1=Rfr1,148, €1=Rfr1,012, US$1=Rfr860 (June 2018)
Main health risk Malaria
Electricity 230/240 volts at 50Hz
International telephone country code 250
Airport Kigali International, Bugesera International (under construction)
Nearest seaports Mombasa (1,760km); Dar es Salaam (1,528km)

Background Information

Rwanda is a landlocked country in Central Africa. Also known as the 'Land of a Thousand Hills', it has five volcanoes, 23 lakes and numerous rivers. Rwanda lies 1,270km west of the Indian Ocean and 2,000km east of the Atlantic – literally in the heart of Africa.

GEOGRAPHY

Rwanda owes its mountainous topography to its position on the eastern rim of the Albertine Rift Valley, a western arm of the Great Rift Valley which cuts through Africa from the Red Sea to Mozambique. The country's largest freshwater body, Lake Kivu, which forms the border with the Democratic Republic of the Congo (DRC), is effectively a large sump hemmed in by the Rift Valley walls, while its highest peaks – in the volcanic Virunga chain – are geologically modern (and in some cases still active) products of the same tectonic process that started forming the Rift Valley 20 million years ago. The Rift Valley escarpment running through western Rwanda is also a watershed between Africa's two largest drainage systems: the Nile and the Congo.

Western and central Rwanda are characterised by a seemingly endless vista of steep mountains, interspersed with several substantial lakes whose irregular shape follows the mountains that surround them. Much of this part of the country lies at elevations of between 1,500m and 2,500m. Only in the far east of the country, along the Tanzanian border, do the steep mountains give way to the lower-lying, flatter terrain of the Lake Victoria Basin. The dominant geographical feature of this part of the country is the Kagera River and associated network of swamps and small lakes running along the Tanzanian border, eventually to flow into Lake Victoria, making it the most remote source of the world's longest river, the Nile (see box, pages 4–5). Much of this ecosystem is protected within Akagera National Park.

NATURAL HISTORY AND CONSERVATION

For more on wildlife in Rwanda, check out Bradt's East African Wildlife. *Get 10% off at* w *bradtguides.com/shop.*

VEGETATION In prehistoric times, as much as a third of what is now Rwanda was covered in montane rainforest, with the remainder of the highlands supporting open grassland. Since the advent of Iron-Age technology and agriculture some 2,000 years ago, much of Rwanda's natural vegetation has been replaced by agriculture, a process that has accelerated dramatically in the last 100 years. The only large stand of forest left in Rwanda today is Nyungwe, in the southwest, though several other small relic forest patches are dotted around the country, notably the recently

The first European to see Lake Victoria was John Hanning Speke, who marched from Tabora to the site of present-day Mwanza in 1858 following his joint 'discovery' of Lake Tanganyika with Richard Burton the previous year. Speke named the lake for Queen Victoria, but prior to that Arab slave traders called it Ukerewe (still the name of its largest island). It is unclear what name was in local use, since the only one used by Speke is Nyanza, which simply means lake.

A major goal of the Burton–Speke expedition had been to solve the great geographical enigma of the age, the source of the White Nile. Speke, based on his brief glimpse of the southeast corner of Lake Victoria, somewhat whimsically proclaimed his 'discovery' to be the answer to that riddle. Burton, with a comparable lack of compelling evidence, was convinced that the great river flowed out of Lake Tanganyika. The dispute between the former travelling companions erupted bitterly on their return to Britain, where Burton – the more persuasive writer and respected traveller – gained the backing of the scientific establishment.

Over 1862–63, Speke and Captain James Grant returned to Lake Victoria, hoping to prove Speke's theory correct. They looped inland around the western shore of the lake, arriving at the court of King Mutesa of Buganda, then continued east to the site of present-day Jinja, where a substantial river flowed out of the lake after tumbling over a cataract that Speke named Ripon Falls. From here, the two explorers headed north, sporadically crossing paths with the river until they reached Lake Albert, then following the Nile to Khartoum and Cairo. Speke's declaration that 'The Nile is settled' met with mixed support back home. Burton and other sceptics pointed out that Speke had bypassed the entire western shore of his purported great lake, had visited only a couple of points on the northern shore, and had not attempted to explore the east. Nor, for that matter, had he followed the course of the Nile in its entirety. Speke, claimed his detractors, had seen several different lakes and different stretches of river, connected only in his own deluded mind. The sceptics had a point, but Speke had nevertheless gathered sufficient geographical evidence to render his claim highly plausible. His notion of one great lake, far from being mere whimsy, was backed by anecdotal information gathered from local sources along the way.

Matters were scheduled to reach a head on 16 September 1864, when an eagerly awaited debate between Burton and Speke – in the words of the former, 'what silly tongues called the "Nile Duel"' – was due to take place at the Royal Geographic Society (RGS). And reach a head they did, but in circumstances more tragic than anybody could have anticipated. On the afternoon of the debate, Speke went out shooting with a cousin, only to stumble while crossing a wall and in the process discharging a barrel of his shotgun into his heart. The subsequent inquest recorded a verdict of accidental death, but it has often been suggested – purely on the basis of the curious timing – that Speke deliberately took his life rather than face up to Burton in public. Burton, who had seen Speke less than three hours earlier, was by all accounts deeply troubled by Speke's death, and years later he was quoted as stating 'the uncharitable [say] that I shot him' – an accusation that seems to have been aired only in Burton's imagination.

Speke was dead, but the 'Nile debate' would keep kicking for several years. In 1864, Sir Stanley and Lady Baker became the first Europeans to reach Lake Albert and nearby Murchison Falls in present-day Uganda. The Bakers, much to the delight of the anti-Speke lobby, were convinced that this newly named lake was a source of the Nile, though they openly admitted it might not be the only one. Following the Bakers' announcement, Burton put forward a revised theory, namely that the most remote source of the Nile was the Rusizi River, which he believed flowed out of the northern head of Lake Tanganyika and emptied into Lake Albert.

In 1865, the RGS followed up on Burton's theory by sending Dr David Livingstone to Lake Tanganyika. Livingstone, however, was of the opinion that the Nile's source lay further south than Burton supposed, and so he struck out towards the lake along a previously unexplored route. Leaving from Mikindani in the far south of present-day Tanzania, Livingstone followed the Rovuma River inland, continuing westward to the southern tip of Lake Tanganyika. From there, he ranged southward into present-day Zambia, where he came across a new candidate for the source of the Nile: the swampy Lake Bangweulu and its major outlet the Lualaba River. It was only after his famous meeting with Henry Stanley at Ujiji, in November 1871, that Livingstone (in the company of Stanley) visited the north of Lake Tanganyika and Burton's cherished Rusizi River, which, it transpired, flowed into the lake. Burton, nevertheless, still regarded Lake Tanganyika as the most likely source of the Nile, while Livingstone was convinced that the answer lay with the Lualaba River. In August 1872, Livingstone headed back to the Lake Bangweulu region, where he fell ill and died six months later, the great question still unanswered.

In August 1874, ten years after Speke's death, Stanley embarked on a three-year expedition every bit as remarkable and arduous as those undertaken by his predecessors, yet one whose significance is often overlooked. Partly, this is because Stanley cuts such an unsympathetic figure, the grim caricature of the murderous pre-colonial White Man blasting and blustering his way through territories where Burton, Speke and Livingstone had relied largely on diplomacy. It is also the case, however, that Stanley set out with no intention of seeking headline-making fresh discoveries. Instead, he determined to test methodically the theories advocated by Speke, Burton and Livingstone about the Nile's source. First, Stanley sailed around the circumference of Lake Victoria, establishing that it was indeed as vast as Speke had claimed (and, incidentally, crossing the so-called 'Alexandra Nile' (Kagera River) into what is now Akagera National Park, where he camped on the shore of Lake Ihema). Stanley's next step was to circumnavigate Lake Tanganyika, which, contrary to Burton's long-held theories, clearly boasted no outlet sufficiently large to be the source of the Nile. Finally, and most remarkably, Stanley took a boat along Livingstone's Lualaba River to its confluence with an even larger river, which he followed for months with no idea as to where he might end up.

When, exactly 999 days after he left Zanzibar, Stanley emerged at the Congo mouth, the shortlist of plausible theories relating to the source of the Nile had been reduced to one. Clearly, the Nile did flow out of Lake Victoria at Ripon Falls, before entering and exiting Lake Albert at its northern tip to start its long course through the sands of the Sahara. Stanley's achievement in putting to rest decades of speculation about how the main rivers and lakes of East Africa linked together is estimable indeed. He was nevertheless generous enough to concede that: 'Speke now has the full glory of having discovered the largest inland sea on the continent of Africa, also its principal affluent as well as its outlet. I must also give him credit for having understood the geography of the countries we travelled through far better than any of us who so persistently opposed his hypothesis'.

gazetted Gishwati and Mukura forests. Patches of true forest still occur on the Virungas, though most of the natural vegetation on this range consists of bamboo forest and open moorland. Outside of Nyungwe and the Virungas, practically no montane grassland is left in Rwanda; the highlands are instead dominated by the terraced agriculture that gives the Rwandan countryside much of its distinctive character. The far east supports an altogether different vegetation: the characteristic African 'bush', a mosaic of savannah woodland and grassland dominated by thorny acacia trees.

FAUNA Rwanda naturally supports a widely varied fauna, but the rapid human population growth in recent decades, with its by-products of habitat loss and poaching, has resulted in the extirpation of most large mammal species outside of a few designated conservation areas. Rwanda today has four national parks – Volcanoes, Akagera, Nyungwe, and Gishwati-Mukura (which was only gazetted in 2015 and was not yet open for tourism at the time of writing) – along with a few smaller forest reserves. Each of the three established national parks protects a very different ecosystem and combination of large mammals, for which reason greater detail on the fauna of each reserve is given under the appropriate regional section. Broadly speaking, however, Akagera supports a typical savannah fauna dominated by a variety of antelope, other grazers such as zebra, buffalo, giraffe and rhinoceros, the aquatic hippopotamus, and plains predators such as lion, leopard and spotted hyena.

Nyungwe and Volcanoes national parks probably supported a similar range of large mammals 500 years ago. Today, however, their faunas differ greatly, mostly as a result of extensive deforestation on the lower slopes of the Virungas. The volcanoes today support bamboo specialists such as golden monkey and mountain gorilla, as well as relict populations of habitat-tolerant species such as buffalo and elephant. The latter two species are extinct in Nyungwe (buffalo were hunted out nearly 30 years ago, while no elephant spoor has been detected since the last known carcass was found in late 1999), but this vast forest still supports one of Africa's richest varieties of forest specialists, ranging from 13 types of primate to golden cat, duiker and giant forest hog. Despite the retreat of most large mammals into reserves, Rwanda remains a rewarding destination for game viewing: the Volcanoes Park is the best place in the world to track mountain gorillas, while Nyungwe offers visitors a good chance of seeing chimpanzees and 400-strong troops of Angola colobus monkeys – the largest arboreal primate troops in Africa today.

Rwanda is a wonderful destination for birdwatchers, with an incredible 700 species recorded in an area smaller than Belgium and half the size of Scotland. Greater detail is supplied in regional chapters, but prime birdwatching destinations include Nyungwe (310 species including numerous forest rarities and 27 Albertine Rift Endemics) and Akagera (480 species of savannah bird, raptor and water bird). Almost anywhere in the country can, however, prove rewarding to birders: an hour in the garden of one of the capital's larger hotels is likely to throw up a variety of colourful robin-chats, weavers, finches, flycatchers and sunbirds.

HISTORY

EARLIEST TIMES Even back in the **ice age**, Rwanda was showing its typically green and fertile face; a part of the Nyungwe Forest remained uncovered by ice, so that animal and plant life could survive there. Excavations undertaken from the 1940s onwards identified several **early Iron-Age** sites in Rwanda and neighbouring Burundi, yielding fragments of typical 'dimpled' pottery (see *Africa in the Iron*

Age, Roland Oliver and Brian M Fagan, Cambridge University Press, 1975). At Nyirankuba in what is now South Province, a site of **late Stone-Age** occupation (without pottery) underlay a later occupation level containing both pottery and iron slag. Iron-smelting furnaces at two other sites in southern Rwanda (Ndora and Cyamakusa) gave radio-carbon datings of around AD200–300. Oliver and Fagan describe these furnaces as being some 5ft in diameter, built of wedge-shaped bricks. Other sites in the area of Rwanda, Burundi and Kivu show late Stone-Age occupation sites underlying early Iron-Age occupation. The early Iron-Age pottery was later succeeded by a different and coarser type, apparently made by newcomers from the north who were cattle raisers – but archaeological investigation in Rwanda has been sparse, and there must be much still awaiting discovery. Some artefacts are displayed in the National Museum in Huye (formerly named Butare).

Rwanda's earliest inhabitants were pygmoid **hunter-gatherers**, ancestors of the *Twa* (the name means, roughly, 'indigenous hunter-gatherers'), who still form part of the population today and are still known for their skill as potters. Gradually – the dates are uncertain, but probably before about 700BC – they were joined by Bantu-speaking **farmers**, who were spreading throughout Central Africa seeking good land on which to settle. Fertile Rwanda was a promising site. The arrival of these incomers, known as *Hutus*, was bad news for the Twa; now a minority, they saw some of their traditional hunting grounds cleared to make way for farming, and retreated further into the forests. Then Iron-Age technology developed tools – such as hoes – which enabled the farmers to grow more crops than were needed for subsistence and thus to trade.

Next came the **cattle raisers**, taller and lankier people than either the pygmoid Twa or the sturdy farmers, who may have come from either the north or the northeast. With only oral tradition to guide us, there's no hard historic evidence for the timing of their arrival – some say before the 10th century AD, others after the 14th. Gradually, whether by conquest or by natural assimilation, a hierarchy emerged in which the cattle raisers (known as *Tutsis*, meaning 'owners of cattle') were superior to the farmers and a master–client relationship known as *ubuhake* developed. Then most of Rwanda was a monarchy ruled by a Tutsi king or *mwami* – although there remained outlying areas where the farming groups did not accept his authority.

Note The three groups are more correctly called Batwa, Bahutu and Batutsi, while individuals are a Mutwa, a Muhutu and a Mututsi. However, we have opted for the forms Twa, Hutu and Tutsi because outside Rwanda they are commonly used. The plural of mwami (sometimes spelt mwaami) is *bami*. The language spoken by all three groups is Kinyarwanda.

THE KINGDOMS OF RWANDA Rwanda has a rich oral history, which was maintained primarily by members of the Rwandan royal court. According to this history the founder of Rwanda's ruling dynasty, Abanyiginya, was not born naturally like other humans, but was born from an earthenware jar of milk. The grandmother of Rwandans lived in heaven with Nkuba (thunder) who was given the secret of creating life. He made a small man out of clay, coated him with his saliva, and placed him in a wooden jar filled with milk and the heart of a slaughtered bull. The jar was constantly refilled with fresh milk. At the end of nine months the man took on the image of Sabizeze. When Sabizeze learned of his origin, he was angry that his mother had revealed the secret and decided to leave heaven and come to earth. He brought with him his sister Nyampundu, his brother Mututsi, and a couple of Batwa. Sabizeze was welcomed by Kabeja who was of the Abazigaba clan and king of the region (in the present-day Akagera National Park). Sabizeze then had a son named Gihanga who was to found the Kingdom of Rwanda. A Rwandan historian, Alexis Kagame, estimates that Gihanga ruled as King of Rwanda in the late 10th or early 11th century.

Before the arrival of Europeans, Rwandans believed they were the centre of the world, with the grandest monarchy, the greatest power and the highest civilisation. Their king or mwami was the supreme authority and was magically identified with Rwanda. There was a strong belief that if the ruling monarch was not the true king, the people of Rwanda would be in danger. The well-being of Rwanda was directly linked to the health of the king. When he grew old, Rwanda's prosperity was compromised. Only when the ageing ruler died and a new, stronger king was enthroned did the country restabilise.

The centralised control by the king was balanced by a very powerful queen mother and a group of dynastic ritualists: the *abiiru*. Queen mothers could never come from the same family clan as the king and rotated among four different family clans. The abiiru, who were also drawn from four different clans, could reverse the king's decisions if they conflicted with the magical Esoteric Code, protected and interpreted by the abiiru. They also governed the selection and installation of a new king. Any member of the abiiru who forgot any part of his assigned portion of the Esoteric Code was punished severely. Members of the abiiru and other custodians of state secrets who revealed the secrets of the royal court were forced to drink *igihango*, a mixture containing a magical power to kill traitors or anyone who failed in his duty. While the king could order the death of a disloyal member of the abiiru, he was required to replace the traitor with a member from the same family clan.

Rwanda's dynastic drums, which could be made only by members of one family clan from very specific trees with magical elements, had the same dignity as the king. The genitals of the enemies of Rwanda killed by the king hung from the drum. The capture of a dynastic drum from an enemy country normally signified annexation, with the group whose drum was stolen losing all faith in itself. This tradition is shared among many Bantu-speaking peoples in Africa. When Rwanda's royal drum Rwoga was lost to a neighbouring kingdom by King Ndahiro II Cyaamatare in the late 15th century, Rwanda was devastated. Rwoga was eventually replaced by Karinga, the last dynastic drum, when King Ruganzu II Ndori regained Rwanda's pride through his military exploits. The fate of Karinga is unknown. It is reported to have survived the colonial period, but disappeared soon after Rwanda's independence.

The origin of the division between Tutsis and Hutus is still being debated, but oral history portrays a feudal society with one group, the Tutsis or cattle herders, occupying a superior status within the social and political structure, and the other group, the Hutus or peasant farmers, serving as the serfs or clients of a Tutsi chief. The hunter-gatherer Twa were potters and had various functions at the royal court – for example, as dancers and music makers.

The complex system known as *ubuhake* provided for protection by the superior partner in exchange for services from the inferior: ubuhake agreements were made either between two Tutsis, or between a Tutsi and a Hutu. While ubuhake was a voluntary and revocable private contract between two individuals, with subjects able to switch loyalty from one chief to another, a peasant could not easily survive without a patron. Cattle could be acquired through ubuhake as well as by purchase, fighting in a war, or marriage. A Hutu who acquired enough cattle could thus become a Tutsi and might take a Tutsi wife, while a Tutsi who lost his herds or otherwise fell on hard times might become a Hutu and marry accordingly. A patron had no authority over a client who had gained cattle, whether Hutu, Tutsi or Twa. Whereas Hutus and

Tutsis could and did sometimes switch status, a Twa seldom became a Tutsi or Hutu. In the rare instances when this did occur, it would be because the king rewarded a Twa for some act of bravery by granting him the status of a Tutsi. He would then be given a Tutsi wife and a political post within the royal court. Meanwhile the three groups spoke the same language (Kinyarwanda, a language in the Bantu group), lived within the same culture and shared the same recent history.

Rwandan nobles were experts in cattle breeding and an entire category of poetry was devoted to the praises of famous cows. Cattle were bred for their beauty, rather than utility. Between AD1000 and 1450, herders in the Great Lakes region invented no fewer than 19 words for the colourful patterns of their animals' hides. As elsewhere in Africa, cattle were closely associated with wealth and status.

AD1000–1894 Whatever the exact timespan may have been, Rwanda (or the larger part of it) was ruled over by a sequence of Tutsi monarchs, each with his various political skirmishes, battles and conquests. Oral tradition shows us a colourful bunch of characters: for example, Ndahiro II Cyaamatare who catastrophically lost the royal drum; Mibambwe II who organised a system of milk distribution to the poor, ordering his chiefs to provide jugs of milk three times a day; and Yuhi III Mazimpaka, the only king to compose poetry – and to go mad. From the 17th century onwards the rulers seem to have become more organised and ambitious, using their armies to subjugate fringe areas. The royal palace was by then at Nyanza – and can still be seen, carefully reconstructed, today.

The mwami was an absolute monarch, deeply revered and seen to embody Rwanda physically. The hierarchy beneath him was complex and tight-knit, with different categories of chief in charge of different aspects of administration. His power covered most of Rwanda, although some Hutu enclaves in the north, northwest and southwest of the country clung to their independence until the 20th century. The country was divided into a pyramid of administrative areas: in ascending order of size, from base to apex, these were the immediate neighbourhood, the hill, the district and the province. (These are echoed in today's administrative pyramid of Commune, Sector, District and Province.) And through this intricate structure ran the practice and spirit of ubuhake, the master–client relationship in which an inferior receives help and protection in return for services and allegiance to a superior.

Beneath the mwami, power was exercised by various chiefs, each with specific responsibilities: *land chiefs* (responsible for land allocation, agriculture and agricultural taxation), *cattle chiefs* (stock-raising and associated taxes), *army chiefs* (security) and so on. While Hutus might take charge at neighbourhood level, most of the power at higher administrative levels was in the hands of Tutsis.

Since our only source of information about these early days is oral tradition, which by its nature favours the holders of power, we cannot be certain to what extent the power structure was accepted by those lower down the ladder, to what extent they resented it and to what extent they were exploited by it. But, whether harsh, benevolent or exploitative (or possibly all three), it survived, and is what the Europeans found when they entered this previously unknown country.

Rwanda had remained untouched by events unfolding elsewhere in Africa. Tucked away in the centre of the continent, the tiny kingdom was ignored by slave traders; consequently Rwanda is one of the few African countries that never sold its people, or its enemies, into slavery. There is no record of Arab traders or Asian merchants, numerous in other parts of East and Central Africa, having penetrated its borders, with the result that no written language was introduced and oral tradition remained the norm until the very end of the 19th century.

THE DISCOVERY OF THE MOUNTAIN GORILLA

The mountain gorilla was first discovered on 17 October 1902, on the ridges of the Virunga Mountains, by German explorer Captain Robert von Beringe, then aged 37. Captain von Beringe, together with a physician, Dr Engeland, Corporal Ehrhardt, 20 Askaris, a machine gun and necessary porters set off from Usumbura on 19 August 1902 to visit Sultan Msinga of Rwanda and then proceed north to reach a 'row of volcanoes'. The purpose of the trip was to visit the German outposts in what was then German East Africa in order to keep in touch with local chiefs and to confirm good relations, while strengthening the influence and power of the German government in these regions. On arriving at the volcanoes, an attempt was made to climb Mount Sabinyo.

Captain von Beringe's report of the expedition (below) is adapted from *In the Heart of Africa* by Duke Adolphus Frederick of Mecklenburg (Cassell, 1910).

From October 16th to 18th, senior physician Dr. Engeland and I together with only a few Askaris and the absolutely necessary baggage attempted to climb the so far unknown Kirunga ya Sabyinyo which, according to my estimation, must have a height of 3,300 metres. At the end of the first day we camped on a plateau at a height of 2,500 metres; the natives climbed up to our campsite to generously supply us with food. We left our camp on October 17th taking with us a tent, eight loads of water, five Askaris and porters as necessary.

After four and a half hours of tracking we reached a height of 3,100 metres and tracked through bamboo forest; although using elephant trails for most of the way, we encountered much undergrowth which had to be cut before we could pass … After two hours we reached a stony area with vegetation consisting mainly of blackberry and blueberry bushes. Step by step we noticed the vegetation becoming poorer and poorer, the ascent became steeper and steeper, and climbing became more difficult – for the last one and a quarter hours we climbed only over rock. After covering the ground with moss we collected, we erected our tent on a ridge at a height of 3,100 metres. The ridge was extremely narrow so that the pegs of the tent had to be secured in the abyss. The Askaris and the porters found shelter in rock caverns, which provided protection against the biting cold wind.

From our campsite we were able to watch a herd of big, black monkeys which tried to climb the crest of the volcano. We succeeded in killing two of these animals, and with a rumbling noise of falling rocks they tumbled into a ravine, which had its opening in a north-easterly direction. After five hours of strenuous work we succeeded in retrieving one of these animals using a rope. It was a big, human-like male monkey of one and a half metres in height and a weight of more than 200 pounds. His chest had no hair, and his hands and feet were of enormous size. Unfortunately I was unable to determine its type; because of its size, it could not very well be a chimpanzee or a gorilla, and in any case the presence of gorillas had not been established in the area around the lakes.

On the journey back to Usumbura, the skin and one of the hands of the animal that von Beringe collected were taken by a hyena but the rest (including the skull) finally reached the Zoological Museum in Berlin. It was classified as a new form of gorilla and named *Gorilla beringei* in honour of the Captain. Later it was considered to be a subspecies and renamed *Gorilla gorilla beringei*.

The Kingdom of Rwanda was isolationist and closed to foreigners (also to many Africans) until the 1890s. The famous American explorer, Henry Stanley, attempted to enter several times and did penetrate as far as Lake Ihema in 1874, but was then forced to retreat under arrow attack. Trade with neighbouring countries was extremely limited and Rwanda had no monetary system.

GERMAN EAST AFRICA Unlike most African states, Rwanda and Burundi were not given artificial borders by their colonisers – they had both been established kingdoms for many centuries. At the Berlin Conference of 1885, they – under the name of Ruanda-Urundi – were assigned to Germany as a part of German East Africa, although at that stage no European had officially set foot there. The first to do so formally was the German Count Gustav Adolf von Götzen on 4 May 1894 (an Austrian, Oscar Baumann, had previously entered privately from Burundi in 1892 and spent several days in the south of the country). Von Götzen entered Rwanda by the Rusumo Falls in the southeast and crossed the country to reach the eastern shore of Lake Kivu. On the way he was received by the mwami, King Kigeli IV (Rwabugiri, page 233) – apparently causing consternation among the watching nobles when he, a mere mortal, shook the sovereign by the hand. They feared that such an affront might cause disaster for the kingdom. At this stage the mwami had no idea that his country had theoretically been under German control for the past nine years.

Von Götzen subsequently became Governor of German East Africa, into which Ruanda-Urundi was formally absorbed in 1898; the same year that the mountain gorilla was first recorded by a European (see box, page 10). At this time the kingdom was larger, stretching as far as Lake Edward in the north and beyond Lake Kivu in the west; it was reduced to its present area at the Conference of Brussels in 1910.

The Germans were surprised to find that their new colony was a highly organised country, with tight, effective power structures and administrative divisions. They left these in place and ruled through them, believing that support for the traditional chiefs would render them and their henchmen loyal to Germany. Meanwhile various religious missions, Roman Catholic at first and then Protestant, began setting up bases in Ruanda-Urundi and establishing schools, farms and medical centres. In 1907, the colonisers opened a 'School for the Sons of Chiefs' in Nyanza, as well as providing military training.

Allowing for the blurring caused by intermarriage and the switching of status between Tutsi and Hutu, the power structures encountered by the colonisers were linked – and this proved to be a matter of great anthropological fascination – to three very visibly different groups of inhabitants: the tall, lanky Tutsi chiefs and nobles; the shorter, stockier Hutu farmers (who formed the majority); and the very much smaller Twa. The Duke of Mecklenburg, visiting the country in 1907, noted:

> The population is divided into three classes – the Watussi, the Wahutu, and a pygmy tribe, the Batwa, who dwell chiefly in the bamboo forests of Bugoie, the swamps of Lake Bolero, and on the island of Kwidschwi on Lake Kiwu.
>
> The Watussi are a tall, well-made people. Heights of 1.80, 2.00 and even 2.20 metres are of quite common occurrence, yet the perfect proportion of their bodies is in no wise detracted from ... The primitive inhabitants are the Wahutu, an agricultural Bantu tribe, who look after the digging and tilling and agricultural economy of the country in general. They are a medium-sized type of people ... Ruanda is certainly the most interesting country in the German East African Protectorate – in fact in all Central Africa – chiefly on account of its ethnographical and geographical position. Its interest is further increased by the fact that it is one of the last negro kingdoms governed

1

autocratically by a sovereign sultan, for German supremacy is only recognised to a very limited extent. Added to this, it is a land flowing with milk and honey, where the breeding of cattle and bee-culture flourish, and the cultivated soil bears rich crops of fruit. A hilly country, thickly populated, full of beautiful scenery, and possessing a climate incomparably fresh and healthy; a land of great fertility, with watercourses which might be termed perennial streams; a land which offers the brightest of prospects to the white settler.

In 1911–12, the Germans joined with the Tutsi monarchy to subjugate some independent Hutu principalities in the north of the country which had not previously been dominated. Their inhabitants, who had always been proud of their independence, resisted vigorously, overrunning much of what is now Northern Province before they were defeated and brought under the mwami's control. Their resentment and deep sense of grievance were to endure for the next half-century.

Germany had little time to make its mark in the colonies; in 1916, Belgium invaded Ruanda-Urundi and occupied the territories until the end of World War I; Belgium was subsequently officially entrusted with their administration under a League of Nations mandate in 1919, to be confirmed in 1923.

THE BELGIAN ERA In its adjoining colony of the Congo, Belgium had full control, but for Ruanda-Urundi it remained responsible first to the League of Nations and then (after 1945) to the United Nations Organisation. Annual reports had to be submitted and no important changes could be made without agreement from above. Despite these constraints, and despite the fact that Ruanda-Urundi had far less potential wealth than the Congo, Belgium took its charge seriously, and by the time of independence some 40 years later its material achievements (increased agricultural production, roads, schools, training centres, hospitals and dispensaries, administrative infrastructures) were considerable. In terms of human beings it did far less well, as later events demonstrated.

Priorities Rwanda had always suffered periodic famines, to such an extent that some were named and absorbed into history as milestones of time: such-and-such a child was born 'just after the *Ruyaga* famine' (1897), or a man died 'just before the *Kimwaramwara* famine' (1906). Most had climatic origins, but some which occurred around the time of the Belgian takeover (in 1916/17 and 1917/18) could also be blamed on World War I, as precious foodstuffs were shipped overseas to feed the troops. At the same time the new Belgian authorities complained that local chiefs made little attempt to prevent famines recurring, or to get emergency relief to the worst-hit areas. They therefore introduced a strict overall food strategy to make supplies less precarious.

The peasant farmers were first of all encouraged (by field workers) to maximise their production using traditional methods. They were then given help to improve their existing techniques, for example by using higher-yielding varieties of their normal crops. From 1924 the cultivation of food crops was made compulsory, including foreign species such as manioc and sweet potatoes. Next the distribution channels were upgraded, with a new road network and the development of markets and co-operatives. Storage facilities were set up; high-grade seed was distributed; the use of manure and fertiliser was promoted; the problem of erosion (caused by overuse of vulnerable land) was tackled; farmers were required to set aside a small emergency hoard of beans, peas or cereals each year; and various new types of stock breeding were initiated. Factories and processing plants were built.

Finally, the farmers were encouraged to grow crops (especially coffee) for export, so that they could earn cash with which to buy extra food in times of hardship.

These measures – not easily implemented, because of the farmers' understandable initial resentment and resistance to change – proved more-or-less successful, helped by a regulated but controversial and sometimes harsh policy of forced labour (*uburetwa*), avoidance of which could incur severe punishment. Famine did recur in 1942–44 and resulted in thousands of deaths, but this could be blamed partly on the shortage of manpower and of efficient machinery caused by World War II.

By the time of independence, large areas of farmland had been better protected against erosion and per-hectare crop yields had risen substantially. The scale of anti-erosion terracing on the hillsides was massive: first horizontal ditches were dug, following the contours; then, directly below these, hedges were planted. Water running down the hillside was trapped by the ditch, and then seeped through it to irrigate the hedge on the lower side; while the roots of the hedge secured the soil and strengthened first the ditch and then the hillside. By 1960, mainly in Rwanda but also to some extent in Burundi, around 570,000km of this protective terracing had been installed, benefiting some 750,000ha of land. However, because much of the work had been carried out under uburetwa, local people tended to see it as a colonial intrusion rather than a useful acquisition; after independence, except on the land of a few enlightened farmers, maintenance lapsed, hedges were destroyed and ditches crumbled. More than 50 years later, an extensive scheme of terracing is underway once more and proving its agricultural worth.

Agricultural research was also important. The Belgian Institut National pour l'Etude Agronomique du Congo Belge (INEAC), although based mainly in the Congo, ran a large Agricultural Research Station in Rubona, as well as the Rwerere Experimental Station (working on food and industrial crops, cropping trials and animal husbandry) and the Karama Planning Centre, focused mainly on animal husbandry, pasture research and crop yields.

Alongside the extensive public, educational, physical and administrative provisions, the agricultural programmes and improvements were probably colonisation's most helpful input to Rwanda. Whatever the shortcomings of the colonial administration, many of the technical personnel (agronomists, engineers, medical staff, etc) working 'in the field' simply wanted to do a good job and benefit the country. Belgium's impact on the relationship between the country's long-term inhabitants was unfortunately far less positive.

Power structures Like the Germans before them, the Belgians decided to retain and use the existing power structures, but unlike their predecessors they then proceeded to undermine the authority of the mwami and his chiefs and to forbid some of their traditional practices, introducing their own Belgian experts and administrators at every level. This interference did not make for easy collaboration. In any case the mwami in power at the time of Belgian accession, Mwami Musinga, was hostile to colonisation and also resented the missionaries, since their innovations undermined the established order and worked against the subjugation of Hutus. In 1931, he was forced by the Belgians to abdicate in favour of his son, the more amenable and Westernised Mwami Mutara Rudahigwa (Mutara III). Until well into the 1950s, although the traditional structures keeping them in a subservient position were somewhat weakened, the Hutus still got a bad deal and remained 'second-class citizens' in almost all respects. So both Hutus and Tutsis – and indeed the minority Twas too, because they received virtually no recognition or privilege – reacted to colonisation with varying degrees of grievance.

Education The Germans had established a few government schools in Rwanda and the Belgians followed suit, but the main source of education was always the Church. In the 1930s, the Catholic Bishop Léon Classé, who had arrived in Rwanda almost 30 years earlier as a priest and worked his way up through the hierarchy, entered into an agreement with the Belgian administration by which the Catholic Church took over full responsibility for the educational system. He may not have been entirely without financial motive, since the government then subsidised the church to the tune of 47 francs per pupil and 600 francs per qualified teacher.

The Church broadened its curriculum to cover more secular subjects such as agronomy, medicine and administration; however, the main beneficiaries of this were still largely Tutsis, although Hutus were not entirely neglected and many attended primary school. Some did make good use of the limited educational openings available to them but could not easily progress beyond a certain level. Of those who trained in the Catholic seminaries (which they could enter more easily than secular educational institutions), some went on to become priests, while others switched back to secular careers. Less than one-fifth of the students attending the Groupe Scolaire in Astrida (later known as Butare and still later as Huye) from 1945 to 1957 – and emerging as agronomists, doctors, vets and administrators – were Hutus. The School for the Sons of Chiefs originally opened by the Germans in Nyanza had a minimum height requirement which effectively reserved it for Tutsis.

In 1955, there were some 2,400 schools of various types and levels (the majority were primary) in Rwanda, with around 215,000 pupils. Of the 5,500-odd teachers, over 5,000 were Rwandan.

Categorisation Size mattered. Like the Germans before them, the Belgians were intrigued by the sharply differing physical characteristics of their colony's inhabitants, and enthusiastically measured, recorded, compared and commented on the facial and bodily proportions of Rwanda's three indigenous groups. For the more timid of the Rwandans, this 'attack' with callipers, measuring tapes, scales and other paraphernalia proved a fearsome ordeal. So man dehumanises his brothers...

Most tellingly, in the early 1930s the Belgians, with their passion for lists and classification, embarked on a census to identify all indigenous inhabitants, on the basis of these physical characteristics, as either Hutu, Tutsi or Twa, and in 1935 issued them with identity cards on which these categories ('ethnic groups' or, in French, *ethnies*, although the accuracy of this term is debatable) were recorded. If, even after strenuous measuring, someone's *ethnie* was not immediately clear, having been blurred by intermarriage or a change of status, those who were reasonably wealthy and/or had more than ten cattle were generally recorded as Tutsis. Still in use at the time of the genocide in 1994, these divisive cards provided an extra pointer (if one were needed) as to who should or should not die. Today there is a tendency to blame them directly for the genocide, but the reality was more complex: power, personalities, demographic differences and pre-colonial history also played their parts. It should be remembered that under Belgian rule Rwanda and Burundi were one country – Ruanda-Urundi – and subject to the same laws, yet they followed different paths after independence.

In 1945, the United Nations Organisation was created, with its charter promising the colonised peoples of the world justice, protection and freedom. Formerly a League of Nations mandate, Ruanda-Urundi now became a UN Trust Territory and Belgium was responsible to the UN's trusteeship council, which was to preside over all colonies' transition to independence. In 1948, a UN mission visited Ruanda-Urundi, and its report was critical of the administration, particularly regarding the inferior status of the Hutus and Twa by comparison with the Tutsis. All too often, compulsory labour was harshly enforced, and the educational system remained heavily biased in favour of Tutsis, although many priests and missions were starting to veer more towards the Hutus.

At the same time, the observers were surprised by the completeness and intricacy of the social and political hierarchy which, if used properly, would offer a sound framework for democratic development. All the necessary command structures were in place, but badly oriented.

Subsequent visits gave rise to similarly critical reports. The Belgians introduced elections at local and administrative levels – which Tutsis won, except in the far north where resentment still smouldered after the 1912 defeat. Throughout Africa, colonies were becoming restless and the scent of independence was in the air, but in Ruanda-Urundi far too little preparation had yet been made, in terms of both political awareness and practical training. Nothing was ready.

THE RUN-UP TO INDEPENDENCE From about 1950, as the numbers of educated Hutus increased, the Hutu voice grew stronger. Hutu leaders such as Grégoire Kayibanda began to demand recognition for the majority. In 1954, the system of ubuhake was officially abolished, although in reality it lingered for a few more years. In 1957, the Superior Council of Rwanda (which had a huge Tutsi majority) called for independence preparations to be speeded up.

In 1956, Mwami Rudahigwa had called for total independence and an end to Belgian occupation. Just before another UN visit in 1957, a *Hutu Manifesto* drawn up by a group of Hutu intellectuals was presented to the Vice Governor General, Jean-Paul Harroy. It challenged the whole structure of Rwanda's administration, called for political power to be placed in the hands of the Hutu majority, pointed out injustices and inequalities, and proposed solutions. Little official action was taken.

The Catholic Church, now pro-Hutu, encouraged Grégoire Kayibanda and his associates to form political parties: APROSOMA (Association pour la Promotion Sociale des Masses) was openly sectarian, championing Hutu interests strongly, while RADER (Rassemblement Démocratique Rwandais) was more moderate. Whereas Tutsis, comfortably in a position of power, were calling for immediate independence without any changes to the system, Hutus wanted change first (to a more democratic system, recognising the fact that they were the majority) and then independence. Buffeted by conflicting claims and struggling to keep pace with the speed of political change in both Ruanda-Urundi and Congo, Belgium, having supported the powerful Tutsi minority for the past 40 years, now switched its allegiance to the Hutu majority, ostensibly in response to the criticisms made by the UN trusteeship council.

The wind of independence was blowing strongly in colonial Africa. More political parties sprang up. UNAR (Union Nationale Rwandaise) was formed by the proponents of immediate independence under the Rwandan monarchy, while PARMEHUTU (Parti du Mouvement de l'Emancipation Hutu) was established under the guidance of the Catholic Church by those favouring delayed independence. MSM (Mouvement Social Muhutu) was created by Grégoire Kayibanda to support Hutu interests, while UNAR (page 16) was a pro-monarchy and anti-Belgium party.

In July 1959, Mwami Rudahigwa fell ill suddenly and died in hospital in Bujumbura (then Usumbura). Confused reports of his death rightly or wrongly fuelled rumours of Belgian involvement, and tensions escalated. His half-brother Jean-Baptiste Ndahindurwa, aged only 23, was named as his successor, but amid the political upheaval was not formally enthroned until October 1960, becoming

Mwami Kigeli V (see box, page 33). Meanwhile there were arrests and some sporadic small-scale violence – which erupted on a larger scale on 1 November, when a Hutu sub-chief belonging to PARMEHUTU was attacked and beaten in Gitarama (now Muhanga) by young members of UNAR. Within 24 hours, highly organised Hutu gangs were out on the streets of towns and villages throughout the country, burning, looting and killing. Then Tutsis began to retaliate. Within about two weeks things were calm again – around 300 had died, and 1,231 (919 Tutsis and 312 Hutus) were arrested by the Belgian authorities. The country was placed under military rule headed by the Belgian Colonel Guy Logiest, who quickly began replacing Tutsi chiefs with Hutus. He was strongly pro-Hutu, claiming to be righting the injustices of colonisation, and played a virtually unconcealed part in anti-Tutsi attacks.

The 'revolution' had begun; Tutsis started to flee the country in large numbers, and outbursts of violence continued. Chronicling this turbulent time in his *l'Histoire du Rwanda de 1853 à 1972* (published 1975; page 362), eminent Rwandan historian Alexis Kagame comments wryly that it needs not just a chapter but an entire book. However, it is worth remembering that it was the first occurrence of organised violence between the two groups and that it happened barely 60 years ago, so those who speak of a long-drawn-out feud originating before colonisation are mistaken.

PARMEHUTU won hastily manipulated elections in 1960. Belgium, the reins of power slipping rapidly from its grasp, organised a referendum on the monarchy under the auspices of the United Nations. In January 1961, Rwanda's elected local administrators were called to a public meeting in Gitarama, Grégoire Kayibanda's birthplace. They and a massed crowd of some 25,000 declared Rwanda a republic – and the United Nations had little option but to accept this ultimatum. The mwami left the country, never to return. However, the UN did not recognise the 1960 elections so more were held in September 1961, under UN supervision. Again they were won by PARMEHUTU, with Grégoire Kayibanda at its head. Later that year, some 150 Tutsis were killed in the Astrida area, 5,000 homes were burned and 22,000 people were displaced. In July 1962, Rwanda's independence was finally confirmed with Kayibanda as its new president, heading a republican government. Astrida, so named in 1935 after Queen Astrid of Belgium, reverted to its local name Butare. Violence against Tutsis continued; by now about 135,000 had fled as refugees to neighbouring countries and the number was growing. Among those who left in 1960 was a three-year-old child named Paul Kagame, of whom much more would be heard later.

It is true that Belgium emerged from the fiasco with little credit. But it is equally true that, even without colonisation, some kind of revolution would inevitably have occurred sooner or later, for the tightly stratified hierarchy of the 19th century could not have held firm indefinitely against the pressures, promises and potentials of the modern world.

The trend today in Rwanda is to hold the colonial administration responsible for the subsequent genocide. Indeed, without colonisation the explosion might well, as a Rwandan friend said to me, 'have happened differently', and perhaps the magnitude of the genocide makes the apportioning of blame a necessary part of the recovery process. But to claim – as is also the trend today – that before the arrival of the Europeans all was peace and harmony may simply reflect the fact that oral tradition tends to favour those in power.

1962–94 The situation became yet more tangled and yet more sensitive. Readers who want a fuller picture than a guidebook allows will find several good sources on pages 364–6. John Reader's *Africa* (Penguin, 1998) is particularly recommended, as is Gérard Prunier's *The Rwanda Crisis – History of a Genocide* (Hurst, 1998). They (among others) have been used as sources in this chapter.

Once in power, the government sought to reinforce its supremacy. 'Quotas' were introduced, giving the Tutsis (who were a minority of about 9% of the population) a right to only 9% of school places, 9% of jobs in the workforce and so on. Small groups of Tutsi exiles in neighbouring countries made sporadic commando-style raids into Rwanda, leading to severe reprisals. In late 1963, up to 10,000 Tutsis were killed. The pattern of violence continued.

In 1964, the Fabian Society (London) published a report entitled *Massacre in Rwanda*, commenting on events since 1959. Also – chillingly, in view of what happened 30 years later – a report entitled *Attempted Genocide in Rwanda* appeared in the March 1964 issue of *The World Today* (vol 20, no 3).

In 1965, Kayibanda was re-elected president and Juvenal Habyarimana was appointed Minister of Defence. In 1969, Kayibanda was again re-elected and PARMEHUTU was renamed the MDR (Mouvement Démocratique Républicain). But Kayibanda's regime was becoming increasingly dictatorial and corrupt. The 'quotas' and other 'cleansing' measures began to be enforced so rigidly that even Hutus became uneasy. In 1973, ostensibly to quell violence following a purge of Tutsis from virtually all educational establishments, Major General Juvenal Habyarimana toppled Grégoire Kayibanda in a military coup.

In 1975, a single party, the MRND (Mouvement Révolutionnaire et National pour le Développement), was formed. For a while, there were signs of improvement, although this tends to be forgotten in the light of subsequent events. Despite initial optimism and a period of relative stability, however, the regime eventually proved little better than its predecessor. Some educational reforms were undertaken, with the object of 'Rwandanisation' – revaluing Kinyarwanda and Rwandan culture. Habyarimana was reconfirmed as president in 1978, 1983 and 1988 – unsurprisingly, since he was the only candidate. The Hutu–Tutsi conflict was to some extent replaced by conflict between Hutus from the south and those from the north (Habyarimana was a northerner, so was accused of favouring 'his own'). Meanwhile, in the international sphere, rising oil prices and falling commodity prices were bringing the country's economy close to collapse and, among all but the privileged elite, dissatisfaction grew.

In 1979, a group of Rwandan exiles in Uganda established the RRWF (Rwandan Refugee Welfare Foundation) which in 1980 became RANU (Rwandan Alliance for National Unity), whose name explains its aim. In 1981, in Uganda, one Yoweri Museveni, later to become Uganda's president, started a guerrilla war against the oppressive regime of Dr Milton Obote – among his men were two Rwandan refugees, Paul Kagame and Fred Rwigyema. Obote was hostile to the Rwandan refugees in Uganda and political youth groups were encouraged to attack them and their property. As a result of such attacks in 1982–83, there was massive displacement of the refugees in southern Uganda and large numbers tried (or were forced) to return to Rwanda. The Rwandan government quickly closed its borders with Uganda and confined those who had already entered to a small and inhospitable area in the north, where many of the young and the old died of hunger and disease.

In 1986, also in Uganda, Yoweri Museveni's National Resistance Army (which contained a number of Rwandan refugees) overthrew Obote, and Museveni assumed power. In 1987, RANU was renamed the RPF (Rwandan Patriotic Front), and was supported not only by exiled Tutsis but also by a few prominent Hutus opposed to Habyarimana's regime.

In 1987/88, a military coup in Burundi and consequent ethnic tensions caused a wave of Burundian refugees to flood into Rwanda. In 1989, the price of coffee, Rwanda's main export, collapsed, causing severe economic problems. Censorship rules were flouted, new politically oriented publications emerged and reports of corruption and mismanagement appeared openly. In July 1990, under pressure from Western aid donors, Habyarimana conceded the principle of multi-party democracy and agreed to allow free debate on the country's future. In practice, little changed.

Then, on 1 October 1990, the RPF (led by Major General Fred Rwigyema), invaded the northeast of Rwanda from Uganda, with the stated objective of ending the political stalemate once and for all and restoring democracy. French, German and Zairean troops were called in to support the Rwandan national army and the incursion was soon suppressed; but the government now took the RPF threat seriously. Habyarimana enlarged the Rwandan army from around 5,000 in 1990 to about 24,000 in 1991 and 35,000 in 1993. Various overseas countries (France, South Africa, the US) provided arms. Additionally, the 1990 RPF invasion was followed by severe reprisals: thousands of Tutsi and southern Hutu were arrested and held in prison for some months. Several were tried and sentenced to death but the sentences were not carried out, although, as one of those arrested later wrote, 'many died of the hunger and the beatings'. Sporadic unrest continued throughout the country.

Political solutions were sought, both nationally and internationally, with several Western countries now involved. In November 1990, Habyarimana agreed to the introduction of multi-partyism and the abolition of 'ethnic' identity cards, but nothing was implemented. The Rwandan army began to train and arm civilian militias known as *interahamwe* ('those who stand together'). It was later estimated that up to 2,000 Rwandans (Tutsis or anti-government Hutus) were killed by their government between October 1990 and December 1992.

The RPF – now led by Major Paul Kagame, since the charismatic Rwigyema had died in the October 1990 invasion – continued its guerrilla raids, striking at targets countrywide. By the end of 1992 it had expanded to a force of almost 12,000 and was growing rapidly. Its stated aim was always to bring democracy to Rwanda rather than to claim supremacy. Meanwhile, French troops were supporting the government forces. In the face of increasing violence, international pressure was applied more strongly and the Arusha Agreement (so named because it was drawn up in Arusha, Tanzania) committed Habyarimana to a number of reforms, including the establishment of the rule of law, political power-sharing, the repatriation and resettlement of refugees, and the integration of the armed forces to include the RPF. A 70-member Transitional National Assembly was to be established. The Agreement was signed in August 1993 and should have been implemented within 37 days, overseen by a United Nations force. But the process, unpalatable to both Tutsi and Hutu hardliners, stalled. Hostilities deepened. Radio stations poured forth inflammatory propaganda. Rwanda's Radio-Télévision Libre des Mille Collines, in particular, insistently and viciously identified Tutsis as 'the enemy' and 'cockroaches', in dehumanising and vilifying terms. Scattered outbursts of violence rumbled on.

On 21 October, the Hutu president of neighbouring Burundi, Melchior Ndadaye, elected only a few months previously, was killed in a military coup, fuelling ethnic tensions in Rwanda. The UN began sending UNAMIR (UN Assistance Mission for Rwanda) forces to the country. Politics were deadlocked. A sense of impending danger grew and, by March 1994, vulnerable (or well-informed) citizens were starting to evacuate their families from Kigali.

On 6 April 1994, a plane carrying Rwanda's President Habyarimana and Burundi's new president Cyprien Ntaryamira was shot down by rocket fire near Kigali airport. Both men died. The source of the attack has never been confirmed. Within hours, the killing began.

THE GENOCIDE It had been well planned, over a long period. Roadblocks were quickly erected and the army and interahamwe went into action, on a rampage of

THE 'GENOCIDE AGAINST THE TUTSI' *Janice Booth*

Until a few years ago, the events of 1994 were spoken of in Rwanda purely as 'the Genocide'. Now you will often hear the phrase 'the Genocide against the Tutsi', a clarification introduced because a scattering of former *génocidaires* and their supporters maintain either that it was not genocide but rather a civil war; or that a 'double genocide' occurred, with Hutu *en masse* targeted also; or that it was simply a spontaneous uprising of Rwandans angry at their president's death.

The prolonged and systematic campaigns of anti-Tutsi vilification carried out in the Rwandan media and elsewhere well before April 1994 powerfully contradict these claims, as does reading the many carefully researched books on the subject and visiting the genocide memorials in Rwanda. Linda Melvern, author of (among others) *A People Betrayed: the Role of the West in Rwanda's Genocide*, speaking at a high-level conference in Stockholm in April 2012, explained that the denials, as with the Holocaust, had started directly after the massacres began. 'The final stage of genocide is denial, where evidence is destroyed, investigations are blocked, and the death toll is manipulated. With the Holocaust, the first deniers were the Nazis themselves. The pattern was repeated with the Genocide in Rwanda.' What engulfed the country in April 1994 was indeed a 'genocide against the Tutsi'.

During and after the 100 days of bloodshed, Hutus in Rwanda – both innocent and guilty – did of course die: some during the repression of the genocide, some at the hands of the interahamwe for refusing to kill, and others in the surprisingly few reprisal or targeted killings that did occur. Later, many who had fled to the DRC succumbed to the hardship of the refugee camps, and those interahamwe who continued to cause trouble in and around the camps were pursued. But the scale of Hutu deaths was only a tiny proportion of that of the Tutsi.

Amid the terror and carnage, there were many acts of heroism by Hutu villagers who had no heart for slaughter. Some hid Tutsi neighbours in their homes while the fighting raged across the countryside, knowing that discovery meant certain death; or sent the killers on false trails. Others looked after Tutsi children orphaned or separated from their parents. Some refused to kill when ordered, so they or their families paid the price. Local officials, ostensibly transporting Tutsis to their deaths, in fact took them to safety; when discovered, they were dispatched without mercy. A group of schoolgirls were ordered to divide themselves into Tutsi and Hutu, with the implication that the Tutsis would die; they refused, saying they were all Rwandans, so all were killed together. Much unsung courage was displayed by Hutus, and these village heroes were equally victims of the 'Genocide against the Tutsi'. Many of them are remembered annually, on Heroes' Day.

death, torture, looting and destruction. Tutsis and moderate Hutus were targeted. Weapons of every sort were used, from slick, military arms to rustic machetes. Orders were passed briskly downw ard from *préfecture* to *commune* to *secteur* to *cellule* – and the gist of every order was: 'These are the enemy. Kill.'

A painfully detailed account, which includes many eyewitness testimonies and brings home the full horror of the slaughter, is given in the 1,200 pages of *Rwanda – Death, Despair and Defiance* (African Rights, London, 1995). In *A People Betrayed: the Role of the West in Rwanda's Genocide*, L R Melvern analyses the political and international background (Zed Books, London & New York, 2000), as does Gérard Prunier in *The Rwanda Crisis* (page 365). A condensed overview of events is given below.

In three months, up to a million people were killed, violently and cruelly. A great, surging tide of slaughter spread across the country, leaving barely a family untouched. The international media suddenly found Rwanda newsworthy. Chilling images filled our TV screens and the scale of the massacre was too great for many of us to grasp.

On 8 April, just two days after the plane crash, the Rwandan Patriotic Front (RPF) launched a major offensive to end the genocide. As they advanced from Uganda, they rescued and liberated Tutsis still hiding in terror from the killers. Meanwhile, however, a new Hutu government, based on the MRND and supporting parties, was formed in Kigali and later shifted to Gitarama (now Muhanga).

The United Nations' UNAMIR force was around 2,500 strong at the time. They watched helplessly, technically unable to intervene as this would breach their 'monitoring' mandate. After the murder of ten Belgian soldiers the force was cut to 250. On 30 April, the UN Security Council spent eight hours discussing the Rwandan crisis – without ever using the word 'genocide'. Had this term been used, they would have been legally obliged to 'prevent and punish' the perpetrators. Meanwhile tens of thousands of refugees were fleeing the country. In May the UN agreed to send 6,800 troops and police to Rwanda to defend civilians, but implementation was

CHILDREN OF THE GENOCIDE

Child survivors of the 1994 genocide are now Rwanda's young adult generation. A National Trauma Survey by UNICEF in 1995 estimated that 99.9% of them had witnessed violence, 79.6% experienced death in the family, 69.5% saw killing or injury inflicted (in many cases by machete), 31.4% witnessed rape or sexual assault, and 61.5% were threatened with death themselves. Many orphaned youngsters, or those whose parents were too traumatised or damaged to cope, had to become carers of their younger siblings. Babies born later were raised in broken families still grieving deeply for their dead.

The years of recovery and reconstruction have been as hard for these children as for adults, but many of them today have positive and successful lives. They include college graduates, technicians, administrators and medical personnel. Others have found the struggle tougher and need continued help – of which much remains available, from governmental support to international aid. For all of these young survivors, no matter how 'normal' their lives now appear, the background shadow of genocide still lingers. It's only the children of this generation, unborn in 1994 but now of school age, who can at last break free.

delayed by arguments over who would cover costs and provide equipment. The RPF army had taken control of Kigali airport and Kanombe barracks and was gaining ground elsewhere. In June, France announced that it would deploy 2,500 peacekeeping troops to Rwanda (*Opération Turquoise*) until the UN force arrived. These created a controversial 'safe zone' in the southwest.

On 4 July, the RPF captured Kigali and set up an interim government. The remnants of the Hutu government fled to Zaire, followed by a further tide of refugees. The RPF continued its advance westward and northward. Many thousands of refugees streamed into the French 'safe zone' and still more headed towards Zaire, cramming into makeshift camps on the inhospitable terrain around Goma. The humanitarian crisis was acute, later to be exacerbated by disease and a cholera outbreak which claimed tens of thousands of lives.

On 18 July 1994, the RPF announced that the war had been won, declared a ceasefire, established a broad-based Government of National Unity and named Pasteur Bizimungu as president. Faustin Twagiramungu was appointed prime minister. The following day, RPF commander Major General Paul Kagame was appointed defence minister and vice president. By the end of July, the UN Security Council had reached a final agreement about sending an international force to Rwanda. By the end of August *Opération Turquoise* was terminated and UN forces had replaced the French. Internationally, it had now been accepted that a 'genocide' had indeed taken place – and it was over. At sites of the worst massacres, memorials now commemorate the dead and remind the world that such an atrocity must never, never be allowed to occur again.

THE AFTERMATH The 70-member Transitional National Assembly provided for in the 1993 Arusha Agreement became operational in December 1994. In November 1994, the UN Security Commission set up the International Criminal Tribunal for Rwanda (ICTR), whose brief was to prosecute those who were guilty, between 1 January and 31 December 1994, of genocide and other violations of international humanitarian law; by the end of 1996 suspects were being brought to trial.

Sporadic bursts of violence were to continue for a further three years or so, with killings on both sides, as tensions in and around refugee settlements persisted and hardline Hutus who had fled across the border mounted guerrilla raids. But the RPF army and the new government remained in control. UN forces left the country in March 1996. Refugees returned home, in massive numbers. Problems of insecurity posed by former Rwanda government forces and interahamwe troops caused Rwanda to become militarily involved with the Democratic Republic of the Congo (DRC).

In 1999, local elections were held at sector and cellule level, and the Lusaka Agreement, to end the war in the DRC, was signed.

In March 2000, President Pasteur Bizimungu resigned and in April Major General Paul Kagame was sworn in as the fifth president of Rwanda, exactly four decades after his flight as a three-year-old refugee.

In July 2000, the Organisation of African Unity (OAU) recommended that the international community should make payments to the government and people of Rwanda in reparation for the genocide. Later the same year, the Rwandan government launched a census to determine the true and total number of genocide victims – irrespective of whether they were Hutus, Tutsis, Twa or foreigners.

In June 2002, with some 115,000 genocide suspects still in gaol after eight years and the country's regular courts unable to clear the backlog, the *Gacaca* Judicial System was launched. Gacaca (pronounced Ga-cha-cha, with a hard g) means 'grass', and was based on the traditional form of Rwandan justice where villagers used to gather together on a patch of grass to resolve conflicts between families, with heads of household acting as judges.

In June 2003, Rwanda's new Constitution was signed, marking the end of the transition period that followed the genocide and replacing various documents referred to as the Fundamental Law. The presidential elections held – entirely peacefully – in August 2003 saw Paul Kagame returned as president for a term of seven years, with 3,544,777 votes or 95.05% of the total. Parliamentary elections followed in September 2003 in which women took 48.8% of the seats, making Rwanda the country with the highest number of women in its parliament at the time, a statistic which still holds true today, and at least in part reflects a belief that women would never allow the sort of mass killing that has occurred in the past, and many others hold high positions in both state and private institutions.

Rwanda has qualified for debt relief under the Highly Indebted Poor Countries Initiative and benefited from economic reform and development programmes supported by the IMF, the World Bank, the African Development Bank and the EU Mission in Rwanda. Huge amounts of foreign aid have been provided – and the fact that these grants have been ongoing since the genocide demonstrates international satisfaction about how the money is used. Donors (the UK is among the largest) renew their contracts. In 2011, Rwanda and Tanzania were the only two countries out of 78 worldwide to receive an 'A' rating from the Organization for Economic Cooperation and Development (OECD) for using aid effectively. The economy keeps growing. In 2017, Transparency International's *Corruption Perceptions Index* named Rwanda as the fourth least corrupt African country, beaten only by Mauritius, Cape Verde and Botswana, and also in 2017 the World Bank '*Doing Business*' Report named it as the second easiest African country in which to do business, behind only Mauritius.

Rwanda's international links have also strengthened steadily. In 2006, it was accepted into the East African Community, and in November 2009 it became the 54th member of the Commonwealth, in which it and Mozambique are the only two member countries to have had no British colonial connections. In 2018, Paul Kagame began a one-year term as Chair of the African Union. A contingent from the Rwandan army has played an active part in the peacekeeping force in Sudan's troubled Darfur region; in addition to normal peacekeeping duties, it has built and equipped a village school for more than 500 pupils and supported other community development. A contingent of Rwandan police officers served in Haiti after its disastrous earthquake, and the current UN peacekeeping forces in South Sudan and the Central African Republic both have a strong Rwandan component.

The country's second round of democratic parliamentary elections was held in September 2008, with the RPF under Kagame gaining 79% of the vote, while the remainder was divided between the minority Social Democratic and Liberal Parties. Five years later in 2013, the third parliamentary elections were cast in a similar mould, and Kagame's RPF went home with a tidy 76% of the votes. By law, at least a third of parliamentary representatives must be female, but in 2008 a remarkable 45 of the 80 seats were won by women. Rwanda is now one of only two countries in the world whose parliament contains fewer males than females (the other being Bolivia; the USA and UK have about 20% and 30%, respectively).

In August 2010, the country held its second presidential election. The RPF once again dominated, with Kagame winning 93% of the vote, while his closest rival, Jean Damascene Ntawukuriryayo of the Social Democratic Party, took a mere 5.15%. The election was conducted peacefully, but some opposition and human rights groups claimed the result was tainted by intimidation and lack of credible competition. Certainly, the two months prior to the election were marked by violent attacks on critics and opponents of Kagame, among them the attempted assassination of Lt-Gen Faustin Nyamwasa in Johannesburg (whose colleague, former intelligence head Patrick Karegeya, was killed here in 2014, and who has, since 2010, survived two further assassination attempts himself), the shooting of the outspoken journalist Jean-Leonard Rugambage, and the murder and partial beheading of André Kagwa Rwisereka, a founder and Vice President of the Democratic Green Party. Were the RPF responsible? Or opponents hoping to cast suspicion on them? Or personal vendettas? In these days of mafia-style killings and political skullduggery worldwide, it's anyone's guess.

After a petition with 3.7 million signatures triggered a parliamentary debate on term limits in 2015, both houses of parliament voted in favour of a constitutional amendment which would abolish term limits and allow Kagame to contest the next elections. Any constitutional amendment must also be approved by national referendum, however, and just such a referendum was held in December of the same year; the proposed changes sailed through with 98% of the vote. These changes cleared the way for Kagame to contest another round of elections, and in August 2017 he was duly returned to Urugwiro Village (Rwanda's state house) with an overwhelming 99% majority vote in an election the African Union Election Observation Mission described as 'peaceful, orderly and transparent'. The remaining 1% of votes were shared between the Green Party (almost 33,000 votes) and independent candidate Philippe Mpayimana (almost 50,000). Thus, Kagame and the RPF seem set to dominate Rwandan politics for the foreseeable future, with parliamentary elections scheduled for late 2018 and the next presidential elections not due until 2024, at the conclusion of Kagame's third seven-year term.

Since the year 2000, a guiding principle of government strategy in Rwanda has been *Vision 2020*, a progressive and consultative set of policies that aim to transform the country's economy to that of a middle-income country. Vision 2020 also places strong emphasis on gender equality, anti-corruption, sustainable management of natural resources, technological progress centred on the IT field, private sector-led economic and infrastructural development, and regional economic integration. An important development in this regard has been the laying of fibre-optic cables throughout the country, making Rwanda a regional leader in internet technology.

The Vision 2020 pro-poor targets seemed ambitious when first set: reducing poverty from 60% of the population to 25%, while increasing per-capita income to US$900, life expectancy to 65 years and literacy to 90%. At the time of writing, progress so far seems positive, and was boosted in mid 2017 when the UK (Rwanda's second-largest bilateral donor) agreed a two-year multi-million-pound partnership aimed at fast-tracking the country's development initiatives and spurring growth at both national and individual levels.

Of course, tensions within the country still exist, the government inevitably has its critics, and the gap between the 'haves' and the 'have-nots' remains too wide. Indeed, many Rwandans still live in economic conditions that are far from ideal. Mental health problems resulting from the genocide, although reducing as time passes, still affect many survivors, particularly during the annual month of mourning. Unemployment is a problem, particularly for the young. However, the government works energetically to combat the deficiencies, and there's a growing feeling of security and optimism.

Considering the size and resources of Rwanda, what happened there in 1994, and the inherent problems faced by almost all countries in sub-Saharan Africa, even without the aftermath of a genocide, the achievements of the past 20-odd years

Functioning effectively in Rwanda today are the **Community Mediators**, locally known as Abunzi, people of integrity chosen by and from their own communities, who are responsible for amicably settling small local disputes between villagers. In many cases this avoids recourse to local courts. The selection process is careful and the mediators then serve a five-year term. Apart from financial disputes they may find themselves dealing with issues such as deception, defamation, damage or excessive noise.

The latest selection process, in July 2015, took place after the monthly **Umuganda**, a morning of community work held on the last Saturday of every month. Businesses close and much work elsewhere stops while communities gather together to do jobs that are useful to their area (digging, painting, repairing, clearing, maintaining ...); it has also become a time when they can discuss their current concerns and plan future improvements. Rwandans abroad, for example those in the UN Peacekeeping Force in Darfur and the Rwandan police contingent in Haiti, have introduced forms of Umuganda there too, with valuable results.

have been amazing, and are witness to a huge amount of energy, courage, goodwill and sheer hard work. Progress has been dramatic and durable. Kigali has become a bustling modern capital city, with some striking contemporary architecture and top-class international conference facilities; tourism is booming; and Rwanda today is a vibrant and forward-looking country, well able to cope with the demands and technologies of the 21st century.

PEOPLE

Rwanda today probably contains inhabitants raised in a greater number of countries than most other African nations, as long-term exiles returned after the genocide from Uganda, Kenya, Tanzania, Burundi, Europe, the USA and more. But of course Rwanda is their origin and their home.

Following the disruptive ethnic clashes of the post-colonial years, which culminated in the 1994 genocide, the current focus is to stress Rwandan unity: the fact that before the arrival of the colonisers Rwandans were living together on the same hills, speaking the same language and practising the same culture.

In fact, matters may not be quite so clear-cut and the insistence on 'same-ness' should not be carried to the extent of concealing historical individuality. But there's no doubt that the people of Rwanda in general are committed to overcoming any awkward or damaging differences. One genocide survivor wrote: 'Before the genocide, Hutus and Tutsis lived together. I remember we used to play with Hutu children and share everything. There were even intermarriages. The only time when we felt discriminated against was when a place at school, or a job, was given to a Hutu, even if there was a Tutsi more qualified for it. But this was no reason for hatred between the two groups.'

Of course, personal attitudes may vary from place to place and old differences may sometimes persist. What is impressive is how thoroughly they are being tackled, in all strata of society. Determined and touchingly courageous efforts at reconciliation and peaceful coexistence are visible nationwide, extending from government level down to rural groups and individuals. Genocide perpetrators and genocide survivors live together (whether closely or uneasily) as neighbours, and local disputes can be settled communally. The passing of time has helped.

Rwanda is also currently hosting tens of thousands of refugees from Burundi and the eastern DRC, and has expressed willingness to accept a generous number of the assorted African migrants stranded in appalling conditions in Libya. Some of these incomers will inevitably be absorbed into the permanent population, so the Rwanda of the future may turn out to be a far more multi-racial country than it is today.

LANGUAGE

The local language is Kinyarwanda, but almost all Rwandans speak a little of at least one international language. In rural areas, this is most likely to be KiSwahili, a coastal Bantu language with strong Arabic influences which, thanks largely to the 19th-century slave caravans, has come to serve as the lingua franca of East Africa. Depending on their age, most educated Rwandans who were brought up within the country also speak passable to fluent French or English, with older generations generally favouring French and younger speakers English. Additionally, many returned long-term exiles were educated in Uganda, Kenya or Tanzania or another Anglophone territory, and don't know any French, but do speak fluent English.

The upshot of this is that French speakers will have no difficulty getting by in the towns, and should always be able to find somebody who can speak French in rural areas. English speakers will get by almost as easily in Kigali and other large towns, but less so in rural areas. Travellers who know some Swahili will also find this very useful, particularly in rural areas. The potential for chaos is, of course, immense: in Musanze/Ruhengeri, I regularly tried my faltering Swahili in a bar or hotel to no avail, followed up on this in my even more limited French, only to have the person I was addressing ask me whether perhaps I spoke English?

In 2008, the government controversially replaced French with English as the main language of education from primary school onwards. This move was intended to help Rwanda integrate into the (Anglophone) East Africa Community, and in the long term it will no doubt result in the spread of English at the expense of French. However, critics complain that the transition was unworkably abrupt, since many experienced teachers (not to mention their pupils) are less than conversant in English, making it almost impossible for them to pursue the official curriculum in any language other than Kinyarwanda. In 2011/12, English-speaking teachers were brought in from Kenya and Uganda to help out, and the first classes of Rwandan students to have completed their education entirely in English are now beginning to graduate.

The national language, spoken by everyone, remains Kinyarwanda, and for the sake of friendliness and courtesy you should try to take on board a few words. At the very

| WHAT THE 'ELL ...? | *Janice Booth* |

The transposition of r and l can be tongue-twisting as well as confusing. I have friends named Hilary and Florence – in Rwanda aka Hiraly and Frolence. The multiple mwamis or kings of Rwanda – *les rois* – can be called *les lois* (the laws); while the queen (*la reine*) can sound like *la laine* (the wool!). In an email once, a young girl asked me to 'play' for her – which, unmusical as I am, would be difficult. She meant 'pray'. And New Year greetings wished me the 'fun and floric of the festive season'. Fortunately I've never heard the transposition applied to gorilla.

least aim for *yégo* (yes), *oya* (no), *murakozé* (thank you), *muraho* (hello, good morning/ afternoon), *bitesé?* (how are you?) and *byiza* (good). For me, an essential phrase in any language is 'What's your name?', to be used on children; their faces light up and they start to take you seriously! Then point to yourself and say your own name, and the introduction is complete. In Kinyarwanda it's easy – *Witwandé?* The above words are written phonetically – the value of consonants may change a bit in different parts of the country; for example 'b' may sometimes sound more like 'v' or 'w'. If you're linguistically ambitious, turn to the more comprehensive vocabulary on pages 356–60.

PLACE NAMES In Kinyarwanda, as in most African languages, place names are more-or-less phonetic, so that the town of Base, for instance, is pronounced *Bah-say*. But the transcription of place names in Rwanda displays some other quirks that I've not encountered anywhere, namely the occasional pronunciation of 'g' as 'j' (Kinigi, for instance, is pronounced *Kiniji*), and of an initial 'k' as 'ch' and 'cy' as 'sh' (Kigali = Chigali, Cyangugu = Shangugu). Further complication is created by the African tendency to treat 'r' and 'l' as interchangeable, and the local custom of distinguishing certain towns from the synonymous region by adding the French word *ville* to the end of the town's name. Hence, when you hear a bus conductor yelling *Chigari-ville* at the top of his voice, he is in fact referring to the city of Kigali!

The names of nine main towns were changed in 2006; for details see box, pages 40–1.

RELIGION

The Christian religions are a powerful force in Rwanda today, as witnessed by the great number of active churches throughout the country. According to statistics released in 2006, Roman Catholicism leads the field with 57% adherence (hence Pope John Paul II's visit to Rwanda in 1990), followed by 26% for Protestantism, and 11% for Seventh Day Adventism. There is a small (less than 5%) Muslim population, leaving only 2% of the population claiming no religious affiliation or following traditional beliefs.

TRADITIONAL RELIGION AND BELIEFS Rwandans traditionally believe in a supreme being called *Imana*. While Imana's actions influence the whole world, Rwanda is his home where he comes to spend the night. Individuals hold informal ceremonies imploring Imana's blessing. There is a tradition that, before retiring, a woman may leave a pitcher of water for Imana in the hope he will make her fertile.

Since words can have a magical impact, the name of Imana is often used when naming children, also in words of comfort, warnings against complacency, blessings, salutations, and during rites associated with marriage and death. Oaths take the form of 'May Imana give me a stroke', or 'May I be killed by Imana'. In instances when a long-desired child is born, people say to the new mother, 'Imana has removed your shame'. Tales of Imana granting magical gifts to humans, who then lose these gifts through greed and disloyalty, are common.

There is a special creative act of Imana at the beginning of each person's life. Impregnation in itself would not be sufficient to produce a new human being, so the young wife, at evening, leaves a few drops of water in a jar. Imana, as a potter, needs water to shape the clay into a child in her womb. Then after birth, Imana decides whether life for that individual is to be happy or unhappy. If, later on, a man is miserable, poverty-stricken or in bad health, it is said that he was created by Ruremakwaci, a name given to Imana when his creation is not very successful, when 'he is tired', or, for some unknown reason, decides that a certain destiny will be unhappy.

Rwandans traditionally believe that a life force exists in all men and animals. In animals this invisible soul disappears when the creature dies, but in humans it is transformed into *bazimu*, spirits of the dead who live in *Ikuzimu*, the underworld or the world below the soil. While the deceased kings of Rwanda constitute a kind of governing body in the underworld, there are no social distinctions. Life is neither pleasant nor unhappy. The bazimu continue the individuality of living persons and have the same names. Though non-material, they are localised by their activity. They do not drink, eat, or mate but their existence in other respects is similar to that in the world of the living. Bazimu return to the world, often to places where they used to live. Some may stay permanently in the hut where their descendants live or in the small huts made for them in the enclosure around the dwelling. Bazimu are generally bad. They bring misfortune, sickness, crop failure and cattle epidemics because they envy the living the cherished things they had to leave behind. Their power, actuated by the male spirits, or grandfathers, extends only over their own clan. The living members of a family must consult a diviner to discover the reason for the ancestor's anger. Respect to bazimu is shown principally by joining a secret cult group.

The cult of Ryangombe Ryangombe is said to be the chief of the *imandwa*, Rwandans who are initiated into the cult of Ryangombe. According to Rwandan legend, he was a great warrior who was accidentally killed by a buffalo during a hunting party. To share their hero's fate, his friends threw themselves on the bull's horns. Imana gave Ryangombe and his followers a special place, the Karisimbi Volcano in the Virunga volcano chain, where they have a notably more agreeable afterlife than the other bazimu. The cult of Ryangombe became an important force of social cohesion, with Tutsi, Hutu and Twa being initiated into it. Ryangombe is propitiated by the *babandwa*, a politico-religious fraternity, who perform rituals, chants and dances in his honour. They meet only once a year, during July, at which time initiation takes place. During their festival the members of the fraternity paint themselves and decorate the spirit huts. A member of the group appears as the personification of the spirit of Ryangombe, carrying his sacred spear. After a ritual is performed, all members purify themselves at the stream. While involvement in the cult is not common today, Rwandans can recall when their grandfathers or fathers participated in the Ryangombe festival and a popular Rwandan song recounts Ryangombe's exploits as a warrior and lover. Also see box, page 247.

EDUCATION

More children are attending school in Rwanda today than at any time in the country's history, and today the country boasts not only the highest primary school enrolment rate in Africa at 97%, but gender parity among the students as well. Although access to schools is very high, the issue of quality education remains, and a number of international organisations are working with the Rwandan government to ensure that children, once in school, have an appropriate syllabus. As well as traditional learning, there's an increasing focus now on encouraging children to think creatively and equipping them for their future in today's rapidly changing world.

EDUCATION FOR GIRLS   *With thanks to Marie Chantal Uwimana*

Before independence, education – and particularly that of girls – had not been greatly developed in Rwanda. Even after independence, traditionally minded parents tended to believe that girls should not study scientific subjects, or that after primary school they should stay in the family to work at home or on the land.

After the genocide, the political, social and economic structures of Rwanda were at rock bottom. To rehabilitate, reintegrate and reconcile the country was a colossal task for the new government: in every sector, they were starting from scratch. Among the priorities, education initially came below the more urgent needs of food, clothing and health. Also many girls had been orphaned in the killing and had become single 'parents', head of their household and caring for their younger siblings. Eventually the government set in place mechanisms to support and motivate girls to go to school. The statistics began to change rapidly, and by 2003 the number of girls at primary school equalled that of boys. At secondary school, however, girls continued to be oriented towards the more 'feminine' subjects and their drop-out rate was higher than that of boys.

This has gradually been changing, with more girls than boys now continuing to secondary school, and larger numbers opting for technical subjects. The many women around the country already holding high positions in technical fields can act as role models. FAWE Rwanda, the forward-looking Rwanda chapter of the Forum for African Women Educationalists (w *fawerwa.org*), strongly supports this trend and has a positive relationship with the Ministry of Education. Its assistance includes scholarships and mentoring. Also Rwanda's First Lady, Mrs Jeannette Kagame, has worked very actively to support and motivate girls to make the most of their lives. Their future looks bright.

The state provides 12 years of free education. Some supplementary costs may be incurred (towards food, materials, registration...) but parents in the two lowest income categories are theoretically exempt from these. For others who still struggle, various local and international charities offer support, as do government funding schemes. In addition to state schools, there are many fee-free Church schools that follow the national curriculum. Some (paying) private schools also exist. English is the language of instruction from the third year of primary school; before then it is Kinyarwanda, with English taught as a subject. French is also offered as an option in secondary schools. Before 2009, French was the language of instruction, so the change to English at that point required the many francophone teachers to undergo significant language training.

Better-quality training for teachers in pedagogy, and for school head teachers and district and sector education officers in shool leadership, will really help to support the improved quality of education in Rwanda. Organisations such as VSO (w *vsointernational.org*), UNICEF (w *unicef.org*) and VVOB (w *vvob.be*) are working on these areas, as is the US Peace Corps (w *peacecorps.gov/rwanda*). In addition, the US government is investing heavily in Rwanda's educational sector, specifically to support improved literacy and numeracy in the early years of primary education; while the UK government has done the same more broadly across the whole educational sector. Two areas which have been identified as needing further attention are education for children with special educational needs, and early childhood education.

A noticeable change over the past few years is that far more girls are now attending primary school – in fact their attendance rate outstrips that of the boys – and continuing on to secondary education, also at higher rates than the boys (see box, opposite). In January 2018, the prime minister announced that the double-shift system of state primary schooling, introduced in 2009 to cope with inadequate numbers of teachers, schools and classrooms, is to be phased out, starting immediately at Primary 6 level and extending year-by-year to the lower classes. This means that pupils will now study for 8 hours a day instead of the previous 6 (or in the worst cases only 4), while teachers will work only one daily shift with one group of pupils rather than having two separate (morning and afternoon) groups. There will be heavy investment in buildings and personnel; the stated government plan is to build 28,635 classrooms and to recruit 18,016 primary teachers over seven years.

Further education is also well catered for. In 2013, all Rwanda's institutions of higher learning, including the long-established National University in Huye/Butare, were reorganised under the umbrella of the newly created University of Rwanda system (w *ur.ac.rw*), which today comprises six subject-based colleges spread throughout the country. These consist of agricultural and animal sciences including veterinary medicine, arts and social sciences, business and economics, education, medicine and health sciences, and science and technology. Around 76% of students benefit from full or partial government grants. In some cases distance learning via the internet is possible, enabling students to study in their spare time while holding down a job. There are also several private colleges and institutes, Rwandan and foreign, covering a variety of subjects.

CULTURE

LITERATURE A written language was not introduced until the Europeans arrived in Rwanda at the end of the 19th century, so there is no great tradition of written literature. However, there is a wealth of oral literature in the form of myths, folk stories, legends, poetry and proverbs. These have passed on not only stories but also moral values and historical traditions from generation to generation. Before (and to some extent after) the arrival of the Europeans, the mwami's court was a centre for training young nobles in various art forms, particularly the composition and performance of songs and poems dedicated to valour in warfare and the magnificence of their cattle.

The historian Alexis Kagame wrote extensively about oral poetry and recorded many poems in both Kinyarwanda and French. A display in the National Museum of Rwanda in Huye/Butare (page 158) gives an idea of the intricacy of some poetic structures.

Given the general paucity of Rwandan literature to begin with, it's no great surprise that very little of it has been translated into English, though readers would do very well to check out Scholastique Mukasonga's 2012 novel *Our Lady of the Nile* (*Notre-Dame du Nil*), which was first published in English in 2014, or the autobiographical *Cockroaches* (*Inyenzi ou les Cafards*), first published in 2006 and available in English since 2016.

MUSIC Music is of great importance to all Rwandans, with variations of style and subject among the three groups. Traditionally, Tutsi songs praised excellence and valour; Hutu songs were lighter, sometimes humorous and linked to social occasions; Twa songs related more directly to aspects of their original occupation, hunting. During the time of the monarchy, the court was dominated musically by the royal drummers, and drumming is still of great artistic importance.

A full drum ensemble typically consists of either seven or nine drums. The smallest of these, sometimes called the soprano, which is often (but not invariably) played by the director of the orchestra, sets the rhythm for each tune and is backed up by some or all of the following drums: a tenor, a harmonist alto, two baritones, two bass and two double bass. The other widely used musical instrument is the *lulunga*, an eight-stringed instrument somewhat resembling a harp. It is most often played solo, perhaps as the background to singing or dancing, but may also be used to provide a melodic interlude and/or as a counterpoint to drums.

As far as Rwandan pop goes, much of the music you'll hear in the country comes in from its larger neighbours like Kenya and the DRC, but the country also has a well-loved contemporary music scene of its own that began to coalesce in 1970s' Kigali. It was here that a trailblazing number of (uniformly named) groups like Orchestre Nyampinga, Orchestre Les Fellows, Orchestre Allouette, Orchestre Muhabura, Orchestre Abamararungu, and the most famous by far, Orchestre Impala, played live and recorded numerous cassettes, which are today still regularly dubbed and enjoyed around the country (I very happily found one waiting for me in my rental car). With styles drawing as much influence from traditional Rwandan rhythms and melodies as they did Congolese soukous and rhumba, the bands were wildly popular through the 80s, until the political situation brought about the collapse of Rwanda's music industry and the eventual death of many of the bands' members during the 1994 genocide.

Today, there's a whole crop of new artists in town, and a few older ones as well. Vocalist Cecile Kayirebwa is among the most famous names in Rwandan music, and her retrospectively wistful 1994 album of traditional songs *Rwanda* is her best-known work, but she's been recording and performing ever since. Orchestre Impala, despite having lost all but two of the band's members during the genocide, has even re-formed in recent years to play some dates with younger musicians – you can catch them performing at the Lemigo Hotel in Kigali (page 87) most Friday nights. Closer to the crest of the Rwandan pop wave, the hits of today lean decidedly towards R&B and hip-hop, often with something of a reggae-zouk twist, and young people around the country are sure to have some combination of Kigali's coolest acts like Urban Boyz, Riderman, Butera Knowless, King James, Meddy, and Tom Close on their mobiles; they'll be happy to Bluetooth you some mp3s, assuming you can figure out how.

Finally, though he was born in Belgium, the half-Rwandan francophone pop superstar Stromae is regarded as something of a favourite son in Rwanda, and you're likely to see his videos all over the place as well. While Stromae was a child in Brussels, his father was murdered in the genocide, a tragedy immortalised in the 2013 track '*Papaoutai*' ('Dad, where are you?'). More than 20,000 fans attended his long-anticipated debut concert in Kigali in 2015.

DANCE Dance is as instinctive as music in Rwanda and its roots stretch back through the centuries. As with music, there are variations of style and subject among the three groups. Best known today are the *Intore* dancers, who perform both nationally and internationally. At the time of the monarchy and for centuries before colonisation, the Intore dancers at the royal court were selected young men who had received a privileged education and choreographic training in order to entertain their masters and to perform at special functions. The name *intore* means 'best', signifying that only the best of them were chosen for this honour.

Traditionally their performances consisted mainly of warlike dances, such as the *ikuma* (lance), *umeheto* (bow) and *ingabo* (shield), in which they carried authentic weapons. In the 20th century dummy weapons were substituted, the dances were given more peaceful names and rhythm and movement (rather than warfare) became their main feature. The Intore dancers were divided into two groups. The first group, the *indashyikirwa* or 'unsurpassables', were all Tutsi. The second, the *ishyaka* or 'those who challenge by effort', were Twa led by a Tutsi. A description nearly three-quarters of a century old leads us through a performance:

In the opening movement, the group of Twa advances with measured step. The musicians also are Twa. The dancers form a square or line up in double file. They perform the opening sequence and then a dance representing 'safety'. Next they stand at ease, chanting the exploits of real or imaginary Rwandan heroes. Then come movements representing 'tattooing', 'stability', 'the incomparable' and 'the most difficult case'. At this point the Tutsi dancers leap into the arena, armed, to mingle with the Twa and demonstrate that they deserve the name of 'unsurpassables'. The names of some of their dances translate into English as 'that which puts an end to all discussion', 'the crested crane', 'the exit dance' and 'thanks'.

The costume worn by the Tutsi dancers consists of either a short floral skirt or a leopard skin wound around their legs. Crossed straps decorated with coloured beads are generally worn across the chest. On their heads they wear a fringe of white colobus monkey fur. Depending on the theme of the dance and the region they may carry a bow, a spear or a stick decorated with a long tail of raffia. Around their ankles they wear bells, the sound of which adds to the rhythm of the dance.

The Intore dancers perform regularly today and it's a dramatic spectacle. You may come across them in Kigali, Nyanza, Huye/Butare – or abroad, on one of their tours. Ask at the tourist office in Kigali (page 82) for details of any scheduled performances. The Twa dancers are mainly in the Rubavu/Gisenyi area: ask at the tourist office.

HANDICRAFTS As in other countries, most genuinely traditional handicrafts have a practical use or are decorated forms of everyday objects. An object which gives purely visual pleasure and is unrelated to any function has probably evolved for the tourist market – although it is none the worse for that. In Rwanda the weaving (of bowls, mats, baskets, storage containers, etc) from various natural fibres is particularly fine. The quality of wood-carving is variable, but at best it's excellent. Pottery made by the Twa community is plain but strong and its uncluttered style is attractive. And finally, the starkly geometric *imigongo* paintings (page 299) traditionally made in the far southeast are a uniquely Rwandan art form and make for a visually striking souvenir. For handicrafts in Kigali, see pages 111–13.

The range of non-traditional handicrafts on offer is increasing rapidly, for example stylish bags and other accessories, paintings, jewellery and decorative stationery. In addition, other attractive items are made from recycled materials such as plastic, paper and metal.

SPORT

Football *Chris Frean and Philip Briggs*

Sport is a passion in Rwanda. Volleyball, rugby, swimming, cricket, tennis, golf and even karate are all there, and developing. But the most popular, as throughout most of Africa, is football, whose supporters include President Kagame. In 2018, the RDB even inked a three-year shirt sponsorship deal with London's Arsenal FC.

Several years ago, the future of Rwandan football looked very exciting, with the national side the Amavubi (which translates as 'wasps') qualifying ahead of Uganda and Ghana for the Africa Cup of Nations, and APR reaching the semi-finals of the African Cup Winners' Cup. Since then, unfortunately, Rwandan football has had limited cause for celebration.

The Amavubi finished last in their qualifying group for the Africa Cup of Nations and World Cup (one group for both) in 2006, with the only result of note being a 1–1 home draw to Nigeria. The Wasps fared better in the preliminary rounds of the 2008 Africa Cup of Nations, coming third in their group of four, with two wins in six matches (including a 4–0 home drubbing of Liberia), but still failed to qualify. They started strongly in the 2010 qualifiers for the Africa Cup of Nations, winning three out of four matches in the first round, but failed to quality when finishing last in a strong qualifying group below Egypt, Algeria and Zambia. Rwanda fared even worse in the 2012 qualifiers, conceding 15 goals during the course of losing four out of six fixtures in a relatively weak pool.

With a shock 3-0 victory over Libya and draws with Republic of Congo, Rwanda secured themselves a place at the 2015 Africa Cup of Nations, but they were disqualified shortly afterwards for fielding an ineligible player – perhaps not coincidentally, it was the same one who had scored those all-important goals against Libya. Congo took their place instead, and The Wasps once again sat out the cup; the 2017 Cup proved no better.

Rwanda has enjoyed greater success in the annual CECAFA Cup, which involves 11 East African nations. True, its solitary championship win came way back in 1998, but Rwanda has emerged as runner-up six times between 2003 and 2017, and also taken third place three times since 2001. Despite this, it now stands at a middling 113 in the FIFA World Rankings.

Domestically, the Turbo King National Football League (sponsored by the eponymous brewer) is a popular and hotly contested competition. It has been dominated in recent years by Kigali's APR FC (supported by the president, who sometimes attends home matches), which topped the league 16 times since 1995. The next most successful club is Nyanza's Rayon Sport, which took six of the remaining titles. For details of how to attend a football match in Kigali, see page 109.

Women's rugby Rwanda made history in February 2005 when the inaugural East African international women's rugby match was held against Uganda in the floodlit Amahoro Stadium. A return match was held in Kampala in December of the same year. Unfortunately, Rwanda was thrashed in both matches. However, despite having no dedicated rugby pitches in the country, there's huge enthusiasm nationwide and progress is being made. Rwanda was one of eight teams participating in the inaugural women's tournament staged in Kampala in 2009 by the Confederation of African Rugby, now Rugby Africa (w *rugbyafrique.com*). Young people in Rwanda (both girls and boys) are increasingly being coached and enabled to play; the UK-registered charity Friends of Rwandan Rugby (w *friendsofrwandanrugby.org.uk*; page 68) is strongly involved in this, running an annual Rugby Development Tour to recruit and train new players, and teams from across the country meet regularly at tournaments.

Cricket Occasional and very small-scale cricket was played in Rwanda before the genocide, but the game didn't really catch on until after 1994. Among the thousands of Rwandans who returned home from exile in countries such as Kenya, Uganda and Tanzania, many had grown up playing it, and in 1999 some of them founded the **Rwanda Cricket Association** (RCA). In 2003, Rwanda became an Affiliate Member of the International Cricket Council. The Kigali 'Oval' was the rather bumpy sports field of the Kicukiro Secondary School; to everyone's delight Brian Lara played a brief three-ball innings there in 2009 when visiting Rwanda.

MWAMI KIGELI V (JEAN-BAPTISTE NDAHINDURWA) 1936–2016

The final Mwami of Rwanda, Kigeli V, died in October 2016, aged 80, in the US state of Virginia, after 55 years in exile. Born Jean-Baptiste Ndahindurwa and enthroned as Kigeli V in 1960 amid political turmoil, he reigned for only nine months, leaving Rwanda in 1961 when independence was declared and the monarchy abolished. After finding temporary refuge in various African countries he reached the United States, penniless, in the early 1990s. Initially, as an ex-king, he was something of a novelty: the Monarchist League took him under their wing and he received a few low-key invitations to speak or visit, but Rwanda was little known in the US at the time and interest soon waned.

A humble, genial giant of a man, almost 2.2m tall, Ndahindurwa lived quietly in a complex of low-income housing in Oakton (about 25km west of Washington, DC), dependent on food stamps and Medicaid. The largely working-class neighbours in his apartment block knew him as 'The King of Africa', which caused him gentle amusement, and he kept a supply of chocolates ready for the children who knocked on his door claiming (possibly several times a year) that it was their birthday. The royal court of Rwanda with its ceremonies and adulation must have seemed a universe away.

President Kagame had indicated that he would be welcome back in Rwanda, the land that he loved, with no remnants of his former royal status. Reluctant to return as a commoner but with no taste for the stress of a power struggle that might damage his country, he remained living modestly in Oakton, and as time passed the practicality of a visit receded. He returned home at the very end, however; his body was flown over and taken to Nyanza, ancient residence of Rwanda's kings, where his brother (Mwami Mutara III) is also buried. Jean-Baptiste Ndahindurwa, long ago Mwami Kigeli V of Rwanda, was back where his heart belonged.

In any post-conflict country, sport is an important therapy and unifier. Almost 5,000 Rwandans have now taken up the game, and cricket is played competitively at international, club and school levels. A club league, three club tournaments, a schools competition and a university competition make up the 11-month formal cricketing calendar. In addition, thousands of young Rwandans, both male and female, play cricket in orphanages, primary and secondary schools and universities. The Rwandan boys' and girls' teams compete well within the East and Central African region. Visitors with cricketing prowess are welcome to join in.

In 2011, the **Rwanda Cricket Stadium Foundation** (RCSF; w *rcsf.org.uk*) was formed. (Its website is the source of much of this information.) Run by both Rwandan and British members, it set out to build the country's first dedicated national cricket ground. A suitable space was found just south of Kigali in 2014, and the 4.5ha, US$1.5 million Gahanga Cricket Stadium was triumphantly inaugurated in October 2017, in a grand ceremony with President Kagame and 200 international cricketers on hand to cut the ribbon. Cricket is well rooted in the country now, and looks set to develop as fast as means allow. (Also see the box on page 108.)

2

Practical Information

WHEN TO VISIT

Rwanda can be visited at any time of year. The long dry season, June to September, is the best time for tracking gorillas in the Volcanoes National Park and for hiking in Nyungwe Forest, since the ground should be dry underfoot and the odds of being drenched are minimal. This should not be a major consideration for any reasonably fit and agile travellers unless they are planning to hike to Virunga peaks such as Bisoke or Karisimbi, in which case the rainy season is best avoided. The dry season is also the best time to travel on dirt roads, and when the risk of malaria is lowest.

There are two annual rainy seasons. The big rains run from mid-February to early June, and the small rains from mid-September to mid-December. Rainfall, especially over the mountains, can be heavy during these two periods – particularly from March to May, although it is still perfectly feasible to travel at these times of year, and, for those visiting at short notice, it is far easier to obtain a gorilla permit at the last minute.

As for the two dry seasons, the major one lasts from June to September and the shorter from December to February. However, the climate is not uniform throughout the country: it is generally drier in the east than in the west and north. On occasion, the volcanoes of the north may be capped by snow, and evenings in Kigali can call for a sweater – as do days anywhere in the highlands should you happen to hit a cold snap! Nevertheless, every season is good for swimming and tanning on the banks of Lake Kivu.

An advantage of travelling during the rainy season is that the scenery is greener, and the sky less hazy (at least when it isn't overcast), a factor that will be of particular significance to photographers. The wet season is also the best time to track chimps in Nyungwe (in the dry season they may wander further off in search of scarce food), while the months of November to March will hold the greatest appeal for birders, as resident birds are supplemented by flocks of Palaearctic migrants.

TOURIST INFORMATION AND SERVICES

The **Rwanda Development Board** (RDB; ☏ *0252 576514/502350;* e *reservation@ rwandatourism.com;* w *rwandatourism.com*) doubles as both tourist office and national parks authority. It operates three offices in Kigali, one at its headquarters in a high-rise on the junction of KN 5 Road (Bd de l'Umuganda) and KG 9 Avenue (Nyarutarama Rd), a city-centre office in the Grand Pension Plaza building near the UTC, and one in the airport arrivals hall that was closed for renovations when we researched this edition; it also has offices in Rubavu/Gisenyi, Musanze/Ruhengeri, Kinigi (the headquarters to Volcanoes National Park) and at Nyungwe National Park. These all stock a fair range of booklets and maps, and the offices in Kigali,

Musanze, and Gisenyi can issue permits for gorilla tracking and certain other activities in the national parks (see box, page 60). Regular updates are posted on our website **w** bradupdates.com/rwanda.

TOUR OPERATORS AND TRAVEL AGENTS

All those listed below will arrange gorilla visits plus international travel. Most offer both scheduled tours and tailor-made trips. More will start to cover the rest of Rwanda during the life of this guide. The many operators in neighbouring countries (Uganda, etc) are deliberately not all listed, because readers in those countries are less likely to need them. Tour operators based in Rwanda are listed in the chapter on Kigali (pages 82–3). Alternatively, **w TravelLocal.com** is a reputable UK-based agent whose website allows customers to communicate directly with selected local operators, as well as book their trips.

UK (national code +44)

Aardvark Safaris ✆01980 849160; **e** mail@ aardvarksafaris.com; **w** aardvarksafaris.co.uk

Abercrombie & Kent ✆012 4238 6460; **e** info@ abercrombiekent.co.uk; **w** abercrombiekent.co.uk

Absolute Africa ✆020 8742 0226; **e** absaf@ absoluteafrica.com; **w** absoluteafrica. com. Overland truck & camping safaris.

Africa Travel Centre ✆020 7843 3500; **e** info@ africatravel.co.uk; **w** africatravel.com

Churchill Safaris ✆01844 290000; **m** 07516 409335; **e** gcarr@churchillsafaris.com; **w** churchillsafaris.com

Exodus ✆020 8772 3936; **e** sales@exodus.co.uk; **w** exodus.co.uk

Expert Africa ✆020 3405 6666; **e** info@ expertafrica.com; **w** expert.africa

Gane and Marsall ✆01822 600600; **e** info@ ganeandmarshall.com; **w** www.ganeandmarshall. com. See ad, page 34.

Imagine Africa ✆020 3141 2800; **e** info@imagineafrica.co.uk; **w** www.imaginetravel.com

Inspired Journeys ✆+255 784 554 044; **e** info@ inspired-journeys.com; **w** inspired-journeys.com

Journeys Discovering Africa ✆0800 088 5470; **e** enquiries@journeysdiscoveringafrica.com; **w** journeysdiscoveringafrica.com. See ad, 4th colour section.

Natural World Safaris ✆01273 691642; **e** sales@ naturalworldsafaris.com; **w** naturalworldsafaris.com

Naturetrek ✆01962 733051; **e** info@naturetrek. co.uk; **w** naturetrek.co.uk

Rainbow Tours ✆020 7666 1276; **e** info@ rainbowtours.co.uk; **w** rainbowtours.co.uk. See ad, inside-front cover.

Reef & Rainforest Tours ✆01803 866965; **e** mail@reefandrainforest.co.uk; **w** reefandrainforest. co.uk

Steppes Travel ✆01285 880980; **e** enquiry@ steppestravel.co.uk; **w** steppestravel.co.uk

Terra Incognita Ecotours ✆0800 098 8454; **e** info@ecotours.com; **w** ecotours.com. See ad, 1st colour section.

Tribes Travel ✆01473 890499; **e** info@tribes. co.uk; **w** tribes.co.uk. See ad, page 34.

Volcanoes Safaris UK office: **m** 07554 828321; **e** salesuk@volcanoessafaris.com; **w** volcanoessafaris.com (offices in UK, USA, Uganda & Rwanda – also see details on page 82)

Wildlife Worldwide ✆01962 302086; **e** reservations@wildlifeworldwide.com; **w** wildlifeworldwide.com

Zambezi Safari & Travel Company ✆01752 878858; **e** info@zambezi.com; **w** zambezi.com

USA AND CANADA (national code +1)

Africa Adventure Company ✆800 882 9453 (toll free US & Canada); **e** safari@africanadventure. com; **w** africa-adventure.com

Churchill Safaris US: ✆562 434 0325; **e** info@ churchillsafaris.com; Canada: ✆587 710 4057; **e** chris@churchillsafaris.com; **w** churchillsafaris.com

Expert Africa ✆800 242 2434 (toll free); **e** info@ expertafrica.com; **w** expert.africa

Steppes Travel ✆855 203 7885 (toll free); **e** enquiry@steppestravel.co.uk; **w** steppestravel. co.uk

Terra Incognita Ecotours ✆855 326 8687; **e** info@ecotours.com; **w** ecotours.com

Volcanoes Safaris ✆212 967 5895; **e** salesus@ volcanoessafaris.com; **w** volcanoessafaris.com

AFRICA
Uganda *(national code +256)*
Adventure Trails Ltd ☎312 261 930/704 333 358;
e info@gorilla-safari.com; w gorilla-safari.com
Churchill Safaris ☎705 111 943/704 671
283/703 499 528; e info@churchillsafaris.com;
w churchillsafaris.com
The Far Horizons ☎312 264 894; e info@
thefarhorizons.com; w thefarhorizons.com
Kagera Safaris m 0782 477992; e info@
kagerasafaris.com; w kagerasafaris.com. See ad,
page 304.
Magic Safaris ☎414 342 926; e info@magic-
safaris.com; w magic-safaris.com. See ad, page 129.

The Uganda Safari Company ☎414 251
182/787 433 710; e info@safariuganda.com;
w safariuganda.com. See ad, 4th colour section.
Volcanoes Safaris ☎414 346 464; e salesug@
volcanoessafaris.com; w volcanoessafaris.com

South Africa *(national code +27)*
Ker & Downey ☎21 201 2484; e enquiries@ker-
downeyafrica.com; w ker-downeyafrica.com
Pulse Africa ☎11 325 2290; e info@pulseafrica.
com; w pulseafrica.com. See ad, page 69.
Wild Frontiers ☎11 702 2035; e reservations@
wildfrontiers.com; w wildfrontiers.com
XA African Safaris ☎21 434 7184; e lisa@
xasafaris.com; w xasafaris.com

RED TAPE

Check well in advance that you have a valid **passport**, and that it won't expire within six months of the date you intend to leave Rwanda. Should your passport be lost or stolen, it will generally be easier to get a replacement if you travel with a photocopy of the important pages.

As of 1 January 2018, citizens of all countries can purchase a 30-day, single-entry visitor visa on arrival for US$30 at the airport or any land border with no advance application. Multiple entry and other classes of visa still have to be applied for in advance at a Rwandan mission abroad. More information on alternative visa classes is available at w migration.gov.rw.

A good option for those wanting to explore the region further is the East Africa tourist visa (EAC visa; ☎ *0252 576514/580814*; e *reservation@rwandatourism. com*; w *visiteastafrica.org*). Launched in 2014, this multi-lateral initiative, set up between Rwanda, Uganda and Kenya, allows for unlimited travel between the three countries for 90 days. Note: Tanzania and Burundi are both part of the EAC but were not yet participating in the common visa scheme at the time of writing; this could easily change (Burundi has declared their intention to join for 2019), so check out w bradtupdates.com/rwanda for the latest. Thus, you can cross back and forth between Rwanda, Uganda and Kenya as many times as you like within the 90 days, but unless Tanzania and Burundi join the scheme, a visit to either of these countries will invalidate your EAC visa, and the same is true for a visit to the DRC. Applications for the EAC visa have to be made with the country you will be entering first, and while the cost is a standardised US$100, the application procedure may vary slightly from country to country.

For its part, Rwanda requires travellers from any country who intend to use the EAC visa to apply at either a Rwandan embassy abroad or online before arriving. If your online application is successful, you'll get a confirmation number via email – bring a printed copy of this document to any port of entry, where the visa will be issued. Payment can be made either online when completing the application or in cash upon arrival. More information is available at w migration.gov.rw, and all applications and payments are now made through the new one-stop government services portal at w irembo.gov.rw. Foreigners with a long-term work/residency permit in Rwanda, Uganda, or Kenya are entitled to visa-free travel between the three countries.

To extend your stay, it's usually easiest to pop out to a neighbouring country and buy another 30-day visa on your return. If that's not an option, changes in visa status, extensions, and all other enquiries can be directed to the Directorate General of Immigration and Emigration in Rwanda (m *078 815 2222/889 9971*; e *visa@migration.gov.rw*).

If there is any possibility that you'll want to drive or hire a vehicle while you're in the country, it's worth organising an **international driving licence** (via one of the main motoring associations in a country in which you're licensed to drive), which you may be asked to produce together with your original licence. You may be asked at borders for an **international health certificate** (also known as a yellow card) showing you've had a **yellow-fever shot**.

For security reasons, it's advisable to detail all your important information in one file that you can forward to the email address you use when travelling, and also print and distribute through your luggage. The sort of things you want to include are travel insurance policy details and 24-hour emergency contact number, passport number, details of relatives or friends to be contacted in an emergency, bank and credit card details, camera and lens serial numbers, etc. It's also handy to carry a photo of your suitcase or other luggage, to save trying to describe it if it's misplaced by an airline.

EMBASSIES AND CONSULATES

A comprehensive list of embassies and consulates is available at w embassypages. com/rwanda. Regional embassies and consulates in Kigali are also listed below.

E Burundi KG 7 Av, Kigali; \0252 587940/3/4; e ambabukgl1@yahoo.fr

E Congo, Democratic Republic (DRC) KN 16 Av; \0252 575999; m 078 300 7318; e ambardckigali@yahoo.fr

E Congo, Republic KG 220 St; m 078 991 1026/992 3341, 073 489 0748; e ambacokigali@ gmail.com

E Ethiopia KG 15 Av, Kigali; \0252 601057; w www.kigali.mfa.gov.et

E Kenya KG 7 Av, Kigali; \0252 583334; e info@ kenyahighcomkigali.org; w kenyahighcomkigali.org

E South Africa 1370 KG 7 Av, Kigali; \0252 551300; e kigali.admin@dirco.gov.za; w dirco. gov.za

E Tanzania KG 9 Av; \0252 505400; e tanzrep@tanzanrep.gov.rw/kigali@nje.go.tz; w nje.go.tz

E Uganda KG 569 St, \0252 503537/8; e embassy@ugandaembassy.rw/kigali@mofa. go.ug; w kigali.mofa.go.ug

GETTING THERE AND AWAY

BY AIR The rapidly expanding national airline **RwandAir** (m *078 817 7000*; e *info@ rwandair.com/reservations@rwandair.com*; w *rwandair.com*; *see ad, 4th colour section*) now flies between Kigali and London Gatwick via Brussels three times a week, as well as regularly connecting to Mumbai, Dubai and Guangzhou – there's even talk of a new flight to New York City in 2019. In Africa, RwandAir connects Kigali to Juba (South Sudan), Accra (Ghana), Lusaka (Zambia), Harare (Zimbabwe), Entebbe (Uganda), Johannesburg (South Africa), Nairobi and Mombasa (Kenya), Bujumbura (Burundi), Dar es Salaam, Mwanza and Kilimanjaro (Tanzania), Addis Ababa (Ethiopia), Brazzaville (Republic of Congo), Libreville (Gabon) and Lagos (Nigeria). Their secondary hub is in Cotonou (Benin), from where they connect to a variety of West African capitals. RwandAir has a reservations office in the Union Trade Centre in central Kigali (though this is eventually supposed to relocate across the street to the Ubumwe Grande building), as well as in all the countries to which it flies (see website for contact details), and bookings can also be made online.

Other operators that fly directly to Kigali include **Kenya Airways** (w *kenya-airways.com*), **Brussels Airlines** (w *brusselsairlines.com*), **KLM** (w *klm.com*), **Ethiopian Airways** (w *flyethiopian.com*), **South African Airways** (w *flysaa.com*), **Turkish Airlines** (w *turkishairlines.com*) and **Qatar Airways** (w *qatarairways.com*). All of these carriers operate a good network of intra- and intercontinental flights – travellers coming from Australasia will do best to aim for Johannesburg, Doha, Dubai or Nairobi, while those from Europe and the Americas are best off flying via Brussels, Istanbul or Addis Ababa. For those tagging a visit to Rwanda on to a safari in northern Tanzania, it is worth knowing that **Coastal Aviation** (w *coastal.co.tz*) operates a flight between Kigali and Arusha, Manyara or the Serengeti by inducement.

Kibale International Airport lies less than 10km from central Kigali, and taxis are available to/from the city centre (page 77). Work on the long-planned Bugesera International Airport, about 40km south of the capital (reached along the road to Nyamata), was officially started in August 2017; in truly ambitious Rwandan style the first phase of construction is slated for completion after just over a year, at the end of 2018. Unfortunately, it remains unclear when and in what capacity the new airport might begin to receive flights, so be sure to double-check progress at w bradtupdates.com/rwanda if you'll be travelling in 2019 or beyond.

Air tickets

A number of travel companies are good sources of cut-price tickets, as well as offering various other services. London is the best place for cheap fares, hence the bias of the list below! It isn't exhaustive but should give you a start. As shown on their websites, most of the companies listed also have offices in other countries.

Africa Travel Centre 227 Shepherds Bush Rd, Hammersmith, London W6 7AS; \ 020 7387 1211; e info@africatravel.co.uk; w africatravel.co.uk

Flight Centre \ (booking) 0870 499 0040; w flightcentre.com. Flight Centre has several offices in London & elsewhere in UK. It offers cut-price airfares & insurance services. Also in Australia, New Zealand, South Africa & USA.

STA Travel \ 0333 321 0099; e enquiries@statravel.co.uk; web (very comprehensive): w statravel.co.uk. Has 65 branches in UK & over 450 worldwide.

Trailfinders 194 Kensington High St, London W8 7RG (one-stop travel shop); \ 020 7938 3939; web (very comprehensive): w trailfinders.com. Also in Ireland, Australia, etc.

WEXAS Dorset Hse, 27–45 Stamford St, London, SE1 9NT; \ 020 7590 0610; w wexas.com. There is an annual subscription to WEXAS (*for current details:* \ *020 7581 8768; e mship@wexas.com*) but membership gives you access to a whole range of useful services (good rates for hotels & airport parking, use of airport lounges, travel insurance, visas…) as well as an excellent travel magazine, *Traveller*.

OVERLAND

Four countries border Rwanda: Burundi to the south, the Democratic Republic of the Congo (DRC) to the west, Uganda to the north and Tanzania to the east. Assuming peaceful conditions, frontier formalities aren't too much of a hassle – but nor are they standardised. Smaller crossings are typically open from 06.00 to 18.00, but Kagitumba and Cyanika (both to Uganda) stay open until 20.00, and larger ones like the *Grande Barrière*/*corniche* in Gisenyi (to Goma/DRC), Rusizi (to Bukavu/DRC), Rusumo (to Tanzania), and Nemba (to Burundi) stay open until 22.00. The Gatuna border post with Uganda now operates 24 hours a day. Don't count on official exchange facilities being available; there are likely to be 'black-market' moneychangers around, but you should decide in advance what rate you're prepared to accept.

Owing to the political crisis in Burundi and simmering tensions between the two countries, public transport hasn't been allowed to cross the border since 2016 and all trips to/from Burundi currently (as of 2018) require a change of vehicle at the border. Several companies that previously ran services to Bujumbura will now transport you as far as the Akanyaru or Nemba border crossings a couple of times daily, including Yahoo Car Express (m *072 842 6005/675 0202*) and Volcano Express (m *072 200 0166*). Expect through services to Bujumbura to resume should the situation stabilise.

If the above wasn't already an indicator, do note that while bus travel is generally reckoned to be safe, the security situation in Burundi remains uncertain and it would be worth seeking out up-to-date information locally before setting out.

Despite the ongoing unrest in the DRC, it is normally safe to travel in the immediate Rwandan border area, which includes the Congolese border towns of Goma and Bukavu and their neighbouring national parks, Virunga and Kahuzi-Biega. Still, you're strongly advised to check the current situation first as this can change. Regular minibus services run between Kigali and Rubavu/Gisenyi (for Goma) and Rusizi/Cyangugu (for Bukavu). On both sides of each border there is accommodation reasonably close by. From Goma or Bukavu, it is also currently possible to visit Idjwi Island (page 351). Travelling further into the DRC remains highly risky.

Crossing to and from Uganda is simple. Direct buses and minibus-taxis connect Kampala and Kigali, taking around 12 hours if you do the trip in one leg. The best operator along this route is probably Modern Coast (m *073 888 7333/7555;* w *modern.co.ke*), who connect Kigali to several destinations in Kenya via Kampala. Another option is Jaguar Executive Coaches (m *+256 414 251855/078 281 1128 (Uganda), 078 940 1499/436 6113/340 8791;* e *jaguar6796@gmail.com*), who connect Kampala to both Kigali and Musanze/ Ruhengeri at least twice a day for around Rfr10,000 one-way. There is a limited number of local minibus-taxis along the roughly 50km road between Kisoro in southwest Uganda and Musanze/Ruhengeri in northwest Rwanda (an hour's trip, not allowing for changing vehicles and other delays at the Cyanika border post, which might add another hour to the journey). It is also easy to travel by minibus-taxi between Kabale, the largest town in southwest Uganda, and Kigali, though once again you might have to change vehicles at the border – this trip should take about 5 hours in total. Entering from Uganda in your own vehicle is relatively hassle-free.

Crossing between Rwanda and Tanzania is something of a slog, due to the poor (but improving) state of roads and lack of large towns in northwest Tanzania. The Rusumo border post lies about 160km from Kigali, roughly a 3-hour trip by minibus-taxi, with the possibility of staying the night *en route* at the town of Ngoma, 60km from the border, or at the surprisingly pleasant accommodation on offer in Rusumo itself, on the Rwandan side of the river (page 303). The closest Tanzanian town to the border is Nyakasanza, from where it's 90km to Nyakanazi, where travellers bound for Kigoma branch to the west, and those

Straightforward enough so far, but in practice the transition of names has been a slow and inconsistent process, one that has posed a dilemma to the authors of the guidebook for all subsequent editions. When the fourth edition was researched, most minibus-taxis, for instance, still used the old name, but that has changed completely over subsequent years. By contrast, maps and other references from outside the country still stick almost exclusively to the old name, while most recent publications within Rwanda use the new name (though the RDB map of the Congo-Nile Trail, launched in November 2011, still uses the old names).

Whatever the official situation, our guiding principle for this guidebook has to be pragmatism. For this edition, we have decided to use the new names throughout; though to make this transition easier and more accessible we have regularly included 'reminders', in the form of the new name followed by the old as in Huye/Butare or Musanze/Ruhengeri. It is not the most elegant solution, but it does have the advantage of being easy to use and foolproof. Today the popularity of the new names is inconsistent across the country – some cities, like Cyangugu/ Rusizi and Gisenyi/Rubavu are still more commonly referred to by their old names, whereas others, like Ruhengeri/Musanze, seem to have been more readily adopted. Thus, for reasons of clarity and consistency we have decided to retain the system of 'reminders' across the country for this seventh edition of the guide.

To add to the confusion, street names in Kigali and several major towns have recently been changed to an alphanumeric system and, though the bevy of new street signs on every corner makes navigation much less of a chore, if you need to ask directions you'll still find that Rwandans tend to orient themselves according to landmarks rather than street names, and the old names will be remembered for some time to come.

for Mwanza head east. To Mwanza, it's possible to go via the towns of Geita and Sengerema or a longer route via Kahama. Matunda Express (m *078 846 9632*) connects Kigali and Kahama reasonably regularly for Rfr8,000. Either way, the route is mostly tarmacked and served by some manner of public transport, but get a very early start if you want to cover the 385km from the border to Mwanza in a day, and don't be shocked if it takes two. A rail link between Rwanda and Tanzania is planned, but it will be some years yet before this is up and running.

HEALTH *with Dr Felicity Nicholson*

Rwanda itself isn't a particularly unhealthy country for tourists and you'll never be far from some kind of medical help. The main towns have hospitals (for anything serious you'll be more comfortable in Kigali) and all towns of any size have a pharmacy, although the range of medicines on sale may be limited. In Kigali, the pharmacy at King Faisal Hospital in Kacyiru is open 24 hours.

Away from Kigali, district hospitals and health centres are spread countrywide. A health centre generally has around five nurses, supported by a doctor and community health workers. In rural areas traditional medicine is also widely used. The ratios of about 1,300 inhabitants per nurse and 12,000 per doctor are high; however, in July 2012 former US president Bill Clinton announced a seven-year programme, supported by the medical faculties of 13 US universities, to train up existing medical personnel so that they in turn can train effectively. The growing private sector has more than 310 clinics and dispensaries. The incidence of HIV/ AIDS is hard to estimate accurately but seems at last to be falling, thanks to preventative measures and the wider availability of antiretroviral drugs.

After accidents, the most serious health threat to travellers in Rwanda is malaria. Akagera National Park and other low-lying parts of the east qualify as high-risk malarial areas, especially in the rainy season. The risk exists but is far lower in highland areas such as Kigali, Butare, Nyungwe National Park, the Virunga Mountains and foothills, and the Lake Kivu region. Nevertheless, all visitors to Rwanda should take preventative measures against malaria, and be alert to potential symptoms both during their trip and after they return home.

Other less common but genuine health threats include the usual array of sanitation-related diseases – cholera, giardia, dysentery, typhoid, etc – associated with the tropics, and bilharzia, which can only be caught by swimming in freshwater habitats inhabited by the snail that carries the disease.

If you do get ill in Rwanda, bear in mind that the most likely culprit – as in most parts of the world – will be the common cold, flu or travellers' diarrhoea, none of which normally constitutes a serious health threat. However, travellers with overt cold- or flu-like symptoms might not be allowed to track gorillas or chimpanzees, both of which are susceptible to infectious airborne human diseases and may lack our resistance.

PREPARATIONS Sensible preparation will go a long way to ensuring your trip goes smoothly. Particularly for first-time visitors to Africa, this includes a visit to a travel clinic to discuss matters such as vaccinations and malaria prevention. A full list of current travel clinic websites worldwide is available on w.istm.org. For other journey preparation information, consult w travelhealthpro.org.uk (UK) or w wwwnc.cdc.gov/travel (US). Information about various medications may be found on w netdoctor.co.uk/travel. All advice found online should be used in conjunction with expert advice received prior to or during travel. The Bradt website now carries a health section online (w *bradtguides.com/africahealth*) to help travellers prepare for their African trip, elaborating on most points raised below, but the following summary points are worth emphasising:

- Don't travel without comprehensive medical **travel insurance** that will cover hospitalisation and fly you home in an emergency. Be aware, if you plan to use cycles or motorbike taxis in Rwanda, that not all policies cover you for this form of transport.
- Make sure all your **immunisations** are up to date. Proof of vaccination against yellow fever is needed for all travellers over one year of age entering the country from a yellow-fever endemic area. The risk of yellow fever in Rwanda itself is considered to be low, so for most people it is not necessary to get the yellow-fever vaccine. It is unwise to travel in the tropics without being up to date on tetanus, polio and diphtheria (now given as an all-in-one vaccine, Revaxis), measles, mumps and rubella (MMR). Immunisation against hepatitis A and typhoid will also be recommended, while those against meningitis ACWY, hepatitis B and rabies may be.
- The biggest health threat is **malaria**. There is no vaccine against this mosquito-borne disease, but a variety of preventative drugs are available, including mefloquine, atovaquone/Proguanil (eg: Malarone) and the antibiotic doxycycline. The start and stop times of the malaria tablets vary and can be as little as two days before and seven days after (Malarone) to two to three weeks before and four weeks after (mefloquine). The most suitable choice of drug varies depending on the individual and the country they are visiting, so visit your GP or a travel clinic for medical advice. If you will be spending a long time in Africa, and expect to visit remote areas, be aware that no preventative drug is 100% effective, so carry a cure too. It is also worth noting that no homeopathic prophylactic for malaria exists, nor can any traveller acquire effective resistance to malaria. Those who don't make use of preventative drugs risk their life in a manner that is both foolish and unnecessary.
- Though advised for everyone, a **pre-exposure rabies vaccination**, involving three doses taken over a minimum of 21 days, is particularly important if you intend to have contact with animals, or are likely to be 24 hours away from medical help.
- Anybody travelling away from major centres should carry a **personal first-aid kit**. Contents might include a good drying antiseptic (eg: iodine or potassium permanganate), Band-Aids, suncream, insect repellent, a pain killer such as paracetamol, antifungal cream (eg: Canesten), ciprofloxacin or norfloxacin (for severe diarrhoea), antibiotic eye drops, tweezers, condoms or femidoms, a digital thermometer and a needle-and-syringe kit with accompanying letter from a health-care professional.
- Bring any **drugs or devices relating to known medical conditions** with you. That applies both to those who are on medication prior to departure, and those who are, for instance, allergic to bee stings, or are prone to attacks of asthma. You should also bring a copy of the prescription with you and ensure that your medication is clearly labelled with your name and that it is in the original packaging.
- Prolonged immobility on long-haul flights can result in **deep-vein thrombosis (DVT)**, which can be dangerous if the clot travels to the lungs to cause pulmonary embolus. The risk increases with age, and is higher in obese or

pregnant travellers, heavy smokers, those taller than 6ft/1.8m or shorter than 5ft/1.5m, and anybody with a history of clots, recent major operation or varicose veins surgery, cancer, a stroke or heart disease. If any of these criteria apply, consult a doctor before you travel.

COMMON MEDICAL PROBLEMS

Travellers' diarrhoea At least half of those travelling to the tropics/developing world will experience a bout of travellers' diarrhoea during their trip; the newer you are to exotic travel, the more likely you will be to suffer. By taking precautions against travellers' diarrhoea you will also avoid typhoid, cholera, hepatitis, dysentery, worms, etc. Rule one in avoiding diarrhoea and other sanitation-related diseases is arguably to wash your hands regularly, particularly before snacks and meals, and after handling money. As for what food you can safely eat, a useful maxim is: PEEL IT, BOIL IT, COOK IT OR FORGET IT. This means that fruit you have washed and peeled yourself should be safe, as should hot cooked foods. However, raw foods, cold cooked foods, salads, fruit salads prepared by others, ice cream and ice are all risky. It is rarer to get sick from drinking contaminated water but it happens, so stick to bottled water, which is widely available.

If you suffer a bout of diarrhoea, it is dehydration that makes you feel awful, so drink lots of water and other clear fluids. These can be infused with sachets of oral rehydration salts, though any dilute mixture of sugar and salt in water will do you good, for instance a bottled soda with a pinch of salt. If diarrhoea persists beyond a couple of days, it is possible it is a symptom of a more serious sanitation-related illness (typhoid, cholera, hepatitis, dysentery, worms, etc), so get to a doctor. If the diarrhoea is greasy and bulky, and is accompanied by sulphurous (eggy) burps, one

AVOIDING MOSQUITO AND INSECT BITES

The *Anopheles* mosquitoes that spread malaria are active at dusk and after dark. Most bites can thus be avoided by covering up at night. This means donning a long-sleeved shirt, trousers and socks from around 30 minutes before dusk until you retire to bed, and applying a DEET-based insect repellent to any exposed flesh. It is best to sleep under a net, or in an air-conditioned room, though burning a mosquito coil and/or sleeping under a fan will also reduce (though not entirely eliminate) bites. Travel clinics usually sell a good range of nets and repellents, as well as Permethrin treatment kits, which will render even the tattiest net a lot more protective, and helps prevent mosquitoes from biting through a net when you roll against it. These measures will also do much to reduce exposure to other nocturnal biters. Bear in mind, too, that most flying insects are attracted to light: leaving a lamp standing near a tent opening or a light on in a poorly screened hotel room will greatly increase the insect presence in your sleeping quarters.

It is also advisable to think about avoiding bites when walking in the countryside by day, especially in wetland habitats, which often teem with diurnal mosquitoes. Wear a long, loose shirt and trousers, preferably 100% cotton, as well as proper walking or hiking shoes with heavy socks (the ankle is particularly vulnerable to bites), and apply a DEET-based insect repellent to any exposed skin. If you are particularly prone to mosquito bites you might consider spraying clothes with an insecticide (permethrin), for example EX4 clothing spray, before you go. The permethrin will survive a few washes.

likely cause is giardia, which is best treated with tinidazole (four x 500mg in one dose, repeated seven days later if symptoms persist).

Other insect-borne diseases Although malaria is the insect-borne disease that attracts the most attention in Africa, and rightly so, there are others, most too uncommon to be a significant concern to short-stay travellers. These include dengue fever and other arboviruses (spread by diurnal mosquitoes), sleeping sickness (tsetse flies) and river blindness (blackflies). Bearing this in mind, however, it is clearly sensible, and makes for a more pleasant trip, to avoid insect bites as far as possible (see box, page 44). Two nasty (though ultimately relatively harmless) flesh-eating insects associated with tropical Africa are *tumbu* or *putsi* flies, which lay eggs, often on drying laundry, that hatch and bury themselves under the skin when they come into contact with humans, and jiggers, which latch on to bare feet and set up home, usually at the side of a toenail, where they cause a painful boil-like swelling. Drying laundry indoors and wearing shoes are the best way to deter this pair of flesh-eaters. Symptoms and treatment of all these afflictions are described in greater detail on Bradt's website (w *bradtguides.com/africahealth*).

Skin infections Any mosquito bite or small nick in the skin provides an opportunity for bacteria to foil the body's usually excellent defences; it will surprise many travellers how quickly skin infections start in warm humid climates and it is essential to clean and cover even the slightest wound. Creams are not as effective as a good drying antiseptic such as dilute iodine, potassium permanganate (a few crystals in half a cup of water), or crystal (or gentian) violet. One of these should be available in most towns. Prickly heat is a fine pimply rash that can be alleviated by cool showers, dabbing (not rubbing) skin dry, using talc, and sleeping naked under a fan or in an air-conditioned room. Fungal infections also get a hold easily in hot moist climates, so wear 100% cotton socks and underwear and shower frequently.

Sun damage Overexposure to the sun can lead to short-term sunburn or sunstroke, and increases the long-term risk of skin cancer. Keep out of the sun during the middle of the day and, if you must expose yourself to the sun, build up gradually from 20 minutes per day. Be especially careful of exposure in the middle of the day and of sun reflected off water, and wear a T-shirt and lots of waterproof suncream. Use a sunscreen with an SPF of 25 or more and a UVA of four or more stars when swimming. Cover up with long, loose clothes and wear a hat when you can. The glare and the dust can be hard on the eyes, too, so bring UV-protecting sunglasses and, perhaps, a soothing eyebath.

HIV/AIDS Rates of HIV/AIDS infection are high in most parts of Africa, and other sexually transmitted diseases are rife. Condoms (or femidoms) greatly reduce the risk of transmission.

OTHER DISEASES
Bilharzia or schistosomiasis *with thanks to Dr Vaughan Southgate of the Natural History Museum, London, and Dr Dick Stockley, The Surgery, Kampala*
Bilharzia or schistosomiasis is a disease that commonly afflicts the rural poor of the tropics. Two types exist in sub-Saharan Africa – *Schistosoma mansoni* and *Schistosoma haematobium*. It is an unpleasant problem that is worth avoiding, though can be treated if you do get it. This parasite is common in almost all water sources in Rwanda – even places advertised as 'bilharzia-free', such as Lake Kivu. The most risky shores will be close to places where infected people use water, wash clothes, etc. Ideally, however, you should avoid swimming in any fresh water other than an artificial pool. If you do swim, you'll reduce the risk by applying DEET insect repellent first, staying in the water for under 10 minutes, and drying off vigorously with a towel. Bilharzia is often asymptomatic in its early stages, but some people experience an intense immune reaction, including fever, cough, abdominal pain and an itching rash, around four to six weeks after infection. Later symptoms vary but often include a general feeling of tiredness and lethargy. Bilharzia is difficult to diagnose, but it can be tested for at specialist travel clinics, ideally at least six weeks after likely exposure. Fortunately, it is easy to treat at present.

Other sanitary diseases Travellers in Rwanda are at risk of suffering from a bout of the usual array of sanitation-related diseases – cholera, giardia, dysentery, typhoid, worms, etc – associated with the tropics. Preventative measures are the same as those for travellers' diarrhoea.

ANIMALS
Rabies Rabies can be carried by all mammals (beware the village dogs and small monkeys in the parks) and is passed on to man through a bite, scratch or a lick. You must always assume any animal is rabid, and seek medical help as soon as possible. Meanwhile scrub the wound with soap under a running tap or while pouring water from a jug. Find a reasonably clear-looking source of water (but at this stage the quality of the water is not important), then pour on a strong iodine or alcohol solution of gin, whisky or rum. This helps stop the rabies virus entering the body and will guard against wound infections, including tetanus. Whether or not you underwent pre-exposure vaccination, it is vital to obtain post-exposure prophylaxis as soon as possible after the incident. However, the treatment needed is much simpler (and is more likely to be available in Rwanda) if you have had the vaccine prior to exposure. Death from rabies is probably one of the worst ways to go, and once you show symptoms it is too late to do anything – the mortality rate is 100%.

Snakebite Snakes rarely attack unless provoked and bites to travellers are unusual. You are less likely to get bitten if you wear stout shoes and long trousers when in the bush. Most snakes are harmless and even venomous species will only dispense venom in about half of their bites. If bitten, then, you are unlikely to have received venom; keeping this fact in mind may help you to stay calm. Many so-called first-aid techniques do more harm than good: cutting into the wound is harmful; tourniquets are dangerous; suction and electrical inactivation devices do not work. The only treatment is antivenom. At the time of writing this is only known to be available at the hospital in Kigali.

USEFUL CONTACTS IN KIGALI

⊞ **King Faisal** (or Faycal) ✆ 0252 582421/585397; emergency ✆ 0252 588888; e faisal@rwanda1.com; w kfh.rw

⊞ **Central Hospital of the University of Kigali** ✆ 0252 575406/575555; e chuck. hospital@chuckigali.org; w chk.org.rw

⊞ **Plateau Polyclinic** ✆ 0272 578767; m 078 830 1630; e pcp@mtnonline.rw; w polycliniqueduplateau.rw

⊞ **Polyfam** m 078 887 7225; e polycliniquefamiliale@yahoo.com; w polyfam.co

For emergency dental treatment, contact the **Adventist Dental Clinic** (✆ *0252 582431*), while optometric services are available at **Eye Care Optical** (m *078 886 7121*; e *eyecareoptical.rwanda@yahoo.com*; �006f *Eye Care Optical Rwanda*). For further medical listings, see w www.theeye.co.rw and the US embassy's list of recommended medical professionals in Rwanda at w rw.usembassy.gov/u-s-citizen-services/doctors.

SAFETY

THEFT So far as tourists need be concerned, Rwanda is among the most crime-free of African countries. Kigali is a very safe city, even at night, though it would probably be courting trouble to stumble around dark alleys with all your valuables on your person. Be aware, too, that this sort of thing can change very quickly: all too often, as tourism volumes increase, so too does opportunistic and petty crime.

The following security hints are applicable anywhere in Africa:

- Most casual thieves operate in busy markets and bus stations. Keep a close watch on your possessions in such places, and avoid having valuables or large amounts of money loose in your daypack or pocket.
- Keep all your valuables and the bulk of your money in a hidden money belt. Never show this money belt in public. Keep any spare cash you need elsewhere on your person – a button-up pocket on the front of the shirt is a good place as money cannot be snatched from it without the thief coming into your view. It is also advisable to keep a small amount of hard currency (ideally cash) hidden in your luggage in case you lose your money belt.
- Where the choice exists between carrying valuables on your person or leaving them in a locked room I would favour the latter option (thefts from locked hotel rooms are relatively rare in Africa). Obviously you should use your judgement on this and be sure the room is absolutely secure. Bear in mind that some travellers' cheque companies will not refund cheques which were stolen from a room.
- Leave any jewellery of financial or sentimental value at home.

John Osman

When you bring your vehicle into Rwanda you need to buy a Carte d'Entrée. It's not expensive, but police checkpoints often ask to see this slip of paper, so don't lose it!

Compulsory vehicle insurance is also available at the border, just after you go through Rwandan customs. You may be approached by an insurance salesman even while you're still going through the customs registration for the car, but we preferred to go to one of the official offices set up in that area rather than to deal with a guy on the street. The insurance process is quick and easy. Minimum coverage is for three days, then one week, and so on. Again it is not prohibitively expensive. The procedure is all carried out in English, in case anyone is worried about having to cope in French.

Police at checkpoints on Rwandan roads may ask to see if you have a fire extinguisher and triangles (which you're supposed to set up on the road to warn of an accident) in your car. Luckily we'd been warned of this beforehand, so we'd bought a little Russian-made fire extinguisher in Kampala for around US$6 and a pair of triangles for about US$10. The police were perfectly satisfied with that.

USEFUL CONTACTS
Police 112 or m 078 831 1155
Ambulance 912
Fire brigade 111

OTHER HAZARDS People new to exotic travel often worry about tropical diseases, but it is accidents which are most likely to carry you off. Road travel isn't as dangerous in Rwanda as in some other African countries but still accidents aren't uncommon, and the number of vehicles is increasing; so be aware and do what you can to reduce risks. For example, try to travel during daylight hours and refuse to be driven by anyone who is drunk. Always heed local advice about where you should (or should not) travel, or about areas where you should take particular care. At the time of writing, Rwanda is a relatively safe country– but, sadly, it has been seen elsewhere that an increase in tourism can lead to an increase in opportunistic crime. Be as sensible in Rwanda as (I hope!) you would be in any other strange country about carrying your cash discreetly and not flaunting jewellery, and (particularly in towns) about where you walk after dark. Also be sensible in hotels and guesthouses: don't leave tempting items too readily accessible.

HASSLES
Overcharging and bargaining Tourists may sometimes need to bargain over prices, but this need is often exaggerated. Hotels, restaurants and supermarkets generally charge fixed prices, and deliberate overcharging is so rare that it's not worth challenging a price unless it is blatantly ridiculous. In other situations – mostly markets or in the street – you're bound to be asked a higher price than the vendor will expect, and a certain degree of bargaining is considered normal. It is, however, important to keep this in perspective.

Minibus conductors may occasionally ask tourists for higher fares than normal. The way to counter this is to watch what other people are paying, or to ask a fellow passenger what the fare should be. The main instance where bargaining is essential is when buying handicrafts or curios. However, the fact that a curio seller is open to negotiation does not mean that he or she was initially trying to rip you off. Vendors will generally quote a starting-price knowing full well that you are going to bargain it down – they'd probably be startled if you didn't – and it is not necessary to respond aggressively. It is impossible to say what size of reduction you should expect (some people say that you should offer half the asking price and be prepared to settle at around two-thirds, but my experience is that curio sellers are far more whimsical than such advice allows for). The sensible approach is to ask the price of similar items at a few different stalls before you actually contemplate buying anything.

In fruit and vegetable markets and stalls, bargaining is often the norm, even between Africans, and the healthiest approach to this sort of haggling is to view it as an enjoyable part of the travel experience. There will normally be an accepted price-band for any particular commodity. To find out what it is, listen to what other people pay (it helps if you know some Kinyarwanda) and try a few stalls – a ludicrously inflated price will drop the moment you walk away. When buying fruit and vegetables, a good way to feel out the situation is to ask for a bulk discount or a few extra items thrown in. And bear in mind that the reason why somebody is reluctant to bargain may be that they asked a fair price in the first place.

Above all, don't lose your sense of proportion. No matter how poor you may feel, it is your choice to travel on a tight budget. Most Rwandans are much poorer than you will ever be, and they do not have the luxury of choosing to travel. If you find yourself quibbling with an old lady selling a few piles of fruit by the roadside, stand back and look at the bigger picture. There is nothing wrong with occasionally erring on the side of generosity.

Begging To anyone who knows Africa it should come as no surprise to see beggars on the streets; the surprise, in view of Rwanda's recent past, is that they aren't more numerous. Nor are they often aggressive. For a charity (one of several) helping Kigali's street kids, see *rYico* on page 69. The maimed, handicapped and very old tell an obvious story. I can't advise you what to do about them. It's true that if you give to one you risk being surrounded by a dozen – but sometimes it's hard to walk on by. Rwandans themselves often recommend that you give something; they and the country's budget have little enough to spare. If you don't believe in giving cash, see pages 68–9, which list some charities where your money will be well used.

Bribery and bureaucracy For all you read about the subject, bribery is not the problem to travellers in Africa that it is often made out to be. Those who are most often asked for bribes are people with private transport; but this seldom happens in Rwanda. Visit the DRC, however, and it may become more of an issue.

There is a tendency to portray African bureaucrats as difficult and inefficient in their dealings with tourists. As a rule, this reputation says more about Western prejudices than it does about Africa. A big determining factor in the response you receive from officials, will be your own attitude. If you walk into every official encounter with an aggressive, paranoid approach, you are quite likely to kindle the feeling held by many Africans that Europeans are arrogant and offhand in their dealings with other races. Instead, try to be friendly and patient, and remember that the person to whom you are talking does not speak English (or French) as a first language and may thus have difficulty understanding you. Treat people with respect rather than disdain, in Rwanda as elsewhere, and they'll tend to treat you in the same way.

As a lone female traveller, I have experienced far less hassle and anxiety in Rwanda during my several visits than I have in many other countries. I travelled all over the country by public transport feeling completely safe. There was a refreshing absence of 'smart Alecs' trying to engage me in dubious conversation.

In one town, a young man (Congolese, as it turned out) overheard me asking directions to the guesthouse and spontaneously walked with me, chatting occasionally, to make sure I found it safely. Then he shook my hand and went off. Another day I gave my driver, who had had a long hard morning, Rfr2,000 to go and buy a good lunch, and he spontaneously handed me Rfr1,000 change when he returned. Once I left my unlockable duffel bag with a smiling girl in a small wooden drinks kiosk near a minibus stop while I explored a village; when I returned to collect it, it had been stowed safely in a corner and the girl's baby was gurgling happily on top. I felt a kind of 'sisterhood', particularly with village women – if I smiled it was always reciprocated, although often shyly, and I always asked a woman first if I needed help or directions.

In Kigali I've spent a lot of time walking both in and outside the city centre and never felt threatened, although there are some poorer areas which (and a Rwandan woman friend agrees with me) become scarier after dark. This applies to men too, of course, but women are generally seen – rightly or wrongly! – as a target less likely to put up resistance. The rule here is to take the same sensible precautions you'd take in any capital city, and then relax.

As a matter of courtesy, watch what the local women wear and don't expose parts of yourself that they leave covered, particularly in village areas. In business areas people are smartly dressed; I've been glad of bringing a skirt and some crumple-free tops. Be sensitive to the fact that people here have suffered a great deal; if someone is reluctant to talk or to answer questions, don't push it. Remember that in shops it's polite to give some kind of greeting like 'good morning' or 'hello' (in whatever language) before asking for what you want.

You may not be as fortunate as I've been. Nor do I suggest that you drop your guard and behave overconfidently. There can be bad apples in any barrel. Would-be Lotharios exist in any country and they tend to home in on female travellers. In fact, one night in Kigali a strange man did knock on my bedroom door at 11pm, but it turned out that he needed money to take a sick street kid to hospital (yes, honestly!).

I place Rwanda very high on the list of relatively hassle-free countries where good manners, honesty and trust are the order of the day – and of course this should be a two-way process.

WHAT TO TAKE

In 1907, when the Duke of Mecklenburg set off on an expedition through Rwanda with a group of scientific researchers, he carried (or rather his team of bearers carried) numerous cases of soap, candles, rope and cigars, as well as such items as salt, wire, beads and woollen blankets to barter with the natives. You could probably cut down on this a little.

In fact Rwanda is a relatively well-stocked little country, in terms of clothing, toiletries, stationery, batteries and so forth. Unless you have particularly exotic tastes (or your schedule is too crowded to allow you time for shopping), you should be able to find most of the everyday items a traveller needs, even if the brands are unfamiliar. Obviously you should bring a supply of any personal medication (and some extra, in case your return home is delayed); as well as enough sunscreen. Otherwise, unless you plan to go way off the beaten track (or you need camping/trekking gear, which is in shorter supply), don't feel that you must fill your bag up with a lot of semi-useful items 'just in case'. Buying things locally helps Rwanda's economy!

The comments below apply as much to any neighbouring African countries you may pass through or visit as they do to Rwanda.

CARRYING YOUR LUGGAGE If you are unlikely to carry your luggage for any significant distance, a conventional suitcase is fine. Make sure it is tough and durable, and seals well, so that its contents survive bumpy drives and boisterous baggage handlers at airports. Travellers with a lot of valuable items should use a bag that can be padlocked easily. Of course it can still be slashed open, but that would be highly unusual in Rwanda – you are more likely to encounter casual theft to which a padlock would be a real deterrent.

On public transport, a durable backpack is the most practical solution, ideally with several pockets. A small daypack will be useful for gorilla tracking and other walks, and to stow any breakable goods on your lap during long drives – anything like an mp3 player or camera will suffer heavily from vibrations on rutted roads.

CLOTHES Try to keep your clothes to a minimum, especially if you are travelling with everything on your back. Bear in mind that you can easily and cheaply replace worn items in markets. The minimum is one or possibly two pairs of trousers and/ or skirts, one pair of shorts, three shirts or T-shirts, one light sweater or similar, one heavy sweater or similar, a waterproof jacket during the rainy season, enough socks and underwear to last five to seven days, one solid pair of shoes or hiking boots for walking, and one pair of sandals, flip-flops or other light shoes.

It's widely held that jeans are not ideal for African travel, since they are bulky to carry, hot to wear and take ages to dry. In their favour, however, jeans do have the advantages of durability and comfort, and of hiding the dust and dirt that tend to accumulate during public transport rides – and they are excellent for gorilla tracking and other forest walks. A good alternative is light cotton trousers, which dry more quickly and weigh less, but try to avoid light colours, as they show dirt more easily. Skirts are best made of a light natural fabric such as cotton. T-shirts are lighter and less bulky than proper shirts, though the top pocket of a shirt (particularly if it buttons up) is a good place to carry spending money in markets and bus stations, since it's easier to keep an eye on than a trouser pocket. A couple of sweaters or sweatshirts will be necessary in places such as Nyungwe, which get chilly at night. Remember that mosquitoes and tsetse flies in some areas show a liking for dark blue.

Socks and underwear *must* be made from natural fabrics. Bear in mind that re-using sweaty undergarments will encourage fungal infections such as athlete's foot, as well as prickly heat in the groin region. Socks and underpants are light and compact enough to make it worth bringing a week's supply. As for footwear, only if you're a serious off-road hiker should you consider genuine hiking boots, since they are very heavy whether on your feet or in your pack. A good pair of walking shoes, preferably leather with good ankle support, is a good compromise, and gaiters are recommended for hiking. For gorilla tracking, old gardening gloves can be handy when you're grabbing for handholds in thorny vegetation.

Another factor in selecting your travel wardrobe is local sensibilities. In Rwanda, which is predominantly Christian, this isn't the concern it would be in several other parts of Africa, but modest dress is nevertheless recommended. For women, the ideal garment is a knee-length skirt, though long trousers – while unconventional

WHICH BINOCULARS ARE BEST FOR ME?

Binoculars are a fabulous tool for getting close to nature – seeing animals well without disturbing them. But with hundreds of models available, and prices ranging from £20 to £2,000, selecting the right pair can feel daunting – whether it is an inaugural purchase or an upgrade. This guide aims to help.

BUYING BINOCULARS: THE BASICS To start, three guiding principles. First, what's right for me may not be for you. Binoculars are a personal thing, so never buy without testing. Second, prepare for trade-offs between weight, performance, practicality and price. Third, buy the best you can afford. You get what you pay for. My Swarovski 'bins', bought in 2004, remain as brilliant as on day one.

Binoculars are described in off-putting jargon. So let's explain the basics. Binocular names include two numbers, respectively the magnification factor and objective lens diameter (in mm). An 8x56 binocular magnifies objects by eight times through a 56mm-wide lens. Larger numbers usually mean heavier and more cumbersome binoculars, which are less convenient for travelling. I advise sticking to the ranges 7–10 (magnification) and 30–56 (lens). Avoid apparent marvels such as 20x50 'ex-army' binoculars, which are rubbish and heavy!

The ratio between the two numbers influences how much light the binocular lets in – and thus how bright the image is in dingy conditions. The larger the ratio, generally, the better such low-light performance. I favour a ratio of 1:4 (eg: 8x32) or 1:5 (eg: 8x42); but up to 1:7 (eg: 8x56) may enhance use in shady forests or at twilight.

Numbers aside, binoculars are either 'roof-prisms' (H-shaped, slimline) or 'porro-prisms' (M-shaped, chunky). For tight budgets, porro-prisms arguably offer better value. Although pricier, roof-prisms tend to be better quality, easier to handle and more compact for travelling. All things being equal, they get my vote.

in rural Rwanda – are unlikely to give offence. For men, shorts are fine, but it is considered more respectable to wear trousers. Walking around in a public place without a shirt is unacceptable.

OTHER USEFUL ITEMS Many backpackers, even those with no intention of camping, carry a **sleeping bag** as a fallback for rooms with dirty bedding. A **padlock** is useful if you have a pack that is lockable. Combination locks are reputedly easier to pick than conventional padlocks, but potential thieves in Rwanda will have far less experience with them.

If you're interested in natural history, a pair of compact binoculars is very useful, and it needn't be much heavier or bulkier than a pack of cards. Binoculars are essential if you want to get a good look at birds, or to watch distant mammals in game reserves. For most purposes, 7x21 compact binoculars will be fine, though some might prefer 7x35 traditional binoculars for their larger field of vision. Serious birdwatchers will find a 10x magnification more useful.

Your toilet bag should at the very minimum include **soap** (secured in a plastic bag or soap holder unless you enjoy a soapy toothbrush!), **shampoo**, **toothbrush** and **toothpaste**. This sort of stuff is easy to replace as you go along, so there's no need to bring family-sized packs. Men will probably want a **razor**. Women should carry enough **tampons** and/or **sanitary pads** to see them through at least one heavy period, since these items may not always be immediately available. Nobody should

TESTING BINOCULARS: WHAT TO LOOK FOR Pick them up. Is the weight evenly distributed? Can you hold them steady? Spectacle-wearers need eyecups that roll or slide so that the binocular offers 14–17mm of 'eye relief'. Now look through the optics. You want a wide field of view – but no need to go overboard. Ensure the image is sharp, ideally right to the edge of vision. How close can you focus? If you anticipate watching insects, choose a pair that focuses on your feet. Check that colours look natural – with no blue or yellow cast. Finally, examine a backlit object: if it is fringed yellow or purple, choose another pair.

WHAT MAKES BINOCULARS REALLY GOOD? Consider each candidate binocular's finer characteristics, which sort wheat from chaff across years of service. 'Fully multi-coated' lenses and prisms are recommended; they maximise light transmission, contrast and clarity. Look for an image so sharp it sears your eyes. Extra-low dispersion (ED) or high-density (HD) lenses correct colour fringing. Depth-of-field is important: you want to minimise time spent refocusing from a close animal to a distant one. Durability is key: seek high-strength but ideally lightweight housing. Weatherproofing is vital to keep out dust and water. Finally, if things go wrong, you want the manufacturer to stand by its product, offering a lifetime warranty. There's a reason why my Swarovskis go on … and on …

James Lowen (w jameslowen.com) is a wildlife expert, award-winning writer and author of four Bradt wildlife titles.

forget to bring a **towel**, or to keep handy a roll of **loo paper**, which although widely available at shops and kiosks cannot always be relied upon to be present where it's most urgently needed.

You should carry a small **medical kit**, the contents of which are discussed in the section on health, as are **mosquito nets**. For those who wear **glasses**, it's worth bringing a spare pair, though in an emergency a new pair can be made up cheaply and quickly in most Rwandan towns, provided that you have your prescription available. If you wear **contact lenses**, be aware that the various fluids are not readily available in Rwanda, and, since many people find the intense sun and dust irritate their eyes, you might consider reverting to glasses.

Other essentials include a **torch (flashlight)**, a **penknife** and a compact **alarm clock** for those early morning starts (assuming this isn't already handled by your phone). Some travellers carry **games** – most commonly a pack of cards, less often chess, draughts or travel Scrabble. A lot of washbasins in Rwanda lack **plugs**, so one of those 'universal' rubber plugs that fit all sizes of plughole can be useful.

MONEY

The unit of currency is the **Rwandan franc** (Rfr), which comes in Rfr5,000, 2,000, 1,000 and 500 notes and Rfr100, 50, 20, 10, 5 and 1 coins. The exchange rate at the time of going to print was around Rfr860 to the US dollar, Rfr1,012 to the euro and Rfr1,148 to the British pound, depending on where the transaction took place. Most local services are best paid in local currency, but there are exceptions, such as gorilla-tracking fees and some upmarket hotels, which require payment in US dollars or another hard currency. Throughout this guide, prices are quoted in local currency except where the institution in question quotes rates in another currency such as US dollars or euros, in which case we follow their lead. Prices are correct for 2018, but will almost certainly be subject to inflation during the lifespan of this edition.

ORGANISING YOUR FINANCES Normally there are three ways of carrying money: hard cash, travellers' cheques and credit/debit cards. However, travellers' cheques are of little to no practical use in Rwanda and Visa is the dominant card, though carrying Mastercard is no longer the source of frustration that it once was. There are dozens of ATMs where international Visa cards can be used to draw local currency at branches of Bank of Kigali, EcoBank, Kenya Commercial Bank (KCB), I&M Bank and others all over Kigali, as well as at the same banks in most other large towns. Even so, if the electricity is down, or the computers or server are offline, then this service will be temporarily unavailable. Mastercard is now theoretically (though readers still occasionally report having trouble) accepted at ATMs from three banks: GT Bank, Kenya Commercial Bank (KCB), and Equity Bank, of which GT Bank has the widest network of the three and is represented in nearly all major cities.

It is possible to pay bills with credit cards at many upmarket hotels throughout the country and other main tourist centres, but not elsewhere. If you are relying on using a card, then it's best to check what cards your hotel accepts when you make your booking. It's worth noting here too that the RDB permit-booking process is now handled through the Irembo web portal, which accepts both Visa and Mastercard – see box, page 60.

That leaves cash. The US dollar is the most widely accepted foreign currency, but all main currencies should be exchangeable in Kigali, whether in banks or in official or private forex bureaux. If you do bring US dollars, be aware that US$100 and US$50 bills attract a significantly better rate than smaller-denomination bills, and few if any institutions will accept notes issued before 2009, or that are torn or marked in any way. After the US dollar, the euro and pound sterling are the most widely recognised currencies in Kigali, with the advantage that there are no problems related to changing older notes. Away from Kigali, US dollars cash is the only foreign currency easily exchangeable outside of banks.

This is a changing situation. And if you don't want to carry too much cash, or your budgeting has fallen apart and you need to be bailed out, there are Western Union facilities all over the place. This isn't cheap – the cost depends on the amount being transferred – but it's quick and secure. Any Rwandan francs left over at the end of your trip can be changed back into dollars, euros or whatever by banks, forex bureaux or moneychangers.

FOREIGN EXCHANGE All Rwandan banks have branches in Kigali and there's at least one bank in each other main town, but these generally deal in cash only

CHANGING MONEY AT BORDERS

The black markets that once thrived in East Africa were killed off some years ago, but you might still need to exchange money on the street at some international borders, so that you have enough local currency to pay for transport to the next town, for a room when you get there, and – should you expect to arrive outside banking hours or over the weekend – to cover other expenses until the next banking day. As a rule you won't get the greatest rate of exchange at any border, which is fair enough, considering that moneychangers, like banks, profit by offering different rates of exchange in either direction. So there's no sense in exchanging significantly more money than you'll require before you reach a bank or forex bureau. The only exception is when you have a surfeit of cash from the country you're leaving and no intention of returning there – the border may be the last place you can unload it.

Many private moneychangers are incidental con artists, so be prepared. Check the exchange rate in advance and calculate roughly what sum of local currency you should expect. Put whatever bills you intend to change in a pocket discrete from your main stash of foreign currency before you arrive at the border. And don't stress too much if you are offered a slightly lower rate than might be expected, since pushing too hard for a good rate carries the risk of weeding out the honest guys so you end up dealing with a con artist. And be wary of a quick-talking moneychanger trying to exploit the mind-boggling decimal shifts involved in many African currency transactions.

Should you be surrounded by a mob of yelling moneychangers, pick any one of them and tell him that you will only discuss rates when his pals back off. Having agreed a rate, insist on taking the money and counting it before you hand over, or expose the location of, your own money. Should the amount be incorrect, it is almost certainly phase one of an elaborate con trick, so safest to hand it back and refuse to have anything further to do with that person. Alternatively, if you do decide to continue, then re-count the money after it is handed back to you and keep doing so until you have the correct amount counted in your hand (not theirs!) – some crooked moneychangers possess such sleight of hand they can seemingly add notes to a wad right in front of your eyes while actually removing a far greater number of notes. Only when you are sure you have the right amount should you hand over your money.

and rates tend to be poorer than in the capital. There are also several private bureaux de change (known locally as forex bureaux) in Kigali, which generally offer slightly better rates than banks against cash (especially if you bargain), not to mention a quicker service, but don't handle travellers' cheques. Banking hours are approximately 08.00–noon and 14.00–17.00 Monday–Friday (some banks stay open longer), and 08.00–noon Saturday. Private forex bureaux keep slightly longer hours than banks. Both are closed on Sundays and public holidays.

There are private forex bureaux in several other large towns, particularly those that lie close to a border crossing (eg: Musanze/Ruhengeri, Rubavu/Gisenyi and Rusizi/Cyangugu) and they are usually as efficient as their counterparts in Kigali.

BUDGETING

Any budget will depend so greatly on how and where you travel that it is almost impossible to give sensible advice in a general travel guide. As a rule, readers who are travelling at the middle to upper end of the price range will have pre-booked most of their trip, which means that they will have a good idea of what the holiday will cost them before they set foot in the country. Pre-booked packages do vary in terms of what is included in the price, and you are advised to check the exact conditions in advance, but generally the price quoted will cover everything but drinks, tips and perhaps some meals.

For budget travellers, Rwanda is no longer one of the cheaper countries in Africa. Genuine budget accommodation is thin on the ground; in many towns it can be difficult to find a basic room for much under US$15 and you'll often need to spend two or three times that amount for something less basic. Throughout the country, a soft drink in a local bar or shop will cost you less than US$0.50 and a 700ml beer slightly more than US$1, but these things cost a lot more in a hotel or restaurant that caters primarily to Westerners. Outside of Kigali, a simple meal in a local restaurant might cost around US$3–4 (and often cheaper for a buffet), a main course in a restaurant catering more to Western palates seldom costs less than US$8, while snacks such as brochette and chips fall somewhere in between. Public transport is cheap – typically about US$1.50–2 per 50km – and distances are relatively small. Taking the above figures into account, the most scrupulous budget travellers should bank on spending around US$30 daily (a bit less for couples, as accommodation costs less per person than for single travellers) and more like US$75–100 if you plan on staying in moderate hotels and eating in proper restaurants. This doesn't include expensive one-off activities such as gorilla tracking or visiting other national parks.

GETTING AROUND

BY AIR RwandAir (page 38) operates a daily flight between Kigali and Kamembe (for Rusizi/Cyangugu). They used to also serve Rubavu/Gisenyi, but this route has been cancelled for several years now and there are no other scheduled domestic flights.

Alternatively, depending on how far your budget stretches, **Akagera Aviation** (✆0252 580234; m 078 830 8382; e office@akageraaviation.com; w akageraaviation.com) offers charter helicopter transfers to all corners of Rwanda, along with sightseeing tours over Kigali starting at US$340 for 30 minutes.

SELF-DRIVE Several travel agencies in Kigali rent out saloons and 4x4s, with or without drivers. For their contact details, see pages 82–3. Rates vary according to

APPROXIMATE DISTANCES BETWEEN MAIN TOWNS

In kilometres

	Kigali	Huye	Gicumbi	Muhanga	Ngoma	Karongi	Rubavu	Nyamagabe	Musanze	Rusizi
Kigali		125	60	50	105	125	175	145	120	240
Huye/Butare	125		185	85	175	150	210	29	165	120
Gicumbi/Byumba	60	185		105	160	180	175	210	105	185
Muhanga/Gitarama	50	85	105		150	75	130	100	85	175
Ngoma/Kibungo	105	175	160	150		225	275	250	230	325
Karongi/Kibuye	125	150	180	75	225		85	160	130	105
Rubavu/Gisenyi	175	210	175	130	275	85		225	60	190
Nyamagabe/Gikongoro	145	29	210	100	250	160	225		190	100
Musanze/Ruhengeri	120	165	105	85	230	130	60	190		235
Rusizi/Cyangugu	240	120	185	175	325	105	190	100	235	

whether you'll be driving outside Kigali, and whether fuel is included. A 4x4 can cost from US$120 to US$200 per day including driver, depending on its type/size. If the deal excludes fuel, bear in mind that this is not cheap – more than US$1.25 per litre – and that most 4x4s have a heavy consumption.

If you rent a self-drive vehicle, be aware that Rwanda follows the continental and American custom of driving on the right side of the road. Check the vehicle over carefully and ask to take it for a test drive. Even if you're not knowledgeable about the working of engines, a few minutes on the road should be sufficient to establish whether it has any seriously disturbing creaks, rattles or other noises. Check the condition of the tyres and that there is at least one spare tyre, better two, both in a condition to be used should the need present itself. Ask to be shown the wheel spanner and jack, check that all parts of the latter are present, and ensure that the licence is valid for the duration of your trip. Ask also to be shown filling points for oil, water and petrol and check that all the keys do what they are supposed to do. Once on the road, check oil and water regularly in the early stages of the trip to ensure that there are no existing leaks. See also box, page 48, for further survival tips.

Most trunk roads in Rwanda are surfaced and in reasonable condition, including the main road from Kigali to Rusizi/Cyangugu via Huye/Butare; to Rubavu/Gisenyi and Kinigi via Musanze/Ruhengeri; to Rusumo via Ngoma/Kibungo; to Karongi/Kibuye via Muhanga/Gitarama; to the Ugandan border via Gicumbi/Byumba or Umutara; and the newly completed lakeshore route from Rusizi/Cyangugu to Karongi/Kibuye and Rubavu/Gisenyi. Roads are generally good but there are still some pot-holed sections along most routes which, together with the winding terrain and the tendency for Rwandans to drive at breakneck speeds and overtake on sharp or blind corners, necessitate a more cautious approach than one might take at home.

The unsurfaced roads most likely to be used by tourists include the approach roads to Akagera National Park (and roads within the park) and the roads around lakes

Burera and Ruhondo. All of these are in variable condition, and should be passable in a saloon car when dry, though a 4x4 would certainly be preferable. Among the last significant trunk routes in Rwanda to be surfaced, the Karongi–Rubavu road was completed in 2017 and is now a delightful 65km of winding tarmac.

Do bear in mind that unsurfaced roads tend to vary seasonally, with conditions most difficult during the rains and least so towards the end of the dry season. Even within this generalisation, an isolated downpour can do major damage to a road that was in perfectly good nick a day earlier, while the arrival of a grader can transform a pot-holed 4x4 track into one navigable by any saloon car.

The main hazard on Rwandan roads, aside from unexpected pot-holes, is the road-hog mentality of most drivers. Until recently, minibuses in particular would regularly flout the rules of the road, ignoring speed limits and overtaking on blind corners. Since 2016, however, it's been mandatory for all public transport vehicles to be fitted with speed governors, capping their maximum velocity at 60km/h. Otherwise, speed limits (60–80km/h) are commonly ignored except when enforced by road conditions. On all routes, be alert to banana-laden cyclists swaying from the verge, and livestock and pedestrians wandering blithely into the middle of the road. Putting one's foot to the floor and hooting like a maniac is the customary Rwandan approach to driving through crowded areas; driving rather more defensively than you would at home is the safer one!

When it comes to overtaking (and given Rwanda's topography and winding roads, there's usually plenty of that going on) be aware that cars or trucks in front of you will often use their indicators to signal whether it's (in their estimation) safe for you to pass them or not. A blinking left indicator means that it's not safe to overtake (or that they're overtaking or making a left themselves), while a blinking right indicator is meant to say that you've got room to overtake them, though it always pays to be cautious here, as their definition of enough room and yours may differ!

A peculiarly African road hazard – one frequently taken to unnecessary extremes in Rwanda – is the giant sleeping policeman, which might be signposted in advance, might be painted in black-and-white strips, or might simply rear up without warning like a 30cm-tall macadamised wave. It's to be assumed that the odd stray bump will exist on any stretch of road that passes through a town or village, so slow down at any looming hint of urbanisation.

MOUNTAIN BIKE ROUTES

Long-time Rwanda resident and bicycling aficionado Kaspar Kundert (e *k. kundert@esri.rw*) has compiled an impressively thorough 400+ page guide to mountain biking in Rwanda, which would be an invaluable resource for anyone planning to explore the roads and trails of Rwanda by bicycle (or foot, for that matter). It contains nearly 60 documented tracks downloadable in GPX format, which can then be followed with a GPS. The guide is freely available at the links below:

- Biking in Rwanda Guide as a PDF (15 MB): w bit.ly/18aojnb
- GPX file (containing all tracks in one large file): w bit.ly/1Jk1smH
- Web application 'Find a Bike Route in Rwanda' (no downloadable GPX files): w bit.ly/1Bd2TQ4
- Elevation profiles of the documented tracks online: w bit.ly/1xUx8q0

Rwandans, like many Africans, display an inexplicable aversion to switching on their headlights except in genuine darkness – switch them on at any other time and every passing vehicle will blink its lights back at you in bemusement. In rainy, misty or twilight conditions, it would be optimistic to think that you'll be alerted to oncoming traffic by headlights, or for that matter to expect the more demented element among Rwandan drivers to avoid overtaking or speeding simply because they cannot see more than 10m ahead. It's best to avoid driving at night, since a significant proportion of vehicles lack functional headlights, while others go around with their lights permanently on blinding full beam!

MOUNTAIN BIKING OR CYCLING The relatively short distances between tourist centres and the consistently attractive scenery should make Rwanda ideal for travelling by mountain bike. These cannot easily be bought locally, so you would have to bring one with you (some airlines are more flexible than others about carrying bicycles; you should discuss this with them in advance). More and more Rwandans are using cycles now, and if you ask around you should be able to find some for hire – but check the brakes carefully and carry a repair kit. Most scheduled midibuses in Rwanda today do not have roof racks, but you may be able to purchase enough seats to carry your bicycle inside one should you need to. Minor roads vary in condition, but in the dry season you're unlikely to encounter any problems. Several of the more off-the-beaten-track destinations mentioned in this book would be particularly attractive to cyclists. The best contact for bicycle tours, particularly in the Lake Kivu region, is Rwandan Adventures in Rubavu/Gisenyi (page 217). They offer guided and unguided tours, and also sell reliable new and used bicycles tailored to Rwandan conditions. Rwanda Bike Tours (e *tom@rwandabiketours. com*; w *rwandabiketours.com*) is another excellent operator which runs specialised group cycle trips to Rwanda throughout the year. The Africa Rising Cycling Centre (page 243), just outside of Musanze, offers tours on professional-grade bicycles, often led by members of Rwanda's national cycling team.

HITCHING This is an option on main roads, but you should expect to pay for lifts offered by Rwandans. Some minor roads have little traffic so you could face a long wait.

PUBLIC TRANSPORT
Boat and rail There are no rail services in Rwanda, although a rail link with Tanzania has been under discussion for some time and Rwanda one day also hopes to connect to the standard-gauge railway recently completed between Mombasa and Nairobi.

Public ferry services on Lake Kivu, operated by the COTRALAKI Cooperative, restarted in 2014 and ply the waters between Rusizi/Cyangugu, Karongi/Kibuye, and Rubavu/Gisenyi twice a week (see the individual chapters for details). In the DRC, there are several boats connecting Goma and Bukavu, including the Ihusi Express, a reliable, fast ferry service with two daily departures, which also stops on Idjwi Island.

It's also possible to rent local dugouts for short excursions on the lake, and motor boats are available for hire at Karongi, Rusizi and Rubavu. Small boats can be used to get around the smaller lakes, such as Burera, Ruhondo or Muhazi, by making an informal arrangement with the boat owner.

Road The main mode of road transport is shared **mini-/midibuses**; these connect all major centres (and most minor ones) and leave from each town's dedicated bus station (*gare taxi/minibus*). The larger routes are for the most part all covered by private companies operating scheduled midibuses (Toyota Coasters or something

BOOKING A GORILLA PERMIT

The one thing that almost all tourists to Rwanda want to do is track gorillas in Volcanoes National Park, and it is no longer the case that you can just pitch up in Kigali and be almost certain of obtaining a permit for the next day, or failing that, the day after. Particularly during the peak season of June to September, and again over the Christmas and New Year holiday period, it is now often the case that all 96 gorilla permits available daily are booked up months in advance for several days running – a scenario that is likely to become increasingly normal as greater volumes of tourists visit Rwanda.

What this means is that any visitors with a tight schedule should book their permits as far in advance as possible. If a tour operator arranges your trip, they will also arrange your gorilla permit and will normally include it in the cost of the trip (or specify it as an extra). But if you are travelling independently, you will need to arrange it yourself. There are three approaches to doing this. The first is to get a reliable local tour operator to act as a go-between and buy the permit on your behalf, which can save a lot of hassle, though the operator will add a small (and deserved) service charge to the normal cost of US$1,500.

Independent travellers can book directly through the Rwandan government's new Irembo web portal (w *irembo.gov.rw/rolportal/web/rdb/tourist-permit*). Introduced in 2017, Irembo is a digital e-government platform through which Rwandans can do everything from requesting birth certificates to paying traffic fines. Visitors can use it to book all relevant national park permits. The process is quite straightforward: first choose the activity, date and number of participants. The system will then alert you to how many places remain on the chosen day, and after filling in some biographical details for each participant, online payment can be made with either Visa or Mastercard. If you have questions, RDB staff are available by email and telephone to assist with bookings. It is also possible to book and pay for any other activities and park entrance fees at the same time. Once complete, simply print your confirmation and arrive at your activity at the designated time. Note that we've recently heard of copycat websites springing up claiming to offer gorilla permits, so be very sure to only book through the official Irembo website listed above.

You can also book all permits in person at an RDB office (page 82). As all bookings are now processed through the Irembo system, RDB staff mostly serve to assist with the process and provide further information, should you need. At RDB offices in Rwanda, US dollars are accepted, but Visa and Mastercard are the preferred method of payment.

If you are prepared to take the risk, it does remain possible to pitch up at the RDB office in Kigali until 17.00 on the day before you want to track, and – assuming availability – to buy a permit on the spot. And if you are coming from across the Ugandan border and want to skip Kigali altogether, you can also buy a permit at the RDB offices in Rubavu/Gisenyi, Musanze/Ruhengeri or the Volcanoes National Park headquarters at Kinigi the day before you want to track. There is of course no guarantee that a permit will be available at such short notice, particularly at busy times when there may already be a waiting list, but the odds are reasonable in the main rainy season of March to May.

similar), which hold up to 32 passengers and depart according to a fixed schedule. Heading out into the smaller towns and villages, smaller white-and-green minibuses operated by the Rwanda Federation of Transport Cooperatives (RFTC) take over, which are significantly less comfortable and only depart when full. All of the above are often referred to simply as taxis or minibuses, and while the mini-/midibus distinction is not used in Rwanda, we've distinguished between them in the text because of the significant difference in comfort and quality between the two. Also worth mentioning is the government-backed **Ritco** (m *078 830 9333;* e *ritcoexpress@gmail.com*), which has replaced the now-defunct ONTRACOM and runs regular and reliable **coach buses** to major destinations throughout the country.

No smoking inside is the rule, as it is on all public transport. Departures continue throughout the day but it's best not to wait until too late, in case the last one proves to be full. Fares generally work out at around Rfr1,000 (US$1) per 50km. More precise fares for specific routes are given throughout this book, but do note that they are subject to regular inflation and occasional deflation as a result of fluctuations in the oil price and to a lesser extent the US dollar exchange rate. Travel times along main surfaced roads typically average about 50km/h (and buses are now fitted with speed governors capping them at 60km/h), with frequent pauses to drop off passengers.

If you're carrying luggage, either keep it on your lap (if it's small enough) or else ask for it to be stuffed in at the back or put on the roof. If you have anything fragile, keep it with you. Overloading is not the problem it is in many African countries and nor are tourists routinely overcharged – indeed this would be rather difficult given the prices clearly posted at all ticket offices! On unscheduled minibuses fares are collected just before you alight rather than when you board; you'll see other passengers getting their money ready as their destinations approach. If you're not sure of the fare, ask another passenger.

The private scheduled midibuses running between larger towns described above are all represented with ticket offices at the main bus stations, and you can book seats in advance – a useful feature, since they often sell out. Previously, these would depart from their own offices scattered around town, but they have since been consolidated into centralised bus stations, and as such are considerably more convenient. Given that the price is generally much the same as for public minibuses and they offer the convenience of a fixed timetable without the innumerable stops for embarking and disembarking passengers so common to African road travel, we highly recommend them. Details appear under the relevant towns in *Part Two*.

Two-wheeled taxis Just about everywhere in Rwanda you'll find 'taxis' in the form of motorbikes (motos), or sometimes standard bicycles as well. They're handy for short distances – but be aware that your travel insurance may not cover you for accidents when on either of them. Agree a price beforehand, and check with a passer-by if it seems excessive.

Taxis In larger towns you may find normal taxis – identifiable by a yellow or orange stripe round the side – known as *taxi-voitures* to distinguish them from minibus-taxis. Agree a price in advance and haggle if it seems extortionate. Fares in Kigali are fixed according to distance. None of the international ride-hailing companies is active in Kigali yet, but the home-grown AfriTaxi (w *afritaxirwanda. com*) provides a similar smartphone-based service.

ACCOMMODATION

Accommodation options in Rwanda range from five-star international hotels to dingy local guesthouses, and prices vary accordingly. The main concentration of high-quality accommodation is in Kigali, but there are also facilities to international standards in and around Volcanoes, Nyungwe and Akagera national parks and the Lake Kivu resorts of Rubavu/Gisenyi, Karongi/Kibuye, and Rusizi/Cyangugu. Elsewhere, there are usually mid-range hotels geared to local businesspeople as much as to tourists, and cheaper local guesthouses favoured by genuine budget travellers.

Most accommodation establishments are recognisably signposted as a hotel, *logement*, guesthouse or similar, but some local places are signposted as *Amacumbi* (pronounced 'amachoombi') – which literally means 'Place with rooms' in Kinyarwanda. Note, too, that in the Swahili language – not indigenous to Rwanda but more widely spoken by locals than any other exotic tongue – a *hoteli* is a restaurant, which can create confusion when asking a non-French speaker for a hotel.

All accommodation listings in this guidebook are placed in one of five categories: exclusive/luxury, upmarket, moderate, budget, and shoestring. The purpose of this categorisation is twofold: to break up long hotel listings that span a wide price range, and to help readers isolate the range of hotels that will best suit their budget and taste. The application of categories is not rigid. Aside from an inevitable element of subjectivity, it is based as much on the feel of a hotel as its rates (which are quoted anyway) and placement is also sometimes influenced by the standard of other accommodation options in the same location.

EXCLUSIVE/LUXURY This category embraces a handful of international four- and five-star luxury hotels, as well as a few select smaller lodges and resorts notable less for their luxury than for offering a genuinely exclusive experience. Rates are typically upwards of US$300 for a double, but many cost twice or even several times as much as that. This is the category to look at if you want the best and/or most characterful accommodation and have few financial restrictions.

UPMARKET This category includes most Western-style hotels, lodges and resorts that cater mainly to international tourist or business travellers but lack the special something that might elevate them into the luxury or exclusive category. Hotels in this range would typically be accorded a two- to three-star ranking elsewhere, and they offer smart en-suite accommodation with a good selection of facilities. Rates are typically around US$120–250 for a double, dependent on quality and location. Most package tours and privately booked safaris use accommodation in this range.

MODERATE In Rwanda, as in many African countries, there is often a wide gap in price and standard between the cheapest hotels geared primarily towards tourists and the best hotels geared primarily towards local and budget travellers. For this reason, the moderate bracket is rather more nebulous than other accommodation categories, essentially consisting of hotels which, for one or other reason, couldn't really be classified as upmarket, but are also a notch or two above the budget category in terms of price and/or quality. Expect unpretentious en-suite accommodation with hot water and Wi-Fi, a decent restaurant and some English-speaking staff. Prices for moderate city and beach hotels are generally in the US$50–100 range. This is the category to look at if you are travelling privately on a limited or low budget and expect a reasonably high but not luxurious standard of accommodation.

BUDGET Hotels in this category are aimed largely at the local market and definitely don't approach international standards, but are still reasonably clean and comfortable, and a definite cut above the basic guesthouses that proliferate in most towns. More often than not, a decent restaurant is attached, there are English-speaking staff, and rooms have en-suite facilities with running cold or possibly hot water, mosquito netting, and Wi-Fi. Expect to pay around US$25–50 for a double, less away from major tourist centres. This is the category to look at if you are on a limited budget, but want to avoid total squalor!

SHOESTRING This is the very bottom end of the market, usually small local guesthouses with simple rooms and common showers and toilets. Running the gamut from pleasantly clean to decidedly squalid, hotels in the category typically cost around US$10–20 for a room. It is the category for those to whom keeping down costs is the main imperative.

CAMPING Few formal campsites exist in Rwanda. Some hotels will permit camping in the gardens, but at little saving over the price of a budget room. There are campsites at the Volcanoes, Akagera and Nyungwe Forest national parks, and the Discover Rwanda youth hostels in Kigali and Rubavu/Gisenyi have dedicated campsites as well. At Nyungwe, the campsite is far more attractively located than the resthouse for travellers without a vehicle. A tent may also come in handy for travellers backpacking or cycling through relatively non-touristed rural areas, where you are strongly advised to ask permission of the local village official before setting up camp.

EATING AND DRINKING

EATING OUT Kigali boasts an impressive and growing range of restaurants representing international cuisines such as Indian, Italian, Chinese and French. In most other towns, a couple of hotels or restaurants serve uncomplicated Western meals – chicken, fish or steak with chips or rice. Possibly as a result of the Belgian influence, restaurant standards seem to be far higher than in most East African countries, and Rwandan chips are among the best on the continent. Servings tend to be dauntingly large, and prices very reasonable – around Rfr1,500–3,500 (US$2–4) for a *mélange* (mixed plate) at local eateries and Rfr5,000–10,000 (US$6–12) for a main course at a smarter restaurant.

Buffet or self-service meals are also on offer, often at very inexpensive rates, and are said to originate from a period in the 1980s when the government decreed that civil servants should have shorter lunch breaks. As a result, enterprising restaurants dreamed up this way of enabling them to eat faster. Smarter restaurants, especially in Kigali, may be closed or take a while to rustle up food outside of normal mealtimes.

Wherever you travel, local restaurants serve Rwandan favourites such as goat kebabs (brochettes), grilled or fried tilapia (a type of lake fish), bean or meat stews. These are normally eaten with one of a few staples: *ugali* (a stiff porridge made with maize meal), *matoke* (stewed cooking banana/plantain), *chapatti* (flat bread), and boiled potatoes (as in Uganda, these are somewhat mysteriously referred to as Irish potatoes) – not to mention rice and the ubiquitous chips.

Unless you have an insatiable appetite for greasy omelettes or stale *mandazi* (deep-fried dough balls not dissimilar to doughnuts), breakfast outside of Kigali (where very fine pastries, croissants and coffees are to be had) can be a problematic meal, though this too is changing with the opening of good cafés in cities around the country.

One area in which Rwanda is definitely influenced more by its anglophone neighbours than by its former coloniser is baking: in common with the rest of East Africa, the bread is almost always sweetish and goes stale quickly. In such cases a bunch of bananas, supplemented by other fresh fruit, is about the best breakfast option: cheap, nutritious and filling.

COOKING FOR YOURSELF The alternative to eating at restaurants is to put together your own meals at markets and supermarkets. The variety of foodstuffs you can buy varies from season to season and from town to town, but in most major centres you can rely on finding a supermarket that stocks frozen meat, a few tinned goods, biscuits, pasta, rice and chocolate bars. If you're that way inclined, and will be staying in hotels rather than camping, bring a small electric immersion heater for use in your bedroom (sockets take standard continental two-pin plugs), plus some teabags or instant coffee, so you can supplement your picnic with a hot drink.

Fruit and vegetables are best bought at markets, where they are very cheap. Potatoes, sweet potatoes, onions, tomatoes, bananas, sugarcane, avocados, paw-paws, mangoes, coconuts, oranges and pineapples are seasonally available in most towns.

For hikers, about the only dehydrated meals available are packet soups. If you have specialised requirements, you're best doing your shopping in Kigali, where a wider selection of goods (cheese, local yoghurt…) is available in the supermarkets; there are also a handful of excellent bakeries, with mouthwatering goodies hot from the oven.

DRINKS Brand-name soft drinks such as Pepsi, Coca-Cola and Fanta are widely available, and cheap by international standards. Tap water is debatably safe to drink in Kigali, although the smell of chlorine may put you off; bottled mineral water is widely available if you sensibly prefer not to take the risk. Locally bottled fruit juice (passion fruit, orange, pineapple…) isn't bad and comes in concentrated versions too.

The most widely drunk hot beverage is tea (*icyayi* in Kinyarwanda, sometimes also referred to by the Swahili name *chai*). In rural areas, the ingredients are often boiled together in a pot: a sticky, sweet, milky concoction that is sometimes referred to as African tea, and that definitely falls into the category of acquired tastes. Most Westernised restaurants serve tea as we know it, but if you want to be certain, specify that you want black tea. The milk served separately with it is almost always powdered, but of a type that dissolves well and doesn't taste too bad. Coffee is one of Rwanda's main cash crops, but you'd hardly know it judging by the insipid slop that passes for coffee in some restaurants and hotels – though this may soon be a thing of the past as something akin to café culture has taken hold in Kigali and seems to be spreading throughout the country.

The most popular alcoholic drink is beer, brewed locally near Rubavu. The cheaper of the two local brands is Primus, which comes in 700ml bottles which cost around Rfr800–1,200 in local bars and as much as Rfr3,000 in Kigali's swankiest hotels. The most popular alternative is Mutzig, which tastes little different, costs about 30% more and comes in 700ml or 350ml bottles. Skol and Gatanu are also ubiquitous and rather generic lagers, while fans of darker beers will want to give Turbo King or Virunga Mist a try.

South African and French wines are sold at outrageously inflated prices in a few upmarket bars and restaurants. Far more sensibly priced are the boxes of Spanish or Italian wine sold in some supermarkets. If you want to check out your capacity for locally brewed banana wine (also called *urwagwa*) before ordering it with a meal, most supermarkets and some small grocers/snack bars have bottles on sale.

It comes in many varieties – some have honey added, and I've heard of a kind made in the northeast that contains hibiscus flowers. There's also a banana liqueur.

As for the harder stuff, *waragi*, a millet-based clear alcohol from Uganda, is available everywhere; either knock it back neat or mix it as you would gin. (In its undistilled form it could strip away a few layers of skin!) The illegal Rwandan firewater, *kanyanga*, is also available widely: treat with care.

TIPPING Generally speaking, tipping isn't common, though in upmarket restaurants it's polite to leave behind some change after a meal (think Rfr500–1,500); this isn't necessary at budget eateries. Taxis, motos and other transport services also don't require any gratuity, though if you're travelling with a hired car and driver-guide it's common (though not obligatory) to tip them at the end of your trip together. Around US$10–20/day would be appropriate, assuming you're happy with their service.

PUBLIC HOLIDAYS AND EVENTS

In addition to the following fixed public holidays, Rwanda recognises Good Friday, Easter Monday, Eid al-Adha and Eid-al-Fitr (end of Ramadan).

1 January	New Year's Day
1 February	Heroes' Day
7 April	Genocide Memorial Day
1 May	Labour Day
1 July	Independence Day
4 July	Liberation Day
First Friday in August	Umuganura (Harvest) Day
15 August	Assumption Day
25 December	Christmas Day
26 December	Boxing Day

The week around Genocide Memorial Day is an official week of mourning during which commemorative ceremonies are held and some activities may be reduced.

Two public events may draw crowds large enough to affect the availability of accommodation in some areas: the International Peace Marathon and Fun Run

HEROES' DAY

Various events are held for Heroes' Day, the purpose of which is to commemorate Rwanda's heroes, old and new and to motivate the young to follow their example. There are three categories of 'hero': the highest, *Imanzi*, applies to those who made the ultimate sacrifice of their own lives for the sake of their country. It includes Major General Fred Rwigema, who died on the front line the day after the launch of the Liberation War, and the 'Unknown Soldier', representing all soldiers who lost their lives fighting for Rwanda's liberation. The next category, *Imena*, comprises others who also died in the service of their country or its people. As well as Mwami Mutara III and political victims of violence it includes genocide heroes: for example, a Hutu nun killed for helping Tutsis to escape across Lake Kivu, and schoolgirls who died when they refused to split into Hutu or Tutsi groups. Finally, the *Ingenzi* category consists of heroes from the more recent past who are still alive.

held annually in and around Kigali in May (■ *Kigali International Peace Marathon*; page 114), and the Kwita Izina Gorilla Naming Ceremony and cycle race held near the Volcanoes National Park in June or September (details from the Tourist Board and on page 262).

The last Saturday of any given month is Umuganda (Public Cleaning) Day. Between 08.00 and 11.00 there is a countrywide ban on road traffic, as the whole country embarks on communal work for the public good. This can consist of anything from local street-cleaning to road repairs, tree planting, land clearance and building homes for genocide survivors – and can result in sizeable portions of the workforce being too busy to attend to travellers! Tourists are welcome to join in too. Generally, tour operators' vehicles are permitted to carry on as normal, but it is worth checking with your tour operator. If you need to be at the airport to catch a flight, a passport and valid travel ticket should be enough to secure dispensation in a taxi.

SHOPPING

All basic requirements (toiletries, stationery, batteries and so forth) are available in Kigali, and, away from the capital, most towns of any size have a pharmacy as well as a reasonable supermarket or general store. In Kigali, the Nakumatt supermarkets in the Union Trade Centre and Kigali City Tower are open 24 hours, along with Simba supermarkets in the city centre and opposite parliament in Kacyiru.

For handicrafts you've a very wide range – wood-carvings, weaving, pottery, baskets, clay statues, beadwork, jewellery, masks, musical instruments, banana-leaf products, batik – see pages 31 and 111–13, for more details. CDs or cassettes (cassettes are cool again, if you haven't heard) of Rwandan music make good gifts, as does local honey: buy it in a market and decant it into a screw-top soft-drinks bottle for travelling. (Some countries prohibit the import of foodstuffs, so check local regulations before you take any home.) Some markets stock candles made of local beeswax. Locally made wines, spirits and liqueurs are heavier to carry but generally appreciated! For traditional musical instruments, you need a well-informed local advisor to help you to pick the best and most authentic.

Women can buy lengths of brightly dyed fabric in the market and have street dressmakers make up a garment on the spot; men can similarly kit themselves out with hand-tailored shirts or trousers. And just browsing in any large street market will give you dozens more ideas…

MEDIA AND COMMUNICATIONS

NEWSPAPERS AND MAGAZINES The main English-language newspaper is the daily *New Times* (w *newtimes.co.rw*) which provides reasonably balanced coverage with a pro-government slant. Imported dailies and weeklies from Uganda and Kenya are also available on the streets of Kigali and Huye/Butare. A very limited range of international papers can be bought at the kiosks of upmarket hotels such as the Mille Collines in Kigali. News magazines such as *Time* and *Newsweek* are available from street vendors and some bookshops. The Ikirezi Bookshop in Kacyiru has a good stock as well.

INTERNET, EMAIL AND FAX The electronic communications age has fast gained a foothold in Rwanda, and it has become an regional leader in internet services following the completion of a high-capacity national fibre-optic cable network worth US$50 million. Outside of Kigali, local servers tend to be slower, and some smaller towns have no public internet facilities at all. Wi-Fi is becoming common in all but the cheapest of hotels, and hotels in the moderate and higher brackets will also occasionally (though not reliably) have internet facilities if you don't have a device of your own.

TELEPHONE Rwanda's telephone system is reasonably efficient, though mobile providers tend to be more reliable than land lines. From overseas, it is definitely one of the easier African countries to get through to first time. The international code is 250. Because of the small size of the country, and limited number of phones, no area codes are in use. In 2009, the old six-digit land lines were extended to ten digits.

In Kigali, international phone calls can be made from the central post office and from various other shops and kiosks in the city. For calls within Rwanda the street kiosks and shops with public phones work well – calls are metered and you pay when you've finished, so there's no fussing with coins or tokens. Some of these can handle international calls too. To make an international call out of Rwanda, dial 000 then the country code, area code and local number.

Cell phones (mobiles) have caught on in a big way in Rwanda, and nearly 80% of Rwandans have one. There are three providers: MTN is the largest with some 42% market share, and is definitely the best option for travellers due to its wide national network. The alternatives are Tigo and Airtel, though a proposed merger of the two received regulatory approval in January 2018, which means Airtel will likely be the largest provider by the time you read this.

Cell-phone numbers are recognisable as ten-digit numbers starting with 078 (MTN), 073 (Airtel), or 072 (Tigo). Mobile-phone owners from overseas can buy a local SIM card giving them a local number using the local network for US$1–2. International text messages and phone calls are also surprisingly cheap from local mobile phones, and 4G LTE mobile data coverage is now available in all districts of Rwanda. Data bundles are inexpensive; just ask for your options when getting your SIM set up at an MTN/Airtel service centre. Note that you're required to show ID in order to register a new SIM card.

It's also very much worth noting that the messaging app Whatsapp (w *whatsapp. com*) is wildly popular in Rwanda, and it's very common for businesses to field questions and communicate with clients on the application – just save the number you'd like to reach into your address book to see if they're Whatsapp-enabled and text away. (To do this, numbers are best saved using the international dialling format, ie: with the country code and without the leading zero: +250 7X XXX XXXX.)

The ubiquity and relative efficiency of mobile phones means that many hotels and other organisations in Rwanda no longer bother with land lines. Unfortunately, when it comes to hotels, this means that contact telephone details tend to change more regularly than is the case with fixed lines. For this reason we have included both numbers where they exist – the mobile will usually be easier to get through to, but there's a far greater chance a land line will still be in place in two or three years' time. Readers are welcome to alert us to any such changes by posting on our website w bradtupdates.com/rwanda.

POST Post from Rwanda is cheap and fairly reliable, but it can be slow. Yellow post-buses with *Iposita* on the side shuttle mail around the country. Letterboxes outside post offices have a variety of appellations – sometimes *Boîte aux Lettres,* sometimes (eg: in Huye) *Box of Letters* and sometimes (a Belgian/Flemish relic in Karongi) *Brievenbus*.

RADIO AND TELEVISION The BBC World Service comes across loud and clear, on different frequencies according to the time of day. Local radio stations broadcast in Kinyarwanda, French, English and Swahili. TV is largely piped in from elsewhere, notably by the South African company DSTV, whose bouquet of channels includes CNN, Sky, BBC News et al. For football fans, the Supersport Channel operated by the DSTV shows most international and English Premiership matches and can be seen at bars all around the country.

CULTURAL ETIQUETTE

As in most African countries, Rwandans tend to be tolerant of Westerners' ways and won't easily take offence at mildly inappropriate behaviour. All the same, it is a relatively conservative and by-and-large highly religious society, and visitors should bear in mind that certain behaviours are very unacceptable. This would include public affection between members of the opposite sex (even if they are married), overt drunkenness, skimpy attire (particularly for women), proclamations of atheism, and in some circles smoking. In conversation, extended greetings are normal, and it is considered rude to ask somebody directions or ask for something in a shop or restaurant without first greeting the person and asking after their health. Probably the biggest social gaffe you could make in Rwanda, however, is insensitive probing into matters of ethnicity or perceived ethnicity – in the aftermath of the genocide people understandably avoid referring to themselves or others as Hutu and Tutsi, and it would be wise for visitors to follow suit.

BECOMING INVOLVED   *Janice Booth*

You may leave Rwanda without a backward glance, or you may find that it has affected you more than you realised. It's an amazing country. Many visitors feel that they want to remain – or become more – involved in its people and development. Most of the large mainstream charities have activities there, but those listed below are just a few of the many smaller ones for whom even one new supporter can make a difference; their websites give more details of their work. New ones are appearing all the time: ask around when you're in Rwanda. Also see **Cards from Africa** and the **Meg Foundation** (pages 120–1), **Imbabazi** (pages 224 and 228) and the **Ubushobozi Foundation** (page 246). **Gorilla conservation** organisations are listed on pages 260–1. Several guesthouses and/or local tour operators also support specific causes.

It's worth remembering – although this is in no way a 'charity' – that 10% of the fees you pay for national park permits are earmarked for development in communities living around the parks. This is known as the 'tourism revenue sharing rate'. During the past 12 years, more than 400 community projects have been funded in this way, from schools, clinics and water supplies to mushroom growing, market gardens, brick kilns and beehives; so rural Rwandans you will probably never meet can benefit directly from your visit.

Engalynx w engalynx.org.uk. Based in Essex, this small but energetic & hands-on charity was set up in 1998 to help post-genocide Rwanda rebuild. Since then, it has provided not only funds but also a mass of practical items (computers, sewing machines, shoes, microscopes, tools...), has funded training & medical installations, including

a maternity centre, & is always involved with ongoing projects that need support.
Friends of Rwandan Rugby
w friendsofrwandanrugby.org.uk. Sport binds people – particularly young people – together, a vital requirement for post-genocide Rwanda. FORR is a UK-registered charity supporting school

& community participation in rugby, providing coaching & encouraging young people (girls as well as boys) to play. Many schools are now involved & there's huge enthusiasm to learn. Rugby-minded tourists are welcome to join in a game, offer a bit of coaching, provide some old balls or kit, or just make a donation.

Goboka Rwanda Trust
w thegobokarwandatrust.co.uk. Based in Derbyshire (UK), Goboka works in partnership with local Rwandan organisations to help provide needy rural communities with assorted practical help: sewing schools, cows, roofing, eco-stoves, beekeeping equipment & training, sheep, a health centre, a clean water supply – & more, with the communities actively joining in the work involved.

Msaada w msaada.org. A UK-registered charity founded in 2005 by journalists Fergal Keane & Billy Kelly, Msaada helps widowed survivors of the genocide in East Province by providing them with cows (1 per family) & help with their maintenance. It also assists the Groupe Scolaire Rwamagana with their educational needs, & organises a (tough!) annual local marathon (w *rwandamarathon.com*), whose profits support the cow project.

Rwanda United Kingdom Goodwill Organisation w rugo.org. Registered as a UK charity in 1999, RUGO has been instrumental in building & equipping 2 vocational training institutions & a community centre; provided specialist hospital beds & other medical equipment for use by Kigali Health Institute in a polyclinic; donated computers & books to the National University & other colleges; & has supported numerous local enterprises & charities. Its current innovative project is to bring solar power to a remote village: check out the 'solar grannies' on its website.

Rwandan Youth Information Community Organisation w ryico.org. A dual UK- & Rwanda-registered charity, rYico works in partnership with Rwandans in the UK to spread knowledge & understanding of Rwanda & its history, while in Kigali its Centre Marembo (w *centremarembo.org*) focuses on young victims of gender-based violence. With a clinic, safe homes & a range of appropriate services, it helps victims of abuse, teen & pre-teen mothers & street girls to access education, training, counselling & legal support so that they can build or rebuild their lives. Visitors are welcome (page 121).

INVESTING IN RWANDA

The ultimate involvement in Rwanda is to invest in one of the many opportunities that the country's rapid development has created. The Rwanda Development Board (☏ *+250 0252 585179;* e *investorfeedback@rdb.rw;* w *rdb.rw*) can provide full information, including the generous incentives and concessions available. The mechanisms are straightforward and investor-friendly, with a minimum of red tape.

Openings exist in many sectors; for example food processing (tea, coffee, fruit, vegetables…), financial services, ICT, mining, tourism and hospitality, solar installations, telecommunications, medical services, construction and transport. It's an Aladdin's cave of opportunity. And remember that the 2017 World Bank '*Doing Business*' Report named Rwanda as the second easiest African country in which to do business, after only Mauritius.

Part Two

THE GUIDE

3

Kigali

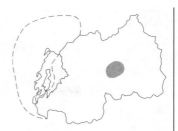

The low-key but attractive Rwandan capital city of Kigali stands in the centre of the country, where it straggles over several hills and valleys, spanning altitudes of around 1,300m to 1,600m. The city was founded in 1907 at a location chosen by Dr Richard Kandt, who built an administrative residence close to the present-day Gakinjiro Market. Two years later, 20 further houses were built (one of which has been restored as a history museum) on the eastern slopes of Nyarugenge Hill, which now forms the commercial city centre.

Kigali remained a small and isolated colonial outpost until 1916, when Belgium ousted Ruanda-Urundi's German colonisers. Under Belgian rule, Kigali retained an important administrative role, but urban growth was very slow and confined mainly to Nyarugenge. Indeed, when Rwanda gained independence in 1962, the population of Kigali stood at no more than 6,000. When Ruanda-Urundi (the capital of which was Usumbura, now named Bujumbura) split into Rwanda and Burundi, the strongest contender to become Rwanda's new capital seemed to be Butare (now known as Huye), which had been the more important administrative centre during colonisation.

However, Kigali's central position and good road links to the rest of the country won out. As a result, while Huye has avoided capital-city brashness and remains relatively calm, Kigali has grown dramatically, with the 2012 census returning the city's first-ever million-plus population count of 1,132,686 people. The commercial city centre is still on Nyarugenge Hill, while the government and administrative quarter is further east on Kacyiru Hill. Between and around these elevated twin centres, empty spaces on the hillsides are filling with new housing, and pollution in the valleys (from the increasing volume of traffic) could soon be a problem.

The centre of Kigali is bustling, colourful and noisy, but impressively clean and safe (indeed, in 2008, Kigali was effectively pronounced the cleanest city on the continent, when it became the first African urban centre to be presented with the Habitat Scroll of Honour award, an annual award launched by the UN Human Settlements Programme in 1989). However, it is undergoing rapid development and change, with shiny

KIGALI *Environs*
For listings, see pages 83–104

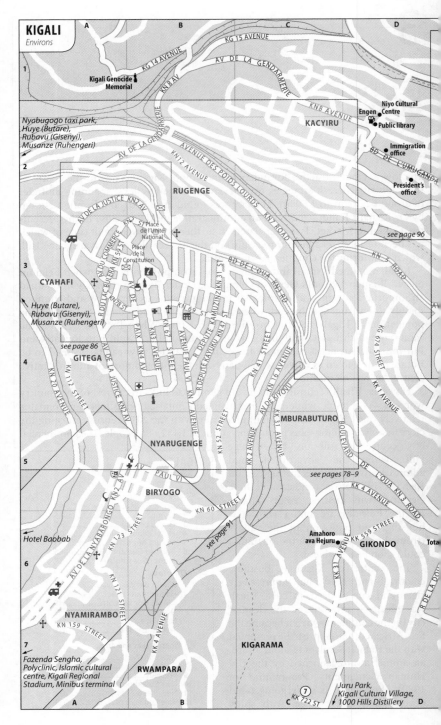

KIGALI
Environs

A   B   C   D

1

KG 15 AVENUE
KG 14 AVENUE
AV DE LA GENDARMERIE
KN 8 AV

Kigali Genocide Memorial

KN8 AVENUE

Niyo Cultural Centre
Engen
Public library
KACYIRU

Nyabugogo taxi park;
Huye (Butare),
Rubavu (Gisenyi),
Musanze (Ruhengeri)

AV DE LA GENDARMERIE

Immigration office
BD DE L'UMUGANDA

AVENUE DES POIDS LOURDS — KN7 ROAD

2

AVENUE DES POIDS LOURDS

President's office

RUGENGE

AV DE LA JUSTICE KN2 AV
KN 12 AVENUE

KN2 AV
Place de l'unité National

KN 5 ROAD

see page 96

Place de la Constitution

BD DE L'OUA KN3 RD

3

CYAHAFI

BD DE L'OUA KN3 RD

KG 674 STREET

Huye (Butare),
Rubavu (Gisenyi),
Musanze (Ruhengeri)

KN8 ST

KN 69 ST

AVENUE PAUL VI KN 7 AVENUE

R DEPUTE KAMUZINZI KN 31 ST

R DEPUTE KAYUKU KN 47

KN 41 STREET

see page 86

GITEGA

AV DE LA PAIX KN4 AV

KN3 ST

KN 67 STREET

4

KN 20 AVENUE

KN 112 STREET

AV DE LA JUSTICE KN2 AV

KN 52 STREET

KK 2 AVENUE

KN 16 AVENUE
AV DE KIYOVU

KK 3 1 AVENUE

MBURABUTURO

KK 1 AVENUE

5

NYARUGENGE

AV PAUL VI

see pages 78–9

BOULEVARD DE L'OUA KN 3 ROAD

KN 2 AV

BIRYOGO

KN 60 STREET

KK 4 AVENUE

Hotel Baobab

AV DE LA NYABARONGO KN2 AV

KN 123 STREET

see page 91

Amahoro
ava Hejuru
GIKONDO

KK 559 STREET

KK 31 STREET

Tota

6

KN 121 STREET

R DE LA DO

NYAMIRAMBO

KN 159 STREET

7

Fazenda Sengha,
Polyclinic, Islamic cultural
centre, Kigali Regional
Stadium, Minibus terminal

RWAMPARA

KIGARAMA

⑦
KK 722 ST

Juru Park,
Kigali Cultural Village,
1000 Hills Distillery

A   B   C   D

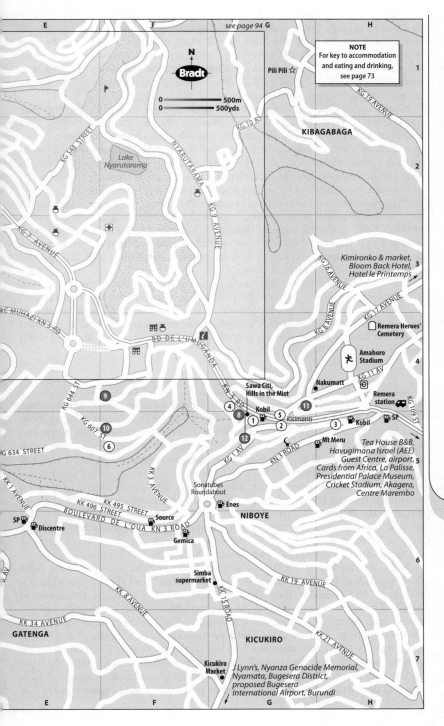

see page 94

NOTE
For key to accommodation
and eating and drinking,
see page 73

Pili Pili ☆

KIBAGABAGA

Lake
Nyarutarama

KG 328 STREET

NYARUTARAMA

KG 9 AVENUE

KG 19 AVENUE

KG 7 AVENUE

KC MUHAZI-KN-3 RD

KG 644 ST

KG 607 ST

G 634 STREET

BD DE L'UMUGANDA

KG 16 AVENUE

KG 8 AVENUE

KG 17 AVENUE

Kimironko & market,
Bloom Back Hotel,
Hotel le Printemps

Remera Heroes'
Cemetery

Amahoro
Stadium

Sawa Citi,
Hills in the Mist

Nakumatt

Remera
station

KG 109 ST

KN 3 RD

Kobil

Kisimenti

Kobil

SP

Mt Meru

KK 1 AVENUE

KK 3 AVENUE

KK 495 STREET

KK 496 STREET

BOULEVARD DE L'OUA   KN 3 ROAD

Sonatubes
Roundabout

Source

Gemica

Enes

NIBOYE

Tea House B&B,
Havugimana Israel (AEE)
Guest Centre, airport,
Cards from Africa, La Palisse,
Presidential Palace Museum,
Cricket Stadium, Akagera,
Centre Marembo

SP

Discentre

Simba
supermarket

KK 8 AVENUE

KK 19 AVENUE

KK 15 ROAD

KK 34 AVENUE

KK 21 AVENUE

GATENGA

KICUKIRO

Kicukiro
Market

J Lynn's, Nyanza Genocide Memorial,
Nyamata, Bugesera District,
proposed Bugesera
International Airport, Burundi

Kigali

3

new shopping malls, hotels and office buildings springing up all over the city; most recently, the construction of a huge new US$12.9 million city hall, and the even larger, US$300 million Kigali Convention Centre, replete with its own five-star hotel, office park and cavernous conference facilities, which was inaugurated in 2016. And while this is all well and good for Kigali's increasingly striking skyline, it remains to be seen if the city's green credentials survive all this development.

Kigali's occupants, from smart-suited businesspeople to scruffy kids hawking newspapers or pirated USB sticks, go purposefully about their activities, only lessening tempo briefly in the middle of the day. Occasional traffic lights, roundabouts, a strictly enforced one-way road system and a cacophony of car horns manage (more or less) to regulate the traffic, although it's heavy and congested at peak times. Peaceful, tree-lined residential streets stretch outwards and generally downwards from the city's heart, and give visitors scope for strolling.

The government and administrative area in Kacyiru quarter is newer and quieter, with wide streets and some striking modern architecture. Kigali was the centre of much fighting during the genocide and offices were ransacked; when workers returned after the end of the war they had virtually no usable typewriters, phones, stationery or furniture and had to start again from scratch. Also files, archives and other documentation had been destroyed.

Kigali doesn't have many tourist attractions and you're unlikely to want to spend many full days there, but it has some good hotels, the services (shops, banks, etc) are plentiful and the ambience is pleasant, making it an excellent base for exploring the rest of Rwanda, all parts of which can easily be reached by road in less than a day. Car hire is available via one of the city's many tour operators and travel agencies (pages 82–3).

GETTING THERE AND AWAY

BY AIR See pages 38–9 for details of flights to and from Rwanda – which means to and from Kigali, since the country's only international airport is situated about 5km from the city centre. There are firm plans to replace this with the larger and more modern Bugesera International Airport near Nyamata, about 40km south of Kigali, which would free the land for further development and bring jobs and opportunities to an underused area, and after several years of delays ground was finally broken on the project in August 2017. As if to prove Kigali's boomtown bona fides, the first phase of construction is slated for completion within just over a year, at the end of 2018. Unfortunately, there was still no information available on how and when the new airport might begin to receive flights when this book went to print in mid 2018, so it would be worth double-checking progress at w bradtupdates.com/rwanda if you'll be travelling in 2019 or beyond.

In the arrivals hall of the current airport (and in offices just outside the front door) you'll find foreign exchange and telephone facilities (MTN is just outside), Wi-Fi, an ATM, various shops and a branch of RDB (Rwanda Development Board) Tourism and Conservation Reservation Office, which is Rwanda's tourism information centre. This office was temporarily closed at the time of writing, but once it reopens you will be able to get a preliminary stock of maps, guides and so forth here. (Alternatively, the main Tourism and Conservation Reservation Office is in the administrative district of Kacyiru.) At present there is no pestering from porters – there aren't any – just grab a trolley from the stack in the baggage reclaim area and deal with your own bags. (Bear in mind that plastic bags are banned in Rwanda; stick to more solid alternatives.)

To get into Kigali town you've got a few options. (Possibly including begging a lift from some fellow traveller who has a vehicle.) If your hotel does airport pickups, you'll have arranged this at the time of booking; give them a ring if no-one has turned up to collect you. If you've very little luggage, you can pick up either KBS bus 104, which runs between the airport and the Bank of Kigali headquarters downtown, or a minibus-taxi (*matatu*) on the road outside the airport. Either will take you to central Kigali for about Rfr350, or a moto would do the same for Rfr1,500, give or take. (Note that KBS buses migrated to a cashless payment system in 2017, so you'll need a Tap&Go card. These are available from agents posted at bus terminals and cost Rfr500.) Otherwise take a taxi-voiture (a normal taxi, as opposed to a minibus-taxi) from the airport (though if you don't have much luggage, these too might be cheaper if flagged down on the road). Either way, agree a price with the driver in advance. At the time of writing, the going rate is about Rfr17,000 or US$20, but rates do legitimately rise over time. If the exchange bureau in the airport is closed, taxi-drivers generally accept US dollars, but check the exchange rate on the list in the window of the bureau (or using w xe.com).

BY ROAD Kigali is a well-connected little city – literally. Good roads and bus services link it to all the main border crossings with neighbouring countries: Uganda, Tanzania, Burundi and the Democratic Republic of the Congo.

In addition, almost all towns within Rwanda are connected to Kigali by regular public minibus-taxis, all of which now leave from Nyabugogo station (*gare routière* Nyabugogo), 2km from the city centre along KN 1 Road. Buses from the city centre to Nyabugogo station leave from the new bus terminal in the city centre [86 B3] or, from further west, there's KBS bus 105 from Remera station via Kacyiru. (Or of course you can always take a moto or taxi-voiture.) Nyabugogo is a huge taxi park and the mini- and midibuses are lined up in ranks, some signposted with destinations, others not – if in doubt, just ask someone and you'll be shown where to buy tickets and wait.

Today, the dominant mode of domestic intercity transport consists of privately operated midibuses (Toyota Coasters, usually) from Nyabugogo to all the major towns in Rwanda. These buses are much faster, more reliable and more comfortable than the matatu-style minibuses that run in parallel and on smaller routes. They leave at scheduled times regardless of the number of passengers on board, but they are invariably full as they are a popular and relatively convenient way to get around, so you may have to wait until there is a bus with seats available. The minibuses (matatus) leave as soon as they've a full complement of passengers – and that does mean *full* as in can of sardines – but everyone gets a seat and there's a non-smoking policy on board.

While you're waiting for your vehicle to leave, vendors of all sorts will be trying to catch your eye and sell you something – including bottled drinks and fruit, as well as fresh bread and cakes. You can even buy hard-boiled eggs, and season them from the salt and pepper pots conveniently provided! If you want something more substantial to eat before you leave, the **Amahoro Restaurant** behind the International and Stella Express bus stands is clean, cheerful and serves hearty plates of African buffet food for Rfr1,500, or you could head to the popular **Mama Boy Restaurant** [78 A2] (m *078 857 0880*), clearly signposted just across the street.

Most of the private bus companies specialise in different geographical areas of the country, with some running multiple routes and others serving only one or two destinations. These times and prices are correct at the time of writing, but naturally may change during the lifetime of this edition. For going to the east of the country,

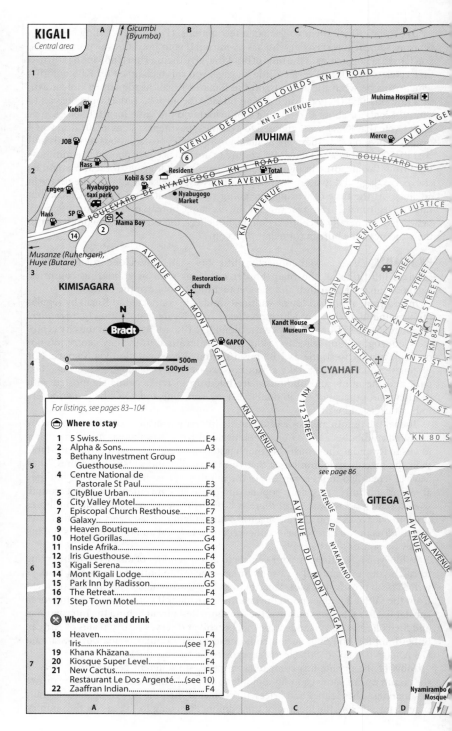

KIGALI
Central area

Gicumbi (Byumba)

Kobil

JOB

Hass

Engen

Nyabugogo taxi park

Kobil & SP

Resident

Hass

SP

Mama Boy

Musanze (Ruhengeri);
Huye (Butare)

KIMISAGARA

N

Bradt

0 .... 500m
0 .... 500yds

MUHIMA HOSPITAL

Muhima Hospital

KN 7 ROAD

AVENUE DES POIDS LOURDS

KN 12 AVENUE

MUHIMA

Merce

AV D LA GEN

BOULEVARD DE

Total

KN 1 ROAD

KN 5 AVENUE

Nyabugogo Market

BOULEVARD DE NYABUGOGO

KN 5 AVENUE

AVENUE DE LA JUSTICE

Restoration church

AVENUE DU MONT KIGALI

GAPCO

Kandt House Museum

AVENUE DE LA JUSTICE

KN 57 ST

KN 82 STREET

KN 2 STREET

KN 76 STREET

KN 74 ST

KN 59 STREET

KN 85 ST

KN 76 ST

CYAHAFI

KN 2 AV

KN 78 ST

KN 80 S

see page 86

KN 112 STREET

KN 20 AVENUE

GITEGA

KN 2 AVENUE

KN 3 AVENUE

AVENUE DE NYAKABANDA

AVENUE DU MONT KIGALI

Nyamirambo
Mosque

For listings, see pages 83–104

Where to stay

1	5 Swiss	E4
2	Alpha & Sons	A3
3	Bethany Investment Group Guesthouse	F4
4	Centre National de Pastorale St Paul	E3
5	CityBlue Urban	F4
6	City Valley Motel	B2
7	Episcopal Church Resthouse	F7
8	Galaxy	E3
9	Heaven Boutique	F3
10	Hotel Gorillas	G4
11	Inside Afrika	G4
12	Iris Guesthouse	F4
13	Kigali Serena	E6
14	Mont Kigali Lodge	A3
15	Park Inn by Radisson	G5
16	The Retreat	F4
17	Step Town Motel	E2

Where to eat and drink

18	Heaven	F4
	Iris	(see 12)
19	Khana Khäzana	F4
20	Kiosque Super Level	F4
21	New Cactus	F5
	Restaurant Le Dos Argenté	(see 10)
22	Zaaffran Indian	F4

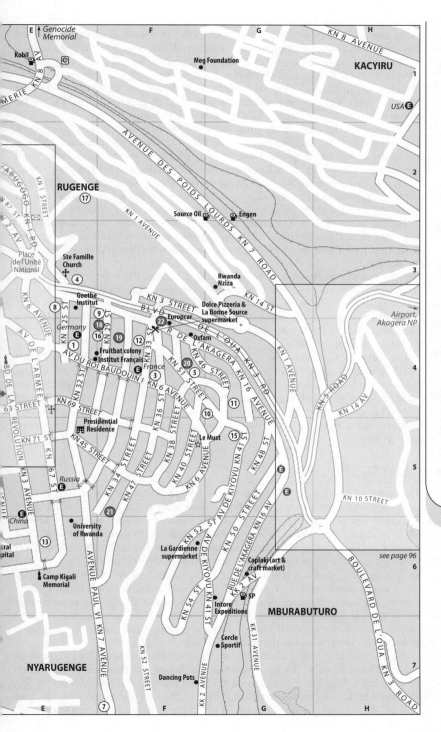

Genocide
Memorial

Kobil

KN 8 AVENUE

KACYIRU

Meg Foundation

1

USA

RUGENGE

(17)

KN 1 AVENUE

AVENUE DES POIDS LOURDS KN 7 ROAD

2

Source Oil

Engen

Place
de l'Unité
National

Ste Famille
Church

(4)

Rwanda
Nziza

KN 14 ST

3

Airport,
Akagera NP

Goethe
Institut

(8)

KN 3 STREET

BLVD

Dolce Pizzeria &
La Bonne Source
supermarket

Germany

(9)

(18)

(22) Europcar

Fruitbat colony

(16) (19)

Oxfam

Institut Français

(12)

France

(3)

(20)

(5)

KN 46 STREET

4

Presidential
Residence

(11)

(10)

KN 14 AV

KN 5 ROAD

Le Must

(15)

Russia

(21)

University
of Rwanda

(13)

5

KN 10 STREET

Camp Kigali
Memorial

La Gardienne
supermarket

Caplaki (art &
craft market)

see page 96

6

SP

Intore
Expeditions

MBURABUTURO

NYARUGENGE

Cercle
Sportif

Dancing Pots

(7)

7

Stella Express (m *078 845 5906*) operates services to Rwamagana, Rfr1,200, every 30 minutes, and Ngoma/Kibungo, Rfr2,100, every 30 minutes. **Select Express** (m *078 917 6907*) and **Matunda Express** (m *078 846 9632*) operate hourly services to Kayonza (*Rfr1,500*) and Rusumo on the Tanzanian border (*Rfr3,200*), and Matunda also goes to Kahama, Tanzania, with several early morning departures (05.00 is the latest) for Rfr8,000. **Yahoo Car Express** (m *072 842 6005/675 0202*) goes to Nyagatare in the far east of the country near Uganda for Rfr3,000 every 30 minutes.

For going to the south of Rwanda, **Volcano Express** (m *072 200 0183*) operates regular services to Muhanga/Gitarama, Rfr1,000, every 15 minutes; Nyanza, Rfr1,800, every 30 minutes; Huye/Butare, Rfr2,600, every 30 minutes; and Nyamagabe/Gikongoro, Rfr3,200, every 30 minutes. **Horizon Express** (m *072 661 8769*) also operates a reliable and regular service to Muhanga/Gitarama, Rfr1,000, every 15 minutes; and Huye/Butare, Rfr2,600, every 30 minutes. **Omega Car** (m *078 880 8795*) goes hourly to Rusizi via either Karongi or Huye for about Rfr5,300.

For the north and west, **Virunga Express** (m *078 830 8620*; w *virungaexpress. net*) operates services to Gicumbi/Byumba, Rfr1,100, every 30 minutes; Musanze/ Ruhengeri, Rfr1,800, every 30 minutes; and Rubavu/Gisenyi, Rfr3,100, every 30 minutes.

Also worth mentioning is the government-backed **Ritco** (m *078 830 9333*; e *ritcoexpress@gmail.com*), which has replaced the now-defunct ONTRACOM and runs regular and reliable coach buses to all of the destinations mentioned above.

Thanks to ongoing political tensions, Burundi-bound public transport has been forbidden to cross the border since 2016 (page 151), so you'll have to pick up an onward vehicle at the crossing.

For travel to Kampala, Dar es Salaam, or Nairobi, **Modern Coast** (m *073 888 7333*; w *modern.africa*) has three departures daily (09.00, 17.00 and 20.00) and you can pay with a credit card. Their office is just north of the main Nyabugogo station, across the road. **Jaguar Executive Coaches** (m *+256 414 251855/078 281 1128 (Uganda), 078 940 1499/436 6113/340 8791*; e *jaguar6796@gmail.com*) also operates a morning and an afternoon service to Kampala from Nyabugogo for Rfr10,000.

GETTING AROUND

The centre of Kigali – for shopping, banks, airline offices, tour operators, etc – is tiny; once you're there, you'll never be far from what you're looking for. It's based around two streets, KN 3 Avenue (Boulevard de la Révolution) and KN 4 Avenue (Avenue de la Paix), and the various roads branching off them. (Note that KN 4 Avenue is open to pedestrian traffic only between Place de la Constitution and KN 78 Street, near the Ecole Belge.) However, if you ask directions you'll soon become aware that people don't go much on street names, rather on well-known landmarks. The **Union Trade Centre (UTC)** [86 D4] is a good landmark to ask for in the city centre. It is within walking distance of most places and all taxi and moto drivers know it. Note that large stretches of the KN 3 and KN 5 roads are closed during morning hours on the fourth Sunday of every month, when people are encouraged to walk, run, or cycle on the traffic-free streets.

A good free map of Kigali city (and an Rfr8,500 foldout one of Rwanda) can be obtained from the RDB (Rwanda Development Board) Tourism and Conservation Reservation Office, but if you plan on spending more than a few days in the city, we would highly recommend you get a copy of the excellent second edition map of Kigali (w *mapofkigali.com*) published by Living in Kigali (w *livinginkigali.com*)

If you get lost in Kigali, or it starts to rain, you will never be far from a moto – the local name for a motorbike taxi. Always agree the price for a moto ride in advance, and check the helmet – they are often good for decorative purposes only, as the buckles and straps are broken or far too loose. If you protest, the driver will usually try to readjust the strap for you, or as likely as not offer you his own, usually rather hot and greasy …! Most drivers speak a smattering of French or English, so if you know the name of your destination they will get you there. But don't be fooled by the maps – road names (even the new ones) are rarely used. People navigate by buildings and local landmarks, so try using these instead.

Alternatively, there are now two ride-hailing apps working with moto drivers in Kigali: SafeMotos (w *safemotos.com*) and YegoMoto (w *yegomoto. com*), both of which track rides and charge metered fares. SafeMotos also offers Uber-style pickup service.

in 2017. It costs Rfr8,000 and is available in bookshops, hotels and cafés all over town. There's a network of urban **minibuses** (minibus-taxis, commonly called taxis or sometimes matatus) serving all areas of the city, and plenty of **taxis** (saloons, commonly called taxi-voitures and recognisable by the yellow/orange stripe along the side) – they park, among other places, in KN 3 Avenue (Boulevard de la Révolution) and at the top of Place de la Constitution, and also cruise the streets waiting to be flagged down.

There is a new **central bus station** [86 B3] in downtown Kigali next to the CHIC Complex, with vehicles departing for all parts of the city. It's predictably clean and orderly, and if you ask someone, you'll be pointed to the bus that you need. Since 2013, the official citywide bus network has been served by three operators: Kigali Bus Services (KBS; w *kigalibusservices.com*) running lines starting with 1**, Royal Express running lines starting with 2**, and the Rwanda Federation of Transport Cooperatives (RFTC; w *rftc.rw*) running lines starting with 3** and 4**. It's generally Rfr250 per ride, but note that KBS buses migrated to a cashless payment system in 2017, so you'll need a Tap&Go card to travel on them. These are available from agents posted at bus terminals and cost Rfr500. To get you started, route 104 goes between the airport and the central bus station, and route 105 connects Nyabugogo and Remera taxi parks via Kacyiru. Detailed route maps and further information on the bus system in Kigali is available at w *bus-planet.com/aworldofbuses/buses-in-africa-nw/rwanda/kigali-2*.

STREET NAMES Starting in 2011, Kigali began a citywide renaming of streets (which is in the process of expanding around the country), replacing the ad-hoc system of named (and often unnamed) streets with a number-and-letter code (somewhat similar to a zip code) linking the street to a grid of the city. Thus today, all signage in Kigali reflects the new numbering system, which consists of Roads (the largest), Avenues (slightly smaller), and Streets (the smallest). In Kigali, street numbers begin with either KN (Kigali Nyarugenge), KG (Kigali Gasabo), or KK (Kigali Kicukiro), depending on which area of town you're in. In addition to their new codes, the streets categorised as 'roads' officially retain their previous names and designations, as most are national roads connecting to other towns. All others have been changed over entirely, but we've tried to retain some of the more important names, as local people will still continue to remember and use the old names for a long while – but in any case tend to orient themselves according to popular landmarks rather than roads. (Elsewhere in Rwanda, the names of nine towns were changed in 2006; for details see box, pages 40–1.)

TOURIST INFORMATION

The **RDB (Rwanda Development Board) Tourism and Conservation Headquarters** (📞 *0252 502350;* e *reservation@rwandatourism.com;* w *rwandatourism.com/rdb. rw*) is situated on the ground floor of the Rwanda Development Building on KN 5 Road (Boulevard de l'Umuganda) [94 D5] in Kacyiru. The staff here can inform you about current events in Kigali, and you can get a free map of Kigali and other tourist areas in Rwanda including the national parks and Lake Kivu region. There is also a good selection of books about Rwanda. RDB also has a **city centre office** [86 C4] (📞*0252 576514*) at the Grand Pension Plaza on KN 4 Avenue (Avenue de la Paix). Permits to track gorillas in Volcanoes National Park (pages 257–84) can be booked at either office, and this is best done before you set off for the park as the tickets are in high demand, especially in the summer months of July and August. The staff here can also give advice on travel to neighbouring countries including Tanzania and the DRC.

An excellent source of information on Kigali for visitors and expatriates alike is the website Living in Kigali (w *livinginkigali.com*). In addition to their fabulous map of Kigali (page 122), they publish guides to living in different areas of the city, restaurant reviews, a calendar of events and have a forum to post questions. Another good source of information is *The Eye* (m *073 501 7019/078 980 0932;* e *editorial@theeye.co.rw;* w *theeye.co.rw*), a quarterly magazine distributed free at several outlets in Kigali; it includes (as does its website) extensive listings of hotels, restaurants, shops and other facilities in Rwanda and Burundi. Last, hopefully not least, check out the updates, or contribute your own, on our website w bradtupdates.com/rwanda.

TOUR OPERATORS

All of the operators listed below can organise day excursions or longer safaris, as well as vehicle hire, accommodation, airport transfers, gorilla-tracking permits, and so forth. All have English-speaking staff. In addition there are several more travel agents, who can deal with national and international travel but don't necessarily obtain gorilla permits (which are issued by the RDB Tourism and Conservation Reservation Office). For those seeking to hire a car, **Europcar** [79 F4] is situated on KN 16 Avenue (📞*0252 571355;* e *reservations@europcar.rw;* w *europcar.com*). The top two listings here offer particularly good services while the rest are also efficient and experienced operators.

Bizidanny Tours & Safaris [96 B1] Cozy Safari building, KG 621 St, Kimihurura; m 078 850 1461; e infobizidanny@yahoo.fr; w bizidanny. com; ⓕ Bizidannny Tours. Universally praised by readers of previous editions, this small & professional operator offers relatively budget-friendly tailor-made trips. As well as all the standard trips he also offers visits to schools, women's co-operatives, local development

projects, etc. Their offices have recently moved to the new Cozy Safari hotel (page 89), which they also own. See ad, page 285.
Volcanoes Safaris [86 D4] Hotel des Mille Collines; 📞0252 502452; m 078 830 2069; e salesrw@volcanoessafaris.com; w volcanoessafaris.com. This well-established company is among the longest-running in Rwanda & also has 3 superb lodges in Uganda. It specialises

in gorilla trips (including fly-in visits & 2-country trips), & its Virunga eco-luxury safari lodge near Volcanoes National Park has one of the most beautiful locations in Rwanda.

A Step Into Nature Tours [86 D2] KN 2 Av; m 072 883 8109; e info@astepintonature.com; w astepintonature.com. See ad, 4th colour section.

Abacus Rwanda Safaris m +256 772 331332 (Uganda); e info@rwanda-safari.com; w rwanda-safari.com. See ad, 4th colour section.

Amber Expeditions 1000 Av de L'Akanyaru; ℡0280 306090; e info@amberexpeditions.com; w amberexpeditions.com

Concord/Magic Safaris Rwanda Bd de l'Umuganda, c/o Ninzi Hill Hotel; ℡0252 588444/+256 414 342 926 (Uganda); m 078 259 6570; e info@magic-safaris.com; w magic-safaris.com. See ad, page 129.

Discover Rwanda m 078 372 0790; e info@discoverrwanda.com; w discoverrwanda.net. See ad, 4th colour section.

The Far Horizons Kigali Business Centre; ℡0280 658777; e info@thefarhorizons.com; w thefarhorizons.com

Go Kigali Tours [86 D7] Kigali Marriott Hotel, KN 3 Av; ℡+250 788 316 607; m 078 831 6607; e info@gokigalitours.com; w gokigalitours.com. See ad, page 72.

Great Lakes Safaris Rwanda Irembo Bldg, KG 5 Rd, Remera; m 078/073 852 1866; e info@greatlakessafaris.com; w https://www.greatlakessafaris.com

Hills in the Mist Tours Irembo Bldg, KG 5 Rd, Remera; m 072/078 850 4756; e info@hillsinthemisttours.com; w hillsinthemisttours.com

Individual Tours PO Box 4218; m 078 835 2661; e contact@individualtours.net; w individual-tours.net. See ad, 4th colour section.

International Tours & Travel ℡0252 578831; m 078 830 0256; e info@itt.co.rw; w www.itt.co.rw

Intore Expeditions 47 KN 41 St; m 078 835 3736; e info@intoreexpeditions.com; w intoreexpeditions.com. See ad, 4th colour section.

Jambo Travel & Tours [86 C6] Chadel Bldg, KN 78 St; m 078 683 1900/906 1729; e info@jambotoursrwanda.com; w jambotoursrwanda.com

Primate Safaris 4 KG 548 St; ℡0252 503428; m 078 973 4384; e info@primatesafaris.info; w primatesafaris.info. See ad, page 189.

Rwanda Eco-tours [86 C6] RUMA Bldg, KN 4 Av; ℡0280 500331; m 078 835 2009; e info@rwandaeco-tours.com; w rwandaeco-tours.com

Thousand Hills Africa 1000 Av de l'Akanyaru, Kiyovu; ℡ 0280 301000; m 078 835 1000; e rwsales@thousandhillsafrica.com; w thousandhillsafrica.com

Wildlife Tours Rwanda KG 11 Av, Kimironko; m 078 835 7052/852 7049; e info@wildlifetours-rwanda.com; w wildlifetours-rwanda.com

World Fusion Tours e worldfusiontours@gmail.com; w worldfusiontours.com. Kigali & Brisbane, Australia.

There are several more around the city offering various levels of service, and new ones are always opening. We can't list them all – so by all means try some out and tell us about them for the next edition! Also, away from Kigali, see **Green Hill Eco-Tours** and **Rwandan Adventures** (page 217).

WHERE TO STAY

Virtually all of the Kigali hotels in the 'Luxury' to 'Middle' categories can arrange airport pickups – just ask (and check the cost, if any) at the time of booking. Generally speaking, all of these hotels will also accept credit card payment (and many budget hotels are beginning to do so as well). Unless otherwise specified, bedrooms in all of the Kigali hotels listed here have en-suite facilities with either bath or shower. Hotels in the Remera suburb are closer to the airport than those in the centre.

LUXURY *(Over US$200 double)*

Kigali is served by a rapidly growing number of luxury hotels that conform to international standards at every level. These hotels tend to be somewhat impersonal & they cater mainly to business travellers; however, they offer an excellent range of facilities. In terms of quality of service & facilities, the **Serena** was long the obvious pick, but the **Marriott** next door & **Radisson Blu** at the Kigali Convention Centre, both opened in 2016, have raised the bar when it comes to luxury & style. If you've got business in Kacyiru, Remera or Nyarutarama, the Radisson Blu is undoubtedly the pick, but the **Gorillas Golf Hotel** & **Grand Legacy Hotel** both have excellent facilities & very good-quality rooms as well. The **Hôtel Des Mille Collines**, made famous by the film *Hotel Rwanda*, has long been something of a Kigali institution & also makes a worthy place to stay right in the heart of the city. Looking forward, **Sheraton** has plans for a lakeside hotel in Nyarutarama as part of the Century Park Hotel & Residences development, slated to open in 2020.

🏠 **Gorillas Golf Hotel** [94 D4] (83 rooms) m 078 817 4000; e reservation@gorillashotels. com; w gorillashotels.com. This relatively new hotel which is part of the Gorillas chain is situated in the peaceful, upmarket suburb of Nyarutarama, between the airport & the city centre. It boasts excellent views of the city & golf course & the staff appear to be very friendly, professional & attentive. The hotel has very good facilities including a fitness centre, bar, 100-seat conference centre & a swimming pool with a sweeping panoramic view. Rooms are smart, spacious & well maintained with DSTV, Wi-Fi, minibar, shower & tub, safe, tea/coffee-making facilities. The hotel restaurant serves upmarket French & continental cuisine, although a snack menu is also available. The hotel is a short walk from the MTN centre & some good restaurants. *US$175/200 sgl/dbl; US$200/225 deluxe; US$300 upwards for suites; discounts possible for stays longer than 7 days.*

🏠 **Grand Legacy Hotel** [75 H5] (43 rooms) 0280 408080; m 078 830 3483; e info@ grandlegacy.rw; w grandlegacy.rw. Opened in 2014, this new multi-storey hotel in Remera is far & away the most upmarket option in the neighbourhood, & it also stacks up quite well against the other luxury options throughout Kigali. The carpeted rooms come with a long list of amenities, including AC, flatscreen DSTV, phone, safe, tea/ kettle, carpet, scale, hairdryer, & a computer in every room. Décor is conservative & comfortable throughout, & there are 2 restaurants (1 with a baby grand piano!), a steam room, sauna & gym, & a swimming pool all on the premises. *US$200/240 sgl/dbl or twin; US$420/460 sgl/dbl suite.*

🏠 **Hôtel des Mille Collines** [86 D4] (112 rooms) 0252 576530; m 078 819 2000/072 802 3067; e reservations@millecollines.rw; w millecollines. rw. This Kigali institution was founded in 1973 & gained international fame for its role as a refuge during the genocide, which was chronicled in the film *Hotel Rwanda* (although the film was not made there). Despite its convenient location, a 5min moderately sloping walk from the city centre, it lies in attractive grounds that offer some enjoyable urban birdwatching, dominated by a large swimming pool & a massive fig tree that looks as if it's been there since time began, but is only 40-odd years old. A series of planned upgrades were abandoned in 2016, but the rooms nonetheless remain very smart & all come with flatscreen DSTV, minibar, Wi-Fi, & safe. The hotel also has a good poolside restaurant, a pricey bar, a tennis court, conference & business facilities & various boutiques. Credit cards accepted. *US$260/280 city view sgl/dbl; US$280/300 garden view sgl/dbl; US$300/320 panorama view sgl/dbl; suites US$360 and up; all rates B&B.*

🏠 **Kigali Marriott Hotel** [86 D7] (254 rooms) 0222 111111; e mhrs.kglmc.fo@marriotthotels. com. Opened in 2016 just a block over from the Serena (see below), this is the new kid on the block when it comes to 5-star accommodation in central Kigali, & it does not disappoint. The grand, marble-clad entrance hall hosts a relaxed bar that's become a popular central meeting point, & opens on to the large Soko restaurant, which itself spills out into the splendid gardens where another bar & a large, squiggle-shaped swimming pool can be found. The Cucina Italian restaurant rounds out the culinary offerings. The rooms are classical & elegant, with big bathtubs, floor-to-ceiling windows overlooking Kigali, & wood & marble accents throughout. There's a spa & steam room, along with beauty salon & several boutiques on site, including the excellent Go Kigali Tours (page 116). *Dbls from US$200, plus tax.*

🏠 **Kigali Serena Hotel** [79 E6] (148 rooms) 0252 597100; m 078 818 4500; e kigalireservations@serena.co.rw; w serenahotels.com. This top-notch 5-star hotel opened as the InterContinental in 2003 on the site of the former Diplomates, & was bought by the Kenya-based Serena Group in 2007. It lies on the tree-lined KN 3 Av, a flat 10min stroll from the city centre. The large carpeted rooms are some of the best on offer in Kigali, & come with king-size beds, DSTV, Wi-Fi, minibar, tea/coffee-making facilities, safe, hairdryer, combined tub/shower, & 24hr room service. Other facilities include a 550-seat conference centre, gym, spa, several boutiques, top-class cuisine at 2 restaurants & 24hr business services. The compact green grounds contain a large swimming pool & the relaxed poolside Sokon Café. *US$440/490 sgl/dbl; US$480/530 superior; US$515 upwards for suites; all rates inc a superb buffet b/fast.*

🏠 **Radisson Blu Hotel & Convention Centre** [94 B5] (291 rooms) ☎0252 252252/253253; e info.kigali@radissonblu.com; w radissonblu.com. Opened in 2016 along with the new Kigali Convention Centre, this is not only Kigali's most prestigious new hotel, but also its most identifiable landmark – its trademark multi-coloured illuminated dome can be seen from all over the city & makes quite a useful navigation aid. It's now become the address in town for visiting VIPs (the Estonian president was also staying here during our last visit), & the facilities are correspondingly plush. There are 2 restaurants (one, *Fillini*, serving fine Italian fare), 2 bars, a large outdoor swimming pool, spa, fitness centre, & a range of colourful & handsomely equipped rooms (starting at 36m²) with minibar, safe, tea/coffee facilities, flatscreen satellite TV, 24hr room service & balconies overlooking the city or pool. *US$270 dbl; US$330 superior dbl; suites from US$500.*

🏠 **The Retreat** [79 F4] (11 rooms) m 078 200 0001; e theretreat@heavenrwanda.com; w theretreatrwanda.com. Opened in early 2018, this is Kigali's newest luxury property & easily one of its most appealing. The row of whitewashed, vault-ceilinged villas all come with balconies out front & private garden areas with outdoor rainfall showers. Inside, the custom teak furnishings & canopy beds are accented with African art & wax-print fabrics. There's a heated saltwater swimming pool in the gardens, along with a spa with sauna, steam room, massage & fitness centre. They've recruited a Mauritian head chef for the exclusive African fusion restaurant, & the whole affair is under the same affable & active management as the Heaven Restaurant & Boutique Hotel next door (page 87). *US$575/675 sgl/dbl; US$775/875 sgl/dbl suite; all rates B&B.* See ad, 4th colour section.

🏠 **Ubumwe Grande** [86 D5] (153 rooms) m 078 374 4755/335 3984; e info@theapdl. com; w ubumwegrandehotel.com. It seems 2016 was a bumper year for upmarket accommodation in Kigali &, while this new addition isn't in the same class as the Radisson or Marriott, the rooms are nonetheless modern, well equipped & comfortable, with all the expected amenities. Set in a 12-storey tower just steps from the Union Trade Centre, facilities here include a gym, spa, & guests-only rooftop swimming pool. Even if you're not staying here, the 12th-floor rooftop restaurant & bar is emphatically worth a stop, with perhaps the best views in Kigali & a continental menu with mains from Rfr8,000 to Rfr15,000. *US$190/230 sgl/dbl; US$220/260 deluxe sgl/dbl; suites from US$240/280; all rates B&B.*

UPMARKET (*US$130–230 double*)
This header covers a wide variety of hotels offering high-quality accommodation at rates more likely to be affordable to non-business travellers. It's difficult to pick favourites, but the **Hotel le Garni du Centre** stands out as a smaller owner-managed hotel with a useful location & likeable character, while the suburban **Manor Hotel** has very smart rooms & good facilities.

🏠 **5 Swiss Hotel** [79 E4] (14 rooms) m 078 551 1155; e info@5swisshotel.com; w 5swisshotel.com. With all the fixtures imported from Switzerland, it's no surprise that this new Kiyovu address has a cool, modern feel. The minimalist rooms are bright & airy, with flatscreen TV, minibar, balcony & *imigongo* accents on the walls. The leafy gardens have views over the adjacent valley, & meals can be taken here or at the guests-only resto-bar inside. *US$100/120 sgl/dbl; US$130/150 sgl/dbl with view or kitchenette; all rates B&B.*

🏠 **CityBlue Embassy Row** [94 A3] (15 rooms) m 073 330 4142; e embassyrow.kigali@ citybluehotels.com; w citybluehotels.com. This smart hotel in Kacyiru has been rebranded under the CityBlue umbrella, & there are single rooms with ¾ bed, netting, DSTV, fridge, balcony & tiled bathrooms, similar double rooms with king-size beds, & immense suites with a large sitting room, 2 TVs, a kitchen & a dining area. The ordinary rooms seem indifferent value, but the suites are pretty attractive at the price, especially for self-caterers. The popular garden restaurant keeps long hours. *US$120/150 sgl/dbl room; US$150/180 sgl/dbl suite.*

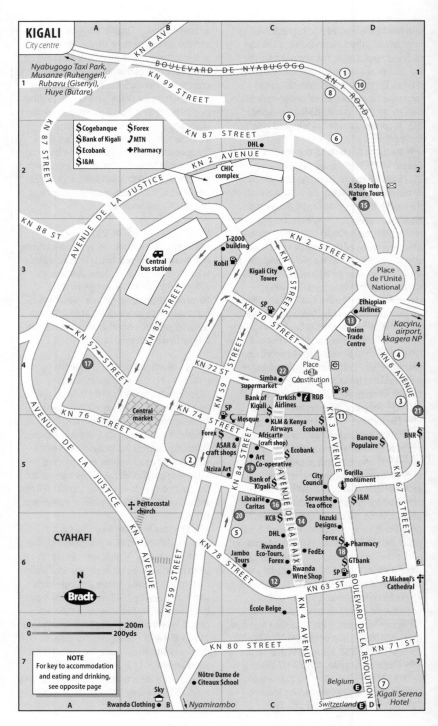

KIGALI
City centre

Nyabugogo Taxi Park,
Musanze (Ruhengeri),
Rubavu (Gisenyi),
Huye (Butare)

BOULEVARD DE NYABUGOGO

KN 8 AV

KN 99 STREET

KN 1 ROAD

KN 87 STREET

$ Cogebanque $ Forex
$ Bank of Kigali   ♪ MTN
$ Ecobank   ✚ Pharmacy
$ I&M

KN 2 AVENUE

CHIC
complex

DHL

A Step Into
Nature Tours

KN 88 ST

AVENUE DE LA JUSTICE

KN 2 STREET

T-2000
building

Kobil

Central
bus station

Kigali City
Tower

Place
de l'Unité
National

KN 82 STREET

KN 81 STREET

KN 70 STREET

SP

Ethiopian
Airlines

Union
Trade
Centre

Kacyiru,
airport,
Akagera NP

KN 57 STREET

KN 72 ST

KN 59 STREET

Simba
supermarket

Place
de la
Constitution

SP

Central
market

KN 76 STREET

KN 74 STREET

Bank of
Kigali

Turkish
Airlines

RDB

KLM & Kenya
Airways

Ecobank

Banque
Populaire

BNR

SP

Mosque

Forex

Africarte
(craft shop)

Ecobank

ASAR &
craft shops

Art
Co-operative

Nziza Art

Bank of
Kigali

City
Council

Gorilla
monument

I&M

AVENUE DE LA JUSTICE

KN 84 STREET

Librairie
Caritas

Sorwathe
Tea office

AVENUE DE LA PAIX

CYAHAFI

Pentecostal
church

KN 2 AVENUE

KCB

DHL

Inzuki
Designs

Forex

Pharmacy

N

Bradt

Jambo
Tours

Rwanda
Eco-Tours,
Forex

FedEx

KN 3 AVENUE

GTbank

SP

KN 67 STREET

St Michael's
Cathedral

0   200m
0   200yds

Rwanda
Wine Shop

KN 63 ST

BOULEVARD DE LA REVOLUTION

École Belge

KN 4 AVENUE

KN 71 ST

NOTE
For key to accommodation
and eating and drinking,
see opposite page

KN 80 STREET

KN 59 STREET

KN 78 STREET

Nôtre Dame de
Citeaux School

Sky

Belgium

Kigali Serena
Hotel

Rwanda Clothing

Nyamirambo

Switzerland

🛏️ **Where to stay**

❌ **Where to eat and drink**

🏠 **CityBlue Urban** [79 F4] (34 rooms) m 073 351 0510; e urban.kigali@citybluehotels.com; w citybluehotels.com. With an excellent location at the heart of Kiyovu, this is the flagship location of the CityBlue chain & would be a good choice for higher-end travellers seeking a somewhat more personal experience than at the larger hotels. Rooms are large, bright & modern, & all come with flatscreen DSTV, coffee/tea facilities, private terrace, writing desk, & carpeting. The rooftop restaurant & bar is a huge perk, & it would be easy to while away some hours up here with a cocktail or 2, but one downside for more active travellers would be the lack of a swimming pool or gym facilities. *US$130/160 sgl/dbl; US$160/190 deluxe sgl/dbl in new building; all rates B&B & negotiable.*

🏠 **Galaxy Hotel** [79 E3] (40 rooms) \0252 500230; m 078 838 2553; e reservations@galaxyhotelrwanda.com; w galaxyhotelrwanda.com. Just between the Mille Collines & the Garni du Centre, this is another comfortable & businesslike central option, though it must be said that it suffers from an acute paucity of character. Still, rooms are nicely equipped with flatscreen DSTV, private balcony, minibar, phone, wardrobe, hairdryer, AC, & a bit of contemporary décor. There's a swimming pool & thatched resto-bar, & an impressive selection of crafts on sale. *US$170–200 dbl depending on size.*

🏠 **Garr Hotel** [94 C2] (28 rooms) m 078 383 1292/830 5165; e reservations@garrhotel.com; w garrhotel.com. Set a short hop north of the MTN Centre in Nyarutarama, regular visitors to Kigali swear by this place. Rooms are furnished in dark wood, spotlessly clean & all come with big beds & mosquito net, writing desk, fan, flatscreen DSTV, wardrobe & very modern en-suite ablutions. There's a trim little garden & swimming pool out back, along with a steam room & massage parlour. Meals are by request. *Excellent value at US$95/120/160 sgl/dbl/suite; all rates B&B.*

🏠 **Heaven Boutique Hotel** [79 F3] (22 rooms) m 073 788 6307; e boutiquehotel@heavenrwanda.com; w heavenrwanda.com. Centrally located & attentively managed, this is a pleasant & reliable option in Kiyovu that's happily attached to one of the best restaurants in town (page 99). Rooms here come in a variety of configurations, from rather small queen-bed rooms in the main building to spacious garden chalets & king-bed rooms next to the restaurant. All come with flatscreen TV, coffee/tea facilities, mosquito nets & free Wi-Fi. Leisure facilities include an indulgent saltwater pool, brand-new fitness centre & guests-only dining area with food from the main restaurant menu. *US$115/145 queen sgl/dbl; US$135/165 king sgl/dbl; US$150/180 garden chalet; all rates B&B.* See ad, 4th colour section.

✳️ 🏠 **Hotel le Garni du Centre** [86 D4] (11 rooms) \0252 572654; m 078 856 9080; e hotelgarnikigalirwanda@gmail.com; w garnirwanda.com. This commendable small hotel, tucked away down a side street near the better-known Hotel des Mille Collines, is an unqualified gem. The quiet, comfortable rooms, which come with TV, free Wi-Fi, phone & minibar, are simply but stylishly decorated, & overlook the garden & small swimming pool. Lunch & dinner are available by request; the Restaurant Chez Robert & Mille Collines are only a few mins' walk away. There's a log fire in the lounge for chilly evenings, & the Swiss owner-manager – who lives on the premises – is very obliging. It's deservedly popular so book in advance (this can be done online). *US$125/155 sgl/dbl; US$150/180 exec sgl/dbl; US$165/195 studio apt sgl/dbl, all inc a superb buffet b/fast, with discounts for longer stays.*

🏠 **Lemigo Hotel** [94 C5] (176 rooms) m 078 404 0924/534 0741; e info@lemigohotel.com; w lemigohotel.com. Located on the edge of

Kacyiru near several international organisations & somewhat bland & impersonal, nevertheless this hotel has very good facilities & everything you would need for a comfortable stay in Kigali. It has a swimming pool & spa/gym, conference centre, nightclub/bar (where Orchestre Impala plays on Fri nights) & restaurant. Rooms have large TVs with DSTV, Wi-Fi, safe, hairdryer & AC, & a large new wing of rooms opened in 2016. *US$150/180 sgl/dbl; US$200/230 deluxe sgl/dbl; all rates B&B.*

✱ 🏠 **The Manor Hotel** [94 C1] (23 rooms) m 078 665 4435/665 0129; e info@ themanorrwanda.com; w themanorrwanda.com. Located off the Nyarutarama road down a cobbled street, this hotel has a lovely swimming pool & views across the city & Chinese, Indian, Italian & Irish restaurants within the hotel grounds. Rooms are smart, carpeted & have big balconies, DSTV, minibar, Wi-Fi, tea/coffee-making facilities, & very well-maintained bathrooms with tub & shower. There is also a bakery, hairdresser, & boutique shops. Expats from the local community sometimes come for the day to use the swimming pool (Rfr4,000 non-guests) & other facilities which gives the hotel a livelier atmosphere at w/ends. Service is friendly & professional if a little slow at times. *US$150/200 sgl/dbl; upwards of US$300 for exec rooms.*

🏠 **Ninzi Hill Hotel** [94 B4] (15 rooms) ☎0252 587711–5; e ninzihill@yahoo.fr. This long-serving mid-range hotel facing the new Kacyiru roundabout was closed as of early 2018 for a total overhaul. Its new incarnation is likely to be considerably more upmarket, & is in easy walking distance from Kigali Heights & the new Kigali Business Centre.

🏠 **Park Inn by Radisson** [79 G5] (161 rooms) m 078 813 2500; e reservation.kigali@ rezidorparkinn.com; w parkinn.com. Opened in May 2017, this is an excellent new 4-star option with a fine location in Kiyovu & international-standard facilities for either business or leisure visitors. The trim rooms start at 26m² & all come with desk, safe, minibar, & flatscreen TV; many have excellent views over Kigali. There's a large outdoor swimming pool, pool bar, & fitness centre, along with a lobby restaurant & bar keeping long hours (with an interesting assortment of wooden *chukudu* bicycles on the walls), & a nightclub in the basement that stays open quite late at w/ends. *US$160 dbl; US$190 superior dbl; US$400 suite.*

🏠 **Ubuki Residence Hotel** [94 C5] (8 rooms) m 078 990 6424; e reservation@ubukihotel. com; w ubukihotel.com. With a rather secluded location behind the parliament, this new lodge skilfully cultivates an intimate & familial feeling while offering professional facilities of a very high standard. Rooms here are well equipped, & all have high ceilings with large bathrooms, AC, TV, safe, & fridge. The secluded rear terrace is home to a swimming pool & guests-only restaurant serving French- & Mediterranean-inspired meals for Rfr13,000–25,000. The **Select Boutique Hotel** [94 C4] (m *078 609 8109;* w *selectboutiquehotel. com) next door is very similar in standard & price. US$200/230 sgl/dbl B&B.*

🏠 **Umubano Hotel** [94 B4] (100 rooms) ☎0252 593500; m 078 840 4065; e reservations@ umubanohotel.rw; w umubanohotel.rw. Formerly part of the Novotel chain (& still frequently referred to by that name), this large hotel has a quiet & attractive location in leafy 4ha gardens in Kacyiru, but is otherwise looking increasingly past its prime these days. The staff are friendly & it's very popular with local people for functions, but the rooms are shabby & overdue for an update, with faded blue carpeting & outmoded bath facilities. The hotel has a good patisserie in the foyer, plus poolside restaurant & bar, swimming pool, tennis courts, fitness centre, Wi-Fi & various boutiques. *Overpriced at US$155/185 sgl/dbl; US$200–230 suite.*

MODERATE (*US$60–120 double*)

Cheaper & generally of lower quality than the upmarket options listed on page 85, hotels listed in the moderate category mostly still cater routinely to bona fide tourists. That said, it's difficult to draw a clear qualitative line between some hotels listed as upmarket & the best of those in the moderate bracket, so we've settled on a cut-off price of US$120 for a standard double, which means that the best hotels in the moderate category – strikingly, **Inside Afrika**, **Tea House B&B**, **Yambi Guesthouse** & the **Iris Guesthouse** – represent some of the best value in town.

🏠 **Amaris Hotel** [96 C1] (20 rooms) m 078 830 4627/865 0250; e amarishotelrwanda@gmail. com; w amarishotel.rw. Just next to Cozy Safari in Kimihurura, this newish place offers clean & well-kept en-suite rooms with fridge, TV, & safe. Some rooms come with balconies. It's not particularly characterful, but it's reasonably priced & there's a very appealing top-floor restaurant & bar with great views over the city & meat & fish dishes for Rfr6,000–7,000. *US$60/80 sgl/dbl with no AC; US$70/90 sgl/dbl with AC; all rates B&B.*

🏠 **Bloom Back Hotel** [75 H3] (26 rooms) m 078 945 3025/855 2224; e bloombackhotels@gmail.com. Set 900m north of the Kimironko Market on KG 11 Av, this likeable hotel lies in large grassy gardens dotted with plastic tables & benches. The bright & spacious en-suite rooms have queen-size or twin beds, DSTV & combined tub/shower; there is Wi-Fi & a restaurant serving European & African cuisine. *Good value at Rfr25,000/40,000 sgl/dbl; Rfr40,000/50,000 sgl/dbl exec; all rates B&B.*

🏠 **Civitas Hotel** [75 G5] (23 rooms) m 078 888 7823; e info@civitashotelrwanda.com; w civitashotelrwanda.com. This somewhat anonymous-seeming hotel on the airport road opposite Chez Lando has smart, spacious & clean rooms with TV, en-suite bathrooms with tub & shower, minibar & Wi-Fi. Prices are somewhat negotiable, especially if you'll be staying a few days. Good restaurant with an outside patio area that is a popular local hangout. *Fair value at US$70/80 sgl/dbl B&B.*

🏠 **Cozy Safari** [96 B1] (12 rooms) m 078 572 1900; e info@cozysafari.com; w cozysafari.com. Under the same ownership as Bizidanny Tours & Safaris (page 82), this new hotel is managed with the same attention & care as their highly recommended tour company, whose offices are also located here. The sleek & modern en-suite rooms come with bathtub & satellite TV, & many come with their own balconies. There's a swimming pool & sauna, plus rooftop restaurant-bar with indoor/outdoor seating & fabulous views over the city. *US$100–150 dbl B&B.*

🏠 **Gloria Hotel** [86 B5] (45 rooms) m 078 893 0233/536 3180; e info@gloriahotelrwanda.com; w gloriahotelrwanda.com. The rooms at this very central option are a bit cramped but nonetheless well managed & well equipped, with modern furnishings, flatscreen TV, Wi-Fi, & tea/coffee facilities. The terrace restaurant is a great spot to watch the busy streets below, & some rooms have balconies with views. *US$70/90 sgl/dbl.*

🏠 **Grazia Apartments** [94 C5] (26 rooms) m 078 886 2351; e graziaparts@gmail.com; w graziaapartments.com. Opened in 2014 just around the corner from the Lemigo Hotel, this is a modern & well-managed mid-range option, with very good facilities including a large swimming pool with views over the city, fitness centre, steam room, spa & complimentary laundry service. Rooms are large & equally well equipped, with mini-fridge, flatscreen TV, microwave, & kitchenette in the apartments. There's a poolside restaurant & bar on site serving good grills & draught beer. *US$100/120 sgl/dbl; US$130/150 sgl/dbl suite; all rates B&B.*

🏠 **Hotel Beauséjour** [75 G4] (35 rooms) ☎0252 580760; m 078 838 8885; e info@beausejourhotel.rw; w beausejourhotel.rw. Not to be confused with the nearby & affiliated Auberge Beau Séjour, this hotel is located next to the Sole Luna restaurant on the airport road. Rooms are well maintained, with great views overlooking the city & all come with DSTV, fan, Wi-Fi, fridge & en-suite hot shower & tub. It has a good restaurant too, which serves weekly culinary themes & African speciality foods. The hotel runs a free airport shuttle service & the staff seem helpful & friendly. *US$60/80 sgl/dbl B&B.*

🏠 **Hotel Chez Lando** [75 G5] (82 rooms) ☎0252 582 050; m 078 838 5300; e info@chezlando.com; w chezlando.com. Founded in the 1980s, this well-established family hotel lies in green grounds just off the main road through the suburb of Remera, an easy taxi or minibus-taxi ride from town. The spacious rooms have satellite TV, Wi-Fi, private balcony, & en-suite tub & shower. The indoor La Fringale restaurant does a good buffet b/fast but can be slow & cheerless for other meals; for these the outdoor, downstairs restaurant is brisker & livelier. Several good restaurants & shops lie within easy walking distance of the hotel, as do several banks & a sauna/massage centre. Rooms in the new wing are better value overall. *US$71/94 sgl/dbl in the old building; US$118/153 in the new extension; all rates B&B.*

🏠 **Hotel Gorillas** [79 G4] (31 rooms) m 078 817 4000/820 0511/848 7777; e reservation@gorillashotels.com; w gorillashotels.com. This calm & efficient hotel, about 1km east of the city centre, has small & somewhat dated but comfortable rooms & a highly rated continental restaurant, with indoor & outdoor seating, & draught beer on tap. Facilities include Wi-Fi & TV in all rooms, some of which have tubs & others showers, so state your

3

preference if you have one. The downhill walk to the hotel from the centre of town is manageable but the uphill walk into town is quite steep, but plenty of taxi-voitures ply the route & minibus-taxis run nearby. *US$70/100 sgl/dbl B&B*.

🏠 **Hotel le Printemps** [75 H3] (20 rooms) 📞0252 582142; m 078 830 7133; e info@ leprintempshotel.rw; w leprintempshotel.rw. Set in pleasant gardens opposite Kimironko taxi park, this small suburban hotel offers a variety of spotlessly clean accommodation, including tiled singles & larger suites, all with TV, phone & en-suite hot shower. There's Wi-Fi & a decent restaurant with outdoor seating. *A bit overpriced at US$35/45 sgl/dbl B&B*.

🏠 **Hotel Okapi** [86 D2] (39 rooms) 📞0252 571667; m 078 147 1041/733 5162; e reservations@okapihotel.com; w okapihotel. com. This 5-storey hotel on KN 87 St is a popular central choice in this price range, & convenient for public transport. While there is a slightly confusing array of different room categories, it is worth paying extra for one of the comfortable tiled rooms in the main building, which have queen-size or twin beds, netting, fridge, DSTV & en-suite combination tub/shower, as their cheaper & gloomier counterparts in the downstairs annexe represent truly poor value for money. The restaurant offers a decent selection of Indian, Rwandan & continental dishes in the Rfr3,000–5,000 range, & vegetarians are well catered for. It also has a panoramic view across the Kigali landscape. *US$60/80 in the main building; US$35/50 in the annexe; US$90/110 sgl/dbl suite*.

🏠 **Inside Afrika Boutique Hotel** [79 G4] (9 rooms) m 072 250 3698/078 850 3698; e info@ inside-afrika.com; w inside-afrika.com. Situated on KN 46 St around the corner from the Gorillas Hotel, this attractive boutique hotel has large rooms with stylish contemporary ethnic décor, king-size or twin beds with net, flatscreen satellite TV, & en-suite hot showers. Although it has no restaurant, there are several good eateries within easy walking distance. Facilities include free Wi-Fi throughout, a tempting swimming pool, & a good b/fast. *US$100 dbl B&B*.

🏠 **Iris Guesthouse** [79 F4] (19 rooms) m 072 850 1181/078 580 6300; e irisguest1@ gmail.com; w irisguesthouserw.com. Situated on KN 33 St downhill from the city centre, this well-managed guesthouse has been popular with NGO

workers & other regular visitors to Kigali since it opened in 2001, & as a result it is often full, so try to book in advance. It stands in pleasant grounds in a shady street away from the traffic, & the neat rooms all come with double or twin bed with netting, phone, DSTV, Wi-Fi, private terrace with seating, & en-suite hot tub. You can eat indoors or alfresco at the attached restaurant, which serves a varied selection of grills, sandwiches, salads & pasta dishes in the Rfr4,000–7,000 range. *US$75/93 sgl/dbl; US$150/180 2-/3-bedroom apt; all rates B&B*.

🏠 **La Palisse Hotel** [75 H5] (77 rooms) m 078 838 5505/830 6111; e palisseho@yahoo.fr. Situated 2km from the airport along the Akagera road, La Palisse is the least urban hotel in Kigali, set in sprawling wooded grounds that harbour a varied birdlife, as well as a swimming pool, children's playground, & outdoor bar & barbecue. Though the standalone en-suite *rondavels* (round huts) are spacious, with king-size or twin beds with net, TV, & minibar, they're looking rather threadbare these days & are in need of an update. The cheaper standard rooms in the main 4-storey building are similar but smaller & less outdoorsy. *US$70/80 standard sgl/dbl room or bungalow; US$100 suite*.

🏠 **New Impala Hotel** [86 C1] (20 rooms) m 078 831 0003/830 1315; e infonewimpalahotel@ gmail.com; w newimpalahotel.com. Situated a few doors down from the Okapi, this 3-storey place is under new management as of late 2017 & can be recognised by the garish statues of gazelles (rather than impalas) that adorn the front parking. The tiled rooms have king-size or twin beds, DSTV, phone, Wi-Fi, en-suite hot shower & a nice little balcony offering great views on the non-street side. Nothing special, but conveniently central & fair value. *US$50 standard dbl; US$70 deluxe dbl*.

🏠 **Romalo Guesthouse** [75 F5] (10 rooms) m 078 830 1453/842 1208; e romalo1@yahoo. com; f Romalo Guesthouse. Tucked away in the sloping backstreets below the convention centre, this small family-run guesthouse around the corner from Inka Steakhouse is a little isolated so only really convenient for those with private transport. Set in a large 2-storey house with a wide balcony overlooking a green compound, the large, clean, tiled rooms come with king-size or twin beds, fridge, TV, Wi-Fi & en-suite hot shower. *Good value at US$40–60 dbl B&B*.

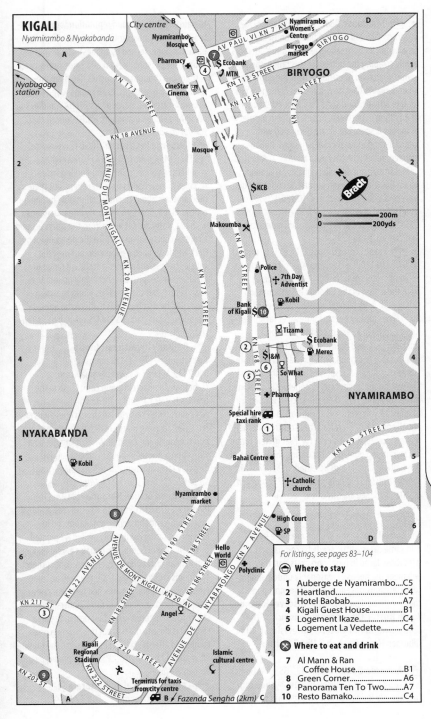

KIGALI
Nyamirambo & Nyakabanda

City centre

Nyabugogo station

KN 173 STREET

KN 18 AVENUE

AVENUE DU MONT KIGALI

KN 20 AVENUE

KN 173 STREET

Nyamirambo Mosque

Pharmacy

CineStar Cinema

AV PAUL VI KN 7 AV

Ecobank

MTN

KN 113 STREET

KN 115 ST

Mosque

KCB

KN 169 STREET

Makoumba

Police

7th Day Adventist

Kobil

Bank of Kigali

Tizama

Ecobank

Merez

I&M

So What

KN 168 STREET

Pharmacy

NYAMIRAMBO

Special hire taxi rank

KN 159 STREET

NYAKABANDA

Kobil

Bahai Centre

Catholic church

Nyamirambo market

High Court

SP

Hello World

Polyclinic

Angel

KN 190 STREET

KN 188 STREET

KN 186 STREET

AVENUE DE MONT KIGALI

KN 20 AV

KN 22 AVENUE

KN 211 ST

KN 220 STREET

KN 183 STREET

AVENUE DE LA NYABARONGO

KN 2 AVENUE

KN 203 ST

Kigali Regional Stadium

KN 222 STREET

Terminus for taxis from city centre

Islamic cultural centre

Fazenda Sengha (2km)

Nyamirambo Women's Centre

Biryogo market

BIRYOGO

BIRYOGO

KN 123 STREET

Brack

0   200m
0   200yds

N

Kigali   WHERE TO STAY

3

For listings, see pages 83–104

Where to stay
1 Auberge de Nyamirambo....C5
2 Heartland..................................C4
3 Hotel Baobab..........................A7
4 Kigali Guest House................B1
5 Logement Ikaze.....................C4
6 Logement La Vedette..........C4

Where to eat and drink
7 Al Mann & Ran
   Coffee House.......................B1
8 Green Corner.........................A6
9 Panorama Ten To Two..........A7
10 Resto Bamako.......................C4

✳ 🏠 **Tea House B&B**   [75 H5] (7 rooms, 1 dorm) m 078 218 1209; e bnbteahousekigali@gmail.com; w bnbteahousekigali.com. With rates barely scraping the bottom of this range, this new owner-managed guesthouse near the airport is an undeniable bargain & is a quiet & friendly pick for late arrivals, long stays (ask about discounts), or anything in between. Rooms come in a variety of shapes & sizes, but all are decorated with lots of Rwandan weaving & paintings. Italian-inspired meals (the chef used to work at Alberto's in Musanze) are available to guests for around US$6–10, & there's even a small dorm for budget travellers. *US$25pp dorm bed; US$40/50 sgl/dbl using shared ablutions; US$45/55 en-suite sgl/dbl; US$55/65 deluxe sgl/dbl; all rates inc a generous b/fast.* See ad, page 129.

✳ 🏠 **Yambi Guesthouse**   [74 C7] (10 rooms) m 078 830 1800; e booking@yambihotel.com; w yambihotel.com. Though it's set rather far from the action in the Gikondo neighbourhood, this superb & social new guesthouse opened in 2015 & has rapidly become a traveller favourite. Rooms come in a variety of sizes & shapes (including a 4-bed dorm), but all are characterful & comfortably equipped, with local art & sculpture (some of it for sale) displayed all over the place. The restaurant serves tasty & generously portioned meals for about US$10 (or the kitchen is open to guests if you prefer), & the included b/fast is equally plentiful. There's a fitness centre & homely-feeling lounge, & plans exist for a set of new rooms & a swimming pool, possibly during the lifespan of this edition. Credit cards accepted. *US$50/70/100 sgl/dbl/trpl; US$120 family suite; US$25 dorm bed; all rates B&B.* See ad, 4th colour section.

BUDGET (US$25–50)

The hotels listed in this section are more basic & in some cases a little seedy by comparison with those laced in higher brackets, but they will meet the needs of reasonably undemanding cost-conscious travellers. By far the most popular choice with backpackers is the **Discover Rwanda Youth Hostel**. Other good options include the central **Dream Inn Motel** & **Hotel Isimbi**, & the suburban **Hotel Baobab** & **Hotel Hilltop**.

🏠 **Auberge Beau Séjour**   [75 G5] (19 rooms) 📞0252 582527; e beausejourhotel@yahoo.com. This homely lodge lies just off the main road to the airport & has a good reputation locally. The rooms are very pleasant, & come with TV & hot bath. Dinner is served by request. The owner supervises personally & takes a pride in the place – there are thoughtful touches like drinking-water in the bedrooms, & all rooms lead out to the well-cared-for garden. *Rfr21,000/30,000 sgl/dbl with a shared bathroom; Rfr30,000/38,000 sgl/dbl en suite, B&B.*

🏠 **Auberge la Caverne**   [86 D1] (20 rooms) 📞0252 574549; m 078 875 4110/821 0000; e aubecav@yahoo.fr. This long-serving lodge receives mixed reports from travellers, but there's no doubt it is about the most affordable option in central Kigali. Spacious & mostly en-suite rooms with hot water are set away from the traffic around a central courtyard on KN 1 Rd (Bd de Nyabugogo). Back windows have a good view out over the valley. The restaurant does a standard range of meals. It's a steepish but short walk up into the town centre, but the hotel lies along the main road used by minibus-taxis to/from the intercity Nyabugogo taxi park. *US$16/25 sgl/dbl; US$30 en-suite dbl with TV.*

🏠 **Bethany Investment Group Guesthouse**   [79 F4] (30 rooms) m 078 600 7439; e bethanykiyovu@gmail.com; w bethanyinvestmentgroup.com. Close to the Gorillas Hotel, a 10min walk downhill from the city centre, this Presbyterian church guesthouse is a clean, relaxing place with cheerful rooms, a good-value dining room, & Wi-Fi. It can get busy with church guests so book in advance. Good monthly rates are available. *Rfr20,000 basic sgl; Rfr30,000/35,000 standard sgl/dbl; all rates B&B.*

🏠 **Centre d'Accueil Hosanna**   [94 A4] (16 rooms) m 078 838 0961/218 2371; e cenhosanby@gmail.com/centrehosanna@gmail.com. Set in Kacyiru but rather confusingly owned & operated by the Diocese of Goma, this remains a solid budget option in an increasingly expensive neighbourhood. The rooms are simple, tiled, & en suite, & all come with mosquito nets. The attached resto-bar does a popular lunch buffet & à la carte dinners. The standard rooms, among the best deal in the area, seem a bit close to the bar, but this is a church-run compound after all, & they should switch the music off around 22.00. *Rfr20,000/35,000 standard/deluxe dbl inc B&B for 1.*

🏠 **Centre National de Pastorale St Paul**   [79 E3] (60 rooms) m 078 528 5341;

e cnpsaintpaul@yahoo.fr. Situated alongside the Eglise Saint-Famille, about 200m east of the Pl de l'Unité Nationale, this was long the most central shoestring option in Kigali, but they've recently phased out their budget rooms & were constructing a huge new wing of smarter rooms in 2018. Their standard rooms come in double or twin configurations, & all have hot showers. The pretty gardens are very relaxing to sit in & the restaurant serves the usuals, though the staff can be rather uninterested on the whole. *Rfr17,000/24,000 sgl occupancy/dbl or twin.*

🏠 **City Valley Motel** [78 B2] (19 rooms) m 078 857 8197. Situated on KN 7 Rd a few hundred metres from Nyabugogo taxi park, this is a pleasant hotel with a decent-looking garden bar & restaurant attached, as well as a nightclub. The location, on a road used by heavy trucks, is potentially noisy, so best to ask for a room facing away from the traffic. The large rooms all have fan, net, TV & a balcony. *Rfr12,000 dbl using common showers; Rfr20,000 en suite with hot water.*

🏠 **Discover Rwanda Youth Hostel** [96 B1] (8 rooms, 3 dorms) m 078 226 5679; e info@hostelkigali.com; w discoverrwanda. net or 🟦 DiscoverRwandaYouthHostel. Kigali's backpacker Mecca, this welcoming hostel provides budget travellers with a genuinely relaxed focal point from which to explore the city & the rest of the country, which has now become even easier since they opened another branch in Rubavu (page 214). Recently relocated to KN 14 Av in Kimihurura, facilities include a sociable balcony with comfortable seating overlooking a large green garden, Wi-Fi, hot showers, movie nights, & affordable meals, including a good variety of Rwandan staples. They're also developing a range of tours around the city & country that are budget-friendly & easily booked at the front desk. Rooms range from dorms to en-suite doubles, & the hostel is operated by the Aegis Trust (see *Kigali Genocide Memorial*, page 117) & all proceeds go towards its Peace-building Education Programme for genocide survivors. *US$16/19 6–8/4-bed dorm; US$23pp twin; US$30/45 sgl/dbl using shared ablutions; US$50/60 en-suite dbl; US$10pp camping; all rates B&B.*

🏠 **Havugimana Israel (AEE) Guest Centre** [75 H5] (18 rooms) m 078 566 8836/868 3756; e higuestcenter@aeerwanda. rw; w aeerwanda.rw/guesthouse. This large &

bright pastoral centre is located in Remera, close to the airport, down a side road now marked as KK 228 St. It has basic but clean & cheerful rooms with nets, towels & a desk. The shared bathrooms have showers & flush toilets, & some have hot water. The staff are always friendly & helpful & although it is a religious institution there is no curfew. The guesthouse has spacious gardens & sitting areas for guests to meet in, & there is also a conference room & free Wi-Fi available. Although it is a distance from the city centre, it is a 10min walk from Remera bus park where buses go very frequently to all parts of the city. A very good option for those wanting an inexpensive place to stay near the airport. *Rfr8,500/15,000 sgl/dbl using shared ablutions; Rfr20,000/30,000 en-suite sgl/ twin; b/fast Rfr2,000pp.*

🏠 **Heartland Hotel** [91 C4] (20 rooms) m 078 857 0674/991 0711; e heartlandhotel2@ gmail.com. Situated in the lively suburb of Nyamirambo, south of the city centre, this 3-storey hotel (formerly known as the Mount Kigali) has comfortable accommodation in the form of singles (1 double bed) & doubles (2 ¾ beds). There are 4 categories of room ranging from basic twins with nets & shared bathrooms to rooms with DSTV & en-suite shower. A restaurant & sauna/massage are attached. *Basic rooms Rfr15,000/20,000 sgl/dbl; superior rooms Rfr30,000 dbl.*

🏠 **Hotel Baobab** [91 A7] (9 rooms) 📞0252 575633; m 078 850 4629/572 2894; e stanisibomana@aol.com. This great place is full of character but some distance from the city centre, down in Nyakabanda suburb in the southwest near Mount Kigali & the Stade Régional de Kigali. If you have your own transport (or don't mind taking taxis), do consider it. The area is peaceful, with widespread views across the valley & to Mount Kigali, & the possibility of quite rural walks. The restaurant (mostly outdoor) has a good reputation locally. Rooms are en suite with hot water, phone, TV & Wi-Fi. A large block of new rooms was under construction in 2018. *US$45 dbl B&B.*

🏠 **Hotel Isimbi** [86 C6] (20 rooms) m 078 609 0557; e isimbihotel@hotmail.com. The most central hotel in this range, situated on KN 84 St just a few mins' walk from KN 4 Av (Av de la Paix), this is an efficient, clean, business-type hotel with a vintage feel about it. The unpretentious en-suite rooms with hot water are very good value (the back ones are quietest), & there's a non-

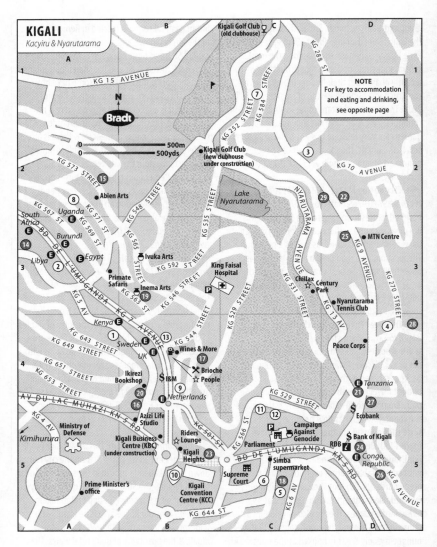

KIGALI
Kacyiru & Nyarutarama

Kigali Golf Club
(old clubhouse)

NOTE
For key to accommodation
and eating and drinking,
see opposite page

KG 15 AVENUE

Bradt

0   500m
0   500yds

Kigali Golf Club
(new clubhouse
under construction)

Lake
Nyarutarama

KG 288 ST

KG 252 STREET

KG 584 STREET

KG 10 AVENUE

Abien Arts

Uganda

South
Africa

Burundi

Libya

Egypt

Ivuka Arts

Primate
Safaris

Inema Arts

King Faisal
Hospital

Chillax

Century
Park

Nyarutarama
Tennis Club

MTN Centre

Kenya

Sweden

UK

Wines & More

Brioche
People

Ikirezi
Bookshop

I&M

Netherlands

Azizi Life
Studio

Ministry of
Defense

Kimihurura

Kigali Business
Centre (KBC)
(under construction)

Riders
Lounge

Kigali
Heights

Prime Minister's
office

Kigali
Convention
Centre (KCC)

Supreme
Court

Parliament

Campaign
Against
Genocide

Simba
supermarket

Peace Corps

Tanzania

Ecobank

Bank of Kigali

RDB

Congo,
Republic

Primate

KG 573 STREET

KG 567 STR

KG 571 ST

KG 569 ST

BD DE L'UMUGANDA

KG 5 AV

KG 7 AVENUE

KG 565 STREET

KG 548 STREET

KG 592 STREET

KG 563 ST

KG 546 STREET

KG 544 STREET

KG 529 STREET

KG 535 STREET

KG 531 STREET

KG 13 AV

KG 9 AVENUE

KG 270 STREET

KG 643 STREET

KG 649 STREET

KG 651 STREET

KG 653 STREET

AV DU LAC MUHAZI KN 5 RD

KG 4 AV

KG 561 ST

KG 566 ST

KG 529 STREET

BD DE L'UMUGANDA

KN 5 RD

KG 6 AV

KG 8 AVENUE

KG 644 ST

NYARUTARAMA AVENUE

smoking snack-bar & restaurant for main meals (up to around Rfr5,000), as well as room service. *US$40/45 sgl/dbl exc b/fast.*

K-Town Motel [86 D1] (17 rooms) m 078 127 6383; e ktwn.motel@gmail.com. This smart hotel opposite the venerable Auberge la Caverne is under new management but remains a reliable budget pick. The tiled rooms are clean, comfortable & reasonably modern, with nets, TV, Wi-Fi & fridge, along with a good-value restaurant & bar downstairs. It's also very central, within walking distance of several restaurants, & plenty of

public transport passes right by the door. *US$35/40 sgl/dbl; US$60 suite; B&B.*

Mamba Club [96 C4] (8 rooms) m 078 030 3463; e info@mambaclub.net; f MambaClubRW. Though mostly known as a hangout for bowling, swimming, & drinking, this Kigali standby has a few rooms for rent as well, including a large 12-bed dorm that opens on to a nice 1st-floor balcony. All rooms come with hot showers & Wi-Fi, but most are above the bar so you might want to steer clear at w/ends if you're sensitive to noise. *Rfr12,000 dorm bed;*

Rfr25,000 dbl using shared ablutions; Rfr30,000 en-suite dbl.

✳ 🏠 **Mijo Hostel** [96 C3] (2 rooms, 6 dorms) m 078 746 3008; e mijolimited@gmail.com. Bright, modern & breezy, this newly opened hostel, furnished with a variety of cleverly recycled & upcycled materials, is easily the prettiest in Kigali, with lovely views from the rear terrace & an array of traveller-friendly facilities on offer, including free purified water & a budget-friendly laundry service. Dorms here range from 4 to 12 beds & are segregated by gender, but couples are generally allocated a room of their own when possible. Indeed, the only drawback here is probably the lack of private rooms – there's only 1 double & 1 single available. The rooftop terrace resto-bar was still under construction when we checked in, but should be serving up Rwandan staples by the time you read this. *US$12—20pp dorm bed; US$25/45 sgl/dbl; all rates B&B.*

🏠 **Murugo Hostel** [94 A2] (5 rooms) m 078 845 6953/739 5019; e david@murugohostel.com; w murugohostel.com. Run by a long-time veteran of the hospitality industry in Rwanda who struck

out & started his own business, this welcoming little place, recently relocated to Kacyiru, is simplicity itself, with no-frills en-suite tiled rooms kept sparklingly clean. The grounds are trim & pleasant (including a sunny roof terrace), staff are eminently helpful & engaging, & it's an easy place to arrange car hire & travel throughout the country. There's a good menu of meals at Rfr2,500–4,000 & a lunch buffet Mon–Fri. *US$25pp in 3-bed dorm; US$40/50 sgl/dbl using shared ablutions; US$50/60 sgl/dbl en suite; all rates B&B.*

🏠 **Step Town Motel** [79 E2] (25 rooms) 📞 0252 500042/56; m 078 500 5662/846 0075; e stepst22@yahoo.com; w step-town.com. This amenable place just north of the city centre gets rave reviews, & the attentive management see to it that it stays that way. The tiled en-suite rooms are split over 3 buildings in the green compound, & all are simple & meticulously clean, with nets, fans, TV & Wi-Fi. There are plentiful views over the city, & a resto-bar serving the usual favourites either inside or out on one of the terraces. *US$55/60/75 sgl/dbl/twin with discounts for residents; all rates B&B.*

SHOESTRING   (*Below US$20 double*)

The lodgings listed in this section are all on the basic side, with rooms using common showers or cold water only – or both! Most cater primarily to the local market, though they are also suitable for backpackers & other travellers on a rock-bottom budget. Unusually for an African capital, there are very few real cheapies in the city centre. Instead, they're mostly clustered south of the city centre in the lively & characterful quarters of Nyamirambo & Nyakabanda, between Nyamirambo Mosque [91 B1] & the Kigali Regional Stadium [91 B7]. Probably the best choices in this category are the **Kigali Guest House**, & for single travellers, **Auberge de Nyamirambo**, which has the added advantage of being close to a cluster of similarly priced options you could fall back on if it's full. To reach Nyamirambo & Nyakabanda on foot from the city centre, walk south on KN 2 Av for about 15mins. Alternatively, pick up bus 401 from the new central bus station opposite the CHIC Complex – this runs towards the stadium, passing within 100m of most of the listed hotels. There are also a couple of decent cheapies near Nyabugogo station, also listed below, should you want to stay nearby for an early departure.

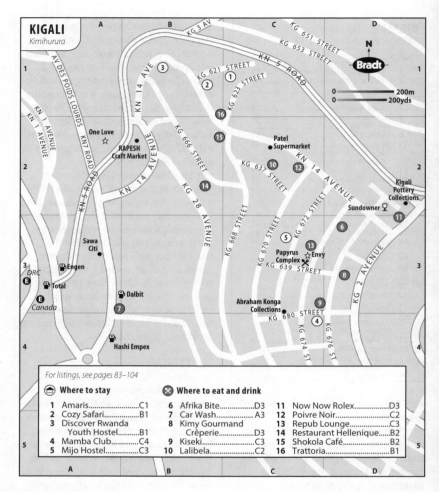

KIGALI
Kimihurura

For listings, see pages 83–104

🛏 **Where to stay**

1	Amaris	C1
2	Cozy Safari	B1
3	Discover Rwanda Youth Hostel	B1
4	Mamba Club	C4
5	Mijo Hostel	C3

❌ **Where to eat and drink**

6	Afrika Bite	D3	11	Now Now Rolex	D3
7	Car Wash	A3	12	Poivre Noir	C2
8	Kimy Gourmand Crêperie	D3	13	Repub Lounge	C3
			14	Restaurant Hellenique	B2
9	Kiseki	C3	15	Shokola Café	B2
10	Lalibela	C2	16	Trattoria	B1

🏠 **Alpha & Sons** [78 A3] (20 rooms) m 078 824 7081; e alphonseniyitegeka@gmail.com. On the top 2 floors of a commercial building just opposite Nyabugogo bus park, this place has basic tiled en-suite rooms in surprisingly good nick (mosquito nets too), linked by corridors adorably crammed with potted plants. Drinks are available on site & there's a balcony for watching the chaos below. *Rfr12,000/15,000/20,000 sgl/dbl/twin B&B.*

🏠 **Auberge de Nyamirambo** [91 C5] (9 rooms) m 078 943 0663/851 0353; e auberge. nyamirambo@yahoo.fr. This homely 2-storey lodge is one of the best-value options in Kigali for those wanting a single room: the *auberge* has clean en-suite rooms & a convenient location on the main road out of town towards the Islamic Centre. 6

rooms are in the main building, some en suite & some using common showers, & the other 3, all en suite, are in a little streetside annexe. The rooms in the annexe are marginally nicer but look slightly less secure, as you don't have to pass through reception to reach them. There's no in-house restaurant or bar, but there are a handful of decent options within 500m. Note that now there are no double rooms available so the following prices are for single rooms. *Rfr10,000 full en suite; Rfr8,000 sink & shower but shared toilet; Rfr5,000 shared bathroom facilities.*

🏠 **Episcopal Church Resthouse** [79 F7] (21 rooms) m 078 884 7592; e eardkguesthouse@ gmail.com. Part of the St Etienne Church on Av Paul VI in Biryogo (aka Bilyogo) District some 500m east of Nyamirambo Mosque, this church guesthouse is not that convenient as far as location, but it's been spruced up considerably in recent years & the trim rooms with nets represent quite good value. Deluxe rooms are set in the new wing, & the gardens out front are green & tranquil. Inexpensive meals are available on site. *Rfr10,000 dbl or twin using shared ablutions; Rfr15,000/25,000 en-suite standard/deluxe dbl; Rfr5,000 dorm bed; b/fast Rfr3,000.*

🏠 **Kigali Guest House** [91 B1] (16 rooms) m 078 731 4301/849 9506; e kigaliguest10@ yahoo.com. Situated a block past the mosque at the corner of KN 2 Av & KN 113 St, this is a good-value hotel, offering accommodation in small en-suite rooms with hot water, phone, Wi-Fi & TV. There's no restaurant or bar, so it's pretty quiet – if you can ignore the passing traffic & early morning mosque calls! There are plenty of other eateries & bars in the area. Minibus-taxis from central Kigali stop right opposite – ask for 'Chez Mayaka' or the mosque. *Rfr8,000/10,000/12,000 sgl/dbl/twin.*

🏠 **Logement Ikaze** [91 C4] (8 rooms) m 078 842 9985. The least inviting of the lodges in Nyamirambo, this place has spacious rooms, but the overall feel is rather dingy & some rooms are in quite a bad state of disrepair. *Rfr7,000 for all rooms.*

🏠 **Logement La Vedette** [91 C4] (14 rooms) m 078 847 6075/768 2277. Situated around the corner from the Auberge de Nyamirambo, this unpretentious guesthouse, which now incorporates the former Home St Bernard, has comfortable large rooms, some en suite, others with sinks & clean common showers – nothing special but fine at the price. *Rfr8,000/10,000 dbl using shared/en-suite ablutions.*

🏠 **Mont Kigali Lodge** [78 A3] (10 rooms) m 078 896 2968. All the rooms at this basic place near Nyabugogo station use shared ablutions, but these are kept very clean & the rooms (with mozzie nets) are too. There's no food, but plenty is available in the neighbourhood & you can hardly argue with the price. *Rfr6,000/7,000/9,000 sgl/ dbl/twin.*

🏠 **Smart Inn** [86 D1] (20 rooms) m 078 483 5602. This newish place on KN 1 Rd looks pretty sharp from the outside, but it's rather more blasé once you're inside. Nonetheless, the small rooms here are clean & perhaps the cheapest you'll get this close to the city centre. Rooms all come with nets & en-suite ablutions, plus B&B for 1. *Rfr17,000 dbl.*

← WHERE TO EAT AND DRINK

This section was put together with the assistance of Kirsty Henderson, long-time Kigali resident and curator of both the excellent Living in Kigali website (w *livinginkigali.com*), and its partner site, Eating in Kigali (w *eatinginkigali.com*), both of which contain a treasure trove of information on Kigali's dining and drinking scenes. What follows is a cross-section of the city's better eateries in various price categories, aimed mainly at short-term visitors, and organised according to suburb rather than price, with the top few picks for each area generally listed first. Most hotels offer acceptable food so, if you prefer to eat wherever you're staying, you won't necessarily miss out, though it's also very much worth noting that delivery from more than 60 restaurants around Kigali, including a number of places listed here, can now be arranged through Jumia Food (w *food.jumia.rw*).

CITY CENTRE AND NYAMIRAMBO

The **city centre** boasts an excellent selection of cafés, snack bars & coffee shops, & restaurants serving more traditional fare. For a coffee, snack or filled baguette, **La Galette** is still arguably the best place in the city centre though the somewhat pricier **Bourbon Café** provides it with some trendier competition. The city centre is also a great place to join Kigali's office workers at lunchtime & try the traditional Rwandan buffet, otherwise

known as a mélange. **Fantastic Restaurant** stands out for the size of its buffet & great downtown atmosphere. Formal restaurants are thin on the ground; the best options are in the upmarket **Marriott**, **Serena** & **Mille Collines** hotels, but all are very pricey & there's a far more interesting selection of dedicated eateries within easy walking distance in Kiyovu, the suburb sloping eastward from the city centre. To the south, Nyamirambo is home to a number of unpretentious restaurants

& bars, including the duelling fish grillers at **Green Corner** and the unexpected West African flavours of **Bamako Restaurant**.

✘ Al Mann & Ran Coffee House   [91 B1]
m 078 306 9120; **f**; ⏰ 08.00–23.30 daily.
One of several good local eateries dotted along the one-way roads around Nyamirambo Mosque, this has become something of a hub in the neighbourhood, & they do a range of cheap coffees & snacks, with prices starting at around Rfr1,000, as well as an assortment of curries & larger meals at around Rfr4,000.

✘ Blue Note   [86 C6] **m** 078 852 0638;
⏰ 08.00–late daily. Situated opposite the Belgian school on Rue des Mille Collines, this restaurant has a nice outdoor garden to sit in & serves a big selection of pizzas & pasta dishes for Rfr4,000–7,500, accompanied by cold draught beer. There's an active schedule of live music & performance here, with open mic on Wed evenings & live jazz Thu nights.

✘ Bourbon Coffee   **m** 078 977 7771;
w bourboncoffee.rw; ⏰ 07.00–22.00 daily. This popular coffee chain has branches in the Union Trade Centre [86 D4], the Kigali City Tower [86 C3], the MTN centre [94 D3] & Kigali International Airport. The coffee is pretty good & a fair selection of light meals, snacks & sandwiches are available, mostly around Rfr5,000–7,000. Free Wi-Fi.

✘ Camellia Tea House & Restaurant   [86 C6 & D6] **m** 078 830 9808/850 6645; **w** camellia. rw; ⏰ 07.00–22.00 daily, buffet 11.30–close. Though the entrances are on opposite sides of the block from each other, these conjoined eateries are under the same management. Head to the tea house for a genuinely impressive 40-odd types of tea & coffee in the Rfr1,000–2,000 range & a selection of salads, sandwiches, pizzas, light meals, & fresh juices starting around Rfr2,000 in a hodgepodge café that's always bustling. The restaurant has much the same menu, except this is where they bring out the cornucopian buffet every day at 11.30, & the steam trays heave with all the Rwandan food you can eat for Rfr2,500.

✘ Fantastic Restaurant   [86 D2] **m** 078 876 7036/583 3605; **e** fantasticrwanda@yahoo. com; ⏰ 07.00–11.00 for b/fast, 10.00–18.00 for the buffet. Recently relocated to an unmissable, pink new location on KN 2 Av, this restaurant has quickly become a Kigali institution because it serves the biggest & best Rwandan buffet in town & for a very reasonable Rfr2,000. The African music & chatter of lots of locals enjoying some time out from work gives it a bustling, jovial atmosphere. The streetside terrace is an ideal place to watch city life & soak up the vibe of downtown Kigali.

✘ Green Corner   [91 A6] **m** 078 884 1342 (DeLuxe), 078 885 3457 (House). Once united but now Solomonically split in 2, these warring twin restaurants, now known as Green Corner DeLuxe and Green Corner House, are both known for their grilled 'big fish', which are the perfect choice for an evening with friends when you've nowhere else to be – preparation takes a while, but there's plenty of beer to keep you entertained. Seating is either in the courtyard or the sheltered booths surrounding, & the fish run to Rfr10,000–15,000 depending on size. Goat, chicken & rabbit are also available if you're feeling contrarian.

✘ La Galette   [86 A4] ☎0252 575434;
⏰ 07.30–19.30 daily. To combine sustenance with shopping, try the snack-bar attached to this excellent supermarket near the corner of KN 57 St & KN 76 St. This is a popular meeting place for expats & NGO workers, & there are notice boards listing various items (cars, dogs, homes, motorbikes, TVs, garden hoses …) wanted or for sale. The supermarket stocks a good selection of fresh & imported groceries; the snack-bar serves fresh filled baguettes for around Rfr2,000, salads & light meals in the Rfr3,000–5,000 range & draught beer, as well as pastries (including croissants) & good coffee – b/fast nirvana!

✘ Lamane   [86 D6] **m** 078 830 6649/300 6098; ⏰ 07.00–16.00 Mon–Fri, 07.00–15.00 Sat. Formerly La Sierra, this is a more low-key & central equivalent to La Galette, combining a good supermarket with a pleasant although somewhat characterless terrace snack-bar on Bd de la Révolution. Burgers, sandwiches & light meals are available throughout the day for Rfr2,000–4,000; it also serves samosas, burritos, pancakes & waffles, & is a good spot for b/fast. Somewhat pricier is the Indian-influenced lunchtime buffet, which costs Rfr5,000 & runs over noon–14.30.

✘ Le Panorama   [86 D4] ☎0252 576530;
⏰ 18.00–21.30 Mon–Sat. On the top floor of the Hotel des Mille Collines, this exclusive place has an appropriately panoramic view over the city, & background music is supplied by a pianist & saxophonist. Official dinners & banquets are

often held here & as it stands now, a 3-course dinner checks in around Rfr27,000. There is also a comprehensive wine list.

✖ Panorama Ten To Two [91 A7] m 078 424 0222; ⏱ 11.00–late daily. Although this restaurant is not particularly close to the city centre as it is on the edge of Nyamirambo District on the same road as Hotel Baobab, the fish served here has come highly recommended by other travellers. There is a lovely terrace to sit on & it is a great place to go for an evening meal or drink, especially if you are staying in Nyamirambo District or you have your own transport.

✖ Preet Fast Food [86 C5] m 078 311 5997; ⏱ 08.00–20.00 Mon–Sat, 08.00–14.00 Sun. As for ambience, it doesn't get much simpler than this ascetically decorated 1-room diner, but they serve up a short menu of authentically Indian, all vegetarian, & deliciously cheap snacks & light meals that will be a welcome sight if you're on the hunt for a cheap lunch but can't bear another buffet. **Fat Mama's Kitchen** [86 C5] (m *073 641 6032*) on the next block is another good bet for vegetarian Indian & is similarly priced.

✖ Prince Fast Food [86 C6] m 073 459 5338–40; ⏱ b/fast, lunch, & dinner daily. This 1st-floor mum-&-dad Indian joint above the much less interesting Camellia Fast Food is open nearly all the time & the friendly proprietors do a variety of samosas, curries & biryanis, with a few more unusual specialties like *haleem* (mince & lentil stew) available on a rotating basis. The menu is 50/50 veg & non-veg, & it feels a bit like a crowded apartment because it is – & nothing on the menu cracks Rfr4,000.

✖ Resto Bamako [91 C4] m 078 851 4391/511 8331; ⏱ 06.00–midnight daily. Though the menu is far from extensive, if you're after a plate of West African style *poulet yassa* (chicken in a lemon-onion sauce) with a savoury rice pilaf for Rfr3,000 & served on a Skol-branded plastic table, this is your place. There's a full bar & football on TV & there were shisha pipes until the government banned them in Dec 2017.

✖ Simba Café [86 C4] m 078 830 7200; ⏱ 07.00–11.00 daily. This efficient, busy & conveniently located café attached to the Simba Supermarket is a great place to pick up a quick lunch or snack & provides some welcome respite from shopping on Kigali's busy streets. Service is swift & the food is filling & tasty. The menu

includes a range of burgers, snacks & light meals for Rfr2,000–5,000. They have another location in Kacyiru, opposite the parliament [94 C5], serving a similar menu.

KIYOVU

This leafy suburb on the eastern verge of the city centre is blessed with a fine selection of top-quality restaurants, a fortunate situation given that many of the city's most popular tourist hotels also lie in the area. Coming from the city centre, the closest restaurant is the rather unremarkable Chez Robert, but if you are prepared to walk a bit further – or to take a taxi – top recommendations are **Heaven Restaurant** for ambience, **Khana Khäzana** & **Zaaffran** for some Asian flavour, & **Dolce** & **Iris** for affordability.

✳ ✖ Heaven Restaurant [79 F4] m 078 848 6581; w heavenrwanda.com; ⏱ 07.00–22.00 daily. This justifiably popular restaurant inspires a feverish loyalty in its devotees, and it's not hard to see why. The dining area is centred on a massive wooden deck scattered with wooden tables & chairs, set below a cane roof & offering good views over suburban Kigali. The main restaurant has an atmospheric alfresco ambience & delicious fusion cuisine in the Rfr8,000–20,000 range that uses 95% local Rwandan ingredients. There is also a bar menu with chapattis, burgers & other light meals at around Rfr5,000. There's a rotating schedule of events including live music, kids' programming & cooking classes, & it's also home to a gallery featuring artwork from Niyo & Abien Arts (page 112), & a boutique carrying fair-trade products from Azizi Life in Muhanga (page 135). They've got a selection of fine rooms for rent as well, either at their Heaven Boutique Hotel (page 87) or The Retreat (page 85), both located next door to the restaurant on either side.

✖ Iris Restaurant [79 F4] m 072 850 1181; ⏱ 07.00–21.00 daily. Situated in the same part of town as the Indian Khäzana, the terrace restaurant at this popular guesthouse has a giddying choice of (mainly) continental dishes & grills. The superb pasta dishes are mostly around Rfr5,000, while salads & sandwiches cost Rfr3,000–5,000 & more substantial meat & fish dishes are in the Rfr5,000–8,000 range.

✖ Khana Khäzana Restaurant [79 F4] m 078 849 9600; w khanakhazana.rw; ⏱ noon–15.00

& 18.00–22.30 daily. This superb & popular Indian restaurant is situated on KN 31 St, a 10min walk downhill from the Mille Collines & the city centre. Most main courses are in the Rfr6,000–9,000 range & the Indian bread is excellent. There's a new branch in Nyarutarama serving the same menu [94 D4].

✖ Kiosque Super Level [79 F4] Situated next to the CityBlue Urban, this welcoming but no-frills local drinking hole serves the cheapest drinks in Kiyovu – around Rfr900 for a large Primus, which is a third of the price charged by most of the restaurants & hotels in this posh suburb.

✖ New Cactus Restaurant [79 F5] ☎0252 572572; m 078 867 8798; ⊕ noon–14.00 & 18.00–22.30 daily. Situated on KN 47 St (near the Hotel Gorillas) this is a super place, particularly for pizza-lovers – it's very welcoming, with a pleasant outdoor terrace giving a beautiful view over Kigali, good food (French cuisine as well as pizzas), & free Wi-Fi. Steak & fish main dishes around Rfr8,000. There's also a take-away pizza service – phone beforehand & it'll be ready for you to collect.

✖ Restaurant Chez Robert [86 D4] m 078 488 8825; ⊕ 09.00–midnight daily. Situated on the eastern border of the city centre opposite Hotel des Mille Collines, this restaurant is easily distinguished by the 2 elephantine statues marking its walk-in entrance (the drive-in entrance is actually a block east, on KN 25 St). It serves a good selection of continental dishes for around Rfr8,000, & brochettes, pasta & other light meals from Rfr4,000 upwards. There's a very nice lunch buffet for Rfr7,000, & you can eat indoors, or outdoors in a large garden with several niches.

✖ Restaurant Le Dos Argenté [79 G4] ☎0252 501717; ⊕ 07.00–22.00 daily (bar stays open late). On the ground floor of the Hotel Gorillas, this smaller restaurant – whose name translates as silverback – is a member of the *Chaîne des Rôtisseurs* & the food usually lives up to its reputation. Main dishes (French cuisine) go up to around Rfr13,000, desserts to Rfr5,000. There's indoor & outdoor seating, draught beer, & a good wine list. Service is relaxed.

✖ Zaaffran Indian Restaurant [79 F4] m 078 304 2504; 🇫 Zaaffran Restaurant; ⊕ noon–15.00 & 18.00–22.30 daily. Located on KN 16 Av (Rue de l'Akagera) near La Bonne Source Supermarket, this restaurant serves Indian cuisine that is flavoursome & good quality for around Rrf 5,000–9,000. The

Rwandan waiters clad in Indian costume give the restaurant an interesting multi-cultural twist & the décor is suitably bright & cheerful. The naan bread is delicious & they have some good vegetarian options on the menu, including paneer & vegetable-based curries.

KIMIHURURA

A variety of restaurants has mushroomed in this sedate residential suburb to the east of Kiyovu, & it's become something of a dining & nightlife destination in its own right, though they can sometimes be a touch tricky to find & somewhat isolated unless you have a private vehicle or take a taxi. There are no duds listed below, but the lunchtime buffet at **Afrika Bite** stands out for those wanting to sample Rwandan food at its finest.

✳ ✖ Afrika Bite [96 D3] m 078 343 7727/850 3888; ⊕ noon–15.00 & 18.00–22.30 Mon–Sat. Widely regarded as the city's leading purveyor of Rwandan cuisine, this homely restaurant on KG 674 St in Kimihurura has indoor & outdoor garden seating & oodles of character. The legendary buffet costs Rfr3,500 & it's served for both lunch & dinner.

✖ Kimy Gourmand Crêperie [96 D3] m 078 679 2388; 🇫; ⊕ 11.30–22.00 Tue–Sun. Kigali's 1st crêperie, this cosy Kimihurura hideaway serves a tasty selection of sweet crêpes, waffles, & ice cream starting around Rfr1,500, plus savoury crêpes & salads for closer to Rfr3,500. There's indoor/outdoor seating, & there are smoothies & alcoholic drinks available.

✖ Kiseki [96 C3] m 078 140 3829/236 9246; w kisekirwanda.com; ⊕ 07.00–17.00 & 18.00–23.00 Tue–Sun. Offering a full menu of sushi, sashimi, & other Japanese mains, this comfortable & unpretentious restaurant located opposite the Mamba Club is serious about their cuisine (the chef has more than 20 years' sushi experience), but not afraid to branch out & try something new – as such, it might be the only restaurant in the world serving matoke tempura & goat teriyaki. It's surprisingly affordable, with rolls starting at Rfr4,000, & even a Japanese lunch buffet for Rfr5,000.

✖ Lalibela [96 C2] m 078 850 5293/855 5079; ⊕ 10.00–23.00 daily. This Ethiopian restaurant now located near Shokola Café serves traditional Ethiopian fare including *injera*, big, flat savoury pancakes, & spicy *wat* stews. Mains cost Rfr4,000–5,000 & there is also a very good buffet for Rfr5,000.

✕ Now Now Rolex [96 D3] m 078 045 8158; ⓕ; ⏱ 08.00–23.00 Mon–Thu, 08.00–04.00 Fri & Sat, 11.00–23.00 Sun. Just opened at the start of 2018, this is a cool new place serving Ugandan-style hot chapatti wraps with a global twist for Rfr2,000–4,000. They all start with eggs & chapatti, but diverge from there – brie, mozzarella & feta all make an appearance on the menu, along with guacamole & gouda. They stay open late at the w/end – ideal if you're crawling out of Sundowner around the corner.

✕ Poivre Noir [96 C2] m 073 582 3282; ⓕ; ⏱ noon–14.30 & 18.00–21.30 Mon–Sat. This tranquil residential compound hides a very juicy secret: Kigali's best burger. Served with cheddar or blue cheese, bacon should you fancy it, & a side of Belgian-style *frites*, it's worth the Rfr8,500 price tag (& there's a veggie version too). The other creative, continental-style mains are no less worthwhile, & they're also known for their excellent beef *filet* (*Rfr12,000*). Most mains (among them a unique pulled-rabbit ravioli) check in between Rfr9,000 & Rfr13,000.

✕ Restaurant Hellenique [96 B2] m 078 851 2342/856 9497; w helleniquehotel.onlc.fr; ⏱ 11.30–14.00 & 17.00–22.00 Mon–Sat. This is tucked away on KG 666 St in a residential part of Kimihurura not far from Shokola Café or Trattoria – taxi-drivers will know it & it's signposted. The food is Greek/International with some Mediterranean favourites & a good wine list; the ambience is relaxed & there's a pleasant terrace as well. Service is attentive but may be slow. Government VIPs & ambassadors often come here. Mains cost around Rfr6,000–9,000. They've also got 12 very tidy & well-priced rooms (*US$50/60 sgl/dbl B&B*) facing the guests-only swimming pool & offering views over Kigali.

✳ ✕ Repub Lounge [96 C3] m 078 830 3030; ⓕ; ⏱ 18.00–late Mon–Sat. Always among Kigali's most stylish eateries (which shows no sign of changing since their 2015 move to Kimihurura), this popular meeting spot is earthy, funky & cool, packed with African art, & the 2-level deck here stays busy even on w/day nights. The menu is as inspired as the décor, with main dishes checking in between Rfr6,000 & Rfr10,000. There's live music at w/ends.

✕ Shokola Café [96 B2] m 078 309 3039; ⓕ; ⏱ 07.30–21.00 daily. Set in a leafy corner of Kimihurura, this tranquil café has a laid-back, cool vibe with lots of comfortable sofas, a small library, terrace seating & free Wi-Fi. The menu has a Middle-Eastern flavour & includes hummus, *harira* soup & lemon & herb grilled chicken. They also run the rooftop café at the Kigali Public Library.

✕ Trattoria [96 B1] m 078 846 8696; ⏱ 11.00–late daily. On the site where the original Papyrus nightclub used to be, Trattoria is a café, restaurant & wine bar rolled into one, serving a decent range of pasta, pizza & continental cuisine in the Rfr3,000–6,000 range. It was closed for renovations in 2018, but will hopefully have reopened by the time you read this.

🍷 Car Wash [96 A3] m 078 882 6195; ⏱ lunch–late daily; ⓕ Car Wash Kigali. At the edge of Kimihurura & also known as the Royal or Executive Car Wash, this makes for a rather unlikely but nonetheless excellent place to sit out in the open air & nosh on a plate of *nyama choma*, sip a cold Primus, catch the latest football & yes, should you so desire, get your car washed. Brochettes start at Rfr1,500, & a whole rack of barbecued goat ribs will set you back Rfr8,000.

KACYIRU AND REMERA

This area of the city has a diverse restaurant scene ranging from the tasty fast food of **Meze Fresh** & **New Fiesta** to the haute cuisine at **Restaurant Brachetto**. Elsewhere, **Sole Luna** & the **Kigali Great Wall of China Restaurant** serve good Italian & Chinese respectively, while the restaurant in **Civitas Hotel** serves some of the best brochettes in Kigali. The café at **Inzora** is a delight, & **CocoBean** next door has, almost overnight, become one of Kigali's most popular hangouts. Several good restaurants have recently opened in the Rugando neighbourhood just south of the convention centre as well, including **The Hut** and **Inka Steakhouse**.

✕ Asian Kitchen [75 G5] m 078 433 7288; ⏱ 11.00–16.00 Tue, 11.00–22.00 Wed–Mon. For authentic Thai flavours in a brisk & informal environment, head straight for this breezy new café, situated on KN 5 Rd just as you enter Remera. The menu includes Thai & Vietnamese favourites like red, green, & *massaman* curries, *pad thai*, & pho noodle soups (*Rfr5,500–7,500*), with a welcome selection of tofu dishes, & Vietnamese coffee with sweetened condensed milk rounding out the offerings.

✖ **Brachetto** [94 A3] m 078 717 8133; f Brachetto Restaurant-Tapas Bar; ⏲ 11.30–14.30 & 19.00–21.30 Mon–Fri, 19.00–21.30 Sat. Opened in 2014, the carefully curated selections of wine (including sangria), cocktails, & dessert here make this Italian-run eatery a worthy destination even if you don't feel like splashing out for a full meal (*Rfr13,000 & up*), but the food confirms their position among Kigali's most cultivated addresses. The menu skews Italian, but Mediterranean flavours are *de rigueur* overall, & homemade tagliatelle, foie gras, beef tartare, & scallops all make an appearance on the menu. Additionally, they do what has to be the nicest lunch buffet in town (*starting at Rfr7,500*) & occasional wine tasting sessions with the owner-sommelier. You won't regret calling ahead for a table.

✳ ✖ **Casa Keza** [94 A2] m 078 838 2581; f; ⏲ 08.00–23.00 Mon–Sat, 10.00–21.00 Sun. Combining a café, Spanish cultural centre & tapas bar, this intimate garden restaurant in Kacyiru manages to do all 3 with aplomb. Mornings are brunch territory – pancakes, *shakshuka* & granola are all on the menu – then there's Wi-Fi to get some work done in the afternoon, & evenings are for tapas, sangria & the occasional garden bonfire – don't be surprised if some tables get pushed aside for salsa dancing after a few mojitos. There's a small craft shop here too, along with a studio apartment for rent at a very simpatico US$32/dbl. Excellent paella is available with advance notice & Spanish-language courses are available throughout the year.

✖ **Civitas Restaurant** [75 G5] m 078 888 7823; ⏲ 06.30–midnight daily. On the ground floor of the Civitas Hotel, this restaurant has a good selection of mains including steaks, spaghetti dishes & arguably the tastiest brochettes in Kigali. The restaurant has a very pleasant leafy outdoor patio area where you can watch the chef grilling brochettes on the open barbecue.

✖ **CocoBean** [94 B4] m 078 340 6442; w www. cocobean.biz; ⏲ 07.00–late daily. This new place next to the Ikirezi Bookshop does it all – café in the morning, restaurant by day, & nightspot after the sun goes down (& well beyond that). They serve a huge menu with everything from Hawaiian pizza to crêpes, pasta, grills & more, plus pan-African favourites like Senegalese *thiéboudiène* rice & Ivorian *kédjénou* stew (*Rfr6,000–10,000*), all served on

a lovely upstairs wooden deck, capped with a tall thatched roof. Downstairs is the lounge-bar, situated around the swimming pool & at the time of writing one of the hottest hangouts in Kigali, with a drinks menu of juices, coffees, milkshakes, cocktails & shots that's almost as impressive as the food menu upstairs & equally popular.

✖ **Georgie's Grill & BBQ** [94 B4] m 078 202 7579; ⏲ 08.00–midnight daily. This restaurant, tucked away around the corner from the Ninzi Hill Hotel, has indoor & outdoor seating & is known around Kigali for its East African *nyama choma* barbecue, which checks in at just over Rfr7,000 for a portion serving 2 or 3. There's football on the TV, & karaoke on Thu nights, & cheap drinks aplenty.

✖ **Great Wall of China Restaurant** [94 C5] m 078 792 1256; ⏲ lunch & dinner daily. In a new location near the Lemigo Hotel, this conspicuously signposted & consistently popular Chinese restaurant has been operating in Kigali for close to 20 years now. The vibe is friendly & there's a great atmosphere in the evening when everything is lit up by lots of red Chinese lanterns. The food is good value & the sizzling hotplates are especially recommended.

✖ **The Hut** [75 F4] m 078 341 9980/996 6006; f thehutrwanda; ⏲ 11.00–22.30 daily, later at w/ends. This colourful new bamboo-built open-sided restaurant behind the convention centre boasts an intimidatingly huge menu covering most of the globe – lebanese lamb kofta (*Rfr9,000*), prawn curry (*Rfr15,000*), pizza (*from Rfr5,000*), fish tacos (*Rfr6,000*), nicoise salad (*Rfr8,000*), sweet potato fries (*Rfr5,000*) & tom yum soup (*Rfr8,000*) all make an appearance, plus a good selection of drinks, dessert, & wine. Not only that, but they can actually make everything they offer. If that's not enough, they've also got 4 good rooms for rent at US$80/120 queen/king bed, & a swimming pool diners can use for a small fee.

✖ **Inema Café** [94 B3] m 078 318 7646; w inemaartcenter.com; ⏲ 08.00–17.00 daily, till later on Thu. The café at this popular arts centre does a good selection of coffee-based drinks & fruit smoothies throughout the day. While it certainly makes a colourful & welcoming spot to hang out for a bit & peruse the art or chat with the artists, it's best known as the site of Inema Arts' happy hour, which takes place every Thu evening, is catered by Meze Fresh (see opposite), & is the place to go to meet travellers, expats, & trendy young Rwandans.

✖ Inka Steakhouse [75 F5] **m** 078 030 2666; **f**; ⊕ noon–15.00 & 17.00–22.00 Tue–Fri, 12.30–23.00 Sat, 12.30–21.00 Sun. If all the cattle wandering around Rwanda leave you feeling carnivorous, this new place south of the convention centre may be just what the doctor ordered. The menu is meaty, as might be expected, but there are seafood dishes to be had as well. Their *pièce de résistance* is probably the 900g bone-in ribeye for Rfr17,000, available with a variety of sauces, including an Argentina-inspired *chimichurri*. They run a variety of evening specials from 17.00 to 22.00, with deals on burgers, beers, cocktails, pork ribs, or *filet mignon* depending on the day.

✻ ✖ Inzora Rooftop Café [94 B4] **m** 078 953 9764; **w** inzoracafe.com; ⊕ 08.30–20.00 Mon–Fri, 10.00–18.30 Sat & Sun. Set at the back of the commendable Ikirezi Bookshop, this is a popular spot for Rwandans & foreigners alike to hang out over a coffee, & both the lower floor & rooftop areas are consistently buzzing with students, professionals, embassy workers, book club meetings, & more. The coffee is excellent & so are the cakes, pastries & sandwiches, starting at around Rfr1,000.

✻ ✖ Meze Fresh [94 B5] **m** 078 557 7009/160 2591; **f** MezeFresh; ⊕ 11.00–23.00 Mon–Sat, 11.00–21.00 Sun. The owners here spent some years in the USA, & their take on Chipotle-style Tex-Mex tacos & burritos is bang on the money. It's Rfr3,000–4,000 for a burrito depending on your choice of meat, & the mere presence of guacamole & a selection of salsas on the menu will set North American tongues salivating. There's 2 floors of seating, the building is an unmissable lime green, & they've got Mexican beers & margaritas to wash down any unexpected homesickness.

✖ New Fiesta (Tasty's) [75 G4] **m** 078 545 7922/839 7620; ⊕ 08.00–21.00 daily. This bright, cosmopolitan little restaurant located close to the Chez Lando hotel has excellent, speedy service & it has become deservedly very popular among Kigali's office workers & expats who want a quick & tasty lunch or b/fast. The chicken & Greek salads are delicious, as are the hot sandwiches. Mains cost around Rfr3,000–5,000. Next door to the restaurant is a small shop selling freshly baked La Galette bread, pastries, snacks & samosas & other essentials.

✖ Sole Luna [75 G5] ✎ 0252 583062; **m** 078 885 9593; **w** soleluna-rwanda.com; ⊕ 18.00–23.00 Mon, noon–23.00 Tue–Sat. Slightly cheaper

than most upmarket eateries in Kigali, out along the airport road at the edge of Remera, this long-serving Italian restaurant has a good range of pizzas & pasta for around Rfr5,000–8,000 – with many ranking it as Kigali's best pizza – & a beautiful view over the city from its vine-shaded terraces. Service is friendly & reasonably brisk.

NYARUTARAMA

This small upmarket suburb of Kigali between Remera & Kacyiru has some expensive but nonetheless very good restaurants. **Zen** tops the list for its delicious Thai fusion cuisine, while simple but stylish **Sakae** is a good place for a plate of Japanese sushi, the unremarkable garden setting at **Monmartsé** belies the excellent quality of Korean food on offer. For b/fast, the pastries & coffee at **RZ Manna** can't be beaten.

✻ ✖ Monmartsé [94 D5] **m** 078 914 6799/073 814 6799; ⊕ 10.30–23.00 daily. Just across from RDB, this unpretentious Korean restaurant serves up generous mains of authentic Korean fare like *bulgogi, galbi* & *bibimbap* for Rfr5,000–8,000 in a green garden with a likeable backyard vibe, & you can even grill it all up right at your table. The affable chef makes sure everything is done to perfection, & you can knock back a couple of glasses of *soju* or a Korean beer with your meal.

✖ Mr. Chips [94 D3] **m** 078 455 7420; **f** Mr. Chips Kigali; ⊕ 10.00–22.00 daily. In a new location just opposite the MTN Centre, this well-loved place serves some of the best fast food in Kigali & is rightfully very popular. Its menu includes authentic American-style cheeseburgers, fish & chips & pulled pork sandwiches accompanied by onion rings & garlic mayonnaise, all priced around Rfr3,000–5,000. They've also got a falafel sandwich, some cream soups & sub sandwiches, should you be in the mood for something (a bit) healthier.

✖ O'Connell's Irish Bar & Pub [94 C1] **m** 072 769 0030. This (sort of) Irish-themed bar found inside the Manor Hotel serves pub-style food such as club sandwiches, fishcakes, burgers & chicken wings for around Rfr5,000. It also has a good range of whiskies, a pleasant panoramic view of the city, & a variety of themed nights throughout the week, from Bollywood to Ragga.

✖ Question Coffee [94 D5] **m** 078 279 0403; **w** questioncoffee.com; ⊕ 07.00–18.00 Mon–Fri,

Set on KK 30 Avenue, not far from Juru Park and about 8km south of central Kigali, the new **1000 Hills Distillery** [74 D2] (m *078 831 6723*; e *info@1000hills.com*; w *1000hills.com*; f *1000HillsDistillery*; ⏱ *17.00–22.00 Mon–Thu, noon–23.00 Fri–Sun*) is East Africa's first craft small batch distillery, and they've been making triple-distilled rum, gin, vodka, whisky and coffee liqueur in Kigali since 2015. The hour-long tours (including a tasting session) cost US$25 per person, or can be booked in combination with a taco dinner and a cocktail afterwards for US$40 per person. In keeping with the owner's Texan background, the restaurant serves a variety of Tex-Mex favourites, and while drop-in customers are welcome for meals and drinks, the tours must be booked in advance, either via telephone or online.

08.00–17.00 Sat & Sun. The café that's taking Rwanda by storm: everybody seems to be talking about this new place & many of Kigali's high-end establishments are now serving their brew. The café is a touch hidden away behind the RDB on KG 8 Av but makes a fine place to while away a few hours once you've made it out here. The menu is appropriately coffee-centric, but there are some muffins, pretzels & the like available to accompany your cuppa. If you'd like to dig deeper into the Rwandan coffee scene, this is also the place to do it: with a bit of advance notice, they arrange coffee master classes covering everything from production (there are coffee plants right in the garden) to roasting (which also takes place on site), & a lesson on barista skills & brewing. Day trips to their partner coffee farms can also be arranged.

✗ **RZ Manna** [94 D4] m 078 918 4448; f Bakery RZ Manna; ⏱ 08.00–20.00 daily. With all of the excellent cafés springing up in Kigali, choosing a favourite has become a considerably more difficult job than it once was, but this Nyarutarama gem is a strong contender for pick of the litter. The bakery here does cookies, cakes, scones, croissants & all manner of tempting pastries, & there's a selection of Korean-inspired meals & snacks as well. Cold drinks run the gamut from mango to mocha, & there's a fine variety of hot tea & coffee. Seating is in the cool, modern interior or on the small terrace.

✗ **Sakae Japanese Restaurant** [94 D4] m 078 457 8435/7738; f; ⏱ noon–15.00 & 18.00–23.00 Mon–Sat. This simple, elegant restaurant can be found down a side street signposted from the beginning of the main Nyarutarama road. It serves the best Japanese food in Kigali & it has an impressive range of sushi including sushi set menus & roll sushi. A la carte sushi is Rfr3,000–8,000 & set menus, while many different types of sushi are Rfr14,000–20,000. There is also a good selection of Korean & Japanese noodle dishes, as well as a full Chinese menu.

✗ **Zen** [94 D2] m 078 258 8593; w zenkigali. com; ⏱ noon–15.00 & 18.00–midnight daily. Located on the main Nyarutarama road, a short distance from the MTN centre, this smart & tranquil restaurant serves an enticing range of oriental cuisine including Thai curries & soups & Chinese dim sum dumplings. Mains start around Rfr8,000. Rather strangely, the dining area is hidden through a car park & around the back of a building, so don't be put off when you look through the gates & fail to see the restaurant.

♀ **Le Poete Bar** [94 D2] m 078 850 3268; ⏱ 10.00–02.00 daily. A cheap bar in an expensive neighbourhood, this no-nonsense place opposite Zen on the main road through Nyarutarama is a strategic spot for the skint, & a pleasant place for a few beers in a plastic picnic chair before working out your wallet at the surrounding white-collar hangouts.

NIGHTLIFE

For a capital city, Kigali isn't over-rich in nightclubs and discos. The newest and hippest is probably **People** [94 B4] (m *078 865 0014*; ⏱ *09.00–06.00 daily*) in Kacyiru, which is where Kigali's cool kids (and adults) come out to drink, dance, and play under the laser lights until daybrea[...] everyone else is, and don't forget to bring Rfr3,000 for th[...] theme nights throughout the week, including Latin/Salsa Sat[...] a VIP section if you'd rather order bottle service and watch the a[...]

Also located in Kacyiru, though not strictly a nightclub and with a [...] more bohemian vibe, the **Inema Arts Center** [94 B3] (m *078 318 7646/865 [...]* f *inemaartscenter*) has rapidly become one of the city's foremost cultural centres, and their Thursday happy hour is a must. They also put on regular concerts and other evening events – it's well worth calling or checking their Facebook page to see what's on. Continuing into town, the cool and unpretentious **Cocobean** [94 B4] (page 102) has become a new go-to spot for kicking back with club tunes and a cocktail. A short walk away, **Riders Lounge** [94 B5] (m *078 483 6839;* f *ridersloungerw*) isn't typically the spot for a raucous party, but they're open 24/7 and can always be relied on for a cold draught beer. In the other direction towards Nyarutarama, **Chillax Lounge** [94 C3] (m *078 761 2222;* f *Lounge Chillax*) is part of the luxury Century Park Hotel & Residences project, with a high-class vibe to match and DJs every weekend. Further out, in the Kibagabaga neighbourhood, **Pili Pili** [75 G1] (*12 KG 303 St;* f *pilipilirwanda*) is known as a place to chill out with a cocktail and perhaps dip your feet in the pool; every Wednesday is Ladies' Night.

Less fashion-conscious than any of the above, the **Blue Note Bar** [86 C6] in the city centre has a dance floor and disco at weekends, but its days as the go-to spot seem to be in the past; worst case, you can still order a pizza. Nearby in Kiyovu, **Le Must** [79 F5] (m *078 8246543/3050580*) is hot and crowded with mostly local revellers from Thursday night on. Continuing east into Kimihurura, **Sundowner Bar** [96 D2] (m *078 739 5868/350 4455*) is a Kigali nightlife stalwart, and gets reliably raucous on weekend nights, but the epicentre of Kigali's night-time scene must be the **Papyrus Complex** [96 C3], a massive multi-storey entertainment complex with stellar views over the city. On the top floor, many start their evening at the stylish, Asian-inspired **Oriental Gourmet** (m *078 670 0108;* w *restaurant. papyrusrw.com*) restaurant and bar, before eventually making their way to **Envy Nightclub** (m *078 710 3990;* f *envynightlifepapyrus;* ⏱ *20.00–06.00 Thu–Sat*) in the basement, where the laser lights are always on and the tunes are always cranked. (The ground floor is **Waka Fitness** (w *wakafitness.com*), where you can sweat out last night's hangover.)

A popular out-of-town drinking hole is **Green Corner** [91 B6] restaurants (page 98), a side-by-side outdoor set-up in Nyakabanda offering cheap chilled beers, grilled fish, and great views towards Mount Kigali. In Kiyovu, **Heaven** [79 F4] is a relaxed spot for excellent cocktails, while the more down-to-earth **Kiosque Super Level** [79 F4] next to CityBlue Urban is a great place to enjoy a few cheap beers in company with local Rwandans.

If you want to try something a bit different, the **Mamba Club** [96 C4] in Kimihurura (page 94) has a fun vibe at the weekends with very reasonably priced cocktails and a five-lane bowling alley, table tennis, volleyball net and swimming pool. Burgers and snacks are also available for Rfr2,000–4,000.

ARTS AND ENTERTAINMENT

CINEMA For a Hollywood fix, **Century Cinemas** [86 C3] (m *078 912 2222;* w *centurycinemas.rw*) at Kigali City Tower shows the latest (or reasonably recent) blockbusters, while the decidedly less glitzy **CineStar cinema** opposite the Kigali

ɔnally shows somewhat dated Western and Premiership football fixtures; better ɔook out the whole theatre for a screening ...nimum four people).

...ι music festival (w *kigaliup.com;* f), first held ...a roundabout, has since then probably become ...e year. They feature multiple stages showcasing the ...can music. The festival is spearheaded by Rwandan- .../opo and his Planet Folk NGO (e *cmurigande@rogers.* ...p with the festival as a volunteer.

ι ...arts are represented on Kigali's growing cultural calendar as well, a... **a Film Festival** (w *rwandafilmfestival.net*) or Hillywood, as it's often kno. ...ds pop-up theatres and takes over existing venues around Kigali and aroun.. the country every July to screen numerous documentaries, shorts, and feature films from around the continent and the globe. Also held in July is the first of Kigali's two week-long celebrations of style, **Kigali Fashion Week** (f *Rwandafashioncouncil*), where dozens of designers from around Rwanda and around the world come together to showcase their latest wares. A few steps further down the catwalk in September, the **Rwanda Cultural Fashion Week** (w *rcfs.rw*) puts on a similar programme.

Finally, for the last couple of years, the **Mutzig Beer Festival** (f *Mutzig Rwanda*) has been held in October at Juru Park, though organisation is a bit nebulous and it's hard to say where it'll pop up next – regardless, live music and beer remains a winning combination.

MUSIC AND DANCE Performances of traditional dancing and music take place from time to time in various venues around the city – these are publicised on local radio and in the local press. The RDB Tourism and Conservation Reservation Office should also have a list of forthcoming events. One worth trying is the **RwaMakondera** (Rwandan Horns) Children's Dance Troupe, which was formed by **Ivuka Arts Studios** [94 B3] (page 112); this was founded by Collin Sekajugo to provide skills, income and a sense of belonging to orphans and other children from disadvantaged backgrounds.

The **Institut Français du Rwanda (IFR)** [79 F4] (f) puts on a regular calendar of cultural events, often in collaboration with the German **Goethe-Institut** [79 E3] (f *goethe kigali*), at various locations in Kigali. Recent performers have included West African stars like Tiken Jah Fakoly and Habib Koité, along with Ugandan singer Maurice Kirya who won the Radio France International music award and the acclaimed Cameroonian opera singer Jacques-Greg Belobo. Check either of their websites for the latest happenings. The ever popular **Inema Arts Center** [94 B3] (m *078 318 7646/865 3683;* f) is another good place to catch a concert, and generally speaking it's the newest must-visit on Kigali's cultural circuit.

In addition to the above, the authoritative website w livinginkigali.com has a monthly calendar that lists events in Kigali including events held by the Goethe-Institut, concerts and live music, karaoke, salsa dancing classes and movie nights.

LIBRARIES The **Kigali Public Library** [74 D2] (m *078 850 0777;* w *kplonline.org;* ⊕ *08.00–20.00 Mon–Fri, 08.00–17.00 Sat, 08.00–noon Sun*) opened in 2012 in a stylish modern building in Kacyiru, and is already well established; see the box opposite. There's free Wi-Fi and computer use, a branch of Shokola Café on the roof, and a rapidly increasing stock of books and other media. Exhibitions, workshops and other activities are held and the website is comprehensive. If you have leftover books in good condition at the end of your visit, do ask about donating them.

SPORT

Kigali caters for both golfers and cricketers. For **cricket**, see box, page 108. The 18-hole **Kigali Golf Club** [94 C1] (m *078 859 0242;* f *Kigali Golf Club*) is in an attractively green corner of northeastern Kigali just off KG 13 Avenue, and though only nine holes are currently active, it's a steep Rfr40,000 for visitors to hit the links, plus Rfr6,000 for clubs, should you need them, and Rfr4,000 for a mandatory caddy. A golf pro is available should you want lessons, and the serene and very pleasant restaurant-bar at the clubhouse dishes up simple meals and cold drinks until late and is open to all. An unexpectedly flash new clubhouse is under construction 1km to the south of the current one as part of an ongoing multi-million-dollar rehabilitation of the course. Nearby is the **Nyarutarama Tennis Club**

KIGALI PUBLIC LIBRARY

In 1999, the Rotary Club of Kigali-Virunga decided to build a public library, its first major project as a chartered Rotary Club. Rwanda was seriously short of books, and consequently lacked any strong culture of reading. Rotary's decision proved to be no mere daydream: the embryonic library received generous financial support both from overseas and from local Rwandan companies. Secondhand Book Sales (a 'first' for Kigali) were among various events held to raise funds.

In 2002, a young Rwandan boy named Sam called into the office of the Library Project's Chairman – who initially thought he had come to ask for school fees, a common practice among Rwanda's youth. However, Sam was in fact a prospective donor, and handed over 200 Rwandan francs (less than 50 US cents, but for him a large sum). He'd discovered the project through one of the book sales, and wanted to contribute in order to make sure the library would be completed.

A site near the US embassy was found and construction work started in 2002, but later stalled through lack of funds. However, by 2009 the campaign had received donations and pledges of approximately US$2 million from individuals, businesses and corporations, foundations, governments, and intergovernmental organisations, and money continued to trickle in. Finally, in 2012, the brand-new library opened its doors. After waiting ten years to see the results of his donation, we can but hope that Sam was among its first visitors.

Now, after a steady programme of improvements and expansions, the library buzzes with activity, and extends its services throughout Rwanda via the internet. It also provides books to schools. In its light and airy building there are children's and teenagers' sections, reference sections, study and reading areas, computers and an internet café. Exhibitions and workshops are held, and opening hours have been extended to meet the needs of workers as well as students. Its branch of Shokola Café (page 101) has made it a social meeting venue too, though it's an enjoyable place to visit in itself. Well done Rotary, for this valuable addition to Kigali life. More information is available at w kplonline.org.

Although the country only really seems to have shifted to a pro-English bent since 1994, cricket has been played for several years in Rwanda. In Butare, the University boys, under Professor Singh, had been playing for quite some time before then. There was a match on a volcanic field in Rubavu/Gisenyi in the 1990s, which finally received appropriate recognition in *Wisden Cricketers' Almanack 2004*. Further reports have been recorded in the *Cricket Round the World* sections of *Wisden*.

By 2003, the RCA managed to get the ground at the Ecole Technique Officielle in the Kicukiro District of Kigali into a good enough condition for regular matches. The ground is basically the school's sports field, so is not exclusive to the Rwanda Cricket Association. Games are subject to regular interruptions, some of the more unusual having been unannounced athletics meetings and the 2004 filming of the BBC feature film *Shooting Dogs*.

Early attempts to bring in kit proved a headache, as Lillywhites has yet to open a branch in Kigali. The Rwanda Revenue Authority, anxious to squeeze whatever they could from persons perceived to have money to burn, decided that a rubber matting pitch supplied free of charge by the ICC was in fact a carpet, and should be subject to duty. Months of wrangling and negotiation failed to convince them. We could only assume a member of RRA staff wanted it to carpet her home.

After achieving ICC membership, Rwanda came 7th in the African Affiliates Championships in 2004 and in 2006 came 6th in Division Three of the African region of the ICC World Cricket League. In 2009, the RCA entered an U13 team in a regional ICC tournament in Uganda. In the event the team could not travel, but it's the desire that matters. Also in 2009, international cricket icon Brian Lara played a brief three-ball innings at Kicukiro 'Oval', as part of a one-day visit to Rwanda.

In 2011, the Rwanda Cricket Stadium Foundation (w *rcsf.org.uk*) was formed, run by both British and Rwandan members, and made it their mission to provide Rwanda's first dedicated national cricket ground – a permanent location was finally secured in 2014, and the 4.5ha, US$1.5 million Gahanga Cricket Stadium was triumphantly inaugurated in October 2017, in a grand ceremony with President Kagame and 200 international cricketers on hand to cut the ribbon. See page 34 for details.

Excitingly, in February 2011, Rwanda won the ICC Africa Division 3 title in Ghana, beating Seychelles, Lesotho, Morocco, Gambia, Cameroon, Mali and St Helena. This secured it a place in the Division 2 qualifier for the 2012 ICC Twenty20 World Cup, where unfortunately it finished bottom of the nine-team league, winning just one of its eight matches, against Malawi. Rwanda hasn't qualified for Division 2 since, but they did take third place in the 2014 ICC Africa Division 3 competition.

Nationwide, around 5,000 Rwandans have now taken up the game, and cricket continues to flourish in Kigali. Matches of 40 overs a side are played on Sundays almost throughout the year, several tournaments have been held, and the national side participates in International Cricket Council competitions. Pitch availability, early sunsets, the superiority of ball over bat and the weather all combine to mean that 20/20 has often been the best format – long before it caught on elsewhere.

[94 D3] (📞 *0252 587009/119947*; ⬛), where you can practise your serve on the illuminated courts, or take a dip in the pool for Rfr4,000. The more central **Cercle Sportif** [79 G7] (📱 *078 850 2140*; w *cerclesportifdekigali.com*) in Lower Kiyovu has facilities for tennis, table tennis, basketball, volleyball, badminton, darts, swimming, and even squash.

Keen equestrians, along with those who simply like a good view, should head straight for **Fazenda Sengha** [91 B7] (📱 *078 855 1787/440 6340*; e *fazenda@sengha. com*; w *sengha.com*; ⬛; ⏰ *09.00–18.00 Wed–Mon*), set on the slopes of Mount Kigali just south of Nyamirambo, where you can go out on a 90-minute trail ride with fantastic views over the hills of Kigali for Rfr25,000 per hour, or even practise your skills with a bow and arrow at their archery range. As of 2017, they're also home to Rwanda's very first **ziplines** (*Rfr7,500 pp*), open to kids and adults. It's best to phone in advance of your visit.

Also check out the current **football** fixtures – enthusiast Chris Frean explains how:

Going to a football match in Kigali is simple as long as you know that it's on. Matches generally take place at the Amahoro Stadium on Sunday afternoons at 4pm, sometimes preceded by each side's reserves' match on the same pitch. Fixtures are generally advertised in the New Times during the week beforehand. It is, however, pretty simple to find out if something is about to happen at Amahoro. Just go up to Kisimenti crossroads – the one by Chez Lando – and check the activity. If you see matatus with fans, and police on the crossroads holding up ordinary traffic for dignitaries, then something is on. Domestically the Kigali teams APR and Rayon Sports dominate. You can tell by the colours who is playing. Black and white means APR; blue and white Rayon; green and white Kiyovu.

Inside the ground, you shouldn't expect anything like a programme or team info; although with the Rwanda Premier League now sponsored by the beer Turbo King, you can actually buy a drink in the ground. For the World Cup qualifiers, tents were set up outside the stands, and a barbeque too.

International match tickets are easy enough to come by too, and priced towards the local market, so not expensive, especially for the terraces. Just go up to the main Amahoro stadium in the hours before kick-off. But beware: you're not allowed to take a mobile phone into the main stand for an international. For one Angola match, I had to submit to a metal detector and was told my phone was not allowed. This, the police later told me, was because people might use phones in the ground to contact hooligans outside and cause problems. However, this policy is only in place when the President is likely to attend a match.

There's more on football (and rugby) on pages 32–4.

SHOPPING

Large shopping centres seem to be opening at a frantic pace in Kigali, with two entirely new complexes, Kigali Heights and the CHIC Complex, opening since the last edition of this book was published. The new **Kigali Business Centre (KBC)** [94 B5] may also be open by the time you read this. **Kigali Heights** [94 B5], sat just opposite the new convention centre and the Radisson Blu hotel, was definitely the most fashionable mall in Kigali as of 2018, with a couple of cafés (including a branch of the Kenyan Java House chain and an Italian-style *gelateria*, Delizia Italiana), multiple ATMs, a local fashion boutique called Made in Kigali (⬛), Simba Supermarket, and the Riders Lounge restaurant and bar (page 105), which, along with Simba, is open 24/7 – a sure a sign as any that this once-somnambulant city becomes a bit more 'city that never sleeps' by the day. The large **CHIC Complex** [86 B2/C2] in the town centre is a bit less, well, chic, but is a useful address nonetheless, with ATMs, a barber shop, beauty salon, forex bureaux, supermarket, and MTN Service Centre all represented.

Older shopping standbys in Kigali include the **Union Trade Centre (UTC)**, **Kigali City Tower** and a couple of standalone **Simba** supermarkets. The **Union Trade Centre** [86 D4] dominates the eastern side of KN 4 Avenue between Place de l'Unité Nationale and Place de la Constitution. The centrepiece of this two-storey mall is an immense 24-hour branch of the Kenyan Nakumatt supermarket chain, by far the best-stocked shop of its type in Kigali (urban legend has it that more than one expatriate wept for joy outside when it opened, a story which, even if untrue, demonstrates the supermarket's impact on resident shoppers). In addition to a wide range of imported goods and electrical and other household items, the supermarket has an excellent bakery (freshly baked bread, croissants and other pastries) and meat-and-cheese counter. Sometimes referred to as the Nakumatt Centre, the UTC also hosts several fast-food outlets, a Bourbon Café for fresh coffee and light meals, an efficient forex bureau, a fast internet café, an MTN shop, a RwandAir booking office, several boutique shops, and several ATMs. The public toilets here are very clean and a nominal fee is charged to use them.

The newer **Kigali City Tower** [86 C3] also has a branch of Nakumatt Supermarket of a similar size to the store in the UTC. In addition, the Kigali City Tower has a branch of Bourbon Café which has a spacious terraced area overlooking Kigali's busy shopping streets. There is also Mr Price, a large shop selling new Western-style clothing and homewares, an authorised Apple dealer and an electrical store, as well as fast-food restaurants. Lots of boutique shops are opening and there's a cinema on the top floor.

Simba Supermarket has five branches, in Kicukiro [75 G6], Kimironko, Kigali [94 B5] Heights, opposite the parliament [94 C5], and opposite the UTC [86 C4], all of which stock a large range of goods including Western clothing and shoes, household items and electrical goods. The branches at Kigali Heights and opposite parliament are open 24/7. They've got good bakeries, butchery and grocery sections, and very good cafés where you can pick up a quick lunch or snack (page 99). The newest entrant into Kigali's supermarket scene, **Sawa Citi** [75 G4], is equally well stocked and has two branches: one on KN 7 Road near Car Wash and the other on KN 5 Road in Remera. Otherwise, most of the shops that are of interest to tourists lie within a rough rectangle formed by Boulevard de la Révolution (KN 3 Avenue), Avenue du Commerce (KN 2/76 streets), Avenue des Mille Collines (KN 63/69/78 Street, depending on where you are) and Rue de l'Epargne (KN 74 Street).

In **Boulevard de la Révolution** (KN 3 Avenue), south of the UTC, the large I&M Bank is on the eastern side [86 D5], almost on Place de l'Indépendance (where the gorilla roundabout is). Looking across the road from the bank you have, alongside the new city council building, a number of small shops/offices, including the Inzuki Designs boutique, Camellia Restaurant, a 24-hour pharmacy, the Lamane Café and Supermarket [86 D6], a GT Bank ATM and a filling station [86 D6].

Turn right at the petrol station into Avenue des Mille Collines (KN 63 Street), then right again into the now-pedestrianised **KN 4 Avenue** (Avenue de la Paix). On the opposite side of KN 4 Avenue before it reaches KN 76 Street (Avenue du Commerce) [86 C6], you have (not necessarily in order), an excellent wine shop, a forex bureau, various clothing and stationery shops, post (DHL) and internet facilities, and a few tour operators and travel agents.

The first road running west from here is **KN 76 Street** (Avenue du Commerce), where the Librairie Caritas bookshop [86 C5] stands a little way down on the left. The next junction is with **KN 74 Street** (Rue de l'Epargne) [86 C5], where you'll find a cluster of excellent handicraft shops, including **Africarte** [86 C5], **COOPAR** [86 C5] and ASAK. Another block down KN 74 Street (Rue de l'Epargne), you'll find Kigali's main cluster of forex bureaux [86 B5], most of which will change cash in any hard currency. Further west is the **central market** [86 B4] (sometimes called Nyarugenge market, after the neighbourhood), reopened in 2015 after extensive renovations and host to a dizzying array of businesses over its seven storeys. Finally, just a block further west, **La Galette** [86 A4], hosts the city's best delicatessen and butchery, as well as a great café serving fresh coffee, filled baguettes and light meals, and makes for a good place to refuel after a morning's shopping.

The biggest suburban mall in Kigali is the **MTN Centre** [94 D3] on KG 9 Avenue (Nyarutarama Road) about 1km north of its junction with KN 5 Road (Boulevard de l'Umuganda). Though it is not as well equipped as the malls listed on pages 109–10, it does have a good bookshop, a butcher and delicatessen affiliated to La Galette in the city centre (and of a similar quality), a branch of Bourbon Café, an MTN Shop, and a sports bar, and the perennially popular Mr. Chips (page 103) is just across the street.

Be aware that plastic bags have been banned in Rwanda since 2005, following a city clean-up in which almost a million old bags or remnants were discovered. This ban is strictly enforced, so it's best to carry your own (non-plastic!) shopping bag if you plan to make many purchases.

HANDICRAFTS AND ART A wide range of handicrafts are sold in Kigali and there's great scope for browsing.

The biggest craft market (as opposed to a unified shop) in town is the **Caplaki handicrafts co-operative** [79 G6] (m *078 856 8596;* e *gerardmuhizi@yahoo.fr*), near the Cercle Sportif. As part of a Kigali clean-up operation some years ago, the clutter of craft stalls and pavement vendors in the city centre had to move (though the handful of **craft shops on KN 74 Avenue** are still worth a visit). A group of about 35 craftspeople approached the Kigali City Council asking for a piece of land where they could relocate. In line with the government's policy of encouraging small-scale income-generating projects, land was allocated. The craftspeople contributed by building the 30-odd wooden huts and stalls.

The complex isn't too far from the city centre, on the Gikondo/Nyenyeri minibus-taxi route. There's parking space inside and outside for a few cars. The stallholders, men and women of all ages, between them sell a huge variety of goods. Carvings, weaving, sculpture, batik, pottery, metalwork, semi-precious stones, palm-fibre items, musical instruments, leather, fabrics, toys, stationery, small furniture, novelties … there's every chance you'll find it at Caplaki. You can visit as part of the Kigali City Tour (page 116), catch a minibus-taxi or take a taxi-voiture. Don't be afraid to bargain hard.

While you're in the city centre, it would also be worth poking your head into a couple of the high-end galleries selling designer jewellery, artwork, clothing, and home goods to be found here – **Inzuki Designs** [86 D6] (m *078 160 0160;* w *inzuki. com*) and **Rwanda Clothing** [86 B7] (m *078 613 4128;* w *rwandaclothing.com*) both stand out for their elegant and up-to-date interpretations of traditional Rwandan motifs. Nearby in the new Kigali Marriott, the **Go Kigali Boutique** [86 D7] (m *078 831 6607;* w *gokigalitours.com*) stocks a finely curated selection of clothing, bags, jewellery and art from more than 35 Rwandan artisans and designers, including

Angaza (m *078 487 2385;* w *angazarwanda.com*) who specialise in upcycling waste products like old vinyl banners and rice sacks into chic designer accessories like wallets, purses and laptop cases.

Outside of the centre, **Abraham Konga Collections** [96 C3] (m *078 556 1626/849 2546;* w *abrahamkonga.com*) in Kimihurura is easily one of the finest new boutiques in Kigali, with affordable but very modern and stylish jewellery designed by the owner himself and fashioned from beads, brass (from melted-down padlocks!), silver and cow horns. They also stock a good and fairly priced selection of more typical Rwandan crafts. Also in Kimihurura, **Kigali Pottery Collections** [96 D2] (m *078 786 3923;* w *kigalipotterycollections.com*) stocks a very appealing collection of dishware, candleholders, figurines and other items made from clay by co-operatives near Kigali in a style very similar to the pottery found at Gatagara near Huye (page 141). They also have a nice in-shop café serving coffee and tea.

The most active of Kigali's galleries has to be the admirable **Inema Arts Center** [94 B3] (m *078 318 7646/865 3683;* e *inemaart@gmail.com;* w *inemaartcenter.com*), where there's an impressive calendar of concerts, poetry readings, classes (yoga, Intore dance) and evening events several times a week in addition to the daytime painting classes for children in the surrounding communities and exhibitions from their 13 artists-in-residence. There are two floors of gallery space, a women's craft co-operative and shop, and a simple café on site as well.

Just a couple of blocks away, **Ivuka Arts** [94 B3] (m *078 862 0560;* e *ivukaarts. kigali@gmail.com/info@ivukaarts.com;* f *ivukaarts;* ⏲ *08.00–19.30 daily*), founded by Collin Sekajugo and named after the Kinyarwanda word for birth, provides a workshop and showcase for more than a dozen up-and-coming Rwandan artists whose innovative work typically blends tradition and contemporary styles.

There are a few other art centres and gallery spaces around Kigali worth checking out, including **Niyo Cultural Centre** [74 D1] (m *078 893 2111;* w *niyoculturalcentre. org*) behind the public library, which was founded by a former street child and today raises money for disadvantaged children through traditional drum and dance performances, along with visual arts. Nearby in Kacyiru, the collective of artists at **Abien Arts** [94 A2] (m *078 899 3414;* w *abienarts.com*) produces sculpture, handicrafts, and paintings, including some large murals around Kigali.

Weaving is one of the specialities of Rwanda – baskets, mats, hangings and pots appear in a variety of shapes and sizes, with carefully interwoven traditional patterns. They are sold by some street vendors, and there's a good selection (including woven hammocks) in the craft shop called **ASAR** [86 C5] (*Association des Artistes Rwandais;* ✆ *0252 504491*). This excellent little shop combines the work of several craft-making co-ops; some items are very touristy but others are traditional and all make good gifts. As well as the weaving there are carvings, musical instruments, pottery, beadwork, palm-leaf crafts (including decorated notepaper and cards) and even stuffed toys. Prices are marked, so you needn't worry about bargaining – but a reduction for quantity would be legitimate.

Amahoro ava Hejuru [74 C6] (m *078 886 9295;* w *amahorocoop.com*) is a peace-building women's sewing co-operative, whose goal is to provide sustainable income generation to women. They make a variety of high-quality fabric items such as purses, backpacks, laptop bags, aprons, place mats, quilts and toys. If you have two or three days they can make any custom item you like, from clothing to draperies. The co-operative is located in Gikondo; look for their blue gate and sign on the left of the road about 100m uphill from the roundabout, or call the manager Grace on m 078 875 1878 for directions. The **Nyamirambo Women's Centre** [91 C1] is another collective producing excellent clothing, jewellery and crafts – see page 117 for details.

You'll also find street vendors selling most kinds of small handicrafts – carvings, jewellery, woven baskets, masks, musical instruments, notepaper and postcards decorated with palm fibres – and so on.

BOOKSHOPS Two good bookshops in Kigali, both of them stocking a wide range of books on the history and culture of Rwanda, the background to the genocide and an assortment of other relevant themes, are the **Librairie Caritas** [86 C5] (☏ *0252 574295/576503;* e *librairiecaritas1@gmail.com;* w *caritasrwanda.org*) in KN 76 Street (Rue du Commerce) just downhill from its junction with KN 4 Avenue (Avenue de la Paix), and the fantastic (and far superior) **Ikirezi Bookshop** [94 B4] (☏ *0252 571314;* m *078 856 0358;* e *info@ikirezi.biz;* w *ikirezi.biz; see ad, page 72*) on KG 5 Avenue in Kacyiru, behind the Dutch embassy. The Ikirezi, which is also home to the Inzora Rooftop Café and sometimes holds book signings and other events, is open 08.00–20.00 Monday–Friday and 09.30–18.30 Saturday and Sunday; while Caritas keeps normal shop hours, but is closed on Saturday afternoon and Sunday. Also, both branches of Nakumatt (Kigali City Tower and Union Trade Centre) stock a small range of fiction and non-fiction books in English, including books with an African theme. The RDB Tourism and Conservation Reservation Office in Kacyiru has a selection of books relating to Rwanda.

MARKETS In all market areas, take care – crowds are popular with pickpockets and opportunistic thieves, and instances of crime, though far from common, have been reported. Also be tactful about taking photos; for every dozen people who don't object to being in a picture, there'll be someone who does. Respect their privacy.

Kimironko market [75 H3] is a short bus journey from the city centre or Remera and is one of the main markets in the city. You can get a bus there from the central bus station (route 302) or Nyabugogo via Kacyiru (route 305), or either will pick you up at Kisimenti roundabout opposite Chez Lando. There is a dazzling array of goods for sale from fresh fruits and vegetables to shoes and handbags, household items, clothes and kitchen equipment. You can choose from a huge selection of colourful fabrics and visit one of the many tailors who will measure you up and make it into whatever you want in a few days. There is also a large section which sells the cheapest handicrafts in the city – jewellery, clothing, sculpture, you name it – if you are prepared to bargain! Also worth a look and smack in the city centre, the remodelled **Central market** [86 B4/5] (also known as Nyarugenge market) is an bustling affair with an equally bewitching array of merchandise spanning e basement up through several storeys of its new multi-level complex.

If you've got a taste for marketplace frenzy, the frenetic market across the road from the Nyabugogo bus station is another worthwhile stop; it's like a human kaleidoscope – a changing, shifting mass of colours and noise. A few minutes being jostled by these brisk crowds, determinedly going about their own business, may be enough for you – but it's a typical and non-touristy experience which it would be a pity to miss completely. See the walk *To Nyabugogo market* on page 124.

KIGALI FOR CHILDREN While Kigali isn't overly rich in things for little ones to do, there are a few places where they can go to play. For starters, the **Mamba Club** [96 C4] (m *078 030 3463;* f *Mamba Club Kigali;* ⊕ *noon–23.00 daily, later at w/ends*) in Kimihurura, while not explicitly oriented to children, is family-friendly and has enough open space to play, along with some playground equipment, a trampoline,

---

INTERNATIONAL PEACE MARATHON

This colourful and energetic event is an initiative of the European Federation of Soroptimists (w *soroptimisteurope.org*), aimed at giving people from other countries the chance to run shoulder to shoulder with Rwandans in the name of peace. After long and careful preparations by the Soroptimists and Rwanda's Ministry of Youth, Sports and Culture, the first International Peace Marathon took place in Kigali on 15 May 2005. On that bright, hot Sunday morning, 2,000 runners from 20 different nations flocked into the Amahoro Stadium. Among them were 500 children, who set off with the less athletic participants on the accompanying 5km Fun Run.

Ever since that day the Kigali Peace Marathon has become a popular annual event attracting participants from the USA, UK, Italy, France, Finland, Belgium, Germany, Austria, Netherlands, Greece, Luxembourg, Malta, Morocco, Kenya, Ethiopia and other African countries. There are many children selected to take part in the fun run from schools all over Rwanda. Many are from underprivileged backgrounds, and the Soroptimists have raised funds to provide each with a commemorative T-shirt, a contribution to his/her school fees for a year, and a backpack with some school equipment. The Ministry of Sport looks after their transport and accommodation.

At the Peace Marathon held in May 2017, Kenyans swept up nearly all the honours, winning the men's and women's marathon and men's half marathon, but a Rwandan runner, Salome Nyirarukundo, took first in the women's half marathon and another Rwandan, John Hakizimana took third in the men's half. Over 3,500 runners took part. There is a great atmosphere of good humour, energy and enthusiasm on the streets of Kigali on marathon day, but as you might expect in the 'Land of a Thousand Hills', the marathon itself is inevitably, hilly! And Kigali's altitude of 1,500m can cause breathlessness among some runners from lower countries. If you choose to take part, bring plenty of water, and remember that you may need more breaks because of the altitude and heat.

Check out the details on w kigalimarathon.org. You have to register to take part before the event and you must go to collect your race number from the Amahoro Stadium in Kigali at least three days beforehand. And you should start training now…

volleyball court, bowling, and a swimming pool. South of town near Mount Kigali, **Fazenda Sengha** [91 B7] (m *078 855 1787/440 6340*; e *fazenda@sengha. com*; w *sengha.com*; f *Fazendasengha*; ☉ *09.00–18.00 Wed–Mon*) has horseriding lessons for youth and children, along with an archery range, trampoline, ziplines, and plenty of open space for running around. It's also on the way up Mount Kigali if the kids are old enough for a hike.

Creative kids are well catered for at the art centres (ie: Inema Arts, Ivuka Arts), which offer regular arts and music classes for children (painting, drumming, etc), and represent a great opportunity for your kid to meet local children as well.

About 15km east of Kigali on the road towards Rwamagana is **Bambino Supercity** (m *078 851 2246*), with a swimming pool, gardens and some play equipment for children. Also, many hotels in Kigali, including the Hotel des Mille Collines, Park Inn, Gorillas Golf, Grand Legacy and La Palisse, have swimming pools which the general public can use for a small fee (*generally Rfr4,000–6,000*); the same is true for the Cercle Sportif and Nyarutarama Tennis Club. **Kidzmania** (m *073 345 5013*; f) is a new dedicated play space at Kigali Heights shopping centre designed for children three and up.

OTHER PRACTICALITIES

COMMUNICATIONS The main **post office** [86 D2] at the top of KN 1 Road (Boulevard de Nyabugogo) in the city centre has a counter for international phone calls and, should the need arise, an efficient fax office. If you want someone to send a fax to you there, the number is ☎+250 252 514091. There's also a philatelic counter.

Internet Cyber cafés are reasonably common, but are in many cases being replaced by cafés and restaurants offering free Wi-Fi. One hour at a cyber café typically costs around Rfr400–600, with faster facilities such as CyberLink Café inside the UTC generally charging slightly higher rates. All but the cheapest of hotels today offer Wi-Fi. Public business facilities generally close on Sundays.

Telephone You can find **public telephones** in shops and kiosks all over Kigali – they are metered, so you pay when you've finished and don't need handfuls of small change. Calls to mobile phones from these are more expensive than those to normal phones, although calls from mobile to mobile are cheaper. Rwanda is now said to have one of the most modern telephone systems in East Africa.

You can buy a local SIM card to convert most imported **mobiles** for use in Rwanda; these cost around Rfr1,000 from any MTN, Airtel or Tigo shop – one or all of these can be found in most of Kigali's shopping centres (Kigali Heights, UTC, etc) and there's an MTN shop at the airport as well. If you need voicemail and international texting, check that your card includes this; some don't, though in Rwanda these services have been largely superseded by WhatsApp. Then it's a pay-as-you-go system: you buy cards in denominations of Rfr500 upwards to top up the airtime balance in your account. Note that if you plan to use data for web browsing, WhatsApp, etc, it's important to buy a dedicated **data bundle** using the airtime balance in your account – using the airtime alone for data purposes is prohibitively expensive. With MTN, it costs Rfr2,000 for 1GB of data valid for one month (price current in 2018), and bundle options can be checked by dialling *345#.

You can also buy either a USB modem or portable Wi-Fi router, both of which take a SIM card in the same way as your mobile phone and use the same pay-as-you-go system of airtime and data bundles as described above.

MEDICAL FACILITIES For additional medical listings, see the US embassy's listings at w rw.usembassy.gov/u-s-citizen-services/doctors.

Hospitals

✚ **Central Hospital of the University of Kigali** [79 E6] 📞 0252 575406/575555; e chuck. hospital@chuckigali.org

✚ **King Faisal** (or Faycal) [94 C3] 📞 0252 582421/585397; emergency 📞 0252 588888; e faisal@rwanda1.com; w kfh.rw

Clinics and laboratories

✚ **Plateau Polyclinic** 📞 0272 578767; m 078 830 1630; e pcp@mtnonline.rw; w polycliniqueduplateau.rw

✚ **Polyfam** m 078 887 7225; e polycliniquefamiliale@yahoo.com; w polyfam.co

MONEY Assuming you arrive with hard-currency cash (ideally, US dollars, euros or UK pounds sterling), the easiest option is to change at a private **bureau de change** (known locally as **forex bureaux**), whch are scattered around the city centre. These are mostly clustered along the east end of KN 74 Street (Rue de l'Epargne), and have current exchange rates chalked up on blackboards outside. You might want to shop around a bit, and bargain, if you're changing large amounts, and you should keep your wits about you. If the touts that hang out here seem intimidating, there is also an efficient forex bureau nearby in KN 4 Avenue (Avenue de la Paix) as well as on the top floor of the Union Trade Centre (UTC) [86 D4]. There are counters in most hotels and banks, and at Kigali International Airport. Forex bureaux offer a significantly lower rate of exchange for US dollar bills smaller than US$50, and the same applies to low-denomination bills in other currencies. US dollars printed before 2009 are unlikely to be accepted.

Travellers' cheques are practically useless in Kigali. The I&M Bank in KN 3 Avenue (Boulevard de la Révolution) [86 D5] may change up to US$200 worth per day, but this is a tedious procedure and you may be required to produce proof of purchase. BCR also has **Western Union** facilities for transfers from abroad, but bear in mind that these transfers attract a hefty charge.

It is now possible to draw local currency from **ATMs** just about everywhere in the country, and the main banks represented throughout Rwanda include **Bank of Kigali** (w bk.rw), **Ecobank** (w ecobank.com), **Kenya Commercial Bank (KCB)** (w kcbbankgroup.com), **GT Bank** (w gtbank.co.rw), **Cogebanque** (w cogebank.com), **Banque Populaire du Rwanda** (w bpr.rw), and **I&M Bank** (w imbank.com), among others. Of these, all have ATMs accepting international Visa cards, but only KCB and GT Bank work with Mastercard.

WHAT TO SEE AND DO

For a capital city, Kigali doesn't offer a great deal in terms of buildings, museums and historical/cultural sites, but it is a pleasant place for strolling and people-watching. If you want to see the best of the city in an organised manner, this can be arranged through the RDB Tourism and Conservation Reservation Office [94 D5] (page 82), which runs **guided tours** of Kigali from Monday to Saturday at US$20/40 per person with your own/RDB transportation. The tour takes in several places covered below, including the Museum of Natural History, Nyamirambo (the oldest quarter of Kigali), Caplaki Handicrafts Co-operative, Gisozi Genocide Memorial and the Heroes' Cemetery, as well as the Parliament Building and Kigali Institute of Science and Technology. The guided tours from Go Kigali (*based at the Marriott hotel;* m *078 831 6607;* w *gokigalitours.com; from US$60pp*) also come highly recommended, and can be done in a full or half day; these are less landmark-focused and take in a trip up

Mount Kigali, coffee tasting, local markets, a milk bar visit and water-taxi ride, plus lunch and the genocide memorial on the full-day tour.

Another great way to get beyond the landmarks and into day-to-day African life is with the **Nyamirambo Women's Centre** [91 C1] (m *078 211 1860;* e *nwcoffice. kigali@gmail.com;* w *nwc-kigali.org;* ⏰ *08.00–17.00 Mon–Fri, 09.00–17.00 Sat*), which offers guided tours of the neighbourhood with several different focuses, all of which serve as an excellent introduction to the vibrant culture of contemporary urban Rwanda in Nyamirambo, the city's oldest and arguably most multi-cultural suburb. Their original tour sees the women of Nyamirambo take visitors to a local hair salon and tailor, as well as the Muslim quarter and market, and finally a private home for a cooking lesson and traditional lunch, while 'Tastes of Nyamirambo' focuses specifically on cooking, and 'The Art of Sisal' takes in a session making traditional *agaseke* baskets with an expert weaver. Whichever tour you choose, they last about 2½ hours plus lunch, it's Rfr15,000 per person plus Rfr3,000 per person for lunch, and 70% of proceeds go straight to the community.

MEMORIALS
Kigali Genocide Memorial [74 B1] (m *078 465 1051;* e *team@kgm.rw;* w *kgm. rw;* f; ⏰ *08.00–17.00 daily, last entry 16.00*) This dignified memorial has been constructed in Gisozi, the burial site of over 250,000 people killed in a three-month period during Rwanda's 1994 genocide. It opened fully for the tenth anniversary of the genocide in April 2004. You can see it across the valley – a large, white, modern building with terraces in front – on the right as you go downhill on KN 1 Road (Boulevard de Nyabugogo). To drive there is easy as it's in sight for much of the way – take a right turn halfway down KN 1 Road on to KN 8 Avenue, continue downwards into the valley, and when you're a little way past the memorial take a left turn across the valley on to KG 14 Avenue, then (at a T-junction) go sharp left (staying on KG 14 Avenue) and you'll come to the gate.

Importantly, the memorial centre is not just a mass grave and exhibition. At the request of Kigali City Council, it was created – and is managed today – by the UK-based Aegis Trust (a non-sectarian, non-governmental genocide prevention organisation; w *aegistrust.org*). Aegis operates a Rebuilding Lives programme to help widows and orphans of the genocide, and a peace-building education programme (hosted at the memorial) educating a new generation about the dangers of prejudice and helping to establish trust between the children of survivors and perpetrators.

The memorial centre is now also home to the Genocide Archive of Rwanda, which is open to the public. The purpose of the archive centre is to illuminate genocidal ideologies and their impact. The archive collection includes photographs, official documents and geographical data.

Entry is free but contributions are very much welcomed because the centre relies on proceeds for the upkeep of the mass graves and the exhibitions. Recently it has developed an audio tour which costs Rfr12,000 (less for residents, students, etc). The audio tour is currently available in English, French, Dutch and German, Italian and Spanish. It is comprehensive, and is particularly helpful for understanding the outside exhibits such as the gardens and mass graves. There is also a bookshop that sells a good selection of films, music and books on the theme of genocide and prevention. Further to this, there's now a café on site selling a good range of snacks, sandwiches and drinks (including premium Rwandan coffee) from about Rfr2,000, and proceeds from this also go towards the upkeep of the museum and its educational outreach work.

To maximise accessibility – particularly for those whose loved ones are buried here – there is no charge for entry to the Kigali Genocide Memorial. However, its operation – and Aegis's programmes in Rwanda – are entirely dependent on donations and revenue from Aegis Social Enterprises (including services provided both on site and at the Discover Rwanda Youth Hostel – page 93), so visitors are invited to make a donation of at least US$15 if choosing not to spend money on any of the centre's services or facilities.

See also the box below.

Nyanza Genocide Memorial [75 G7] In April 2014, this stark memorial overlooking KK 15 Road (Bugesera Road) in the suburb of Kicukiro was the site of the official Genocide Memorial Day ceremony on the 20th anniversary of the Rwandan genocide. An estimated 10,000 victims of the genocide are buried in mass graves here, covered in large slabs of concrete. Many of these victims were Tutsis who, when the killing started, took refuge in the Ecole Technique Officielle (ETO), which fell under the protection of Belgian troops from the United Nations Assistance Mission for Rwanda (UNAMIR). Tragically, UNAMIR withdrew the Belgians from Rwanda, and the interahamwe descended on the ETO to massacre the thousands of refugees gathered there. To get there, take a bus to Kicukiro and

RESPONSES TO THE KIGALI GENOCIDE MEMORIAL

You are the stone on which we will build a Rwanda without conflict.
Bernard Makuza, Rwandan Prime Minister, 2004.

Since my own visit to Rwanda's genocide memorial site, I have been talking to many colleagues in the United Nations…. Anyone who goes there cannot come out without crying, without being very humble about how the international community failed to react to this.'
Ban Ki-moon, UN Secretary-General, speaking at the UN Headquarters in New York at the launch of the Aegis Trust/UN exhibition 'Lessons from Rwanda', 30 April 2007.

Finally, a beautiful and profound memorial.
Alain Destexhe, Senator, Belgium.

I want to thank the local government and the Aegis Trust and all the people who've worked on this. This is in some ways the most moving memorial of its kind I've ever seen, simply for the power and simplicity of it… it faithfully, honestly, painfully presents the truth of the Rwandan genocide. It is a profoundly important contribution to the ability of this country to go on with its life, and it's an important contribution to the recent history of the world that no-one can afford to forget. We are all in debt to everyone who had anything to do with the creation of this magnificent museum, and I urge those of you who can to see it and to support it.
Former US President Bill Clinton at the Kigali Memorial Centre, Rwanda.

Before our colleagues visited the Memorial, there were some students who had lost their parents or siblings during the genocide and who had the feeling that someone who prevented your parents from living is your enemy; but now, we have learnt and things changed.
Student response to Aegis Rwanda's genocide education programme.

above   With over 100 individuals, Akagera National Park's elephant population is the largest it's been in more than half a century (HK/AMC) pages 310–11

right   Thousands of buffalo call Akagera National Park home, and the park's wide-open savannahs are the best place in Rwanda to spot them (SH/AMC) page 309

below left   Though rarely spotted by visitors, leopards still reliably prowl the savannahs of Akagera National Park (JH/AMC) page 308

below right   Since the reintroduction of lions in 2015, 11 cubs have been born in Akagera (SH/AMC) page 309

above left Maasai giraffe were first introduced to Akagera from Kenya in 1986; the original herd of two males and four females has now multiplied to a population of around 80 (WT/S) page 309

above right Hippo are present in impressive numbers in Akagera National Park; some lakes support several hundred (JG/AMC) page 309

middle Akagera is the only place in Rwanda where zebra still roam in the wild (SH/AMC) page 309

below Vehicle safaris in Akagera National Park cover everything from swamps to savannahs, and the year-on-year increase in animal populations means that game viewing here has never been better (MT/AMC) pages 319–22

above left   The topi tends to be seen in open habitats (AZ) page 310

above right   The common duiker is usually seen alone or in pairs (AZ) page 311

right   Reedbuck are almost always spotted in pairs, and most easily found in Akagera's Mutumba Hills (JG/AMC) pages 310–11

below left   Often seen in large groups, the impala is the most common antelope found in Akagera National Park (SH/AMC) page 310

below right   Known for its attractively shaggy coat, the waterbuck can be spotted near the lakes of Akagera (SH/AMC) page 310

above left	The great blue turaco can be seen gliding clumsily between the trees in flocks of up to ten birds (PO/MP/FLPA) page 175
above right	The grey crowned crane is usually associated with marshes and moist grassland (AZ) page 290
right	The lakes of Akagera support a prodigious number of fish eagles (AZ) page 312
below left	Known to haunt the skies above Akagera's Lake Ihema, the unmistakeable marabou stork has a face to remember (AZ) page 320
below right	Regal sunbird (SS) page 176
bottom	Open-bill storks forage in the shallows of Lake Hago (AZ) page 321

above left Canoe trips on the Mukungwa River take in the lush countryside outside Musanze and offer ample opportunity for birding (SV/KJ) page 243

above right Rwanda's newest national park, Gishwati-Mukura protects two relict forest patches that were nearly wiped out but are now on the rebound (MJR) pages 222–3

left Dangling 40m above a streambed on the forest floor, East Africa's only canopy walkway is found in Nyungwe Forest National Park and offers spectacular views over the riot of greenery below (AZ) pages 182–5

below Rugezi Birding Site on Lake Burera is the place to see large water-associated birds (AZ) pages 246–55

above Running along the Congolese border for 90km, the stunning Lake Kivu has long served as a popular weekend getaway for residents of this otherwise landlocked country (AZ) pages 191–229

right These distinctive crafts, consisting of three dugouts lashed together with bamboo poles, are the vessel of choice for Lake Kivu's many fishermen and known as *amato* ('boat') in Kinyarwanda (AZ) page 201

below In villages up and down Lake Kivu, young girls head to the lakeshore to fetch water, socialise, and take care of the day's washing (AZ)

above   Tea and coffee are the most important export crops for Rwanda, and the intensively cultivated hillside terraces are a magical sight (AZ)

left   The Maraba coffee co-operative, based in Huye, has excelled in international taste tests (AZ) page 163

below   Grown largely by smallholders on hills throughout Rwanda, tea is always plucked by hand and Rwanda's produce enjoys a growing reputation for excellence around the world (SS)

stay on until you reach the main Nyanza bus park. Then look for ETO; it's just across KK 15 Road from the bus park. Bus 108 comes here from Remera via Sonatubes, and bus 204 from Nyabugogo via KN 7 Road. For a meal in the area, **Oasis of Peace** (m *078 488 8770;* f *restoasisofpeace;* ⊕ *08.00–23.30 daily; mains US$8*) is a new restaurant a few hundred metres away on KK 432 Street; it was founded to provide employment opportunities for Burundian refugees in Kigali.

Remera Heroes' Cemetery [75 H4] Situated on KG 17 Avenue (Kimironko Road) a few hundred metres past Amahoro Stadium, Heroes' Cemetery is another site associated with the 1994 genocide. Three graves here are of particular significance. The first is the grave of **Fred Gisa Rwigyema**, the co-founder and leader of the RPF, who was killed in battle on 2 October 1990 during a failed invasion of Rwanda. The second is the grave of **Agathe Uwilingiyimana**, the first (and thus far only) female prime minister of Rwanda, who was less than a year into her term when she was assassinated by the interahamwe on 7 April 1994, within hours of the plane crash that killed President Habyarimana. The third is the **Tomb of the Unknown Soldier**, whose anonymous occupant symbolises all those who died in the civil war.

Unfortunately, a permit is now required to visit. This can be obtained at the Chancellery For Heroes And Decorations Of Honour (CHENO) (m *078 785 9090*; e *info@cheno.gov.rw;* w *cheno.gov.rw*) office in Remera (near Chez Lando Hotel) before setting out.

Camp Kigali Memorial [79 E6] Now the University of Rwanda Nyarugenge Campus, Camp Kigali is where ten Belgian UNAMIR peacekeepers, deployed to guard the house of Prime Minister Agathe Uwilingiyimana, were executed brutally by the Presidential Guard on the first day of the genocide. The former military camp now hosts a memorial and small museum that still bears the scars of grenade shrapnel. In the garden, ten stone obelisks have been erected, each with the initials of one of the soldiers carved into the base, and horizontal slashes indicating his age.

For memorials outside Kigali, see *Ntarama and Nyamata genocide memorials* on pages 126–7.

MUSEUMS
Presidential Palace Museum [75 H5] (✪ S 1°58.554, E 30°10.346; KK 106 St; m *073 074 1093*; w *museum.gov.rw;* ⊕ *08.00–18.00 daily except 7 Apr & 11.00–18.00 on Umuganda days; entrance Rfr6,000 non-residents, Rfr5,000 foreign residents, Rfr3,000 students & non-resident children*) The whitewashed state house situated about 4km from Kigali International Airport was the home of the former Rwandan president Juvenal Habyarimana until his death in 1994, and it was then occupied by his successor, President Pasteur Bizimungu, until 2000.

The house has been left largely unchanged since it was last occupied in 2000, including the threadbare sofa rumoured to be the place where Habyarimana's wife, Agathe, was sitting at the moment her husband's plane was shot down on 6 April 1994. A reader recently reported that the information boards describing various aspects of Rwandan culture have been taken down, so today the quality of your visit will depend largely on the enthusiasm of your guide, which can be variable. In showing you around the property, guides talk you through some of the decisions made by the Habyarimanas during their 20-year stay in the palace and how these decisions contributed to the Rwandan genocide.

Camilla Gore

In the past few years, a number of individuals and NGOs (Non-Governmental Organisations) have been seeking to help Rwandans, particularly young orphans, underprivileged children and abandoned or widowed women, to develop their skills and lift themselves out of poverty and into education and a better future. The places mentioned in this box all work towards empowering Rwandans to learn and use new skills and they invest profits back into local communities in Kigali. All are very welcoming towards visitors and show the many positive changes that are happening across the city. Other travellers have reported that visiting one of these projects is a particularly powerful experience after going to the Gisozi Genocide Memorial Centre.

J. LYNN'S [75 G7] (m *078 840 8308*; w *jlynnskigali.blogspot.com*; *J.Lynn's*; *08.00–16.00 Mon–Fri, 08.00–14.00 Sat*) Formerly known as the African Bagel Company and tucked away on a little street (*KK 25 Av*) on the left up the hill past Kicukiro market (and signposted from the main road), this cosy café was founded several years ago to help local young people and women get into employment and education and off the streets. Other than the owners and a few volunteers, all of the staff are local Rwandan people, and they serve mouthwatering bagels, doughnuts and chocolate chip cookies; some of the delicious bagel options include the hot pizza bagel, bagel chips with hummus or barbecue sauce and bagels with vegetables and cream cheese. On Saturdays, doughnuts are cooked outside on a traditional charcoal stove. You can also buy handicrafts from local disabled artisans at the café.

CARDS FROM AFRICA [75 H5] (m *078 865 8158*; w *cardsfromafrica.com*; *09.00–15.00 Mon–Fri*) These beautiful, textured paper cards are made by young people in the Kigali area who have lost both of their parents. The young people are trained to make the cards, and the work provides them with an income for supporting their families or getting an education. If you visit their workshop in Kigali near the airport, you can take a guided tour and see the card-making process from making the paper pulp to assembling the cards. To get to Cards from Africa by public transport, go to the Remera crossroads and stand so you are on the road opposite the bus park with the MTN shop on your left. Walk a short way down the

Outside, in the extensive grounds of the museum, lie the remains of the plane crash that killed Habyarimana. Looking at the scattered remains of the plane is a poignant and sobering experience, and serves as a powerful reminder of how Rwanda fell apart during the events of April 1994.

Kandt House Museum [78 C4] (m *073 074 1093/078 457 7776*; w *museum.gov.rw*; *08.00–18.00 daily except 7 Apr & 11.00–18.00 on Umuganda days; entrance Rfr6,000 non-residents, Rfr5,000 foreign residents, Rfr3,000 students & non-resident children*) Standing alongside KN 90 Street just west of KN 2 Avenue (Avenue de la Justice), this museum is set in Kandt House, which was built by Richard Kandt in 1907, restored with German aid over 2004–05, and opened as a museum in 2007. Kandt House, probably the oldest in Kigali, is a moderately interesting example of German colonial architecture, set in pretty gardens with a lovely view over the valleys. Effectively the founder of Kigali, Kandt embarked on his first journey

road until you see a blue taxi sign and get a bus to Kabeza town. Stay on the bus for about 10 minutes until you reach its terminus. Walk a couple of hundred yards down the road and you should see Cards from Africa just down the hill on your left (there's a useful map on their website).

THE MEG FOUNDATION [79 F1] (m *078 579 1008;* e *info@kinambaproject.org.uk;* ⏰ *08.00–17.00 Mon–Fri*) The Meg Foundation was founded by former VSO volunteer Meg Fletcher in 2007 to provide educational opportunities for underprivileged children in the Kinamba area of Kigali, a small area tucked behind the US embassy. Visitors are most welcome. In the mornings, visitors can join the nursery children in their daily activities including, singing, reading, painting and playing games. In the afternoons, the foundation runs an after-school club for primary children who attend local government schools. The foundation also provides literacy and skills training for local women and their handicrafts can be bought at the site. There are also sometimes longer-term volunteering opportunities available. To get to the centre, ask for a moto or taxi to Kinamba Jehova and the foundation is opposite; or turn left at the roundabout by the US embassy, then take the first right cobbled road and walk for 1km until you see the blue-and-white building on the left.

CENTRE MAREMBO [75 H5] (m *078 850 5355;* e *centremarembo@gmail.com;* w *centremarembo.org;* f *centremarembo*) Centre Marembo focuses on vulnerable young (female) victims of abuse and violence, teen mothers, pregnant girls and street girls. It has a clinic and two safe homes, and a range of services and skills (training in various crafts, education, health and childcare teaching ...) that enable them gradually to rebuild their lives. There's an organic gardening project, and the health-care services (including HIV/AIDS education) are also available to the community. Visitors are welcome and the staff are happy to show you around. Handicrafts made by the girls are on sale, as well as organic food products and medicinal plants. If you've got leftover first-aid equipment or other useful items at the end of your trip, consider lightening your suitcase by donating them here. The centre is about 7km east of Remera (towards Kibale airport) in Ndera sector, an area with a lot of new building; the road as yet has no name or number but is known locally as Caraes Street. Best to phone in advance for directions. See also page 69.

to Rwanda in 1897 in search of the most remote source of the Nile, and he was appointed first Resident Governor of Rwanda upon his return in 1907. An ardent naturalist, he was the first westerner to visit Nyungwe Forest, and he also discovered several plant and animal species, among them the localised golden monkey. Thus, when the museum opened in 2007, it quite logically served as Rwanda's natural history museum, with displays covering archaeology, geology, biology and more. Most of these exhibits, however, have now been incorporated into the much larger Museum of the Environment in Karongi (page 207), with the Kandt House Museum undergoing something of a rebranding at the time of writing, with permanent exhibitions closed to the public in late 2017.

Once it reopens (likely by the time you read this), the new exhibits will focus on a social, economic, and political history of pre-colonial and colonial-era Rwanda, with a focus on the history of Kigali and its development into Rwanda's capital city, including a gallery of rare monochrome photographs of the settlement on

Nyarugenge Hill in the city's early days. No matter the content inside the museum, one of the best reasons to visit is for the excellent view of Kigali from the terrace at the back of the building, which makes an ideal place to take photos of the city.

Campaign Against Genocide Museum

[94 C5] (m *078 307 0131*; w *museum. gov.rw*; ⊕ *08.00–17.00 daily except 7 Apr & 11.00–17.00 on Umuganda days; entrance Rfr6,000 non-residents, Rfr5,000 foreign residents, Rfr3,000 students & non-resident children; no photography*) Set inside the parliament building and opened to the public in July 2017, this new museum provides a forensic-feeling, event-by-event breakdown of modern Rwandan history from the civil war through the Arusha peace accords and the 1994 genocide, with a particular focus on the military measures taken by the RPF against the *génocidaires*. Through nine rooms, a series of the RPF's political and military movements are explained, including the well-known shelling, siege, and rescue of RPF troops and newly installed parliamentarians who were stranded in the parliament building itself. The liberation of Kigali and a handful of other rescue missions are also explained, and military history buffs will appreciate the detailed troop movement schematics provided for several of the missions.

Exhibits are largely contemporary photos and text, with a few supplementary battlefield reconstructions. The tour continues through a tiny, grim room, formerly used as an operating theatre for injured RPF troops, and concludes on the parliament's rooftop, where a statue of a gunner defending the building overlooks the city. The museum is well worth a visit for those who seek a better

---

WALKING AND CYCLING AROUND KIGALI   *Caroline Pomeroy*

Sprawling over numerous hills and valleys, with roads that wind crazily around and across the contours, Kigali can be a confusing city to navigate. Just when you think you know where you are going, your destination appears on the horizon in another direction! However, it's a fairly compact city and, assuming that you aren't put off by the idea of steep slopes, over-friendly children and changeable weather, walking is a fantastic way to get about. If you have just arrived, don't forget that Kigali lies at an altitude of around 1,600m, so take it easy on the hills!

Although the geography of the city is confusing, you can nearly always spot a landmark to help you find your way to your destination. Many buildings offer great views across Kigali, so if you plan to explore on foot you will do well to start by getting to grips with the geography, map in hand, from one of these: the panoramic top-floor bar of the Ubumwe Grande in the centre; Bourbon Café in the MTN Centre, Nyarutarama; the terrace of the Kandt House Museum; and Bourbon Café in the UTC. If you don't have a map, go get the brilliant Map of Kigali published by w livinginkigali.com; it's available at hotels and bookshops for Rfr8,000 and is worth every centime.

As well as walking as a means of getting about town, there are plenty of good hikes on the hills which ring the city. These offer spectacular views and can be surprisingly peaceful away from the constant calls of 'muzungu'. You could start your walk by taking a minibus-taxi from the centre of town – these are very cheap and are all labelled with their eventual destination (and now, in most cases, with route numbers as well).

At 1,850m, Mount Kigali is the highest peak around the city, and it can be climbed from Nyamirambo. Catch bus 401 from the central station to the terminus

understanding of the events leading up to the 1994 genocide, and the entrance fee includes an English- or French-speaking guide. Visitors must show ID at the parliament's entry gate.

NYARUTARAMA LAKE [94 C2] Situated at the south end of the Kigali Golf Club in the valley between Nyarutarama and Kacyiru Hills (and near the new golf clubhouse that's under construction), this small artificial lake and surrounding patchwork of exotic and indigenous woodland offers the best nature walk and birdwatching opportunity within Kigali city limits. The open water and its margins frequently support a variety of ducks, pelicans, herons and egrets, along with black crake, African jacana and pied and malachite kingfisher. The handsome long-crested eagle also appears to be resident, and the rank grasslands around the lake host widow birds, weavers, waxbills and seedeaters such as African citril.

The lake can be approached from two directions, either by following KG 546 Street downhill from KG 7 Avenue near King Faisal Hospital, or by following KG 9 Avenue (Nyarutarama Road) north from the junction with KN 5 Road (Boulevard de l'Umuganda), then taking the first major intersection left on to KG 13 Avenue and continuing northwards past the Nyarutarama Tennis Club for about 1.5km. These two main roads are connected by a vehicle-width track (KG 531 and 533 streets) that runs through the woodland south of the lake, a promising area for barbets, cuckoos and other acacia-associated species. KG 531 Street intersects KG 535 Street at the southwest corner of the lake and runs back north to KG 13 Avenue, forming the border between the golf course and the lake.

opposite the stadium, then keep walking along the main cobbled road until it eventually peters out to dirt. There are many routes up the mountain – follow your nose or ask locals to direct you (the signs for Fazenda Sengha are a good guide as well). At the top, there's a path along a wooded ridge, with very few people about. Beware that as you head north, you will encounter a military camp and be asked to turn back.

The hills above Gikondo and Kicukiro can be reached by taking buses 109 (from Remera), 205 (from the central bus station) or 206 (from Nyabugogo station). Get off at the last stop, and then keep walking uphill on KK 31 Avenue. When you reach the ridge, veering left on to KK 30 Avenue will bring you to **Juru Park**, a laid-back outdoor park and restaurant with pleasant gardens and views over the city. There are numerous roads and tracks all over this ridge, many with spectacular views in all directions. The new **Kigali Cultural Village** (see box, page 125) is being constructed just south of here. KK 30 Avenue continues 3.5km to Kicukiro and the Nyanza Genocide Memorial (page 118), from where you can catch bus 108 back to Sonatubes and Remera or bus 204 towards KN 7 Road and Nyabugogo.

While the heat, the hills and the traffic mean that cycling in Kigali is not for the faint-hearted, it can be an exhilarating and rewarding experience. Heading out of town in any direction will soon lead you to a huge network of dirt tracks and paths, offering a great insight into rural Rwandan life. A good direction to start is to the east and south of the city (head for Kibagabaga, Kimironko, Remera, Kicukiro or the airport, and keep going) where the terrain is a little flatter. Kaspar Kundert's *Biking in Rwanda* guide (page 58) provides detailed route information and no small bit of inspiration.

Just south of the lake along KG 13 Avenue, the new US$200 million Century Park Hotel & Residences project is now under construction and will eventually host luxury apartments and villas, as well as the new 136-room Sheraton Hotel, so you can expect big changes in this neighbourhood in the coming years.

STROLLING ROUND KIGALI If you don't mind the unavoidable hills, Kigali offers some good strolls. There are plenty of places where you can stop for a snack or a drink if you need to cool off. Two walks which could each fill up a morning, depending on how often you stop on the way, are given below; but just look at a map of the whole city and you'll see that there are plenty more.

To the mosque and Nyamirambo District

One way of getting to the big mosque in the Muslim quarter is to walk southwards along KN 2 Avenue (Avenue de la Justice), with views out across the valley to your right; the mosque is at the junction where KN 75 Street (Rue de la Sécurité) joins from the left [91 B/C2]. Continue for a few minutes and you're in a lively, busy district (Nyamirambo) of small streets and colourful little local shops. The atmosphere has a touch of London's Soho about it. This is said to be the part of the present-day city where people first settled, long ago. There's a lot of small-scale activity going on here, and small bar/cafés where you can stop for a drink.

To return to the centre, you can either catch bus 401, which follows KN 2 Avenue back up to the central bus station (look out for the yellow signs indicating bus stops), or easily flag down a moto or taxi-voiture. (Note that a short stretch of KN 2 Avenue is one-way.) Or else retrace your steps towards the mosque and look out for KN 7 Avenue (Avenue Paul VI) on your right – follow this upwards and it'll bring you on to the area covered by the map on pages 78–9. Or – be adventurous and find your own variations!

To Nyabugogo market

This takes you through an area of many small shops and market stalls, finishing at the busy market opposite Nyabugogo station [78 A2]. If you can cope with seething crowds and a lot of jostling, try it (but don't take photos without the permission of the subjects).

Starting at the new central bus station, walk down to KN 2 Avenue (Avenue de la Justice), crossing the road on to the the unsurfaced KN 87 Street (Rue du Mont Huye), which runs downhill at a sharp angle just opposite. Take this and follow it – you'll pass homes, small shops, an enclosed market area off it to your right, and (after zig-zagging a few times on to KN 93 Street and KN 5 Avenue) you arrive at the bottom – and the lively Nyabugogo market. Just look at the variety of people here – you'll see so many different bone structures, shades of colour, styles of clothing …

If you cross over into the minibus-taxi station (which is a 'market area' all of its own, with vendors offering everything from leather shoes and hi-fi equipment to – improbably – plastic hair curlers and freshly baked bread) you can get a minibus-taxi back to the central station or else take a taxi-voiture; they park just by the main gate. Or turn right up the main road as you leave the market; this upward hill is KN 1 Road (Boulevard de Nyabugogo) and will take you back to Place de l'Unité Nationale and the centre of town; bus 401 plies this route between the central bus station and Nyamirambo via KN 1 Road and KN 20 Avenue.

EXCURSIONS FURTHER AFIELD

Rwanda is such a small country that almost any of the towns and other attractions covered in this guidebook make for a feasible day or overnight trip from the capital.

A sizeable government-backed initiative is being constructed next door to Juru Park atop Rebero Hill, and when finished will boast a variety of facilities highlighting Rwandan history, traditional lifestyles, the natural environment, and traditional and contemporary art forms. Kigali Cultural Village will take the form of a large hilltop campus consisting of open green space interspersed with educational and artistic exhibitions, indoor/outdoor auditoriums, several restaurants, a new ecolodge, camping area, and natural and cultural interpretive trails crossing the grounds. It's not yet clear when this will be finished, but construction was underway as of 2018. See the Bradt Rwanda updates website (w *bradtupdates.com/rwanda*) for the latest.

This is certainly true for **Huye** (formerly Butare) and the National Museum of Rwanda (page 158), as well as the former royal capital of **Nyanza** along the same road (pages 141–7), though it would be a push to squeeze both sites into a one-day outing from Kigali. Travelling to Huye by public transport, you'll find that the museum and the new bus station are conveniently only a couple of hundred metres apart. If you leave early and check the return times, you should be able to visit the attractive little lakeside town of **Karongi** (formerly Kibuye, pages 201–9) as a round trip from Kigali as well.

Of the national parks, **Akagera** (*Chapter 11*) can technically be visited from Kigali in a day, but you'll need your own transport, a very early start, and would get a lot more from the exercise by overnighting in or near the park. The mountain gorillas in **Volcanoes National Park** (*Chapter 9*) can also be visited as a day trip from Kigali, but you'd need a very early start (before 05.00) in a private vehicle to reach the park headquarters by the check-in time of 07.00. **Nyungwe** (*Chapter 6*) really is too far away for a day trip, but it could be visited as an overnight trip, though two nights would be more realistic.

The following suggestions are closer to Kigali.

BUGESERA DISTRICT The relatively hot and low-lying part of Rwanda running directly south from Kigali to the Burundi border at Nemba now forms the administrative district of Bugesera, which is centred upon the town of Nyamata, some 35km south of the capital. Bugesera was severely affected by the genocide. At least 80% of the local Tutsi population was killed (actual numbers are unknown), and many of the victims were thrown into the Nyabarongo River, eventually to wash up on the Uganda shore of Lake Victoria. Two of the most brutal massacres in Bugesera are commemorated at the genocide memorials at Ntarama and Nyamata (page 126).

Although Bugesera receives a relatively low rainfall and is prone to periodic droughts, its dominant geographic feature is the Nyabarongo River, the country's longest, a tributary of the Akagera that rises in Nyungwe and feeds a wetland area comprising at least a dozen lakes and several large areas of swampland. Listed as one of Rwanda's seven Important Bird Areas, these vast wetlands are of special interest for waterbirds, including localised papyrus-associated species such as papyrus gonolek, Carruthers's cisticola, white-winged scrub-warbler, papyrus yellow warbler, northern brown-throated weaver, papyrus canary and possibly even shoebill. In addition to boasting immense potential for birding tourism, several of the lakes also host hippos and crocodiles (indeed, wild elephants still roamed the area until 1975, when the last 26 elephants were rounded up and transported to Akagera National Park).

Until recently, road access to Bugesera was poor, and few tourists visited the area. But this has changed following the construction of an excellent surfaced road from Kigali to the Burundi border in 2008, and the area is likely to gain greater prominence as and when the proposed Bugesera International Airport opens outside Nyamata to replace the current international airport in Kigali (page 76).

Two attractive hotels have opened on the shores of lakes Rumira and Mirayi, to the east of Nyamata, making a promising start for future tourist development in this underrated part of Rwanda; expect plenty more to spring up as the new airport nears completion.

All distances below are given from the Sonatubes roundabout on KG 1 Avenue (OAU Road) in Kigali.

Nyabarongo Bridge (⊕ S 2°03.261, E 30°05.243) The nippy modern bridge that spans the Nyabarongo River 12.5km south of Sonatubes forms the northern boundary of Bugesera. It also offers a superb viewpoint over the river and associated patches of papyrus swamp and acacia woodland, which it fringes for about 1km to form probably the best birding spot in the immediate vicinity of Kigali (only 15 minutes' drive away). You might easily record a few-dozen species in the space of 2 hours with an early-morning start – among the more interesting species we picked up were pink-backed pelican, common moorhen, African jacana, three types of weaver, marsh flycatcher and black-headed gonolek – and it looks like good potential territory for the eagerly sought papyrus gonolek.

Nyamata and Ntarama genocide memorials Co-written with Rachel J Strohm
The Catholic church at **Nyamata** (⊕ S 02°08.928, E 30°05.655; w *genocidearchiverwanda.org.rw*), about 26km from Sonatubes in Kigali, was the scene of a horrific massacre during the genocide. Many people from the town and surrounding areas took refuge in the church, thinking that they were safe there. But on 10 April 1994, members of the interahamwe and army attacked the church compound and killed the 10,000 people who had gathered there. Today, the victims' clothing and personal belongings are piled up on every single pew in the church, and the altar has a machete on it, as well as a rosary in a glass box, which is said to have been blessed by John Paul II and given to the memorial a few years ago. Two underground crypts hold the bodies of 41,000 people who died in the church massacre and elsewhere in Nyamata. Visitors can enter both of the crypts with a guide, though many will prefer not to be underground in an unlit chamber with skulls piled on four layers of shelves all around them. The remains of genocide victims are still being exhumed around the country today, and on most days there's a bag or two of bones in a corner of the church right next to the door (under the wall where babies were smashed to death), waiting to be added to the piles in the crypts. The guides who work at the site all lost family members in the attacks there.

There is another genocide memorial at **Ntarama** (⊕ S 02°06.773, E 30°02.988; w *genocidearchiverwanda.org.rw*), about 1km down a right-hand fork that branches off the Nyamata road at Kuri Arete 21km outside Kigali. As was the case at Nyamata, people fled to the church here seeking safety. A sign outside the gate records that around 5,000 victims died there. The church interior is now piled with the clothes of victims, similar to Nyamata, although it's even eerier because a good deal of the clothing is hanging from the rafters near the doorways. Two sets of large metal shelves, at the front and back of the church, hold the skeletons and personal belongings (ID cards, jewellery, toys, etc) of a number of victims from the site. Outside, a memorial garden has been planted, with a 500m walking path and a wall of names being inscribed whenever they find money to do it. The single guide at Ntarama now is English-speaking.

Both memorials are grim, and go some way to conveying the appalling scale of the tragedy. There's no charge for entry to the sites and the guides do a difficult job with dignity. A donation is requested (a few thousand Rwandan francs or US$5–10 would be appropriate), as the memorials are almost entirely dependent on such contributions for their basic operations and salaries.

Getting there and away It is easy to visit either site, or both, as a day trip from Kigali. Now that the road is paved, the drive takes about 30 minutes. For visitors who didn't rent a car or don't wish to hire a private taxi at a cost of about Rfr25,000 for the round trip, minibus-taxis bound for Nyamata leave from the Nyanza/Kicukiro stand in Kigali every hour on the hour. (Bus 108 comes here from Remera via Sonatubes, and bus 204 from Nyabugogo via KN 7 Road.) Easier still, the usual companies run comfortable minibuses to Nyamata every half hour from Nyabugogo taxi park. The trip costs Rfr500 one-way, and buses stop directly in central Nyamata. The memorial at Ntarama is 1.8km from the main road, along a feeder road signposted a few hundred metres south of the town centre. The easiest way to get to Ntarama from Nyamata is by moto-taxi (or you could conceivably hire a moto from Kigali to do the entire trip for around Rfr10,000).

Where to stay

🏠 **Golden Tulip La Palisse Kigali** (185 rooms) `\`0220 101000; e reservation@ goldentuliplapalissekigali.com; w goldentuliplapalissekigali.com. This rather confusingly named hotel became part of the French hotelier group Golden Tulip in Apr 2015, & you would do well not to confuse it with either the La Palisse in Gashora or the one near the airport in Kigali. Either way, it's certainly the most upmarket accommodation in Nyamata, & rooms come with writing desk, flatscreen DSTV, phone, AC & balcony. There are a couple of restaurants & bars, along with sports facilities aplenty – there's an Olympic-sized swimming pool, gym, spa, & courts for tennis, volleyball & basketball. *From US$135/165 sgl/dbl.*

🏠 **Heaven Motel** (7 rooms) m 078 848 3208; e heavenmotel2011@gmail.com. This is a quite modern hotel with rooms set around a large courtyard bar & restaurant 100m from the main road. The clean rooms have a double bed, & en-suite cold showers. *Rfr15,000 dbl.*

🏠 **Palast Rock Hotel** (40 rooms) m 078 830 1068/831 6060; e info@palasthotelrwanda.com; w palasthotelrwanda.com. This multi-storey place seems squarely aimed at the conference market, or at least it does until the new airport opens. Rooms are comfortable but characterless, & come with minibar, flatscreen DSTV, & balcony. There's also a resto-bar, swimming pool, sauna & kids' playground. *US$70/80 sgl/dbl; US$120/150 sgl/dbl exec; all rates B&B.*

🏠 **Peace Motel** (18 rooms) m 078 856 8007. This basic place on the left side of the main road coming from Kigali is attached to an internet café & the best restaurant in town. *Rfr7,000/9,500 sgl/ dbl, or Rfr15,000 for a VIP room with ¾ bed.*

Gashora and environs The small and rather nondescript town of Gashora lies at the heart of the Nyabarongo Wetlands, where it is flanked by Lake Rumira to the north and Lake Mirayi to the south. The La Palisse Hotel, 2km from the town centre, is a superb location in its own right, set on the reed-lined shore of Lake Rumira, and it also forms the ideal base for exploring the surrounding wetlands. This one hotel (and the new Lakeside Fish Farm) aside, the area is poorly developed for tourism, but the possibilities are boundless. Plenty of local footpaths surround Lake Rumira itself, and it's also possible to walk to Lake Mirayi, which lies about 500m south of Gashora town centre.

Further afield, follow the Ngoma/Kibungo road (NR6) out of Gashora for about 2km, and you'll find yourself on an elevated causeway running through the dense papyrus swamp that divides the two lakes – potentially a superb spot for papyrus endemics. With a sturdy vehicle, it should be possible to follow this road for 50km to rejoin the tar road at Ngoma/Kibungo, passing through several areas of swamp and within eyeshot of a trio of lakes: Birara, Mugesera and Sake.

Further south, Rweru (also known as Rugweru) is the largest lake in the Nyabarongo Wetlands, extending over some 100km², of which four-fifths lies within Burundi. A shallow sump set at an altitude of around 1,350m, it is nowhere more than 4m deep, and much of its marshy shoreline is difficult to access. A motorable track to the Rwandan part of the lakeshore branches left from the surfaced road to the Burundi border about 57km south of Kigali (and 3km before the border post). It's a rather circuitous 18km drive, and after 7km you need to turn right (downhill) in a small trading centre called Mayuboro. You reach the lakeshore at a village called Nyiragiseke, where it is easy enough to arrange to be taken out in a local dugout, and there's even a motorboat available if you can supply the fuel.

Getting there and away The town lies 53km from Kigali along a dirt side-road to the left signposted 48km along the surfaced road to the Burundi border (the junction is at Ramiro, ✪ *S 2°15.081, E 30°12.861*). The drive shouldn't take longer than 45 minutes in a private vehicle, though you might want to stop at the Nyabarongo Bridge and Nyamata on the way. On public transport, first aim for the Nyanza/Kicukiro terminus in Kigali, from where minibus-taxis bound for Ramiro and/or Gashora depart. From the Ramiro junction, it's 5.5km to Gashora town (7km to La Palisse), and just over 4km to Lakeside Fish Farm (bear left for Gashora, right for the fish farm). There are plenty of moto-taxis available.

You can drive via Gashora and Sake to Ngoma/Kibungo on fairly good, and picturesque, unsealed road. If coming the other way – from Ngoma/Kibungo to Kigali – don't be put off by the sign saying a bridge is closed. They fixed the bridge ages ago but forgot to remove the sign!

Where to stay

Lakeside Fish Farm m 078 569 6606/583 7416; e visit@lakesidefishfarm.com; w lakesidefishfarm.com; lakesidefishfarm. Run by a Rwandan-American couple, this unexpected 16ha property at the southern end of Lake Mirayi is mostly a fish farm (they supply fish to a number of Kigali restaurants), but also offers budget- & family-friendly accommodation in either their small guesthouse or a number of standing tents sleeping up to 8. In addition to the fish farm, which visitors can tour (*US$10/5 adult/child*), the idyllic property is full of animals – cows, guinea fowl, pigs, goats, turkeys, rabbits & ducks – and an organic farm as well. Meals (sourced from the aforementioned farm) are available at US$4 b/ fast & US$6 lunch/dinner, or barbecue facilities & a firepit are available for self-caterers. Finally, there's a treehouse overlooking the lake & kayaks are available for guests. Follow the signs for about 4km from the Gashora turn-off at Ramiro. *US$25–40 dbl; US$5pp camping in standing tent.* See ad, opposite.

La Palisse Hotel & Clubhouse (52 rooms) ✪ S 2°11.805, E 30°14.414; m 078 830 6111/838 5505; e palisseho@yahoo.fr; ClubHouseLaPalisseHotels. This resort on the south shore of Lake Rumira makes for an attractive place to stay outside of the city, & its popularity is likely to soar as & when the international airport relocates to Bugesera. (Don't confuse it with its sister property, La Palisse Hotel, 2km from the current airport, listed on page 90.) Spread across large green gardens rattling with birdlife, the tiled rooms have king-size or twin beds with netting, satellite TV, fridge, wardrobes & a large en-suite bathroom with shower & tub. There are also larger suites designed in the shape of a traditional royal palace. A lakeside restaurant with indoor &

outdoor seating serves a varied selection of mains in the Rfr4,000–6,000 range. But the setting is the real attraction here: the lake supports hippos, crocs & a varied birdlife, including the magnificent African fish eagle & an array of colourful weavers & bishops. *US$60/70 sgl/dbl B&B; US$100 suite.*

 Mirayi Lake Hotel (10 rooms) ⊕ S 2°13.652, E 30°15.323; m 078 488 9778/830

7454/878 5898. Reached via a 6.5km road that branches southeast from the junction for Gashora, this sleepy lodge on the south shore of Lake Mirayi offers accommodation in clean tiled cottages with double bed, en-suite hot shower, net & balcony. There is a restaurant & a beach with a jetty, but it feels a little neglected. *Rfr20,000 dbl.*

4

The Road to Huye (Butare)

The surfaced 136km road between Kigali and Huye (formerly Butare) can usually be covered in about 2 hours, partly depending on how often you get stuck behind trucks on the steeper slopes, and how aggressively your driver attempts to overtake such obstacles. The largest town *en route*, Muhanga, sprawls alongside the main road for several kilometres either side of the junction westward to Karongi. Nearby tourist attractions include the Kabgayi Cathedral and associated museum on the outskirts of Muhanga, as well as the former royal compound at Nyanza, which lies about halfway between Muhanga and Huye, and is now a museum. Any of these sites can be visited as a day trip out of Kigali or *en route* to Huye.

For details of town name changes (Huye, Muhanga, Karongi, etc) see the box on pages 40–1.

MUHANGA (GITARAMA)

The scattered capital of Muhanga District, often still referred to by its pre-2006 name Gitarama, is a rather unfocused but nonetheless important trading centre, with a 2012 population of 50,000 and growing, making it the fifth-largest city in the country. Thanks to its strategic location at the junction of the roads running southward to Huye and westward to Lake Kivu, Muhanga is passed through by a great many tourists, but explored by few. And, with the exception of the cathedral and associated museum at nearby Kabgayi (pages 135–9), there really is very little to do or see in this workaday town, though the everyday hustle and bustle of ordinary Rwandans going about their lives can be a change from more intensive tourism.

Despite its unassuming appearance, Muhanga has often been involved in Rwanda's recent history. It is famous as the location of the historic gathering on 28 January 1961 at which the people first declared Rwanda a republic, and it was the probable starting point for the violence that led to the imposition of martial law under Colonel Guy Logiest in November 1959. It was also the birthplace of Rwanda's first president Grégoire Kayibanda, whose modest tomb now stands in the town centre alongside a disused open-air auditorium built during his rule. On 12 April 1994, it replaced Kigali as the seat of the Provisional Government that presided over the genocide, prior to its capture by the RDF on 13 June 1994.

If you do opt to explore Muhanga, you'll find a Bank of Kigali just around the corner from the main transport park in the town centre [132 A3], together with a handful of small shops and bar/restaurants. The post office [132 C1] is about 1km away: turn right as you leave the minibus stand and keep straight on; you'll come to it on the left just after the Rwanda Revenue Authority. There's no shortage of moto-taxis in town, especially around the bus park.

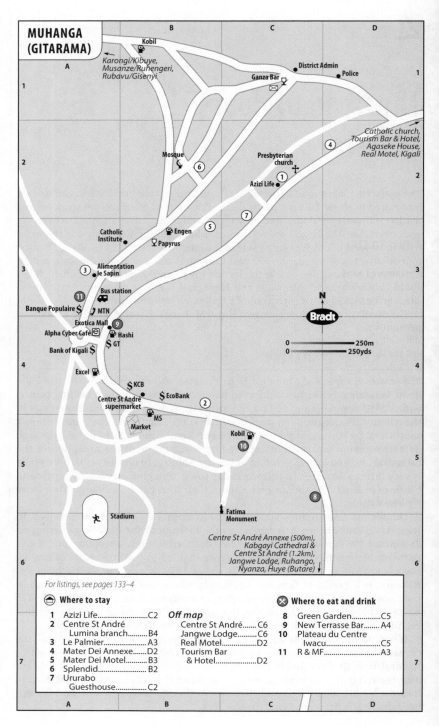

MUHANGA (GITARAMA)

Kobil

← Karongi/Kibuye,
Musanze/Ruhengeri,
Rubavu/Gisenyi

District Admin
Police

Ganza Bar

④

Catholic church,
Tourism Bar & Hotel,
Agaseke House,
Real Motel, Kigali →

Mosque
⑥

Presbyterian
church

① Azizi Life

⑦

⑤

Catholic
Institute

Engen
Papyrus

③ Alimentation
le Sapin

N

⑪ Bus station
MTN
Banque Populaire $

Bradt

Ekotica Mall
⑨
Alpha Cyber Café
Hashi
$ GT
Bank of Kigali $

0 ————— 250m
0 ————— 250yds

Excel

$ KCB
$ EcoBank
Centre St André
supermarket
②
MS
Market
Kobil
⑩

⑧

Stadium

Fatima
Monument

Centre St André Annexe (500m),
Kabgayi Cathedral &
Centre St André (1.2km),
Jangwe Lodge, Ruhango,
Nyanza, Huye (Butare) ↓

For listings, see pages 133–4

Over the last decade or so, the town has experienced a noticeable drift in development from its old town centre (already a busy conglomeration of small buildings and bustle) to the main Kigali–Huye road, which is now lined with tall modern buildings, including several hotels and the Exotica Mall [132 A4], which houses a restaurant, pharmacy, supermarket, sauna/massage centre, and nightclub. Also on the main road, further in the direction of Kigali, the main tourist focus in Muhanga is Azizi Life [132 C2], a committed fair-wage handicraft exporter that runs a worthwhile craft shop, offers popular full-day village visits, and since 2015 offers simple and pleasant accommodation as well (see below).

GETTING THERE AND AWAY Muhanga lies about 50km south of Kigali, a drive that shouldn't take longer than an hour except in very heavy traffic. Regularly scheduled midibuses connect the centrally located bus station [132 A3] to Kigali (*Rfr1,000*), Karongi/Kibuye (*Rfr2,000*), Huye (*Rfr1,500*), and Musanze/Ruhengeri or Rubavu/Gisenyi via Ngororero for Rfr3,000.

WHERE TO STAY
Upmarket
🏠 **Jangwe Lodge** [132 C6] (6 rooms) ✿ S 2°08.532, E 29°47.005; m 078 506 6081/821 6829; e georges.kamanayo@gmail.com/lydie. becart@gmail.com. This beautiful peaceful retreat makes an excellent w/end getaway from Kigali, with its attractive location amid green rolling hills, good Belgian food, & the only swimming pool in this part of the country. To get there follow the Huye road out of Muhanga for 2km, then take the dirt road signposted for Shyogwe to the left. It is about 6km from the turn-off to the lodge, passing through Shyogwe about halfway. Booking is recommended, whether you want to stay or just to pop in for a meal. *Rfr55,000 sgl inc b/fast & swimming.*

Moderate
🏠 **Real Motel** [132 D2] (7 rooms) m 078 350 6551/827 5807/785 2736; e realmotel@gmail.com. This small hotel stands in neat gardens alongside the main Kigali road about 4km from the town centre. There are 3 large rooms with hot tub & shower, TV, built-in cupboard, balcony & double bed with netting, & 4 smaller twins & doubles using shared showers. A ground-floor bar & restaurant serves a typical selection of snacks & meals in the Rfr1,200–3,000 range. *Rfr20,000 en-suite dbl; Rfr 7,000/10,000 sgl/dbl with shared ablutions.*
🏠 **Splendid Hotel** [132 B2] (45 rooms) m 078 830 1894/842 1573; e splendidhotel1@ yahoo.fr; w splendidhotelrwanda.com. With 2 multi-storey wings directly across the street from each other, this is likely the best-value &

most appealing option in this range, with a quiet but central location around the corner from the mosque & cultural centre. Opened in 2014, the new wing is all work & no play, but probably has the sharpest rooms in town, all of which come with big beds, writing desks, & flatscreen TVs. On the original side, rooms with hot shower are clean, spacious & comfortable (though you might want to test the mattress for sagginess), & there's a ground-floor bar & 1st-floor restaurant serving excellent steak & other dishes at around Rfr3,000. *Rfr15,000–25,000 dbl in old wing & from Rfr35,000 dbl in new wing.*

Budget
🏠 **Azizi Life** [132 C2] (4 rooms) m 078 304 9665/578 1146; e info@azizilife.com; w azizilife. com. On the main road just north of the town centre, this place has for years been at the centre of just about anything tourism-related in Muhanga, & they've well cemented that position since starting to offer rooms in 2015. All of the rooms use clean shared ablutions & there are currently 2 dorms & twin rooms on offer, along with camping space. It's obvious to stay here if you're planning to go on one of their excellent village trips, but it's a perfectly good budget option if you're just passing through Muhanga as well. Note that it's popular with groups, so it's worth calling ahead to see that it's not booked out. *US$15pp B&B; Rfr6,000/8,000pp camping with/without b/fast.*
🏠 **Centre St André** [132 C6] (121 rooms) ☎0252 562812/562348; m 078 842 1378; e saintandrekabgayi@yahoo.fr;

w saintandrekabgayi.com. Situated alongside Kabgayi Cathedral about 3km south of central Muhanga & some 200m or so off the Huye road, this large & reasonably priced church-run guesthouse is undoubtedly the best place to stay in the area, assuming that you don't mind the non-central location. Rooms range from basic doubles using common showers to comfortable mini-suites, while facilities include a restaurant, bar (serving beer as well as soft drinks), Wi-Fi, & well-equipped business centre. They now have 2 annexes closer to the town centre: rooms using shared facilities are next to the Gemeca garage at the south end of town, while additional en-suite rooms can be found at the new **Lumina branch** [132 B4] just south of the St André Supermarket. *Rfr8,000/10,000 sgl/dbl using common showers; Rfr15,000/20,000 en-suite sgl/dbl; Rfr35,000 mini-suite, B&B. Meals around Rfr3,000.*

🏠 **Mater Dei Motel** [132 B3] (16 rooms) m 078 846 3006/492 5492. The best central option in its range is this clean lodge set in a quiet garden only 100m from the bus station. Rooms are nicely kept, & there are larger apartments in an annexe [132 D2] on the main road. A pleasant terrace bar & popular restaurant is attached. *Large tiled dbls with king-size bed & en-suite hot tub Rfr25,000; smaller en-suite dbls Rfr20,000; dbls using common shower Rfr15,000.*

🏠 **Ururabo Guesthouse** [132 C2] (9 rooms) m 078 281 6444/883 4818/370 8704; e carimuhoza@yahoo.fr. An easy walk from the centre on the main Kigali–Huye road, this unassuming place sits in a little garden & has a modest smattering of tiled rooms in varying shapes & sizes, all of which are kept reasonably neat & trim. They can do the usual array of meals at command, & it's fair value overall. *Rooms using shared ablutions Rfr 6,000–8,000 without b/fast; en-suite rooms Rfr15,000–20,000 B&B.*

Shoestring

🏠 **Le Palmier** [132 A3] (5 rooms) m 072 626 4317. More of a last resort than anything else, this place has barely adequate rooms opposite the main taxi park, but it's mostly a resto-bar serving basic meals & drinks. *Dbl with common shower Rfr5,000; en-suite dbl Rfr8,000.*

🏠 **Tourism Bar & Hotel** [132 D2] (8 rooms) ⊕ S 02°04.551, E 029°46.1679, 1,880m; m 072 541 5319. Situated about 3km from the town centre alongside the main road to Kigali, this is a pleasant, peaceful place with large but rundown rooms & concrete-dominated grounds. There's a bar but no restaurant, though it does serve evening brochettes & the like by request. *Rooms with net & cold water Rfr7,000.*

✕ WHERE TO EAT AND DRINK

Most of the hotels offer meals of a sort, with the **Splendid Hotel** undoubtedly the best option for meat dishes (assuming you don't mind a bit of a wait), and the restaurant at Mater Dei Motel is also quite popular. Other options include the following:

✕ **Green Garden** [132 C5] m 078 163 4583; ⊕ 11.00–late daily. Set a few hundred metres out of town past Brothers Inn, this is a great spot for a drink at sunset, thanks to its hillside location, & it also serves tasty brochettes & other snacks. There's no sign, but it's directly opposite the Ecole Technique de Kabgayi.

✕ **R & MF Restaurant** [132 A3] m 078 856 2564/072 722 2415; ⊕ 07.00–21.00 daily. Better known as Tranquillité, this long-serving & popular local eatery consists of a cheerful courtyard, with assorted shapes & sizes of tables, energetic waitresses serving customers briskly, & a blackboard with the dishes of the day chalked on it. The food is simple (meat, fish or chicken with chips/salad, fresh fruit for dessert) but good, & cheap. There's also usually a lunch buffet.

🍷 **New Terrasse Bar** [132 A4] m 078 350 2331; ⊕ noon–midnight daily. Set in a large open-sided thatch building behind the Exotica Mall, this is now more of a bar than an eatery, though it does serve inexpensive brochettes, grilled chicken & chips. There's a TV & a decent sound system, occasionally supplemented by karaoke or live music at w/ends, but the toilets are rather grotty. The attached Orion Nightclub opens its doors at around 23.00 at w/ends, & keeps going throughout the night.

🍷 **Plateau du Centre Iwacu** [132 C5] m 078 849 7243/869 4282; ⊕ 08.00–late daily. Also known as Bar Magnificat, this spacious & popular garden bar behind the Kobil Filling Station serves excellent & reasonably priced grilled whole fish, among other barbecue options.

OTHER PRACTICALITIES

Banks and money There are no dedicated forex bureaux in town, nor is there any real call for them with Kigali being so close. However, if you do need to draw money there are several banks with Visa-enabled ATMs in town, including a branch of GT Bank that also accepts Mastercard.

Internet The Alpha Cyber Café [132 A4] opposite the GT Bank is a good central place to check internet. None of the bespoke restaurants had Wi-Fi when we dropped in, though you might be able to get connected at the Mater Dei Motel's terrace restaurant.

Supermarkets There are also two supermarkets worth checking out: the **Alimentation le Sapin** [132 A3] opposite the bus station also doubles as a bakery selling tasty fresh bread, while the better-stocked **Centre St André Supermarket** [132 B4] opposite the market has an excellent selection of imported goods, including wines and spirits, as well as a butchery, bakery, and restaurant out back.

Handicrafts In addition to Azizi Life (see below), there are two other good craft outlets in town. The better of the two is **Agaseke House** [132 D2] (**m** *078 871 9521/072 871 9521;* **e** *uwanastas@yahoo.fr*), a salmon-coloured building which lies on the right as you enter Muhanga from Kigali, opposite the prominent St André Cathedral. Adorned with a huge, faded *agaseke* (a traditional Rwandan basket with its distinctive conical lid) painted on the side, this is the showroom for the 400 members of the Coopérative de Production d'Artisant d'Art du Rwanda (COPARWA) and sells a varied stock of good-quality basketwork, wood sculptures, mats, beadwork and other traditional artefacts.

WHAT TO SEE

Azizi Life [132 C2] (**m** *078 304 9665/578 1146;* **e** *info@azizilife.com;* **w** *azizilife. com*) Situated just off the Kigali–Huye road near the Presbyterian Church, Azizi Life is a faith-based social enterprise dedicated to supporting artisans by providing them with fair wages, market connections, and resources for developing their art, business, faith, and life as a whole. Through these fair-trade relationships, Azizi Life offers visitors a fine array of handcrafted goods and agricultural products from more than 30 partnering artisan groups in their on-site boutique (and their new studio in Kigali; page 113). It also offers a variety of village visits and community-based cultural experiences designed to connect visitors with rural Rwanda, by joining in with local artisans and their families doing seasonal agricultural activities, cooking and sharing a midday meal, learning to make banana juice and about local coffee and apiculture (including candle making), producing *imigongo* art, building a traditional home, or weaving a simple object in sisal, all with expert tuition (⊕ *08.00–18.00 daily except 7 Apr & 11.00–18.00 on Umuganda days*). (See box, page 138.) Most excursions cost US$75 per person for a full day (slightly more for single visitors), while it's US$52 per person for a drumming and dancing session and US$39 for a guided hike with up to five hikers. There are discounts for children, East Africa residents, groups, and multi-day packages. Much of the fee directly benefits the co-operative members and their families, with 5% being set aside for non-profit activities. They also offer good budget accommodation (page 133).

Kabgayi Cathedral and Museum [132 C6] The **Kabgayi Mission**, which lies a couple of hundred metres from the Huye road just 3km south of Muhanga

With its distinctive tall green stem topped by a luxuriant clump of thick, wide leaves, the banana (or plantain, known locally as *insina*) is an integral feature of the Rwandan landscape, occupying a full 35% of the country's cultivated land. Grown at a wide range of altitudes – from as low as 800m to above 2,000m – the banana thrives in Rwanda's characteristically moist climate, and is unquestionably the most important cash crop countrywide, accounting for 60–80% of the income of most subsistence-level households.

So it might come as a surprise to many visitors to learn that the banana is not indigenous to Rwanda – or anywhere else in Africa for that matter. One Ugandan legend has it that the first banana plant was brought to the region by Kintu, whose shrine lies on a hill called Magonga (almost certainly a derivative of a local Ugandan name for the banana) alongside a tree that is said to have grown from the root of the plant he originally imported. If this legend is true, it would place the banana's arrival in East-Central Africa in perhaps the 13th–15th century, probably from the Ethiopian Highlands. Most botanists argue, however, that the immense number of distinct varieties grown in the region could not have been cultivated within so short a period – a timespan of at least 1,000 years would be required.

Only one species of banana, *Musa ensete*, is indigenous to Africa, and it doesn't bear edible fruit. The more familiar cultivated varieties have all been propagated from two wild Asian species, *M. acuminata* and *M. balbisiana* and hybrids thereof. Wild bananas are almost inedible and riddled with hard pits, and it is thought that the first edible variety was cultivated from a rare mutant of one of the above species about 10,000 years ago – making the banana one of the oldest cultivated plants in existence. Edible bananas were most likely cultivated in Egypt before the time of Christ, presumably having arrived there via Arabia or the Indian Ocean. The Greek sailor and explorer Cosmas Indicopleustes recorded that edible bananas grew around the port of Adulis, in present-day Eritrea, circa AD525 – describing them as 'moza, the wild-date of India'.

The route via which the banana reached modern-day Rwanda is open to conjecture. The most obvious point of origin is Ethiopia, the source of several southward migrations in the past two millennia. But it is intriguing that while the banana is known by a name approximating the generic Latin *Musa* throughout Asia, Arabia and northeast Africa – *'moz'* in Arabic and Persian, for instance, or *'mus'* or *'musa'* in various Ethiopian languages and Somali – no such linguistic resemblance occurs in East Africa, where it is known variously as *'ndizi'*, *'gonja'*, *'matoke'*, *'insina'* et al. This peculiarity has been cited to support a hypothesis that the banana travelled between Asia and the East African coast either as a result of direct trade or else via Madagascar, and that it was entrenched there before regular trade was established with Arabia. A third possibility is that the banana reached East-Central Africa via the Congolese Basin, possibly in association with the arrival of Bantu-speakers from West Africa.

However it arrived, the banana has certainly flourished there, forming the main subsistence crop for most people in the region – indeed, Rwanda's mean banana consumption of almost 2kg per person per week ranks among the highest in the world. Some 50 varieties are grown in the region, divided into four broad categories based on their primary use – most familiar are sweet bananas, eaten raw as a snack or dessert, while other more floury varieties are used especially for boiling (like potatoes), roasting, or distillation into banana beer or wine.

The banana's uses are not restricted to feeding bellies. The juice from the stem is traditionally regarded to have several medicinal applications, for instance as a cure for snakebite and for childish behaviour. Pulped or scraped sections from the stem also form very effective cloths for cleaning. The outer stem can be plaited to make a strong rope, while the cleaned central rib of the leaf is used to weave fish traps and other items of basketry. The leaf itself forms a useful makeshift umbrella, and was traditionally worn by young girls as an apron. The dried leaf is a popular bedding and roofing material, and is also used to manufacture the head pads on which Rwandan women generally carry their loads.

The banana as we know it is a cultigen – modified by humans to their own ends and totally dependent on them for its propagation. The domestic fruit is the result of a freak mutation that gives the cells an extra copy of each chromosome, preventing the normal development of seeds, thereby rendering the plant edible but also sterile. Every cultivated banana tree on the planet is effectively a clone, propagated by the planting of suckers or corms cut from 'parent' plants. This means that, unlike sexually reproductive crops, which experience new genetic configurations in every generation, the banana is unable to evolve mechanisms to fight off new diseases.

In early 2003, a report in the *New Scientist* warned that cultivated bananas are threatened with extinction within the next decade, due to their lack of defence against a pair of fungal diseases rampant in most of the world's banana-producing countries. These are *black sigatoka*, an airborne disease first identified in Fiji in 1963, and the soil-borne Panama Disease, also known as *Fusarium Wilt*. Black sigatoka can be kept at bay by regular spraying – every ten days or so – but it is swiftly developing resistance to all known fungicides, which in any case are not affordable to the average subsistence farmers. There is no known cure for Panama Disease.

So far as can be ascertained, Panama Disease does not affect any banana variety indigenous to Rwanda or neighbouring countries, but it has already resulted in the disappearance of several introduced varieties. Black sigatoka, by contrast, poses a threat to every banana variety in the world. It has been present throughout Uganda for some years, where a progressive reduction exceeding 50% has been experienced in the annual yield of the most seriously affected areas, and reports suggest it is spreading into parts of Rwanda and the DRC. In addition to reducing the yield of a single plant by up to 75%, black sigatoka can also cut its fruit-bearing life from more than 30 years to less than five.

International attempts to clone a banana tree resistant to both diseases have met with one limited success – agricultural researchers in Honduras have managed to produce one such variety, but it reputedly doesn't taste much like a banana. Another area of solution is genetic engineering – introducing a gene from a wild species to create a disease-resistant edible banana. Although ecologists are generally opposed to the genetic modification of crops, the domestic banana should perhaps be considered an exception, given its inability to spread its genes to related species – not to mention its pivotal importance to the subsistence economies of some of the world's poorest countries, Rwanda among them.

Ever wanted to experience life in a welcoming rural village community for a day? Well now you can. **Azizi Life**, an initiative founded in 2007 to support independent artisan groups, now offers day visits to the rural communities they work with, allowing you to join in with all aspects of their life. The following account is my experience of a village visit to the Abarikumwe ('People who are together') Association in the village of Cyeza.

When our car arrived at Cyeza, a small village perched precariously on a hillside, we were warmly greeted by the women of the Abarikumwe Association. This group of women of various ages meet regularly to make handicrafts, namely earrings and bracelets out of the sisal plant, cultivate their fields and generally talk about daily life. We were welcomed into our host Yusta's home, and dressed for the field in fabric wraps. Then, hoes in hand, we walked down into the valley to a nearby cassava field to help the women to harvest the cassava. We joined in with the harvest and Jeannine, our translator, helped us to understand what to do. The women talked about their homes and their lives as they worked, and helped us with our hoeing technique! We tried to carry our harvest back to the house on our heads which was a great experience and the women helped us when our loads began to wobble.

Then we peeled the cassava roots together, again listening to tales of Rwandan village life as we did so. We fetched some water together from the village tap, and on our journey we passed through fields of coffee plants, banana trees, maize and bean crops, all with the stunning green hills of Muhanga District in the background. After finishing our work for the day, we were treated to a home-cooked lunch of fresh avocados, cassava, beans and rice, and we enjoyed the company of the women over lunch. The women laughed as we ate and with the help of our translator we shared stories about our homes.

After this hearty lunch, the women taught us how to make our own earrings and bracelets out of the sisal plant. Berthilde, my teacher, was very patient and guided me with her expert skill. We were shown the farm animals by our hosts' friendly children and then we danced outside in the sun. It was a real privilege to spend a day with these lively, vivacious and welcoming women and we learned so much about rural life in Rwanda from our experience. We felt as if we were part of the group as the women were so keen to involve us in everything they did. When I arrived back at the Azizi Life headquarters I felt tired but very content after such a wonderful day out in the Rwandan hills.

Azizi Life is based in Muhanga (page 135), where it also has accommodation, a handicrafts shop, and is busy developing other experience days. As of today, they offer not only an agriculture and artisans excursion as described above, but also outings focused on banana-juice making, beekeeping, traditional art and construction methods, cooking, drumming and dancing, and guided hikes – call or check their website for the latest information.

(see *Centre St André* under *Where to stay*, page 133), was founded by Catholic missionaries in 1906, and it became the seat of the first Catholic bishop of Ruanda-Urundi, for which reason nearby Muhanga (then known as Gitarama) was once seriously considered as the colonial capital. Built in 1925, the massive Cathedral Basilica of Our Lady at Kabgayi, with its red-brick exterior, stained-glass windows, and huge and tranquil interior, is the oldest and most historically important in the country, and worth a visit, especially now that the roof has been restored following a destructive earthquake in April 2008. During the colonial era, a hospital and various training schools were set up in Kabgayi – for midwives, artisans, printers, carpenters and blacksmiths, among others.

In the early stages of the genocide, Kabgayi, situated within walking distance of the Provisional Government headquarters at the then Gitarama, provided refuge to tens of thousands of civilians, many of whom died of disease or starvation. The full extent of the genocide killings at Kabgayi emerged in February 2009, when a report compiled by 18 Gacaca judges revealed that at least 64,000 people who sought refuge in the church grounds were killed there, with the probable complicity of local church leaders and Red Cross workers, who allegedly buried many victims alive. A genocide memorial stands alongside the hospital, where at least 6,000 victims are currently buried in a mass grave consisting of three concrete pits.

The **Kabgayi Museum**, tucked away in the Evêché (Archdeacon's residence) alongside the cathedral, is theoretically open from 08.00 to 17.00 Monday to Friday, though in practice you may need to ask around to locate the caretaker. Saturday and Sunday visits are also possible if booked in advance. A nominal entrance fee is charged. Within the very small interior are many historically and culturally interesting items such as:

- Ancient hand tools and weapons: knives, hoes, spears, arrows, etc
- Tools and implements connected with the iron industry
- Ancient examples of clothing: bark cloth, etc
- Musical instruments
- Methods of transportation used for chiefs, high-born women and the sick
- Clay pots and pipes
- Baskets – ornamental and for domestic use
- The prestigious Milk Bar and jugs from the palace of the last queen mother
- Old indoor games such as *igisoro*, which are still popular in Rwanda and neighbouring countries
- Ancient military officers' costumes and pips
- A national drum captured from Idjwi Island (Kivu, DRC) in 1875, thereby effectively annexing it to Rwanda
- Information about traditional medicines, and tokens (*kwe*) formerly used as currency
- Modern clothing and historical photographs

RUHANGO

Straddling the Huye road about 25km south of Muhanga, and connected to it by regular public transport, the eponymous capital of Ruhango District is another nondescript but well-equipped and surprisingly substantial town. The 2012 census gave its population as just under 20,000, making it the 13th largest in the country. It is of limited interest to tourists except on Friday mornings, when it hosts one of the largest markets in the country. Previously it was held out in the open, a buzzing stretch of colour and activity visible from the road, but now it is contained in a large purpose-built market building. Vendors trek in for the occasion from far afield, carrying their wares, and an astonishing range of merchandise is on sale, from livestock and vegetables to hi-fi equipment, household goods and swathes of

A NEW VERSION OF AN ANCIENT TALE It happened during the reign of Mwami Mibambwe II Sekarongoro II Gisanura, who ruled Rwanda almost four centuries ago. He was a fair and just ruler. Among other innovations, he required his chiefs to bring jars of milk from their own cows to the court – and these were then distributed to the poor and needy, three times a day: morning, noon and evening. Some chiefs grumbled at this, although they were careful to do so out of earshot of the mwami; others admired his generosity, and sometimes brought small gifts of vegetables or meat in addition to the milk. Wise and observant as he was, he knew well which chiefs resented his laws, which had true kindness in their hearts and which tended to misuse or misdirect their powers.

One day, so the story goes, a man was convicted of stealing from the mwami, which was considered a most serious crime. The mwami called two of his chiefs to the royal court, selecting them carefully, and asked each of them to devise a suitable punishment.

The chief named Mikoranya thought for many days and then scratched a careful diagram on the ground; it represented a shaft of wood extending from a hut, on which the thief would be slowly tortured in full view of the populace. His cries would echo far and wide. The chief named Kamageri, on the other hand, remembered a large flat rock that lay close to his home place in Ruhango; he proposed to the mwami that this rock should be heated until it was red hot, and the criminal should then be spread-eagled across it with his wrists and ankles securely tied, so that he roasted to a lingering death. The mwami then asked the chiefs to demonstrate their ideas, so that he could decide which should be used, and eagerly they set to work.

---

brightly coloured cotton fabric. You could consider spending a Thursday night here and then watching activities unfold the next morning. There's also an important church service held here on the first Sunday of the month, again attracting large crowds. Otherwise, the area is notable mainly for *Uratare rwa Kamageri* (Kamageri's Rock – see box, above), which is signposted by the roadside 10 minutes' walk south of the town centre, and for the Poterie Locale de Gatagara described below. Minibuses to/from Kigali cost Rfr1,600, and both Banque Populaire and Bank of Kigali are represented here with ATMs.

🏠 WHERE TO STAY AND EAT

🏠 **Eden Palace Hotel** (13 rooms) m 078 859 7483/072 379 3920; e edenpalacehotelltd@ gmail.com. Set in a large rambling compound & decorated with loads of delightfully wonky concrete animal statues, this newish mid-range hotel is the only tourist-class accommodation in town. Rooms are set in a couple of large multi-unit bungalows, & all are tiled & en suite with mosquito nets. There's a resto-bar on site & some playground equipment scattered about too. It's well signposted, some 600m west of the main road. No Wi-Fi. *Rfr20,000 dbl; Rfr30,000 twin.*

🏠 **Hotel Pacis** (8 rooms) m 078 859 7483/877 8733, 072 390 2327. In a bright yellow building near the bus depot, this adequate hotel has basic but clean double rooms with net & en-suite cold shower. *Rfr5,000 dbl.*

🏠 **Hotel Umuco** (12 rooms) m 078 788 7584. Centrally located, & arranged around a pleasant courtyard, this sensibly priced hotel provides travellers with basic but clean accommodation close to the taxi park, as well as inexpensive meals such as goat brochettes & chips or beef stew & rice. *Sgl using common shower Rfr5,000; Rfr8,000 dbl; meals Rfr1,000.*

After much hammering and hauling, the torture rack was in position. Mikoranya refused to pay his labourers, and two of them were whipped when they complained, but grudgingly they finished the task. For a whole week Kamageri's rock was piled with brushwood fires which were kept burning day and night (some women came under cover of darkness to use the embers for cooking), although those tending the flames were burned and choked by smoke. At last the rock glowed crimson and the heat was unbearable from many yards away. Paths leading to the area were crammed with people – men come straight from tending their cattle, old women leaning heavily on canes, young women with babies on their backs, scampering children getting under everyone's feet – all excited to see the spectacle. The chiefs sent word to the mwami, and he arrived with his retinue.

'Is everything ready?' he asked Kamageri and Mikoranya, and they nodded proudly, expecting praise and possibly some reward. The mwami called forward his guards, to whom he had already explained what would happen. 'Take them,' he ordered. 'And subject them to the punishments they have devised! Let Kamageri roast on his rock and Mikoranya suffer his own torture. These were cruel men. They took pleasure from brutality. There is no place for such in my kingdom.' The guards seized the two chiefs and cast them to their fate; and from the watching crowd a great cheer rose into the sky, as the people acknowledged the wisdom and goodness of their ruler.

The rock can still be seen today, at Ruhango on the Muhanga–Huye road. Tourists stop to photograph it and guides recount various versions of the story. And on the blackest nights, when the moon is hidden by cloud and stars cannot pierce the thick velvet of the sky, you may still – if you lift your head to the wind and breathe as lightly as thistledown – smell the faint ashiness of smoke drifting from Kamageri's ancient fire.

WHAT TO SEE

Poterie Locale de Gatagara (m *078 865 6271/852 0872*; w *www.ada-zoa. org/?p=4270*; ⊕ *09.00–noon & 13.00–17.00 Mon–Sat*) Marked by an inconspicuous blue signpost to the right of the Huye road about 10km south of Ruhango, this ceramic workshop lies alongside a locally well-known church centre for the disabled (*Home de la Vierge des Pauvres* (HVP); w *gatagara.org*), though the two organisations are apparently unaffiliated. Using foot-driven wooden treadle wheels, the dozen or so artisans working at Gatagara – some since its opening in 1977 – produce much of the pottery you see for sale in craft shops in Kigali, but items can be bought more cheaply here at the source, from a shop piled high with bowls, mugs, teacups, vases and other ceramic wares. Note that the wares produced at Gatagara are not overtly ethnic in style, but the quality is high. You can watch the Batwa potters throwing, baking and glazing the pottery, and see the clay in all its stages, or you can ask to pay for a short 'pottery course' (*about US$15*) where you make your own creation.

NYANZA

Sometimes known as Nyabisindu, the unassuming town of Nyanza lies about 20km south of Ruhango, along a surfaced feeder road that branches westward from the main Huye–Kigali road at Kubijega (literally, 'Place of Storage', in reference to a trio of nearby metal warehouses). With its wide dusty streets, waist-deep gullies caused by water erosion, and rather unfocused layout, Nyanza has something of a Wild West feel, and until just a few years ago it boasted few tourist

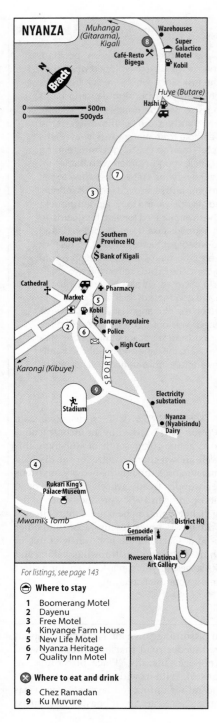

NYANZA

Muhanga (Gitarama), Kigali

Warehouses

Café-Resto Bigega

Super Galactico Motel

Kobil

Huye (Butare)

Hashi

0 ———— 500m
0 ———— 500yds

⑦

③

Mosque

Southern Province HQ

Bank of Kigali

Cathedral

Market

Pharmacy

⑤

Kobil

Banque Populaire

② ⑥

Police

High Court

Karongi (Kibuye)

SPORTS

⑨

Electricity substation

Stadium

Nyanza (Nyabisindu) Dairy

④

①

Rukari King's Palace Museum

Mwami's Tomb

District HQ

Genocide memorial

Rwesero National Art Gallery

For listings, see page 143

Where to stay

1 Boomerang Motel
2 Dayenu
3 Free Motel
4 Kinyange Farm House
5 New Life Motel
6 Nyanza Heritage
7 Quality Inn Motel

Where to eat and drink

8 Chez Ramadan
9 Ku Muvure

facilities. All the same, it's a reasonably substantial town (in fact, a population of 28,000 makes it the eighth largest in the country), and it seems destined to expand further following its surprise selection ahead of Huye as the capital of Southern Province in the administrative shake-up of 2006.

The elevation of Nyanza to provincial capital is not without historical precedent. In 1899, Mwami Musinga Yuhi V, his sense of absolute authority undermined by the growing colonial presence in Rwanda, decided to break with the royal tradition of mobility that had led to his predecessor having had an estimated 50–60 residences scattered through the kingdom. The recently enthroned Musinga selected Nyanza Hill as the site of the first permanent royal capital, a role it would retain throughout both his reign and that of his son Rudahigwa Mutara III until the traditional monarchy was abolished in 1961. Today, the traditional palace built by Musinga and first house built by Mutara III have been restored to form the highly worthwhile Rukari Palace Museum, while the newer house built by Mutara III is now the Rwesero Art Museum – both well worth the minor diversion from the Huye road, whether you use private or public transport.

GETTING THERE AND AWAY Nyanza lies 2km west of Kubijega junction (⊕ S 02°20.749, E 029°46.001, 1,811m) on the main Kigali–Huye road, less than 2 hours' drive from Kigali and just 45 minutes' drive from Huye. A good surfaced road leads all the way to the Rukari King's Palace Museum. Scheduled midibuses to/from Huye, Muhanga and Kigali with Volcano Express (m 078 507 8908) and Horizon express (m 072 261 3272) leave from the town centre, adjacent to the market, but it is also pretty easy to pick one up at Kubijega – transport in either direction stops alongside the Hashi filling station at the junction.

Moderate

🏠 **Dayenu Hotel** (42 rooms) m 078 884 9845/855 9220; e dayenuhotel@yahoo.com; f. This 3-storey hotel in the town centre has good facilities including a garden bar, restaurant & swimming pool. The standard rooms are large & tiled with nets & TV, but they only have a ¾ bed. VIP rooms come with a proper double bed & a second sitting area with flatscreen TV. It is a decent set-up & good value. *Rfr25,000/35,000 sgl/dbl; Rfr50,000 VIP room.*

🏠 **Nyanza Heritage Hotel** (25 rooms) 📞 0252 533295; m 078 933 0702; e lenimaheritagehotel@yahoo.fr; w nyanzaheritagehotel.com. Though swimmers should head for its neighbour, this central hotel next to the Dayenu is still a fine pick, with a 1st-floor balcony restaurant serving mains in the Rfr3,500–5,000 range & accommodation in clean tiled rooms with private balcony, king-size bed with net, small writing desk, DSTV & en-suite hot shower. *Rfr31,500/45,500 sgl/dbl.*

Budget

🏠 **Boomerang Motel** (14 rooms) m 078 852 6617. Very convenient for both of Nyanza's museums, this simple but welcoming guesthouse sits about two-thirds of the way along the road from the town centre. The clean & brightly decorated rooms have ¾ beds, nets & hot showers, & a restaurant-bar serves typical local fare for around Rfr2,000 per main course. *Rfr8,000/10,000 sgl/dbl using shared ablutions; Rfr10,000/12,000 sgl/dbl en suite; Rfr15,000 VIP room.*

🏠 **Free Motel** (17 rooms) m 078 877 3285/722 6767; e jacquelineashimwe@yahoo. fr. More-or-less opposite the Quality Inn, this adequate hotel has spacious but rather gloomy rooms with double beds, nets, tiled hot showers, & a decent garden bar. Some room renovations were underway when we visited in 2017. *Rfr8,000 dbl using shared ablutions; Rfr12,000 en-suite dbl.*

🏠 **Kinyange Farm House** (10 rooms) m 072 207 2584, 078 517 8916/201 3675. The quiet hillside location next to the king's palace here is one of the nicest in town, & while the accommodation doesn't quite live up to the locale, rooms are nonetheless simple & clean, with nets & en-suite hot showers. It seems a bit disorganised, but you should also be able to request meals with advance notice. Camping is also available at a nominal fee. *Rfr15,000 dbl.*

🏠 **New Life Motel** (10 rooms) m 078 223 8937. There's nothing special about this basic guesthouse, but it's cheap, very central, seems clean enough, & has a basic bar & restaurant in front. *Rfr7,000 dbl using shared ablutions; Rfr10,000 en-suite dbl.*

🏠 **Quality Inn Motel** (8 rooms) m 078 221 3909. This pleasant & sensibly priced hotel is situated on the left side of the feeder road halfway between Kubijega junction & the town centre. The airy rooms all have double beds with netting, tiled bathrooms, ample cupboard space & a phone, while the balcony offers an attractive view over cultivated hills surrounding Nyanza. A garden bar serves brochettes, omelettes & the like. *Rfr15,000/20,000 sgl/dbl; Rfr30,000 for a twin with 2 dbl beds; all rates B&B.*

✖ **WHERE TO EAT AND DRINK** It must be said that Nyanza is something of a gastronomically limited corner of Rwanda, but most of the hotels listed above serve decent to good local fare, along with the places listed below.

✖ **Chez Ramadan** m 078 861 9899/863 4450, 072 567 5828. Known throughout southern Rwanda for having the best brochettes around (& this in a country that clearly knows its brochettes), this unassuming roadside stop in Kubijega does indeed produce some fabulous grilled goat, chicken, or beef & roast potatoes. Even better, you can call them from the road & they'll have your order waiting.

✖ **Ku Muvure** m 078 879 3741. This low-key local restaurant opened in 2017 & the friendly manager here serves up typically Rwandan meals & snacks for Rfr1,000–3,000, along with cold beer, in the pleasant roadside garden or more workaday interior.

WHAT TO SEE

Rukari King's Palace Museum (m *078 457 7773/073 074 1093;* w *museum.gov. rw;* 🕐 *08.00–18.00 daily except 7 Apr & 11.00–18.00 on Umuganda days; entrance*

BARK CLOTH

In 1862, when Speke prepared for his first audience with King Mutesa of Buganda (part of modern-day Uganda), he put on his finest clothes, but admitted that he 'cut a poor figure in comparison with the dressy Baganda [who] wore neat bark cloaks resembling the best yellow corduroy cloth, crimp and well set, as if stiffened with starch'.

Known as *impuzu* in Rwanda, the stiff, neat bark-cloth cloak described by Speke was then the conventional form of attire in this part of Africa. Exactly how and when the craft arose is unknown. One tradition has it that King Wamala of Bacwezi Kingdom (legendary precursor to both Rwanda and Buganda) discovered bark cloth by accident on a hunting expedition, when he hammered a piece of bark to break it up and instead found that it expanded laterally to form a durable material.

Bark cloth can be made from the inner bark lining of at least 20 tree species. The best-quality cloth derives from four species of the genus *Ficus*, known locally as *umutaba, umuhororo, umurama* and *umugombe*, all of which were extensively cultivated in pre-colonial times. Different species of tree yielded different textures and colours, from yellow to sandy brown to dark red-brown.

The common bark-cloth tree can be propagated simply by cutting a branch from a grown one and planting it in the ground – after about five years the new tree will be large enough to be used for making cloth. The bark will be stripped from any one given tree only once a year, when it is in full leaf. After the bark has been removed, the trunk is wrapped in green banana leaves for several days, then plastered with wet cow dung and dry banana leaves to help it heal. If a tree is looked after this way, it may survive 30 years of annual use.

The bark is removed from the tree in one long strip. A circular incision is made near the ground, another one below the lowest branches, then a long line is cut from base to top, before finally a knife is worked underneath the bark to ease it carefully away from the trunk. The peeled bark is left out overnight before the hard outer layer is scraped off, then it is soaked. It is then folded into two equal halves and laid out on a log to be beaten with a wooden mallet on alternating sides to become thinner. When it has spread sufficiently, the cloth is folded in four and the beating continues. The cloth is then unfolded before being left to dry in the sun.

There are several local variations in the preparation process, but the finest cloth reputedly results when the freshly stripped bark, instead of being soaked, is steamed for about an hour above a pot of boiling water, then beaten for an hour or so daily over the course of a week. The steaming and extended process of beating are said to improve the texture of the cloth and to enrich the natural red-brown or yellow colour of the bark. Although it is used mostly for clothing, bark cloth can also serve as a blanket or a shroud, and is rare but valued as bookbinding.

Oral tradition has it that the cloth was originally worn only by the king and members of his court. Ironically, however, this historical association between bark cloth and social prestige was reversed during the early decades of colonial rule, when clothing made from cotton and other fabrics became a status symbol. By the 1950s, bark cloth had practically disappeared from everyday use.

Rfr6,000 non-residents, Rfr5,000 foreign residents, Rfr3,000 students & non-resident children; no photography) This is the top touristic reason for visiting Nyanza, situated on a hilltop about 2km southwest of the centre, and well signposted (⊕ *S 02°21.468, E 029°44.395, 1,805m*). The traditional ancient palace of the mwami has been reconstructed, together with some other buildings, 3–4km away from its original site, beside the newer Western-style palace built for Mwami Rudahigwa Mutara III in 1932. In olden times, Nyanza was the heart of Rwanda and seat of its monarchy, background to the oral tradition of battles and conquests, power struggles and royal intrigues. It is where the German colonisers came, at the end of the 19th century, to visit the mwami – and contemporary reports tell of the great pomp and ceremony these visits occasioned, as well as the impressive size of the mwami's court.

The capital of the kingdom was composed of a group of huts, an ephemeral town of some 2,000 inhabitants, well organised as far as the administration of the country and the comfort of the nobility were concerned... At his court the Mwami maintained the following retinue: the *'Ntore'*, adolescent sons of chiefs and notables, who formed the corps de ballet; the *'Bakoma'*, soothsayers, magicians and historians; the *'Abashashi'*, keepers of the arsenal, the wardrobe and the furniture; the *'Abasisi'* and *'Abacurabgenge'*, mimes, musicians and cooks; the *'Abanyabyumba'*, palanquin bearers and night watchmen; the *'Nitalindwa'*, huntsmen and runners; the *'Intumwa'*, artisans working for the Mwami; and finally the hangmen, attentive servants of jurists, ever ready to respond to the brief order to fetch and kill.

Traveller's Guide to the Belgian Congo and Ruanda-Urundi, Tourist Bureau for the Belgian Congo and Ruanda-Urundi, Brussels, 1951

The traditional palace has been carefully reconstructed and maintained, and contains the king's massive bed as well as various utensils. English- and French-speaking guides are available to relate the history and traditions of the royal court – there is even significance attached to some of the poles supporting the roof; for example, the one at the entrance to the king's bed is named 'do not speak of what happens here' and another conferred sanctuary on anyone touching it.

The newer palace is a typical colonial-era building with its spacious rooms and wide balcony. The *Traveller's Guide* above also states: 'In certain circumstances, and with the permission of the local authorities, he [the mwami] may be visited at his palace which is built on modern lines, furnished in good taste and richly decorated with trophies in an oriental manner.' In more recent times, the rundown palace served for several years as the part-time home of Rwanda's National Ballet (the Intore dancers, page 31). Now fully restored, it reopened in May 2008 as a museum whose exhibits relate to the two rulers who lived here during the early to mid 20th century, as well as the more ancient history of the Rwanda Empire. Several original items of royal furniture decorate the interior, and the walls are adorned with monochrome photographs. Other displays depict the palace when it was in use, and chart the history of Rwanda from the 5th century onwards. They've also reintroduced several long-horned *Inyambo* cattle to the complex and, as of early 2018, are developing interpretive materials and a garden space at the burial site of Mutara III and his wife Queen Rosalie Gicanda, signposted less than 1km away.

The museum can also arrange Intore dance performances by prior notice. The performances can start at any time from 08.00 to 20.00 and last for about 2 hours. Between 08.00 and 16.00 on normal weekdays, the cost is Rfr50,000 for one or two

HOLLYWOOD COMES TO NYANZA *Rosamond Halsey Carr*

My introduction to the mwami and his royal court was in 1956, when the Hollywood film *King Solomon's Mines* was shown to the king and queen and the royal courtiers. The movie, which was partially filmed on location in Ruanda and starred Stewart Granger and Deborah Kerr, contains some of the most authentic African dance sequences on film, including a dazzling depiction of the dance of the Intore.

The showing was arranged by the American consulate in Léopoldville and held in the royal city of Nyanza. Many of the European residents of Ruanda were invited, myself included. The mwami and his queen, their courtiers, and the Tutsi nobles who took part in the film were all present. It was a mild, clear night, charged with an air of excitement and wonder. A large screen was erected in the middle of a wide dirt road. On one side of the screen, chairs had been set up for the invited guests. On the other side (the back side), a huge crowd of Banyaruanda sat with expectant faces waiting for the movie to begin.

The king and his entourage made a ceremonial entrance. One would be hard-pressed to find a more majestic figure than this giant of a monarch who could trace his family dynasty back more than four hundred years. Rudahigwa and his courtiers were dressed in traditional white robes with flowing togas knotted at their shoulders, and his queen, Rosalie Gicanda, was wrapped in billowing layers of pale pink ...

The soundtrack for the film was in English and, as a result, the Africans were unable to understand the dialogue. Restlessness and murmurs of disappointment rippled through the crowd until the action sequences progressed to the familiar landscape of Ruanda. From that point on, the spectators provided their own soundtrack with cheers and improvised dialogue, as they followed the safari adventure across the desert to the royal city of Nyanza, shouting with glee each time they recognised friends – and in some instances themselves – on the big movie screen.

The city of Nyanza was almost entirely devoid of Western influence, as the Belgian administration had refrained from intruding upon the royal seat of the Tutsi monarchy. There were no hotels, and outside visitors were discouraged. When the movie ended, the mwami and his entourage and most of the invited guests assembled at the one small restaurant in town for sandwiches and drinks.

From Land of a Thousand Hills: My Life in Rwanda *by Rosamond Halsey Carr with Ann Howard Halsey, Viking, 1999* (page 366).

people, Rfr70,000 for up to five people, then another Rfr20,000–30,000 for each additional group of up to five people. The price rises by Rfr20,000 from 16.00 to 18.00 and by another 25% after 18.00. An additional levy of 50% is charged on weekends and public holidays. If that's too steep, a DVD of the same drum/dance troupe performing at the Festival Pan-African de la Danse (FESPAD) in 2008 is theoretically available for purchase, though in reality is now often sold out (the art gallery may also have copies).

Rwesero National Art Gallery (*0252 553131;* **m** *073 074 1093;* **w** *museum.gov.rw;* 🕘 *08.00–18.00 daily except 7 Apr & 11.00–18.00 on Umuganda days; entrance*

Rfr6,000 non-residents, Rfr5,000 foreign residents, Rfr3,000 students & non-resident children; no charge for photography) Prominently perched atop Rwesero Hill (⊕ *S 02°22.050, E 029°44.452, 1,834m*) about 1km south of Rukari, this striking building was constructed for Mutara III Rudahigwa over 1957–59, but he died in July 1959 before he could take up residence. Later used as a Supreme Court and Appeals Court, the palace fell into disuse for several years before being renovated and reopening as an arts museum in 2006. It now hosts a combination of permanent and temporary displays, featuring a fascinating combination of traditional and contemporary Rwandan paintings and sculptures dating from the 1950s onwards, though most postdate the genocide. In my estimation, this is one of the finest exhibitions of its type anywhere in Africa, and in many respects it is more interesting and rewarding than the nearby palace museum.

Nyanza (Nyabisindu) Dairy (✎ *0252 533022/533266*) On the way to the palaces you'll pass this state-owned dairy, the largest in Rwanda, which was founded by the Belgian colonists in 1937 and is still going strong today. In theory you can just turn up and ask for a free tour, but in practice it's courteous to ask about this on your way out to the palaces and then have your tour (if convenient) on the way back.

UPDATES WEBSITE

Go to **w** bradtupdates.com/rwanda for the latest on-the-ground travel news, trip reports and factual updates. Keep up to date with the latest posts by following Philip on Twitter (🐦 *@philipbriggs*) and via Facebook (f *pb.travel. updates*). And, if you have any comments, queries, grumbles, insights, news or other feedback, you're invited to post them directly on the website, or to email them to Philip (e *philip.briggs@bradtguides.com*) for inclusion.

5

Huye (Butare)

Set at an altitude of 1,755m some 30km north of the border with Burundi, the pleasant, businesslike town of Huye (formerly Butare) is often referred to as the country's 'intellectual centre': the first secondary school in what is now Rwanda opened here in 1928, and it has been the site of the national university since 1963. Founded in the early colonial era, its name was originally Butare, but in 1935 it was renamed Astrida in tribute to Queen Astrid, the 29-year-old Swedish wife of Belgium's King Leopold III, who died in a car accident.

The town served as the administrative centre of the northern half of Ruanda-Urundi in the colonial era, when it was popular with Belgian settlers, and it was the second-largest town in the joint territory, after the capital Bujumbura (in modern-day Burundi). It reverted to the name Butare in 1962, and served as the administrative capital of the eponymous province prior to the administrative reorganisation of 2006, when it was renamed Huye (after Mount Huye, which rises to 2,278m about 10km west of town).

At the time of independence, it seemed almost inevitable that Huye would become the capital city of Rwanda. In the end, however, Kigali was favoured for its more central location. So while Kigali has mushroomed, Huye remains peaceful and compact – though it is still the fourth-largest town in Rwanda, with a population estimated at around 55,000 in 2018 and its neatly laid-out centre still displays strong architectural evidence of its favoured status during the colonial era. For better or worse, many of the city's colonial-era buildings are slated to meet the wrecking ball soon as part of an ongoing redevelopment scheme meant to give the city a fully modern sheen, and all new construction on the main drag is required to be two storeys or higher. As such, in 2017, Huye's main street was pockmarked with shuttered businesses awaiting redevelopment, with their replacement structures yet to materialise.

During term-time Huye has probably the country's greatest concentration of students, in relation to its size – not only at the university but also at technical and training schools and colleges. It's something of a religious centre, too, with its massive cathedral and other churches. Its most prominent tourist attraction is the National Ethnographic Museum of Rwanda, which lies on the northern outskirts of town alongside the Kigali road, but the surrounding countryside also hosts several interesting cultural sites.

GETTING THERE AND AWAY

Huye lies 136km south of Kigali, a 2-hour drive along good tarred roads. All public transport arrives and departs from the new bus station on the northern edge of town [150 C1] where the Kigali and Rusizi roads meet. It's probably the smartest transport terminal in Rwanda, with a large parking area and multi-storey plaza

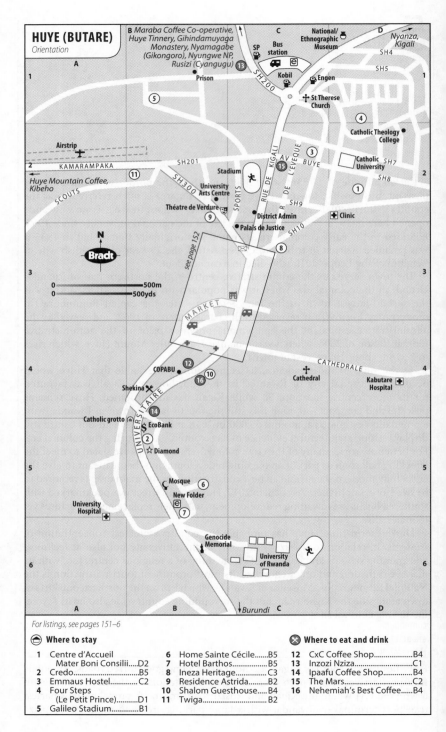

HUYE (BUTARE)
Orientation

B Maraba Coffee Co-operative, Huye Tinnery, Gihindamuyaga Monastery, Nyamagabe (Gikongoro), Nyungwe NP, Rusizi (Cyangugu)

National/Ethnographic Museum

Bus station

Kobil

SP

Prison

Engen

St Therese Church

Airstrip

Catholic Theology College

KAMARAMPAKA

SH201

Huye Mountain Coffee, Kibeho

SCOUTS

Stadium

University Arts Centre

Théatre de Verdure

Catholic University

BUYE

RUE DE KIGALI

R DE L'EVEQUE

SPORTS

District Admin

Palais de Justice

Clinic

Bradt

N

0 — 500m
0 — 500yds

see page 152

MARKET

CATHEDRALE

COPABU

Shekina

Catholic grotto

EcoBank

Diamond

Cathedral

Kabutare Hospital

Mosque

New Folder

University Hospital

Genocide Memorial

University of Rwanda

Burundi

Nyanza, Kigali

SH4

SH5

SH200

SH7

SH8

SH9

SH10

SH300

For listings, see pages 151–6

Where to stay

1 Centre d'Accueil
  Mater Boni Consilii.....D2
2 Credo.................................B5
3 Emmaus Hostel...............C2
4 Four Steps
  (Le Petit Prince)...........D1
5 Galileo Stadium..............B1
6 Home Sainte Cécile.......B5
7 Hotel Barthos.................B5
8 Ineza Heritage................ C3
9 Residence Astrida..........B2
10 Shalom Guesthouse.....B4
11 Twiga...............................B2

Where to eat and drink

12 CxC Coffee Shop...................B4
13 Inzozi Nziza...........................C1
14 Ipaafu Coffee Shop..............B4
15 The Mars................................C2
16 Nehemiah's Best Coffee......B4

with many shops, cafés, offices and other facilities. Volcano Express (m *072 200 0166*), Horizon Express (m *072 267 3799*) and Alpha Express (m *078 992 3072*) all run scheduled midibuses between Huye and Kigali every 30 to 60 minutes between 05.00 and 19.00 (*Rfr2,500*), while Alpha Express and Omega Car Express (m *078 881 3681*) connect to Rusizi/Cyangugu hourly from 05.00 to 19.00 (*Rfr3,000*). Any Kigali-bound vehicle can also drop you in Muhanga/Gitarama for Rfr1,500. Volcano Express and Horizon Express both also offer frequent connections to Nyanza for Rfr700.

Vehicles also head south to the Burundi border at Akanyaru/Kanyaru Haut (Burundi), but simmering political tensions between the two countries mean buses have been forbidden to cross since 2016, so you'll have to pick up an onward vehicle at the border.

GETTING AROUND

The National Museum and the University are no more than about 5km apart, so everything is manageable on foot. If you need transport, however, plenty of motos and taxi-voitures can be found at the turning from the main street leading to the market [152 A6/7], and at other strategic points in the town centre.

WHERE TO STAY

With your own vehicle, the Gihindamuyaga Monastery (page 160) about 6km outside of town makes for a peaceful rural alternative to staying in the city.

UPMARKET

Casa Hotel [152 D6] (24 rooms) m 078 170 5910/388 8836; e casahotel250@gmail. com; w casahotel.rw. Conveniently located between the market area & the main commercial street to the north, the whitewashed rooms at this newly constructed hotel aren't exactly dripping with character, but they're perfectly comfortable for the price & all come with hot water, flatscreen TV & mosquito nets, & some also have balconies. The popular attached restaurant has good meals & bar snacks plus indoor & balcony seating. *Solid value at Rfr25,000/30,000 dbl without/with balcony, Rfr50,000 junior suite; all rates B&B.*

Centre d'Accueil Mater Boni Consilii [150 D2] (100 rooms) m 078 377 7626/828 3903/877 7455; e management@ mbcrwanda.com; w mbcrwanda.com. A strong contender for the smartest hotel in town & just about nudging into the upmarket category, this recently expanded landmark is owned & managed by the Abiszemariya Sisters & profits are used to help take care of orphans, the disabled, & other marginalised people. Situated 1km from the new bus station & about

the same distance from the city centre, it has a good restaurant, high-speed Wi-Fi, conference facilities, a chapel, & well-tended en-suite rooms with hot showers & DSTV. *Sgls are fair value at Rfr30,000; Rfr60,000/70,000 larger VIP dbl/twin; all rates B&B.*

Four Steps (Le Petit Prince) Hotel [150 D1] (25 rooms) m 078 835 8681/348 1572; e fourstepshotel@yahoo.fr; w fourstepshotel.com. Set in large manicured gardens in the northern suburbs opposite the Catholic University, a few mins' walk from the National Museum, this private hotel isn't quite up to the standard of the Centre d'Accueil (see left), but is still a fine pick. The smartest & most expensive rooms are mini-suites with double bed, lockable built-in cupboards, fridge, tiled bathroom with tub, satellite TV, phone & balcony. The cheapest rooms are smaller & some have rather awkward shapes, but still come with TV & en-suite showers. Rooms are very variable in price, size & layout, so it is worth asking to see one before you take it. Facilities include Wi-Fi, & a restaurant bar that stays open from 10.00 to 23.00. They've rebranded as Four Steps, but remain better known around town as Le Petit Prince. *Rfr30,000–40,000*

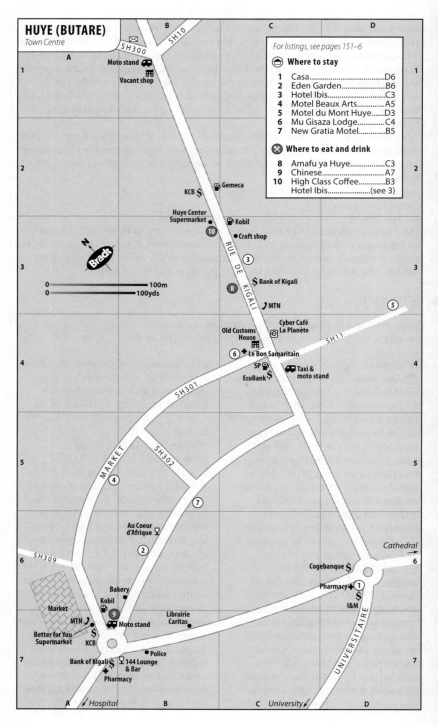

HUYE (BUTARE)
Town Centre

A   B   SH10   C   D

SH300

1   Moto stand   1
Vacant shop

2   Gemeca   2
KCB $

Huye Center
Supermarket   Kobil
10   Craft shop

3   RUE DE KIGALI
3   3
$ Bank of Kigali
8   ♪ MTN   5

Cyber Café
Old Customs   🖳 La Planète
House   SH11
6   + Le Bon Samaritain   4
4   SP 🚌   🚐 Taxi &
EcoBank $ moto stand

SH301

5   SH302   5
4

7

Au Coeur
d'Afrique 🍸
6   2   Cathedral
SH309   Cogebanque $ 6
Pharmacy + 1
Bakery $
Kobil   I&M
🖳
Market   9   Librairie
MTN ♪   🚌 Moto stand   Caritas
Better for You
Supermarket $
7   KCB   • Police   UNIVERSITAIRE   7
Bank of Kigali $ 🍸 144 Lounge
+   & Bar
Pharmacy

A   ↙ Hospital   B   C   University ↙   D

0   _____   100m
0   _____   100yds

N   Bract

sgl; Rfr45,000 dbl/twin; Rfr75,000 mini-suite; all rates B&B.

🏠 **Galileo Stadium Hotel** [150 B1] (26 rooms) **m** 078 764 7565/858 7844; **e** galileostadiummrwanda@gmail.com; **w** galileostadiumhotel.com. In an appealingly landscaped (though somewhat crowded) compound just north of the airstrip, this pleasant new hotel has rather cramped singles & doubles, more comfortably sized junior suites & twin rooms, & a thoroughly ostentatious VIP room replete with multi-coloured lights & walls. All rooms come with canopy beds, nets, TV, & fridge. The bar-restaurant does a variety of meat & fish dishes for Rfr5,000–6,000 &, quite uniquely, the menu gives an estimated prep time for each dish (most clock in at around 30mins). *Rfr30,000/50,000/60,000 sgl/dbl/twin; US$100 VIP room; all rates B&B.*

MODERATE

🏠 **Credo Hotel** [150 B5] (58 rooms, more under construction) **** 0252 530505/530855; **m** 078 850 4176/434 7705; **e** credohotel1@ gmail.com; 📘. Situated 500m from the town centre along the road to the university, this was once the smartest option around, & it is still the only hotel with a swimming pool. Unfortunately it is also rather characterless, with dazzling labyrinthine corridors that make excessive use of bright white tiles. All rooms are en suite, with impeccably clean WC & showers, & most also have a TV, phone & balcony. There's a peaceful view across fields at the back, while facilities include a swimming pool, restaurant & outdoor poolside restaurant-bar. Their new wing, 4 storeys of blue glass & balconies, remains closed after several years of delays, but will aim to reclaim the title of smartest digs in town once it finally opens, so expect rates on this side of the hotel to be significantly higher than those listed here. *Rfr25,000–60,000 sgl; Rfr35,000–70,000 dbl; all rates B&B.*

🏠 **Hotel Barthos** [150 B5] (26 rooms) **m** 078 830 5618/602 2299; **e** barthoshotel2000@yahoo. fr. Probably the pick in its range, this comfortable & friendly 4-storey hotel has an attractive façade with Art-Deco influences, & lies at the south end of town near the university campus. The large rooms are simply furnished with handcrafted wood, & have an en-suite hot shower & TV. Ask for a room

at the back of the hotel because the front side is near the busy road. *Good value at Rfr25,000/30,000 B&B for a tiled sgl/dbl with king-sized bed, net, writing desk, satellite TV & large en-suite bathroom. Also smaller rooms at Rfr15,000/20,000 & Rfr20,000/25,000 sgl/dbl.*

🏠 **Hotel Ibis** [152 C3] (11 rooms) **** 0252 530335; **m** 078 832 3000; **e** campionibis@ hotmail.com; 📘 Hotel Ibis Butare. Established in 1942, this centrally located, family-run hotel is something of a local institution, though it's become rather rundown of late & the neighbouring Motel du Mont Huye (page 154) has taken over the rear block of rooms. The remaining old-fashioned rooms all come with en-suite ablutions & TV, & most have 1 double & 1 single bed. Though the rooms have gone downhill, the streetside terrace bar & restaurant remains a solid bet (page 155). *US$20–40 sgl & US$25–50 dbl, depending on room size.*

🏠 **Shalom Guesthouse** [150 B4] (35 rooms) **m** 078 388 0153/871 9604; **e** rusodilo@ yahoo.fr. Run by the Anglican (EER) Diocese of Huye & situated on the south side of the town centre, this is a hotel in 2 parts: older, very basic rooms out front & a smart, more recent 2-storey block at the back. The older rooms are tiny, with just enough space for a bed (with net), with either shared or en-suite bathrooms. The newer building boasts very large tiled rooms with big windows, lockable built-in cupboards, king-size or twin beds, nets, en-suite showers & access to a ground-floor lounge with TV/DVD. The new rooms are among the best deals in this range, while the old ones are trim enough & just about the cheapest in town. Nehemiah's Best Coffee (page 156) shares the same compound. *Rfr4,000/5,000 sgl/dbl with shared ablutions; Rfr5,000/6,000 sgl/dbl en suite; Rfr30,000 exec dbl; all exc b/fast.*

BUDGET

🏠 **Emmaus Hostel** [150 C2] (14 rooms) **m** 078 886 5736/874 8649; **e** emmaushostel@ gmail.com. On a quiet suburban road close to the stadium & a reasonably short walk from the new bus station, this agreeable church-run hostel is centred around a neat green courtyard & offers a variety of spacious & spotless tiled en-suite rooms. *Great value starting at Rfr10,000/13,000/25,000 sgl/dbl/suite.*

The intellectual and cultural spirit of Huye – or Butare, as it was then – was so strong that initially it seemed that it could resist the madness of slaughter that erupted elsewhere in the country on 6 April 1994. For decades Hutus and Tutsis had lived and studied peacefully together there. When the killing started, people flocked to Butare from outlying areas believing that they would find safety – as indeed they did, for a while. The prefect of Butare, Jean-Baptiste Habyarimana (no relation to the late president), was the only Tutsi prefect in Rwanda at the time of the genocide. He took charge, welcoming the refugees, reassuring parishioners, and demonstrating such authority that, for two weeks while the killing raged elsewhere, relative calm prevailed in Butare, punctuated by only isolated instances of violence.

It couldn't last. Because of his defiance, Habyarimana was sacked from his post and murdered, to be replaced by a hardline military officer, Lieutenant Colonel Tharcisse Muvunyi, and an equally hardline civilian administrator. Under their orchestration, paramilitary units from Kigali were airlifted to Butare, and the killing started immediately. Ultimately, the massacres in and around Butare proved to be some of the worst of the genocide, and the death tally of 220,000 was the highest of any prefecture.

After the genocide, Tharcisse Muvunyi fled to Britain, where he was tracked down and arrested in February 2000. In September 2006, the International Criminal Tribunal for Rwanda (ICTR) sentenced him to 25 years' imprisonment. This ruling was annulled on appeal in August 2008 and retrial with regards to one count of the indictment commenced in June 2009. In February 2010, the ICTR found Tharcisse Muvunyi guilty of direct and public incitement to commit genocide, and he was given a 15-year sentence, with credit on time spent in custody since his arrest ten years earlier. In March 2012, he was granted early release, having served more than 80% of his jail term.

🏠 **Motel du Mont Huye** [152 D3] (30 rooms) 📱 078 830 2359/840 1228. Arguably the best budget option, this centrally located but peaceful spot lies along a side road away from the main street & its traffic. The clean, tiled, comfortable en-suite rooms with 1 or 2 ¾ beds all have hot water & a small balcony opening on to a central garden, & a more than adequate restaurant serves meals & snacks in the Rfr2,000–5,000 range. It's popular with NGOs, etc, so it's best to book in advance, though they've recently absorbed 12 rooms formerly belonging to the neighbouring Ibis Hotel, & they've got another annexe on the university road about 100m past the Hotel Credo. Wi-Fi. *Fair value at Rfr15,000/26,000 sgl/dbl or twin B&B.*

🏠 **Residence Astrida** [150 B2] (5 rooms) 📱 078 026 9145/598 3006; e residence. astrida@gmail.com. This converted house lies in leafy gardens immediately north of the town centre opposite Théâtre de Verdure. The spacious clean rooms come with double beds, nets, writing desk & en-suite bathroom with shower & tub, & there is a common lounge with TV. *Reasonable value at Rfr20,000/25,000 sgl/ dbl B&B.*

🏠 **Twiga Hotel** [150 B2] (40 rooms) 📱 078 885 5032; e hotel_twiga@yahoo.com. In the northern suburbs, along the road to Kibeho, this place is decorated with garish sculptures of giraffes (twiga in Swahili), gorillas & other wildlife. There is a pleasant-looking garden bar & restaurant, & for rooms you have the choice of small en-suite ones with ¾ bed & hot shower or a 4-bed dormitory, all with mosquito nets. *Rfr10,000/15,000 sgl/dbl; Rfr3,000 dorm bed.*

SHOESTRING

🏠 **Eden Garden Hotel** [152 B6] (13 rooms) 📱 078 899 0632/072 285 5553. In the market area, this hotel, set around a central courtyard, offers adequate accommodation in plain, clean & rather gloomy rooms using en-suite or shared facilities. *Rfr5,000 shared bath dbl; 6,000 en-suite dbl.*

⌂ Home Sainte Cécile [150 B5] (12 rooms) m 078 852 9582. Tucked away on a back road near the university & behind the Barthos Hotel, this neat & carefully landscaped little compound is home to a handful of newish & well-tended rooms in 2 different sizes, all with mozzie nets & hot water. The Inyamibwa Restaurant next door is under the same ownership and does the usual brochettes & such. There's no signboard, but it's the next building downhill from Inyamibwa. *Rfr8,000/10,000 sgl/dbl; 10,000/12,000 larger sgl/dbl.*

⌂ Ineza Heritage [150 C3] (12 rooms) m 078 361 1225/072 261 1225; e vitalmbr@gmail.com. On a side road opposite the post office just north of the city centre, this popular guesthouse has a pretty & secluded garden where you can sit out & eat, or just enjoy the peace & quiet. The en-suite rooms are clean & equipped with mozzie nets, but rather cramped & best suited to single travellers. It serves a variety of snacks & light meals, & it's very close to the centre if you prefer to eat elsewhere. *Rfr6,000 sgl.*

⌂ Motel Beaux Arts [152 A5] (10 rooms) ☏0252 530037; m 078 956 6999/866 6802. The pick of a cluster of inexpensive hotels dotted around the market area, this comfortable & reasonably priced 2-storey place offers clean en-suite twin & double rooms. The restaurant no longer serves meals other than b/fast, but there are plenty of other options for eating out within a couple of hundred metres. *Rfr9,000/12,000 sgl/dbl.*

⌂ Mu Gisaza Lodge [152 C4] (10 rooms) m 078 887 2004. Smack in the centre of town behind Pharmacie Le Bon Samaritain, the condom machine on the wall gives up the game as to some of the clientele here, but the rooms are freshly painted & reasonably clean, if a bit stuffy. There's a simple resto-bar attached. *Rfr6,000/10,000 sgl/dbl.*

⌂ New Gratia Motel [152 B5] (11 rooms) m 078 469 2454. Situated close to the market, this is a reasonably comfortable set-up, with basic but clean en-suite twins (with a solitary net dangling pointlessly above the space between the 2 beds) set round a small, well-watered courtyard garden. There's a (very) popular bar attached. *Not such good value at Rfr6,000/10,000/15,000 sgl/twin/dbl.*

✖ WHERE TO EAT AND DRINK

Plenty of small restaurants round the market offer snacks and good-value mélanges of rice, vegetables and meat for around Rfr1,500–2,500, while most hotels also serve meals in the Rfr4,000–6,000 range. Several more formal restaurants are scattered around town, notably the following:

✖ Amafu ya Huye [152 C3] ⊕ 07.00–22.00 daily. This comfortable 1st-floor standby opposite Bank of Kigali on the main road through town is one of the most popular lunch buffets in town. Expect the usual heaping steam trays of rice, matoke & bean stews, & a rotating variety of meat for Rfr2,000–4,000.

✖ Chinese Restaurant [152 A7] m 078 884 9793/857 4858; ⊕ daily from 08.00 until the last customer leaves. Situated behind the Kobil filling station opposite the central market, this is arguably the best eatery in town, despite the rather scruffy exterior, serving an MSG-laden selection of Chinese fish, meat & vegetarian dishes in the Rfr2,500–5,000 range, as well as more typical grills (beef, chicken, rabbit & fish) at a similar price. You can eat indoors or on the balcony.

✖ Hotel Ibis [152 C3] ☏0252 530335; m 078 832 3000; ⊕ 06.30–22.00 daily. There's hardly a more characterful (or popular) spot for an evening rendezvous in Huye than the terrace of the venerable Hotel Ibis, with its mix 'n' match of contemporary & period décor, & attached indoor bar. It serves the usual range of grills, mostly for around Rfr4,000–6,000, though brochettes & burgers are cheaper. There is also draught beer & a pizza menu.

✖ Inzozi Nziza [150 C1] m 078 841 4091; ▣; ⊕ 07.00–22.00 daily. Translating as 'Sweet Dreams', this charming ice-cream & coffee shop, on the Rusizi road opposite the new bus station, is the only place in town to serve locally produced ice cream, made freshly with local ingredients, & costing around Rfr800–1,500 depending on what toppings are added. It also serves fresh coffee roasted on the premises, fresh fruit juice, milkshakes, sandwiches & light snacks. Proceeds support a co-operative of more than 100 women from the drumming group Ingoma Nshya.

✳ 💻 **CxC Coffee Shop** [150 B4] m 078 612 0712; ⊕ 08.00–19.00 Mon–Sat, 10.00–18.00 Sun. With its minimalist interior dominated by a huge industrial coffee roaster, this friendly & funky spot immediately south of the town centre serves coffees from a variety of farmers in Rwanda, depending on what's currently in season. The delicious espresso, drip coffee, & cappuccino are well worth the Rfr500 outlay, and they've usually also got a couple of pastries on offer. You can buy beans (or ask for them to be freshly ground in front of you) to take home in medium, medium-dark, and dark roasts at Rfr5,000/500g.

💻 **High Class Coffee** [152 B3] m 078 869 2623; ⊕ 07.00–23.00 daily. With a prime location on the main drag, this new café-restaurant-bar has a rather drab interior, but the 1st-floor terrace overlooking the road makes a great spot to hang out & watch the action below. The menu skews towards the usual continental fare, with mains clocking in at about Rfr3,000–4,000.

💻 **Ipaafu Coffee Shop** [150 B4] m 078 485 6885/072 958 5072; ⊕ 07.00–22.00 Mon–Sat, noon–22.00 Sun. Another new entry in Huye's mushrooming café scene, this simple little shop does coffees, milkshakes & smoothies alongside a more prosaic fast-food menu of burgers, pizzas & the like for around Rfr3,000, alongside a few unexpected Chinese dishes. Wi-Fi.

💻 **Nehemiah's Best Coffee** [150 B4] m 078 388 0153; w nehemiahsbestcoffee.org; ⊕ 06.30–22.00 Mon–Sat, noon–22.00 Sun. This American-style coffee shop/job training centre in front of the Shalom Guesthouse isn't quite as shiny as those in Kigali, but it nonetheless serves a good selection of coffee, pastries, smoothies & the like, either inside the shop (where you can catch live music at the w/ends) or out front on their terrace. They've got Wi-Fi as well.

♀ **The Mars** [150 C2] m 078 884 7478/847 5527; ⊕ 24/7. Though the posted opening hours are rather unlikely to be true, this is nonetheless a reliably popular & unpretentious spot to catch the football over a beer & a brochette, with outdoor seating if you'd rather get some air.

NIGHTLIFE

There's not a huge amount of nightlife in Huye. Plenty of small bars are dotted around the market area, the most attractive and upmarket being **144 Lounge & Bar** [152 B7] which overlooks the roundabout from a third-floor perch where you can find a DJ most nights, projector screen with the football, and even occasional karaoke. Significantly downmarket by comparison, the rough-and-ready **Au Coeur d'Afrique** [152 B6] just down the road has a pool table and garden seating out back. **The Mars** [150 C2] (see above) is a more pleasant option on the north side of town.

Otherwise, the terrace bar at the **Hotel Ibis** [152 C3] remains a popular place to while away the evening in the open air as the life of the town goes by. A touch further south at the Credo Hotel, the **Diamond Nightclub** [150 B5] (m *078 850 4176*) is likely the only nightclub worthy of the name, complete with mirrors, disco lights, a VIP section overlooking the dance floor, and a Rfr1,000 cover charge.

SHOPPING

The only **bookshop** is the Librairie Caritas [152 B7] which has a few touristy books and items of stationery, as well as some international magazines and games.

For **self-caterers**, the central market [152 A6/7] is a good place to buy local produce such as fruit and vegetables, and there's a good bakery nearby, alongside the Chinese Restaurant [152 A7]. For imported foods and other goodies, your best bet is the Huye Center Supermarket [152 B3] on the main road or Better For You Supermarket [152 A7] on the ground floor of the main market building.

For **handicrafts**, there's an excellent shop next to the CxC Coffee Shop selling products made by the Coopérative des Producteurs Artisanaux de Huye [150 B4] (*COPABU;* m *078 885 3085;* e *copabu@yahoo.fr;* ☺ *08.00–19.00 Mon–Sat, 09.00– 19.00 Sun*). The items have set prices, but a little gentle bargaining will do no harm, particularly if you're buying more than one. The co-op was set up in 1997 with 47 members, working in banana-leaf products, wood-carving and reed baskets. Three years later it had 954 members (99 individuals and 35 associations) of which 66% were women, and it continued to grow. Handicrafts in the Huye area have been well organised, with the help of German aid.

OTHER PRACTICALITIES

COMMUNICATIONS The **post office** [152 B1] is at the northern end of the main street. Most of Huye's hotels (except those in the shoestring category) now offer Wi-Fi, as do several restaurants and cafés, but there's also the Cyber Café la Planète a few doors down from the Hotel Ibis [152 C4], New Folder near the university [150 B5], and another internet café at the new bus park. There are MTN service centres near the market [152 A7] and on the main road near the Bank of Kigali [152 C3].

MONEY KCB, Bank of Kigali, EcoBank, and others are all represented here with ATMs and offer normal services, but there are no private forex bureaux, so you are generally better off changing money in Kigali or (if you're heading that way) Rusizi/Cyangugu.

WHAT TO SEE AND DO

UNIVERSITY OF RWANDA [150 C6] (m *078 863 4945;* e *info@ur.ac.rw;* w *ur.ac.rw*) Although not really a tourist 'sight', the Huye campus of the University of Rwanda is by far Huye's most important institution. The fetching Art-Deco buildings at the centre of campus date to 1948–49 and first functioned as a White Sisters primary school for colonial children before the land was handed over to found the National University of Rwanda in 1963. Though it began with only 51 students and 16 lecturers, Huye now boasts the largest campus in the University of Rwanda system, with 10,368 students (of 30,445 in the whole UR system) and 457 lecturers (of 1,450). It lost many of its students and personnel during the genocide and suffered considerable damage, but managed to reopen in 1995. It is now a vibrant and forward-looking institution, comprising faculties of agronomy, law, arts and human sciences, medicine, science and technology, economics, social sciences and management, and education, as well as schools of journalism and communication and modern languages. You may run across visiting professors in any of the town's hotels and guesthouses. There is a decent cafeteria serving a buffet for around Rfr1,000, and over the weekend the main auditorium sometimes shows music and Premier League football in the evenings. You may be asked to show ID on entering the campus.

Out by the university is the **Ruhande Arboretum**, started in 1934. Its objective at the outset was to study the behaviour of imported and indigenous species, to determine what silvicultural methods were most suitable, to evaluate the trees' productivity and timber quality, and to develop the best of them. Now, it is of interest for the range and variety of its species – and it's a peaceful, shady place.

The university campus is the best place in Huye/Butare to look for **vervet monkeys**. The security policemen at the arboretum gate will usually allow in visitors who ask to see the monkeys, and will point you towards the football field straight ahead, which is where a troop of around 50–100 often hang out, usually in the surrounding trees, though obviously their presence cannot be guaranteed.

If you have an interest in the arts, you might want to check out whether any student productions are running at the **Théatre de Verdure** [150 B2] (m *078 859 8225;* e *cua_centre@yahoo.com*), part of the Centre Universitaire des Arts, which lies along SH300 behind the post office.

THE NATIONAL/ETHNOGRAPHIC MUSEUM OF RWANDA [150 D1] (m *073 074 1093/854 3550;* w *museum.gov.rw;* ⊕ *08.00–18.00 daily except 7 Apr & 11.00–18.00 on Umuganda days; entrance Rfr6,000 non-residents, Rfr5,000 foreign residents, Rfr3,000 students & non-resident children; no photography*) If you're in Huye, do allow time to visit this beautifully presented collection of exhibits on Rwandan history and culture. As you approach Huye on the Kigali road, you'll see its colourful fence on the right. Opened in 1988, and presented to Rwanda as a gift from Belgium's King Baudouin I, it is situated on more than 20ha of land containing indigenous vegetation and a traditional craft training centre as well as the main 2,500m² museum building, whose seven spacious rooms illustrate the country and its people from earliest times until the present day. At the reception desk, various English-language pamphlets and books are on sale, and most displays are labelled in English as well as Kinyarwanda.

Room 1 (the entrance hall) has space for temporary displays as well as numerous shelves of traditional handicrafts for sale. **Room 2** presents a comprehensive view of Rwanda's geological and geographical background and the development of its terrain and population. In **Room 3** the occupations of its early inhabitants (hunter-gathering, farming and stock-raising) are illustrated, together with the later development of tools and methods of transport. The social importance of cattle is explained and there are even detailed instructions for the brewing of traditional banana beer (see box, page 162). **Room 4** displays a variety of handicrafts and the making of traditional household items: pottery, mats, baskets, leatherwork and the wooden shields of the Intore dancers. **Room 5** illustrates traditional styles and methods of architecture – and a full-scale royal hut has been reconstructed. In **Room 6** traditional games and sports are displayed and more space is given to the costumes and equipment of the Intore dancers. Finally, **Room 7** contains exhibits relating to traditional customs and beliefs, history, culture, poetry, oral tradition and the supernatural.

If you don't fancy the walk from town (about 1.5km from the centre), then a taxi to the museum will cost around Rfr1,500, or more if you ask it to wait. Alternatively, it's only about 300m from the new bus station, so it makes sense as a first or last stop in town, should you not be too weighed down by luggage.

OTHER POINTS OF INTEREST The huge, red-brick, Roman Catholic **cathedral** [150 C4], built in memory of Belgium's Princess Astrid in the late 1930s, is the largest in the country and worth a visit. Its interior is fairly plain, but the atmosphere is tranquil and the size impressive. A service there can be a moving experience, especially if you arrive during mass, or choir rehearsals, and catch the Acapella choir of 30+ Rwandans in song. It's possible to take a turning to the right a short distance east of the Ineza Heritage guesthouse and then to cross twisty tracks through the green and cultivated valley until you reach the cathedral, but ask for directions and advice.

There is some attractive architecture in the city centre, and the tranquil, tree-lined residential streets away from the centre are good territory for strolling. Major colonial landmarks along the main road through the centre of town include the **Old Customs House** [152 C4] (now a financial training centre) opposite the

SP filling station, whose architecture would suggest it was built in the 1930s, and the handsome little blue-and-white **shop** [152 B1] (now vacant), which was erected as a doctor's surgery in the 1950s and later served as a bank. Just down SH300 near the Théatre de Verdure, the **Centre Universitaire des Arts** [150 B2] is another compelling building, this one feeling almost Cape Dutch in style, but the inside is just offices. Most, if not all, of these historic buildings fall afoul of Huye's master plan to modernise the city centre and could well disappear in the coming years.

Spectacular displays of **traditional dance** (Intore) take place in the town and the museum, and can be arranged on request (and for a fee); ask at the museum (see opposite) about this.

EXCURSIONS FROM HUYE

HUYE TINNERY (m *078 864 0923;* e *abmabuye@gmail.com;* f *Etainerie de Huye;* ⏲ *07.00–16.30 Mon–Fri, 07.00–noon Sat*) Established in 1986 by a Benedictine monk who did his internship in Europe and managed by the affable Antoine Bizimana, this interesting tinworks is located about 5km northwest of Huye on the Nyamagabe/Gikongoro road (look out for 'Etainerie Huye' in metal Art-Deco lettering). It uses Rwandan tin made from 99.8% pewter to produce an attractive range of products ranging from gorilla, giraffe, and long-horned inyambo cattle statuettes to household utensils reminiscent of the Carrol Boyes range, but cheaper. Visitors are welcome to watch the artisans at all stages in the process, from making the moulds to pouring, burnishing and welding. Products are sold at the tinnery's on-site shop, as well as through various hotel boutique shops in Kigali.

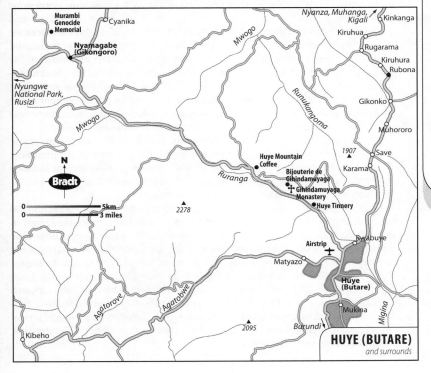

GIHINDAMUYAGA MONASTERY (m *078 852 0243;* e *hotelleriegihinda@yahoo.fr*) Founded in 1958 by Benedictine monks from Belgium's Maredsous Abbey, this welcoming monastery sits cloistered behind a thick grove of eucalyptus just shy of 2km off the main Huye–Rusizi road. Set in grassy, carefully manicured grounds, the campus of brick buildings and covered walkways here was designed and built in the early 1960s by Belgian architect Lucien Kroll; it was selected as Rwanda's entry in *The Phaidon Atlas of 20th-Century World Architecture* in 2012. In addition to the church and other religious facilities, the monastery is home to a jewellery workshop and boutique. The **Bijouterie de Gihindamuyaga** (m *078 852 5661/072 670 9708;* e *bijougihinda@yahoo.fr/gihindabijou@gmail.com;* ⏲ *08.00–noon & 13.00–17.00 Mon–Sat*) sells a small selection of handmade rings, bracelets, pendants and the like made out of silver and gold, in both religious and secular designs, and it's possible to visit the workshops as well.

If you'd like to stay and soak up the contemplative vibes, there are also 30 very trim and good-value guest rooms with hot water and mosquito nets on offer here (*2 dbls & 28 sgls at Rfr12,000/20,000 sgl/dbl*), some of which have balconies

MURAMBI GENOCIDE MEMORIAL   *Phil Vernon*

Arriving at Murambi Hill, one is first struck by the breathtaking beauty of its location. The site of a partially completed technical school in Nyamagabe District in southern Rwanda, it is a tidy array of unfinished classrooms, dormitories and washrooms situated on the grassy crest of a red dirt ridge that falls away on both sides to lush green bottom lands, beyond which rise the steeply cultivated and densely populated hills that hold this place in a close, but in no way comfortable, embrace.

Despite its beauty, however, Murambi was the site of a horrific massacre of Tutsi men, women and children during the 1994 genocide. It is where up to 50,000 Tutsi from all over the region were sent in the early days of the genocide, ostensibly for their safety, only to have their water and the flow of food shut off by the authorities. Local militias sent in to kill the Tutsi were met by fierce resistance and forced to turn back. But the interahamwe returned on the early morning of 21 April, together with the army, to massacre the refugees with guns, grenades, clubs, hoes and machetes. Only a dozen Tutsi are known to have survived.

Murambi, with its history as a killing site, and its unique compelling displays of preserved bodies, is arguably the most important site in Rwanda for confronting the truth of the genocide. The addition of an exhibition locating Murambi's story within that of the 1994 genocide against the Tutsi provides both a national and a local context for understanding what happened here.

After the massacre, the authorities used bulldozers to dig mass graves; upon later exhumation hundreds of the buried bodies were found mummified by the heat of decomposition. These bodies, preserved with lime, can now be viewed on white-painted racks in the dormitory blocks. The humanity of individual corpses – their torment still visible in the frozen cry of a child, the chopped skull and severed leg tendons, the missing limbs – is the grim legacy of Murambi.

On 26 May 2011, Murambi Genocide Memorial became the second commemorative site in Rwanda (the other being the Kigali Genocide Memorial) to offer visitors a museum-quality experience, with the official opening of a new exhibition created by Aegis Trust under the auspices of the National Commission for the Fight Against Genocide (CNLG).

overlooking the grounds. The restaurant (with bar) offers breakfast for Rfr2,500, plus lunch and dinner for Rfr4,000 each, and meals can be taken independently or with the monks in the refectory. It makes a memorable alternative to staying in Huye if you've got your own transport, though they do sometimes book up with retreats and other events, so it's best to call in advance.

To get here from Huye, take the unsigned right-hand turning 350m after the tinnery, then follow the earthen access road (keeping left at the fork) past farm fields and brick kilns, and through the eucalyptus grove to reach the monastery after 1.8km.

KIBEHO Before the genocide, Kibeho hit the headlines because of the visions of the Virgin Mary allegedly seen there by young girls from 1981 onwards, starting with that of teenager Alphonsine Mumureke in November 1981. Her prophesies have been said to reflect the subsequent genocide. The phenomena were reported both nationally and internationally, and the small, remote community became a centre of pilgrimage and faith, as believers travelled from all over Rwanda and further afield

The Murambi exhibition comprises 350m² of exhibit space, complete with floor-to-ceiling displays of archival photos, interpretive text in Kinyarwanda, English and French, video installations, and an interactive GPS display of killing sites. The testimonies of survivors, of those who risked their own lives to shelter those targeted, and of the perpetrators themselves, provide a window into the stark emotions and inner struggles of Rwandans coming to terms with the genocide.

Incorporating recent scholarship and archival material, the Murambi exhibition traces the history of the genocide from colonial times – the cycles of anti-Tutsi violence and discrimination ushered in with independence, the escalation of propaganda and attacks against Tutsi by successive Hutu regimes – revealing how plans for extermination were prepared and carried out by the authorities at all levels, by the army and militia during the genocide, and what was done – and not done – to stop it.

Following the broad narrative of the genocide are exhibits that focus specifically on the events at Murambi. With chilling clarity, the story of what unfolded during the night of 21 April 1994, is told in the words of those few who survived. Visitors then pass through rooms of family photos mounted larger-than-life upon the walls – the smiling faces seeming to refuse the brutal fact of their slaughter – where glass-covered burial crypts, built but not yet in use at the time of writing, will hold preserved bodies: adults in one chamber, and children in another.

'There are those who feel that only reburial can offer dignity for the dead, but some survivors ask what dignity there is in being forgotten,' reports Freddy Mutanguha, East Africa Director of Aegis Trust: 'They fear that unless the ultimate evidence is there to see, the genocide could be denied and perhaps one day happen again.'

A final room displays the important stories of people who risked death and suffered themselves to rescue Tutsi and to preserve human life.

The exhibition ends with a challenge to visitors: Now that you have heard the story of Murambi, what is in your heart, and what are you moved to do? Visitors are invited to write on slips of coloured paper and to post them on a bulletin board for others to read.

5

to witness the miracles. During the genocide Kibeho suffered appallingly: hospital, primary school, college and church were all attacked. The church was badly burned while still sheltering survivors and has been rebuilt; a genocide memorial stands beside it.

The road to Kibeho heads west from near Huye's stadium, and Horizon Express (m *072 267 3799*) runs an hourly service from Huye between 06.00 and 19.00 for Rfr850. It's a beautiful drive through a mixture of high ground with extensive views, wooded valleys, farmland and tea plantations, on an unmade road. The surface isn't bad, at least in the dry season – there are small wooden 'bridges' where streams run across the road – but high clearance is advised. There's not a great deal to see at Kibeho, apart from the church and genocide memorial, but it's a pleasant town with open views. If you want to spend the night, clean, comfortable, safe and inexpensive accommodation and decent meals are available by prior arrangement at the **Regina Pacis Hospitality House** (\ *0252 530242;* m *078 326 1736;* e *benebikira@yahoo.fr;* w *benebikira.net*), run by the Benebikira Sisters of Rwanda, a charitable order dedicated to creating sustainable revenue-generating projects for local communities. It's a friendly place, and the restaurant is open to non-residents too. Good accommodation can also be had with the **Pallottine Fathers** (*Pallotti Hse;* m *078 830 7376;* e *pallottihouse@gmail.com;* w *kibeho-sanctuary.com*) or the **Pallottine Sisters** (m *078 386 7718;* e *pallotines.sisters@gmail.com;* w *kibeho-sanctuary.com*), both of whom also have restaurants.

COFFEE COUNTRY The fertile slopes around Mount Huye, west of the town, lie at the heart of the region's coffee-growing country: one of the most scenic parts of Rwanda, all rolling green hills swathed in coffee shrubs and other lush vegetation. You could explore it either as a day excursion from Huye (by car or bicycle), or *en route* from Huye to Nyungwe or Rusizi/Cyangugu.

A good place to start is the **Cyarumbo Coffee Washing Station**: follow the main road west from Huye towards Rusizi/Cyangugu for 12km to Maraba trading centre, continue for another few hundred metres across a bridge, and it is clearly signposted to the left down a 1.5km dirt track.

THE PREPARATION OF BANANA BEER   *(Free translation by Janice Booth)*

- When the bunches of fruit are ready, cut them.
- Cover the bunches with banana leaves and leave them in the courtyard to ripen for two to three days.
- Clean out the pit in which the fruit ripened.
- Lay banana branches across the top of the pit.
- Place the bananas on top of the branches.
- Wrap the bananas in fresh banana leaves and then scatter a layer of earth on top.
- Put leaves in the ditch under the bananas and set the leaves alight. Leave for three days.
- Peel the fruit, then crush it, then mix a little water into the pulp.
- Press the pulp and filter the juice.
- Grind up a small amount of sorghum.
- Pour the juice into a large jar and add the sorghum to it.
- Leave to ferment for three days.
- The beer is ready to drink.

Here the coffee beans are dried, washed and sorted. Back on the Huye–Rusizi road, 1km past the turn-off to Cyarumbo, you'll pass the **National Speciality Coffee Quality Laboratory & Training Centre** (known locally as 'the Laboratory') on the right. Another 500m past this, a good dirt road to the right reaches the tiny trading centre of Simbi after 2km, then continues deeper into the hills to the shambas where the coffee is grown – a wonderfully scenic area with great potential for hiking and cycling.

Maraba Bourbon gourmet coffee

The Maraba Bourbon coffee from this area is one of Rwanda's success stories. A special type of Arabica from Bourbon coffee trees; it has a smooth, full-bodied flavour with no astringency or after-taste. The beans have excelled in international taste tests and are marketed actively in the UK and US.

The coffee plantation is run by the **Abahuzamugambi Co-operative**, set up in 2001, many of whose members are women widowed in the genocide who were struggling to support their families. This income has enabled them to pay school fees, improve their homes and acquire livestock. Support from a number of international organisations, including USAID and the UK's Comic Relief, has provided new washing stations and improved equipment, and the area has acquired a new clinic, bank and market as well as schools and other ancillary shops and services. From an initial 200 members in 2001 there are now around 1,500; including their families and children, up to 6,000 people benefit directly or indirectly. In the UK, Maraba Bourbon is available from w unionroasted.com (Union Coffee Roasters).

Traditionally, Arabica coffee had always been Rwanda's principal export, but quality and quantity declined seriously after the genocide when production fell to about half its previous level. In true Rwandan fashion, the coffee industry's recovery has been remarkable, and other plantations around Rwanda are achieving similar success with different brands, particularly in the north and the Lake Kivu area. Abahuzamugambi offers ad-hoc visits to the plantation and facilities, but coffee enthusiasts would be better off heading to **Huye Mountain Coffee** nearby, where thorough and informative tours and tastings are easily arranged (see box, below).

NYAMAGABE (GIKONGORO)

This modestly sized town, administrative capital of Nyamagabe District, whose name was changed from Gikongoro to Nyamagabe

HUYE MOUNTAIN COFFEE

Since June 2015, Huye Mountain Coffee [150 A2] (m *078 830 3678/852 4967/564 3913/763 0689, 073 294 3913;* e *rubanzangabo@yahoo.fr;* w *huyemountaincoffee.com*) has been inviting tourists to experience every aspect of their coffee production process, from crop to cup, at their spectacularly situated plantation about 8km from Huye, along the road to Nyamagabe. On a walking tour lasting between 1 hours and 3 hours (there are some uphill stretches – bring water), vivacious tour guide Tuyisenge Aloys brings the local history and fast-growing industry to life. Visits explain local coffee legends, as well as all the steps of the growing, roasting, and tasting processes (with a parting gift of some beans to brew up at home). Come between February and June to see the harvesting, washing and drying of the coffee cherries in full swing. Transport and accommodation can be arranged too – see their website for details. Highly recommended.

in 2006, sprawls uneventfully along a green ridge on the Rusizi/Cyangugu Road almost 30km west of Huye. There's not a lot to see around here except for a few shops and some beautiful, dramatically hilly landscapes. But if the area appeals and you feel like some steepish strolling, there's decent accommodation at the three-storey **Golden Monkey Hotel** (*23 rooms;* m *078 830 6080/848 4849;* e *info@ goldenmonkeyhotel.com;* w *goldenmonkeyhotel.com*), which lies alongside the main road and charges US$30/37/42 single/twin/double for a smart room with netting, tiled floors, lockable built-in cupboards and en-suite hot shower and toilet. There's a bright and colourful restaurant on site, and they can also arrange for forex, massages, and cars to Nyungwe (*US$100*). Just around the corner, **Bar-Resto La Fraicheur** (m *078 282 2833*) is another good bet for beer, stews and barbecued meat. If you need cash, Cogebanque and Bank of Kigali both have ATMs in the centre of town. To get here, any vehicle going between Huye/Butare and Rusizi/Cyangugu can drop you off, and **Horizon Express** [152 D6] (m *072 258 8690*) connects regularly from here to Kigali via Huye and Muhanga/Gitarama.

About 2.5km north of Nyamagabe, **Murambi Genocide Memorial** (see box, pages 160–1) is one of Rwanda's starkest. More than 1,800 bodies, of the 27,000-odd exhumed from mass graves here, have been placed on display to the public in the old technical school. They people the bare rooms, mingling horror with poignancy, as a mute but chillingly eloquent reminder that such events must never, ever, be allowed to recur.

6

Nyungwe Forest National Park

The largest remaining tract of montane rainforest in eastern Africa, Nyungwe extends for 1,015km² over the mountainous southwest of Rwanda, forming a contiguous forest block with Burundi's 400km² Kibira National Park. The park is the most important catchment area in Rwanda, supplying water to 70% of the country, and its central ridge divides Africa's two largest drainage systems, the Nile and the Congo – indeed, a spring on the slopes of the 2,950m Mount Bigugu is now regarded to be the most remote source of the world's longest river (see box, page 184).

As with other forests along the Albertine Rift (the part of the Rift Valley that follows the Congolese border with Uganda, Rwanda, Burundi and northwest Tanzania), Nyungwe is a remarkably rich centre of biodiversity. More than 1,050 plant species have been recorded, including 200 orchids and 250 Albertine Rift Endemics (AREs), along with at least 120 butterfly species. The vertebrate fauna includes 85 mammal, 310 bird, 32 amphibian and 38 reptile species, of which about 15% are AREs.

Statistics aside, Nyungwe is simply magnificent. The forest takes on a liberatingly primal presence even before you enter it. One moment the road is winding through a characteristic rural Rwandan landscape of rolling tea plantations and artificially terraced hills, the next a dense tangle of trees rises imperiously from the fringing cultivation. For a full 50km, the road clings improbably to steep forested slopes, offering grandstand views over densely swathed hills that tumble like monstrous green waves towards the distant Burundi border. One normally thinks of the rainforest as an intimate and confining environment, and Nyungwe's dank interior certainly possesses those qualities. But as viewed from the main road, Nyungwe is also a gloriously expansive sight.

For most visitors, primates are the main attraction. All 13 species are represented, including a chimpanzee population estimated at around 500, which can usually be tracked at short notice, but several other monkeys are readily seen, including the acrobatic Ruwenzori colobus and the localised L'Hoest's monkey. Nyungwe is also highly alluring to birders, botanists and keen walkers, with its 130km network of walking trails, and is the site of the region's only suspended canopy walk.

Bisected by the surfaced trunk road between Huye and Rusizi/Cyangugu, Nyungwe is unusually accessible by car. Despite that, it features on relatively few tourist itineraries. Partly, this is because the forest trails require more stamina than their counterparts in Volcanoes National Park, without the enticement of mountain gorillas to justify the effort. Another factor was the lack of any genuine tourist-class accommodation prior to the opening of Nyungwe Forest Lodge in 2010 (which, in step with the current trend in Rwandan tourism, has now been upgraded once again and joined the ultra-luxurious One&Only family of resorts as Nyungwe House in 2018).

Furthermore, in keeping with the RDB's aim of attracting high-cost low-volume tourism, Nyungwe makes few concessions to independent or budget travel.

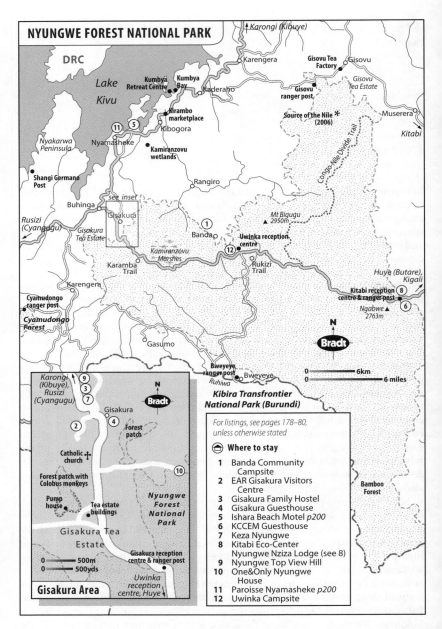

NYUNGWE FOREST NATIONAL PARK

↑*Karongi (Kibuye)*

DRC

Lake Kivu

Karengera

Kumbya Retreat Centre
Kumbya Bay
Kaderaho

Gisovu Tea Factory
Gisovu

Gisovu Tea Estate

Gisovu ranger post

Kirambo marketplace

(11) (5) Kibogora

Nyamasheke

Nyakarwa Peninsula

Kamiranzovu wetlands

Shangi Germano Post

Rangiro

Source of the Nile ✳ (2006)

Congo-Nile Divide Trail

Muserera

Kitabi

Buhinga

see inset

Gisakura

Rusizi (Cyangugu)

Gisakura Tea Estate

Banda

(1)

Mt Bigugu ▲ 2950m

Uwinka reception centre

(12)

Kamiranzovu Marshes

Karamba Trail

Karengera

Rukizi Trail

Huye (Butare), Kigali

Kitabi reception centre & ranger post (8)
(6)

Ngabwe ▲ 2763m

Cyamudongo ranger post

Cyamudongo Forest

Gasumo

N

Bradt

Bweyeye ranger post
Ruhiwa
Bweyeye

0 ———— 6km
0 ———— 6 miles

Kibira Transfrontier National Park (Burundi)

Gisakura Area inset

Karongi (Kibuye), Rusizi (Cyangugu)

(9)
(3)
(7)

Gisakura

N

Bradt

(2)

(4)

Forest patch

Catholic church ✝

Forest patch with Colobus monkeys

Pump house

Tea estate buildings

Gisakura Tea Estate

(10)

Nyungwe Forest National Park

Gisakura reception centre & ranger post

0 ———— 500m
0 ———— 500yds

Gisakura Area

Uwinka reception centre, Huye ↓

Bamboo Forest

For listings, see pages 178–80, unless otherwise stated

🛏 Where to stay

1 Banda Community Campsite
2 EAR Gisakura Visitors Centre
3 Gisakura Family Hostel
4 Gisakura Guesthouse
5 Ishara Beach Motel *p200*
6 KCCEM Guesthouse
7 Keza Nyungwe
8 Kitabi Eco-Center
   Nyungwe Nziza Lodge (see 8)
9 Nyungwe Top View Hill
10 One&Only Nyungwe House
11 Paroisse Nyamasheke *p200*
12 Uwinka Campsite

Fees for guided activities are high, unguided exploration is forbidden, and until relatively recently there were few affordable accommodation options in the vicinity. Getting around without private transport is tricky, but the road between Huye and Rusizi does see a fair bit of traffic so, with a bit of flexibility and a willingness to hitch, you can usually make it work (though chimpanzee tracking may be another story). Still, Nyungwe is probably not worth visiting on a daily budget of much less than US$150 per person – and even then, your options will be restricted if you are dependent on public transport.

ORIENTATION

Nyungwe is a large park, and facilities and attractions are widely spaced out along the 50km stretch of the surfaced Huye–Rusizi road that bisects it. As a result, exploration tends to entail lots of driving to-and-fro for those with private transport, and can be problematic (though not impossible) for those without.

Coming from Huye, Kitabi Entrance Gate, site of the park headquarters and a reception/booking office, lies on the park's eastern boundary. Also here is a growing complement of accommodation, including the Kitabi Eco-Centre and the Kitabi College of Conservation & Environmental Management (KCCEM) guesthouse, both offering some of the more affordable accommodation in or around the park. Kitabi is the base for the little-used Ngabwe Trail, but it is somewhat remote from Nyungwe's key attractions, making it a potentially frustrating base without your own vehicle.

About 45 minutes' drive further west, the park's most ambitious tourist development is the Uwinka Reception Centre, which lies alongside the main road and is well signposted 90km from Huye and 54km from Rusizi/Cyangugu. This is the starting point for several trails, including the canopy walkway, and it is also very close to some good sites for general birdwatching and primate viewing. The campsite and canteen are found here, too, but there's no other accommodation nearby.

The main cluster of facilities lies 18km west of Uwinka, immediately outside the park boundary, close to the Gisakura Tea Estate. Nyungwe House, Gisakura Guesthouse and Nyungwe Top View Hill Hotel (among others) all lie close to the 2km stretch of road running from Gisakura Tea Estate to the eponymous village. Two activities can easily be undertaken from Gisakura without a private vehicle: the superb Isumo (Waterfall) Trail, and a visit to the monkey-rich relict forest patch in the nearby tea estate.

Trails and activities can be booked at any of the three reception centres: Kitabi (m 078 831 7028/9), Uwinka or Gisakura (m 078 831 7027); the last is no longer next to Gisakura Guesthouse, but now sits at the park boundary a further 2.5km towards Huye. (A fourth reception centre, at Gisovu in the north of the park (page 187), is scheduled to open in 2018.) In most cases, the trailheads lie somewhere alongside the 50km road between Kitabi and Gisakura, which makes them difficult of access without a private vehicle, though any public transport between Rusizi and Huye will drop you along the way. You'll have to pay the full ticket price, and make sure to keep your eyes out and tell the driver where you're stopping so that you don't accidentally miss it. Chimp tracking isn't possible on public transport, as it usually entails a 05.30 rendezvous at Gisakura Reception Centre, then at least 1 hour's drive to the starting point. You can try to hitch a lift with other travellers going chimp tracking (and the rangers at Gisakura can let you know if there are other groups booked on a given day), but this is obviously not a guarantee. Park staff can arrange vehicles for chimp tracking at around US$100 per vehicle.

PARK FEES

An entrance fee is no longer charged, but fixed fees apply to all activities, and many independent travellers find them prohibitively high. The somewhat Byzantine fee structure (though it was thankfully simplified slightly a few years back) also comes across as the brainchild of somebody with way too much time on their hands, and

ACTIVITY FEES

Activity	Days	NR ($)	RF ($)	RFc ($)	EACr ($)	EACn ($)	EACc ($)	RC (Rfr)	RCc (Rfr)
Nature	1	40	30	20	30	5	3	3,000	1,500
walks	2+	20	15	10	15	2.50	1.50	1,500	750
Isumo (Waterfall) Trail	1	50	40	20	40	10	5	5,000	2,000
Chimp tracking	1	90	60	30	60	10	5	5,000	2,500
Other primate tracking	1	60	40	20	40	10	3	5,000	1,500
Birding	1	50	40	20	40	10	5	5,000	2,000
walks	2+	25	20	10	20	5	2.50	2,500	1,000
Canopy Walkway	1	60	50	25	50	10	5	5,000	5,000
Congo-Nile Divide Trail	3–4	100	70	35	70	20	10	10,000	5,000

a limited understanding of what a typical tourist might want to do over the course a few days' stay.

Different fees apply to five categories of adult visitor: non-residents (NR), resident foreigners (RF), residents of other East African Community countries (EACr), nationals of other East African Community countries (EACn), Rwandan citizens (RC). Lower student/children fees are charged to foreign residents (RFc), East African Community nationals (EACc) and Rwandans (RCc). There's no category for student/child resident foreigners of other EAC countries, but they can reasonably expect to pay the Rwandan foreign resident student/child price (RFc on the chart). There doesn't appear to be any discount for non-resident children and students.

Discounted fees are charged to those who spend more than one day in the park, but only for hiking and birding, which are charged at a 50% rate for every day after the first. Chimpanzee tracking, canopy walk, and other primate treks are always the same price.

In addition to paying activity fees, it is customary to tip your guide and trackers. The table above sums up the various activity fees.

NATURAL HISTORY

Nyungwe is a true rainforest, typically receiving in excess of 2,000mm of precipitation annually. It is also one of the oldest forests in Africa, which is one reason why it

ALBERTINE RIFT ENDEMICS

Most of Rwanda's forest inhabitants have a wide distribution in the DRC and/or West Africa, while a smaller proportion consists of eastern species that might as easily be observed in forested habitats in Kenya, Tanzania and in some instances Ethiopia. A significant number, however, are Albertine Rift Endemics (AREs): in other words their range is more-or-less confined to montane habitats associated with the Rift Valley escarpment running between Lake Albert and the north of Lake Tanganyika. The most celebrated of these regional endemics is of course the mountain gorilla, confined to the Virunga and Bwindi mountains near the eastern Rift Valley escarpment. Other primates endemic to the Albertine Rift include several taxa of smaller primates, for instance the golden monkey and Ruwenzori colobus, while eight endemic butterflies are regarded as flagship species for the many hundreds of invertebrate taxa that occur nowhere else.

Of the remarkable tally of 37 range-restricted bird species listed as AREs, roughly half are considered to be of global conservation concern. All 37 of these species have been recorded in the DRC, and nine are endemic to that country, since their range is confined to the western escarpment forests. More than 20 AREs are resident in each of Uganda, Rwanda and Burundi, while two extend their range southward into western Tanzania.

All but two of the 29 endemics that occur on the eastern escarpment have been recorded in Rwanda's Nyungwe Forest. Largely inaccessible to tourists for some years now, the Itombwe Mountains, which rise from the Congolese shore of northern Lake Tanganyika, support the largest contiguous block of montane forest in East Africa. This range is also regarded as the most important site for montane forest birds in the region, with a checklist of 565 species including 31 AREs, three of which are known from nowhere else in the world. The most elusive of these birds is the enigmatic Congo bay owl, first collected in 1952, and yet to be seen again, though its presence is suspected in Nyungwe based on unidentified owl calls recorded in 1990 by Dowsett and Dowsett-Lemaire.

Several forest-dwelling AREs share stronger affinities with extant or extinct Asian genera than they do with any other living African species, affirming the great age of these forests, which are thought to have flourished during prehistoric climatic changes that caused temporary deforestation in lower-lying areas such as the Congo Basin. The Congo bay owl, African green broadbill and Grauer's cuckoo-shrike, for instance, might all be classed as living fossils – isolated relics of a migrant Asian stock superseded elsewhere in Africa by indigenous genera evolved from a common ancestor.

Among the mammalian AREs, the dwarf otter-shrew of the Ruwenzori is one of three highly localised African mainland species belonging to a family of aquatic insectivores that flourished some 50 million years ago and is elsewhere survived only by the related tenrecs of Madagascar. A relict horseshoe bat species restricted to the Ruwenzori and Lake Kivu is anatomically closer to extant Asian forms of horseshoe bat and to ancient migrant stock than it is to any of the 20-odd more modern and widespread African horseshoe bat species, while a shrew specimen collected only once in the Itombwe Mountains is probably the most primitive and ancient of all 150 described African species.

boasts such a high level of biodiversity. Scientific opinion is that Nyungwe, along with the other forests of the Albertine Rift, was largely unaffected by the drying up of lowland areas during the last ice age, and thus became a refuge for forest plants and animals which have subsequently recolonised areas such as the Congo Basin. Nyungwe's faunal and floral diversity is a function not only of its antiquity, but also of the wide variation in elevation (between 1,600m and 2,950m above sea level), since many forest plants and animals live within very specific altitudinal bands.

Vast though it may be, Nyungwe today is but a fragment of what was once an uninterrupted forest belt covering the length of the Albertine Rift. The fragmentation of this forest started some 2,000 years ago, at the dawn of the Iron Age, when the first patches were cut down to make way for agriculture – it is thought, for instance, that the isolation of Uganda's Bwindi Forest from similar habitats on the Virunga Mountains occurred as recently as 500 years ago.

It is over the past 100 years that the forests of the Albertine Rift have suffered most heavily. The Gishwati Forest in northwest Rwanda, for instance, extended over an area comparable to Nyungwe's in the 1930s, but by 1989 it had been reduced to two separate blocks comprising 280km². Today it covers less than 15km² but, encouragingly, has recently been gazetted as part of Rwanda's newest national park (page 222). Nyungwe has fared well by comparison. It was first protected in 1933 as the 1,140km² Forêt Naturelle de Nyungwe, which was reduced in area by about 15% between 1958 and 1979, thanks to encroachment by local subsistence farmers, who also harvested it as a source of honey, bush meat, firewood and alluvial gold (an estimated 3,000 gold panners worked the Nyungwe watershed in the mid 1950s).

Nyungwe's extent has remained reasonably stable since 1984, when a co-ordinated forest protection plan was implemented under the Wildlife Conservation Society. This in turn led to the establishment of research projects by the likes of Amy Vedder (Angola colobus) and Beth Kaplin (L'Hoest's and blue monkeys), the creation of a vast network of tourist trails in the late 1980s, and the first reasonably comprehensive biodiversity survey as undertaken by Robert Dowsett and Françoise Dowsett-Lemaire in 1990. The tragic events of 1994 had little long-term effect on Nyungwe, which was formally accorded national park status in 2004.

FLORA The forest contains at least 200 tree species. The upper canopy in some areas reaches 50–60m in height, dominated by slow-growing hardwoods such as *Entandrophragma excelsum* (African mahogany), *Syzygium parvifolium* (water-berry), *Podocarpus milanjianus* (Mulanje cedar), *Newtonia buchananii* (forest newtonia) and *Albizia gummifera* (smooth-barked albizia). A much larger variety of trees makes up the mid-storey canopy, of which one of the most conspicuous is *Dichaetanthera corymbosa*, whose bright purple blooms break up the rich green textures of the forest.

Of the smaller trees, one of the most striking is the giant tree-fern *Cyathea mannania*, which grows to 5m tall, and is seen in large numbers along the ravines of the Isumo (Waterfall) Trail. Also very distinctive are the 2–3m-tall giant lobelias, more normally associated with montane moorland than forest, but common in Nyungwe, particularly along the roadside. Bamboo plants, a large type of grass, are dominant at higher altitudes in the rather inaccessible southeast of the forest, where their shoots are favoured by the rare and elusive owl-faced monkey. Nyungwe also harbours a huge variety of small flowering plants, including around 200 varieties of orchid and the wild begonia.

Within Nyungwe lie several swampy areas whose biology is quite distinct from that of the surrounding forest. The largest of these is the 13km² Kamiranzovu

Marsh, sweeping views of which are offered along the main road between Uwinka and the Gisakura – and which can also now be explored on the guided Kamiranzovu Marsh Trail. Formerly a favoured haunt of elephants, this open area is also rich in epiphytic orchids and harbours localised animals such as the Congo clawless otter and Grauer's rush warbler. The higher-altitude Uwasenkoko Marsh, bisected by the main road towards Huye/Butare, is dominated by the Ethiopian hagenia and protects a community of heather-like plants sharing unexpected affinities with the Nyika Plateau in distant Malawi.

MAMMALS The most prominent mammals in Nyungwe are primates, of which 13 species are present, including the common chimpanzee (see box, pages 172–3) and eight types of monkey (see below). In total, however, an estimated 86 different mammal species have been recorded in Nyungwe, including several rare forest inhabitants.

Of the so-called 'Big Five', elephant, buffalo and leopard were all common in pre-colonial times. Buffalo and elephant are now extinct. The last buffalo was shot in 1976. By contrast, between six and 20 elephants still lived in the forest as recently as 1990, but no spoor have been seen since November 1999, when the corpse of what was presumably Nyungwe's last elephant was found by rangers, cause of death unknown. Leopard, by contrast, are still present in small numbers, and regularly seen by local villagers, but as a tourist you'd be very lucky to encounter one.

A number of smaller predators occur in Nyungwe, including golden cat, wild cat, serval cat, side-striped jackal, three types of mongoose, Congo clawless otter, common and servaline genet, and common and palm civet. Most of these are highly secretive nocturnal creatures which are infrequently observed.

The largest antelope found in Nyungwe is the bushbuck. Three types of duiker also occur in the forest: black-fronted, yellow-backed and an endemic race of Weyns's duiker. Formerly common, all the forest's antelope species have suffered from intensive poaching as bush meat. Other large mammals include giant forest hog, bushpig, several types of squirrel (including the monkey-sized giant forest squirrel), Derby's anomalure (a large squirrel-like creature whose underarm flaps enable it to glide between trees) and the tree hyrax (a rarely seen guinea-pig-like animal whose blood-curdling nocturnal screeching is one of the characteristic sounds of the African forest).

Monkeys The primate species recorded in Nyungwe represent about 20–25% of the total number in Africa, a phenomenal figure which in East Africa is comparable only to Uganda's Kibale Forest. Furthermore, several of these primates are listed as 'Vulnerable' or 'Endangered' on the IUCN red list, and Nyungwe is almost certainly the main stronghold for at least two of them.

Disregarding the chimpanzee (see box, pages 172–3), the most celebrated of Nyungwe's primates is the **Ruwenzori colobus** (*Colobus angolensis ruwenzori*), a race of the more widespread Angola colobus restricted to the Albertine Rift. The Ruwenzori colobus is a highly arboreal and acrobatic leaf-eater, easily distinguished from any other primate found in Nyungwe by its contrasting black overall colour and snow-white whiskers, shoulders and tail tip. Although all colobus monkeys are very sociable, the ones in Nyungwe are unique in so far as they typically move in troops of several hundred animals. A semi-habituated troop of 350, resident in the forest around the campsite, is thought to be the largest troop of arboreal primates anywhere in Africa – elsewhere in the world, only the Chinese golden monkey moves in groups of a comparable number.

You'll hear them before you see them: from somewhere deep in the forest, an excited hooting, just one voice at first, then several, rising in volume and tempo and pitch to a frenzied unified crescendo, before stopping abruptly or fading away. Jane Goodall called it the 'pant-hoot' call, a kind of bonding ritual that allows any chimpanzees within earshot of each other to identify exactly who is around at any given moment, through the individual's unique vocal stylisation. To the human listener, this eruptive crescendo is one of the most spine-chilling and exciting sounds of the rainforest, and a strong indicator that visual contact with man's closest genetic relative is imminent.

It is, in large part, our close evolutionary kinship with chimpanzees that makes these sociable black-coated apes of the forest so enduringly fascinating. Humans, chimpanzees and bonobos (also known as pygmy chimpanzees) share more than 95% of their genetic code, and the three species are far more closely related to each other than they are to any other living creature, even gorillas. Superficial differences notwithstanding, the similarities between humans and chimps are consistently striking, not only in the skeletal structure and skull, but also in relation to the nervous system, the immune system, and in many behavioural aspects – bonobos, for instance, are the only animals other than humans to copulate in the missionary position.

Unlike most other primates, chimpanzees don't live in troops; instead they form extended communities of up to 100 individuals, which roam the forest in small socially mobile subgroups that often revolve around a few close family members such as brothers or a mother and daughter. Male chimps normally spend their entire life within the community into which they were born, whereas females are likely to migrate into a neighbouring community at some point after reaching adolescence. A high-ranking male will occasionally attempt to monopolise a female in oestrus, but the more normal state of sexual affairs in chimp society is non-hierarchical promiscuity. A young female in oestrus will generally mate with any male that takes her fancy, while older females tend to form close bonds with a few specific males, sometimes allowing themselves to be monopolised by a favoured suitor for a period, but never pairing off exclusively in the long term.

Within each community, one alpha male is normally recognised – though coalitions between two males, often a dominant and a submissive sibling, have often been recorded. The role of the alpha male, not fully understood, is evidently quite benevolent – chairman of the board rather than crusty tyrant. This is probably influenced by the alpha male's relatively limited reproductive advantages over his potential rivals, most of whom he will have known for his entire life. Other males in the community are generally supportive rather than competitive towards the alpha male, except for when a rival consciously contests the alpha position, which is far from being an everyday occurrence. One male in Tanzania's Mahale Mountains maintained an alpha status within his community for more than 15 years between 1979 and 1995!

Prior to the 1960s, it was always assumed that chimps were strict vegetarians. This notion was rocked when Jane Goodall, during her pioneering chimpanzee study in Tanzania's Gombe Stream, witnessed them hunting down a red colobus monkey, something that has since been discovered to be common behaviour, particularly during the dry season when other food sources are depleted. Over subsequent years, an average of 20 kills has been recorded in Gombe annually, with red colobus being the prey on more than half of these occasions, though young bushbuck, young bushpig and even infant chimps have also been victimised and eaten. The normal modus operandi is for four or five adult chimps to slowly encircle a colobus troop, then for another chimp to act as a decoy, creating deliberate confusion in the hope that it will drive the monkeys into the trap, or cause a mother to drop her baby.

Although chimp communities appear by-and-large to be stable and peaceful entities, intensive warfare has been known to erupt once each within the habituated communities of Mahale and Gombe. In Mahale, one of the two communities originally habituated by researchers in 1967 had exterminated the other by 1982. A similar thing happened in Gombe Stream in the 1970s, when the Kasekela community as originally habituated by Goodall divided into two discrete communities. The Kasekela and breakaway Kahama community coexisted alongside each other for some years. Then in 1974, Goodall returned to Gombe Stream after a break to discover that the Kasekela males were methodically persecuting their former community mates, isolating the Kahama males one by one, and tearing into them until they were dead or terminally wounded. By 1977, the Kahama community had vanished entirely.

Chimpanzees are essentially inhabitants of the western rainforest, but their range does extend into the extreme west of Tanzania, Rwanda and Uganda, whose combined population of perhaps 7,000 individuals is assigned to the race *P. t. schweinfurthii*. The Rwandan chimp population of fewer than 1,000 individuals is now largely confined to Nyungwe National Park (including a small community in the Cyamudongo Forest), but a small population still survives in the more northerly and badly degraded Gishwati Forest, where conservation plans are beginning to take shape after the area was gazetted as a national park in 2015. Although East Africa's chimps represent less than 3% of the global population, much of what is known about wild chimpanzee society and behaviour stems from the region, in particular the ongoing research projects initiated in Tanzania's Gombe Stream and Mahale Mountain National Parks back in the 1960s.

An interesting pattern that emerged from the parallel research projects in these two reserves, situated little more than 100km apart along the shore of Lake Tanganyika, is a variety of social and behavioural differences between their chimp populations. Of the plant species common to both national parks, for instance, as many as 40% of those utilised as a food source by chimps in the one reserve are not eaten by chimps in the other. In Gombe Stream, chimps appear to regard the palmnut as something of a delicacy, but while the same plants grow profusely in Mahale, the chimps there have yet to be recorded eating them. Likewise, the 'termite-fishing' behaviour first recorded by Jane Goodall at Gombe Stream in the 1960s has a parallel in Mahale, where the chimps are often seen 'fishing' for carpenter ants in the trees. But the Mahale chimps have never been recorded fishing for termites, while the Gombe chimps are not known to fish for carpenter ants. Mahale's chimps routinely groom each other with one hand while holding their other hands together above their heads – once again, behaviour that has never been noted at Gombe. More than any structural similarity, more even than any single quirk of chimpanzee behaviour, it is such striking cultural differences – the influence of nurture over nature if you like – that bring home our close genetic kinship with chimpanzees.

Most of the other monkeys in Nyungwe are guenons, the collective name for the taxonomically confusing *Cercopithecus* genus. Most guenons are arboreal forest-dwelling omnivores, noted for their colourful coats and the male's bright red or blue genitals. The most striking of Nyungwe's guenons is **L'Hoest's monkey** (*Cercopithecus l'hoesti*), a large and unusually terrestrial monkey, whose cryptic grey and red coat is offset by a bold white 'beard' which renders it unmistakable. As with the Ruwenzori colobus, L'Hoest's monkey, also known as mountain monkey, is more-or-less confined to the Albertine Rift, and is very scarce elsewhere in its restricted range. In Nyungwe, it is the most frequently encountered monkey, with troops of five–15 animals often seen along the roadside, within the forest, and even in the campsite.

Likely to be encountered along the road, around the campsite, and in the grounds of Nyungwe Forest Lodge, the **silver monkey** (*C. doggetti*), formerly considered to be a race of blue monkey (*C. mitis*), is similar in build and general appearance to L'Hoest's monkey, but it is plainer grey in colour with a conspicuous white line along the brow, and it lacks the diagnostic white beard. The silver monkey typically lives in small family parties, though solitary males are also often encountered in Nyungwe. Some sources list the closely related golden monkey (*C. kandti*) for Nyungwe, but this appears to be an error – though it is not impossible that a small population of this ARE inhabits the remote bamboo forests close to the Burundi border.

These southerly bamboo forests definitely provide refuge to the rare and secretive **owl-faced monkey** (*C. hamlyni*), another ARE whose modern range is restricted to a handful of montane forests. This thickset, plain-grey, pug-faced monkey was first recorded in the Nshili sector of Nyungwe as recently as 1992, and it remains the least-known of the reserve's monkeys – the 1999 WCS survey was unable to locate a single individual despite searching around Nshili for three days, but researchers in 2009 had better luck and managed 15 direct observations, though this was while covering an intensive 185km of transects. Locals also still see them occasionally, most often when they emerge from the depths of the bamboo forest to raid crops on the surrounding fields.

Another guenon whose status within Nyungwe is uncertain is the **red-tailed monkey** (*C. ascanius*), a small and highly active arboreal monkey most easily distinguished by its bright white nose. Generally associated with low-elevation forest, the red-faced monkey now faces extinction within Nyungwe owing to much of its habitat having been cleared for cultivation over recent decades. The solitary individual that hangs out with a colobus troop on the tea estate is presumably unlikely ever to find a breeding partner, though we have been told that a small but viable population of red-tailed monkeys survives on the fringes of the forest reserve near Banda.

Dent's monkey (*C. denti*), formerly considered to be a race of mona monkey (*C. mona*), is widespread within Nyungwe, and occurs at all elevations. It is distinguished from other monkeys in the forest by its contrasting black back and white belly, blue-white forehead, and yellowish ear tufts. It often moves with other guenons, and is mostly likely to be seen in the forest patch in the Gisakura Tea Estate or at Karamba, along the road to Uwinka not far from the Gisakura Guesthouse. Some sources incorrectly list the **crowned monkey** (*C. pogonias*) for Nyungwe, but this is a West African lowland species, considered by some to be a race of mona monkey.

Unlikely to be seen within the forest proper, the **vervet monkey** (*C. aethiops*) is a grizzled grey guenon of savannah and open woodland, with a distinctive black face mask. Probably the most numerous monkey in the world, the vervet is occasionally encountered on the forest verge and around the Gisakura Guesthouse, where it is often quite tame and regularly raids crops.

Another savannah monkey occasionally seen along the road through Nyungwe is the **olive baboon** (*Papio anubis*), a predominantly terrestrial primate which lives in large troops. After the chimpanzee, this is by far the largest and stockiest of the forest's primates, with a uniform dark olive coat and the canine snout and large teeth characteristic of all baboons. The olive baboon is very aggressive and, like the vervet monkey, it frequently raids crops.

Intermediate in size between the olive baboon and the various guenons, the **grey-cheeked mangabey** (*Cercocebus albigena*) is an arboreal monkey of the forest interior. Rather more spindly than any guenon, the grey-cheeked mangabey has a uniform dark-brown coat and grey-brown cape, and is renowned for its loud gobbling call. It lives in small troops, typically around ten animals, and is localised in Nyungwe because of its preference for lower altitudes.

Other primates In addition to chimpanzees and monkeys, Nyungwe harbours four types of prosimian, small nocturnal primates more closely related to the lemurs of Madagascar than to any other primates of the African mainland. These are three species of **bushbaby** or galago (a group of tiny, hyperactive wide-eyed insectivores) and the sloth-like **potto**. All are very unlikely to be encountered by tourists.

BIRDS Nyungwe is probably the single most important birdwatching destination in Rwanda, with 310 bird species recorded, of which the majority are forest specialists. This includes 27 Albertine Rift Endemics, of which three (Albertine owlet, red-collared babbler and Rockefeller's sunbird) are unrecorded elsewhere on the eastern side of the Albertine Rift. Birdwatching in Nyungwe can be rather frustrating, since the vegetation is thick and many birds tend to stick to the canopy, but almost everything you do see ranks as a good sighting.

You don't have to be an ardent birdwatcher to appreciate some of Nyungwe's birds. Most people, for instance, will do a double-take when they first spot a great blue turaco, a chicken-sized bird with garish blue, green and yellow feathers, often seen gliding between the trees along the main road. Another real gem is the paradise flycatcher, a long-tailed blue, orange and (sometimes) white bird often seen around Gisakura Guesthouse. Other birds impress with their bizarre appearance – the gigantic forest hornbills, for instance, whose wailing vocalisations are almost as comical as their ungainly bills and heavy-winged flight. And, when tracking through the forest undergrowth, watch out for the red-throated alethe, a very localised bird with a distinctive blue-white eyebrow. The alethe habitually follows colobus troops to eat the insects they disturb, and based on our experience it sees humans as merely another large mammal, often perching within a few inches!

The priorities of more serious birdwatchers will depend to some extent on their experience elsewhere in Africa. It is difficult to imagine, for instance, that a first-time visitor to the continent will get as excited about a drab Chubb's cisticola as they will when they first see a paradise flycatcher or green pigeon. For somebody coming from southern Africa, at least half of what they see will be new to them, with a total of about 60 relatively widespread East African forest specials headed by the likes of great blue turaco, Ross's turaco, red-breasted sparrowhawk and white-headed wood-hoopoe.

From an East African perspective, however, it is the Albertine Rift Endemics that are the most alluring. Depending on your level of expertise, you could

CHAMELEONS

Common and widespread in Rwanda, but not easily seen unless they are actively searched for, chameleons are arguably the most intriguing of African reptiles. True chameleons of the family Chamaeleontidae are confined to the Old World, with the most important centre of speciation being the island of Madagascar, to which about half of the world's 130 described species are endemic. Another two species of chameleon occur in each of Asia and Europe, while the remainder are distributed across mainland Africa, with at least eight species recorded from Rwanda, most of which are forest species associated with Nyungwe National Park.

Chameleons are best known for their capacity to change colour, a trait that is often exaggerated in popular literature, and which is generally influenced by mood more than the colour of the background. Some chameleons are more adept at changing colour than others, the most variable being the common chameleon *Chamaeleo chamaeleon* of the Mediterranean region, with more than 100 colour and pattern variations recorded. Many African chameleons are typically green in colour but will gradually take on a browner hue when they descend from the foliage in more exposed terrain, for instance while crossing a road. Several change colour and pattern far more dramatically when they feel threatened or are confronted by a rival of the same species. Different chameleon species also vary greatly in size, with the largest being Oustalet's chameleon of Madagascar, known to reach a length of almost 80cm.

A remarkable physiological feature common to all true chameleons is their protuberant round eyes, which offer a potential 180° vision on both sides and are able to swivel around independently of each other. Only when one of them isolates a suitably juicy-looking insect will the two eyes focus in the same direction as the chameleon stalks slowly forward until it is close enough to use the other unique weapon in its armoury. This is its sticky-tipped tongue, which is typically about

reasonably hope to tick off half of these over a few days in the forest. Of the 27 avian AREs found in Nyungwe National Park, the following are reasonably common: handsome francolin, Ruwenzori turaco, red-faced woodland warbler, collared apalis, mountain masked apalis, yellow-eyed black flycatcher, Ruwenzori batis, stripe-breasted tit, regal sunbird, blue-headed sunbird, purple-breasted sunbird, dusky crimsonwing and strange weaver. Also common but rather more localised, Grauer's rush warbler and red-collared mountain babbler are respectively confined to Kamiranzovu Swamp and Mount Bigugu. The nocturnal Ruwenzori nightjar and secretive creeper-loving Grauer's warbler are both common but difficult to observe. Short-tailed warbler, Shelley's crimsonwing, red-throated alethe, Kungwe apalis, Archer's robin-chat, Kivu ground thrush, dwarf honeyguide and Albertine owlet are uncommon, and Rockefeller's sunbird is very rare.

The guides at Nyungwe are improving and some are excellent, but others have only limited knowledge. For this reason, you will be highly dependent on a field guide, and without a great amount of advance research you are bound to struggle to identify every bird that you glimpse. Given the above, relict forest patches and the road verge are often more productive than the forest interior, since you'll get clearer views of what you do see.

OTHER CREATURES While monkeys and to a lesser extent birds tend to attract the most attention, Nyungwe's fauna also includes a large number of smaller animals.

the same length as its body and remains coiled up within its mouth most of the time, to be unleashed in a sudden, blink-and-you'll-miss-it lunge to zap a selected item of prey. In addition to their unique eyes and tongues, many chameleons are adorned with an array of facial casques, flaps, horns and crests that enhance their already somewhat fearsome prehistoric appearance.

In Rwanda, you're most likely to come across a chameleon by chance when it is crossing a road, in which case it should be easy to take a closer look at it, since most chameleons move painfully slowly and deliberately. Chameleons are also often seen on night game drives, when their ghostly nocturnal colouring shows up clearly under a spotlight – as well as making it pretty clear why these strange creatures are regarded with both fear and awe in many local African cultures. More actively, you could ask your guide if they know where to find a chameleon – a few individuals will be resident in most lodge grounds.

The flap-necked chameleon *Chamaeleo delepis* is probably the most regularly observed species of savannah and woodland habitats in East Africa. Often seen crossing roads, the flap-necked chameleon is generally around 15cm long and bright green in colour with few distinctive markings, but individuals might be up to 30cm in length and will turn tan or brown under the right conditions.

Characteristic of East African montane forests, the horned chameleons form a closely allied species cluster of some taxonomic uncertainty. They are typically darker than the savannah chameleons and, significantly, the males of all taxa within this cluster are distinguished by up to three nasal horns that project forward from their face. In Rwanda, the cluster is represented by the Ruwenzori three-horned chameleon *C. johnstoni*, a range-restricted ARE that can grow up to 30cm long and is reasonably common in Nyungwe National Park, where it supplements a diet of insects with more substantial fare such as small lizards.

With only 12 species recorded, snakes are relatively poorly represented, due to the chilly climate – probably good news for most visitors – but colourful lizards are often seen on the rocks, and at least five species of chameleon occur in the forest. Nyungwe also harbours more than 100 different types of colourful butterfly, including 40 regional endemics. Look out, too, for the outsized beetles and bugs that are characteristic of all tropical forests. Equally remarkable, but only to be admired at a distance of a metre or so, are the vast columns of army ants that move across the forest trails – step on one of these columns, and you'll know all about it, as these guys can bite!

FURTHER INFORMATION   A basic fact-sheet and map of the forest is available from any RDB office (though don't be surprised if they've run out), and an excellent book entitled *A Trail Guide for Rwanda's Nyungwe National Park* is sold for around Rfr7,000. here as well. A useful website about the park, though somewhat academic in tone, is **w** bit.ly/2FUVJMj, maintained by the Antioch University of New England. Similar content can be found on the RDB website **w** rwandatourism.com.

The combination of a good East African field guide and the *Birds of Rwanda: An Atlas and Handbook* (page 363) should be all that birdwatchers need in order to come to terms with the forest's avifauna. A more esoteric publication, of interest primarily to researchers, is the WCS Working Paper *Biodiversity Surveys of the Nyungwe Forest Reserve in Southwest Rwanda* (Plumptre, Andrew, 2002), which can (among others) be downloaded from **w** programs.wcs.org/Rwanda.

GETTING THERE AND AWAY

Unless you have private transport, the easiest way to visit the park is as part of an organised tour or in a 4x4 with driver hired in Kigali. Either option is quite costly and we would advise a minimum of two nights, better three, to get the most from a visit. The drive takes about 4–5 hours from Kigali, 2–3 hours from Huye/Butare, and less than 1 hour from Rusizi/Cyangugu.

It is also possible to get to the forest using the regular midibuses that connect Huye to Rusizi, dropping off either at Kitabi, Uwinka or Gisakura, depending on whether you plan to camp or stay at one of the lodges. However, it must be emphasised that exploring the park is difficult without private transport. Furthermore, when you decide to leave, most public transport will be full when it comes past; so you'd need either to try hitching a lift or to ask the people at reception to phone through to a minibus company in Huye or Rusizi to arrange for a seat to be reserved for you (at full fare). That said, it's only 3km from Gisakura (and 4.5km from Gisakura Guesthouse) to the junction village of Buhinga where the newly completed road to Karongi/Kibuye begins. This road has a decent amount of traffic on it and a fair few villages in which public transport makes stops (meaning potentially open seats), so you might have an easier time picking up transport along this route without advance arrangement.

There has long been talk that the section of the main road between Huye and Rusizi that passes through Nyungwe will be closed to non-touristic traffic – including all public transport – with the completion of the Karongi–Rusizi road, but there are no signs that such a move is imminent.

WHERE TO STAY AND EAT   *Map, page 166*

LUXURY

One&Only Nyungwe House (22 rooms) ✤ S 02°26.877, E 029°05.205; ☎ +44 800 169 0530 (UK), +1 855 271 9494 (US); e reservations@ oneandonlyresorts.com; w oneandonlyresorts. com. Though already opulent in its previous incarnation as the Nyungwe Forest Lodge, One&Only Resorts put their uber-luxurious stamp on things when they took it over in 2017, & few would argue with our rating this among the top lodges in the country. It has a fantastic setting within the Gisakura Tea Estate, right on the forested park boundary, where patches of relict forest support a semi-resident troop of silver monkeys along with some prodigious birdlife, & you might well also hear the thrilling pant-hoot call of chimpanzees. The large airy dining & sitting area combines clean modern lines with attractive ethnic décor & tall windows offering views across neat rows of tea bushes to the forest gallery. Accommodation is in spacious state-of-the-art wooden chalets with king-size beds, AC, fireplace, flatscreen satellite TV, bathroom with a welcome hot tub & shower, & a balcony only metres from the forest edge. Expect excellent meals & service; other facilities include a stunning heated infinity pool staring into the forest, a good spa, mountain bikes & a gift boutique. Packed b/fasts & lunches can be arranged for those on activities in the forest. The lodge is situated about 2km from the main Rusizi road, along a dirt road signposted to the right (coming from Huye) between the junction to Gisakura Tea Estate & the Gisakura Guesthouse. *From US$780 dbl FB.*

UPMARKET

Nyungwe Top View Hill Hotel (12 rooms) m 078 710 9335; e nyungwetopview@ gmail.com; w nyungwehotel.com. This welcoming & well-managed hotel bridges the price & quality gap between the plush Nyungwe Hse & the budget options listed opposite. Situated about 1km from Gisakura Village along a newly surfaced access road, it is set on an isolated hilltop with stunning panoramic views eastward over the forest & west to Lake Kivu. Accommodation is in stone chalets with a king-size bed, en-suite bathroom with hot combination shower/tub, large sitting room with fireplace, & a balcony with lake or forest view. The common area (with Wi-Fi) is a striking circular 2-storey building with a wide balcony on the 1st floor, *imigongo* walls, & a tall thatched roof in traditional style. The décor is a touch bare & lets it down slightly, but that's a small quibble at the price. *US$135/200/300 sgl/dbl/trpl B&B, with 3-course lunches & dinners at US$15 each.*

MODERATE

🏠 EAR Gisakura Visitors
Centre (4 rooms) m 078 441 7866/827 8766; e gisakuravisitors16@yahoo.com. Set in a patch of forest about 400m from the main road at the south end of Gisakura, this quiet & budget-friendly guesthouse (formerly the Nyungwe Eagle's Nest, which has since moved to an inferior location up the road) has been run by the Anglican Church since 2016. The neat & trim rooms are set in en-suite cottages a few steps from the central restaurant, where meals are available for around Rfr3,000. There are plans for a large expansion afoot, of 20 more rooms, possibly during the lifespan of this edition. Camping is also available at Rfr10,000/tent. No alcohol. *Rfr25,000/30,000 sgl/dbl.*

🏠 Gisakura Guesthouse (12 rooms)
✪ S 02°26.281, E 029°05.548, 1,931m; m 078 867 5051/853 0716, 072 853 0716; e ghnyungwe@yahoo.com/ghgisakura@ gmail.com; w gisakuraguesthouserw.com. Once the only place to stay at Nyungwe, this former government guesthouse, now privately managed, stands 2km outside the forest close to the Gisakura Tea Estate. Although it lies 18km from Uwinka, it has a convenient location for the excellent Isumo Trail & for visits to the colobus troop on the Gisakura Tea Estate. It's less convenient now that the Gisakura reception centre has moved 2.5km down the road, but chimp-tracking guides can still meet you here on request (though you will still need private transport to get to the starting point for the actual tracking). The Wildlife Conservation Society (w *wcs.org*) now has offices in the former reception centre. Vervet monkeys occasionally pass through the grounds, & a fair variety of birds are present in the small patch of forest in front of the guesthouse. It serves good meals for Rfr8,000 & a selection of wine, beers & sodas, & there's now Wi-Fi in the

restaurant as well. The one large flaw is that it seems chronically overpriced for what you get: a bone-bare guesthouse room using communal showers & toilets. Given the newer, cheaper guesthouses nearby & the relocation of the park reception, it's no longer the only (or indeed, best) option for travellers without private transport. *US$35/55/75 sgl/dbl or twin/trpl; all rates B&B.*

🏠 Nyungwe Nziza Lodge m 078 830
6080/848 4849; e info@goldenmonkeyhotel. com; w goldenmonkeyhotel.com. Situated on a hillside right at the park entrance in Kitabi, this new lodge was still under construction when we passed through. It's under the same ownership as the Golden Monkey Hotel in Nyamagabe (page 164), so you can expect a similar standard of accommodation when it opens, hopefully during the lifespan of this edition. *Rates in Nyamagabe are US$30/37/42 sgl/twin/dbl.*

BUDGET

🏠 Gisakura Family Hostel (6 rooms)
m 078 820 3748; e moniquemubyeyi@gmail. com. 2 doors up from Keza Nyungwe, this homely guesthouse opened in 2017 & offers basic & bright rooms, most of which come with individual bathrooms that are not en suite; all have mosquito nets. Meals are also available at Rfr3,000–4,000. *Rfr30,000/45,000 dbl/trpl.*

🏠 KCCEM Guesthouse (25 rooms) m 078
494 3252/350 6432; e booking@kccem.ac.rw; w kccem.ac.rw. The Kitabi College of Conservation & Environmental Management, set next to the Kitabi reception centre on the eastern park boundary, about 45mins' drive from Uwinka & twice as far from Gisakura, operates a reasonably priced guesthouse & canteen. The small but clean rooms are arranged in 6 blocks, & come with en-suite toilet & hot shower, & pretty views over a valley covered in tea plantations & forest. Reservations are not usually required, but it sometimes hosts training & other events that use all of the rooms, so it is advisable to call ahead. The canteen charges Rfr3,000 for lunch or dinner & Rfr2,000 for b/fast. Despite being so close to the reception centre, it can be surprisingly tricky to find: there's an unmarked footpath from the reception centre, & the vehicle turn-off (signed for Kitabi Tea Company) is 350m to the east – follow this for another 550m to reach the entrance gate. *Rooms Rfr12,000/18,000/20,000/25,000 sgl/dbl/twin/trpl.*

Kitabi Eco-Center (3 rooms) m 078 726 0016; e kitabiecocenter@gmail.com; w kitabiecocenter.com. Set on a hilltop 300m from the main road, just opposite the Kitabi reception centre, this admirable new project offers uniquely rustic accommodation with views over both the forest & tea plantations in sizeable thatched huts built in the style of the king's palace at Nyanza, and space for campers (with 2- & 4-person tents for hire, including sleeping bag, sleeping pad, & pillow). The thatched palaces come with queen beds & a traditional fireplace, & if you're looking for an authentic cultural experience, there's everything from beekeeping tours to Intore dances on offer. B/fast, lunch & dinner are available at Rfr2,000/4,000/5,000, & on Fri nights they fire up the pizza oven. Dinners are eaten communally, followed by drinks around the central campfire. *US$15/25 sgl/dbl camping with own tent; US$20/30 sgl/dbl camping with their tent; US$30/40 sgl/dbl prince's palace; US$50/75/100 sgl/dbl/quad king's palace.*

Uwinka Campsite ✪ S 02°28.696, E 029°12.007, 2,442m; m 078 974 6759/072 606 5744. Set in the heart of the forest, yet only a couple of hundred metres from the main road, the campsite here has a perfect (albeit rather chilly) location on a high ridge, with 2 levels of thatch-roofed tent platforms & fire pits a short walk from the visitors' centre. Tents (with sleeping bag, mat, & pillow) are available for Rfr10,000/night, should you not have your own. The campsite here is also the most convenient base for hikes, particularly if you have no vehicle, as the trailhead for the coloured Uwinka Trails, for tracking the 350-strong troop of colobus, & for the Canopy Walk. It also offers good monkey viewing, with L'Hoest's & silver monkeys the most regular visitors, & a variety of forest birds is present. The main road adjacent to the campsite is also worth exploring, for the great views & variety of birds. There's a little canteen here serving up drinks, snacks & meals (*Rfr3,000*) during the day, so you don't have to worry as much about packing food, but you'd do well to bring sufficient warm clothing to offset the chilly night temperatures at high altitude. See box, page 168, for rates.

SHOESTRING

Banda Community Campsite (2 rooms) m 078 512 0737/843 6763; e bandacamp@yahoo. fr; w bandacommunity.blogspot.com. Set in a grassy compound in the remote village of Banda, the impressively built thatch huts here are built in the same style as the king's palace at Nyanza, & it's possible to either stay in one of these or pitch your own tent. Village tours, weaving, banana-beer making, dance performances, & more are all on the agenda, & they do traditional meals at request. It's about a 2hr walk north from Uwinka, or less in a 4x4, but the road is in poor shape. Costs are nominal. Also in Banda village, the Kageno Eco-Lodge (e harejaphet@yahoo.fr; w kageno.org) remains under construction, but simple rooms can be arranged at US$75pp FB. Call for rates.

Keza Nyungwe (6 rooms) m 078 339 6666; e nyirijecla@gmail.com. Just 400m from the ranger post at the base of the hill in Gisakura Village, the rooms here are tiny & basic, but they're acceptably clean & come with mosquito nets. Rather illogically, it's the same price for an en-suite double as it is for a twin using shared ablutions, but however you slice it, it's the cheapest option on this side of the park. Meals in the attached restaurant start at Rfr2,000. *US$25 dbl.*

TRAILS AND ACTIVITIES

A varied selection of walking possibilities and other excursions is available within Nyungwe. Visitors with a private vehicle, sufficient interest, and deep pockets could easily keep themselves busy for a week without significantly retracing their steps. The options for travellers without private transport are more limited, and depend greatly on which accommodation option they choose. All forest trails are steep and often very slippery, so dress accordingly. Jeans, a thick shirt and good hiking shoes are the ideal outfit. A waterproof jacket is useful too, especially during the rainy season.

Uwinka Reception Centre is the trailhead for the Canopy Walkway and several other trails, and is a good site for primate-and birdwatching. There are also some good walking options out of Gisakura Reception Centre, while one trail runs within walking distance of the Kitabi Reception Centre. All reception centres are open 07.00–17.00 daily. Chimp tracking is best booked ahead, through either your tour operator, the RDB head office (✆ 252 580388; e reservation@rwandatourism. com), or the Rwandan government's new Irembo web portal (w irembo.gov.rw/rolportal/web/rdb/tourist-permit). Other activities can be arranged on the spot.

Unguided exploration of the park is forbidden, and a fee is charged for all activities (see box, page 168). All activities leave at fixed times. Most leave at 09.00, but in theory there are further departures for medium-length hikes at 13.00 and for shorter hikes at 11.00, 13.00 and 15.00. Exceptions are dedicated birding excursions, which usually leave at 06.00 or 14.00 to coincide with the most productive birding hours, and the Canopy Walkway Trail, which leaves at 08.00, 10.00, 13.00 and 15.00. In practice, don't bank on doing any activities in the afternoon, unless you're prepared to do them in the rain.

The trails and activities on the following pages are covered from east to west, starting with the Ngabwe Trail near Kitabi Entrance Gate on the road from Huye and ending with chimpanzee tracking, which normally takes place in the Cyamudongo Forest, a western annexe to the main national park.

NGABWE TRAIL (*4.7km, 3hrs, moderate*) Set on the slopes of Ngabwe near the park's eastern boundary, this circular trail is the only straightforward option open to people staying at the KCCEM Guesthouse or Kitabi Eco-Centre without their own transport, since the trailhead lies about 200m down a side road on the left of the main road only 3km past Kitabi Entrance Gate. The trail passes through a wide variety of vegetation zones over a relatively short distance, including patches of mature forest rich in strangler figs, as well as shrubbier heath communities, and there is a spectacular camping/picnic site with a toilet and benches at the summit. L'Hoest's, silver and colobus monkeys are common here, while mangabey, chimpanzee and black-fronted duiker are seen occasionally. The trail, which can be extended to an 8-hour walk through Kitabi Tea Plantation, ends 1.2km closer to the gate than where it starts.

BIGUGU TRAIL (*6.7km in either direction, 6hrs, difficult*) Aimed squarely at the 'because it's there' fraternity, the steep and slippery 7km trail leads to the 2,950m Bigugu Peak, which is the highest point in Nyungwe National Park. Suitable only for reasonably fit walkers, the trail starts about 4km from Uwinka along the Huye/Butare Road (the trailhead is clearly marked). Birders come here to see the localised red-collared mountain babbler, but the area also boasts some wonderful wildflowers, ranging from red-hot pokers and orchids to giant lobelias.

BIRDING AND MANGABEY TRACKING ON THE RANGIRO ROAD The dirt road to Rangiro, which leaves the main tar road about 1km east of Uwinka, is regarded as the best excursion for dedicated birdwatchers. This is because the road passes through both high- and low-elevation forest within a relatively short distance, and affords good views into the canopy in several places. The road is also the only reliable place to see grey-cheeked mangabey, since a habituated troop lives in a forest patch 5–10km past the junction with the main road. The troop is usually monitored by researchers on Monday and Friday, the best days to visit. L'Hoest's, silver and colobus monkeys are also often seen in this area. A 4x4 vehicle is essential to explore this area, and a visit will generally be charged as a specialist birding or primate activity.

The Nile is the world's longest river, flowing for more than 6,650km (4,130 miles) from its most remote headwaters in Burundi and Rwanda to the delta formed as it enters the Mediterranean in Egypt. Its vast drainage basin occupies more than 10% of the African mainland and includes portions of ten countries: Tanzania, Burundi, Rwanda, the DRC, Kenya, Uganda, Ethiopia, Sudan, South Sudan and Egypt. While passing through South Sudan, the Nile also feeds the 5.5 million hectare Sudd or Bar-el-Jebel, the world's most expansive wetland system.

A feature of the Nile Basin is a marked decrease in precipitation as it runs further northward. In the East African lakes region and Ethiopian Highlands, mean annual rainfall figures are typically in excess of 1,000mm. Rainfall in south and central Sudan varies from 250mm to 500mm annually, except in the Sudd (900mm), while in the deserts north of Khartoum the annual rainfall is little more than 100mm, dropping to 25mm in the south of Egypt, then increasing to around 200mm closer to the Mediterranean.

The Nile has served as the lifeblood of Egyptian agriculture for millennia, carrying not only water, but also silt, from the fertile tropics into the sandy expanses of the Sahara. Indeed, it is widely believed that the very first agricultural societies arose on the floodplain of the Egyptian Nile, and so, certainly, did the earliest and most enduring of all human civilisations. The antiquity of the name Nile, which simply means river valley, is reflected in the Ancient Greek (Nelios), Semetic (Nahal) and Latin (Nilus).

Over the past 50 years, several hydro-electric dams have been built along the Nile, notably the Aswan Dam in Egypt and the Owen Falls Dam in Uganda. The Aswan Dam doesn't merely provide hydro-electric power, it also supplies water for various irrigation schemes, and protects crops downriver from destruction by heavy flooding. Built in 1963, the dam wall rises 110m above the river and is almost 4km long, producing up to 2,100 megawatts and forming the 450km-long Lake Nasser. The construction of the Aswan Dam enforced the resettlement of 90,000 Nubians, while the Temple of Abu Simbel, built 3,200 ago for the Pharaoh Rameses II, had to be relocated 65m higher.

The waterway plays a major role in transportation, especially in parts of the Sudans between May and November, when transportation of goods and people is not possible by road due to the floods. Like other rivers and lakes, the Nile provides a variety of fish as food. And its importance for conservation is difficult to overstate. The Sudd alone supports more than half the global populations of Nile lechwe and shoebill (more than 6,000), together with astonishing numbers of other water-associated birds – aerial surveys undertaken between 1979 and 1982

UWINKA TRAILS AND CANOPY WALK Uwinka Reception Centre forms the trailhead for the park's most extensive network of trails, as well as being the site of a worthwhile Interpretation Centre and Canopy Walkway developed by USAID. The Uwinka Trails are a relict of the earliest attempt to develop tourism at Nyungwe in the late 1980s, and each of the six routes was designated by a colour until a new set of names was adopted – both names are provided in the table on page 185. The footpaths are all well maintained and clearly marked, but don't underestimate the steepness of the slopes or – after rain – the muddy conditions, which can be fairly tough going at this high altitude.

counted an estimated 1.7 million glossy ibis, 370,000 marabou stork, 350,000 open-billed stork, 175,000 cattle egret and 150,000 spur-winged goose.

The Nile has two major sources, often referred to as the White and Blue Nile, which flow respectively from Lake Victoria near Jinja and from Lake Tana in Ethiopia. The stretch of the White Nile that flows through southern Uganda is today known as the Victoria Nile (it was formerly called Kiira locally). From Jinja, it runs northward through the swampy Lake Kyoga, before veering west to descend into the Rift Valley over Murchison Falls and empty into Lake Albert. The Albert Nile flows from the northern tip of Lake Albert to enter South Sudan at Nimule, passing through the Sudd before it merges with the Blue Nile at the Sudanese capital of Khartoum, more than 3,000km from Lake Victoria.

The discovery of the source of the Blue Nile on Lake Tana is often accredited to the 18th-century Scots explorer James Bruce. In fact, its approximate (if not exact) location was almost certainly known to the ancients. The Old Testament mentions that the Ghion (Nile) 'compasseth the whole land of Ethiopia', evidently in reference to the arcing course followed by the river along the approximate southern boundary of Ethiopia's ancient Axumite Empire. There are, too, strong similarities in the design of the papyrus 'tankwa' used on Lake Tana to this day and the papyrus boats depicted in ancient Egyptian paintings. Furthermore, the main river feeding Lake Tana rises at a spring known locally as Abay Minch (literally 'Nile Fountain'), a site held sacred by Ethiopian Christians, whose links with the Egyptian Coptic Church date to the 4th century AD. Bruce's claim is further undermined by the Portuguese stone bridge, built circa 1620, which crosses the Nile a few hundred metres downstream of the Blue Nile Falls and only 30km from the Lake Tana outlet.

By contrast, the source of the White Nile was for centuries one of the world's great unsolved mysteries. The Roman emperor Nero once sent an expedition south from Khartoum to search for it, but it was forced to turn back at the edge of the Sudd. In 1862, Speke correctly identified Ripon Falls as the source of the Nile, a theory confirmed by Stanley in 1875. Only as recently as 1937, however, did the German explorer Burkhart Waldecker locate the most remote of the Nile's headwaters in Burundi: a hillside spring known as Kasumo which forms the source of the Ruvyironza River, a tributary of the 690km-long Kagera, the most important river to flow into Lake Victoria. Remarkably, however, the absolute location of the most remote source of the Nile still remains up for grabs in the early 21st century – as you can see in the box on page 184.

Based partially on text kindly supplied by Laura Sserunjogi, of the Source of the Nile Gardens in Jinja, Uganda.

The most popular hike at Uwinka is now the short Igishigishigi Trail, site of a canopy walkway – similar to the famous one in Ghana's Kakum National Park – that opened in October 2010. Suspended between higher slopes and giant trees about 1km from Uwinka, the metallic walkway is almost 200m long, with a maximum height of around 40m, and it offers superb bird's-eye views into and over a steep streambed lined with tall trees and ferns. It can feel quite unstable, especially in windy weather, and may be unsuitable to those with a poor head for heights.

The slopes below Uwinka pass through the territory of a habituated troop of 300-plus colobus monkeys, and these might easily be seen on any of the trails.

ASCEND THE NILE

On 19 September 2005, three men set out to make a complete ascent of the Nile from the sea to the source.

Known as the Ascend the Nile Expedition, Neil McGrigor, Cam McLeay and Garth McIntyre took to the water in Rashid in Egypt and travelled in tiny inflatable boats ('Zap Cats'), just 4m long and with outboard engines, for the entire length of the river, over 6,700km. Their journey took them through five challenging countries: Egypt, Sudan, Uganda, Tanzania and finally Rwanda.

The expedition was self-sufficient but did receive some support from Fortnum & Mason, the famous store based in London's Piccadilly, which had previously supplied Stanley's 1875 expedition with goodies such as thick-cut marmalade, humbugs and sardines. Hampers were delivered to the team throughout their journey.

They faced enormous difficulties on the way, not least ascending the many river rapids, facing crocodiles head on and avoiding numerous pods of hippos. The weather ranged from searing heat to continuous rain, while the river changed from a wide blue delta in Egypt to a muddy puddle at its source in Rwanda.

Apprehension and frustration turned to real fear and sorrow when, in November 2005, the men came under attack from rebels in Uganda. A close friend of the team was killed and the remaining members were injured. But the team decided to continue to their goal.

On 3 March 2006, they resumed, crossing Lake Victoria and reaching the border of Tanzania and Rwanda. It was this part of the journey that offered unexpected challenges: larger-than-predicted rapids, cold nights and achingly slow progress on foot through the Nyungwe Forest as the team edged ever closer to the Nile's new source that they were so determined to find.

Finally, on 31 March 2006, they reached their goal at the headwater of the Rukarara River, a tributary of the Akagera which in turn drains into Lake Victoria. With their patient guides, the team planted a flag to mark the spot on the slopes of Mount Bigugu and the celebrations began. News of the expedition and its findings made its way across the world, reaching as far as China and Russia.

Using research and modern navigation equipment, they have been able to demonstrate that they discovered another, longer source than that pinpointed by Dr Kandt in 1898. Kandt had not had the benefit of either the maps drawn by the Belgians in 1937 or the Global Positioning System from which the team had remeasured the entire length of the Nile – which turns out to be some 107km longer than previously recorded! It's possible to walk to the source; page 187.

The co-ordinates of the new longest source, deep in Rwanda's Nyungwe Forest, are: Latitude S 02°16'055.962"; Longitude E 29°19'052.470"; Elevation 2,428m.

However, if you want to seek the colobus actively on the Uwinka Trails, you will need to pay extra for a dedicated primate visit. In addition to colobus, you can reasonably expect to see some primates along any of the trails, as well as a good variety of forest birds, though the latter requires patience and regular stops where there are open views into the canopy. The Umugote Trail is regarded as especially

New name	Old name	Length & grading	Meaning
Imbaraga Trail	Red trail	9.8km, 6hrs, difficult	Imbaraga means strength, reflecting how difficult the trail is
Umuyove Trail	Pink trail	5.5km, 3½hrs, moderate	Umuyove is a mahogany, many large specimens of which are seen on this trail
Umugote Trail	Blue trail	3.6km, 3hrs, moderate	Umugote is a Syzygium tree, which is common on this trail
Igishigishigi Trail	Green trail	2.4km, 1½hrs, easy	Igishigishigi means a tree fern, a common plant along this trail, which also leads to the Canopy Walkway
Buhoro Trail	Grey trail	2km, 1½hrs, easy	Buhoro means slow, and this short trail is an easy slow walk
Irebero Trail	Yellow trail	3.6km, 3hrs, moderate	Irebero means a viewpoint, and there are some magnificent ones on this trail

good for primates and birds, while the Imbaraga Trail passes four waterfalls and also sometimes offers a seasonal opportunity to see chimpanzees.

Dedicated birdwatchers, rather than following the trails deep into the forest, are advised to explore the main road close to Uwinka, which offers some great views into the canopy and the likelihood of a greater variety of birds than from anywhere within the forest. Birding here will be charged as a birding activity rather than a standard trail, so make sure you ask for a specialist bird guide. About 500m east of Uwinka, the road offers some stunning views over the forested valleys, and passes a stand of giant lobelias.

KAMIRANZOVU MARSH TRAIL (*6km, 3hrs, moderate*) This botanically exciting trail leads from the forested main road downhill to the relatively low-lying Kamiranzovu Marsh, which is the park's largest wetland habitat, set within a caldera-like depression. It was the favoured haunt of Nyungwe's elephants before they became extinct, and it remains fabulously rich in orchids, particularly during the rainy season, and localised swamp-associated birds such as Grauer's rush warbler and Albertine owlet (the latter is most likely to be seen on a nocturnal visit, with a guide who has a recording of its call).

KARAMBA BIRDING TRAIL (*4km, 3hrs, easy*) One of the easiest walks in Nyungwe, and the best trail for birdwatching, this circular trail ascends through a relatively flat and open area to a 360° viewpoint. The absence of big trees is largely because of human disturbance, first as a gold mine and market, then as a quarry for road-building material, and most recently as an army camp. The footpath is on quartzite rock, so it's less muddy than other trails at Nyungwe, but it forms a stream after rain. About 500m into the walk, there is a large hole offering a perfect cutaway view of all rainforest strata. Plants here include white *Satyrium* orchids and giant tree ferns normally seen in moist, rainforest valleys. At the viewpoint is a bench where you can look out for birds and monkeys. Karamba area is the best part of Nyungwe for Dent's monkey, and the large troop that lives here sometimes keeps company with red-tailed monkeys.

GISAKURA TEA ESTATE Arguably the most rewarding activity in Nyungwe for those with limited time, funds and/or mobility – even if it will be charged as a primate or birding excursion – is a relict forest patch situated in the Gisakura Tea Estate only 20 minutes' walk from either the Gisakura Reception Centre or Gisakura Guesthouse. The forest here supports a very habituated troop of around 40–50 Ruwenzori colobus monkey, and the relatively small territory makes them easy to locate and to photograph.

The forest patch in the tea estate also seems to serve as a refuge for lone males of various other primate species, possibly individuals that were rejected by their original troop and now hang around with the colobus troop. Over the course of researching seven editions of this guide we have always seen at least one and sometimes three other monkey species in the forest patch (most often red-tailed monkey but also sometimes silver, Dent's and red-tailed/Dent's hybrids).

Particularly in the early morning, the forest here is an excellent birdwatching site, since it lies in a ravine and is encircled by a road, making it easy to see deep into the canopy. Most of what you see are forest fringe or woodland species (as opposed to forest interior birds), but numerically this proved to be the most rewarding spot in Nyungwe, with some 40 species identified in an hour, notably black-throated apalis, paradise and white-tailed crested flycatcher, Chubb's cisticola, montane oriole, green pigeon, olive-green cameroptera, three types of sunbird, two greenbuls and two species of crimsonwing.

Tours of the factory itself give a fascinating insight – from the weighing stations and machinery used to dry the leaves, to the grading of the leaves ready for sale and the furnaces which power the drying processes. Tours start at US$20 per person and are best arranged at the Nyungwe Cultural Village Cooperative (m *078 661 1886/868 5393/863 6663;* e *info@nyungwecommunity.org.rw;* w *nyungwecommunity.org.rw;* f *nyungweculturalvillage*) on the main drag in Gisakura village.

ISUMO (WATERFALL) TRAIL (*10.6km, 4hrs, moderate*) This superb trail starts at the Gisakura Guesthouse (or reception centre, if you prefer), making it the favoured option for people staying in Gisakura without private transport (though for those with a car, the length can be reduced by driving the first 3km to the forest edge – the park can also arrange motos). The first part of the trail – in essence following the road to the car park – passes through rolling tea plantations dotted with relict forest patches, which are worth scanning closely for silver and other monkeys, as well as birds. The trail then descends into the forest proper, following flat contour paths through a succession of tree-fern-covered ravines, and crossing several streams, before a sharp descent to the base of a pretty but small waterfall. Monkeys are often seen along the way (the Angola colobus seems to be particularly common) and the steep slopes allow good views into the canopy. This trail can be very rewarding for true forest interior birds, with a good chance of spotting AREs such as Ruwenzori turaco and yellow-eyed black flycatcher.

CHIMP TRACKING (CYAMUDONGO/BANDA) Covering an area of about 6km², Cyamudongo is an isolated patch of montane forest situated about an hour's drive southwest of Gisakura via the Shagasha Tea Estate. Protected as an isolated annexe to Nyungwe National Park, Cyamudongo harbours a community of around 40 chimpanzees that are now the most usual goal of daily chimp-tracking excursions out of Gisakura. Chimp tracking here is altogether more hit-and-miss than gorilla tracking in the Virungas, partly because these smaller and less sedentary apes are usually found either feeding high in the trees or moving swiftly along the ground. Nevertheless, the success rate of chimp tracking at Cyamudongo is now pretty high (most visitors will at least get a glimpse) and if you find them in the right location, they can be quite relaxed viewing subjects.

At some times of year, depending on seasonal movements, trackers will not be taken to Cyamudongo but to the village of Banda, reached by a dirt road running north of Uwinka. Usually this happens when fruiting trees lure another habituated community, known as the Mayebe group, to within a kilometre of Banda. For those without a vehicle (or when the Banda road is impassable, as may be the case after heavy rain), it is also possible to track the chimps from Uwinka, but be prepared for a very tough hike on steep slippery slopes!

Whichever venue is used, chimp tracking is limited to one daily group of eight participants (who must be aged 16 or older). These days it is often heavily subscribed by tour groups, especially in the high season, so it is advisable to book well in advance. If you arrive without a reservation, it is still possible to go if there are places available, but you will need to arrange it the day before. For the best chance of locating chimps quickly, you need to be at the forest edge as early as possible, so trackers usually convene at around 05.30 at Gisakura Reception Centre (or Gisakura Guesthouse by advance request), from where it is about 1 hour's drive to Cyamudongo and somewhat further to Banda.

CONGO-NILE DIVIDE TRAIL (*42.2km, 3–4 days, difficult*) Not to be confused with the Congo-Nile Trail that runs along the Lake Kivu shore (see box, pages 224–5), the Congo-Nile Divide Trail is the only multi-day trek in Nyungwe. Cut in 2007, it follows the spectacular ridge that forms the continental divide between the Congo and Nile watersheds. It's a challenging but rewarding wilderness hike, and includes a visit to a sedge marsh identified as the source of the White Nile by Richard Kandt a century before *Ascend the Nile* identified a more remote source in 2006. There are stunning views most of the way, switchback ascents to several tall peaks, and the trail passes through a cross-section of the park's main habitats, including bracken fields, primary and secondary forest, bamboo forest, ericaceous shrub, marsh and open fields swathed in wildflowers. The park authorities recommend traversing from north to south, starting at a trailhead near Musarara about 3 hours north of Gisakura on a rough dirt road, and three overnight stops is ideal, though fit hikers could cut it back to two. The trail ends on the main road between Huye and Rusizi, 7km west of Uwinka.

SOURCE OF THE NILE It is possible to visit the newly identified source of the Nile (see box, page 184) near Gisovu Tea Factory by advance arrangement with the RDB. It is an easy walk, taking 45–60 minutes in either direction from the trailhead, but the drive there from Gisakura or Kitabi takes 3–4 hours in either direction on rough dirt roads. The trailhead is more quickly reached from Karongi, a 2-hour drive following the Rusizi/Cyangugu Road southward then taking the signposted turn-off for Gisovu Tea Factory. The post has recently been refurbished and there are nine guest rooms (along with a restaurant and campsite) scheduled to open here, but they had yet to find an operator at the time of writing. Until the post is fully operational (hopefully during the lifespan of this edition) you'll need to ring through to Kitabi in advance to arrange for a guide to meet you at the Gisovu ranger post. There are also plans to offer birding and tea plantation tours from the new ranger post, as well as hikes to visit a recently habituated group of chimps nearby.

Currently, if you'd like to stay out this way (and once you've made the effort to get here, why not!), there's good accommodation and great views at the **Gisovu Tea Estate** (*3 rooms;* m *078 457 5503;* e *harjot.brar@mcleodrussel.com;* w *silverbacktea. com*) for US$125/150 single/double full board (with good Indian-inspired meals), including a compelling and complimentary 90-minute tour of the tea plantation and factory (*US$15pp for walk-ins*). It's best to ring them and see if there's space (for both rooms and tours) before you make the trek out here – it's about 90 minutes from Karongi on a rough road, passing the Bisesero Genocide Memorial (page 208) *en route.*

MUZIMU TRAIL (*5.2km, 3½hrs, moderate*) This remote trail lies in the northeast of the park, and the trailhead lies 2 hours' drive from Gisakura. It passes through an area dominated by open heath-like vegetation and tangled scrub, and is particularly rewarding for wildflowers and non-forest birds. It is notable for offering several 360° panoramic views over the park, with Lake Kivu shimmering below, and – on a clear day – the volcanic peaks of the Virungas on the distant horizon.

7

Lake Kivu

Running along the Congolese border for 90km, the 2,370km² Lake Kivu is one of a string of 'inland seas' that submerge much of the Albertine Rift floor as it runs southward from Sudan to Zambia. It is a very beautiful lake, hemmed in by steeply terraced escarpments containing several peaks of 2,800m or higher, including the smoking outline of volcanic Nyiragongo in the far north, and it has long served as a popular weekend getaway for residents of this otherwise landlocked country.

Kivu has a smaller surface area than the two most expansive Albertine Rift lakes, the more southerly Tanganyika and more northerly Albert. Nevertheless, a maximum depth of 480m and total water content of 333km³ places it among the world's 20 deepest and 20 most voluminous freshwater bodies. In addition, the 285km² Idjwi Island, which falls entirely within Congolese territory, is the second-largest inland island in Africa and tenth largest in the world.

A shallower and larger incarnation of Kivu probably formed about two million years ago as a result of the same tectonic activity that created the Albertine Rift and other associated lakes. Back then, Kivu would have been contiguous with the lower-lying Lake Edward on the Uganda–DRC border, and it was thus part of the Nile watershed (as Lake Edward still is today). About 20,000 years ago, however, a natural dam created by lava from the Virungas isolated Lake Kivu from Lake Edward. As a result, Kivu's surface rose to its present-day altitude of 1,470m, the Rusizi River – which had formerly drained out of Lake Tanganyika into the southern tip of Kivu – reversed its flow, and the lake became part of the Congo watershed.

Kivu supports an impoverished fauna by comparison with other large Rift Valley lakes, as a result of an unusually high level of volcanic activity. The geological record suggests that the release of methane trapped below the lake's surface has resulted in regular mass extinctions every few thousand years. As a result, fewer than 30 fish species are known from the lake and, while this does include 16 endemics, it pales by comparison with the many hundreds of species recorded from lakes Victoria and Tanganyika. High methane levels probably also explain the complete absence of hippo and croc, and are also cited by those who claim that the lake has no bilharzia (a claim contradicted by certain anecdotal reports from expatriates).

Kivu's attractively irregular shoreline, with its verdant slopes and sandy beaches, is served by three main resort towns. The most northerly of these, Rubavu/Gisenyi, has the best tourist facilities, partly because of its proximity to Volcanoes National Park. Karongi/Kibuye, further south and with the advantage of being far closer to Kigali, also has a few decent lakeshore hotels. At the southern end of the lake, overlooking the exit point of the Rusizi River, Rusizi/Cyangugu can easily be visited in conjunction with Nyungwe National Park and Huye/Butare, and now also boasts accommodation meeting international standards. (For details of town name changes – Rubavu, Karongi, Rusizi, etc – see box, pages 40–1.)

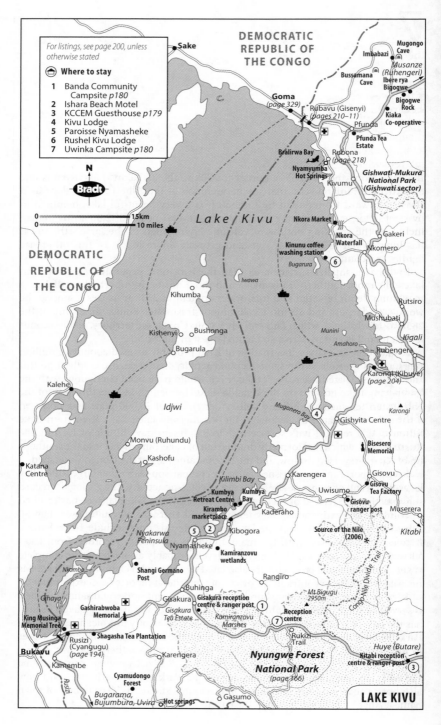

For listings, see page 200, unless
otherwise stated

Where to stay

1 Banda Community
   Campsite *p180*
2 Ishara Beach Motel
3 KCCEM Guesthouse *p179*
4 Kivu Lodge
5 Paroisse Nyamasheke
6 Rushel Kivu Lodge
7 Uwinka Campsite *p180*

N

Bradt

0   15km
0   10 miles

Sake

**DEMOCRATIC
REPUBLIC OF
THE CONGO**

Mugongo
Cave
Imbabazi

Bussamana
Cave

Goma
(page 329)

Rubavu (Gisenyi)
(pages 210–11)

Musanze
(Ruhengeri)
Ibere rya
Bigogwe

Bigogwe
Rock

Kiaka
Co-operative

Pfunda

Pfunda Tea
Estate

Bralirwa Bay

Rubona
(page 218)

**Nyamyumba
Hot Springs**

Kivumu

*Gishwati-Mukura
National Park
(Gishwati sector)*

Lake Kivu

Nkora Market

Nkora
Waterfall

Gakeri

Nkomero

**Kinunu coffee
washing station**

Bugarura

6

Iwawa

Kihumba

Kishenyi

Bushonga

Bugarula

Munini

Amahoro

Mushubati

Kigali

Rutsiro

Rubengera

**DEMOCRATIC
REPUBLIC OF
THE CONGO**

Kalehe

Idjwi

Monvu (Ruhundu)

Kashofu

Katana
Centre

Karongi (Kibuye)
(page 204)

Karongi

Mugonero Bay

4

Gishyita Centre

Bisesero
Memorial

Gisovu

Gisovu
Tea Factory

Karengera

Uwisumo

Gisovu
ranger post

Muserera

Kilimbi Bay

**Kumbya
Retreat Centre**

**Kumbya
Bay**

**Kirambo
marketplace**

Kaderaho

**Source of the Nile
(2006)**

Kitabi

*Nyakarwa
Peninsula*

5 2

Kibogora

Nyamasheke

**Kamiranzovu
wetlands**

Rangiro

Mt Bigugu
2950m

Nkomba

**Shangi Germano
Post**

Buhinga

Gisakura

**Gisakura reception
centre & ranger post**

1

**Reception
centre**

7

Gihaya

**Gashirabwoba
Memorial**

*Gisakura
Tea Estate*

*Kamiranzovu
Marshes*

Rukizi
Trail

**King Musinga
Memorial Tree**

Shagasha Tea Plantation

Rusizi
(Cyangugu)
(page 194)

Bukavu

Kamembe

Karengera

Nile Divide Trail

Huye (Butare)

**Kitabi reception
centre & ranger post**

3

**Cyamudongo
Forest**

*Bugarama,
Bujumbura, Uvira*

Hot springs

Gasumo

**Nyungwe Forest
National Park**
(page 166)

LAKE KIVU

RUSIZI (CYANGUGU)

The most southerly of Rwanda's Lake Kivu ports, Rusizi (formerly Cyangugu, pronounced 'Shangugu') is also the most amorphous, sprawling along a 5km road through the green hills that run down to the lakeshore. A district capital, it consists of discrete upper and lower towns whose combined population of 30,000 makes it the seventh-largest settlement in the country.

The upper town, Kamembe, which stands some 150m above the lakeshore at an altitude of 1,620m, is a lively business centre, and the site of the main taxi stand, market, banks and supermarkets, as well as a clutch of local guesthouses and restaurants. It has also seen a spate of new developments over the past decade, in the form of several multi-storey complexes and other such buildings under construction, giving it the feel of a genuine small town rather than the incidental market centre it was some years back. Nevertheless, aside from the marvellous views of the lake, and a couple of flaking colonial-era buildings, Kamembe is all energy and no character, with little to distinguish it from any other African town of comparable size.

Far more intriguing, the lower town – Rusizi/Cyangugu proper – consists of little more than one pot-hole-scored main road, yet within its abrupt confines it does have a decidedly built-up feel, suggesting it must once have been more grand and prosperous than it is today. Overhung with an aura of tropical ennui, and overlooking the Rusizi River as it flows out of the lake, this small urban enclave possesses a vaguely cinematic quality, like some semi-abandoned West African riverside trade backwater dotted with several forex bureaux and market stalls. The river, spanned by a soon-to-be-redundant narrow bridge and its much wider replacement, not only forms the border between Rwanda and the DRC, but separates Rusizi from the much larger Congolese settlement of Bukavu (pages 342–7), which sprawls across the hills of the lakeshore opposite.

During the genocide, what was then the prefecture of Cyangugu was the site of the second most extensive extermination of Tutsis (after Karongi/Kibuye). It is estimated that 85–90% of Tutsis here died before the French set up their 'safe zone', and many communities were wiped out completely. More recently, on 4 February 2008, the town was hard hit by an earthquake that measured 6.1 on the Richter Scale and was felt throughout the great lakes region. Several houses collapsed, and 30 people were killed when a church roof collapsed at Shangi, about 5km north of Kamembe.

Unless you are thinking of crossing into the DRC and Bukavu, Rusizi has to be classed as something of a dead end in travel terms (though to be completely accurate, there is a border crossing south of here at Bugarama that leads to Bujumbura via Burundi's restive Cibitoke region). It is, however, the closest town to Nyungwe, and might therefore make an attractive alternative base for budget self-drive visitors to this national park. The lakeshore setting is lovely, too, and the atmospheric old town forms a good base from which to explore more off-the-beaten-track destinations such as the Bugarama hot springs and islands of Gihaya and Nkombo.

GETTING THERE AND AWAY

By air RwandAir runs a once-daily flight between Kigali and Kamembe.

By road The road from Huye/Butare to Rusizi is surfaced in its entirety but some parts west of Nyamagabe/Gikongoro can get a bit pot-holed. Regular midibuses connect Kigali and Huye to the main bus station in Kamembe [194 D5]. The fare

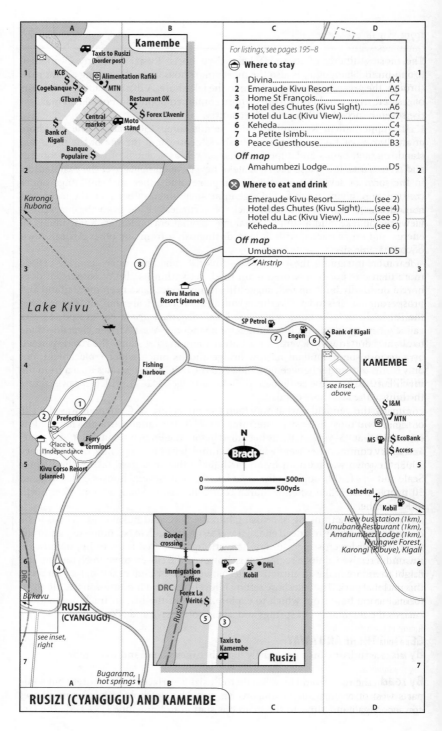

Kamembe (inset)

- Taxis to Rusizi (border post)
- Alimentation Rafiki
- KCB
- MTN
- Cogebanque
- GTbank
- Restaurant OK
- Central market
- Forex L'Avenir
- Moto stand
- Bank of Kigali
- Banque Populaire

Karongi, Rubona

For listings, see pages 195–8

Where to stay

1. Divina...A4
2. Emeraude Kivu Resort.........................A5
3. Home St François...............................C7
4. Hotel des Chutes (Kivu Sight)............A6
5. Hotel du Lac (Kivu View)....................C7
6. Keheda..C4
7. La Petite Isimbi.................................C4
8. Peace Guesthouse..............................B3

Off map
    Amahumbezi Lodge..........................D5

Where to eat and drink

    Emeraude Kivu Resort....................(see 2)
    Hotel des Chutes (Kivu Sight)........(see 4)
    Hotel du Lac (Kivu View)................(see 5)
    Keheda..(see 6)

Off map
    Umubano...D5

Lake Kivu

Airstrip

Kivu Marina Resort (planned)

SP Petrol
Engen
Bank of Kigali

KAMEMBE

see inset, above

Fishing harbour

I&M
MTN

Prefecture
Place de l'Indépendance
Ferry terminus

MS
EcoBank
Access

Kivu Corso Resort (planned)

N

Bradt

0 ———— 500m
0 ———— 500yds

Cathedral
Kobil

New bus station (1km), Umubano Restaurant (1km), Amahumbezi Lodge (1km), Nyungwe Forest, Karongi (Kibuye), Kigali

DRC

Bukavu

RUSIZI (CYANGUGU)

see inset, right

Bugarama, hot springs

Rusizi (inset)

Border crossing
Immigration office
SP
DHL
Kobil
DRC
Forex La Vérité
Rusizi

Taxis to Kamembe

Rusizi

RUSIZI (CYANGUGU) AND KAMEMBE

from Kigali is around Rfr5,300 and from Huye around Rfr4,000, though this fluctuates with the current fuel price. Omega Car (m *078 841 2155*) and Alpha Express (m *078 992 3073*) are among the companies serving Kamembe, and the last Kigali-bound vehicle of the day departs at 16.00.

With the lakeshore road complete all the way north, it's also now possible to connect directly from Kamembe to Karongi/Kibuye and Rubavu/Gisenyi. Several companies, including Omega Car and Ugusenga Express (m *078 637 1421*), serve Karongi multiple times daily (*Rfr2,200*), with buses often continuing to Kigali. To go all 220km up the lake to Rubavu/Gisenyi (*Rfr 4,500*), Kivu Belt (m *078 492 7432*) has three daily departures at 06.30, 08.30, and 13.30. All depart from the main bus station in Kamembe.

A steady stream of minibus-taxis run back and forth between Kamembe and the border post at Rusizi, at about Rfr200 for the 5km trip (alternatively, a moto is about Rfr500). The Peace Guesthouse [194 B3] and Hotel des Chutes [194 A6] both lie within 50m of the taxi route, as does the main harbour and port.

By boat Scheduled (though rather infrequent) lake ferries serve the Rwandan side of Lake Kivu. Calling at Rusizi/Cyangugu, Karongi/Kibuye, and Rubona (for Rubavu/Gisenyi), boats (m *078 856 3431/199 6764, 072 896 3431*) make the northbound trip from Rusizi twice weekly, departing at 07.00 on Tuesdays and Fridays and charging Rfr2,500 to Karongi (*6hrs*) and Rfr5,000 to Rubona (Rubavu). Boats head south from Rubona on Wednesdays and Sundays. The boats may also call at other lakeshore communities (ie: Kinunu, etc) if there are passengers wishing to alight there. In Rusizi, the Emeraude Kivu Resort (see below) is the best place to arrange tourist boat trips and private lake transport.

WHERE TO STAY Though it's well behind the other two main lakeshore resorts in terms of accommodation choices, Rusizi is today home to considerably more comfortable digs than it was even a few years ago, and this trend seems set to continue, with at least two large new hotels under construction in 2018. The Emeraude Kivu Resort is a fabulous spot by any measure, while the Home St François stands out as the best budget choice (and a relatively cheap base from which to visit Nyungwe Forest National Park).

Upmarket

✳ 🏠 **Emeraude Kivu Resort** [194 A5] (29 rooms) m 078 701 0900; e emeraudekivu@ gmail.com; w emeraudekivuresort.rw. Opened in 2013, this is far & away the smartest option in town, & its views over the lake & peninsulas of Bukavu are worth the price of admission alone. Rooms, all of which have lake views, are done up in colourful modern décor & come with flatscreen TV, canopy bed, modern bathroom, safe & wardrobe. Rooms in the new block are slightly larger, but all are equally smart & meticulously cared for. The terrace restaurant is among the best in town (try the *sambaza* – small, sardine-like fish) & a fitness centre with spa, massage & sauna facilities was under construction at the time of writing. They also arrange boat trips to the nearby islands.

US$100/120 sgl/dbl; suites from US$170/190 sgl/ dbl; all rates B&B.

Moderate

🏠 **Keheda Hotel** [194 C4] (29 rooms) m 078 240 7529/154 4157; e info_keheda@yahoo.fr; 🄵. Situated in the heart of Kamembe, a location that has little going for it aside from its proximity to the bus station, this modern 3-storey block is a smart enough option, despite a glaring deficit of character. The large tiled en-suite rooms, though a little frayed at the edges, come with nets, TV, fan, private balcony, hot water & some have lake views. Other facilities include a good restaurant & rooftop bar, along with room service, massages & a sauna. The echoing passages might make you vulnerable to noise from other guests, & things

Shortly before midnight on 15 August 1984, villagers living around Cameroon's Lake Monoun recall being awoken by an explosive noise emanating from within the lake. Come dawn the next morning, 37 residents of a nearby low-lying valley lay mysteriously dead, their skin damaged and discoloured, the surrounding air overhung with the remnants of a pungent smoky cloud; bizarre circumstances that gave rise to any number of macabre and implausible theories: a vicious terrorist attack, a chemical weapon test gone horribly wrong, the malicious work of an angry lake spirit …

The truth was somewhat more prosaic, yet no less frightening. And even before scientific investigators were able to release their tentative findings, it happened again, only 100km further northwest, when an acrid cloud of gas erupted from beneath the surface of a 200m-deep crater lake called Nyos on 22 August 1986. Within the space of hours, 1,750 local villagers living in the surrounding valleys had suffocated to death, together with thousands of animals, with the furthest casualty occurring a full 27km from the lakeshore.

In March 1987, a UNESCO conference was held at Yaounde to discuss the previously unknown phenomenon, unique to very deep lakes, which investigators called a *limnic eruption*. What seemed to have happened, in simplistic terms, is that carbon dioxide of volcanic origin seeps continuously into the lower strata of a deep lake, where its high solubility allows it to accumulate in volumes up to five-times heavier than normal water, becoming increasingly volatile as it approaches saturation point – the carbonated pressure at the bottom of the lake might be three-times greater than that of a sparkling wine or soda! By now, the time bomb is ticking. All it takes is a seemingly innocuous external trigger – a light landslide, a heavy storm, an otherwise inconsequential subterranean volcanic activity – to upset the lake's stratification. Then, suddenly, a cloud of noxious carbon dioxide will belch out from the lake surface, diffusing into lower-lying areas and effectively suffocating all oxygen-dependent creatures in its path until finally it dissipates.

Over the next few years, a French research team travelled around Africa trying to establish whether any other very deep lakes might be at similar risk to Monoun and Nyos. And as it turned out, the only contender for this unwanted distinction is

---

can get very noisy on Fri/Sat when the nightclub continues until the early hours. *Rfr30,000 sgl; Rfr40,000/50,000 sgl/dbl with a lake view.*

🏠 **Peace Guesthouse** [194 B3] (55 rooms) m 078 852 2727; e peaceguesthouse3@yahoo. com; w earpeaceguesthouse.com. Overlooking the lake about 1km from Kamembe along the scenic road towards Rusizi proper, this popular guesthouse was constructed by the Anglican Church in 1998 & offers a wide selection of accommodation, ranging from en-suite bungalows that can sleep 4 to simple en-suite rooms & suites with balconies overlooking the lake. Several Rwandan VIPs – including the president – have stayed here, & overall it's an attractive option, particularly the very sharp new buildings. Adequate meals are

available in the restaurant, but no alcohol is served. They can also arrange boat trips. *Rfr15,000/20,000 sgl/dbl; Rfr25,000/30,000 lake-view sgl/dbl; from Rfr50,000/60,000 sgl/dbl bungalow; from Rfr35,000/45,000 sgl/dbl in new building.*

Budget
🏠 **Divina Hotel** [194 A4] (20 rooms) m 072 863 1333/078 476 9755. On the inland side of the same peninsula as Emeraude Kivu Resort, this sleepy guesthouse is clean & quiet, with several categories of double rooms, all set around a little grass courtyard & with en-suite ablutions. Cold drinks are available, but meals should be requested well in advance. *Rfr10,000/15,000 sgl/dbl, Rfr20,000–25,000 deluxe dbl; Rfr50,000 suite; all rates B&B.*

Kivu, whose lower strata, below around 260m, are infused with 60km^3 of dissolved methane gas and 300km^3 of carbon dioxide, a mix potentially made doubly unstable by the high level of volcanic activity around the northern lakeshore. Indeed, it seems more than likely that the periodic faunal extinctions punctuating Kivu's fossil record can be attributed to prehistoric limnic eruptions, and experts regard another such incident as inevitable – though there is no immediate risk, since the water pressure is currently twice the gas pressure, and it might not happen for hundreds or thousands of years!

The Cameroonian lakes have been equipped with 'degassing' systems – a procedure that involves laying a pipe to the lowest strata of the lake and pumping the pressurised water so that it shoots out from the lake surface in a spectacular 50m-high fountain to release the carbon dioxide safely into the atmosphere. Some fear that the degassing process might itself trigger another disaster, but monitoring by the 2011–16 Cameroonian–Japanese SATREPS IRGM Project indicated drastic reductions of gas concentrations in both lakes.

As for Kivu, experts believe that the best way to minimise the risk of future disaster is to extract the lake's practically inexhaustible reserves of methane as a source of fuel and energy for local and possibly international consumption. Prior to 2004, this took place only on a very small scale to fuel the Bralirwa Brewery near Rubavu/Gisenyi, a project that is still in operation today. However, following several trial extractions elsewhere on the lake, the Rwandan government has now committed to the large-scale extraction of methane for conversion to electricity at a new plant built outside Karongi/Kibuye as part of the US$325 million KivuWatt Project, which was formally awarded to the international company ContourGlobal in March 2009. After many delays, the plant's gas extraction barge was launched in 2015, producing 26MW of electricity for the local grid by the end of the year. A planned expansion will see the plant produce 100MW by 2020, and it's hoped that eventually the lake will produce up to 700MW of electricity, leaving a large surplus for sale to neighbouring countries.

For further information about methane extraction at Lake Kivu, check out w contourglobal.com/asset/kivuwatt.

🏠 **Hotel des Chutes (Kivu Sight)** [194 A6] (17 rooms) m 078 434 3191; e kivu.sight@yahoo. com. Set on a rise about 500m back from the border post, this reasonable hotel has an attractive location overlooking the lake, & the shady balcony is fun for a drink or snack. The rooms were once among the best in town, & though they're feeling a bit shabbier these days, are still for the most part clean & comfortable, with TV, netting, hot bath, & in some instances a lake-facing private balcony. The restaurant serves good meals & snacks, but overall the places closer to the border seem a better deal for the money. *Rfr15,000–30,000 en-suite dbl depending on size & view.*

🏠 **Hotel du Lac (Kivu View)** [194 C7] (20 rooms) m 073/078 830 7576; e kivuview@

yahoo.fr. Once upon a time the smartest option in Rusizi, this wonderfully located hotel overlooks the river immediately south of the border post with the DRC. Unfortunately, the rooms, although impressively clean, are rather artless & a touch pricey in comparison with other hotels in this range – though they were getting a bit of a facelift at the end of 2017. The hotel's best feature is the open-air riverfront bar & restaurant, which serves excellent brochettes & grilled chicken, as well as more substantial meals, if you don't mind a wait. There's also a large swimming pool but with water this murky, you're better off swimming in the lake. *Rfr12,000 en suite with ¾ bed, cold water & fan; Rfr20,000 en suite with dbl bed; Rfr50,000 VIP dbl with TV.*

🏠 **La Petite Isimbi** [194 C4] (25 rooms)
m 078 984 7205/850 0564. At the beginning of the built-up part of town as you enter Kamembe from the north, this is a comfortable & friendly budget pick, with a variety of simple en-suite rooms, all of which come with hot water & Wi-Fi, & some with small balconies overlooking the lake way down below. *Rfr10,000/15,000 sgl/dbl, Rfr20,000 dbl with lake view; Rfr35,000 suite; all rates B&B.*

Shoestring

🏠 **Amahumbezi Lodge** [194 D5] (16 rooms)
m 078 260 3862/885 1291. Just opposite the bus park, this is a surprisingly pleasant budget option that could make a good pick if you're trying to catch an early departure. It's right next to the Umubano Restaurant & Trump Bar, so ask for a room in one of the standalone buildings further back. *Rfr8,000/10,000 sgl/dbl or twin.*

🏠 **Home St François** [194 C7] (50 rooms)
m 078 409 3490; e rusizicentrede39@yahoo.fr. Situated directly opposite the Hotel du Lac, this homely church-run lodge is possibly the most savoury option in Rusizi despite the low price – in fact it's as good a deal as you'll find anywhere in Rwanda. The rooms are spacious, clean & secure, some with en-suite hot shower, others with access to a common hot bath (& Wi-Fi all around!). Meals are very cheap but nothing to shout about, so you are probably better off eating at the nearby Hotel du Lac or up the hill a bit at Emeraude Kivu. *Rfr5,000/8,000 sgl/dbl using shared showers; Rfr8,000/15,000 en-suite sgl/dbl.*

🍴 **WHERE TO EAT AND DRINK** By far the nicest place to eat is the lakefront terrace at the **Emeraude Kivu Resort** [194 A5], which has the best views and most sophisticated cuisine in town, with plates starting around Rfr6,000. Another riverside favourite is the **Hotel du Lac (Kivu View)** [194 C7], which also has a pleasant terrace, and charges Rfr3,000–5,000 for à la carte dishes, including superb barbecued whole fish, peri-peri chicken and brochettes. Also recommended is the terrace restaurant at **Hotel des Chutes (Kivu Sight)** [194 A6], which has a reasonable menu in a similar price range. Up in Kamembe the restaurant at the **Keheda Hotel** [194 C4] is adequate but a bit boring (their terrace overlooks the road, not the lake), while **Restaurant OK** (m *078 841 0607*) near the market does a good local buffet for an unbeatable Rfr1,500. All these places are open for breakfast, lunch and dinner daily. If you need a bite near the bus station, **Umubano Restaurant** [194 D5] (m *078 856 0425*) across the street does all the local staples.

OTHER PRACTICALITIES

Internet There are a couple of internet cafés dotted along the main road through Kamembe, though most guesthouses now offer Wi-Fi.

Money There are no fewer than five banks here with ATMs, including KCB and GT Bank, both of which at least ostensibly accept Mastercard. Banks also provide the normal **foreign exchange** services at the usual snail's pace. There are also a couple of forex bureaux dotted around the border post and market area, offering an instant service for cash, generally at better rates than the banks. (These are also a good place to get Congolese francs if you're headed to Bukavu.)

WHAT TO SEE AND DO Rusizi forms the obvious base from which to explore the far southwest of Rwanda, a region which sees very few tourists. The southwest boasts a couple of points of interest in the form of the Bugarama hot springs and islands of Gihaya and Nkombo, though you could argue that these landmarks provide a good pretext to explore a remote corner of Rwanda as much as they rank as worthwhile goals in their own right. With access to a private vehicle, this area can easily be explored as a day trip out of Rusizi, and recent improvements in both road conditions and public transport mean it's now feasible without your own wheels as well, assuming you're feeling adventurous and prepared for some waiting on the roadside and a fair bit of walking.

Note that some old travel guides refer to the **Rusizi Falls** (Les Chutes de Rusizi) on the Rusizi River along the border with the DRC. In reality, whatever waterfall may once have existed here is now submerged beneath the waters of the Mururu Dam, which was built in 1958 about 10km south of Rusizi as a source of hydro-electric power and also serves as an obscure border crossing into the DRC.

Bugarama hot springs Situated slightly less than 60km from Rusizi by road, the Bugarama hot springs lie at the base of a limestone quarry, 5km from the Cimerwa Cement Factory, in a lightly wooded area dotted by large sinkholes. The springs bubble up into a large green pool which, as viewed from the roadward side, is initially somewhat disappointing. You can, however, follow a path around the edge of the pool, past a large sinkhole to your left, then leap over the outlet stream to the base of the cliff. Here you are right next to the main springs, which bubble into the pool like a freshly shaken and opened fizzy-drink bottle, and are sizzling hot to the touch.

In a private vehicle the springs can be reached in about 60 minutes from Rusizi. The first part of the trip involves following the surfaced road towards the junction town of Bugarama, about 40km away. At the main roundabout in Bugarama, you need to take a sharp left on to a newly surfaced road heading towards the Cimerwa Cement Factory (✪ *S 2°36.462, E 29°01.008*) in Muganza Village. (Continuing straight at the roundabout brings you to the DRC border at Kamanyola after 800m, and the soft left is for the Ruhwa border with Burundi, 7.5km away.) Continuing through Bugarama and a series of villages along the new road, you'll reach Cimerwa after just under 11km. Here you must make a left to stay on the surfaced road, passing the factory on your right and continue for just over 3km (the tarmac runs out just after the factory), taking the left-hand fork just before you reach a quarry. After 400m, you'll see a kiosk selling snacks and drinks – bear right here, the pools are about 200m beyond (✪ *S 2°35.015, E 29°00.944*). If in doubt, ask for directions to the 'Amashyuza' (aka 'Amahyuza'). From here, it would be possible to continue on the **Cyamudongo Forest** sector of Nyungwe Forest National Park.

Accessing the springs by public transport is a little tricker. Tripartite (m *078 964 8630*) runs minibuses for Bugarama from the main bus park in Kamembe hourly between 04.00 and 15.00 every day for under Rfr1,000. Bugarama itself isn't much to shout about – a hot, dusty small town (with a Bank of Kigali ATM) ringed

Situated about 60 minutes' drive north of Rusizi on the stunning lakeshore road to Karongi, Kumbya is a spectacular 10ha peninsula that has been used as a retreat by Protestant missionaries in the Great Lakes region since the 1940s. As a result, it has been saved from deforestation, and it protects around 100 bird species, as well as otters and vervet monkeys. Today it's home to the **Kumbya Retreat Centre** (✪ *S 02°17.578, E 29°09.083*), where an annual missionary conference is held every July, but the cabins and camping areas on the peninsula are open to guests year-round. There's long been talk of developing it into a more formal eco-resort, but as things stand the cabins can be hired on arrival from the missionary agencies themselves – see w kumbya.net for the latest.

by plantations of plantains and pines. Its transport park sits alongside the main roundabout mentioned on page 199, and the occasional minibus heads towards Cimerwa from here, but there's no public transport for the 3.7km beyond the factory. Even so, the terrain is largely flat and the remaining walk shouldn't take longer than an hour in either direction.

Gihaya and Nkombo islands A short boat ride away from Rusizi, this pair of islands in Lake Kivu makes for a diverting half-day outing, and forms a good excuse to get out on to the lake, without really qualifying as an essential excursion. Gihaya is the smaller island, best known as the site of a derelict mansion set in large shady lawns that locals variously claim was built as a holiday home for King Baudouin II of Belgium or for President Juvenal Habyarimana. The 20km-long Nkombo Island, which was badly hit by the 2008 earthquake, offers plenty of opportunity for exploration, but the main attraction seems to be a rather impressive fruit-bat colony near a jetty at the south end of the island. The lake itself is very pretty, with sweeping views to the heavily settled Congolese shore around Bukavu, and there is plenty of birdlife to be seen, notably cormorants and pelicans, as well as the unusual

Paroisse Nyamasheke Roughly 40km from Rusizi; ✪ S 02°20.116, E 29°05.553; m 078/072 214 9531, 078/072 864 0914; e paroissenyamasheke@yahoo.fr. Very pleasant budget rooms with mosquito nets & hot water though not much in the way of lake access. *Rfr7,000 sgl/10,000 dbl en suite.*

Ishara Beach Motel (27 rooms) Gataka Village; ✪ S 02°20.057, E 29°06.554; m 078 822 1876/830 7433; e isharabeach. motel@yahoo.fr. Simple but well-kept en-suite double rooms available. The lush hilltop compound leads down to a small private beach & is a popular w/end getaway for Rwandans. *Rfr15,000–50,000.*

Kivu Lodge (20 cottages) ✪ S 02°08.756, E 29°15.392; m 078 830 5708; e info@3bhotels.com; w 3bhotels. com. Sits on its own diminutive peninsula at the end of a rough 7.5km access road, reached from the turn-off at ✪ S 02°10.666, E 29°17.311. (There's also a helipad if that's more your style.) It's under the same ownership as the Mountain Gorilla View Lodge in Kinigi (page 266), & offers attractively decorated cottages of a similar standard to their sister property, along with an infinity pool & fire pit overlooking the lake. *US$250/300 sgl/dbl FB.*

Rushel Kivu Lodge (4 suites plus standing tents) North shore; ✪ S 01°54.370, E 29°17.040; m 078 882 5000/352 3660/830 2278; e rushelkivu@ gmail.com; w rushelkivu.wixsite.com/ home; f rushelkivu. This beachfront lodge sits in wide, grassy gardens next to Kinunu Village (page 227) about 65km north of Karongi & 60km south of Rubavu. By road it's reachable along a rough 10km access route from a signposted turn-off at Nkomero Village (✪ S 01°53.568, E 29°20.292), but it's also possible to get here by boat, or along the Congo-Nile Trail. The beach is good for swimming & there are canoes you can take to the banana-shaped Bugarura Island just offshore. *US$60/70 well-equipped en-suite sgl/dbl B&B; standing tents starting at US$30/45 sgl/dbl B&B.*

local *amato* – the Kinyarwanda word for boat – which comprise three widely spaced dugouts bound together with bamboo poles.

Motorboats taking eight to ten passengers are usually available at Rusizi fishing harbour [194 B4], and local dugouts with paddlers can also be arranged; just ask around. Prices depend on where you arrange your boat – it's Rfr40,000 with Emeraude Kivu (who also work with a women's craft co-operative on the island), but you could go for considerably less than that (probably in a considerably less comfortable vessel) directly from the harbour. Perhaps this is obvious, but the trip over is far quicker with a motor: around 20 minutes each way as opposed to 1 hour.

KARONGI (KIBUYE)

The capital of Western Province, Karongi – known as Kibuye prior to 2006 – is also the most conventionally pretty of Rwanda's three main lake ports, a modestly sized town (population 15,000) that sprawls attractively across a series of hills interwoven with the lagoon-like arms of the lake. Karongi is now the most quickly accessible lakeside town from Kigali, to which it is linked by a good surfaced road through Muhanga/Gitarama, but it hasn't yet caught on with foreign tourists the way Rubavu/Gisenyi has. Nevertheless, it now boasts a decent selection of accommodation at all levels, and it is a popular weekend beach retreat for families living elsewhere in Rwanda. Hills planted with pines and eucalyptus give the locale a pristine, almost alpine appearance, in contrast to the atmosphere of fading tropical languor which to some extent afflicts the other ports. It's a green, peaceful and appealing place, whose sudden views of the lake sparkling amid overhanging trees are true picture-postcard material.

It's hard to believe, amid today's sunlight and tranquillity, that the prefecture then known as Kibuye experienced the most comprehensive slaughter of Tutsis anywhere in Rwanda during the genocide. Previously there had been around 60,000 in the prefecture, an unusually high proportion of about 20%. When the French troops arrived afterwards they estimated that up to nine out of every ten had been killed. Whole communities were annihilated, leaving no witnesses to the crime. Near the sports stadium you will see just one of the mass graves, with a sign announcing: 'More than 10,000 people were inhumated here. Official ceremony was presided over by H E Pasteur Bizimungu, President of the Republic of Rwanda. April 26th 1995.' Now birds chirp on the surrounding wall and the laughter of children in the nearby primary school echoes across the enclosure. Here and throughout Rwanda, memories of the genocide remain acute but daily life carries on determinedly around them. As does tourism.

Looking ahead, Karongi is growing into its role as provincial capital, as well as reaping benefits from two other recent government initiatives. The first is the methane extraction plant, which lies about 3km south of town (see box, pages 196–7), and started producing electricity in 2008, a move that has given the local economy a genuine shot in the arm. The second development is the recent completion of two new surfaced roads: the first heads south to Rusizi and the second north to Rubavu, and both have rapidly expanded access to Karongi's isolated lakeside hinterland and integrated Rwanda's three major lake ports as never before.

GETTING THERE AND AWAY

By road The main access is by the road from Kigali via Muhanga/Gitarama, started by the Chinese in 1990 and now starting to show its age with a few pot-holed stretches throughout. The drive takes at least 2 hours in a private vehicle. Numerous scheduled midibuses from Capital Express (m *073 230 0271*), Omega

A NEW VERSION OF AN ANCIENT TALE Long, long ago, before the beginning of what we now remember, there was nothing but a dry, grassy plain covering the area where Lake Kivu lies today. It was a hard, hot place, whose people had to work ceaselessly to scrape a living from the land. One of these people was a man whose heart was kind; he helped his older neighbours to till their ground and to gather in their crops. His wife scolded him for this, saying: 'Why do you spend so much time filling their grain-stores when our own lies empty?' But Imana had seen his good deeds and was pleased, and wanted to reward the man, so he gave him a cow whose udders yielded milk, millet, beans and peas. Imana warned the man that he must not speak of his special cow to others, lest they envy him and try to steal it, so the man milked his cow in secret and carried home the produce to his wife who began to scold him a little less.

A day came when the man was called away to work at the Mwami's court. Anxiously, he asked Imana what he should do about his cow. Imana said that his wife might be told, and might milk it in the meantime, but that she must not pass on the secret of the cow to others.

With her husband away from home, the woman invited a young man to her house. He dined off the milk and the millet and the beans and the peas, and he wondered how her poor land could produce so much. He searched all round her homestead for an extra storeroom or piece of land but he found nothing, and the cow looked just like an ordinary cow. Insistently the young man questioned the woman, using all kinds of persuasion to discover her secret, and eventually she weakened. She milked the cow in front of him and he was so amazed that he ran to the neighbours, crying: 'Here is an animal that will feed us all – we need work on the land no more!'

Imana heard this, and he frowned deeply, and that night he prepared a punishment. Before going to bed, the woman went out into her field to empty her bladder as usual, thinking to take only a few moments. But the flow was unstoppable. On and on it went, flooding her house and her fields and the land around about. Deeper and deeper it became, until the woman herself was drowned in it and even the trees were covered. Her household utensils – her wooden bowl and her woven mat and the gourd which held her grain – floated away into the distance, broke into bits and became islands. And as the morning sun rose into the sky it lit the new and shining surface of Lake Kivu as it is today.

When the man returned from working at the mwami's court he found a lake of sweet water lapping at the edge of his fields. The land had become soft and fertile. Fish swam in the lake, and waterbirds bobbed on the wavelets. Of the cow there was no sign, but she had left behind a big heap of millet and peas and beans which he then planted, and his crop and all those after it grew richly on the irrigated land.

And Imana smiled.

Express (m *078 890 8343*) and others are available from Nyabugogo bus station and cost Rfr2,500 (or Rfr1,500 coming from Muhanga/Gitarama).

Travelling from elsewhere on the lakeshore, both the 115km trip to Rusizi and 105km to Rubavu can now be done in less than 2½ hours in a private vehicle, thanks to the surfacing of the northern and southern lakeshore roads. Both roads are considerable feats of engineering, cutting through hillsides and teetering around steep valleys, and they offer spectacular views over the lake and surrounding hills.

All transport in Karongi starts and stops in the bus park behind the market in the tiny town centre. Kivu Belt (m *078 866 5656*) runs hourly midibuses to Rubavu/Gisenyi for Rfr2,500 between 05.00 and 17.30 daily, and Ugusenga Express (m *078 307 5083*) has close to hourly daily departures between 06.15 and 19.00 to Rusizi/Cyangugu for a similar price.

If you're self-driving, note that the junction of the Rusizi–Nyungwe Road and the road to Karongi is at Buhinga Village (✪ *S 02°25.355, E 29°04.196*), while the trip to Rubavu involves following the Kigali road east for 17km as far as Rubengera (✪ *S 02°02.916, E 29°24.849*), then taking a clearly signposted left. In Karongi itself, the main surfaced loop road encircling the sprawling town is one-way in an anti-clockwise direction.

By boat Public lake ferries serve the Rwandan side of Lake Kivu, calling at Rusizi/Cyangugu, Karongi/Kibuye, and Rubona (for Rubavu/Gisenyi), plus a few other villages if there's demand. Boats head north between Rusizi and Rubona (Rubavu) on Tuesdays and Fridays, stopping in Karongi at (roughly) 13.00 before continuing north, while boats heading south from Rubona call here on Wednesdays and Sundays around 10.00. Tickets are purchased on the boat (m *078 856 3431/199 6764, 072 896 3431*), which departs from the fishing harbour on the west side of town. It's Rfr2,500 to Rusizi (*6hrs*) and Rfr2,000 to Rubona (*3hrs*).

It's still of course possible to charter a boat of your own should you be so inclined, and the Cotralaki Cooperative has about a dozen covered passenger boats for hire on the stretch of lakeshore near the Bralirwa depot. Carrying up to 15 people, these boats charge around Rfr140,000/230,000 one-way/return to/from Rusizi, a 5–6-hour trip, in either direction and Rfr120,000/200,000 one-way/return to/from Rubavu, which takes 2–3 hours one-way. The Home St Jean also has boats for hire linking Karongi to Rusizi and Rubavu; these are a little faster than the Cotralaki boats but also about 25% more costly. Plans exist to eventually open an official border crossing to Idjwi Island in the DRC as well. Contact Idjwi Ecolodge (page 354) for the latest information.

WHERE TO STAY *Map, page 204*
Upmarket

✳ 🏠 **Cormoran Lodge** (7 rooms) m 072 860 1515; e contact@cormoranlodge.com; w cormoranlodge.com. Situated on an isolated private beach about 3km out of town, this is the most stylish lodge in the vicinity of Karongi, set in steeply sloping lawns that run down to the palm-lined lakeshore & jetty. Constructed mainly with wood, it offers accommodation in large en-suite rooms with king-size bed, walk-in nets, flatscreen DSTV, Wi-Fi, teakettle, hot water & private balcony with lake view. The restaurant is well known for its pizzas, but it also serves a variety of meat & fish dishes in the Rfr6,000–8,000 range. Activities on offer include kayaking, waterskiing & boat trips to the islands. *US$135/180 sgl/dbl (non-residents), US$90/130 (residents); all rates B&B.*

🏠 **Moriah Hill Resort** (20 rooms) m 078 851 2222/830 7660; e info@moriah-hill.com; w moriah-hill.com. The smartest hotel in Karongi prior to the opening of Cormoran Lodge, this remains a very pleasant option, boasting an isolated location further along the same peninsula as the Hotel Centre Béthanie. Spanning 4 storeys, the bright white main hotel building is somewhat intrusive, but it has been designed so that all rooms have large balconies with views across the lake to a nearby forested peninsula, & are perfectly positioned to catch the sunset. The rooms are large & comfortable, if a bit dated, with double beds, Wi-Fi, satellite TV, fridge, seats & table, & a spacious bathroom with tub & shower. The restaurant, in a separate building, has plenty of indoor & outdoor seating, good service, & an unusually imaginative

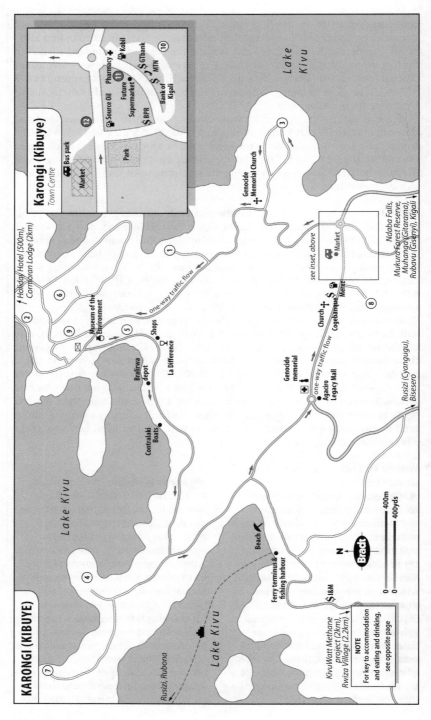

KARONGI (KIBUYE)

Karongi (Kibuye)
Town Centre

Lake Kivu

Holiday Hotel (500m),
Cormoran Lodge (2km)

Museum of the
Environment

one-way traffic flow

Shops

La Difference

Bralirwa
depot

Contralaki
Boats

Lake Kivu

Beach

Ferry terminus &
fishing harbour

Rusizi, Rubona

Lake Kivu

KivuWatt Methane
project (2km),
Rwiza Village (2.2km)

NOTE
For key to accommodation
and eating and drinking,
see opposite page

Genocide
Memorial Church

Lake
Kivu

Genocide
memorial

see inset, above

Market

Ndaba Falls,
Mukura Forest Reserve,
Muhanga (Gitarama),
Rubavu (Gisenyi), Kigali

Genocide
memorial

one-way traffic flow

Agaciro
Legacy Mall

Church
Cogebanque

Merez

Rusizi (Cyangugu),
Bisesero

N

Bradt

0   400m
0   400yds

Bus park

Pharmacy
Kobil

Source Oil
MTN
GTbank

Future
Supermarket

Bank of
Kigali

BPR

Market

Park

204

🛏 **Where to stay**
1 Centre d'Accueil Sainte Marie
2 Delta Resort
3 Home St Jean
4 Hotel Centre Béthanie
5 Hotel Golf Eden Rock
6 Macheo Eco-Lodge
7 Moriah Hill Resort
8 Mulberry Guesthouse
9 Rebero Kivu Resort
10 Romantic

Off map
   Cormoran Lodge
   Holiday
   Rwiza Village

😋 **Where to eat and drink**
   Home St Jean (see 3)
   Hotel Centre Béthanie (see 4)
   Hotel Golf Eden Rock (see 5)
11 Joyce
   Moriah Hill Resort (see 7)
12 New Umunyina House

Off map
   Rwiza Village

menu with main courses falling in the Rfr8,000–12,000 range. There's a sauna, private swimming beach, & a motorboat & kayaks for hire. *US$96/126 sgl/dbl; US$125/155 sgl/dbl exec; US$170 family room; all rates B&B with discounts around 15% for residents.*

Moderate

🛏 **Delta Resort Hotel** (20 rooms)
m 078 398 1000; e deltaresort@yahoo.com; w deltaresorthotel.com. This new terraced block facing the lakeshore at the north end of town doesn't have much character, but the rooms are trim & modern & have large private balconies with full views over the water. The appealing thatch-roofed restaurant & bar opens out into a small garden & serves a variety of pizzas, fish & meat dishes for Rfr4,000–8,000. *Rfr40,000 dbl; Rfr80,000 deluxe dbl; all rates B&B.*

🛏 **Holiday Hotel** (28 rooms) m 078 732 0326/835 4343; e holidayhotel01@yahoo. fr. Situated on the lakeshore about 1km north of the Golf Eden Rock, this hotel comprises a circular 3-storey building & a row of chalets set in uninspired gardens running down to the lakeshore. The rooms in the main building are poorly designed to accommodate a king-size bed, but they do have TV, large tiled en-suite bathroom with tub, & a small balcony. The semi-detached rooms in the chalets are also small & overall quite

similar, but they seem less awkwardly laid out. Either way, it feels like poor value. *Rfr45,000 for a dbl with lake view or Rfr40,000 without.*

🛏 **Hotel Centre Béthanie** (42 rooms)
m 078 495 7945; e bigltdbethany@hotmail.fr; w bethanyinvestmentgroup.com. This friendly Presbyterian lodge has a beautiful lakeshore position on a wooded peninsula, though it seems a shame that most of that wood consists of eucalyptus, pine & other exotic trees. The brick chalet-style rooms are a bit cramped together, but very clean, & they come with hot showers, netting & a view of the lake. A decent restaurant overlooking the lake serves a good selection of main dishes in the Rfr5,000–6,000 range, & a selection of lighter meals & snacks for around Rfr2,000. Normally there is plenty of space but it can fill up if there's a religious gathering or seminar, so it's safer to book in advance. A bit overpriced for what you get. *Rfr25,000/35,000 sgl/dbl; Rfr35,000/45,000 lakefront deluxe sgl/dbl; all rates B&B.*

🛏 **Hotel Golf Eden Rock** (76 rooms)
m 078 723 8320/853 1339/855 5574; e info@golfedenrockhotel.com; w golfedenrockhotel. com. Situated opposite the waterfront close to the post office, this large hotel has a great location, with excellent views over the lake, & pleasant en-suite rooms with a double bed, netting & polished floor. Ask for a room that leads on to the lower balcony. Facilities include an internet café/Wi-Fi & decent restaurant with indoor & outdoor seating. *Rfr20,000/25,000 dbl without/with lake view; inc B&B for 1.*

🛏 **Rebero Kivu Resort** (15 rooms) m 078 830 6025/830 6171. In school-like brick buildings just uphill from the Museum of the Environment, this new place hadn't fully begun operations at the time of research, but the completed rooms seem adequate, if rather bare. The lake views from the shared terraces in front of the rooms are undoubtedly fine, however, & meals can be arranged at request. *Rfr35,000 dbl.*

☀ 🛏 **Rwiza Village** (10 rooms) m 078 971 4551/830 7356; e info@rwizavillage.org; w rwizavillage.org. A few km outside town towards the KivuWatt plant, this country-chic place is arranged around lush gardens on a steep hillside sloping down to the lake, where you'll find a floating pier for swimming. Rooms are in appealing thatched A-frame cottages built into the hillside, all of which come with private balconies, en-suite bathrooms, big mozzie nets & decorative stone accents. It's both very comfortable & very characterful, & the conference room is built to mirror the king's palace in Nyanza. The terrace restaurant (also with fabulous lake views) does a good menu of seafood & meat, along with a surprising number of veg options. Boat trips are also easily arranged. *US$60/70/85 sgl/dbl/twin B&B*. See ad, 4th colour section.

Budget

⌂ **Home St Jean** (26 rooms) m 078 472 5107; e homesaintjean@ymail.com; w homesaintjean.com. Arguably the best-value option in Karongi, this Catholic guesthouse is tucked away down a lane to the right-hand side of the large hilltop church that you see as you enter town. Its most attractive feature is the tremendous hilltop views of the lake, & access to a small swimming beach via a steep footpath through neat gardens. A small restaurant with DSTV & Wi-Fi serves brochettes, pizzas & more substantial meals in the Rfr3,000–7,000 range, & it has a well-stocked bar. The rooms are all comfortable at the price, the nicest being the en suites (with ¾ bed) in the newer block facing the lake. *Rfr8,000 dorm bed; Rfr11,000/16,000/18,000 sgl/dbl/twin using common shower; Rfr15,000/20,000 sgl/dbl en suite; Rfr25,000/30,000 deluxe sgl/dbl en suite; all rates B&B*.

⌂ **Macheo Eco-Lodge** (3 rooms) m 078 717 2821; e reception@macheoecolodge.com; w macheoecolodge.com. Built into a hillside with expansive views over the large bay to the east of Karongi, this new backpacker-friendly wood-&-bamboo outpost is less than 500m from the main road but manages to feel delightfully remote. Of the 3 rooms, 2 have shared bathrooms, but the 1 en-suite room is the same price, so ask if it's available; all come with solar hot water. The camping area is spectacularly positioned for a scenic sunrise, & the resto-bar does a typical selection of Rwandan favourites for Rfr2,000–5,000. *Rfr30,000 dbl & trpl; Rfr15,000/20,000 camping in your/their tent*.

⌂ **Romantic Hotel** (28 rooms) m 078 206 6860. Though there's nothing particularly amorous about it, this is a centrally located & sensibly priced option with very tidy rooms set over 3 floors, many of them with balconies. There's an easy-going terrace resto-bar downstairs. Wi-Fi. *Rfr20,000–30,000 dbl, inc B&B for 1*.

Shoestring

⌂ **Centre d'Accueil Sainte Marie** (20 rooms) m 078 874 2303. Although it is a bit out of the way unless you have private transport, this clean little guesthouse run by Catholic Sisters is a pretty good option for single travellers (no doubles are available). There's a basic resto-bar on site. *The cheapest rooms, using common showers, cost Rfr5,000–6,000 & en-suite rooms cost Rfr10,000–20,000 depending on size & facilities*.

⌂ **Mulberry Guesthouse** (10 rooms) m 078 841 0408/620 2500. This is the cheapest central option in Karongi, & seems quite clean, pleasant & secure, set in a small green compound not far from the market & bus station. *Rfr5,000/6,000/8,000 en-suite sgl/dbl/twin with cold water & net*.

✗ **WHERE TO EAT AND DRINK** Most of the hotels listed above serve food. The **Moriah Hill Resort** offers a good variety of mains at reasonable prices, but it isn't so convenient for people staying elsewhere (unless you have a car – the same goes for **Rwiza Village**, which has a good selection of vegetarian options, but is several kilometres out of town). Elsewhere, the **Hotel Golf Eden Rock** serves snacks and meals in the Rfr5,000–7,000 range, but service is on the slow side, and nobody seems overly concerned about serving you the meal you actually ordered. The restaurants at **Béthanie** and **Home St Jean** are also good, with standard menus, and more efficient. In the town centre, **Joyce Restaurant** (m *078 863 0666*) is the place to go for a tasty lunch buffet, and the **New Umunyina House** (m *078 935 1348*) is a cheap, cheerful and bright blue resto-bar serving grills and Rwandan favourites; it's perched on a rise next to the bus station and market.

OTHER PRACTICALITIES The **post office** has international telephone facilities, and there's at least one **internet café** in the town centre. Otherwise, all but the cheapest hotels in town offer Wi-Fi. There is no forex bureau, but Bank of Kigali, GT Bank and Cogebanque all have **ATMs** in the centre, and there's an I&M Bank branch on the way out towards Rwiza Village.

WHAT TO SEE AND DO

Around town Karongi is such a relaxed, pleasant town that it's enjoyable just strolling and watching life unfold. There's a big **market** on Fridays, in an open area just beyond the hospital, when people come in from outlying villages and across the lake from Idjwi Island. The week-long market in the centre of town hasn't a huge range but is still worth a browse. The **Museum of the Environment** (m *073 346 0602*; w *museum.gov.rw;* ⊕ *08.00–18.00 daily except 7 Apr & 11.00–18.00 on Umuganda days; Rfr6,000 non-residents, Rfr5,000 foreign residents, Rfr3,000 students & non-resident children*) finally opened in 2015 and has largely taken over from Kandt House in Kigali (page 120) as Rwanda's natural history museum. Indeed, many exhibits have been moved from there, including displays on minerals, hydrology, fossils, artefacts, wildlife and volcanism in Rwanda, and a collection of stuffed animals and mounted butterflies from the various national parks, including a 600kg Nile crocodile that turned up with an undigested pair of shoes in its belly. The attractive rooftop gardens function as a living exhibition on traditional medicine in Rwanda, with a wide variety of native plants identified by placards detailing their uses. Unless you've a specialised interest, the exhibits are likely to only be modestly diverting, but the English-speaking guides are enthusiastic about the exhibits in their charge and can provide an in-depth tour, included in the ticket price. The collection should soon be boosted by artefacts from an archaeological excavation started in late 2017 on the nearby site of the old royal residence of Mwami Kigeri IV Rwagubiri, who in 1854 hosted the German explorer Gustav Adolf von Götzen (page 233). Ritual pots and other small items have already been discovered, as well as postholes that should make it possible to identify the layout of the site and buildings. The plan is then to develop it into a tourist attraction.

As the town map shows, you can do a **circular walk** along the main one-way road around Karongi. This offers some beautiful views across the lake and can be stretched to fill a couple of hours or so, depending on how often you stop to photograph, watch birds, or just enjoy the surroundings. Views are slightly better going clockwise rather than anticlockwise – with the added advantage that you'll be facing any oncoming traffic, so can take evasive action more quickly! Once you've passed the hospital on your way up to the Béthanie there's nowhere to get a drink until you're back down by the Golf Eden Rock, so you may want to carry some water.

Genocide memorial church As you enter Karongi from the east, you'll see a large church perched on a hill above the town. During the genocide, over 11,400 died there. Lindsey Hilsum caught the stark horror of it in an article in *Granta* issue 51:

> The church stands among trees on a promontory above the calm blue of Lake Kivu. The Tutsis were sheltering inside when a mob, drunk on banana beer, threw grenades through the doors and windows and then ran in to club and stab to death the people who remained alive. It took about three hours.

For some time the church remained empty and scarred. Then gradually work started – new mosaics were sketched out and then completed, and new stained glass filled the broken windows. New hangings adorned the altar. A memorial has been built outside by the relatives of those who died there and nearby. During the week it is generally empty, for anyone who wants to go to reflect peacefully on the past, but on Sundays now it is filled with worshippers and their singing wafts out across Lake Kivu. Sometimes commemorative services are held. A memorial of this kind is arguably more evocative and moving than the skulls of Nyamata or the corpses of Murambi. Here there is an echoing beauty, which is no bad accompaniment to thoughts of death. Try to find time for a few reflective minutes in this deeply memorable place.

Boat trips Apart from longer trips to Rusizi/Cyangugu and Rubavu/Gisenyi (page 203) there are possibilities for trips on Lake Kivu and to nearby islands. The steep-sided Napoleon's Island, said to be shaped like its namesake's hat, supports quite a number of birds as well as a colony of thousands of fruit bats, which rise from the slopes like a massive chattering cloud when disturbed. By contrast, tiny Amahoro (Peace) Island was once a popular chill-out spot with a restaurant and camping. This has now shut down, but the short walking trail around its rocky northern extension remains worth a look. The Hotel Centre Béthanie and Moriah Hill Resort

BISESERO *Janice Booth*

In the hills high above Karongi, often shrouded in mountain mist, Bisesero is a place of great sadness and great heroism. Of the estimated 800,000 or so people who lost their lives throughout the whole country during the genocide, more than 6% were slaughtered here in this one area; but the resistance they mounted against the killers – and maintained for almost three months – was the strongest and most courageous in all of Rwanda.

When the genocide began on 7 April 1994, Tutsis from the whole surrounding region converged on Bisesero for refuge, numbering around 50,000 at their height. Then the killers came, an assortment of military, trained interahamwe and villagers, heavily armed and equipped with vehicles. The people of Bisesero had machetes and other rudimentary weapons and managed to survive relatively well until mid-May, killing a number of their attackers and repulsing others. But it was bitterly cold in the hills and raining heavily, and they were short of food.

On 13 May, the attackers returned in full force, including many militia and soldiers, and with weapons that the refugees in Bisesero could not match, although they did their best to group themselves effectively and fought fiercely hand-to-hand. The battle raged for 8 hours and resumed the next day. By the end, around half of the refugees had died. The exhausted survivors had little choice but to hide in the forest and put up what sporadic resistance they could. The attacks continued relentlessly. By the time the French arrived at the end of June, only around 1,300 of the 50,000 were still alive. But – they had survived.

Set on a hillside about 30km from Karongi along route NR12, Bisesero Genocide Memorial (✪ S 02°11.508, E 29°20.480), maintained by the National Commission for the Fight Against Genocide (w *cnlg.gov.rw*), comprises nine small buildings, each of which represents one of the nine communes that formerly made up the province of Kibuye. Within these buildings are a chilling collection of human bones and skulls, along with other related documents. The site of the memorial is now called the 'Hill of Resistance' because of the heroic events that took place there. It's a sad, moving and evocative place, where the sense of history is very strong.

(page 203) both have motorboats for hire, but it is cheaper to make arrangements at Cotralaki, near the Bralirwa Depot, which charges around Rfr25,000 per hour for groups of up to 15 people. Because the charge for motorised boats is per hour, you'll pay a lot more if the boat waits for you at one of the islands than if you are dropped and arrange to be collected later.

Chutes de Ndaba

One of the largest waterfalls in Rwanda, Ndaba lies at an altitude of 2,150m about 26km from Karongi along the Muhanga/Gitarama road (✥ S 02°02.874, E 29°28.184). It is not easy to see, as the top of the waterfall lies just below the road, but look out for an (unrelated) signboard just past the falls (on the right coming from Karongi) reading 'Nyange Heroes' Mausoleum'. In the rainy season it's an impressive 100m cascade, in the dry season a fairly unimpressive straggle. Either way, a rough footpath leads to the base of the waterfall (some children will doubtless guide you, hoping for a tip), where you get a far better view than from along the road.

Mukura Forest (Gishwati-Mukura National Park)

This 12km² relict forest patch to the northeast of Karongi, formerly part of a continuous belt of forest connecting Nyungwe in the south to Gishwati in the south, remains one of the most extensive in Rwanda, despite having lost 50% of its area since it was gazetted in 1951. A true montane rainforest, it lies high on the Rift Valley wall, with an average altitude of 2,600m, and an annual precipitation of around 1,500mm, though much of the vegetation is badly degraded due to logging and encroachment. The most important component of the forest's fauna is its birdlife, which comprises more than 150 recorded species including 17 AREs, all of which it shares with Nyungwe. Although Mukura is not yet formally developed for tourism, 1,988ha of the forest were officially protected as part of the Gishwati-Mukura National Park in 2015, along with a 696ha buffer zone. As it stands now, there are no authorised activities here, but the forest is accessible from the road connecting Karongi to Muhanga, heading north at either Rwimpiri (✥ S 02°03.042, E 29°26.753) on to road DR21, or at Nyange (✥ S 02°03.240, E 29°36.144) on to road DR18, then left after 2.2km on to road DR19. Both are dirt roads that lead close to the forest edge.

RUBAVU (GISENYI)

The largest port on the Rwandan shore of Lake Kivu, Rubavu (formerly Gisenyi) is an attractive resort town situated about 110km north of Karongi by road, and 60km west of the gorilla-tracking base of Musanze/Ruhengeri. It is the second-largest town in Rwanda, with a population estimated at 140,000, and it lies a mere 6km from the smaller lakeside village of Rubona, with its burgeoning concentration of bona fide beach resorts. This combination of good tourist facilities – arguably the best of any urban centre outside the capital – and a seductive tropical ambience make Rubavu the ideal place to chill out for a few days after tracking gorillas.

In 1907, the Duke of Mecklenburg wrote of the then Gisenyi:

> Kissenji possesses an excellent climate, for by virtue of its 1,500 metres above sea level all enervating heat is banished. The natural coolness prevalent in consequence makes a visit there a very agreeable experience. The man who has this place allotted to him for his sphere of activity draws a prize. In front are the swirling breakers of the most beautiful of all the Central African lakes, framed in by banks which fall back steeply from the rugged masses of rock; at the rear the stately summits of the eight Virunga volcanoes.

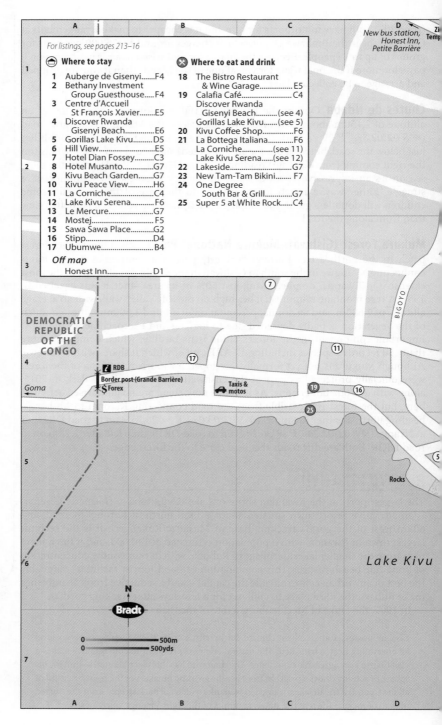

For listings, see pages 213–16

Where to stay

1	Auberge de Gisenyi	F4
2	Bethany Investment Group Guesthouse	F4
3	Centre d'Accueil St François Xavier	E5
4	Discover Rwanda Gisenyi Beach	E6
5	Gorillas Lake Kivu	D5
6	Hill View	E5
7	Hotel Dian Fossey	C3
8	Hotel Musanto	G7
9	Kivu Beach Garden	G7
10	Kivu Peace View	H6
11	La Corniche	C4
12	Lake Kivu Serena	F6
13	Le Mercure	G7
14	Mostej	F5
15	Sawa Sawa Place	G2
16	Stipp	D4
17	Ubumwe	B4

Off map

Honest Inn..................... D1

Where to eat and drink

18	The Bistro Restaurant & Wine Garage	E5
19	Calafia Café	C4
	Discover Rwanda Gisenyi Beach	(see 4)
	Gorillas Lake Kivu	(see 5)
20	Kivu Coffee Shop	F6
21	La Bottega Italiana	F6
	La Corniche	(see 11)
	Lake Kivu Serena	(see 12)
22	Lakeside	G7
23	New Tam-Tam Bikini	F7
24	One Degree South Bar & Grill	G7
25	Super 5 at White Rock	C4

New bus station, Honest Inn, Petite Barrière

DEMOCRATIC REPUBLIC OF THE CONGO

RDB
Border post (Grande Barrière)
Forex

Goma

Taxis & motos

Rocks

Lake Kivu

N

Bradt

0 — 500m
0 — 500yds

Airport (1km)

Airport (1.5 km)

E   F   G   H

1

Umuganda   Om

Pentecostal
church

15

Islamic
school

Delta

2

Mosque

MILITANTE

POISSONS   Cogebanque

Bank of   Boulangerie
Kigali   de Gisenyi

New market   Engen
(under
construction)   Banque
Moto stand   Populaire

1

Kobil   Forex bureau

EcoBank   Iby' Iwacu

Pharmacy

3

MTN   I&M

2   KCB

GTbank

Nyiragongo
Expedition   14

INDUSTRIE   MARCHE

COPROVEPA
shop

3

Catholic church

Presbyterian
church

4

5

ubavu District
Admin   Access

6

INDEPENDANCE

Police

CO-OPERATION

20

Cultural centre   Green Hills Eco-Tours
& Kingfisher Journeys

4

Police   African Art   Catholic
21   Gallery   Grotto

EcoBank   Merez

12   SP

Jetty   Gemera   10

Swimming Beach   RUHENGERI

PRODUCTION

Football
field

Volcanoes National Park,
Musanze (Ruhengeri),
Kibuye (Karangi), Kigali

23   9

7

Fish market

24

13   8

22

Rubona hotels & ferry   H

E   F   G

Split into an upper and a lower town, Rubavu today still has most of the attributes extolled by the duke a century ago. This is particularly so for the lower town, which comprises a leafy and spaciously laid-out conglomeration of banks, government offices, old colonial homesteads and upmarket hotels separated from the lakeshore by a neat park where children dive and swim, and courting couples walk hand-in-hand below shady trees. Indeed, with its red sandy beaches, mismatched architectural styles and shady palm-lined avenues, this part of Rubavu has the captivating ennui of a slightly down-at-heel tropical beach resort, except that the relatively high altitude means it has a more refreshing climate. Though several of the more characterful old waterfront buildings have been knocked down in the name of urban renewal, so far the streets along the waterfront have managed to retain the easy-going tropical character that makes them so appealing.

Altogether livelier is the upper town, which consists of an undistinguished grid of busy roads centred around the central market but has some useful facilities for travellers, including the main bus station and several supermarkets, internet cafés, forex bureaux and banks. In clear weather, the northern skyline of the upper town is dominated by the distinctive volcanic outline of Nyiragongo, whose active crater often belches out smoke by day and glows ominously at night.

Rubavu offers little in the way of formal sightseeing, but its singular atmosphere makes it the sort of town that you could easily settle into and explore at random, whether your interest lies in the prolific birds that line the lakeshore, the fantastic old colonial buildings that dot the leafy suburban avenues, lazing around on the beach, or mixing in to the hustle and bustle of the market area. And once you have exhausted the town itself, there's always the 6km walk or minibus drive to **Rubona**, which now acts as a kind of satellite resort to Rubavu itself.

Further afield, the Congo-Nile Trail, which runs south along the lakeshore to Rusizi/Cyangugu, officially starts at Rubona, which is also the base for popular cycling trips pioneered by Rwandan Adventures (page 217). Other day-tripping possibilities include the Imbabazi Foundation, the Gishwati Forest portion of the new Gishwati-Mukura National Park, and the 'birding area' centred on lakes Karago and Nyarakigugu on the Musanze/Ruhengeri road. More ambitiously, you could cross from Rubavu into the DRC to explore Goma and the magnificent Virunga National Park (page 325).

GETTING THERE AND AWAY All buses and minibus-taxis leave from the bus station [210 D1] at the north end of town near the *Petite Barrière*. The main port for Rubavu is at Rubona, about 6km south of town; the two are connected by regular minibuses.

To/from Kigali and Musanze/Ruhengeri Rubavu lies approximately 60km from Musanze by road, and 160km from Kigali. The road is sealed and in good condition, and the direct drive from Kigali should take about 3 hours. Regularly scheduled midibuses connect the three towns; the fare from Rubavu to Musanze is Rfr1,200 and to Kigali Rfr3,000. The most reliable service is Virunga Express (m *078 830 8620/830 0169/838 0982;* w *virungaexpress.net*), which departs every 30 minutes between 05.00 and 19.00.

To/from Karongi/Kibuye and Rusizi/Cyangugu To drive from Rubavu to Karongi, you first need to head out along the Musanze road for about 10km to Pfunda, before turning right at a well-signposted junction (✛ *S 1°41.962, E 29°19.081*) on to the newly surfaced road that leads to Rubengera on the surfaced road between Kigali and Karongi. It's a drive of about 105km in all, and can be done in about 2 hours. The road runs parallel to Lake Kivu, offering occasional glimpses down to the water and more consistently thrilling views of the surrounding mountain scenery, plus relic patches of Gishwati Forest (page 222). From Karongi, it's another 115km of newly surfaced road to Rusizi.

On public transport, scheduled midibuses with Kivu Belt (m *078 272 5229*) run from Rubavu to Karongi hourly throughout the day (*Rfr2,500*), with three continuing to Rusizi (*Rfr4,500*) at 06.30, 08.30, and 13.30.

As for lake transport, ferries ply the Rwandan side of Lake Kivu, calling at Rusizi/Cyangugu, Karongi/Kibuye, and Rubona (for Rubavu/Gisenyi). The boats (m *078 856 3431/199 6764, 072 896 3431*) make the southbound trip from Rubona twice weekly, departing at 07.00 on Wednesdays and Sundays and charging Rfr2,000 to Karongi (*3hrs*) and Rfr5,000 to Rusizi (*9hrs*). Boats head north from Rusizi on Tuesdays and Fridays.

WHERE TO STAY Rubavu has a range of accommodation to suit most tastes and budgets, with the smartest options generally situated on the waterfront and the cheaper ones set back in the upper town closer to the bus station (with the notable exception of Discover Rwanda Gisenyi Beach). For genuine beach resorts, however, you are better heading to Rubona, which lies 6km away, and is covered separately on pages 218–22.

Luxury

Lake Kivu Serena Hotel [211 F6] (66 rooms) 0252 541100; m 078 820 0430; e kivu@ serena.co.rw; w serenahotels.com. Acquired by the prestigious Kenyan-based Serena Group in 2007, the former Kivu Sun is among the only urban hotels outside of the capital that truly conforms to international standards, & it forms a justifiably popular w/end retreat for Kigali-based expatriates & NGO workers. The green & well-wooded lakeshore grounds lead down to a sandy swimming beach; the spacious & comfortable en-suite rooms all have AC, minibar, safe, DSTV & en-suite bathroom with tub/shower. Other facilities include a sparkling swimming pool, a fitness centre with spa & massage facilities, a gift shop, well-trained English-speaking staff, free Wi-Fi access throughout the building, & a highly rated restaurant with indoor & outdoor tables & a varied menu serving grills, curries & salads in the Rfr8,000–15,000 bracket. Visa & Mastercard accepted. *US$210/275/425 sgl/dbl/suite B&B.*

Upmarket

Gorillas Lake Kivu Hotel [210 D5] (35 rooms) m 078 820 0522–4; e reservation@ gorillashotels.com; w gorillashotels.com. This modernistic upmarket hotel on the Rubavu waterfront doesn't match the Serena in terms

of class, but it feels like a reliable & efficient choice at less than half the price. The bland but neat rooms come with a twin or king-size bed, writing desk, built-in wardrobes, flatscreen DSTV, & a small bathroom with combined tub/shower. Other facilities include a massive swimming pool (*Rfr4,000 for non-guests*), free Wi-Fi, & an excellent restaurant with a varied selection of main courses in the Rfr6,000–12,000 range. Decent value. *US$80/100/120 sgl/dbl/twin B&B.*

Hill View Hotel [211 E5] (49 rooms) m 078 034 5858/073 434 5858/072 354 5094; e info@ hillviewhotelkivu.com; w hillviewhotelkivu.com. The newest accommodation on Rubavu's *corniche*, this large complex is broadly similar in price & standard to the other 2 upmarket options, but with the advantage of newer facilities. That said, the standard rooms are surprisingly small (gold & silver rooms are considerably larger), but all are nonetheless well equipped. There's an appealing swimming pool & thatched resto-bar in the gardens out front. *US$80/100 standard sgl/dbl; US$110/130 'silver' sgl/dbl; US$150/170 'gold' sgl/ dbl; all rates B&B.*

Stipp Hotel [210 D4] (26 rooms) m 078 830 4335/6; e management@stipphotelrwanda. com; w stipphotelrwanda.com Boasting a suburban location about 1km northwest of the Serena, this renovated colonial building lies in attractive landscaped grounds overlooking the lake, but is separated from the shore by a road & a tall wall. It is of similar standard to the Gorillas Hotel, but a lot smaller, with smart modern décor, a more personalised feel, & reasonable rates. There is a large, clean swimming pool, the restaurant serves a varied selection of meals for around Rfr6,000–12,000 per main course, the large carpeted en-suite rooms all come with DSTV & (in most cases) a lake view, & facilities include a gym, sauna & free Wi-Fi. *US$100/120/140 sgl/dbl/ twin B&B.*

Moderate

🏠 **Hotel Dian Fossey** [210 C3] (29 rooms) m 078 830 5511/851 7591; e dianfosseyhotel1@ yahoo.com. This suburban lodge, set in a cluttered compound decorated with large Disney-on-acid animal sculptures, would be few people's choice on aesthetic grounds. Otherwise, it is an agreeable enough set-up, with friendly staff, & the tiled en-suite rooms represent good value for money in this range. *Rfr25,000 sgl with ¾ bed & net; Rfr30,000 dbl with queen-size bed, TV, tub & ample cupboard space; Rfr45,000 suite with king-size bed, sofa, TV & fridge.*

🏠 **Hotel Musanto** [211 G7] (23 rooms) m 078 834 6434/304 7180; e hotelmusanto@ yahoo.fr; w hotelmusanto.com. Just opposite the string of restaurants at the beginning of the road to Rubona, this is a very pleasant & well-tended address, with trim whitewashed rooms set on 2 floors around a green garden area. Upper-floor rooms have balconies & all come with nets, hot water, TV & Wi-Fi. It's under the same management as the New Tam-Tam Bikini across the road, but meals & drinks are also available on site should you prefer a quiet night in. *US$30/35 basic sgl/dbl; US$35/40 standard sgl/dbl; US$45 twin; US$40/45 deluxe sgl/dbl; all rates B&B.*

🏠 **Kivu Beach Garden** [211 G7] (6 rooms) m 078 561 2169/072 249 6928; e kivubeachgarden@gmail.com; 🔲 Beach Garden BnB. At the start of the road to Rubona, this is a small new guesthouse with several slightly under-furnished but lovingly decorated rooms with low beds & en-suite hot-water ablutions. They only serve b/fast but plan to expand to other meals; in the meantime there are a number of good restaurants just across the street. *Rfr30,000/35,000 dbl/twin B&B.*

🏠 **Kivu Peace View Hotel** [211 H6] (32 rooms) m 078 832 6330; e info@kivupeaceviewhotel.com; w kivupeaceviewhotel.com. Built into the hillside at a variety of dizzying angles, this new diocese-owned hotel at the entrance to town has an Escher-esque surfeit of stairs heading in seemingly all directions, but good-quality rooms (all en suite with mosquito nets & TV, many with balconies) once you reach them. The pricing structure is almost as complicated as the architecture, but all the rooms represent excellent value & the top-floor restaurant & bar is uniquely well situated for commanding views over the lake. *Rfr15,000/20,000 sgl/dbl inc b/fast for 1; Rfr30,000 dbl & twin B&B; Rfr40,000 deluxe dbl B&B.*

🏠 **Mostej Hotel** [211 F5] (20 rooms) ☎0252 540486; m 078 302 6757/835 0366; e mostejhotel@yahoo.com; 🔲. Boasting an indifferent location between the market & the lakeshore, this solidly built & modern-looking hotel feels rather bland, functional & probably a touch overpriced. All rooms are en suite with hot shower & DSTV, but the cheaper rooms are quite cramped & have a ¾ bed, whereas more expensive rooms have a king-size bed, small balcony & large bathroom. *US$32 small sgl; US$50/57 large sgl/dbl; all rates B&B.*

Budget

🏠 **Centre d'Accueil St François Xavier** [211 E5] (30 rooms) m 072/078 448 8576; e nyundocasfx@yahoo.fr; w nyundodiocese.info/ Divers.html. Situated on a back road between the town centre & waterfront, this church-run hostel has surprisingly pleasant & clean twin rooms, each with 2 ¾ beds & en-suite hot shower. There's a bar-resto serving up the usuals on site & free Wi-Fi. Good value. *Rfr2,500 dorm bed; Rfr5,000/7,000 sgl/ dbl using shared ablutions; Rfr10,000/15,000 sgl/ dbl en suite.*

✳ 🏠 **Discover Rwanda Gisenyi Beach** [211 E6] (5 rooms) m 078 158 6272; e hostelgisenyi@ discoverrwanda.org; w discoverrwanda.org; 🔲. There's a delicious historical irony in the former colonial governor's mansion being turned into a youth hostel, & that's before you even realise you're also right next door to the most expensive hotel in town. Set in wide, manicured gardens as would befit the building's historical pedigree & just across the street from the beach, this breezy place is under the same management as the Discover

Rwanda hostel in Kigali, & has rightfully become the go-to spot for tourists & locals alike since it opened here in 2014. The rooms & dorms are all spotlessly clean & brightly decorated in wax prints & Rwandan handicrafts, while the popular restaurant does a rotating menu of Rwandan favourites starting around Rfr3,500. There's plenty of space for campers, & they can help arrange trips throughout the region. *US$40/50 sgl/dbl using shared ablutions; US$50/60 sgl/dbl en suite; US$19pp twin; US$17pp 8-bed dorm; US$10pp camping; all rates B&B.*

🏠 **La Corniche** [210 C4] (11 rooms) m 078 489 6949/832 2234; e motel.la.corniche@gmail.com; w lacornichemotel.com. Set alongside a pleasant garden bar & restaurant a short walk north of the lakeshore, this is an adequate & homely lodge. Most rooms have 1 single & 1 double bed, & an en-suite hot bath or shower. Some rooms are nicer than others so look before you commit. Wi-Fi. *Rfr21,000–40,000 dbl.*

🏠 **Sawa Sawa Place** [211 G2] (20 rooms) m 078 343 6644/265 1104; e ngaboking@gmail.com. Upstairs, this newish place on the way to the airport has pleasant en-suite tiled double rooms (that are airier & more expensive the higher you go) with Wi-Fi, flatscreen TVs, & private balconies on the top floor. Downstairs, there's an amenable thatched bar-resto dishing up the usuals with football on the flatscreen & beer on draught. *Rfr15,000/20,000 sgl/twin; Rfr50,000 top-floor dbl.*

🏠 **Ubumwe Hotel** [210 B4] (25 rooms) m 078 850 6647/328 5745/850 0601; e ubumwehotel2006@yahoo.fr; w ubumwehotel.rw. Barely 150m from the new border post, this old standby is mostly of note for its convenient location, but the en-suite rooms are well kept, with hot en-suite ablutions, & deluxe rooms have balconies. There's a resto-bar serving a standard menu & a small garden out front. *Rfr20,000/25,000 sgl/dbl; Rfr35,000 deluxe dbl; all rates B&B.*

Shoestring

🏠 **Auberge de Gisenyi** [211 F4] (20 rooms) m 078 404 3049. Situated close to the market, this is a standard local guesthouse & bar/restaurant with small en-suite rooms (cold water, hot buckets by request). *Rfr8,000/9,000/12,000 sgl/dbl/exec.*

🏠 **Bethany Investment Group Guesthouse** [211 G4] (13 rooms) m 078 573 0113; e bigltd@hotmail.fr/contact@bethanyinvestment.com; w bethanyinvestmentgroup.com. This agreeable Presbyterian-affiliated lodge near the market has long been one of the best deals in this range, despite its distance (about a 10min walk) from the lake, with bright & fresh rooms set in spaciously laid-out grounds that also contain a basic but good-value restaurant. *Rfr3,000 dorm bed; Rfr5,000/10,000 sgl/dbl with shared bathroom; Rfr8,000/10,000 en-suite sgl/dbl or twin with nets & hot water.*

🏠 **Honest Inn** [210 D1] (12 rooms) m 078 150 4478/797 6263. At not even 100m away, this is by far the closest accommodation to the new bus station (make a right out the gate & an immediate right at the next street), & unlike most places in such close proximity to a taxi park, it's actually quite pleasant. The en-suite rooms are impressively clean & come with hot water & mozzie nets, & the resto-bar on the other side of the grassy grounds is quite popular, but rooms seem to be far enough removed from the action to avoid major noise issues. *Rfr10,00–15,000 en-suite dbl.*

🏠 **Le Mercure** [211 G7] (6 rooms) m 078 342 4750. This no-frills guesthouse feels like it belongs in a rural village rather than on one of Rubavu's most happening stretches of beach, but if the concrete-floored ambience doesn't put you off, there are good cheap rooms here with mozzie nets, hot water & Wi-Fi, & you couldn't get closer to the water if you tried. It's sandwiched between a couple of popular bars, however, so noise could be an issue at w/ends. *Rfr15,000 dbl; Rfr30,000 deluxe dbl.*

◀ **WHERE TO EAT AND DRINK** Most of the smarter hotels have adequate to good restaurants. For top-notch continental cuisine, the **Gorillas Lake Kivu Hotel** [210 D5] should be your first port of call, but it lacks the outdoor ambience of the almost-as-good **Lake Kivu Serena** [211 F6]. You can also eat well in the pretty gardens of **Discover Rwanda Gisenyi Beach** [211 E6], which is also a popular hangout for a casual drink. There are plenty of budget eateries around the market area, of which the **Auberge de Gisenyi** [211 F4] is recommended. For dedicated clubbers, **Super 5** at **White Rock** [210 C5] has a DJ downstairs and live music upstairs on Friday and Saturday nights.

✗ **The Bistro Restaurant & Wine Garage** [211 E5] ⏲ 10.00–22.00 Sun–Thu, 11.00–23.30 Fri & Sat. Hours listed above are for the kitchen; the bar is open until late daily. This tranquil garden restaurant sits in a leafy compound just off the corniche road & boasts the longest wine list in town, plus a good menu of pizzas & European dishes around Rfr5,000–6,000.

✳ ✗ **Calafia Café** [210 C4] m 078 793 8145; ⓕ; ⏲ 08.00–20.00 Mon–Thu, 08.00–22.00 Fri & Sat, 09.00–18.00 Sun. Set atop a small hill in a restored old colonial house near the lake, this gorgeous new café is reached by a path through the organic gardens where much of their produce is grown. There are several rooms of seating (with Wi-Fi), a long list of coffee beverages, & probably the most inventive menu you'll find outside of Kigali – don't expect to get fish tacos, a gin fizz or a kale & avocado salad anywhere else in Rubavu. Most meals are around Rfr5,000 & there's a children's playground out front.

✗ **Kivu Coffee Shop** [211 F6] m 078 852 8771; ⏲ 08.00–19.00 daily. Situated next to the Green Hills Eco-Tours office, this small & easily missed café serves excellent filter coffee for Rfr1,000, as well as a selection of inexpensive light meals & snacks.

✗ **La Corniche** [210 C4] m 078 489 6949. Set in a pretty suburban garden, this place is notable for its expansive lunchtime buffets, which are great value for the hungry at Rfr3,000–4,000. It functions mainly as a garden bar in the evenings, but a limited selection of affordable snacks is also available.

✗ **Lakeside Restaurant** [211 G7] ⏲ 10.00–22.00 Sun–Thu, 10.00–02.00 Fri & Sat. This beachside hangout is the place to head to for DJs & beach parties at the w/end, & Salsa dancing on Thu nights, plus pizzas & continental dishes throughout the week at around Rfr5,000–7,000.

✗ **New Tam-Tam Bikini** [211 F7] m 078 849 6959; ⏲ 08.00–23.00 daily, later at w/ends. Smack on the beach alongside the Rubona road, this is a great spot for sundowners – indeed for a drink at any time of day – & it's correspondingly popular. They do a short menu of inexpensive meals & grills in addition to cold beverages, & it's the perfect spot to try the Lake Kivu speciality of sambaza (small, sardine-like fish) if you haven't already.

✗ **Super 5 at White Rock** [210 C4] m 078 300 0935; ⏲ 08.00–midnight Tue–Sun, with a downstairs nightclub on Fri & Sat only. Among the most attractive places to eat in Rubavu, this long-serving place is centred on a large covered deck right above the lakeshore, but with indoor seating too, & a pool table, occasional live music, & a nightclub downstairs. The menu, though not extensive, includes snacks for around Rfr3,500, pizzas for Rfr5,000–7,000, a variety of full fish, meat & vegetarian meals at around Rfr6,000–9,000, & a tempting choice of desserts for Rfr5,000–6,000. The bar is well stocked but disproportionately pricey.

✗ **One Degree South Bar & Grill** [211 G7] m 078 553 3000; ⓕ; ⏲ noon–22.00 Tue & Wed, 10.00–22.00 Thu, 10.00–midnight Fri–Sun. The Lebanese-inspired menu of meze makes this a thoroughly exotic option in Rubavu, so if it's *kefta* & *baba ghanoush* you're after, this is the only address you need to know. It's also probably the hippest bar on this stretch of beach, with a long bar to belly up to & a loyal clientele. The meze check in at about Rfr2,500, with larger meals (including a rotating seafood *plat du jour*) more like Rfr4,000–8,000. There's draught beer & a good selection of fresh juices.

♀ **La Bottega Italiana** [211 F6] ⏲ 14.00–midnight daily. Attached to the supermarket of the same name, this is a very pleasant little bar, serving up draught beer in an open courtyard with a big projector screen for movies & likely football.

OTHER PRACTICALITIES

Tourist information and gorilla-tracking permits The Rwanda Development Board (RDB) tourist information and booking office [210 A4] (m *078 831 7031;* ⏲ *07.00–17.00 Mon–Fri, 07.00–14.00 Sat & Sun*) sits inside the Rwandan half of the new Grande Barrière (corniche) border post, just off the lake at the west end of Avenue de l'Indépendance. Gorilla-tracking permits can be booked here (along with RDB offices in Kigali, Kinigi and Musanze) and payments can be made in cash or by Visa card. The office can also supply information about travel elsewhere in the country, and stocks a variety of books, maps and handouts. It is also the place to book and make guide arrangements for the Congo-Nile Trail (unless you are cycling it with Rwandan Adventures; see below), and to arrange guides for other local attractions.

Tour operators

Green Hills Eco-Tours [211 F6] m 078 821 9495/072 222 0000; e rwandacongotours@gmail. com; w greenhillsecotours.com. This operator has been recommended for organised cross-border visits to Goma & Virunga National Park in the DRC, & also offers day excursions out of Rubavu to Batwa communities, Dancing Pots & various other local attractions.

Rwandan Adventures [map, page 218] m 078 657 1414/740 5531; e info@rwandan-adventures.com; w rwandan-adventures.com. This dynamic, flexible & responsive company is operated by a British/Rwandan pair of cycling enthusiasts, and its speciality is cycling tours that follow the Congo-Nile Trail (see box, pages 224–5) in part or in full, & range from half a day to a week in duration. These can be either supported by a chaperone (*US$40pp/day for helmet & bicycle, inc an emergency tool kit & essential spare parts*), or fully guided (*from US$80pp/day*). It also offers guided bicycle & walking tours of Rubavu town, Gishwati Forest, the Kinunu Coffee Estate, lakes Burera & Ruhondo near Musanze, or Mount Rebero near Kigali – see its website for an ever-expanding full list of activities. And if you have any other specialist interest in the Rubavu area, from birding or botany to hiking or caving, this would be an excellent first contact. See ad, page 190.

Rwanda Bike Adventures/Bike Shop \+250 787 136 642; e info@rwandabikeadventures. com; w rwandabikeadventures.com. A new

company offering walking & bike tours as well as bike hire. See ad, page 229.

Kingfisher Journeys [211 F6] m 078 381 1918; e info@kingfisherjourneys.com; w kingfisherjourneys.com. Whether it's for a 4-day excursion down to Karongi or just a half-day paddle around town, this new outfit has the guides & the kayaks to get you out on the lake without the roar of a motor. Details of all their trips are available on their informative website. See ad, page 256.

Nyiragongo Expedition [211 F5] m 078 488 2060; e info@nyiragongoexpedition.com; w nyiragongoexpedition.com. This responsive new agency with an office just downhill from the Mostej Hotel can arrange cross-border trips to the DRC, local excursions & tours along the lake, as well as customisable packages throughout Rwanda.

Okapi Tours m 078 358 9405 (Rwanda), 082 556 6810 (DRC); e okapitoursandtravelcompany@gmail. com/emmanuelrufubya@yahoo.fr; w okapitoursandtravel.org. Represented on both sides of the Goma–Rubavu border, this small agency can arrange anything from city tours of Goma or Gisenyi to excursions deep into the DRC – they know both countries like the backs of their 2 hands. There's no fixed office at the moment, so just give Emmanuel a shout & you can arrange a convenient meeting point. See ad, page 190.

Foreign exchange Most of the banks marked on the map will change US dollars cash, but you'll get better rates and more efficient service at any of several forex bureaux dotted around the market area [211 F/G4]. All the major banks are represented with ATMs along the main road near the market, and the Bank of Kigali [211 F3] also has Western Union.

Internet A few cyber cafés can be found in the market area, and the one directly above the EcoBank [211 F4] has fast and inexpensive access. Discover Rwanda Gisenyi Beach and the new Calafia Café both have Wi-Fi, which you can use for the price of a meal or drink.

Shopping The **Boulangerie de Gisenyi** [211 F3] opposite the market is a very well-stocked supermarket with a good bakery, and **La Bottega Italiana** [211 F6] has a good selection of groceries, along with a small meat and cheese deli. For **handicrafts**, the shop run by the COPROVEPA co-operative [211 G5] on the main road running south from the market is worth a look. The **African Art Gallery** [211 F6] near La Bottega Italiana and the RDB office also carries a good variety of art and souvenirs.

AROUND RUBAVU

Rubona Set on an attractive bay 6km from Rubavu, the bustling little satellite town of Rubona is the main harbour on the northern lakeshore and the site of the Brasseries et Limonaderies du Rwanda (Bralirwa), the country's largest brewery. It's become an important and very likeable tourist focus, with a growing number of mid-priced lakeside resorts making it an attractive retreat both for Kigali residents and for travellers seeking a restful few days by the lake.

Although it is mainly of interest for its beaches, Rubona is fun to stroll around. At times – usually in the early morning or late evening – hundreds of small fishing canoes dot the harbour, some boasting a distinctive catamaran-style design comprising three separate dugouts held together by poles. The fish in this bay have an unusual diet, as dregs from the brewing process at Bralirwa Brewery are thrown into the water regularly, but the fishermen mostly ply their trade further afield, and at night their lanterns can sometimes be seen distantly bobbing on the open water.

RUBONA		

For listings, see pages 219–22

Where to stay

1. Eden Garden Lodge
2. Hakuna Matata
3. Inzozi Beach
4. Inzu Lodge
5. La Bella Lodge & Campsite
6. La Maison St Benoît
7. Nirvana Heights Resort
8. Palm Beach Resort
9. Palm Garden Resort
10. Paradis Malahide
11. Sawa Sawa Beach
12. Sous le Soleil

Where to eat and drink

13. Jacaranda

Most of the lakeshore resorts have boats you can use to explore the lake, but it is also easy enough to arrange an outing in a local dugout.

About halfway along this road, near the village of Gitsamba, a signposted dirt road leads uphill for about 1km to the **Rubona Hill Scenic Viewpoint** (easily located by its twin satellite towers), which offers wonderful views over the lake to central Rubavu and the Congolese city of Goma, with Nyiragongo and some of the other Virungas providing a compelling backdrop.

Getting there and away Rubona is connected to Rubavu by two surfaced roads, but unfortunately the more appealing of these, following the lakeshore in its entirely, is closed to the public due to the presence of an important military installation. The main road between the two towns runs inland, following a scenic route that would make for a pleasant stroll in one or other direction. Regular minibus-taxis run along the Rubavu–Rubona road, charging Rfr300 one-way in either direction. A moto costs around Rfr1,000.

Where to stay *Map, page 218*
There is now a good choice of mid-range beach resorts in Rubona, but genuine budget accommodation is thin on the ground, and travellers seeking a cheap lakeside room are advised instead to head for the Maison St Benoît, which lies in Kigufi about 3km from Rubona traffic circle (page 221).

Moderate

Hakuna Matata (6 rooms) m 078 795 4645/748 4954; e info@hakunamatatalodge. rw; w hakunamatatalodge.rw. The very last stop on the Rubona road, this new place sits in a lush, tree-studded garden that sprawls its way down to the water's edge, with the rooms & open-sided restaurant perched on the very edge of a steep terrace above. As befits the name, the décor is casual & Africa-inspired, with carved wood furnishings throughout & local textile accents. Rooms all come with private balconies overlooking the gardens & lake, & the restaurant does grilled fish & other meals for around Rfr6,000–7,000. *US$100 dbl; US$350 villa sleeping 6.*

Inzozi Beach Hotel (15 rooms) m 078 867 3886. This new stone-built lodge on a bluff above the water is attractive from the exterior but rather overwrought on the inside, with rooms feeling vaguely reminiscent of the interior of an Egyptian pyramid – with more comfortable beds, hot water, & a fine lake view, that is. The boat-shaped restaurant adds to the somewhat contrived feel of the place, but if you can get past the ostentation it's pleasant enough (though unsurprisingly overpriced) & there's beach access & a swimming pool. *US$100/150 sgl/dbl B&B.*

La Bella Lodge & Campsite (5 rooms) m 078 851 0714/337 3400; e labella@labella-

lodge.com; w labella-lodge.com. This relaxed owner-managed resort has a secluded lakeshore setting 2km from the main traffic circle in Rubona, close to the junction for the methane-extraction plant. The shady well-tended tropical gardens, dotted with lounger beds & thatched gazebos (& a new sunbathing deck right over the water), are a delight. The restaurant is one of the best around, serving a varied selection of Rwandan & continental dishes for Rfr4,000–6,000. Comfortable en-suite rooms, set away from the public areas, have a king-size bed, en-suite hot tub, writing desk & private balcony facing the lake. It's a good spot for swimming & sunbathing, & they also have a family villa sleeping 4 close to the Rubona Hill Scenic Viewpoint. *US$100 dbl; US$20/tent camping; US$250 family villa.*

Nirvana Heights Resort (17 rooms) m 078 820 3015/830 6585; e nirvanaheightshotel@gmail.com; nirvanaheights. Atop a steep hill on the inland side of the road, this vertiginous new place has several categories of room, the most basic of which are rather uninspiring, but each category above that is quite comfortable with balcony, fridge, kettle & canopy bed. The restaurant sits on an open terrace next to the dramatic infinity pool, which abuts the cliff edge & provides a genuinely sensational view over the lake & surrounds

(*Rfr4,000 for non-guests*). *US$80/100 sgl/dbl; US$120/150 deluxe/executive dbl.*

🏠 **Palm Beach Resort** (10 rooms) m 078 569 5576/7; e palmbeachrubavu@gmail.com; w palmbeachrubavu.com. Situated about 1.7km along the road from Rubona traffic circle to La Bella Lodge, this attractive beach resort, formerly known as the Palm Garden or the Waterfront Resort (it's had a new name in each of the last 3 editions of this guide) lies in pretty palm-shaded gardens that run down to a swimming beach, above which there's a chilled open-sided restaurant with an Asian-inspired menu in the Rfr5,000–8,000 range. The 'modern' (their nomenclature) rooms have a double bed with net & en-suite hot shower, but they are let down a little by the tacky décor & seem poor value compared with similarly priced options elsewhere in Rubona. By contrast, the pricier & larger 'African' bungalows – with a funky ethnic feel to the décor & great outdoor shower & toilet – are among the best rooms on offer in the area. *US$80/100 'modern'/'African' dbl.*

🏠 **Palm Garden Resort** (9 rooms) m 078 830 6830/883 4800; e info@palmgardenlodge. com; w palmgardenlodge.com. Formerly on the lakeshore just down the road, this relocated lodge is today situated just to the west of Inzu Lodge, in small but attractive gardens across the road from the lake. Rooms here are charming & eminently likeable, with high ceilings, whitewashed brick, bold ethnic prints, & funky accents within, & irresistibly breezy terraces without. All come with nets & en-suite hot shower & the suites are equipped with a kitchen. Good meals are served in the shady gardens. *US$60/120 dbl/suite; all rates B&B.*

🏠 **Paradis Malahide** (12 rooms) m 078 864 8650/875 6204; e parmalahide@yahoo.fr; w paradisemalahide.com. Situated in Rubona, only 800m from the traffic circle, this long-serving & perennially popular beach resort has a rustically beautiful lakeshore setting, complete with secluded swimming beach. Accommodation is either in rooms with double beds, nets & en-suite hot shower, or in circular stone-&-thatch cottages with similar facilities. A terrace restaurant serves adequate meals in the Rfr5,000–7,000 range as well as cheaper snacks such as omelettes & brochettes, & there's a well-stocked bar. The lodge is ideally sited to enjoy sunsets over the lake while kamikaze pied kingfishers dive into the water & local fishermen cruise past. Facilities include

Wi-Fi & a motorboat for hire at US$60/hr, if you want to explore the lakeshore or visit nearby Akeza Island to catch the sunset or enjoy candlelit dinners or a family picnic. Traditional dances are held here at the w/ends. They're also building an upmarket lodge on the lakeshore south of Kigufi which will likely open during the lifespan of this edition. *US$80/90/125 sgl/dbl/trpl B&B; camping Rfr10,000/tent.*

Budget

🏠 **Eden Garden Lodge** (7 rooms) m 078 896 5692/120 9656. Situated in an appealing grassy compound on a tiny nub of a promontory with rooms in a handful of duplex brick bungalows, this long-serving place is institutional feeling & overpriced, but one of the very few budget options in Rubona. The rooms are nothing to shout about but are well positioned to catch the lake breezes. A fish dinner for 2 can be arranged for Rfr6,000. *Rfr25,000 en-suite dbl with cold water; Rfr35,000 en-suite dbl with hot water; rates inc B&B for 1.*

🏠 **Inzu Lodge** (10 standing tents, 1 bamboo house) m 072 525 0101/078 417 9203; e info@ inzulodge.com; w inzulodge.com. About halfway between Palm Beach Resort & La Bella, but on the opposite side of the road to the lake, this scenic & characterful lodge has accommodation in comfortably equipped standing tents set on stone platforms with views over the lake, & a bamboo house that sleeps 3. There's plenty of space for campers as well, & the sustainability minded will appreciate the eco-loos. The restaurant serves brochettes, fish & traditional Rwandan fare, ranging in price from Rfr1,500 to Rfr6,000. The rooms are rightfully popular, so they often get booked up. *Rfr25,000/30,000–35,000/45,000 sgl/ dbl/trpl standing tent; Rfr25,000/35,000/45,000 sgl/dbl/trpl bamboo house; Rfr20,000/own tent camping.*

Shoestring

🏠 **Sawa Sawa Beach** m 078 350 7021/850 1156/847 5358; e sawasawabeach@gmail.com. There's not a whole lot going on at this haphazard campground next to the Inzozi Beach Hotel, but it's set in a nice little patch of grass right on the water & the usual meals & boat trips can be arranged with enough notice. *Rfr10,000/20,000 your/their tent.*

🏠 **Sous le Soleil** (9 rooms) m 078 884 7201. Situated in Rubona, between the brewery & Paradis Malahide, this has a nice lakeshore location & the basic rooms & bunkbed dorms are about as cheap as it gets in this part of Rwanda. Perhaps recognising tourism's growing profile in the area, they now arrange cheap boat tours to the hot springs & have recently built a new bar-resto & beach terrace area, popular locally for beers & grills. The only signboard is one for Primus. *Rfr5,000 dorm bed; Rfr10,000 dbl with ¾ bed.*

✖ **Where to eat and drink** [map, page 218] All the hotels listed on pages 219–21 serve good meals for roughly Rfr5,000. The restaurant at the Palm Beach Resort probably wins out on ambience, but La Bella Lodge serves the most consistently good food, and if you don't fancy eating indoors, there are several gazebos in the lakeshore gardens. There is also one decent standalone restaurant in Rubona:

✖ **Jacaranda** m 078 820 7987/839 1223; ⏰ 07.00–midnight daily. Set in attractive landscaped lakeshore gardens a few gates up from the Paradis Malahide, this pleasant alfresco restaurant, also known as Chez Maman Chakula, serves continental-style meat, rabbit & fish dishes in the Rfr4,000–7,000 range. It also offers a range of cheaper snacks & local dishes, & a bar.

Nyamyumba Hot Springs and Kigufi

A worthwhile short walk out of Rubona follows the lakeshore south via the Nyamyumba Hot Springs to the Kigufi Peninsula, site of the church-run Maison St Benoît, a lovely spot for a pot of tea or a chilled beer in secluded bird-rich gardens running down to the lake. The walk starts at the main traffic circle in Rubona (where the inland and lakeshore roads from Rubavu connect) and follows the third road running south past (through, really) the prominent Bralirwa Brewery to your left. From here, it is perhaps 40 minutes in either direction to Kigufi, but you probably need to add 20 minutes or so for the diversion to the springs, and another 20–30 minutes for an uphill diversion through the village of Rambo.

Perhaps 500m past the brewery, you'll see the unsignposted motorable track that runs downhill for a few hundred metres to the Nyamyumba Hot Springs (⊕ S 01°44.391, E 29°16.441), whose shallow searing waters run into the lake creating a bathing beach with the temperature of a sauna. Bathing in the hot water allegedly has a curative effect, relieving fatigue, curing skin rashes and mending simple fractures. More prosaically, in some places the springs are hot enough – and are used by the villagers – to boil potatoes and cassava. That aside, the springs are not much to look at, and visitors are likely to be mobbed by friendly children who come there to play and swim.

Less than 100m past the turn-off to the springs, you hit a junction where a signpost proclaims the official start of the Congo-Nile Trail. Here, the road to the left climbs through the village of Rambo to the newly surfaced main road connecting Pfunda to Karongi/Kibuye via the Gishwati Forest. If you feel like following this steep road for a short way, you'll be rewarded by some great views to the receding lake over the first kilometre or so. To head to Kigufi, however, you need to carry straight on at this junction, along the older and rougher lakeside road to Karongi/Kibuye, which brings you to La Maison St Benoît after 2km.

Where to stay *Map, page 218*

🏠 **La Maison St Benoît** (28 rooms) ⊕ S 01°44.917, E 29°16.677; m 078 840 9867; e msaintbenoit@gmail.com. This little-known gem, run by friendly Catholic nuns, was originally constructed as the residence of the Bishop of Rwanda in 1947, & was later home of the country's first African bishop Aloysius Bigirumwami, appointed in 1959. Today it is one of the best-value

& most attractive places to stay in the Rubavu area, set in paradisiacal green lakeshore grounds that support plenty of colourful birds & also offer good swimming. The en-suite rooms are very clean & all come with double bed & hot showers. It also serves b/fast (*Rfr2,000*), affordable lunches & dinners (*Rfr3,500 each*) & a selection of beers & soft drinks. *Rfr20,000 dbl.*

Dancing Pots This offers visitors the opportunity to interact with one of three forward-looking Batwa communities who now operate as potters outside Rubavu/ Gisenyi. Hunter-gatherers by tradition, the historically marginalised Batwa comprise less than 0.5% of the population, and suffer from high levels of illiteracy, unemployment and landlessness. At Abatigayubuke outside Rubavu, however, the Batwa have harnessed traditional skills such as pottery and performing arts to make a living and become integrated into the greater community. A visit incorporates traditional dance performances, pottery and the opportunity to talk about the Batwa traditions and lifestyle. To arrange a Dancing Pots visit, the best contact is Green Hills Eco-Tours (page 217).

Gishwati Forest (Gishwati-Mukura National Park)
In the early 20th century, Gishwati was Rwanda's second-largest tract of indigenous forest, extending over 1,000km² along the Albertine Rift escarpment from the base of the Virungas halfway down Lake Kivu. By 1989, when the last forest-dwelling Batwa hunter-gatherers were evicted from Gishwati, the forest comprised two main blocs that collectively covered less than a quarter of its former extent. Further deforestation occurred in the 1980s to make way for a World Bank forestry and livestock development project, and again over 1998–99 to accommodate the land needs of returned refugees. By the turn of the millennium, all that remained of Gishwati was one disjunct 6km² stand of forest with a similar vegetation composition to Nyungwe. Forest biodiversity has been the most obvious victim of this 99% loss in Gishwati's original area, but it has also resulted in several fatal landslides, the drying up of streams fed by the watershed, decreased soil fertility, and flooding that destroyed hundreds of homes in 2008.

A few years back, Gishwati seemed doomed to vanish entirely, and it was widely believed that its once prodigious populations of chimpanzee and golden monkey were either extinct or on the verge of it. Then, in late 2007, President Kagame and the Des-Moines-based Great Ape Trust (GAT) agreed to develop Gishwati Forest Reserve as a proposed 'national conservation park' to be managed by the Gishwati Area Conservation Program (GACP), which has since been replaced by a Rwandan NGO, the Forest of Hope Association (w *fharwanda.org*). The aims of the FHA are not only to preserve the forest that remains, but also to develop sustainable livelihoods for surrounding communities and engage them in the forest's protection. An ambitious reforestation project aims to eventually create a 50km forest corridor connecting it to Nyungwe National Park. Since then it has been established not only that the forest still supports a small chimpanzee (*Pan troglodytes schweinfurthii*) community, but also that improved protection has allowed that population to increase from 13 to 30. Habituation efforts were suspended in 2012, but are likely to resume as tourism in the park develops, eventually allowing visitors to approach the chimps as closely as their counterparts at Nyungwe. Golden and L'Hoest's monkeys are also still quite common, with more than 100 individuals of each species present.

Gishwati is also an interesting destination for birders. Prior to the genocide, some 209 bird species had been recorded there, and, while some of these are probably now locally extinct, a survey undertaken between October and November 2009 recorded 101 species, 14 of which are Albertine Rift Endemics, including Ruwenzori turaco, strange weaver, handsome francolin, red-throated alethe, and four types of sunbird. Other alluring birds resident in Gishwati include black-billed turaco, Doherty's bush-shrike, white-headed wood-hoopoe and African hill-babbler.

After several years of discussions, the new Gishwati-Mukura National Park, encompassing 1,570ha of the Gishwati Forest Reserve (plus a 266ha buffer zone) and 1,988ha of the Mukura Forest Reserve (plus a 696ha buffer zone; page 209), was finally gazetted in 2016, bringing a total of 3,558ha (plus the 962ha of buffer zone) under official protection as Rwanda's fourth and newest national park. Despite the significant developments in the park's protection, with several walking trails having already been cut through the forest (and a further 30km route planned between Gishwati and Mukura forests along the Sebeya and Satinsyi rivers), Gishwati's status as a tourist attraction was somewhat uncertain at the time of writing. As of 2018, the park remained undeveloped for tourism, with no activities officially open to visitors. It will almost certainly open up for tourist activities such as birdwatching, forest walks, and community visits during the lifespan of this edition (with chimpanzee tracking set to resume eventually as well), but as this book went to print there was no timeline for when exactly any of this may happen. For further information on the full range of planned activities, the Forests of Hope Association published a thoroughly informative 24-page guide to the new park in December 2017, which is available at w fharwanda.org/IMG/pdf/gmnp_guidebook.pdf.

The Sunshine Gishwati Research Center (m *078 349 1512;* e *fharwanda2012@ gmail.com*) in Kinihira (Rwambeho) Village was under construction at the time of writing, but should now be able to provide basic accommodation; otherwise the closest accommodation is the basic Good Heart Lodge (Chez Michel) (m *078 199 7608/072 357 2618/073 357 5260*), 10km down the road towards Karongi in in Gakeri Village. In the longer term, it's likely an upmarket hotel concessionaire will be stepping in to develop a luxury lodge at the forest's edge.

The main stand of forest lies about 40km from Rubavu, following the surfaced road from Musanze/Ruhengeri out of town to Pfunda, then turning right on to the main surfaced road towards Karongi/Kibuye. It can also be reached from Rubona by driving out past the Bralirwa Brewery towards Kigufi and turning left (on to the Rambo road) after about 600m. A useful contact for organised visits to the forest is Rwandan Adventures (page 217), who can arrange day and overnight trips there with advance notice. For updates, contact the RDB tourist office in Rubavu (page 216), or check out our updates website w bradtupdates.com/rwanda.

THE MUSANZE (RUHENGERI) ROAD Several points of interest lie along or close to the road connecting Rubavu/Gisenyi to Musanze/Ruhengeri, as follows:

Pfunda Tea Estate [map, page 192] (✆ *0252 540622;* w *mcleodrussel.com*) Situated 9km from Rubavu along the Musanze road, this Fairtrade-certified estate is also a member of the Ethical Tea Partnership and Fairtrade, and in 2011 it became the first plantation in Rwanda to be certificated as having met the stringent criteria balancing ecological, economic and social considerations set by the Rainforest Alliance. It produces excellent tea, too, thanks to its location on the fertile volcanic soils of the Virunga foothills. Tourists are welcome, and visits can be set up either through the RDB office in Rubavu or through Rwandan Adventures (pages 216–17) as part of a full-day cycling excursion on the Pfunda sub-route of the Congo-Nile Trail.

Kiaka Co-operative [map, page 232] (m *078 862 3757/473 5774/319 4444;* e *kiakacoop@yahoo.fr;* f *Coopérative KIAKA;* ⏰ *08.00–17.00 Mon–Sat, 13.00–17.00*

Officially launched in December 2011, the Congo-Nile Trail (not to be confused with the similarly named Congo-Nile Divide Trail in Nyungwe Forest) was developed by the RDB with two main goals: exposing active visitors to the thrilling scenery along the shores and escarpment hemming in Lake Kivu, and generating income for rural lakeshore communities. It is not a purpose-made hiking trail, but one constructed from existing roads and motorable tracks. Indeed, while the northern section, between Rubavu and Karongi/Kibuye, mostly follows a little-used old lakeshore road, the southern sector essentially comprises the main road between Karongi and Rusizi, which is now completely surfaced.

The ten-stage main trail runs roughly parallel to the eastern shore of Lake Kivu for 227km, and can be completed on foot in ten days, by bicycle in five days, and in a 4x4 over two to three days. Although the ten-stage trail is marketed as one entity, it is perfectly possible to do any single stage or sequence of stages in isolation from the others. In addition, for hikers with limited time, three different sub-trails – Pfunda in the north near Rubavu, Gisovu a short distance south of Karongi, and Shangi in the south near Rusizi – can each be completed in 2 days on foot, or 1 day by bike.

The ten stages of the main trail are as follows (and hiking times are on the generous side in good conditions):

Day One	Rubavu/Gisenyi to Rwinyoni, 8 hours
Day Two	Rwinyoni to Kinunu, 8½ hours (arriving at 15.00, in time for an optional tour of Kinunu Coffee Estate)
Day Three	Kinunu to Musasa, 6 hours
Day Four	Musasa to Rubengera junction, 7 hours (Rubengera lies on the surfaced road between Muhanga/Gitarama and Karongi/Kibuye, so it is advisable just to catch public transport from there to Karongi/Kibuye)
Day Five	Rest Day
Day Six	Karongi/Kibuye to Mugonero, 8 hours

Sun) Situated at Kanama, about 15km from Rubavu along the road to Musanze, this Atelier de Menuiserie (Carpentry Shop) showcases the highly regarded work of the Coopérative des Artisans de Kanama. The hefty furniture here is probably of greater interest to expatriates than tourists, but it also stocks a decent selection of basketwork, pottery, carvings and other handicrafts, and you can visit the workshop to watch the craftsmen in action.

Imbabazi [map, page 192] (m *078 883 6558/432 7058/410 6578*; e *imbabazi@ imbabazi.org*; w *imbabazi.org*) Formerly Imbabazi Orphanage, this very positive project, founded by Rosamond Halsey Carr at her plantation in Mugongo in December 1994, originally sheltered some of the many orphans and displaced children left behind after the genocide (pages 19–21). Orphanages have now been closed in Rwanda, and Imbabazi's few remaining children have been settled with families; if you visit Imbabazi today you can see Roz's cottage and much-loved garden, her grave, a small museum of her life, a working farm which provides local employment, and a pre-school for children from surrounding villages (school days/hours only). The gardens are beautiful and peaceful, with striking views of Karisimbi, Mikeno and Nyiragongo volcanoes; some scenes in *Gorillas in the Mist*

Day Seven	Mugonero to Karengera, 6 hours
Day Eight	Karengera to Kibogora, 7½ hours
Day Nine	Kibogora to Shangi, 8 hours
Day Ten	Shangi to Kamembe (Rusizi/Cyangugu), 8 hours

The best place to organise hikes is the RDB tourist office in Rubavu (page 216), ideally with a day or two's notice. However, bicycle tours are better organised directly through the specialist operator Rwandan Adventures (page 217), who are also developing bike-kayak combo trips in partnership with Kingfisher Journeys (page 217). In both cases, itineraries can be tailored to suit your interests, available time, and fitness level. For keen hikers with a few days to spare, a good option would comprise the first four stages running from Rubavu to Rubengera (from where you could bus directly to Karongi or Kigali). A similar route is recommended to cyclists, who could complete it in two days, with the option of an organised boat transfer (or ferry ride if you time it correctly) from Karongi back to Rubavu.

A fixed fee structure is in place for the Congo-Nile Trail. The guide fee is US$50 per day for groups of up to five people, while (optional) porters cost US$30 per day, (optional) pack hire US$30 per day, and an (optional) back-up 4x4 US$100 per day. For accommodation, the guides can arrange either camping at US$5 per person per day, home stays at US$10 per person per day, or (where available) normal lodges and guesthouses at a similar price to the one quoted in this guidebook. Additional activities are overnight fishing (US$20 per person) or visits to coffee or tea estates (US$30 per person each). Theoretically, there's nothing stopping intrepid travellers from striking out and hitting the trail on their own, but unless you're fit, flexible, and prepared for getting lost along the way, a guide is invaluable.

For detailed information on accommodation in villages along the route, see the following excellent trip report from reader Sam Waldock: w bit.ly/2DTzYq1.

were filmed here. Tours of the house, gardens and farm cost Rfr10,000 per person; lunch with home-grown produce can be provided for an extra Rfr5,000; and a performance by the Intore Dancing Group can be arranged (subject to at least four visitors attending) for Rfr5,000 per person. Imbabazi is normally open 10.00 to 16.00 Monday to Friday; also on the last Sunday afternoon of the month there is an Intore performance with tea in the garden (*Rfr10,000*). However, times may vary, and meals and the dance performance need a few days' notice, so it's important to check by phone or email before visiting. To get to Imbabazi from Rubavu, follow the Musanze road out of town for about 20km to Kabari (aka Kabali) junction, then turn left on to a dirt road signposted to Mugongo. Imbabazi is signed and is on the right after 7km. At the first main fork after the turning, take the right-hand road, heading upwards. It's a beautiful drive, winding through farmland and with spectacular views of two of the volcanoes and Lake Kivu. If you decide to walk from the junction, be warned that it's uphill and there's not much shade.

Ibere rya Bigogwe [map, page 192] (⊕ *S 01°38.618, E 29°23.652*) Literally 'Breast Rock', this massive domed outcrop lies a few hundred metres south of the road from Musanze/Ruhengeri and is clearly visible from the stretch between Kabari junction

Tom Tofield of Rwanda Bike Tours (w rwandabiketours.com), which specialises in cycling tours through western Rwanda.

The beautiful lake views and panoramic mountain scenery are a big part of what makes the Congo-Nile Trail such an ideal destination for cycling. But the area also boasts a large network of unsurfaced roads, tracks and single-trails, many used almost exclusively by pedestrians and cyclists, creating a perfect adventure playground for biking. However, this undulating landscape – seemingly countless climbs of up to an hour each, rewarded by a corresponding downhill towards the lake – is not without challenges. And it forces us to take things easy, as a lot of energy is required to make it through the day.

When estimating how much time you need to pedal through each stage, base your first estimate on a riding time of 8km/h, excluding pauses and photo breaks. It is also advisable to get up early and be riding off before 07.00, thus allowing some extra time to repair a puncture or to take a swim without the risk and stress of arriving after dark. Another challenge is making sure you have the right amount of water. Too much and the weight makes the climbs arduous, too little and you risk dehydration.

The trail can be travelled in either direction. In the dry season the winds come from the south, so those wanting the wind in their back should start in Kamembe and those who prefer the wind in their face should start in Gisenyi. Alternatively, for those with insufficient time to cover the whole trail, these towns and villages also make ideal starting points: N'Kora; Kinunu; Karongi/Kibuye; Nyamasheke; and Rusizi. They can all be reached by boat from Rubavu/Gisenyi or Kamembe, and Karongi/Kibuye can also be reached by road from Kigali.

Our trips normally start in the north and as we ride out of Gisenyi and Rubona, the landscape is breathtaking. There are peninsulas and bays, *isambaza* fishing boats with their beams and telescopic poles, and the mountains and volcano on the other side of the lake. We ride through small villages and by fields, backing down to the lake from time to time.

Rwanda's coffee explosion is happening on the slopes next to the lake, while the longer-established tea plantations, in particular Pfunda and Gisovu, are on higher, cooler land with a greater rainfall. After a few hours riding through the coffee plantations and fields, we see a collection of small islands as we descend back down to the lake and to N'Kora, a unique lakeshore market town.

Predominantly Islamic, N'Kora developed after the creation of the eponymous coffee station. Today it has one of the largest beaches on Kivu's shores. In the 1960s, however, when the African Rift lakes were at high-water, this beach did not exist! The market is on Fridays and Tuesdays, and people come from all over – even paddling across the lake from the DRC – to sell and buy. Congolese coffee is bought and dried here, and we often see it laid out on sheets on the beach in the sun, with small children picking out the unwanted small stones.

and the village of Mizingo. Undeveloped for tourism at the time of writing, it has enormous potential as a rock-climbing site – indeed, the main face is still studded with cables and pitons dating from pre-1994, when it was used as a commando training site – and it offers spectacular views over the surrounding farmland to Mount Karisimbi and Nyiragongo.

After an hour or two pedalling from N'Kora we arrive at Kinunu village centre, a good place to buy tasty brochettes and to stock up on bottled water. From here, it's a steep track – from where views encompass Nyiragongo, Karongi/Kibuye and Rubavu/Gisenyi – to the lakeside Kinunu Coffee Station, where rooms and meals are available. People in Kinunu are happy with the coffee explosion, as they have seen their standard of living increase in real terms. During the coffee-harvesting periods, the station employs over 2,000 and operates 24 hours a day!

The section from Kinunu to Mushubati through Musasa is one of my favourite rides in Rwanda. It is challenging and rural, and the landscape is amazing. However, if you want to make Karongi/Kibuye in just one day, it's a tough 60km ride, starting with a steep climb from the coffee station to the village centre, so you need to get going by 07.00 at the latest.

The passage across the river Koko can be very muddy, with slippery soils after rain. After the river crossing, there is a big climb towards Sure and Mushubati, where we join the main road from Rubavu to Rubengera junction, on the surfaced road between Muhanga/Gitarama and Karongi/Kibuye. From here, it's a hilly 20km to Karongi/Kibuye, compensated for by some fantastic views over the islands as the sun sets behind the Congolese mountains west of the lake.

Many tours end in Karongi/Kibuye. But it is also possible to continue south along the main road to Rusizi/Cyangugu. Once again we follow the lake and there are more outstanding views as we ride through Gishyita and down to the lakeside town of Mugonero.

From Mugonero, we sometimes return to Karongi/Kibuye on the Gisovu sub-trail. This is a big ride, and once again, you should head off early. It climbs past the Bisesero Genocide Memorial into tea plantations on the edge of Nyungwe Forest, then returns to Karongi town with a descent of over 1,000m from Mount Karongi!

Alternatively, the base-trail continues southward through the lakeside market town of Kirambo (Saturday is market day here, or Friday if it's Umuganda) on to Nyamasheke, where there are some basic guesthouses and hotels. After a few kilometres, you connect with the road between Huye/Butare and Rusizi/Cyangugu. From here, the options are either to continue directly along the tarmac to Rusizi, or else, close by the Gashirabwoba memorial, to follow the longer historical lakeside Shangi sub-trail there. From the intersection, it's also possible to continue on to Nyungwe (a full day's ride from Nyamasheke).

Rwanda's roads are fun to ride on, even though there are very few flat stretches, and the bumpy and sandy tracks really put the bikes – in particular brakes and gears – through their paces. Outside of the major cities, it is hard or impossible to find simple bike parts, or mechanics familiar with the likes of derailleurs and disc-brakes. So, for those travelling unguided, recommended bike tools and spare parts are as follows: spare inner tube; puncture-repair kit; spare gear and brake cables; some oil and a rag; a multi-tool; tyre-levers; a pump; spare chain links and chain tool; and spare brake pads.

Lake Nyirakigugu [map, page 232] (✵ *S 01°37.293, E 29°29.367*) Accorded official protection as of 2011, this small highland lake, situated at an altitude of 2,350m alongside the village of Jenda 35km from Rubavu, is one of the trio of 'Northern Lakes' (along with Karago and the relatively inaccessible Bihinga) earmarked for development as a formal birding route by the RDB, and there are

A young fashion illustrator in New York City, Rosamond Halsey boldly married a hunter-explorer, Kenneth Carr, and journeyed with him to the Congo in 1949. After their eventual divorce, Kenneth left; Rosamond stayed on. In 1955, she moved to northwest Rwanda to manage a flower plantation, Mugongo, and later bought it. For the next 50 years she witnessed the end of colonialism, celebrated Rwanda's independence and became one of Dian Fossey's closest friends. (In the film *Gorillas in the Mist* she is played by Julie Harris.)

During periods of violence and upheaval, Mrs Carr stayed fast in Mugongo while others fled. But when the genocide began in April 1994 the American embassy finally insisted that she leave. After several months in the US, she learned that Sembagare, her friend and plantation manager for 50 years, had survived three attempts on his life. In August 1994, aged 82, she returned by cargo plane, to find her home in ruins and all her possessions either stolen or destroyed. At Mugongo, she and Sembagare did the only thing that made sense to them: they converted an old pyrethrum drying-house and set up the Imbabazi Orphanage, to care for genocide orphans.

In 1997, the orphanage was forced to move from Mugongo for security reasons and eventually settled in what was then Gisenyi until 2005, when it returned 'home' to Mugongo. The plantation and farm provided the orphanage with fresh vegetables and many Rwandan businesses with fresh flowers.

A novel fundraising scheme, 'Through the Eyes of Children' (w *rwandaproject.org*), began in 2000: using disposable cameras, children at the orphanage took photos of each other and their surroundings. At first these were developed locally, displayed at the orphanage and put into albums. Then the US embassy in Kigali held an exhibition of the children's work, with all proceeds going towards their education. International recognition and awards followed, and the cover of UNICEF's 2003 *State of the World's Children* report showed a photo by an Imbabazi child. The project later featured in several more exhibitions, mostly in the USA. It has now run full circle as some of its former child participants, now adults, are today passing on their photography techniques to children in Rwandan schools.

Rosamond Carr died on 29 September 2006 at the age of 94 (she was officially Rwanda's oldest resident) and was buried at Mugongo. Many Rwandans were among the friends attending her funeral. Up until her death she had lived in her peaceful, tree-shaded house by Rubavu's lakeshore, and still visited the orphanage several times a week to manage its affairs. Roz was also – flatteringly – a great fan of this guide, and was delighted when I took her a copy of the second edition to replace the first; both are still in her bookshelf at Imbabazi. A contribution from her own book (page 366) is on page 146.

Rosamond Halsey Carr is the author of *Land of a Thousand Hills: My Life in Rwanda* (written with her niece, Ann Howard Halsey); page 366. She is also the subject of a short documentary film *A Mother's Love: Rosamond Carr & A Lifetime In Rwanda.*

a handful of signposts up to this effect today. Historically, it is the most reliable site for several waterfowl with a localised distribution in Rwanda, among them the red-knobbed coot, little grebe, maccoa duck and southern pochard, but while the first two species remain common here, the other two have not been recorded for several years. Otherwise, the fringes support a fairly standard selection of ibises, herons, cormorants and small waders, and a pair of augur buzzard appears to nest in the cliffs rising to the east of the lake. The surrounding vegetation, dominated by exotic trees, is rather sterile in terms of birds and other animals. The lake lies only about 100m from the main road to Musanze, on the left coming from Rubavu, and it would be difficult to miss even if it were not clearly signposted (as the 'Home of Red-Knobbed Coot') about 2km before the junction town of Mukamiira.

Lake Karago [map, page 232] Larger than Nyirakigugu, this marsh-fringed lake – also part of the mooted Northern Lakes bird route – lies less than 2km south of Mukamiira. Once an important source of fish and fresh water to local communities, it also served for years as the site of the President of Rwanda's holiday home, but these days it is reputedly threatened by deforestation and terracing of the Gishwati watershed. Despite this, the birdlife is prodigious, with red-knobbed coot, pink-back-pelican and various ducks likely to be observed on the open water, while the swampy surround supports a selection of herons, ibises, wagtails, warblers and waders. To get there from Mukamiira on the main road between Rubavu and Musanze, follow the surfaced road running south to Ngororero and Muhanga/Gitarama for 1.2km, then stop at the signposted dirt track to your left. From here, you can follow an indistinct footpath downhill, then cross a small wooden bridge on to the lake floodplain, reaching the shore after about 10 minutes, depending on how muddy it is.

SEND US YOUR SNAPS!

We'd love to follow your adventures using our *Rwanda* guide – why not
send us your photos and stories via Twitter (@BradtGuides) and Instagram
(@bradtguides) using the hashtag #rwanda? Alternatively, you can upload
your photos directly to the gallery on the Rwanda destination page via our
website (w bradtguides.com/rwanda).

8

Musanze (Ruhengeri) and Surrounds

The third-largest town in Rwanda, with a population estimated at around 65,000, Musanze, formerly known as Ruhengeri, is also the closest town to Volcanoes National Park (*Chapter 9*), and the most convenient urban base from which to track mountain gorillas. Despite this strategic importance, and its status as capital of Musanze District, it is an inherently unremarkable town, sprawling amorphously from the tight grid of roads that surround the new multi-storey central market.

Still, there is much to commend Musanze as a travel base. It boasts a more-than-adequate selection of lodges, a few eateries that rank as exceptional in a Rwandan context, and a friendly hassle-free mood. Set at an altitude of 1,850m, it also has an agreeable temperate climate, and a stirring backdrop in the form of the distinctive volcanic outlines of the three most easterly mountains in the Virunga chain. The mountains and their gorillas are the main local attraction, but there are also some pleasant strolls around town, as well as canoe trips on the Mukungwa River, and the possibility of excursions further afield to lakes Burera and Ruhondo.

GETTING THERE AND AWAY

All transport, including express services to Rubavu/Gisenyi and Kigali operated by the likes of Virunga Express and Kigali Coach, leaves from the bus station [235 F7] at the edge of the compact town centre, a short distance south of the central market.

TO/FROM KIGALI Kigali and Musanze are linked by a good 96km surfaced road, though the combination of outrageous bends and manic minibus drivers necessitates caution. Even so, you should cover the distance in under 2 hours.

Frequent midibuses connect Kigali (Nyabugogo bus station) and Musanze, leaving in either direction every 30 minutes (sometimes sooner if they have a full complement of passengers). Tickets cost Rfr1,800 and the trip takes around 2 hours. The most reliable service to Kigali is with Virunga Express (m *078 830 8620/830 0169/838 0982;* w *virungaexpress.net*), which has departures every 30 minutes between 05.30 and 19.30. If they are full, try the Kigali Coach (m *078 942 9696/072 773 4432*), which operates on the same schedule.

About 45km out of Kigali brings you to **Nyirangarama**, a hugely popular stopover for food and drink where nearly all buses take a quick break, and a kilometre further along is Base (pronounced *Bah-say*), where a turning off to the right is the start of the exceptionally scenic road to Gicumbi (Byumba) and the Sorwathe tea plantation – pages 288–91.

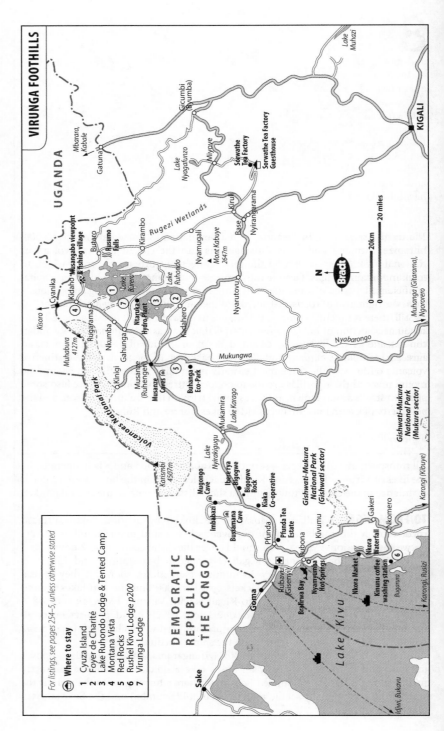

VIRUNGA FOOTHILLS

TO/FROM RUBAVU/GISENYI The 62km drive between Musanze and Rubavu follows a fairly good (and by Rwandan standards unusually straight) surfaced road, and should take no longer than 90 minutes. Scheduled midibuses between the two towns leave regularly and cost around Rfr1,200. As with the Kigali trip, a reliable operator is Virunga Express, which departs hourly from 05.00 to 19.00.

Musanze to Muhanga via Ngororero

A newly surfaced road connects Musanze and Rubavu to Muhanga/Gitarama via Ngororero. It runs south from the Rubavu road at Mukamira, 27km from Musanze, passes Lake Karago (page 229) to the left about 1km later, then continues southwards towards Muhanga, winding high up into the hills and offering breathtaking views. It passes through hamlets and beside tea plantations, so there is human interest too, but the main attraction has to be the wonderfully panoramic landscape. Regular midibuses now cover the route throughout the day for about Rfr3,000.

Situated at an altitude of 1,760m about halfway between Mukamiira and Muhanga, **Ngororero** is a small district capital surrounded by steep hills and notable mostly for the large multi-level market, which lies a few hundred metres downhill from the petrol station and is busiest on Wednesday and Saturday. The former MRND Palace, where 14,500 Tutsis were burnt alive in 1994, is now a genocide memorial.

About 12km from Ngororero, the hilltop site known as Umukore wa Rwabugili (✪ *S 01°52.380, E 029°35.204*) might be of interest to history enthusiasts. It is here, on 30 May 1894, that the powerful King Kigeli IV (birth name Rwabugili) hosted the explorer Gustav Adolf von Götzen (who later became the Governor of German East Africa) at the first official meeting between a European and a Rwandan king (page 11). There is a sign marking the site, and a less than compelling reconstruction of the royal hut, but not much else to see, except for the views, which are quite spectacular from the 2,290m hilltop. To get there, follow the Muhanga road 2.3km south from Ngororero, then turn right, crossing a flimsy bridge after about 50m, and another after 2km, before climbing towards the village of Kageyo. The site lies about 600m past the village.

The Ngororero District government built a **guesthouse** (m *078 841 7801;* e *ngororerodistrict@minaloc.go.rw*) here in 2013, and while it is up and running, there's been talk of auctioning off the concession to a private investor, so contact details are subject to change.

TO/FROM UGANDA The border crossings between Uganda and Rwanda are covered more fully on pages 40–1. There are at least two services a day running directly between Kampala and Musanze with **Jaguar Executive Coaches** [235 H2] (m *+256 41 425 1855/78 281 1128 (Uganda), 078 940 1499/436 6113/340 8791;* e *jaguar6796@ gmail.com*), departing Musanze at 16.00 and 16.30 daily, charging Rfr8,000/10,000 for standard/VIP services, arriving in Kampala in the early morning.

Coming from the west of Uganda, you will have to pass through Kabale. Prior to the surfacing of the road between Kabale and Kisoro, there was a strong case for taking the circuitous but smoother route between Kabale and Musanze via Kigali, crossing into Rwanda at the Katuna border post. These days, however, the quicker option from Kabale is to continue within Uganda along what is now a good surfaced 100km road to Kisoro and cross at the Cyanika border post. Kisoro and Musanze lie approximately 40km from each other along a mostly tarred road. On public transport, you'll have to change vehicles at the border, and can expect to pay around Rfr500 for each leg.

8

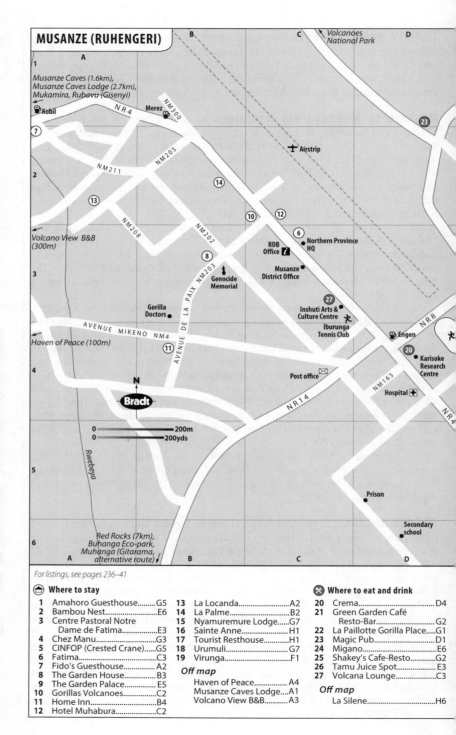

MUSANZE (RUHENGERI)

Volcanoes National Park

Musanze Caves (1.6km),
Musanze Caves Lodge (2.7km),
Mukamira, Rubavu (Gisenyi)

Kobil

Merez

NR 4

NM300

NM211

NM205

Airstrip

Volcano View B&B
(300m)

NM208

NM202

NM203

AVENUE DE LA PAIX

RDB Office

Northern Province HQ

Musanze District Office

Genocide Memorial

Gorilla Doctors

AVENUE MIKENO NM4

Inshuti Arts & Culture Centre

Iburunga Tennis Club

Engen

NR 8

Haven of Peace (100m)

Karisoke Research Centre

Post office

NR 14

NM163

Hospital

Bradt

N

0 ————— 200m
0 ————— 200yds

Rwebeya

Prison

Secondary school

Red Rocks (7km),
Buhanga Eco-park,
Muhanga (Gitarama,
alternative route)

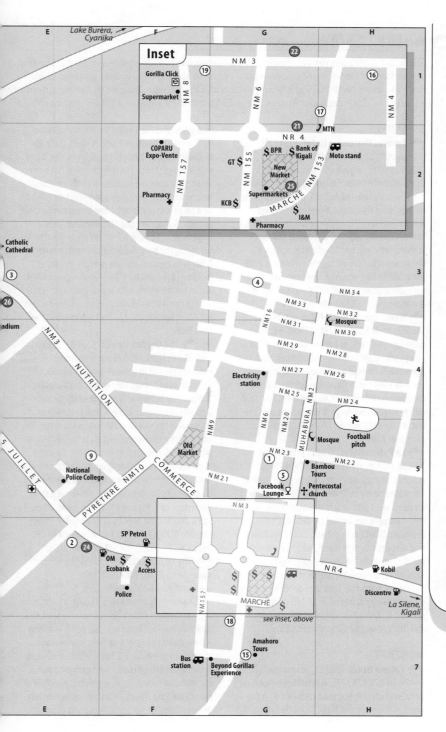

Inset

Lake Burera, Cyanika

NM 3

Gorilla Click
Supermarket

NM 8

NM 6

NM 4

COPARU
Expo-Vente

NM 157

NM 155

NR 4

MTN

BPR

Bank of
Kigali

Moto stand

GT

New
Market

NM 153

Pharmacy

KCB

Supermarkets

MARCHÉ

Pharmacy

I&M

Catholic
Cathedral

adium

NM 3

NUTRITION

NM 33

NM 34

NM 32

NM 31

Mosque

NM 30

NM 16

NM 29

NM 28

Electricity
station

NM 27

NM 26

NM 25

NM 2

NM 24

JUILLET

NM 6

NM 20

Mosque

Football
pitch

National
Police College

PYRETHRE

NM 10

NM 9

Old
Market

MUHABURA

NM 23

Bambou
Tours

NM 22

COMMERCE

NM 21

Facebook
Lounge

Pentecostal
church

NM 3

SP Petrol

OM
Ecobank

Access

NR 4

Kobil

Police

NM 157

MARCHÉ

Discentre

La Silene,
Kigali

see inset, above

Amahoro
Tours

Bus
station

Beyond Gorillas
Experience

8

235

There is a wide selection of moderate, budget or shoestring options in town. The few upmarket options are not of comparable class to the smarter lodges situated close to the Volcanoes National Park headquarters at Kinigi (page 265), or to the sumptuous Virunga Lodge near Lake Burera (page 254), but they are also a lot less expensive.

UPMARKET

🏠 **Gorillas Volcanoes Hotel** [234 C2] (24 rooms) 📞 0252 546700/1; m 078 820 0520/820 0518; e gvolcanoeshotel@yahoo.fr; w gorillashotels.com. Situated directly opposite the venerable Hotel Muhabura, this branch of the Gorillas Hotel chain (also represented in Kigali & Rubavu/Gisenyi) is easily the smartest option in town. Comfortable but somewhat lacking in character, it has good facilities including a restaurant & bar, fitness centre, swimming pool (*Rfr5,000 for non-guests*) & large en-suite rooms with tub or shower, satellite TV, terrace, free Wi-Fi & volcano views. *US$90/110 sgl/dbl*.

🏠 **Home Inn** [234 B4] (17 rooms) 📞 0252 546333; m 078 834 3127/414 1000; e info@homeinnhotel.com; w homeinnhotel.com. Set in a quiet back street southwest of the main road, this agreeable & friendly newish hotel has large tiled en-suite rooms with flatscreen satellite TV, hot combination tub/shower, writing desk, terrace, & rather overbearing décor. If you can get past the last, it's decent value. *US$70/90/120 sgl/dbl or twin/suite B&B*.

🏠 **La Palme Hotel** [234 B2] (48 rooms) 📞 0252 546428; m 078 678 6890/749 5453; e frontdesk@lapalmehotel.net; w lapalmehotel.net. Rated highly by several local tour operators for its efficient service & reasonable prices, this well-managed but ambience-deficient hotel lies in small but green grounds at the northwest end of town. The tiled rooms, which come with minibar, en-suite hot shower, safe, balcony & satellite TV, are nothing special at the price, but the service & food are both very good, & facilities include laundry & free Wi-Fi. *US$50 sgl with queen-size bed; US$70/80 sgl/dbl with king-size bed; US$100/110 sgl/dbl suite; all rates B&B*.

MODERATE

🏠 **Fatima Hotel** [234 C3] (65 rooms) 📞 0252 54665; m 078 875 3875; e info@fatimahotel.rw; w fatimahotel.rw. Not to be confused with the nearby Centre Pastoral Notre Dame de Fatima, this

flashy new diocese-owned hotel dominates the skyline on the northwest side of town. Done up in Miami-esque pinks, yellows & blues, this is not your average church-run guesthouse & has been aiming to corner the business & conference market here in Musanze since they opened in late 2017. It's all a bit devoid of character but seems comfortable enough, & there are good facilities including a large swimming pool, a 2-storey open-sided resto-bar facing the pool, & a 5th-floor rooftop terrace & bar with expansive views over the volcanoes looming in the distance. They've also got the first lifts in town (replete with piped-in smooth jazz), & a big spiral wheelchair ramp for disabled access. *US$70/90 sgl/dbl; US$120/140 deluxe sgl/dbl; all rates B&B*.

☀️ 🏠 **The Garden House** [234 B3] (5 rooms) m 078 842 7200/840 5760; e emgardner1@yahoo.co.uk. Set in tranquil gardens a block off the main road behind the Gorillas Volcanoes Hotel, this low-key hideaway is an eminently pleasant stopover in Musanze & the British proprietress goes out of her way to make you feel at home. The bright & airy rooms open out on to the garden, & all have high ceilings & tasteful décor. There are a few resident pooches welcoming guests to the grounds, & the guests-only restaurant serves very good dinners (by request only) either outside on the terrace or in the homely dining room, where you'll also find the best English-language library this side of Kigali. It often fills up, so best to call ahead. Wi-Fi. *US$60/80/100 sgl/dbl/trpl B&B*.

🏠 **The Garden Place** [235 E5] (23 rooms) m 078 162 6504/157 2091; e info@thegardenplacehotel.com; w thegardenplacehotel.com. Though it's not as flash as the new Fatima Hotel down the road, this new Anglican-run hotel near the police academy is nonetheless a big step up from your average church-run guesthouse & has a selection of clean & comfortable tiled rooms with mosquito nets & en-suite bathrooms. Some rooms come with TV & private balcony. There's an on-site restaurant but no bar (though it's acceptable to bring your own booze). *Rfr35,000/45,000/75,000 sgl/dbl/trpl; Rfr60,000/70,000 VIP sgl/dbl with kitchenette; all rates B&B.*

🏠 **Hotel Muhabura** [234 C2] (30 rooms) m 078 836 4774; e info@hotelmuhabura. com; w hotelmuhabura.com. The oldest tourist lodging in town, this likeable old favourite just celebrated its 60th anniversary & used to serve as Dian Fossey's home base when she came down from the mountains. It lies in green grounds on the northwest side of town along the NR4 in the direction of Rubavu/Gisenyi. With its outmoded décor & wide balcony that comes across like a cross between the Wild West & a Congolese colonial time-warp, it is difficult to believe this was once the smartest hotel within staging distance of the Virungas. Still it is a very characterful & reasonably priced set-up, offering accommodation in spacious tiled en-suite rooms with king-size or twin bed, hot bath & shower, & a small sitting room with TV; larger apartments are also available. There is also a campground. A good bar & restaurant serves a wide selection of continental dishes inside or outdoors in the Rfr5,000–8,000 range & it's a good place to come to use the Wi-Fi. *US$45/55/70 sgl/ dbl/twin; US$100 2-room apt; US$150 Dian Fossey's room; all rates B&B. Camping US$20/tent.*

✳ 🏠 **La Locanda** [234 A2] (9 rooms) m 078 263 7996/844 8943; e lalocandarwanda@gmail. com; w lalocandarwanda.com. Also known as Alberto's after the Italian owner-manager, this is a delightfully warm & welcoming getaway in Musanze, with leafy gardens & individually decorated rooms in a variety of shapes & sizes. These are spread out in 3 buildings across the property, connected by rock-strewn paths, & each is en suite, with twin, double or king beds & sometimes a kitchenette, depending on the room. All are spotlessly clean & most come with private garden terraces as well. The restaurant is among the best in Musanze, with fine brick-oven pizzas, cannelloni & other Italian dishes for US$10. (Non-guests can only eat here with reservations made 24hrs in advance.) *US$35–65 sgl; 60–80 dbl; all rates inc b/fast.*

🏠 **Sainte Anne Hotel** [235 H1] (16 rooms) m 078 838 6971/880 0169/545 0505; e info@ sainteannehotel.com; w sainteannehotel.com. This pleasant 3-storey hotel, set on a quiet side road a block northeast of the new market, has excellent staff, along with neat & clean en-suite

rooms with tiled floor, a queen-size or 2 ¾ beds, DSTV, lockable cupboards, & a compact bathroom with tub or shower as you prefer. There's Wi-Fi in all rooms, & a pleasant terrace & indoor restaurant serving African & Western dishes from Rfr3,500 upwards. Good value. *Rfr25,000/30,000/35,000 sgl/dbl/twin B&B.*

🏠 **Virunga Hotel** [235 F1] (25 rooms) m 078 834 6391/830 1462; e info@virungahotel.com; w virungahotel.com. This efficient multi-storey hotel lies on the same road as the Sainte Anne, & is similar in standard if not in price. The en-suite rooms have a queen-size or 2 ¾ beds, flatscreen DSTV, minibar, terrace, & a compact bathroom with hot shower. There's a decent restaurant on the ground floor & Wi-Fi in all the rooms. A block of 20 new rooms is slated to open sometime in 2018. *Overpriced at US$60/80/100/120 sgl/dbl/ exec/suite.*

BUDGET

🏠 **Amahoro Guesthouse** [235 G5] (7 rooms) m 078 8655223/4424866; e info@ amahoro-tours.com; w amahoroguesthouse. com. Bookable through Amahoro Tours (page 241), this pleasant small guesthouse (also self catering) in the back-roads north of the town centre has neat-tiled twin or dbl rooms that share a bathroom, kitchen & lounge with TV & a small library. *US$35/50 sgl/dbl B&B.*

🏠 **Bambou Nest Hotel** [235 E6] (19 rooms) m 078 551 9481/830 8992. Just off the main road through town, this newish guesthouse is simple, clean & central, with en-suite tiled rooms in 2 sizes over 3 floors & Wi-Fi. Best of all, it's connected to the excellent Migano restaurant (page 241). *Rfr15,000/25,000 small/large dbl.*

🏠 **Centre Pastoral Notre Dame de Fatima** [235 E3] (35 rooms) m 078 832 4033/607 6742; e cpndefatima@yahoo.fr/ info@fatimamusanze.com; w fatimamusanze. com. Among the better deals in this range, by virtue of not having raised prices significantly since it opened in 2004, is this modern-looking hostel situated on the edge of the town centre opposite the stadium & alongside an affiliated Catholic church. Although a bit institutional for some tastes, it has a useful location, very clean rooms, a decent bar & restaurant, curio shop, net café, Wi-Fi, & very reasonable rates. Credit cards accepted. A green campsite is attached.

This 2,643m peak is a pleasant hike, all the more attractive because it can be done easily in a day from Kigali without having to leave before dawn – and you're still back in town before dark. Also, as it's so close to the main road, you can get there by public transport. The hike involves 1,000m of ascent and takes 2–4 hours to the top (a 4–7-hour round trip of about 12km) for most people.

The 'mountain' is visible to the east side of the main road, about an hour out of Kigali or 45 minutes out of Musanze. It stands out as a hill that is bigger than the rest. You may wish to obtain a topographic map (Gakenke, map number 9) from the Ministry of Public Works in Kigali, but it is not necessary as long as visibility is good enough to see the mountain (which it almost always is).

The junction village for Mount Kabuye is Gakenke, which straddles the main surfaced road 31km from Musanze and 63km from Kigali. Just north of this village, turn eastward into what appears to be a paved road signposted 'Hospital Nemba 1km'. The road becomes dirt within 100m and soon after you need to take the first switchback to the left through 'town', which leads to a soccer field on the right after about 1km. After another 300m, you pass the hospital to the right, then 400m further on a downhill fork to the right leads you to another football pitch with a small kiosk-like shop and a wooden footbridge across the river on the far side. The guy who owns the shop will probably offer to guard your car, but if in doubt you could always park in the hospital grounds.

Hikers should cross the wooden bridge and follow the road, climbing steadily to its end (about 2km). After 30 minutes, look for a little shack on the right which (if open) will sell you warm Fanta and you may even be able to arrange for a child to carry some to the top. This is a good way to keep hydrated and support the local economy.

Where the road ends at a pipe, there is an obvious steep section of trail. Above this, there are multiple trails and it is not always easy to pick the best one, but you

---

Rfr12,000/20,000 sgl/dbl using common showers; Rfr30,000/40,000 sgl/dbl with TV; Rfr8,000 dorm bed; Rfr10,000pp camping. All rates B&B except dorms & camping.

🏠 **Fido's Guesthouse** [234 A2] (7 rooms) m 078 847 2460; e fidosguesthouse@yahoo.com; w fidosguesthouse.com. Run by Fidele, a long-time tourist guide in Musanze, this simple place on the outskirts of Musanze has developed a devoted following since it opened in 2013, & it's especially popular with student & volunteer groups. The en-suite rooms are basic but well taken care of, & they can help you set up any aspect of your visit. Meals are available at request (including rabbit at Rfr5,000/plate) & there's a low-key local bar out front. No Wi-Fi. *Rfr19,000 dbl.*

🏠 **Musanze Caves Lodge** [234 A1] (4 rooms, more under construction) m 078 830 3152/831 4510; e muhawe07@gmail.com. Set 900m off the road to Gisenyi & reached by a northbound turning

directly opposite the entrance to the Musanze Caves, this is a pleasant & good-value option, particularly if you've got your own transport. The large rooms come with big wood-frame beds & mosquito nets, & while they're a touch under furnished there are clever decorative accents throughout (a concrete tree built around the shower, for instance). Each room also comes with a private terrace out front, overlooking the green, though largely shadeless, grounds. The on-site resto-bar does meals at Rfr3,000–8,000. *Good value at Rfr30,000 dbl B&B.*

🏠 **Red Rocks** [map, page 232] (5 rooms) m 078 925 4315/868 7448/865 5223; e info@ redrocksrwanda.com; w redrocksrwanda.com. Despite being 7km out of town near Nyakinama Village, this popular place has become Musanze's backpacker hub since it opened here in 2013. Rooms are simple & colourful, & all use the trim shared ablutions. There's free Wi-Fi, nightly campfires, & Rwandan meals on offer (along

can easily readjust on smaller trails if you lose the main one. The best route goes right at the top of the steep section and stays just to the right of the ridge, passing by the local water supply and eventually passing a school (prominently visible from below) in a big clearing. Above the school, the trail follows the right side of the ridge to a T-junction. Turn left and enjoy the short flat stretch before turning right and heading steeply back up the very scenic ridge through farmlands and by houses with the mountain prominently visible above. If the sky is very clear, views of the volcanoes will appear off to the left.

After a while, the trail switches over to the left side of the ridge and soon reaches a flattish place on the ridge proper. Turn right after 50m for a scenic rest on rocks in a eucalyptus grove. You're about two-thirds of the way to the top. After your rest, continue up the steepening ridge toward the summit cone. A short steep section up a grassy patch leads to a rocky trail, which slabs off to the left and eventually swings around the peak to reach the pass on the left (north) side of the summit.

At the pass, leave the main trail by turning right on a smaller one. You're now 15 minutes from the top. Follow this vague path up the ridge, through new eucalyptus trees, to nearly the top. The precise but somewhat indistinct summit (visible *en route* from a prior false top) is reached by leaving the path for the final 20m. If it is very clear, you can see all the Virunga volcanoes and Lake Ruhondo to the north. Just down on the other side of the summit, there is a pine forest which offers shade on a sunny day.

As in all places in Rwanda, expect to be followed by a pack of children, although I have found that each time we go (I have done it five times), there are fewer, as they seem to be getting used to visitors.

Descend the same way, or pick another. The valley off to the right (looking down) is very beautiful, but it adds at least an hour to the descent.

with cooking lessons should you feel the urge). Activities available cover everything from basketry to beekeeping. *US$20/30 sgl/twin B&B; US$6/10pp camping in your/their tent*.

🏠 **Volcano View B&B**   [234 A3] (3 rooms) m 078 487 6354/882 1820; e info@ volcanoviewrw.com; w volcanoviewrw.com. Set in a residential district at the west end of Musanze town, this new guesthouse is run by a Rwandan–British couple and offers 3 cosy en-suite rooms. There are gardens & a gazebo out front, lunch & dinner are available at request, & activities around Musanze can be easily arranged. *Rfr30,000–35,000 dbl B&B*.

SHOESTRING AND CAMPING

Camping is available near the centre of town at both the Hotel Muhabura & Centre Pastoral Notre Dame de Fatima, or further out of town at Red Rocks as listed opposite.

🏠 **Chez Manu**   [235 G3] (14 rooms) m 078 853 7770/631 2008; e chezmanu@gmail.com. At the northern edge of the city centre, this is a fine new budget option with meticulously kept en-suite rooms with hot showers set around a neat front garden & parking area. There's no chance of late-night shenanigans here: alcohol isn't allowed on the premises & couples may even be asked for proof of marriage to share a double room, though we were told this rule isn't typically applied to tourists. B/fast is available at Rfr2,000pp & other meals by request. *Great value at Rfr7,000 sgl, Rfr10,000–15,000 dbl*.

🏠 **CINFOP (Crested Crane)**   [235 G5] (56 rooms) m 078 852 6522; e cinfope@yahoo.fr. Based out of an office & restaurant in the grid of back roads immediately north of the town centre, this rundown establishment consists of 8 different houses whose musty individual rooms are rented out by the night. It looks a bit like an airplane hangar from out front. *Rfr5,000/6,000 sgl/dbl using shared ablutions; Rfr10,000 en-suite dbl.*

🏠 **Haven of Peace** [234 A4] (16 rooms) m 078 372 1260/886 7871/697 0914. At the corner of Av Mikeno (NM4) & NM214, in a residential district of Musanze about 600m from the main NR4 road, this quiet wood-&-brick guesthouse is fittingly named, with well-kept en-suite rooms. They serve b/fast for Rfr2,000pp but no other meals. *Very good value at Rfr8,000/10,000 sgl/dbl.*

🏠 **Nyamuremure Lodge** [235 G7] (9 rooms) m 078 875 3860. This is the closest accommodation to the bus station, & rooms here are tiled & reasonably clean, & are surprisingly decent for the price. The larger Urumuli Hotel [235 G7] just up the block has similar-standard rooms for similar prices, should they be full. *Rfr6,000 dbl using shared ablutions; Rfr10,000 en-suite dbl.*

🏠 **Tourist Resthouse** [235 H2] (6 rooms) ☏ 0252 546635; m 078 522 7990. Centrally located on Rue de Muhabura, this friendly little lodge has clean but cramped en-suite rooms with ¾ bed, net & sporadic hot water. They also do a wildly popular lunch buffet starting around Rfr1,500. *Rfr8,000/10,000 sgl/dbl.*

✖ WHERE TO EAT AND DRINK

As with hotels, there is plenty of choice when it comes to eating out in Musanze. The smarter hotels all serve extensive breakfast, lunch and dinner menus daily. The **Gorillas Volcanoes Hotel** [234 C2] is the pick if you want to splash out, serving high-quality French-influenced cuisine, with most main courses coming in at around Rfr7,000–9,000. Most of the other mid-range hotels, including **the La Palme** [234 B2], **Sainte Anne** [235 H1] and **Virunga** [235 F1], have more than serviceable restaurants, with food in the Rfr5,000–7,000 range, but none really stands out. Far more alluring is **Hotel Muhabura** [234 C2], where a selection of grills, stews and mild curries start at around Rfr5,000 for a heaped plate, and the semi-shaded balcony ranks as high on the ambience front as anywhere in town. Beers and other drinks are only slightly more expensive than at the local bars and restaurants in town. Dropping several rungs in both price and standard, the **Tourist Resthouse** [235 H2] also has an inviting menu, dominated by stews rather than grills.

Surprisingly enough, Musanze is also home to a burgeoning café scene, with several warm and welcoming coffee shops (see below) serving Western-style fare opening in the last couple of years alone.

✖ **Crema** [234 D4] m 078 677 5198; ⏰ 06.00–18.00 Mon–Sat. Set in a lovingly restored old house on the main drag & opened at the end of 2017, this cosy café serves hot & iced coffees & teas, along with American-style bagel sandwiches & b/fast burritos for Rfr2,000–4,000, plus muffins & other baked goods. There's a small selection of local crafts for sale, along with Wi-Fi & a fireplace for cold days.

✖ **Green Garden Café Resto-Bar** [235 G2] m 078 256 4638; ⏰ 08.00–late daily. Centrally located, with shady outdoor seating, this is a pleasant place for a cheap beer after dark, but also good for a lunchtime mélange buffet at the usual Rfr2,000–3,000.

✳ ✖ **La Paillotte Gorilla Place** [235 G1] m 078 552 3561/889 4486; w lapaillottegorillaplace.com; ⏰ 07.00–20.00 daily. Possibly our favourite eatery in Musanze, this clean, efficient, & friendly bakery & café – earthily decorated with basketwork & wood – produces excellent fresh bread & pastries right in front of customers' eyes. Centrally located, it also serves a great selection of sandwiches, pizzas, brochettes & other light meals for around Rfr2,500, with more substantial meals around Rfr4,500. They've also got fresh espresso & cappuccino, & the usual soft & alcoholic drinks.

✖ **La Silene** [234 H6] m 078 378 5399/891 6999/853 5870; e lasilene4@gmail.com. Set about 3km south of Musanze proper along the Mukungwa River, this is the meeting point for canoe trips with Kingfisher Journeys (page 243), but it's also a fine spot for coffee, tea, smoothies & beer, along with brochettes, sandwiches & chapatti wraps for around Rfr3,000. If the riverine ambience strikes your fancy, they've also got 9 neatly tended rooms in the back with nets & hot water for Rfr10,000/15,000 single/double.

✗ Migano [235 E6] **m** 078 551 9481; **f** miganogrill; ⏱ 08.00–22.30 daily. This new café opposite the hospital has recently become a focal point for visitors in Musanze, & rightfully so. They serve a long menu of locally unusual dishes like Thai noodles & burgers, plus an array of b/fast options like pancakes & crêpes (*mostly Rfr4,000–7,000*), along with plenty of coffee- & tea-based drinks. There's also Wi-Fi, a small English-language library & some board games to play.

✗ Shakey's Cafe-Resto [235 G2] **m** 078 884 3210; ⏱ b/fast, lunch & dinner daily. The Rfr1,000–2,000 buffet here has everything from bananas, beans & squash, to goat, beef & chicken. It's a well-loved lunch spot, & recently moved to a new location on the 1st floor of the central market.

✳ ✗ Tamu Juice Spot [235 E3] **m** 078 532 5133/031 9198; ⏱ 08.00–21.30 daily. This tiny café had just opened at the time of research in 2017, but the affable proprietress has helped ensure that it's already regularly packed. They serve a short menu of lip-smacking fresh juices for Rfr500 a glass (try the sugarcane) alongside chapattis, samosas & a few Kenyan rice & stew dishes for around Rfr2,000 – portions are huge so bring an appetite, or a friend.

✗ Volcana Lounge [234 C3] **m** 078 581 8501; ⏱ 11.30–22.00 Tue–Sun. Roughly opposite the Bank of Kigali, this popular & atmospheric 1st-floor restaurant does highly rated pizzas starting at Rfr4,500 depending on your choice of toppings, & there's a selection of salads, pastas, grills & even Moroccan tajines in the Rfr4,000–8,000 range.

♀ Magic Pub [234 D1] At the junction where the roads to Kinigi & Cynika split, this is a popular & pleasant, though unexceptional, local bar with beers & basic meals at bargain-basement prices, along with plenty of plastic seating & a pool table in an open gravel courtyard under the stars.

TOURIST INFORMATION

There's now an RDB office [234 C3] (**m** *078 877 1633/844 9008*) in Musanze proper in addition to the one at Volcanoes National Park headquarters in Kinigi (page 264) and Rubavu/Gisenyi, 60km to the west. Gorilla-tracking permits can usually be booked at any of these offices.

A useful online source of travel information is **w** musanze.com, which hosts pretty detailed and up-to-date accommodation, restaurant and shopping listings.

TOUR OPERATORS As well as those listed, La Locanda and Gorillas Volcanoes Hotel can arrange transport for gorilla tracking and other activities in the area.

Amahoro Tours [235 G7] ☎0252 546877; **m** 078 8655223/8687448; **e** amahorotours@ gmail.com; **w** amahoro-tours.com. Offers community-based tourist activities such as fishing, dancing, drumming, traditional medicine, beekeeping & local cuisine.

Beyond Gorillas Experience [235 G7] **m** 078 849 5604/072 242 8035; **e** beyondgorillasexperience@gmail.com; **w** beyondgorillaexperience.com; **f** Beyond Gorillas. This new operator, with their offices in Musanze bus station, is an enthusiastic & well-connected outfit, offering a wide selection of tours & activities around town & beyond. These include park transfers, boat trips & 4x4 hire, as well as a range of hikes, bike rides & cultural activities, with customisable village visits that include weaving, brewing, cooking, herding, & playing music.

Umubano Tours **m** 078 217 5174/875 7937; **e** info@umubanotours.com; **w** umubanotours. com. Another reputable operator in town, they can arrange trips to all corners of Rwanda & neighbouring countries, as well as specialised birding trips, 4x4 hire, home stays, village visits, & fully customisable excursions on land or water.

Bambou Tours [235 G5] **m** 078 888 4557/605 9431; **e** bamboutours@gmail.com; **w** scoutonweb. be/membres/www.bambou-tours.com. The director here, Patience, is an enthusiastic guide who can help set up all manner of excursions in the area, including village visits, primate tracking, boat trips, hikes & 4x4 hire. They have a new office on NM22. See ad, page 256.

Lava Bike Tours **m** 078 606 7159; **e** yannick. ngabo@gmail.com; **w** lavabiketoursrwanda. com. This new outfit is run by Yannick, a former

Team Rwanda cyclist, & offers a variety of cycle tours in villages surrounding Musanze as well as further afield to lakes Burera & Ruhondo & beyond.

OTHER PRACTICALITIES

SHOPPING Central Musanze was being reorganised at the time of writing in early 2018, with many businesses in the city centre closing their existing locations and migrating to the new multi-storey central market, also known as Goico Plaza [235 G2], in anticipation of the planned demolition and redevelopment of many of the surrounding buildings. At the market itself, traders' stalls occupy the top floors, where you'll find no shortage of tailors, cobblers, and all manner of Chinese-made bric-a-brac, while the lower floors host supermarkets, restaurants, banks and larger shops. The long-standing COPABU Craft Shop recently shut its doors, so today the COPARU Expo-Vente shop [235 F2] on the main road is probably the best place to buy local handicrafts, though the selection is considerably less enticing than what was available at COPABU. For food, Kinara or Zam Zam, both in the new market, are reasonably well stocked, and the old market remains good for fruit and veg. For fresh bread and pastries, you can't beat La Paillotte Gorilla Place [235 G1], though the recently opened Migano and Crema are certainly giving it a shot (page 240). Even if you don't plan to buy, the Inshuti Arts & Culture Centre [234 C3] (m 078 306 3786; f) has an interesting collection of contemporary Rwandan paintings and carvings, though the standard is rather variable.

BANKING AND FOREIGN EXCHANGE All the usual banks are represented here with ATMs accepting Visa, including GT Bank which accepts Mastercard. Otherwise, the branch of the Bank of Kigali [234 G2] in the new central market has foreign exchange and Western Union facilities.

For travellers who arrive from Uganda, there are no private forex bureaux in town, so try to obtain some Rwandan francs when you cross the border. Otherwise, assuming that you have US dollars or euros cash, most of the hotels will sort you out at a rate fractionally lower than the street rate in Kigali, which is probably a safer bet than trying to change money on the street or in the market.

INTERNET There are a couple of **internet** cafés dotted around the town centre, including one at the Centre Pastorale Notre Dame de Fatima [235 E3] and the brilliantly named Gorilla Click [235 F1] on NM8, but if you have your own laptop or phone, free Wi-Fi is available at the Hotel Muhabura for the price of a drink.

SWIMMING There is a clean **swimming pool** at the Gorillas Volcanoes Hotel [234 C2] and it costs Rfr5,000 for non-guests to use it.

CYCLING About 4km up the road towards Kinigi, bicycle enthusiasts should hit the brakes for the **Africa Rising Cycling Centre** (m *072 508 7887;* e *bikeadventuresrwanda@gmail.com;* w *teamafricarising.com*), where you can meet the Rwanda national cycling team and see how they train. They've recently begun offering half-day road and mountain-biking tours at US$150 per person, with a professional-grade bicycle and gear provided, and a member of Team Rwanda as your guide. To get even more of a feel for how Rwanda's superstar cyclists train, there's now a house with kitchen for rent at the centre at US$60/80/100 double/ triple/quad, with prepared meals also available for US$12 per person.

EXCURSIONS FROM MUSANZE

Most people who visit Musanze treat it purely as a base from which to track gorillas (*Chapter 8*). But several local points of interest make for worthwhile day or overnight excursions, notably the little-visited lakes Karago, Burera and Ruhondo. For visitors seeking upmarket accommodation, the Virunga Lodge at Lake Burera and several lodges in Kinigi, including the fabulous new Bisate Lodge, are far more alluring than anything on offer in Musanze itself.

MUKUNGWA RIVER Among the most exciting new tourism developments in Musanze are the canoe trips now offered on the Mukungwa River with Kingfisher Journeys (m *078 381 1918;* e *.info@kingfisherjourneys.com;* w *kingfisherjourneys. com*). With morning and afternoon departures, these half-day excursions (with about 3 hours on the water) in Canadian-style canoes offer a rarely seen view of the heavily cultivated Mukungwa River valley, and the river's leisurely, meandering flow means there's plenty of time to greet farmers tending their crops onshore and marvel at the balance of fishermen passing in their dugouts. There are a couple of gently thrilling whitewater sections, including one where you pass under the main road and every child within shouting distance gathers to watch and see if you'll fall out. (But even if you do, there are neither hippos nor crocs in the Mukungwa.) There's plenty of opportunity for birding as well, and a checklist is available at w kingfisherjourneys. com/mukungwa-wildlife.html. No paddling experience is required, and the qualified guides are available to provide all instruction necessary. Pick up and drop off from Musanze are included in the price (*US$40/30/28 foreigners/foreign residents/ Rwandans, students & volunteers*), and dry bags for valuables are also provided.

A NEW VERSION OF AN ANCIENT TALE Ruganzu II Ndori was one of the greatest of Rwanda's warrior kings. One source puts his reign at 1510–43, another at 1600–24, so … who knows! His father, Ndahiro II, had catastrophically lost the Royal Drum, Rwoga, in battle, causing a time of great hardship for Rwanda: for 11 years the land was tortured by drought, sorghum withered in the ground, cows were barren and women conceived only sickly children. Considering the family cursed, the powerful abiiru (dynastic ritualists) banished Ruganzu from the kingdom – but after Ndahiro's death chiefs traced him and returned him to power.

Immediately rain began to fall on the parched land, sorghum grew fresh and sweet, cows produced rich milk and many calves, and woman became pregnant with fine, healthy sons. Ruganzu introduced the last of the Royal Drums, Karinga, to replace the lost Rwoga. He chose an adoptive Queen Mother from another clan; she was a poet and created a new form of dynastic poem. Ruganzu's conquests were many and much praised.

One day – so the ancient stories relate in various ways – the king and his entourage were visiting a part of Rwanda that today is just off to the right of the Kigali–Musanze road where it crosses the river Base. A sign to Nemba Hospital is nearby – as is a large rock known as 'Bagenge's Rock'.

Bagenge was the local chief in whose home the king was lodging for the night – and he had spent all that day in a state of great anxiety. The cause for his concern was the great rock, which was well known for moving about at night and relentlessly crushing anything that came within its path, whether mice, children, men, cattle or possibly even kings. Bagenge knew that death or injury to the king risked returning Rwanda to its previous state of drought and disaster.

BUHANGA ECO-PARK This unassuming nature park lies 8km outside Musanze (✥ *S 01°34.061, E 029°38.169, 1,628m*); just head out of town past the post office until you reach the Nyakinama College, turn right on to a poorly signposted and rough dirt track after another 500m, and you'll reach it after another 500m or so. Consisting of a small patch of forest dominated by spectacular dragon trees and crisscrossed by lava-block walking trails, this culturally significant site (see box, page 247) is of some interest to birdwatchers too. The exquisite and very seldom seen Angola pitta was recorded here in 2006 and 2008 (both times in May), a Nubian woodpecker sighting several years back is the second for Rwanda, and rather more improbably we've heard unconfirmed reports of the green broadbill (an ARE known only from the Congo and one locality in Uganda).

Some years back, the park was reputedly under private development as a nature trail, with a bar and possibly a hotel. Instead, it has been made into an isolated annexe of Volcanoes National Park, and foreign visitors must now pay a difficult-to-justify entrance fee of US$40 (*US$30 foreign residents, Rfr3,000 Rwandan citizens; all prices inc guided tour*) at the RDB office in Kinigi (page 264) before heading out here – if you arrive without a receipt you will be turned back. There was talk of developing overnight camping here in 2018; check with the RDB to see if it's up and running yet.

MUSANZE CAVES The main entrance to the impressive Musanze Caves lies about 2km from the town centre along the road to Rubavu/Gisenyi. Practically speaking, there are two accessible sets of caves, one just outside Musanze (with five cave

He prepared a great feast, the greatest that the region had seen for some years, and the smell of the spit-roasted meats and pungent spices caused many a nearby villager's mouth to water. There was wine too, in great abundance, and banana beer; and after the feast dancers leaped and drummed and chanted in the firelight. Bagenge's aim was to entertain the king and his entourage until they fell deeply asleep, so that none would wander off and fall victim to the rock.

But kings sleep less than ordinary men. In the quiet of the night Ruganzu awoke. He wanted to feel air fresh upon his face and to plan new conquests in a silence unbroken by the snores of his attendants. He strolled off along the soft mud path and stood in the open, above the valley, looking upwards at the stars.

The ground shook, a shadow blotted out the starlight and the great rock lurched ominously towards the king. Ruganzu raised his staff threateningly and stood his ground. Disconcerted by such courage, the rock hesitated. Gently the king spoke (for he was wise, and knew that soft words hold the greatest power).

'Greetings, my subject. I hail you and I accept the offering you bring: the offering of your size and strength, to use for the good of my kingdom. Guard this village well. Protect the children who play in your shadow. Comfort the weary traveller who leans against you. Shelter the plants growing around your base. Remain in this spot for ever, the friend of all who live nearby. Perform this task well, my subject, and many centuries from now men will still remember you and tell this tale.'

As you will see, if you visit Bagenge's Rock today, it has indeed performed its task well and stayed peacefully in the same spot. All the same, if you wander the paths by night, keep your ears alert for the rumble of a sudden stealthy movement, because Rwanda is a republic now and the power of kings is very much reduced …

segments) and the other closer to Kinigi (with seven). Carved out by Virunga lava flows, each side of the current cave system stretches for about 1km, but the underground portions have long since broken up into short segments, so visits consist of a guided walk along a trail that connects and descends into each cave. The largest cave is at the entrance near Musanze, some 350m long with a hall the size of a cathedral and an impressive bat colony inside. (Though increasing visitor numbers mean many of the bats have decamped to quieter surroundings in recent years.) The large ditch out of which the cave opens is littered with pockmarked black volcanic rubble, and at the opposite end there is a natural bridge which was formed by a lava flow from one of the Virunga volcanoes. Lava block pathways and stairs have been built through all the caves, so it's no longer necessary to do any scrambling to get in and out.

Legend has it that the Musanze Caves were created by a local king, and that they have been used as a refuge on several occasions in history. However intriguing it may be, it's forbidden to enter on your own. The caves were the site of a massacre during the genocide; local people consider it a tomb and don't take kindly to tourists scrambling about inside. As such, access is limited to guided visits and the site is protected and administered through the RDB. Guided visits can be organised at their offices, and cost US$50/30 per person for foreigners/Rwanda residents. A tour of all the caves takes about 2 hours (safety helmet and torch are provided), but as the two sets of accessible caves involve a 20-minute drive to get between them, many people opt to visit the first set only, which finishes just next to the pleasant Musanze Caves Lodge (page 238) and can be done in less than an hour.

Elizabeth Todd

If you are looking for a fantastic off-the-beaten-path excursion in Musanze, the Ubushobozi Project (m *078 475 5712;* e *ubushoboziproject@gmail.com;* w *ubushobozi.org;* f) is a small, grassroots non-profit organisation devoted to educating and training at-risk and orphaned teenage girls. In a stable, social and caring environment, the girls are taught sewing (and have become highly competent), basic computer and business skills, life skills, and attend daily English class. They make beautiful bags (among other items), which are excellent souvenirs/gifts. Each is handmade and all proceeds go directly back into the project so not only are you getting a cool item, you're making a donation. The programme's director and house manager speaks great English, and has a million stories about Rwanda. If you want to see a programme up close and first-hand that's empowering and changing the course of young girls' lives while supporting the women and men of the local community, you won't be disappointed. We visited after gorilla trekking. It's a really nice and interesting way to spend an afternoon. It's most definitely a feel-good excursion.

LAKE BURERA AND RUGEZI BIRDING SITE The largest and most beautiful lake in the vicinity of Musanze, Burera (aka Bulera) is almost entirely neglected by travellers, despite being overlooked by one of Rwanda's top three tourist lodges. With a private vehicle, however, the dirt road that loops around its eastern shore makes for a superb day outing, while adventurous backpackers could happily spend several days exploring the lake using a combination of minibus-taxis, motos, boats, and foot power. As for budget accommodation, the area is dotted with small villages where it shouldn't be a problem to get permission to pitch a tent, and basic lodges now exist in Butaro, the largest town close to the lake, as well as Kirambo, 13km to its south.

With an eccentric shape defined by the incredibly steep hills that enclose it, Lake Burera is visually reminiscent of Uganda's popular Lake Bunyonyi – not too surprising when you realise that these two bodies of water lie no more than 20km apart as the crow flies. The slopes that fall towards the lake are densely terraced and intensively cultivated: very little natural vegetation remains among the fields of plantains, potatoes, beans and other crops, while the most common tree is the eucalyptus, a fast-growing Australian exotic. The stunning and distinctive scenery around the lake is enhanced by the outlines of the Virunga Mountains, the closest of which towers 10km away on the western horizon.

Lake Burera lies at the northern end of the Rugezi Wetland, a vast highland marsh area that runs all the way south to Gicumbi/Byumba, where it is most easily accessed at Lake Nyagafunzo (pages 289–90). However, the RDB has designated the northern part of the wetlands as the Rugezi Birding Site, which now hosts three birding watchtowers along the 13km stretch of road running south of Butaro.

Listed as a Ramsar Wetland and an Important Bird Area, this is a good place to see large water-associated birds such as herons and ibises, but the main attraction here is Grauer's rush warbler, an Albertine Rift Endemic whose nondescript appearance is unlikely to enthuse anybody but the most dedicated of birdwatchers.

Getting there and around
By road For travellers with their own transport, the circuit around the lake is straightforward enough. The road is mostly in good shape, and likely to present no problems provided that your vehicle has reasonable clearance (a 4x4 would be

above A wall at the Kigali Genocide Memorial displaying photographs of some of the victims of the 1994 killings
(EL) pages 117–18

right The bullet-holed walls of Camp Kigali, now a memorial to the ten Belgian peacekeepers executed in the 1994 genocide
(EL) page 119

below The ancient royal palace has been carefully reconstructed at the Rukari King's Palace Museum in Nyanza
(AZ) pages 143–6

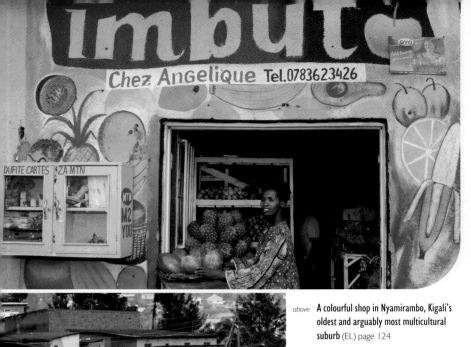

above A colourful shop in Nyamirambo, Kigali's oldest and arguably most multicultural suburb (EL) page 124

left Kigali's undulating topography and countless hills make for some seriously vertiginous neighbourhoods and occasionally confounding routes around town (BSM/S) pages 73–129

below The largest in Rwanda, Huye's Roman Catholic cathedral was built in the 1930s and is today known for the powerful choirs that pack the pews each Sunday (AZ) page 158

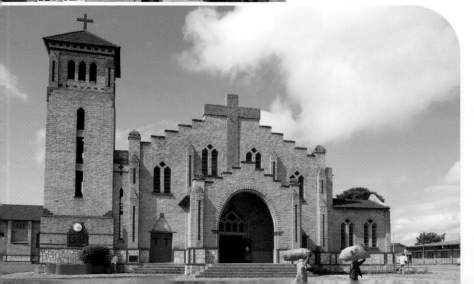

above	Natural-fibre weaving is a Rwandan specialty, and hand-woven bowls, baskets and mats make unusual souvenirs (AZ) pages 31–2
right	Founded some years ago by a Benedictine monk, the Huye Tinnery is known for its appealing and rather unexpected range of hand-crafted tin statues, utensils and more (AZ) page 159
below left	Traditional potter at work at the Poterie Locale de Gatagara, a workshop piled with bowls, teacups, vases and other ceramics (AZ) page 141
below right	On the road from Musanze to Muhanga, and at an altitude of 1,760m, Ngororero is host to a large multi-level market (AZ) page 233

top Towering over the surrounding landscape, the active Nyiragongo Volcano can be seen from miles around (SS) pages 339–40

above left Steep-roofed homes characteristic of the eastern DR Congo crowd the hillsides of Bukavu (L/S) pages 342–7

below left Viewed from above on the volcano's frigid cone, Nyiragongo's endlessly shapeshifting lava lake makes for a dramatic and otherworldly sight (AZ) page 339

below The civilians of the eastern DR Congo have long borne the brunt of the region's many conflicts, but ongoing improvements in security give hope for the future (LM/S)

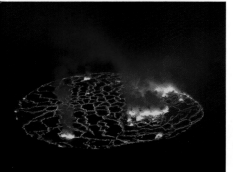

RYANGOMBE AND THE BUHANGA FOREST   *Janice Booth*

A NEW VERSION OF AN ANCIENT TALE   None could shoot an arrow so far and straight as Ryangombe, the greatest warrior and hunter of his time. None could run so fast or stalk so silently. The sun dimmed its rays in respect when he was taking aim and the rain paused as he pursued his quarry. He defended the forest against farmers who would fell trees to make space for their crops, and the branches murmured their thanks as he rested in their shade. Women competed for his favours, opponents feared him, storytellers throughout the realm extolled his exploits and his name was lauded far and wide. So powerful was Ryangombe that he challenged even the mighty King Ruganzu, who ruled Rwanda almost seven centuries ago.

Ryangombe's favourite hunting-ground was the Buhanga Forest, in the volcano foothills not far from what is now Musanze: a place of ancient trees, dark ravines and thrusting rocks, where sunlight throws patterns on the leafy floor and butterflies bask on mossy logs. Birds swoop and perch among the branches and small creatures scuttle in the undergrowth. In this forest is the sacred pool called Gihanga, empty in the rainy season but full to overflowing in the dry season, where Rwanda's early monarchs would come to bathe and drink the water.

It was on a dark, dark day here in the Buhanga Forest that Ryangombe faced his final opponent – no king or fellow warrior but a wild and angry buffalo, which burst upon him from the shelter of the trees. Its horns tore into his flesh and the forest floor was reddened by his blood. His companions, seeing their hero slain and wishing to be at his side in the higher world, taunted the buffalo until it gored them also and trampled their limbs with its hooves. The bodies of the young men lay beneath the great tree Umuvumu, still in the forest today, until Imana raised them to their final home on the slopes of Karisimbi. If you climb the mountain nowadays, you may – if your spirit is fair and you know how to listen with your heart – still hear their voices carried on the breeze as they talk and laugh together.

After Ryangombe's death, traditional healers from throughout the Great Lakes region would journey to the spot in Buhanga Forest where he fell. From the trees in that place they would take a branch back to their homelands, and use it as the base to build a shrine – Ingoro – from which to worship him and send prayers to their gods.

Sit quietly in Buhanga Forest today and you can sense its ancient history. Kings and healers and legendary heroes have walked its paths and felt its power. And – who knows – that sudden rustle that you hear behind you may even be the soft and stealthy footfall of Ryangombe as he stalks some ghostly prey.

advisable during the rainy season). The full round trip from Musanze covers about 120km, most of which is on dirt, and realistically takes a minimum of 5 hours to complete. Better, arguably, to leave after breakfast, carry a picnic lunch, and make a day of it, stopping along the way to enjoy the views and rustic villages.

To follow the circuit, head out of Musanze along the surfaced road towards Cyanika on the Ugandan border, passing the turn-off for Virunga Lodge to your right after 16km, then continuing for another 6km to Kidaho, where there's a good hotel and you need to turn right on to a dirt road signposted for Rugezi Birding Site. After about six relatively flat kilometres, the lake becomes visible to the right: on the shore you'll see a small fishing village, also called Kidaho, and dozens of

For most people, Musanze does not come to mind as a place where one goes birding, but rather as a base for tracking the mountain gorillas. The area has a huge diversity of habitats with altitudes ranging from around 1,600m to the peaks of the Virungas at over 4,500m. The habitats include relic forest (Buhanga Forest), wetlands (Rugezi Swamps and areas along the Mukungwa and Mpenge rivers), eucalyptus plantations/stands, rocky areas (Kinigi) and freshwater lakes (including lakes Burera and Ruhondo).

Musanze town itself and most gardens of hotels and guesthouses there will surprise the keen birder with the number of species they contain, with **bronze**, **variable** and **scarlet-chested sunbirds** being fairly common. Lodge gardens in Kinigi will add **Ruwenzori double-collared sunbird** to this list. **White-eyed slaty flycatchers**, **African paradise-flycatchers** and **white-tailed blue-flycatchers** are often seen hawking for insects while the seed-eaters like **western citrils**, **yellow-fronted** and **brimstone canaries**, **common** and **black-crowned waxbills**, **bronze** and **black and white mannikins**, to name but a few, will undoubtedly make their appearance.

In the gardens, and even in the centre of town, the **red-billed fire-finches** will be around, occasionally with a **village indigobird**, for which the former is a host species. Look out as well for the lovely plumaged **cinnamon-breasted bee-eaters** and their aerial acrobatics, only beaten in complexity, low passes and speed by the **little swifts**. A garden in the middle of Musanze even hosted an **African pitta** for three days in 2006! At night (and in some places during the day), look out for the **spotted eagle-owl** and, easily identifiable during breeding season, **pennant-winged nightjars**.

Contesting the award as the loudest garden bird (other than **hadeda ibis**) will be the **white-browed robin-chat** and **grey-capped warbler** – the latter being more often heard than seen in its hiding places in thick hedges. In more wooded gardens there are **olive** and **grey woodpeckers**, and the noisy but entertaining **spot-flanked barbets**. The **double-toothed barbet** can be seen in Buhanga Forest.

Birds of prey are well represented in the area with the ever-present **black kite** (look out during October to May for the migrant nominate race *Milvus migrans migrans*), but also the **African harrier-hawk**, **augur buzzard** (both white and dark morphs), **long-crested**, **Wahlberg's** and **martial eagle**, **lanner** and **peregrine falcon** and also the rather common (in Musanze) **hooded vulture**. Other sightings have included **gabar goshawk** and **European honey-buzzard**.

small boats used to ferry locals around the lake. A few hundred metres further, a side road leads around the small Musangabo Peninsula, where a platform run by the Episcopal Church offers stunning views in all directions. The church operates a motorboat that can be hired for the 2-hour round trip to the bridge between lakes Burera and Ruhondo.

The largest centre near the eastern lakeshore, Butaro is separated from Musangabo by a genuinely spectacular 17km stretch of road that hugs the cultivated contours about 100–200m above the lakeshore. *En route*, the road passes through the small market village of Umugu. Butaro itself lies a couple of kilometres off the main road, along a side road to Gicumbi/Byumba, signposted for the Rugezi Birding Area. About 50m from this junction, the attractive Rusumo Falls (not to be confused

Stands of eucalyptus trees also boast a huge variety of species, especially where they're not subject to much human activity. Species include **chinspot batis**, **spotted flycatcher** (October–May), **African stonechat** (also in cultivations), **brown-crowned tchagra**, and **yellow-bellied** and **fawn-breasted waxbills**, and there is even the chance of finding **narina trogon** (seen 1.5km from the centre of Musanze). **Klaas's diederik** and **red-chested cuckoos** are heard all the time during October to May.

Mpenge River and its associated wetland area is about 1km from the fuel station (Kobil) at the southern end of Musanze (also the location of a local market twice a week). Early mornings here can produce **black crake**, **cape** and **pied wagtails**, **white-browed** and **red-capped robin-chats**, and a variety of weavers. These include **baglafecht**, **slender-billed**, **northern brown-throated**, **yellow-backed (black-headed)** and **Holub's golden weavers**, which are all easily viewed and identified. The surrounding reed-beds and papyrus are easily accessible for viewing Palearctic warblers during the period from September/October to April/May.

The Rugezi Swamps are another location where the endangered **Grauer's swamp warbler** breeds and a host of reed-bed and papyrus specials can be found. This could also make up part of a journey around lakes Burera and/or Ruhondo, where flooded areas (such as the northern shore of lake Burera) are the scene for the jaw-dropping antics of **pied kingfishers**. **Yellow-billed storks**, **African spoonbills**, **little grebes**, **African jacanas**, **grey herons**, **intermediate**, **cattle** and **little egrets** frequent these areas as well. The **black saw-wings** are particularly obliging here and provide good viewing and photo opportunities.

The road to the southern part of Lake Ruhondo (turning off from the road to Kigali at the stone crushers) follows the Mukungwa River for part of the way, where **malachite kingfishers** can be observed from close proximity. The area is dominated by cultivated land but the irrigation 'ditches' often hide **hamerkop**, **African spoonbill**, **yellow-billed storks** and **sacred ibis**. **Fan-tailed widowbirds** are also seen close to the road. It is ideal for good sightings of swallows such as the **Angola, wire-tailed**, **mosque**, **barn** (October–May), and **lesser-striped** varieties.

A few days birding in and around Musanze can thus be very productive and result in a very respectable bird list which would include quite a few 'specials'.

*Marcell Claassen (*w *http://rwandabirdingguide.blogspot.com) is a birding guide who was based in Musanze/Ruhengeri until 2010.*

with their namesake on the Tanzanian border) used to tumble over a cliff to the fields next to the lake at the confluence of two rivers, one lateritic, the other black. The waterfall has been diverted to feed a small hydro-electric scheme so there is no longer anything much to see.

From the Butaro junction, you have three options: turn back, head southeast towards Gicumbi/Byumba via the Rugezi Wetlands, or head more directly south to Base on the main road between Kigali and Musanze. If getting back to Musanze quickly is your main priority, then the best option is to return the way you came, a trip of around 45km (of which about 25km is on dirt).

The dirt road from Butaro towards Gicumbi is most likely to be of interest to birders wanting to check out the Rugezi Birding Area. Good vantages over the

THE NYABINGI CULT

Traditionally the most popular spirit among the Bakiga of southwest Uganda and neighbouring parts of Rwanda is that of a respected rainmaker called Nyabingi, who – possibly in the mid to late 18th century – was murdered by a rival medium at her home in Mukante in the Bufundi Hills of the Rwanda–Uganda border area. After the death of Nyabingi, legend has it, her attendants were visited by numerous ill or barren Bakiga villagers, who would make sacrifices to the late rainmaker's spirit, which would cure their ailment if it approved of the items offered. Over subsequent decades, the spirit possessed a succession of Bakiga mediums, mostly but not always women, who would be blessed with Nyabinga's powers of healing, rainmaking and curing infertility.

Several Nyabingi mediums incited local uprisings against colonialism. The first such rebel was Queen Muhumusa, of mysterious origin, but possibly a former wife of the late Rwandan king Rwabuguri Kigeri. In 1909, Muhumusa was imprisoned by the German authorities in Rwanda after threatening that her son Ndungutse would capture the throne and boot the colonists out of his kingdom. Upon her release in 1911, the queen crossed the border into Uganda and settled at Ihanga Hill near Bubale, 12km from present-day Kabale on the Kisoro Road. She then announced that she had come in search of a cave wherein was secured a sacred drum which, she claimed, would call up a limitless stream of calves when beaten by her and her son. As the news of the magic drum spread through Kigezi, hundreds of young Bakiga men joined in the quest for its location, hoping for a share of the spoils, and Muhumusa received wide support from local chiefs.

The Christian Muganda chiefs installed by the British in southwest Uganda regarded the growing cult surrounding Muhumusa to be evil and insurrectionist, and refused to have anything to do with it. This angered Muhumusa, who attacked the home of one such chief, burning it to the ground, killing several people, and threatening to impale her victim on a sharpened pole, along with any other disrespectful chiefs she could capture. The colonial authorities responded to this affront by attacking Muhumusa's residence with 50 troops and a cannon. At least 40 of the medium's followers were killed on the spot and buried in a mass grave, and several more died of wounds after fleeing the battle site. Muhumusa was captured and imprisoned in Mbarara, where she remained until her death in 1945. The British authorities then proceeded to criminalise the Nyabingi cult through the Witchcraft Ordinance of 1912.

swamp can be obtained from the birding watchtowers at Mubuga, Murwa I, and Murwa II, which respectively lie 5km, 11km and 13km past Butaro, though you would need binoculars to see much birdlife properly. After passing the last of these watchtowers, it is around 40km to Gicumbi, or you could return to Musanze the way you came.

Alternatively, from the Butaro junction, you could carry on straight past the hydro-electric station to complete the lake circuit, an 75km trip of which 30km is on dirt. Be aware, however, that this road veers away from the lake, so the views are few and far between. (Depending on the route you take, it may, however, veer back.) Assuming that you do decide to sally forth, the next main settlement you will reach, after 10km, is Kirambo.

Here, you can turn left along a side road which leads to the village of Ruyange in a cultivated river valley at the southern tip of Lake Burera (a 20km round trip);

In order to help win over local converts, the earliest Christian missionaries to Rwanda and southwest Uganda used words associated with the Nyabingi cult in their sermons and descriptions of Christian rituals. The Virgin Mary was portrayed as a spiritual icon similar to but more powerful than Nyabingi, and many locals adopted the Mother of Jesus as a substitute for the traditional spirit associated with healing and fertility. By the 1930s, the Nyabingi cult, if not completely dead, had gone so far underground as to be undetectable – while it became increasingly common for locals to claim having seen the Virgin Mary at sites of worship formerly associated with Nyabingi.

At least one former Nyabingi shrine has more recently been adopted by a nominally Christian cult. The Nyabugoto Caves near the small town of Kunungu in southwest Uganda were in times past occupied by a renowned medium who regularly cured barren Bakiga women. In the late 1970s, it was reported that a local woman called Blandina Buzigye witnessed a large rock formation in this cave transform into the Virgin Mary before her eyes. It was in the same Ugandan cave, ten years later, that a former prostitute called Credonia Mwerinde founded a fertility cult that mutated into the doomsday movement whose entire membership was locked inside a blazing church by the leaders in a shocking massacre that attracted world headlines in March 2000.

Oddly enough, the term Nyabingi found its way across the Atlantic to Jamaica, where admirers of the rebellious Queen Muhumusa incorporated what are known as *nyabinghi* chants into their celebrations. Sometimes abbreviated to *bhingi*, the chants and dances were originally performed to invoke 'death to the black or white oppressors', but today they are purely ceremonial. Three differently pitched drums are used to create the nyabinghi beat, which – popularised in the late 1950s by the recording artist Count Ossie – has been a huge rhythmic influence on better-known secular Jamaican genres such as ska and reggae. Nyabinghi is also the name of a fundamentalist but strictly pacifist Rastafarian cult which regards the late Ethiopian emperor Haile Selassie as having been an earthly incarnation of God. Indeed, according to some Rastafarian cultists in Jamaica, the neglected Nyabingi spirit abandoned its home in the Rwanda–Ugandan border area in 1937 and relocated to Ethiopia, where it took possession of Haile Selassie during the Italian Occupation. The present whereabouts of the spirit is unknown.

this road continues, winding its way on to the strip of land between the two lakes, and after 25 rough, switchbacked, and scenic kilometres, will return you to the Cyanika road at Gahunga, 10km from Musanze. Alternatively, you can continue straight south from Kirambo towards Base on the main Kigali–Musanze road. Base lies 20km past Kirambo, and is almost equidistant between Kigali and Musanze.

By public transport It is easy enough to get as far as Kidaho – any Cyanika-bound minibus-taxi can drop you there, though you will probably be expected to pay the full fare of around Rfr500 – from where a motorcycle-taxi will cost under Rfr1,000 to the Musangabo Peninsula and Rfr3,000 all the way to Butaro, Alternatively, there are now a handful of direct minibuses between Musanze and Butaro daily, costing around Rfr1,200 (Rfr1,000 from Kidaho), but an early start is recommended if you want to be certain of getting back to Musanze the same day.

BATWA PYGMIES

We have always lived in the forest. Like my father and grandfathers, I lived from hunting and collecting in this mountain. Then the Bahutu came. They cut the forest to cultivate the land. They carried on cutting and planting until they had encircled our forest with their fields. Today, they come right up to our huts. Instead of forest, now we are surrounded by Irish potatoes!

Gahut Gahuliro, a Mutwa born 100 years earlier on the slopes of the Virungas, talking in 1999.

The Batwa are a pygmy people, found today in pockets of the eastern DRC, Uganda, Burundi – and Rwanda, where they number around 30,000–35,000 and comprise the third so-called 'ethnic' group in Rwanda's cultural make-up. That they are indigenous Rwandans is surprisingly little known; even the 2001 film *100 Days*, the first feature film to be made about the 1994 genocide, mentioned only two groups, despite the fact that an estimated 30% of Batwa lost their lives in the genocide, as against 14% of the population overall. Both currently and historically, their role in Rwanda's culture is as exponents of a strikingly distinctive and highly reputed dance, and they are also known for their attractive and traditionally made pottery. In olden times, some had a niche as dancers and potters at the Rwandan royal court.

Less than two millennia have passed since almost all of eastern and southern Africa was populated by semi-nomadic hunter-gatherers, including the Batwa, living in harmony with nature and doing no harm to the environment. But then, as Gahut Gahuliro describes in the quotation above, five or so centuries ago the forests began gradually to fall victim to encroaching farmers. Later, colonisation introduced new industries and construction. Recognising the threat to the forest, the colonisers gazetted tracts of it as protected reserves: the Batwa could still hunt and forage there, but it now belonged to the government and eventually – some decades later – most Batwa were evicted from conservation areas and, of course, from the new national parks. This condensed sequence of events is described in greater detail in Jerome Lewis's report *Batwa Pygmies of the Great Lakes Region* (Minority Rights Group, 2000, available free at w minorityrights. org), while Colin Turnbull's *The Forest People* (1961, available free at w archive.org/details/forestpeople00turn) gives a human picture of a lifestyle that was soon to disappear.

Some Batwa in and around the Great Lakes region had already developed an alternative occupation: they worked as potters, using the clay found in the marshes that lie between Rwanda's many hills. Today they still use just their feet to trample

There's also supposed to be one early-morning minibus between Butaro and Gicumbi/Byumba daily, but there doesn't seem to be any public transport south towards Base. A moto from Butare to Kirambo should set you back about Rfr2,500.

Lake Burera could also be explored more extensively by boat, but it is an option suitable only for those with a pioneering spirit. The obvious place to start a trip of this sort would be Musangabo, though boats are the main form of transport throughout the area, so it should be easy enough to hire a boat and paddler anywhere. There are at least four large islands in the lake: Bushongo, Batutsi, Munanira, and Mudimba (also known as Cyuza and home to a recommended new campsite; page 254). In theory, it should be possible to boat to the south of Lake Burera, hike across the narrow strip of hilly terrain that separates it from Lake Ruhondo, and then pick up another boat to either Ruhondo Beach Resort on the end of a 6km promontory

it into malleability and then their hands to shape cooking pots, stoves, decorative vases, traditional lamps, candle-holders and little replicas of local animals, from cattle to gorillas. The pots are fired without kilns, largely in hollows in the ground, by burning grasses and natural debris, and sealed with earth.

For a minority group that is both small in number and small in size, life can be tough, and over the years the Batwa have suffered extreme prejudice. Even today, they are often seen by unenlightened sections of the population at large as 'inferior'. Since the post-genocide reconstruction they officially enjoy the same rights as all Rwandans, but old attitudes die hard and their social and economic marginalisation won't vanish overnight. They are still by far the poorest sector of Rwandan society. Very few have stable, regular employment or own enough land to feed their families independently, although a handful have managed to improve their circumstances and more children are attending school now than in the past.

After the genocide, in which division between two ethnic groups played such a lethal part, it was decided that Rwanda's population should see themselves simply as 'Rwandans' rather than as Hutu, Tutsi, Twa or any other historic/ethnic group. A person may still refer individually to his or her own group if he or she so wishes, but it is a crime (known as divisionism) to do so collectively, derogatively or provocatively to someone of a different group. Perversely, this ruling aimed at the common good in fact meant that the Batwa communities then missed out on potential government benefits and welfare schemes, because these were no longer aimed at historically marginalised 'ethnic' groups.

A canny bit of renaming removed the impasse. The Batwa in Rwanda are now known as the **Rwandese Community of Potters**, and as such (with no hint of ethnicity in their name) are able to receive official help. The Rwandan government has taken positive action in the fields of education, health and housing, and the community is supported by charities such as COPORWA (*Community of Potters of Rwanda;* ☏ 0252 502357; m 078 884 1610; e coporwa@yahoo.fr; w coporwa1en. wordpress.com), together with various international bodies.

In addition, tourism is increasingly providing the potters with a showcase for their skills (see *Dancing Pots*, page 222) and some of the men work usefully as porters for gorilla-trackers in Volcanoes National Park. It seems that for this talented group of craftspeople and dancers the tide may at last have turned, and that they will gradually find the stability and acceptance they deserve in Rwandan society.

jutting into Lake Ruhondo, or the Foyer de Charité on the southern shore of that lake (page 256). We've never heard of a traveller who attempted this, so drop us a line to let us know how it goes!

On foot   Keen walkers might also think about exploring the area over a few days. We've not heard of anybody doing this, so it would be uncharted territory, and would probably be practical only if you have a tent and are prepared to ask permission to camp at the many villages and homesteads you encounter. It could well be advisable to carry some food (though fish and potatoes should be easy to buy along the way). It is difficult to imagine that any serious security concerns are attached to hiking in this Ugandan border area; you'll come across loads of local pedestrians for company, and travellers are still something of a novelty in this rural region.

Kaspar Kundert's impressively detailed *Biking in Rwanda* (page 58) would also make an excellent resource for getting around here on foot.

The road to the east of the lake can effectively be viewed as an unusually wide hiking trail: it offers great views the whole way, is used by very few vehicles, and follows the contours for most of its length. The most beautiful stretch for hiking is the 17km between Musangabo and Butaro (which can also be covered by boat), and you would be forced to walk (or perhaps hire a moto) for the last 13km between Butaro and Kirambo. From Kirambo, there is a limited amount of public transport to Base, where it is easy to find a lift on to Musanze or Kigali.

 ## Where to stay

Exclusive

🏠 **Virunga Lodge** [map, page 232] (8 rooms) ✪ S 01°26.694, E 029°44.517; 📞0252 502452; m 078 830 2069; m +44 755 4828 321 (UK), 📞+1 212 967 5895 (US); e salesrw@ volcanoessafaris.com/salesuk@volcanoessafaris. com; w volcanoessafaris.com. Boasting one of the most stunning locations in Africa, this superb lodge lies on a 2,175m hilltop above lakes Burera & Ruhondo. In addition to superb views over the lakes to its southeast, the panorama stretches northwest to embrace 4 of the Virunga volcanoes, providing a magnificent overview of this wild volcanic landscape. If you're after organic bush chic rather than transatlantic luxury, this is one of the top 2 or 3 lodges anywhere in Rwanda, comprising 8 secluded stone-&-wood chalets that are both spacious & stylish, with hardwood floors, ample wood & bamboo in the décor, & private verandas offering superb views either to the volcanoes or to the lakes, depending which side you're on. All rooms have 2 double beds & a walk-in net, spacious bathrooms with hot water, sensor lights at night, & a selection of current magazines for reading. This is an excellent base for gorilla tracking, with the 1 caveat being that the distance from Kinigi enforces an earlier start than other lodges (ideally at 06.00 – but the staff are used to this & organise early wake-up calls, showers & b/fast as a matter of course). The food is excellent, as the selection of complimentary wine is usually, & guests eat dinner at 1 large table. Other activities include guided or unguided nature trails, village visits, & Intore dancing. The lodge lies about 30mins' drive from Musanze, turning right off the Cyanika road after 16km at Nyaragondo junction (✪ S 01°25.073, E 029°43.509). US$1,090/1,820 sgl/ dbl high season; US$500/1,000 sgl/dbl low season; both rates inc all meals, alcoholic & non-alcoholic drinks, laundry, massage, activities around the lodge & all government taxes.

Moderate

🏠 **Montana Vista Hotel** [map, page 232] (24 rooms) m 078 157 4685/464 4499/037 2981; e info@montanavistahotel.com; w montanavistahotel.com. Though it's a few km removed from the lakeshore in Kidaho & they're mostly oriented to business rather than tourist clientele, this is a good address to know if you find yourself up this way & don't want to truck back to Musanze before putting up for the night. The rooms are very sharp; all are clean, comfortable & en suite, & some come with private terraces. *Rfr45,000/50,000 sgl/dbl or twin; Rfr60,000/65,000 executive sgl/dbl; Rfr85,000 suite; all rates B&B & are negotiable.*

Shoestring

🏠 **Cyuza Island** [map, page 232] m 078 552 3561/072 232 2066; e lapaillottegorillaplace@ hotmail.com; w lapaillottegorillaplace.com. Set on a diminutive 14ha island on the north side of Lake Burera, this new campsite is under the same management as La Paillotte in Musanze, & all bookings, etc, need to be done through them. Boat transfers to the island start on the Cyanika road, about 17km from Musanze in Rugarama, where the camp manager will pick you up (on foot or moto then paddleboat). Facilities on the island are basic, but you'd be hard pressed to find a more picturesque slice of rural Rwandan life anywhere. Rudimentary cooking gear is available or you can arrange meals & drinks in advance with La Paillotte. Toilets are of the composting variety, ablutions are in the lake, & tents, mattresses & pillows are available for hire, but you'll need your own sleeping bag. *Rfr10,000pp.*

🏠 **Paradise Medal** (15 rooms) m 078 847 8512; e harelimanaviateur@yahoo.fr. Situated in Kirambo, about 13km south of Butaro, this small establishment is very friendly & helpful, & it also serves meals, including outstanding rabbit & fried potatoes. *Rfr8,000/10,000 for an en-suite sgl/dbl with cold water only.*

☝ **Twiheshe Agaciro Resto-Lodge** (21 rooms) 📱 078 834 9336. The only guesthouse in Butaro, so far as we could ascertain, operates in 2 halves. The restaurant (with the usual buffet options) is in a clearly signed (& bright pink) building next to the ATM-equipped Bank of Kigali, while the somewhat scruffy rooms are 350m down the road in an unmarked green house next to the police station. It's nothing to write home about, but sensibly priced at least. *Rfr5,000/7,000 sgl/dbl using common shower; Rfr10,000/13,000 en-suite sgl/dbl; Rfr3,000 dorm bed.*

LAKE RUHONDO Separated from Lake Burera by a 1km-wide strip of land (thought to be an ancient lava flow from Mount Sabinyo), Lake Ruhondo is, like its more northerly neighbour, an erratically shaped body of water whose shore follows the contours of the tall, steep hills that characterise this part of Rwanda. In common with Lake Burera, Ruhondo's shores are densely cultivated, and little natural vegetation remains, but it is nevertheless a very beautiful spot, offering dramatic views across the water to the volcanically formed cones of the Virunga Mountains looming on the horizon. Ruhondo is also an easy target for an overnight excursion, since good accommodation is available – though availability should be confirmed in advance.

The lake is most accessible from the southwest, where the Foyer de Charité guesthouse has a superb location on a hilltop overlooking the lake, with sweeping views across to the volcanoes in the northwest, and potentially stupendous sunsets. Several footpaths lead down the steep slopes below the mission to the lakeshore, a knee-crunching descent and lung-wrenching ascent. At the end of the long promontory jutting into the lake from the south, the Ruhondo Lodge & Tented Camp is a promising new accommodation option as well. At the lakeshore, it is easy to negotiate a fee to take a pirogue to one of the islands, or to the Ntaruka hydro-electric plant on the opposite shore, where a small waterfall connects Lake Ruhondo with Lake Burera.

Getting around The best route to the Foyer de Charité starts on the main Kigali road about 3km south of Musanze. Coming from Musanze, you need to turn left along a dirt road clearly signed for the Foyer de Charité, which initially leads through a marshy area dotted with traditional brickmaking urns, before following the cultivated Mukungwa River valley (note the small waterfall on your left after 300m). After 2.8km, take a left fork at the electrical facility, then just under 2km after that turn right to cross a bridge over the river, then bear left, following the signposts. The road is flat until this point, but now it starts to ascend gently, with the lake becoming visible to the left about 2.5km past the bridge. Several footpaths lead from this viewpoint to the lakeshore, an easier ascent than the one from the Foyer de Charité. Beyond the viewpoint, the road continues to climb for 3km to the village of Kadahero, where a left turn leads after about 400m to the mission. To get to Ruhondo Lodge & Tented Camp, continue south from here, skirting the edge of a high ridge for around 3km, then bear left to head back north down the other side of the ridge, after which another 10km or so of winding roads will land you at the resort.

This is all straightforward enough provided that you have a vehicle (ideally one with high clearance, though the Foyer de Charité should be accessible by saloon car year-round), and that – if driving along the tar from Kigali – you don't inadvertently take an earlier road signposted for Remera (this road does lead to the mission, but it's longer and rougher). There is no public transport, however, and hitching might prove to be frustrating. One option would be to catch public transport towards Musanze as far as the turn-off to Remera, then to walk the final 10km to the mission (the last 6km would be steep going with a rucksack, and Ruhondo Lodge & Tented Camp would be too far altogether). The alternative is to hire a motorcycle-taxi from Musanze – the going rate is around Rfr2,500 one-way (double this to the resort) – and arrange to be collected at a specified time. A much easier way to get to the resort is with a boat transfer from the Ntaruka hydro-electric plant (page 255).

Where to stay *Map, page 232*

Foyer de Charité (45 rooms) m 078 851 0659/855 5053/672 9385; e vdprw@yahoo.fr/ vdpreception@gmail.com; w foyer-de-charite. com. Established as a religious retreat in 1968, this mission was renovated in 1995 after it had been damaged during the genocide. It remains first & foremost a religious retreat, but respectful lay visitors are usually permitted to stay provided that they make advance arrangements. Comfortable guest rooms with washbasins are available, as are communal solar-heated showers, inexpensive & filling meals made with locally grown produce, & reliably cold beers & sodas. There is little in the way of formal entertainment (the beautiful singing at evening mass in the chapel might qualify I suppose), but it's a lovely place to relax for a couple of days, & there's plenty of room for exploration on the surrounding roads. It is essential to make contact in advance, as the mission closes to lay visitors for special religious events – which probably add up to around 100 days annually. *Room rates are negotiable, but are generally around Rfr15,000–30,000pp B&B.*

Lake Ruhondo Lodge & Tented Camp (10 rooms, 9 tents) ✪ S 1°29.661, E 29°44.526; m 078 857 2697/372 8297/249 7865; e hafashimangervais@yahoo.fr; f Lake Ruhondo Lodge & Tented Camp. With a location that's as remote as it is magnificent, this relatively new hotel, also known as Ruhondo Beach Resort, sits on the waterfront at the end of a long peninsula, deep in the centre of Lake Ruhondo. It's a bit of a trek to get here by car (page 255), but if you phone ahead they can also arrange scenic boat transfers from the Ntaruka hydro plant (*Rfr10,000 round trip for up to 10 passengers*) or elsewhere on the lake. Accommodation is in comfortably equipped en-suite rooms & standing tents, & the resto-bar quite appropriately specialises in fish. There's hot water, Wi-Fi, & a range of hikes & canoe trips possible from here. *Significant low-season discounts. US$80/100/120 sgl/dbl/twin room; US$30/50 sgl/dbl standing tent; all rates B&B.*

9

Volcanoes National Park

The 160km² Volcanoes National Park protects the Rwandan sector of the Virunga Mountains, a range of six extinct and three active volcanoes that straddle the Ugandan and Congolese borders and protect more than half the global population of the charismatic mountain gorilla. Occasionally referred to by its French name Parc des Volcans, it forms part of a contiguous 433km² transfrontier conservation unit that protects the upper slopes of the Virungas in their entirety, and also incorporates the southern portion of the Congolese Virunga National Park and Uganda's Mgahinga National Park. The three national parks function separately today, but prior to 1960 the Rwandan and Congolese sectors were jointly managed as the Albert National Park.

Volcanoes National Park is an immensely scenic and ecologically diverse destination. Indeed, this chain of steep free-standing mountains, spanning altitudes of 2,400m to 4,507m, and linked by fertile saddles formed by solidified lava flows, ranks among the most stirring and memorable of African landscapes. The tallest member of the chain, and the most westerly part of the national park, is Karisimbi (4,507m) on the border with the DRC. Moving eastwards, the other main peaks within the national park are: Bisoke (aka Visoke) on the DRC border; Sabyinyo, at the tripartite border with Uganda and the DRC; and Gahinga (aka Mgahinga) and Muhabura (aka Muhavura) on the Ugandan border.

Tracking mountain gorillas is easily the most popular tourist activity in Volcanoes National Park. However, a wide variety of other hikes and activities are offered, making it possible to spend several days in the area without running out of things to do. The most popular activity after gorilla tracking is a visit to a habituated troop of the rare golden monkey, an Albertine Rift Endemic whose modern range is more-or-less restricted to the Virungas. Also quite popular is the hike to Dian Fossey's former camp and grave on the forested slopes of Karisoke. Fewer visitors embark on the more demanding day treks to the summits of Bisoke (famed for its beautiful crater lake) or Muhabura, and fewer still are up for the overnight hike to the highest point in the range, the summit of Karisimbi.

WILDLIFE

Gorillas and golden monkeys aside, primates are poorly represented by comparison with most other large forests in Rwanda and Uganda. Little information is available regarding the current status of other large mammals in the mountains, but 70-plus species have been recorded in neighbouring Mgahinga National Park, and most probably also occur in the larger Rwanda sector. Elephant and buffalo are still quite common, judging by the amount of spoor encountered on forest trails, but are very timid and infrequently observed. Also present are giant forest hog,

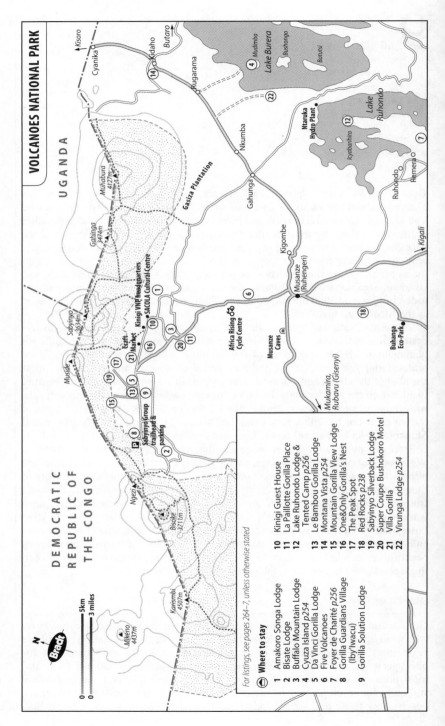

VOLCANOES NATIONAL PARK

For listings, see pages 264–7, unless otherwise stated

Where to stay

1. Amakoro Songa Lodge
2. Bisate Lodge
3. Buffalo Mountain Lodge
4. Cyuza Island *p254*
5. Da Vinci Gorilla Lodge
6. Five Volcanoes
7. Foyer de Charité *p256*
8. Gorilla Guardians Village (Iby'Iwacu)
9. Gorilla Solution Lodge
10. Kinigi Guest House
11. La Paillotte Gorilla Place
12. Lake Ruhondo Lodge & Tented Camp *p256*
13. Le Bambou Gorilla Lodge
14. Montana Vista *p254*
15. Mountain Gorilla View Lodge
16. One&Only Gorilla's Nest
17. The Peak Spot
18. Red Rocks *p238*
19. Sabyinyo Silverback Lodge
20. Super Coupe Bushokoro Motel
21. Villa Gorilla
22. Virunga Lodge *p254*

bushpig, bushbuck, black-fronted duiker, spotted hyena, and several varieties of small predator. Modern extinctions, probably as a result of deforestation, include the massive yellow-backed duiker and leopard.

A bird checklist for Volcanoes National Park compiled in 1980 totalled 180 species. About 15 previously unrecorded species were noted during a 2004 biodiversity survey, but it is possible that several other forest specialists have vanished since 1980. A local speciality is the vulnerable swamp-dwelling Grauer's rush warbler, while at least 16 Albertine Rift Endemics are present, including handsome francolin, Ruwenzori turaco, Ruwenzori double-collared sunbird, Ruwenzori batis, strange weaver, dusky crimson-wing, collared apalis, red-faced woodland warbler and Archer's ground robin.

HISTORY, CONSERVATION AND ECOTOURISM

The ecology of the Virungas remained practically unknown to Western science until 1902, when the German explorer Robert von Beringe ascended Mount Sabyinyo and became the first European to encounter – and to kill – a mountain gorilla (see box, page 10). Over the following two decades, at least 50 individual mountain gorillas were captured or killed in the Virungas, prompting the Belgian government to establish the Albert National Park by decree on 21 April 1925, protecting a triangle formed by the Karisimbi, Mikeno and Bisoke volcanoes.

At the time of its creation, this was the first national park in Africa to be known as such. The Institut du Parc National Albert was created by decree on 9 July 1929. A further decree on 12 November 1935 determined the final boundaries of the Albert National Park, then covering 809,000ha. About 8% of the park lay in what is now Rwanda and today constitutes the Volcanoes National Park, while the rest was in the Congo. At the time of independence, Rwanda's new leaders confirmed that they would maintain the park (the gorillas were already well known internationally), the pressing problem of overpopulation notwithstanding.

SCHALLER AND FOSSEY The gorilla population of the Virungas is thought to have been reasonably stable in 1960, when a census undertaken by George Schaller indicated that some 450 individuals lived in the range. By 1971–73, however, the population had plummeted to an estimated 250. This decline was caused by several factors, including the post-colonial division of the Albert National Park into its Rwandan and Congolese components, the ongoing fighting between the Hutu and Tutsi of Rwanda, and a grisly tourist trade in poached gorilla heads and hands – the latter used by some sad individuals as ashtrays! Most devastating of all perhaps was the irreversible loss of almost half of the gorillas' habitat between 1957 and 1968 to local farmers and a European-funded agricultural scheme.

George Schaller initiated the first study of mountain gorilla behaviour in the 1950s, and his pioneering work formed the starting point for the more recent and well-known study undertaken by American primatologist Dian Fossey. Fossey arrived in Rwanda to study mountain gorillas in 1967, supported by the eminent Kenyan palaeontologist Louis Leakey, who had earlier been responsible for placing Jane Goodall at Gombe Stream in Tanzania. She founded the Karisoke Research Centre on the forested slopes of Mount Karisimbi, and for the next 18 years used it as the base for her studies of Volcanoes National Park's mountain gorillas.

It is largely thanks to Fossey's single-minded and somewhat paramilitary campaign to discourage poaching in Volcanoes National Park that this activity was curtailed while there were still some gorillas to save. For this, she would pay the ultimate price. Her brutal murder at the Karisoke Research Centre in December 1985, though officially unsolved, is widely thought to have been the work of one of the many poachers whom she antagonised in her efforts to save her gorillas. Three years after her death, Fossey's life work was exposed to a mass audience with the release of *Gorillas in the Mist*, a cinematic account of her life that was filmed on location in Volcanoes National Park. The film grossed more than US$60 million worldwide, was nominated for five Academy Awards, and generated unprecedented global interest in mountain gorillas and ecotourism in the Virungas.

GORILLA TOURISM 1979–94 In 1979, Amy Vedder and Bill Weber initiated the first gorilla tourism project in Rwanda's Volcanoes Park, integrating tourism, local education and anti-poaching measures with remarkable success. Initially, the project was aimed mainly at tourists in overland trucks, who paid a laughably

INTERNATIONAL CONSERVATION ORGANISATIONS

Mountain gorillas are the focus of several international conservation organisations; the following are among the largest and most active in Rwanda.

DIAN FOSSEY GORILLA FUND INTERNATIONAL Founded in 1978, the Atlanta-based DFGFI funds and operates the Karisoke Research Centre [234 D4] (w *gorillafund. org*), originally established by Dr Dian Fossey more than 50 years ago, in 1967. Their new US$10m Ellen DeGeneres campus is slated to open in 2020, though the location wasn't yet finalised as this book went to print; see w bradtupdates.com/rwanda for the latest. Based in Musanze, it continues to monitor multiple gorilla groups and to carry out daily anti-poaching patrols from a base outside the park. DFGFI aims to strengthen research and protection efforts through education, local capacity building, and support to a Geographic Information Systems unit based within the national university.

GORILLA DOCTORS (w *gorilladoctors.org*) Gorilla Doctors (Mountain Gorilla Veterinary Project) provides veterinary care to the mountain gorillas. The project's vets monitor the health of individual gorillas in both the research and tourist groups, and are able to intervene in emergency situations, such as a gorilla becoming trapped by a life-threatening snare. Since disease transmission from humans is a serious threat to the gorillas' survival, they also monitor the health of government and project staff working in the park, and organise seminars addressing health and hygiene issues. Gorilla Doctors receives funding from the Morris Animal Foundation and is affiliated to the Maryland Zoo and UC Davis Wildlife Health Centre in the US.

THE GORILLA ORGANIZATION (w *gorillas.org*) Founded in 1992, this London-based organisation, an advocate of community-led conservation, manages several projects designed to integrate traditional conservation and research with economic development and education in Rwanda, Uganda, DR Congo, Cameroon and Gabon. These include:

- Beekeepers, who are supported to develop modern sustainable honey farms at the edge of, rather than inside, the park boundary.
- Fresh water in village schools using local engineering technology to provide water cisterns. Water collection is one of the main causes of encroachment in

paltry – by today's standards – US$20 per person to track gorillas. Even so, gorilla tourism was raising up to ten million US dollars annually by the mid 1980s, making it Rwanda's third-highest earner of foreign revenue, and the industry was given a further boost with the release of the film *Gorillas in the Mist* in 1988.

By that time, Volcanoes National Park was the best-organised and most-popular gorilla sanctuary in Africa, and gorilla tourism was probably Rwanda's leading earner of tourist revenue. What's more, the mountain gorilla had practically become the national emblem of Rwanda, and it was officially recognised to be the country's most important renewable natural resource. To ordinary Rwandans, gorillas became a source of great national pride: living gorillas ultimately created far more work and money than poaching them had ever done. As a result, a census undertaken in 1989 indicated that the local mountain gorilla population had increased by almost 30% to 320 animals.

the gorilla habitat, and children living close to the forest often miss school to collect water for their families.

- Training in sustainable agriculture for farmers in areas adjacent to gorilla habitat.
- Tree planting to alleviate environmental degradation, since most fuel used in households comes from wood.
- Virunga Wildlife Clubs in schools, which organise field trips, tree planting and environment-week activities, and a Conservation Network that links local organisations in the Virunga region.

INTERNATIONAL GORILLA CONSERVATION PROGRAMME (w *mountaingorillas.org*) IGCP is a joint initiative of three organisations: the African Wildlife Foundation, Fauna and Flora International and the World Wide Fund for Nature. Their goal is the sustainable conservation of the world's remaining mountain gorillas and their habitat. IGCP promotes communication and co-operation between protected-area authorities through regional meetings, training programmes, cross-border patrols and contact networks; and advises governments on environmental policy and legislation enforcement. It provides training and support for park staff, and has set up a ranger-based monitoring programme throughout the Virunga region. The African Wildlife Foundation donated 28ha of land to be incorporated into Volcanoes National Park in January 2018.

WILDLIFE CONSERVATION SOCIETY (w *wcs.org*) With strong historic links to the mountain gorillas, WCS's major programme in Rwanda is now the Nyungwe Forest Conservation Project, although it is still involved with the Volcanoes and Akagera national parks. It also implements training programmes in monitoring and research with its partners, including the Rwanda Development Board (RDB); provides direct support to the management of parks and wildlife; and supports the RDB in tackling immediate threats. In addition, the volcanoes fall within the WCS's **Albertine Rift Project** (w *albertinerift.org*). The objective of this programme is to improve conservation by providing information for park managers, better management of these areas, and collaboration across national boundaries. Biological and socio-economic surveys are used to identify priority conservation areas and to plan measures to alleviate poverty in the communities that border them.

Gorilla tourism came to an abrupt halt in 1991, when the country erupted into the civil war that culminated in the 1994 genocide. In February 1992, the park headquarters were attacked, two park employees were killed, and the Karisoke Research Centre established by Fossey had to be evacuated. The park was closed to tourists and, although it reopened in June 1993, it had to be evacuated in April 1994 because of the genocide.

WAR AND THE GORILLAS The Rwandan civil war raised considerable concern about the survival of the gorillas, as land mines were planted there by various military factions, and the mountains provided an escape route to thousands of fleeing refugees. Remarkably, however, when researchers were finally able to return to the park, it was discovered that only four gorillas could not be accounted for. Two of those missing were old females who most probably died of natural causes; the other two might have been shot, but might just as easily have succumbed to disease. It is also encouraging to note that the war had no evident effect on breeding activity, a strong indication that it was less disruptive to the gorillas than had been feared.

But in this most volatile part of Africa little can be taken for granted. Just as Rwanda started to stabilise politically, the DRC descended into anarchy. For years,

KWITA IZINA: THE GORILLA-NAMING CEREMONY

The birth of a child in Rwanda is a big event for the family and neighbourhood, and the naming of the child at the Kwita Izina ceremony is traditionally the chance to welcome him or her into the wider world. The baby is carried outside and shown to the public, and young children suggest names for this infant who has recently joined them. The parents then select one of the names. It's a lively gathering, accompanied by plenty of food, drink and, of course, dancing.

In the past few decades, the Kwita Izina naming tradition has also been applied to young mountain gorillas, with the park guides taking on the role of proposing the names – which are based on the behaviour, circumstances and background of the infants or their mother. This gorilla-naming ceremony was a low-key private affair up until 2004, but in June 2005 it was held publicly at what is now the One&Only Gorilla's Nest resort in Kinigi (page 265), and the official naming of 23 gorillas was followed by a celebration party with traditional music and dancing.

So successful was the inaugural public ceremony that it has now become an annual event, now typically held in early September, when all gorillas born over the past 12 months are given a formal name to the accompaniment of traditional music and dance. In September 2017, 19 baby gorillas were given poetic names like Ubudasa (remarkable) and Imirasire (ray of sun), along with a few more prosaic ones like Ikoranabuhanga (information technology), born 29 December 2016. Visitors are most welcome to attend these events, which are now held at a small area in Kinigi, close to the park headquarters. Kwita Izina raises valuable funds for the protection of the mountain gorillas; tour operators will fit it into your itinerary by request. As well as the naming, there is the opportunity to 'adopt' (sponsor) a gorilla and/or to make general donations to the animals' welfare.

For more information, tickets and details of sponsorship, contact RDB (page 82) or check w rwandatourism.com.

eastern Congolese officials, who lived far from the capital, received no formal salary and were forced to devise their own ways of securing a living, leading to a level of corruption second to none in the region. At least 16 gorillas were killed in three separate incidents in the DRC between 1995 and 1998, since when the Congolese part of the Virungas was effectively closed to tourists and researchers alike prior to reopening in 2005.

Under the circumstances, it is remarkable to learn that a gorilla count undertaken in the Virungas in 2003 showed a continued increase to at least 380 individuals. No further killings were reported between 2003 and 2007, but then at least ten Congolese mountain gorillas were shot in four separate incidents in the space of a few months, culminating in the arrest of the alleged perpetrators in September of that year.

The good news continued through 2010, when another census recorded 480 mountain gorillas in the Virungas, and thanks to intensive conservation efforts, this trend shows no sign of slowing down. The most recent census results were announced in May 2018, counting a total of 604 individuals (41 groups and 14 solitary males) across the Virungas, marking a 25% increase since the last count and the highest figure since the first formal census was undertaken almost 60 years ago. Including the 400 mountain gorillas resident in Bwindi, the global population is now just over 1,000.

PROS AND CONS OF GORILLA TOURISM Any concern about the fate of a few gorillas might seem misplaced in the context of a genocide that claimed a million human lives. But it is these self-same gorillas which have allowed Rwanda to rebuild the lucrative tourist industry that was shattered by the war. Gorilla tracking resumed on a permanent basis in July 1999, and Volcanoes National Park has remained open ever since, a period during which the volume of permits sold annually has increased more than tenfold. Mostly, it's the gorillas that bring tourists to Rwanda, but once there they will usually spend money in other parts of the country, providing foreign revenue and creating employment beyond the immediate vicinity of Volcanoes National Park.

There are those who query the wisdom of habituating gorillas for tourist visits. One area of concern is health, with humans and gorillas being sufficiently close genetically for there to be a real risk of passing a viral or bacterial infection to a habituated gorilla, which might in turn infect other members of its group, potentially resulting in all their deaths should they have no resistance to the infection. Another concern is that habituating gorillas to humans increases their vulnerability to poachers, a theory backed up by the fact that most mountain gorillas poached since the mid 1990s belonged to habituated troops.

Given the above, a reasonable response might be to query the wisdom of habituating gorillas in the first place. The problem facing conservationists is that gorillas cannot be conserved in a vacuum. The park generated more than US$16 million in 2016 and, at current prices, the Rwandan authorities can potentially earn US$144,000 daily in tracking permits alone, much of which is pumped back into the protection and management of the Volcanoes Park or distributed to local communities bordering the park. There are also the broader benefits of job creation through tourism in and around the Virungas. And even in terms of pure conservation, habituation has many positive effects, allowing researchers and rangers to monitor the gorillas on a daily basis, and to intervene when one of them is ill, injured or in a snare.

Put crudely, while tourism is probably integral to the survival of the mountain gorilla, the survival of the mountain gorilla is certainly integral to the growth of

9

Rwanda's tourist industry. Ultimately, it's a symbiotic situation that motivates a far greater number of people to take an active interest in the fate of the gorillas than would be the case if gorilla tourism were to be curtailed.

GETTING THERE AND AWAY

Gorilla tracking and all other activities in Volcanoes National Park start at the RDB office/park headquarters in the sprawling village of Kinigi, which lies at an altitude of 2,200m on the eucalyptus-strewn Virunga footslopes (✿ S 01°25.783, E 029°35.717). Kinigi lies 12km north of Musanze/Ruhengeri, along a surfaced road signposted to the left of the Cyanika Road about 300m past the Centre Pastoral Notre Dame de Fatima. All participants in gorilla tracking and other hikes must be at the park headquarters by 07.00, or they risk invalidating any permit bought in advance.

There is a fair amount of public transport to Kinigi. At least one minibus leaves from the bus station in Musanze every 30 minutes, charging Rfr500 per person, and taking 15–20 minutes to get there, but usually stopping a kilometre or two short of the park headquarters. A one-way taxi ride between Musanze and any of the hotels in and around Kinigi will cost around Rfr10,000, while a moto costs Rfr2,000–3,000.

Most visitors on organised trips stay at one of the mid-range-to-upmarket lodges scattered in and around Kinigi on the night before they go gorilla tracking or do another hike, which eases the pressure to be at the headquarters by 07.00 on the morning of departure. By contrast, budget-conscious travellers tend to use Musanze as a base for gorilla tracking and other activities, though there are also now some genuinely affordable options close to the park headquarters.

Either way, there is no public transport from the park headquarters to any of the car parks from where one enters the forest to start tracking, and, while individuals may be able to beg a lift with another tourist group, this is not foolproof. Which means that even if you get as far as Musanze or Kinigi using public transport, you will need to arrange to rent a 4x4 with driver to get you to the trailhead. This costs around US$100 for transport in both directions, including waiting time, and it can be arranged in advance through Beyond Gorillas Experience in Musanze (page 241) or at most Musanze or Kinigi hotels. If you're really skint after paying for the permit, you could also conceivably arrange with a moto-taxi driver to get you to the trailhead for considerably less cash.

With a private vehicle, it is possible to drive to Kinigi from Rubavu/Gisenyi or Kigali on the day you track, though you would need a very early start to be at the assembly point by 07.00. Allow at least 2 hours from Kigali, or 1 hour from Rubavu. Virunga Lodge (page 254), which overlooks Lake Burera 30–45 minutes' drive from Kinigi, is another popular upmarket base for gorilla tracking and other activities in the park.

 WHERE TO STAY AND EAT *Map, page 258*

There is no accommodation within the national park and overnight camping is forbidden. However, several lodges catering to all budgets are situated within a few kilometres of Kinigi, and are all listed on pages 265–7. Many travellers on a restricted budget overnight in Musanze, and make their way to Kinigi early in the morning, while those with limited time and a high tolerance for very early mornings sometimes base themselves further off at a hotel in Rubavu/Gisenyi.

EXCLUSIVE

✳ 🏠 Bisate Lodge (6 rooms) ☎ +27 11 257 5000/21 702 7500; e enquiry@wilderness.co.za; w wilderness-safaris.com. Set in a handful of otherworldly, dome-shaped villas sprinkled on a 43ha hillside property overlooking Bisate Village & the Virunga range, this new lodge singlehandedly raises the bar for accommodation in Rwanda & would rightfully rank among the finest lodges anywhere in East Africa. The architecture is inspired by traditional Rwandan building methods & everything here has been built from local materials. The pointy-roofed, dual-dome villas are widely spaced & every bit as opulent as you might expect, with jaw-dropping views over the Virunga chain from the sizeable balconies, & a designer interior of lava stone, wood, leather, thatch, & locally fired brick. Rooms all come with dual sinks, shower, & deep soak tub, along with king-size bed, lounge area, fireplace, & a tablet computer packed with information on the park, surrounding areas, & a profile of all the lodge's employees. There's also a radio in every room so you can order food & drink from the comfort of your bathrobe. The main building is home to the restaurant, bar, fireplace lounge, & library, & the plush fur-lined seats & twinkling sea-glass chandeliers make a rather compelling case to put your feet up & stay awhile. In keeping with their mission to engage with the neighbouring communities, much of the produce served in the restaurant is grown locally, guests are encouraged to join a guided visit to Bisate Village, & they've planted nearly 20,000 trees in the area so far. Getting to the lodge requires climbing a number of steps, but it's a piece of cake compared to your gorilla trek. If you're after a bit more walking, there are also 2 nature trails on the property following an eroded crater rim, both of which are excellent for birding. The room rate includes a complimentary 20min massage, village visit, & all food & drink except premium spirits. *US$2,310–2,940 dbl all inclusive.*

🏠 One&Only Gorilla's Nest ☎ +1 954 809 2700; e info@oneandonlyresorts.com; w oneandonlyresorts.com. Situated in a eucalyptus grove at an altitude of 2,295m, between Kinigi & the Volcanoes National Park boundary, this long-serving lodge suffered extensive fire damage in 2011, but was being entirely redesigned & rebuilt at the time of writing. Slated to reopen as part of the exclusive One&Only line of luxury resorts in late 2018, you can expect characterful & locally inspired top-end accommodation, a full-service spa & fitness centre, volcano views & nods to traditional Rwandan culture & cuisine throughout. *Enquire for rates.*

🏠 Sabyinyo Silverback Lodge (8 rooms) ☎ +254 20 273 4000; m 078 838 2030; e reservations@governorscamp.com; w governorscamp.com. This is one of the swishiest lodges in the immediate vicinity of Kinigi, set on community land at an altitude of 2,515m on the footslopes of Mount Sabyinyo, only a 10min drive from the park headquarters. The land is owned by the Sacola Community Trust & leased to Governors' Camp, a long-serving & award-winning Kenyan luxury safari camp operator which built the lodge & also manages it. A community fee of roughly US$100pp/night is levied, & the community also receives a cut of the lodge's profits. Accommodation consists of 5 stone cottages, 2 suites & 1 4-bed family suite, all spread out across the grassy slopes. The stylish & well-equipped rooms were fully redecorated in 2015, & combine ethnically influenced décor with something of a country house feel, & come complete with log fire, minibar, tea/coffee-making facilities, mini-safe, telephone, Wi-Fi, 24hr electricity, & a fabulously earthy bathroom with tub & shower. The restaurant & lounge area is in the main building & serves a choice of 2 3-course set menus daily. In addition to gorilla tracking, it offers birding expeditions, & trips to Musanze & lakes Kivu & Burera. The steep climb from the car park to the accommodation makes this lodge highly unsuited to disabled travellers, though it should be perfectly manageable to anybody fit & supple enough to track gorillas. Rates include full-board accommodation but exclude massage treatments, premium spirits, gorilla-tracking permits, transfers to/from Kigali & community fee. *From US$520/1,040 to US$1,215/1,940 sgl/dbl, depending on season.*

UPMARKET

🏠 Amakoro Songa Lodge (4 rooms) m 078 142 2098/9; e amakoro@songaafrica.com; w songaafrica.com. Built with an eye to sustainability, this bright & modern new lodge opened at the end of 2016 sits about 3km off the road to the Kinigi park HQ & consists of 2 standalone cottages & 2 rooms in the main building with the restaurant & lounge. The grounds are handsomely manicured & crisscrossed by pebble-strewn pathways leading between the rooms, restaurant, outdoor firepit, & picturesque thatch *palapa* hut for outdoor dinners & drinks. Rooms are bright & modern & all come with private terraces & large, luxurious bathrooms. *US$720/960 sgl/dbl.*

🏠 **Five Volcanoes Boutique Hotel** (13 rooms) m 078 992 4969/073 937 3971; e bookings@fivevolcanoesrwanda.com; w fivevolcanoesrwanda.com. Opened at the end of 2016, this welcoming new lodge is the first accommodation you reach entering Kinigi from Musanze & offers a selection of trim & appealing rooms built from lava stones with heating, AC, mini-fridge, tea/coffee facilities, & garden-facing terraces out front. Deluxe rooms come with canopy beds & there are wood-built family cottages on offer as well. The open-sided 1st-floor restaurant-bar does a good selection of Indian- & European-inspired dishes on a rotating basis. There's an outdoor swimming pool & a sauna/steam room is under construction. *US$300/400 sgl/dbl; US$420/530 dbl sgl/dbl; all rates FB.*

🏠 **Mountain Gorilla View Lodge** (41 rooms) m 078 830 5708/564 0438; e info@3bhotels.com; w 3bhotels.com. Set in expansive, grassy grounds, this lodge stands on the breezy open saddle that connects Sabyinyo & Bisoke & offers superb views to all 6 of the volcanoes in the Rwandan part of the Virungas. Accommodation is in large & attractive free-standing cottages with queen-size or twin beds, tea/coffee-making facilities, private balconies, fridge, Wi-Fi, mini-safe, log fire, a spacious bathroom with a hot shower, & dual sinks. The restaurant & bar is a big thatched building with stone floors, where there's a fireplace inside for cool nights & a big wooden terrace outside for hot days. There are a couple of new & extravagant serviced suites here as well. *US$230/300/450 sgl/dbl/trpl FB; US$2,000 serviced suite (sleeps 5).*

MODERATE

🏠 **Da Vinci Gorilla Lodge** (6 rooms, 4 under construction) m 078 308 3901/397 1888; e info@davincigorillalodge.com; w davincigorillalodge.com. Though you're unlikely to mistake the stone bungalow rooms at this new place for anything

designed by the Italian master, they're all certainly comfortable enough & come well equipped with fireplace, kettle, phone, safe & sitting area. The 1st-floor bar & restaurant is a bit hodgepodge in feel, but the staff are eager to please & there's a good menu of Rwandan favourites on offer. *US$250 dbl FB.*

🏠 **Gorilla Guardians Village (Iby'Iwacu)** m 078 835 2009; e info@ibyiwacuvillage.org; w ibyiwacuvillage.org. An interesting alternative to staying in a conventional lodge is the village stay offered by this cultural village bordering Volcanoes National Park. Accommodation is in traditional thatched mud houses, with en-suite long-drop & bathing area, surrounding a replica royal palace (similar to the one at Nyanza) big enough to accommodate more than 100 people. Fresh local food is eaten communally. *US$100pp FB.*

🏠 **Gorilla Solution Lodge** (10 rooms) m 078 729 5758/931 9286; e info@gorillasolutionlodge.com; w gorillasolutionlodge.com. Whether they've solved something for the gorillas, with the gorillas, or something else entirely here remains unclear, & the 2 rows of stone-built bungalows behind the fetching thatched main hall unfortunately don't offer any clues. Also unfortunate is the degree to which the hodgepodge of inappropriate furnishings (more conference hall than safari lodge) brings down the atmosphere in what otherwise seems a likeable enough & well-constructed lodge. The guest rooms are very spacious, making their lack of furnishings all the more conspicuous, but they do all come with kettle, mini-fridge, & the like. The Kenyan chef does a variety of East African dishes, & rates are negotiable depending on the season. *US$170/200 sgl/dbl FB.*

🏠 **Le Bambou Gorilla Lodge** (20 rooms) m 078 830 7374/858 6515; e info@lebambougorillalodge.com; w lebambougorillalodge.com. Adeptly plugging the gap between the upmarket properties listed on page 265 & the more basic options listed opposite, accommodation here is in large stone cottages (some of which have fireplaces) painted in bold geometric patterns, with firm king-size beds, en-suite hot shower, kettle, private balcony & a cluttered & colourful collection of furniture, including a writing desk & wardrobe. As with other lodges in this area the setting of exotic eucalyptus trees is less than inspiring, but this is countered by the well-tended gardens. There is a slightly unfinished feel to the place, especially the incoherently furnished reception, bar & dining area, but this is a minor quibble indeed as the food is good (*US$15 for the 3-course menu*), & the staff very helpful & accommodating. *US$150/200/350 sgl/dbl/trpl FB.*

🏠 **Villa Gorilla** (8 rooms) m 078 859 2924; e info@villagorillarwanda.com; w villagorillarwanda.com. Just a few steps down the road from the craft centre you visit after gorilla tracking, this friendly & likeable place opened in 2014 & offers high-quality but unpretentious accommodation in a pretty garden with views to the mountains. The colourful rooms are carpeted & spotlessly clean, & they come in either a standard configuration or bungalow-style rooms (with sizeable showers!) connected by a wooden walkway out back. The garden is host to sundowners, campfires, & Intore dances nightly, should you so desire, & the engaging owner & staff are happy to take you out on free village tours as well. All other activities & transport can be arranged, there's free Wi-Fi & laundry, & a turkey named Roger that lives in the gardens. *US$175/200 sgl/dbl, US$500 cottage sleeping 4; all rates FB.* See ad, 4th colour section.

BUDGET

🏠 **Buffalo Mountain Lodge** (10 rooms) m 078 852 9550/563 5002; e twagiramanaeric1@gmail.com; w buffalomountainlodge.rw. About 700m towards the park HQ from Kinigi's main junction, the rooms here are set in a series of duplex rondavels behind the surprisingly cheerful open-sided bar, which serves the usual array of Rwandan-style grills & other meals. The basic rooms are a bit short on windows, but clean, trim & otherwise fine for the price, with Wi-Fi & hot water. They've also got a branch in Musanze opposite the CINFOP Guesthouse. *Rfr15,000/20,000 sgl/dbl; Rfr25,000 VIP dbl.*

🏠 **Kinigi Guest House** (11 rooms, 4 dorms) m 078 853 3606/689 2045; e kinigi2020@yahoo. fr; w rwanda-kinigi-guesthouse.com. Situated in peaceful green gardens only 300m from the park headquarters, this likeably low-key lodge is run by the charity ASOFERWA & its en-suite wooden

chalets (with hot showers) have an almost Swiss appearance. There's a craft shop on site, along with comfortable public areas, a good restaurant & bar, & the view of the volcanoes from here is superb. *Good value in this location at Rfr25,000/30,000 sgl/ dbl; Rfr40,000 VIP dbl; Rfr10,000/bed in a 4-berth dorm; all rates B&B.*

🏠 **La Paillotte Gorilla Place** (6 rooms) m 078 552 3561; e lapaillottegorillaplace@ hotmail.com; w lapaillottegorillaplace.com. Affiliated to the eponymous bakery in Musanze, this is the choicest budget option near the national park, about 3km from the park HQ at the junction of the roads from Musanze & Gorilla's Nest. The modest rooms vary greatly in size, but all have en-suite hot showers & double beds. The restaurant-bar has indoor & courtyard seating; it serves a good selection of tasty pizzas, sandwiches & meals in the Rfr2,500–4,000 range & is open from 06.00 to 22.00 daily. *From Rfr15,000/20,000 for the smallest sgl/dbl to Rfr20,000/25,000/30,000 for a larger sgl/ dbl/trpl.*

🏠 **The Peak Spot** (6 rooms) m 078 844 1652; e thepeakspotlodge@gmail.com; w thepeakspotkinigi.com. Set below Mount Sabyinyo at an altitude of around 2,500m, this tranquil place opened in 2015 & has a casual, backpacker-friendly vibe – something of a rarity in this corner of Rwanda. The small but neat rooms are set in stone bungalows around the central gardens (where camping is available), & all come with en-suite hot-water ablutions. The resto-bar does Rwandan favourites for around Rfr8,500, & it's cheerfully decorated with local textiles & basketry throughout. If you call them from Musanze or Kinigi, they'll arrange a moto-taxi to fetch you for around Rfr2,000. *US$75/125 sgl/dbl; US$200 family room sleeping 4; all rates B&B.*

🏠 **Super Coupe Bushokoro Motel** (8 rooms) m 078 830 1060. About 500m from La Paillotte, this basic lodge has large clean tiled rooms with king-size beds & en-suite hot shower. A mediocre restaurant & bar is attached. It's the cheapest place in town, but if your budget stretches just a smidge further, La Paillotte is much nicer. *Rfr5,000/10,000 sgl/dbl.*

GORILLA TRACKING

Tracking mountain gorillas in the Virungas is a peerless wildlife experience, and one of Africa's indisputable travel highlights. It is difficult to describe the simple exhilaration attached to first setting eyes on a wild mountain gorilla. These are enormous animals: the silverbacks weigh about three times as much as the average man, and their bulk is exaggerated by a shaggily luxuriant coat. And yet despite their fearsome size and appearance, gorillas are remarkably peaceable creatures, certainly by comparison with most primates – gorilla tracking would be a considerably more dangerous pursuit if these gentle giants had the temperament of vervet monkeys, say, or baboons (or, for that matter, humans).

More impressive even than the gorillas' size and bearing is their unfathomable attitude to their daily human visitors, which differs greatly from that of any other wild animal. Anthropomorphic as it might sound, almost everybody who visits the gorillas experiences an almost mystical sense of recognition: we regularly had one of the gorillas break off from chomping on bamboo to study us, its soft brown eyes staring deeply into ours, as if seeking out some sort of connection.

Equally fascinating is the extent to which the gorillas try to interact with their visitors, often approaching them, and occasionally touching one of the guides in apparent recognition and greeting as they walk past. A photographic tripod raised considerable curiosity in several of the youngsters and a couple of the adults – one large female walked up to the tripod, stared ponderously into the lens, then wandered back off evidently satisfied. It is almost as if the gorillas recognise their daily visitors as a troop of fellow apes, but one too passive to pose any threat – often a youngster will put on a chest-beating display as it walks past tourists, safe in the knowledge that they'll accept its dominance: something it would never do to an adult gorilla. (It should be noted here that close contact with humans can expose gorillas to fatal diseases, for which reason the guides try to keep their tourists at least 7m away – but the reality is that there is little anybody can do to stop the gorillas from flouting rules of which they are unaware.)

The magical hour with the gorillas is undoubtedly expensive and getting there can sometimes be hard work. The hike up to the mountain gorillas' preferred habitat of bamboo forest involves a combination of steep slopes, dense vegetation, slippery underfoot conditions after rain, and high altitude. For all that, the more accessible gorilla groups can be visited by reasonably fit adults of any age, and in decades of African travel we have yet to meet anybody who has gone gorilla tracking and regretted the financial or physical expense.

PERMITS Eight permits per day are issued for each of the 12 habituated groups in the Volcanoes Park, making a daily total of 96 permits. At the time of writing, all these habituated groups stay within tracking range on a more-or-less permanent basis, but gorillas are not governed by international boundaries and it is always possible that groups which originated in Uganda or the DR Congo might cross there again. Trackers are not allocated a specific group in advance but the guides do generally make an effort to match people to a group based on their apparent fitness – Sabyinyo and usually Agashya (Group Thirteen) being the least demanding hikes and Susa, Isimbi or Karisimbi the most challenging. The strictly enforced minimum age for tracking gorillas is 15.

In May 2017, the cost of a gorilla-tracking permit, including park entrance, was controversially doubled from US$750 to US$1,500 for all visitors. Though there has been a fair bit of grumbling about the move, the price seems likely to hold for the duration of this edition, though any changes will be posted at w bradtupdates.com/rwanda as soon as we become aware of them. The permit is best bought in advance through the RDB office in Kigali or through a tour operator in Kigali or abroad. Depending on availability, permits can also be bought at short notice from other

RDB offices. There is no guarantee a permit will be available on any given day: the likelihood is highest during the main rainy season of April and May, when trekking operates at well under full capacity, but you may need to wait for days or even weeks in the peak season of June to September, when booking 6–12 months ahead is strongly advised. In any event, the procedure regarding last-minute bookings could always change, so you are strongly advised to check this beforehand with RDB in Kigali – see page 82. Either way, it is advisable for independent travellers to visit or ring the RDB office in Kinigi (m *078 877 1633*) the afternoon before they intend to go tracking in order to confirm arrangements. Through June to September, when demand is high, permits for specific days can sell out well in advance, so be sure to book as far ahead as possible.

Trackers are required to check in at the park headquarters at Kinigi at 07.00, where they can enjoy a complimentary cup of tea or coffee and make use of the last clean flush toilets they'll see for a few hours before being allocated to one of the eight habituated groups. If you want to visit or to avoid any specific group, it helps to be there a little early so you have time to chat to the rangers. A briefing is held at around 07.30 after which you must drive to the appropriate trailhead, so the actual tracking generally starts at 08.15–08.30 (or as late as 09.30 for the more distant groups).

HABITUATED GROUPS The most difficult to reach of the permanent groups is the **Susa Group**, the one originally studied by Dian Fossey on the slopes of Mount Karisimbi. Until recently, it comprised more than 40 individuals, including four silverbacks, making it for a time the second-largest group of mountain gorillas in the world. Following a 2010 split into **Karisimbi Group** (with 10 members) and another in 2014 forming **Igisha Group** (28 members), Susu now contains 18 members. Karisimbi group split again in 2012, forming the 16-member **Isimbi Group**. The above groups are generally the first choice of most fit visitors (or where they are likely to be placed, anyway), but it takes about 90 minutes to drive from Kinigi to the starting point, and you should be prepared for a severe hike. The ascent from the car park to the forest boundary, though not as steep as it used to be from the new starting point, will also take the best part of an hour. On a good day, it will take no more than 20 minutes to reach the gorillas from the boundary; on a bad day you might be looking at 2 hours or more in either direction and it has been known to take as long as 7 hours to locate the group in the dry season (the record from the previous day will give an indication of how deep in the gorillas are, as they generally don't move too far in one day).

At the other end of the severity scale is the trek to the **Sabyinyo Group**, whose permanent territory lies within the Volcanoes Park, on a lightly forested saddle between Mount Sabyinyo and Mount Gahinga. Depending on exactly where the gorillas are, the walk from the car park to the forest boundary is flat to gently sloping, and will typically take 20–30 minutes. Once you're in the forest, the gorillas might take anything from 10 minutes to an hour to reach, but generally the slopes aren't too daunting, though they can be slippery after rain. The Sabyinyo Group consists of 17 individuals, with three silverbacks. What's more, the dominant male Guhondo is the heaviest gorilla (of any race) ever measured, at 220kg.

The **Agashya Group** (also known as Group Thirteen) spends most of its time on the same saddle as the Sabyinyo Group. When it is in that area, it is normally as easy to reach as the Sabyinyo Group, but it does sometimes move deeper into the mountains and the hike can then be significantly longer. Group Thirteen's former name dates to when it was first habituated, and numbered 13 gorillas,

The largest living primates, gorillas are widespread residents of the equatorial African rainforest, with a global population of perhaps 150,000–200,000 concentrated mainly in the Congo Basin. Until 2001, all gorillas were assigned to the species *Gorilla gorilla*, split into three races: the western lowland gorilla *G. g. gorilla* of the western Congo Basin, the eastern lowland gorilla *G. g. graueri* in the eastern Congo, and the mountain gorilla *G. g. beringei* living in highland forest on the eastern side of the Albertine Rift. The western race was formally described in 1847, but the eastern races were only described in the early 20th century – the mountain gorilla in 1903, a year after two individuals were shot on Mount Sabyinyo by Robert von Beringe, and the eastern lowland gorilla in 1914.

The conventional taxonomic classification of gorillas has been challenged by recent advances in DNA testing and fresh morphological studies suggesting that the western and eastern gorilla populations, whose ranges lie more than 1,000km apart, diverged some two million years ago. For this reason, they are now treated as discrete species: *G. gorilla* (western) and *G. beringei* (eastern). One distinct western race – the Cross River gorilla (*G. g. dielhi*) of the Cameroon–Nigeria border region – fulfils the IUCN criteria for 'Critically Endangered', since it lives in 11 fragmented populations, only some of which are on protected land, with a combined total of fewer than 250 individuals. In 2000, the Cross River gorilla and mountain gorilla shared the unwanted distinction of being placed on a shortlist of the world's 25 most endangered primate taxa.

Despite also being listed as 'Critically Endangered', the status of the western gorilla is comparatively secure, since it is far more numerous in the wild than its eastern counterpart, and has a more extensive range spanning half-a-dozen countries. In the 1980s, the western gorilla population was estimated at 100,000, but that figure was adjusted to 50,000 circa 2006, largely due to hunting for bush meat and the lethal Ebola virus (which had killed 5,000 gorillas in Central Africa prior to 2006, according to a study published in *Science*. Surveys conducted between 2005 and 2013 recorded a 18.75% drop in the population, roughly a 2.5% loss every year. Encouragingly, however, a Wildlife Conservation Society survey undertaken over 2006–07 found more than 100,000 previously unreported gorillas in the Lake Tele region of the Republic of Congo.

The future of the eastern gorilla – still split into a lowland and a mountain race – is far less certain. In the mid 1990s, an estimated 17,000 eastern lowland gorillas remained in the wild, but is widely thought that the population has dropped to 4,000 or fewer since the outbreak of the Congolese civil war in the DRC. Rarer still, but more stable, is the mountain gorilla, which consists of roughly 1,000 individuals confined to two ranges: the border-straddling Virunga Volcanoes and Bwindi National Park in Uganda.

The first study of mountain gorilla behaviour was undertaken in the 1950s by George Schaller, whose pioneering work formed the starting point for the more recent research initiated by Dian Fossey in the 1960s. Fossey's acclaimed book *Gorillas in the Mist* remains perhaps the best starting point for anybody who wants to know more about mountain gorilla behaviour.

The mountain gorilla is distinguished from its lowland counterparts by several adaptations to its high-altitude home, most visibly a longer and more luxuriant coat.

It is on average bulkier than other races, with the heaviest individual gorilla on record (of any race) being the 220kg dominant silverback of Rwanda's Sabyinyo Group. Like other gorillas, it is a highly sociable creature, moving in defined troops of anything from five to 50 animals. A troop typically consists of a dominant silverback male (the male's back turns silver when he reaches sexual maturity at about 13 years old) and sometimes a subordinate silverback, as well as a harem of three or four mature females, and several young animals. Unusually for mammals, it is the male who forms the focal point of gorilla society; when a silverback dies, his troop normally disintegrates. A silverback will start to acquire his harem at about 15 years of age, most normally by attracting a young, sexually mature female from another troop. He may continue to lead a troop well into his 40s.

A female gorilla reaches sexual maturity at the age of eight, after which she will often move between different troops several times. Once a female has successfully given birth, however, she normally stays loyal to the same silverback until he dies, and she will even help to defend him against other males. (When a male takes over a troop, he generally kills all nursing infants to bring the mothers into oestrus more quickly, a strong motive for a female to help preserve the status quo.) A female gorilla has a gestation period similar to that of a human, and if she reaches old age she will typically have raised up to six offspring to sexual maturity. A female's status within a troop is based on the length of time she has been with a silverback: the alpha female is normally the longest-serving member of the harem.

The mountain gorilla is primarily vegetarian, with bamboo shoots being the favoured diet, though they are known to eat 58 different plant species in the Virungas. It may also eat insects, ants being a particularly popular protein supplement. A gorilla troop will spend most of its waking hours on the ground, but it will generally move into the trees at night, when each member of the troop builds itself a temporary nest. Gorillas are surprisingly sedentary creatures, typically moving less than 1km in a day, which makes tracking them on a day-to-day basis relatively easy for experienced guides. A troop will generally only move a long distance after a stressful incident, for instance an aggressive encounter with another troop. Gorillas are peaceable animals with few natural enemies and they often live for up to 50 years in the wild, but their long-term survival is critically threatened by poaching, deforestation and exposure to human-borne diseases.

It was previously thought that the Virunga and Bwindi gorilla populations were racially identical, not an unreasonable assumption given that a corridor of mid-altitude forest linked the two mountain ranges until about 500 years ago. But DNA tests indicate the Bwindi and Virunga gorillas show sufficient genetic differences to suggest that they have formed mutually isolated breeding populations for many millennia, in which case the 'mountain gorilla' should possibly be split into two discrete races, one – the Bwindi gorilla – endemic to Uganda, the other unique to the Virunga Mountains. Neither race numbers more than 600 in the wild, neither has ever bred successfully in captivity, and both meet several of the criteria for an IUCN classification of 'Critically Endangered'.

This is one of the most frequently asked questions about gorilla tracking in Rwanda. And it is also perhaps the most difficult to answer. So many variables are involved, and if they all conspire against you, you could be in for a genuinely exhausting outing (indeed, on rare occasions, the guides have had to carry tourists down). On the other hand, if everything falls in your favour, the excursion will be little more demanding than the proverbial stroll in the park.

The trek to see the gorillas has two distinct phases. The first is the hike from the closest car park to the forest and national park boundary, which usually takes 30–60 minutes depending on the speed of the party and the group they are visiting. The second is the trek into the forest in search of the gorillas, which will usually have been located by the advance trackers by the time tourists reach the forest edge. This might take anything from 10 minutes to 2 hours, but 20–30 minutes is typical, especially for those groups whose territory lies closer to the forest edge.

The first part of the trek is predictable, and it is usually quite flat and undemanding, unless you are going to the Susa, Karisimbi or Isimbi groups, which involves a longer and steeper ascent. The second part is more difficult to predict, as it will depend on the exact location of the gorillas on the day, and on the steepness of the terrain *en route*. Other factors in determining how tough it will be include the density of vegetation (bending and crawling through the jungle can be tiring, especially if you have to dodge vicious nettles) and whether it has rained recently, in which case everything will be muddier and quite slippery underfoot.

At risk of stating the obvious, age and fitness levels are the key factors in how difficult the hike will feel. Susa and its offshoots aside, moderately fit people under the age of 40 seldom feel any significant strain, but a high proportion of trackers are in their 50s or 60s, in which case the hike might be somewhat tougher. As one reader of a previous edition wrote: 'We think you underestimate how strenuous the gorilla trip is. We are both 61 but fit and well, bicycling to work each day, and still we had to take regular breaks due to problems with breathing.' That said, while many older travellers do find the track quite demanding, it is very unusual that they are so daunted as to turn back.

An important factor in determining how difficult the hike will be is which group you are allocated. As a rule, the hike to Susa and groups nearby is the most demanding, while the Sabyinyo Group is the most reliably straightforward to reach. The hikes to Kwitonda, Hirwa and Agashya (Group Thirteen) are also usually quite undemanding, whereas the hikes to the Amahoro and Umubano groups tend to be more difficult, but not as tough as Susa, Karisimbi or Isimbi. Unfortunately,

but today it numbers 21 individuals, including one promiscuous silverback and all the females taken from the Nyakagezi Group after it fled into Rwanda from Uganda following the arrival there of the Kwitonda Group from the DR Congo in 2006. Agashya seems to be a favourite of many of the guides, probably because its eponymous silverback is more relaxed and approachable than those in other groups.

The **Amahoro Group**, numbering 18, and the more recently habituated **Umubano Group**, with 12 individuals, share an overlapping territory on the slopes of Mount Bisoke. Both of these groups have four silverbacks and the hikes to reach them are typically intermediate in difficulty between those of Susa and Sabyinyo. As their names suggest, the Amahoro (literally 'Peace') and Umubano ('Live Together')

these things aren't set in stone, and any group might be unusually demanding (or easy) to reach on a bad day. Furthermore, nobody can guarantee which group you will be allocated in advance. However, the guides at Kinigi do make a conscious attempt to match individuals to the most suitable group, especially if they are asked to. Generally, the parties for Susa and groups nearby consist of lean-looking under-30s, while the opposite holds true for the Sabyinyo party.

Two further factors are uneven underfoot conditions and high altitude. Most visitors to Africa live in towns and cities where roads and pavements are paved, and parks are serviced by neatly maintained footpaths, so they are unused to walking on the more irregular and seasonally slippery surfaces typical of the ascent paths and forest floor. It will help enormously in this regard to wear strong waterproof shoes or hiking boots with a good tread and solid ankle support. Furthermore, if you think you might struggle in these conditions, there is a lot to be said for avoiding the rainy seasons, in particular March–May, when conditions can be dauntingly muddy.

Don't underestimate the tiring effect of altitude. The trekking takes place at elevations of 2,500–3,000m above sea level, not high enough for altitude sickness to be a concern but sufficient to knock the breath out of anybody – no matter how fit – who has just flown in from a low altitude. For this reason, visitors who are spending a while in Rwanda might think seriously about leaving their gorilla tracking until they've been in the country a week or so, and are better acclimatised. Most of Rwanda lies at above 1,500m, and much of the country is higher – a couple of days at Nyungwe, which lies above 2,000m, would be good preparation for the Virungas. Likewise, if you are coming from elsewhere in Africa, try to plan your itinerary so that you spend your last pre-Rwanda days at medium to high altitude: for example, were you flying in from Kenya, a few days in Nairobi (2,300m) or even the Maasai Mara (1,600m) would be far better preparation than time at the coast.

Guides will generally offer you a walking stick at the start of the hike, and, even if you normally shun such props, it is worth taking up the offer to help support you on those slippery mountain paths. If you have luggage, hire a porter too. Once on the trail, take it easy, and don't be afraid to ask to stop for a few minutes whenever you feel tired. Drink plenty of water, and carry some quick calories – biscuits and chocolate can both be bought at supermarkets in Musanze. The good news is that most people who track gorillas find the hike to be far less demanding than they expect, and in 99% of cases, whatever exhaustion you might feel on the way up will vanish with the adrenalin charge that follows the first sighting of a silverback gorilla!

groups have a quite harmonious relationship despite their territorial overlap, probably because there are strong familial links between them, with several individuals having brothers and sisters in the other group.

One indicator that conservation efforts are now bearing fruit is the proliferation of new gorilla groups, as the increasing population encourages splits in older groups. Several of these new groups are open to tourist visits, including the most recent, Igisha and Isimbi (page 269). The **Hirwa Group**, comprising 18 individuals, was formed in 2006 by a silverback who had broken away from the Susa group about two years earlier, and it usually inhabits the foothills of Mount Sabyinyo on the Gahinga side. At about the same time, the now 29-strong **Kwitonda Group** crossed into Uganda from the DR Congo, probably due to the Congolese civil war, and stayed in Mgahinga National Park for a while, forcing the smaller Uganda-based Nyakagezi Group to cross into Rwanda. The Kwitonda Group crossed into Rwanda in late 2006, and it now inhabits the lower slopes of Mount Muhabura, a relatively easy hike (comparable to that for the Sabyinyo Group). As a result of these territorial shifts, the Nyakagezi Group clashed several times with Agashya/Group Thirteen, whose silverback poached all the Nyakagezi females before the rest of the (now all-male) group beat a retreat back to Uganda. Depending on the movements of the various groups, there are a handful of other groups that are sometimes visited, including Muhoza (ten members, one silverback), Isabukuru (14 members, one silverback), Mafunzo (12 members, one silverback), Musilikare (19 members, three silverbacks), Ntambara (11 members, one silverback), and Pablo (24 members, three silverbacks).

WHAT TO WEAR AND TAKE Put on your sturdiest hiking boots or walking shoes, thick trousers, gaiters and a long-sleeved top as protection against vicious stinging nettles. It's often cold when you set out, so start off with a sweatshirt or jersey (which also help protect against nettles). The gorillas are thoroughly used to people, so it makes little difference whether you wear bright or muted colours. Whatever clothes you wear are likely to get very dirty as you slip and slither in the mud, so if you have pre-muddied clothes you might as well wear them. When you're grabbing for handholds in thorny vegetation, a pair of old gardening gloves are helpful. If you feel safer with a walking stick, you'll be offered a wooden one at the start of the ascent.

Carry as little as possible, ideally in a waterproof bag of some sort. During the rainy season, a poncho or raincoat might be a worthy addition to your daypack, while sunscreen, sunglasses and a hat are a good idea at any time of year. You may well feel like a snack during the long hike, and should certainly carry enough drinking water – at least one litre, more to visit the Susa Group. Especially during the rainy season, make sure your camera gear is well protected – if your bag isn't waterproof, seal your camera gear in a plastic bag.

Binoculars are not necessary to see the gorillas. In theory, birdwatchers might want to carry binoculars, though in practice only the most dedicated are likely to make use of them – the trek up to the gorillas is normally very directed, and walking up the steep slopes and through the thick vegetation tends to occupy one's eyes and mind.

If you are carrying much gear and food/water, it's advisable to hire one of the porters who hang about at the car park in the hope of work. This costs US$10 per porter. Locals have asked us to emphasise that it is not demeaning or exploitative to hire a porter to carry your daypack; on the contrary, tourists who refuse a porter for 'ethical reasons' are simply denying income to poor locals and making it harder for them to gain any benefit from tourism.

You will need to show your passport (or a copy that will be kept by the park) when you check in, so don't forget to bring it along!

REGULATIONS AND PROTOCOL Tourists are permitted to spend no longer than 1 hour with the gorillas, and it is forbidden to eat, urinate or defecate in their presence. It is also forbidden to approach within less than 7m of the gorillas, a rule that is difficult to enforce with curious youngsters (and some adults) who often approach human visitors. Smoking is forbidden anywhere within the national park boundary ('it's unhealthy for the animals', according to one rather earnest guide, which seems to be taking concerns about passive smoking to stratospheric absurdity – more genuine justifications are litter, fire and annoying other tourists).

Gorillas are susceptible to many human diseases, and it has long been feared by researchers that one ill tourist might infect a gorilla, resulting in the possible death of the whole troop should they have no immunity to that disease. For this reason, you should not go gorilla tracking with a potentially airborne infection such as flu or a cold, and are asked to turn away from the gorillas should you need to sneeze.

To the best of our knowledge, no tourist has ever been seriously hurt by a habituated gorilla, but there is always a first time. An adult gorilla is much stronger than a person, and will act in accordance with its own social codes. Therefore it is vital that you listen to your guide at all times regarding correct protocol in the presence of gorillas.

GOLDEN MONKEY TRACKING

Although it's the gorillas that tend to hog the limelight, the little-known golden monkey *Cercopithecus kandti* (sometimes treated as a distinctive race of the more widespread blue monkey *C. mitis*) is also IUCN-listed as 'Endangered', with a similarly restricted range within the Albertine Rift. As such, it's a rare treat for visitors to be able to view a habituated group of about 15 of these delightful creatures in the Volcanoes National Park. Visits can be arranged through any RDB office; they last for 1 hour and are for a maximum of six people. The cost is US$100/80/65 for non-residents/EAC foreign residents/Rwanda foreign residents (and Rfr4,000 for Rwandans), including entry to the park. Booking is seldom necessary, but it would be advisable to do so in advance if you have to track on one specific day.

Endemic to the Albertine Rift, the golden monkey is characterised by a bright orange-gold body, cheeks and tail, contrasting with its black limbs, crown and tail-end. Once quite widespread in the forests of southwest Uganda and northwest Rwanda, it is now near-endemic to the Virunga volcanoes, though a small number still inhabit the long-degraded but recently gazetted Gishwati Forest near Rubavu. Within its restricted range, however, it is the numerically dominant primate, and reasonably common – the number of individuals protected within Volcanoes National Park is a matter of conjecture, but a 2003 survey estimated a population of 3,000–4,000 in its smaller neighbour, Uganda's Mgahinga National Park.

In early 2002, the RDB approached the Dian Fossey Gorilla Fund International (DFGFI) to discuss the possibility of habituating the golden monkeys for purposes of tourism. The DFGFI welcomed the chance to learn more about this little-studied monkey and to help promote tourism in the park. First, two possible groups were selected for habituation – they are in areas of the park that would be suitable as part of a nature trail for tourists. Field assistants were then trained in habituation and data collection techniques, and work could begin.

The first few months were terribly frustrating. Dense vegetation (bamboo) made approaching the groups very difficult and the monkeys would flee at the first sight of humans. In time, the researchers were able to refine their techniques and determine at what time of day the monkeys were most active, which made them easier to locate. Gradually the monkeys came to accept the presence of the observers for longer and longer periods. Meanwhile the researchers were gathering more and more data about their diet, habitat use, social structure and behavioural ecology, all of which must be understood if the project is to succeed in the long term.

The first group was 'opened to the public' in summer 2003 and has delighted visitors ever since. It's a very different experience from gorilla viewing, where the huge creatures are entirely visible as they react and interact. The golden monkeys in their bamboo thicket are smaller, nimbler and can be harder to locate and follow,

THE VIRUNGAS

Straddling the borders of Uganda, Rwanda and the DRC, the Virungas are not a mountain range as such, but a chain of isolated freestanding volcanic cones strung along a fault line associated with the same geological process that formed the Rift Valley. Sometimes also referred to as the Birunga or Bufumbira Mountains, the chain comprises six inactive and three active volcanoes, all of which exceed 3,000m in altitude – the tallest being Karisimbi (4,507m), Mikeno (4,437m) and Muhabura (4,127m).

The names of the individual mountains in the Virunga chain reflect local perceptions. Sabyinyo translates as 'old man's teeth' in reference to the jagged rim of what is probably the most ancient and weathered of the eight volcanoes. Muhabura is 'the guide', and anecdotes collected by the first Europeans to visit the area suggest that its perfect cone, topped today by a small crater lake, still glowed at night as recently as the early 19th century. Gahinga is variously translated as meaning 'pile of stones' or 'the hoe', the former a reference to its relatively small size, the latter to the breach on its flank. Of the other volcanoes that lie partially within Rwanda, Karisimbi – which occasionally sports a small cap of snow, most often in the rainy season – is named for the colour of a cowry shell, while Bisoke simply means watering hole, in reference to the crater lake near its peak.

The vegetation zones of the Virungas correspond closely to those of other large East African mountains, although much of the Afro-montane forest below the 2,500m contour has been sacrificed to cultivation. Moist broad-leaved semideciduous forest dominates up until the 2,800m contour, while the slopes at altitudes of 2,800–3,200m, where an average annual rainfall of 2,000mm is typical, support bamboo forest interspersed with stands of tall hagenia woodland. At higher altitudes, the cover of Afro-alpine moorland, grassland and marsh is studded with giant lobelia, senecios and other outsized plants similar to those found on Kilimanjaro and the Ruwenzori. Above 3,600m, biodiversity levels are very low and the dominant vegetation consists of a fragile community of grasses, mosses and lichens. A total of 1,265 plant species identified across the range to date includes at least 120 that are endemic to the Albertine Rift.

The most famous denizen of the Virungas is the mountain gorilla, which inhabits all six of the extinct or dormant volcanoes, but not – for obvious reasons – the more active ones. The Virungas also form the main stronghold for the endangered golden monkey, possibly the last one aside from the Gishwati Forest, which today covers less than 1% of its original extent but has recently been declared a national park (page 209). Estimates based on dung surveys tentatively place the buffalo population at close to 1,000, while the total number of elephants might be anything from 20 to 100. Other typical highland forest species include yellow-backed duiker, bushbuck and giant forest hog. The mountains' avifauna is comparatively poorly known, as evidenced by sightings of 36 previously unrecorded species during a cross-border biodiversity study

though they are a lot more relaxed these days than they were a few years back, and the quality of sightings can be superb. The benefits of this project are mutual; for tourists, the pleasure of observing a rare species of monkey; for researchers, the satisfaction of learning more about a little-known species; and for the endangered golden monkeys, far less threat of extinction, as they are studied, protected and better understood.

undertaken in early 2004, bringing the total checklist for the Virungas to 294, including 20 Albertine Rift Endemics. Still in their geological infancy, none of the Virunga Mountains is more than two million years old and two of the cones remain highly active – indeed, they are together responsible for nearly 40% of documented eruptions in Africa. The most dramatic volcanic explosion of historical times was the 1977 eruption of the 3,465m Mount Nyiragongo in the DRC, about 20km north of the Lake Kivu port of Goma. During this eruption, a lava lake that had formed in the volcano's main crater back in 1894 drained in less than 1 hour, emitting streams of molten lava that flowed at a rate of up to 60km per hour, killing an estimated 2,000 people and terminating only 500m from Goma airport.

In 1994, a new lake of lava started to accumulate within the main crater of Nyiragongo, leading to another highly destructive eruption on 17 January 2002. Lava flowed down the southern and eastern flanks of the volcano into Goma itself, killing at least 50 people. Goma was evacuated, and an estimated 450,000 people crossed into the nearby Rwandan towns of Rubavu and Musanze for temporary refuge. Three days later, when the first evacuees returned, it transpired that about a quarter of the town – including large parts of the commercial and residential centre – had been engulfed by the lava, leaving 12,000 families homeless. The lava lake in Nyiragongo's crater remains active, with a diameter of around 50m, and, although there has been no subsequent eruption, the crater rim still glows menacingly above the nocturnal skyline of Rubavu, and a new lava lake has started to form about 250m below the level of the 1994 one.

Only 15km northwest of Nyiragongo stands the 3,058m Mount Nyamuragira, which also erupted in January 2002. Nyamuragira vies with Ol Doinyo Lengai in Tanzania as probably the most active volcano on the African mainland, with more than 40 eruptions recorded since 1882. Only the 1912–13 incidence resulted in any known direct fatalities, though 17 people were killed and several pregnancies terminated as a result of ash-contaminated drinking water in the 2000 eruption. Nyamuragira most recently blew its top in January 2010 and November 2011, spewing lava hundreds of metres into the air, along with plumes of ash and sulphur dioxide that destroyed large tracts of cultivated land and forest.

It is perhaps worth noting that these temperamental Congolese volcanoes pose no threat to visitors to the mountain gorillas, as the relevant cones are all dormant or extinct. That might change one day: there is a tradition among the Bafumbira people that the fiery spirits inhabiting the crater of Nyamuragira will eventually relocate to Muhabura, reducing both the mountain and its surrounds to ash. Another Bafumbira custom has it that the crater lake atop Mount Muhabura is inhabited by a powerful snake spirit called Indyoka, which lives on a bed of gold and need only raise its head to bring rain to the surrounding countryside.

OTHER HIKES

Several non-primate-related hikes are now offered to visitors to Volcanoes National Park. Most of these are day hikes, attracting a charge of US$75–100 for non-residents and US$60–75 for foreign residents, including park entrance, but the overnight ascent of Karisimbi is a two-day excursion costing US$400 for a party of one and US$300

IBIRUNGA, A LOVE STORY On my first visit to northern Rwanda to track the Susa Group of gorillas in 2002, I was immediately taken with the towering volcanoes of the Virunga chain, known in Kinyarwanda as *ibirunga* – five of which fall along Rwanda's borders. In the years since, I've climbed both Bisoke and Karisimbi (page 280), and for my 50th birthday I set myself the goal of completing my Rwandan quartet, where there were two volcanoes left, Muhabura and Gahinga. (Volcano number five, Sabyinyo, can only be approached from Uganda.)

ASCENDING MUHABURA It's an early morning in August 2014, and I'm trying to prepare myself to climb and descend 1,700m before nightfall. Even with a 07.05 start, we have to hurry; I have bad memories about rainforests in the dark of the night. The 35km ride to the trailhead takes longer than expected, and by 08.30, we've lost our way in the potato fields at the foot of the mountain and decide to just start walking, as every minute counts. We're at about 2,400m and right in front of us is a terrifying volcanic giant. We pick up five armed rangers who are going to protect us in the park, supposedly against buffaloes and elephants, and a local man with a *panga* who accepts to carry my pack for US$10. Hence, five Kalashnikovs and a machete will go with me into the forest. No wonder I feel safe.

Along eucalyptus trees and little walls made of volcanic stones we head for the park boundary, where the forest really begins. We cross a ditch and almost immediately the trail gets very steep. I feel the sweat under my shirt but I am reassured when I see the guide, porter and rangers sweating just as much. This hike is tough. Two hours in, the forest starts to clear, giving way to moorland with giant heathers. We walk through high grasses and start to feel the wind, although it is not really cold. Fortunately the trail is dry. The wind disappears several times as we pass each of the several false summits. We continue straight along a large ridge, which is getting progressively rockier.

We must be above 4,000m now. In my mind I hear Captain Beefheart singing 'Zig-Zag Wanderer'. A signboard to my right indicates a trail down to Uganda. Two minutes later, we reach the Rwandan–Ugandan border at 4,127m – the summit! It is 13.09, so it took us 4 hours and 45 minutes to climb the 1,700m. When you gain almost 350m per hour, you can imagine how steep it is.

Here, near the lovely little crater lake, a signboard says we are in the Afromontane belt, at an altitude of 4,137m. Ten metres above the official summit! How high can you get? We all share some biscuits and wander around the lake, staying at the summit for an hour. The weather is fine, but the clouds in the west don't allow me to see any of the other nearby volcanoes.

---

per person for two or more (US$250/200 for residents). The RDB will provide guides for all hikes, but trekkers should have suitable clothing and (if overnighting on Karisimbi) bring their own camping equipment. Hikes can be booked through the RDB office in Kigali, Rubavu, Musanze or Kinigi. All hikes depart from the park headquarters at Kinigi at around 07.30 (check-in time 07.00), the same departure time as for gorilla tracking, which means that visitors can undertake only one activity per day within the park. Porters can be hired at a daily rate of US$10.

One popular hike is to **Dian Fossey's tomb** and the adjacent gorilla cemetery at the former Karisoke Research Camp. This trek involves a 30-minute drive from the park headquarters to the trailhead at the village of Bisate (now home to the

We start the descent at 14.10, and looking down I can distinguish Kidaho and Lake Burera, along with Kisoro and Lake Bunyonyi in Uganda. But fatigue sets in and I soon start to lose my focus. I start to slip over loose stones and wonder how this descent can take so awfully long. At this rate, I'll be remembered as 'the muzungu who was faster going up than down'. After a nerve-wracking 3½ hours, we reach the park boundary at 17.40 and take a rest before continuing through the potato fields to civilisation. Despite the time, scores of children greet us with shouts of 'muzungu, good morning!'.

ASCENDING GAHINGA Another early start sees us leaving Kinigi shortly after 07.00 for the 50-minute drive to the trailhead, where our altimeter reads 2,330m – we have 1,140 vertical metres ahead of us. Today four armed soldiers assure my protection. After an hour, the potato fields give way to an undulating meadow, and at 09.00 we cross a ditch and enter the forest.

Although the two volcanoes are very close to each other, they are not similar. There is much more bamboo forest on the Gahinga trek, but the main difference is the trail. Muhabura is hard because of the steep climb, but the challenge on Gahinga is the trail itself – muddy, narrow, and densely vegetated almost until the summit. Sometimes it runs through streambeds, making rain trousers a very wise idea. The higher we get, the more my porter has to use his machete to hack through the branches and leaves obscuring the trail. It almost looks like we are the first visitors here since the late Dian Fossey arrived in the Virungas. (Later I was told RDB recorded just 34 Gahinga tourists in the whole of 2014, and Muhabura 125. To compare, when I summited Kilimanjaro, there were more than 200 persons arriving at the top that same day!).

At 11.38, we reach the summit, at the rim of a marshy crater surrounded by giant groundsels and giant lobelias. A total of 1,140m up in 3 hours 45 minutes, making for an altitude gain of about 300m per hour. Big Brother Muhabura is towering above us; the other volcanoes hide themselves, but I know where they are.

The descent is slippery. Going up, I had eliminated all thoughts as I was only concentrated on making it to the top, but now my brain starts working again: I think about Bruce Chatwin's book, *What Am I Doing Here?* At 15.25, after a 3-hour descent, we arrive at the car and it starts to thunder. From inside we can see the rain pouring down, as if Imana, the God of Rwanda, wants to wash away my footsteps, so that only memories remain. My Virunga quartet is complete, and my goal is reached. I know I will return to Rwanda to admire the ibirunga, but now only from a distance.

spectacular Bisate Lodge; page 265), which lies at 2,610m close to the forest boundary. From here, assuming you stop in the village (rather than continuing by car along the rutted road to the nearby car park), the 1.7km hike to the entry point into the forest, climbing steeply in parts to 2,820m, should take around 25 minutes. Once in the forest, a gently climbing path leads after 1km to the 2,970m clearing where Fossey used to take a break *en route* to her camp, and most hikers emulate her example. Depending on your fitness, and how often you stop to enjoy the scenery, this should take around 20–30 minutes, and it is then another 45–60 minutes to the camp itself, following a contour path that gains little in altitude. Fossey's old living quarters – which she nicknamed the mausoleum – are now in ruins, and several

4 JANUARY This was not my first visit to the Virungas. I had visited the Susa Group back in 2002, the golden monkeys in 2004 and hiked Bisoke in 2006. But now my eyes were set on Karisimbi, at 4,507m the sixth-highest mountain in Africa, after Kilimanjaro, Mount Kenya, Ruwenzori, Mount Meru (Tanzania) and Ras Dashen in Ethiopia's Simien Mountains.

Before heading for Musanze, I visited RDB in Kigali twice for information. And twice I was told that I did not have to make an advance reservation for the Karisimbi hike, I must just pitch up at the RDB headquarters at Kinigi and pay. But once in Musanze, I called the park warden and he confirmed that normally you must book a Karisimbi trek a couple of days ahead so that they can make preparations.

Finally, I was told they would make an· exception: I could leave the next morning. I did not have to be at Kinigi at 07.00, the normal reporting time, but at 08.30. Just before darkness fell, the sky cleared after an afternoon shower, and the magnificent volcanoes appeared – Muhabura, Gahinga, Sabyinyo, Bisoke and Karisimbi – though the summit of Rwanda's highest remained hidden in the clouds, as if it wanted to tell me: *I won't reveal myself to you entirely, you have to conquer me first.*

5 JANUARY At Kinigi, I paid them the standard fee for the two-day trek, plus US$10 to rent a tent, and I met my guide, who spoke perfect English and French. The drive from Kinigi to the trailhead was 16km and took 30 minutes. At 10.15 we arrived at the car park at Bisate, the same trailhead that is used for hikes to Bisoke and Dian Fossey's tomb. There we met the porters; one for me and one for the guide, at Rfr5,000 per day, not included in the price. I paid my porter after the trip. The guide paid for his own porter. Both guide and porters wore rubber boots: not a bad idea compared with my mountain shoes, as the trail is very muddy.

We set off at 10.20, starting at around 2,600m altitude. The guide carries a phone for communication with rangers/soldiers patrolling the park. At 10.30, we cross the stone wall that separates the park from the potato fields. Now we are in the jungle. Here, several armed soldiers join us, as protection against buffalo and elephants. We walk the same trail as for the Bisoke climb. With my binoculars I see a group of tourists approach the Amahoro Group. There is a lot of fresh buffalo dung on the trail.

After an hour's gradual ascent, we reach a junction, with some benches, at the site where Dian Fossey reputedly rested *en route* to her camp. We go left. A light rain starts falling. We walk close to Dian Fossey's tomb and gorilla graveyard, but don't visit, which would involve paying extra. I put on my rain trousers, also good protection against the stinging nettles that hem in the narrow trail. The rain trousers become essential to combat the mud, which is everywhere – not so much a mountain hike as a swamp walk! We see a squirrel, and hear what the guide reckons to be a gorilla research group not normally visited by tourists.

other landmarks in the camp are signposted. The hike offers a good opportunity to see birds and other creatures typical of the Virungas on the way.

Far more demanding is the day hike to the rim of the 3,711m **Mount Bisoke**, which is topped by a beautiful crater lake. It departs from Bisate, a trailhead it shares with the hike to Dian Fossey's tomb, and follows the same route as far as the

We cross different vegetation zones: bamboo and wild celery on the lower slopes, ideal food for gorillas. Then hagenia forest, with old-man's-beard moss on the branches. Then, above 3,000m, the marvellous giant groundsel and giant lobelia. At 15.50 we reach camp (3,700m), a similar altitude to Bisoke, which can be seen behind us. So today we climbed 1,100m in 5½ hours. I don't feel the effect of the altitude, but my legs are tired.

The staff pitch my tent. At 17.00 the sky clears and I finally see a glimpse of the top of Karisimbi, as well as Mikeno Volcano in the Congo. I count how many we are now: one guide, two porters and seven soldiers, for just one muzungu! The wood is damp, so it's difficult to make a good fire and my porter uses the opening of his rubber boots to blow air into it. Around the fire we share the food we brought. At 20.00 I head to my tent for a deserved rest.

6 JANUARY Dawn at 05.30. I eat biscuits and drink water. Beautiful morning light. We leave at 06.10. The trail gets steeper, while the fog closes in. Sometimes I have to use my hands to crawl over the labyrinth of trees and branches above the muddy ground, which I would not like to fall into. On several occasions my porter has to give me a hand to pull me up. The terrain is more difficult than I had expected.

At about 4,000m we are above the tree line. The slope becomes more exposed and a cold wind blows. My guide already wears a hat and gloves; I put them on now too. The last couple of hundred metres we walk on volcanic scree (fortunately not loose, more like grey gravel). The wind gets harder and visibility drops to 25m. I see more and more junk and rubbish lying on the ground, and wonder where all this dirt comes from. Metal pipes, empty cans, etc. Suddenly I realise I don't climb any more. It is 08.45 and we are on the summit!

The rubbish is construction waste, left by the builders of the huge telecom mast at the summit. The Congolese border must be somewhere here, but the fog is so thick I don't have a clue where. There are two abandoned huts for the builders of the mast. One is open and we use it as a shelter. I put on all my warm clothes and take pictures outside, while my Rwandan companions, unused to this bitter cold, remain inside. The temperature is maybe 0°C, but the wind chill factor makes it feel much colder. My guide hugs and congratulates me: 'You are very strong, many people don't make it to the summit.'

At 09.15, we start the descent, arriving in camp at 11.00. The warm clothes can be taken off again. It is basically the same way down. *En route*, the sun starts shining, for the first time in two days. We spot a beautiful reedbuck and cross the stream where Dian Fossey was amazed to see gorillas looking at their own reflection in the water. At 15.10 we are at the car park, so today we hiked for about 9 hours, including breaks: 800m up and 1,900m down. We pay the porters and get into the car. I turn around for a last quick look at Karisimbi, but Rwanda's roof has vanished in the clouds again. Did I really conquer her heart? Although she is invisible and far away once more, I know for sure she conquered mine.

resting point mentioned in the paragraph on page 279, which you should reach in 45–60 minutes. It's only 2km from here to the rim, but the path is very steep (it gains about 650m in altitude from the resting place), so it normally takes at least 1½ hours, and might take twice as long, depending on your fitness, how you respond to the altitude, and underfoot conditions (muddy at the best of times, and outright treacherous after heavy rain, when you'll be sinking to your knees in the bog with ever other step). However, the atmospheric vegetation of giant lobelias and hagenia woodland is fantastic, as is the view over the crater lake when you reach the rim. You reach the rim at 2,635m, so if bagging peaks is important to you, you might want to circle the crater rim to the highest peak. Note, however, that the crater lake is often obscured by clouds during the rainy season, so this is one walk best suited to drier times of year. The descent takes about 2 hours in normal conditions, but it might take longer after rain, when you'd spend a lot of time sliding down on your bottom! Allow for 6–8 hours in all, so bring food and plenty of water, and don't refuse the walking stick that will be offered to you at the car park. Porters are available at Bisate.

Recommended only to dedicated hikers, the overnight trek to **Karisimbi** (see box, pages 280–1) is even more demanding but, as the highest peak in the range, it also offers the greatest vegetation diversity, rising through clumped bamboo and aromatic hagenia forest to the spectacularly otherworldly vegetation of the sub-alpine and Afro-alpine zones, which are dominated by clumped moss and heather and stands of giant senecio and lobelia. Be warned that you will be camping in near-freezing conditions, so good camping gear and plenty of warm clothing are prerequisites, and you'll need to be self-sufficient when it comes to food and water.

Karisimbi's inaccessibility stands to lessen considerably in the next few years though, as there are RDB-approved plans afoot for a cable car all the way up to the crater, where trails, rock climbing and ziplining have been proposed, and another stop on the summit, where the new Rwanda Climate Observatory is set to be built in partnership with the Massachusetts Institute of Technology. Negotiations with investors were ongoing when this book went to print, so check in with RDB for all the latest.

Finally, though only a few-dozen visitors per year make the attempt to tackle them, it's now also possible to summit **Gahinga** and **Muhabura** as well (*US$200/160 foreigner/foreign resident for the 2-day trip*) – see box, pages 278–9, for details.

GORILLA GUARDIANS VILLAGE (IBY'IWACU)

Situated next to the car park at the trailhead for the Sabyinyo Group and Agashya Group (Group Thirteen), this award-winning venture was founded in 2004 by Edwin Sabuhoro of Rwanda Eco-Tours to help improve the livelihood of communities living around Volcanoes National Park, thereby reducing human pressure on the park's resources. The village, still better known by its former name of Iby'Iwacu Cultural Village, is essentially the public flagship for an ambitious project that provides legitimate employment in areas such as vegetable and mushroom farming, beekeeping and tourism to about 1,000 former and potential poachers.

Best arranged a day or so in advance, Gorilla Guardians offers a busy programme that lasts about 2 hours and slots in ideally after a morning's gorilla tracking. The setting is a fantastic wood-and-thatch replica of a traditional Rwandan palace, second only in size to the restored palace at Nyanza Museum, and an ideal stage

SABYINYO COMMUNITY LIVELIHOOD ASSOCIATION (SACOLA)

Just around the corner from the Volcanoes National Park HQ, this community-run organisation (the same one that owns the land for Sabyinyo Silverback Lodge) offers a variety of possible post-tracking activities in a similar vein to Gorilla Guardians/Iby'Iwacu at their Kinigi Cultural Centre, clearly signposted just before you reach the park HQ. At the centre itself, there's a small replica of a traditional king's dwelling, and visits here usually continue on to nearby villages, where guests are introduced to artisans and practitioners of traditional skills and livelihoods. Tours introduce you to medicinal plants, blacksmithing, weaving, traditional carpentry, and both banana *and* sorghum beer brewing (no word on if you'll need a designated driver after all this homebrew).

Other sights include some of the economic and social projects that income via Sabyinyo and their tourism offerings have funded, including a school and several animal husbandry projects. Nature walks around the perimeter of the park are also possible and birders are catered to as well.

A tour of the cultural centre is US$20/10/5 for foreigners/foreign students and children/Rwandans, village walks are US$30/15/15, and nature walks are US$40/20/7. They should be open most days, but it wouldn't hurt to set up your visit in advance: call **m** 078 885 4067/508 2729/646 9730 or email **e** sacolakinigi@yahoo.fr. More information is available at **w** sacola.org.

for traditional Intore dancers to share their drumming and dance routines. Also on offer are a short community walk, a church visit, a consultation with a traditional healer, shooting a bow and arrow with one of the local Batwa pygmies, and demonstrations of activities such as grinding millet and sorghum, making banana beer and harvesting potatoes and other crops.

Although Rwanda Eco-Tours plays a role in marketing and advising Gorilla Guardians, the cultural village is owned entirely by local communities, and the fee is split so that 40% goes directly to community members who perform and do other activities, while 60% goes to a village fund managed by a committee that channels it into various charitable efforts, from buying seeds for farmers to sponsoring schoolchildren and buying scholastic materials. Day visits cost US$35 per person, inclusive of all activities, which include a guided walk to visit village elders, women, children and various community projects. An overnight stay costs US$100 per person (page 266). (For further details and bookings, contact m 078 835 2009; e info@ibyiwacuvillage.org; w ibyiwacuvillage.org.)

Volcanoes National Park   GORILLA GUARDIANS VILLAGE (IBY'IWACU)

9

285

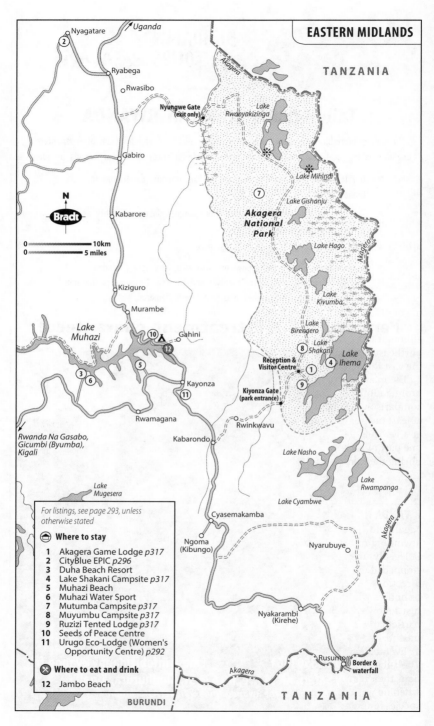

EASTERN MIDLANDS

For listings, see page 293, unless otherwise stated

Where to stay

1 Akagera Game Lodge *p317*
2 CityBlue EPIC *p296*
3 Duha Beach Resort
4 Lake Shakani Campsite *p317*
5 Muhazi Beach
6 Muhazi Water Sport
7 Mutumba Campsite *p317*
8 Muyumbu Campsite *p317*
9 Ruzizi Tented Lodge *p317*
10 Seeds of Peace Centre
11 Urugo Eco-Lodge (Women's Opportunity Centre) *p292*

Where to eat and drink

12 Jambo Beach

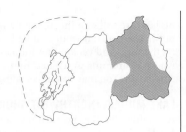

10

Eastern Rwanda

East of Kigali, the highlands of the Albertine Rift descend towards the western rim of the Lake Victoria Basin, a relatively flat and low-lying region marked by a distinctly warmer and more humid climate than the rest of Rwanda. Geographically, the most significant feature of eastern Rwanda is probably the **Akagera River**, which forms the border with Tanzania and feeds the extensive complex of lakes and marshes protected within **Akagera National Park** – the most important attraction in eastern Rwanda, covered in the next chapter.

Akagera aside, the east of Rwanda lacks any major tourist attractions. Other landmarks include the **Rusumo Falls** on the Tanzanian border and **Lake Muhazi**, both of which are diverting enough if you are in the area, but not worth making a major effort to reach, although the drive along the northern shore of Lake Muhazi is attractive. The handful of towns that dot the region are uniformly on the dull side, although some have lively markets, and the breezy highland town of **Gicumbi** in the northeast is surrounded by extensive tea plantations, as well as offering access to the vast Rugezi Wetlands.

The main roads through eastern Rwanda are surfaced and covered by the usual proliferation of scheduled midibuses. Accommodation options are limited by comparison with those in other parts of the country, but all the main towns have at least one reasonably comfortable – and reasonably priced – hotel. Because it lies at a lower altitude than the rest of the country, the Tanzanian border area is the one part of Rwanda where malaria is a major rather than a minor risk, particularly during the rainy season.

THE GICUMBI (BYUMBA) ROAD

RWANDA NA GASABO The first substantial right turn off the main road between Kigali and Gicumbi (formerly Byumba), about 25km out of Kigali, takes you on a winding route to Rwanda Na Gasabo or the original Rwanda hill. This is where (allegedly) the first of the ancient kings, travelling to Rwanda from the northeast, stopped at the top and set up his kingdom. It's high, with a flat top and a view in all directions. After leaving the main road, continue for a short distance to a cluster of houses where there's a sharp left turn on to a narrow road that climbs steeply. Just follow this upwards and you'll reach the top of the hill. (A 4x4 is advisable, particularly after rain.) People are generally around, so ask directions if you're unsure. The view is spectacular.

Eventually the site may be developed for tourism, because it's rich with legends. The ancient King Gihanga (see box, page 302) is said to have left two of his cows here; their names were Rugira and Ingizi. Another king threw a branch at an animal when he was out hunting; the tip sank into the ground and took root, becoming a species found nowhere else in Rwanda, and the great trees planted as the gateway to his land are still standing today. Perhaps. Then again, there was a magic earthenware pot in the court; it would fill with water of its own accord to signify that rain was on the way. And yet another monarch had a very special group of royal drummers, whose drumming awakened him in the morning and sent him to sleep at night. And so on. You may well meet someone up there who will tell you other tales.

LAKE MUHAZI (NORTHWEST SHORE) About 5 minutes further up the Gicumbi road after the Gasabo turning, another right turn at Cyamutara (⊕ S 1°46.707, E 30°7.778), signposted for Lake Muhazi and the village of Rwesero, leads to the northwest tip of Lake Muhazi. This western part of the lake was much studied by the Germans as they explored their new territory. Writing in 1907, a Doctor Mildbraed rather crossly commented:

> The west end of Lake Muhazi terminates in a papyrus swamp, and therefore promised rich spoils for zoological treasure-hunters. We were all the more keenly disillusioned to find the fauna far more meagre in character in this great water basin – the first we had explored in Africa – than we had been led to suppose in Germany. In spite of the luxurious vegetation at this part of the lake, the most diligent search was needed before we found a few sponges and polypi attached to some characeous plants.

About 15 minutes (8km) along this road (longer if you stop to look at birds and enjoy the lakeside views), you'll come to Rwesero, where the church-run **Rwesero Beach** (m 078 788 0398/510 7765) does Rwandan-style grills and other meals on the lakeshore. They've also got simple rooms and camping space to let and can arrange boat trips around the lake or a transfer across the water to the **Kingfish Beach Hotel** (m 078 702 1958), where there are similar offerings and a swimming pool as well. By road, Kingfish Beach is best reached via the Gasabo turn-off, after which it's a 10km drive. Back on the north shore of the lake and about 5km east of Rwesero Beach is the waterfront **AGS Country Club** (m 078 830 9252/073 100 0310; e info@ agsholidays.com; f AGScountryclub), which has pleasant lakeside cottages and a bar/restaurant serving a varied selection of Indian-inspired snacks and meals in the Rfr3,000–7,000 range. You can eat indoors or on a floating wooden deck suspended above the lake. There's also a picnic place, children's playground and campsite. Any of the above would make a good pick for day trippers seeking a lakeside snack or drink. All have boats, so you can also fish on the lake. There's plenty of birdlife around too, including pied and malachite kingfishers and fish eagle, and otters are sometimes seen in the area.

Past Rwesero, a beautiful (but sometimes rough) road, offering a succession of tranquil watery views (and numerous birds), follows the northern bank of the 60km-long Lake Muhazi in an easterly direction to emerge at **Gakenke** near Gahini on the main surfaced road flanking Akagera National Park. Allow a half-day, including stops, to travel this full route – you can do it in less, but it's a shame to hurry and the road is sometimes quite rutted. It also crosses several small creeks on rough wooden 'bridges' so is best done in a 4x4 during the dry season. It may well become impassable in a couple of places when the lake rises: ask local advice about this. Hitching could be difficult; transport comes in from either end but doesn't necessarily go right through.

GICUMBI (BYUMBA) The sprawling town of Gicumbi (formerly Byumba), which lies about 75km north of Kigali, some 7km off the main road to Kibale (Uganda), is the sixth largest in Rwanda (population estimated at 38,000) and the capital of

Northern Province, It is the country's highest settlement of note, perched at an altitude of 2,220m above the Mulindi Valley, whose rich volcanic soils lie at the heart of a burgeoning tea industry that has assumed a growing economic importance in recent years. More than 20 million kilograms of tea is exported from Rwanda yearly, much of it to the UK and Pakistan, with annual earnings of US$74.5 million over 2016–17, a nearly fourfold increase since 2004. The only potential tourist attractions are Lake Nyagafunzo, which lies about 12km out of town in the heart of the bird-rich Rugezi Swamp, and, to a lesser extent, the National Liberation Park Museum in Mulindi, some 25km to the north.

There is plenty of transport from Kigali as well as from Gatuna, the border post with Uganda. If you have trouble getting a lift, there's loads of passing traffic along the main road at Rukomo. The 50km or so of soon-to-be-surfaced road from Base (on the Kigali/Musanze road) to Gicumbi, with its spectacular bird's-eye views down to the multi-green tea plantations in the valleys, wasn't served by any transport at the time of writing, but this will surely change with the completion of the road surfacing during the lifespan of this edition. It's rightfully known as one of Rwanda's most beautiful roads. Heading east, there are plans for a surfaced link to Nyagatare via Rukomo and Ngarama; ask locally for a status update.

The town itself is a bustling, attractive and prosperous-looking place, with enough small shops and eating places to warrant stretching your legs there.

Where to stay

Hotel Ubwuzu (5 rooms) m 078 842 8353; e blandineka06@gmail.com; f ubwuzu. This commendably friendly guesthouse is set in a big white house & operated by the same people who are trying to develop tourism at Lake Nyagafunzo. They relocated in Nov 2017 & can now be found 200m from the transport park, visible across a cultivated valley as you exit the station. The en-suite rooms are clean & bright, & come with hot water & woven floor mats. A restaurant with indoor & outdoor tables serves good buffets in the Rfr1,500–2,500 range. *Rfr15,000/20,000 sgl/dbl or twin B&B.*

Hotel Urumuli (30 rooms) m 078 450 0242/879 6313; e hotelurumuli@yahoo. fr; w hotelurumuli.weebly.com. This radically renovated stalwart is the smartest option on offer. Single, double & twin rooms with DSTV, phone & en-suite hot shower are available, & there's also a 2-bedroom suite. Facilities include Wi-Fi & a decent bar-restaurant serving the usual Rwandan fare. The hotel lies at the top of the long main street, about 2.7km from the public taxi park, but is served by private minibuses. *Rfr30,000/45,000 sgl/ dbl or twin; US$100 apt; all rates B&B.*

Around Gicumbi The primary tourist attraction is Lake Nyagafunzo in the Rugezi Swamp, but the neat green tea plantations of Sorwathe – and those that blanket the countryside closer to Gicumbi – are very pretty, and you could well spend a couple of days here just walking and enjoying the expansive views. Until further development takes place, the National Liberation Park Museum in Mulindi can only really be recommended for diehard Rwandan history buffs.

Lake Nyagafunzo [map, page 232] Situated at an elevation of around 2,050m about 12km west of Gicumbi, Nyagafunzo is one of the few substantial expanses of open water in the Rugezi Wetlands, an 80km² swamp that extends northward all the way to Lake Burera. Listed as a Ramsar Wetland and Important Bird Area, this headwater of the Nile came close to vanishing completely after a hole was blasted in the rocks that held in its water in 1979, order to feed a commercial sunflower scheme. During the course of the 1980s, the high rate of water drainage from the swamp caused large mammals such as the sitatunga antelope to become extinct, and it also had a negative impact on the water level of lakes Burera and Ruhondo, reducing their capacity to produce electricity. The hole in the rocks was eventually dammed, but as recently as 2000 the swamp was still only half its original area, and little or no papyrus remained. Since 2006, however, the concerted efforts of the Rwandan Environmental Management Authority (REMA) has helped regenerate the swamp close to its full former extent, and the northern part of the swamp is under development as the Rugezi Birding Area, by the RDB (pages 246–54).

Set scenically among tall terraced slopes offering distant views to Mount Muhabura in clear weather, Lake Nyagafunzo is one of the most worthwhile sites in Rwanda for water-associated birds. The big draw for serious birders is the presence of Grauer's rush warbler, an Albertine Rift Endemic that might easily be confused with several more widespread warblers found in the area. But the reed-fringed lake also supports a wide variety of more striking birds, among them the spectacular grey-crowned crane, great white pelican, African spoonbill, African marsh harrier, long-toed lapwing, and breeding colonies of black-crowned night heron and purple heron.

The lake is best explored by boat, which can be arranged through the Hotel Ubwuzu in Gicumbi. Guided tours inclusive of transport from Gicumbi, a boat trip and guide cost Rfr50,000 for parties of up to four people, and Rfr60,000 for five to ten passengers. For those with their own transport, the charge is Rfr25,000 for up to six people, including the boat trip and guide, and Rfr35,000 for larger groups. The round day trip from Gicumbi would be fun on a bicycle, so you could ask the hotel management about renting one for the day. At the moment there is no accommodation on the lakeshore, but RDB-approved plans to start work on a private ecolodge on the slopes above the launching point have existed for some years; check our update website to see if they've made any progress.

To get there from Gicumbi, follow the surfaced road out towards the Catholic Cathedral for a few hundred metres, then after about 800m (✆ S 01°34.449, E 030°03.463), shortly before you would reach the cathedral, turn left on to a good dirt road that leads after 7km to the junction for the village of Yaramba (✆ S 01°33.697, E 030°01.253). Turn left here, keep going straight, and after another 5km you'll reach the lakeshore (✆ S 01°34.466, E 029°59.171).

Coming from Musanze/Ruhengeri, it is also possible to reach Lake Nyagafunzo via Lake Burera, Butaro, and the north end of the Rugezi Wetland (pages 289–90), passing the Mubuga, Murwa I, and Murwa II birding watchtowers, then continuing for another 30km to the junction for Yaramba.

Sorwathe Tea Plantation [map, page 232] (m 078 830 0532/830 2645; e sorwatheadm@gmail.com/sorwathe@gmail.com; w teaimporters.com/sorwathe; ✆ S 01°40.449, E 029°58.738) Perched on a high ridge with expansive tea-filled valleys below, the Sorwathe factory began producing tea in 1978, and today accounts for some 12% of all Rwanda's tea production. It's a typically beautiful slice of Rwandan countryside, and the receptive management is happy to have visitors. **Factory and plantation tours** (with tasting) are available with advance booking and start at 10.00 Tuesday to Sunday during high production season (*Mar–May & Oct–Jan*) and irregularly throughout the rest of the year. The Rfr2,000 entry fee goes to support genocide survivors. It's also a fine place to spend the night, with ten simple **rooms** (R*fr40,000/50,000/70,000 sgl/dbl/trpl B&B*) in a two-storey guesthouse overlooking the fields, plus a tennis court at Rfr2,000 per hour. Reservations can be made by email, phone, or at their office on KN 3 Avenue in Kigali.

To get here from the Kigali–Musanze road, take a right turn at Base and continue for 19 well-signposted kilometres until you reach the factory. From Gicumbi, head 20km towards Base until you reach a four-way junction at Miyove, where you'll take a left and continue for 8km to Kinihira Village and the factory.

National Liberation Park Museum (m *078 555 9584;* ⏱ *08.00–17.00 Mon–Fri, 08.00–noon Sat & Sun; entrance Rfr6,000/10,000 without/with visit to Kagame's bunker;* ✪ *S 01°28.661, E 030°02.170*) Situated in a handful of unassuming buildings atop a steep hill at the edge of Mulindi, this was once the RPF's most significant in-country operating base, and served as their headquarters from June 1992 until the genocide, when the RPF gained control of Kigali. Though it was officially dedicated as a museum in 2012, there was still nothing in the way of exhibits here at the time of writing in early 2018. Thus, visits consist of a walk-through of several empty meeting and sleeping rooms where the guide can tell stories of what took place, and a visit to Paul Kagame's bunker – a small wood-panelled room at the centre of an artificial mound, with enough room for a few people to stand and little else. There are a few detached houses where visiting dignitaries were hosted (again, empty), and plans for a canteen. You can also visit the pitch where the Armée Patriotique Rwandaise Football Club (APR) got their start in 1993.

If you do decide to make the trip, head north from the Rukomo junction, where the road to Gicumbi begins, for 20km towards the Gatuna border crossing and take a right turn at Maya Village, heading into a valley of tea fields. Continue for 3.5km, taking a left to climb towards Mulindi after 800m, then a right after 2.3km when you reach the village centre. It's a further 500m to the museum and neighbouring Mulindi tea factory.

THE NYAGATARE ROAD

RWAMAGANA Superficially just another unremarkable small Rwandan town, Rwamagana is in fact the capital of Southern Province, though it seems to have few of the associated trappings. This aside, it is unlikely to generate much excitement in passing travellers, especially as it lies only 60km from Kigali (no more than an hour's drive on a good surfaced road), and the limited accommodation seems overpriced for what it is. Regular midibuses to Rwamagana leave Kigali from the Nyabugogo bus station and call at Remera bus station *en route*.

MUTWA BASEBYA

In pre-colonial times, the Rugezi Wetland is where unmarried girls who became pregnant were customarily abandoned or drowned. One such victim was a teenage girl called Nyirantwari, who was reputedly raped and impregnated by a local chief in the 1880s, and then abandoned to die on an island in the heart of the swamp. She was rescued by a group of Batwa, however, and gave birth to a son, who grew up to become an important local chief known as Mutwa Basebya. In 1908, together with some powerful local Tutsi leaders, Mutwa Basebya led a rebellion against the German colonials, one that ultimately led to the subjugation of several semi-autonomous chieftaincies in the Gicumbi/Byumba area under central German rule. Mutwa Basebya was captured and shot by the Germans in 1912, but several of his descendants still live in the Rugezi area.

Where to stay and eat

Centre D'Accueil Sainte Agnes (20 rooms)
m 078 281 3656/830 6512; e sainte_agnes@
yahoo.fr. Situated right next door to the Dereva,
this certainly looks the part with its neat exterior
& pleasant dining area, but overall the plain en-
suite rooms with hypothetical hot water seem
overpriced. The restaurant is very good, though, &
one of the few places outside Kigali to serve fajitas.
*Rfr15,000/25,000 sgl/dbl occupancy for a room with
a dbl bed; Rfr20,000/30,000 sgl/dbl occupancy of
a twin.*

Dereva Hotel (60 rooms) m 078 567
9246/830 6512; e derevahotel@yahoo.fr. Set in
large green grounds alongside the main road,
the Dereva offers what are probably the most
commodious lodgings in this part of Rwanda,
though it does feel overpriced. The attached
restaurant serves large meals in the Rfr3,000–
5,000 range; it's a great place to try the traditional
groundnut stew called *igisafuriga*. *US$35/45 sgl/
twin; US$45/55 queen sgl/dbl; US$50/70 king sgl/
dbl; all rates B&B.*

KAYONZA This small, rather scruffy settlement is situated 78km from Kigali, at the junction (✚ S 01°53.975, E 030°30.454) of the main north–south road connecting Kagitumba on the Ugandan border to Rusumo on the Tanzanian border. Kayonza is, if anything, even less remarkable than Rwamagana, though once again, particularly since the 2014 opening of the Urugo Eco-Lodge at the Women's Opportunity Centre, it serves as a good base for exploring Lake Muhazi and Akagera National Park, and it's readily accessible from Kigali on public transport, with midibuses leaving from Nyabugogo bus station. Bank of Kigali, GT Bank and KCB all have ATMs clustered around the main junction here, and the bus station is set just a few metres along the road to Nyagatare. If you're hanging out in the area, volunteers working in Kayonza reckon there is some good walking to be had by heading out of town in the general direction of Akagera National Park.

Where to stay

Eastland Hotel (25 rooms) m 078 700
3924/867 3683; e eastlandhotel@yahoo.com;
w eastlandhotel.rw. Situated in a deceptively
large garden about 500m from the main junction
along the Kigali road, this is theoretically
the smartest place to stay in Kayonza proper
(assuming you don't want to hike the 3km down
to Urugo), but a lack of maintenance means
standards have taken a tumble. The en-suite
rooms are on the scruffy side, with unreliable
Wi-Fi & hot showers. A courtyard bar & restaurant
serves chilled drinks & hot snacks & meals. They
also manage the ominously named Silent Hill
Hotel a stone's throw down the road towards
Kigali. *Rfr15,000/25,000/40,000 sgl/dbl/exec.*

 **Urugo Eco-Lodge (Women's
Opportunity Centre)** [map, page 286]
(7 rooms) ✚ S 1°55.217, E 30°29.711; m 078 835
0577; e info@urugowoc.com; f urugoecolodge.
Run in conjunction with (& signposted as) the
Women's Opportunity Centre, this place on the
east side of the road towards Rusumo (3km south
of the main junction in Kayonza) is just one part
of a larger organisation promoting women's

economic empowerment through a variety of
community-based programmes. The wide hillside
grounds boast long views over the surrounding
farms & valleys, & are home to a series of modern
workshop spaces, an organic garden, & a small
restaurant doing tasty interpretations of the
usual meat & fish favourites, with the added
bonus of fresh produce from the garden. Double/
twin rooms are in deluxe standing tents with
en-suite hot shower & eco-loo, writing desk,
wardrobe, & wax-print décor, while the 4-bed
dorms come with nets & lockers & are spotlessly
clean; all are solar-powered & have Wi-Fi. Since
its opening in 2014, it's become a preferred
staging point for visits to Akagera National Park
(*Rfr90,000/120,000 per day for a 4x4 with a max
of 4/7 pax*), but they also offer village tours to
community projects around Kayonza. There's a
new café & market out front selling good coffee
& pastries alongside fruit, veg, & handicrafts.
*US$50/60 sgl/dbl en-suite deluxe standing tent;
US$25pp dorm bed; US$10pp camping; all rates inc
a hearty b/fast.*

LAKE MUHAZI (EASTERN AND SOUTHERN SHORES) In common with most lakes in Rwanda, Muhazi is an erratically shaped body of water whose shores follow the contours of the surrounding hills. Roughly 60km long but nowhere more than 5km wide, Muhazi is a classic 'flooded valley' type of lake, its serpentine shape broken by numerous tendrils stretching northward or southward along former tributaries. It is a pretty spot, not as beautiful perhaps as the lakes around Musanze/Ruhengeri but – at least for travellers dependent on public transport – with the added virtue of easy accessibility. The birdlife here is highly rewarding, and the lake harbours an unusually dense population of spotted-necked otter, though no other large mammals are found in the area. The eastern tip of Lake Muhazi lies beside the surfaced Nyagatare road, about 8km north of Kayonza, opposite the turn-off to the small but attractive little town of Gahini, set high above the lake.

Where to stay and eat *Map, page 286*

🏠 **Duha Beach Resort** (7 rooms) m 078 830 2824/583 7043; e info@duhabeachresort.com; w duhabeachresort.com. Along the southern lakeshore, these brick-built cottages sit just steps from the water & are either duplex bungalows with double rooms or a 3-bedroom family house with kitchen (sleeps 6). There are kayaks, canoes & pedal boats available for guests, as well as a badminton court. Meals are available by advance arrangement, or you can head to Muhazi Water Sport, less than 300m away. *Great value at Rfr30,000 dbl; Rfr80,000 family house; all rates B&B.*

🏠 **Muhazi Beach Hotel** (68 rooms) m 078 838 9978. Ostensibly the most upmarket accommodation on the lakeshore, this large resort complex is long on location but short on character, & we've had reports of lacklustre maintenance & indifferent staff. The en-suite rooms are set either in a long main block or in bungalows staggered along the shoreline. Coming from Kigali, look for a signposted left-hand turn-off 8km before you reach Kayonza junction & continue straight for 5km. *From US$50 dbl B&B.*

🏠 **Muhazi Water Sport** (11 rooms) m 078 280 9080/743 7822; w muhazi-watersport. weebly.com; ✦ S 01°53.077, E 030°21.352. This relatively new reader-recommended spot sits in a garden compound along the lake's southern shore. The simple tiled rooms come in a variety of colours, all with en-suite bathrooms & hot water. There's a

large deck overhanging the lake & an open-sided resto-bar on shore. About 35km after leaving Kigali, take a left on to the signposted DR 18 towards Muhazi & Musha & continue for a rather rough 10km. *Rfr40,000 dbl.*

🏠 **Seeds of Peace Centre** (40 rooms) ✦ S 01°50.502, E 030°28.496, 1,460m; m 078 881 8018/072 613 6028; e gahini@rwanda1. com/sylvestrenduwayezu@gmail.com. Run by the Episcopal Church, this pretty lakeshore resort, opposite the turn-off to Gahini, is intermittently well organised for tourism, offering boating, swimming, birdwatching, a (booze-free) restaurant with fresh lake fish, camping, a picnic place & 2 reconstructed traditional dwellings. It also has rondavels, each with 2 bedrooms, bathroom, kitchen & lounge, & a new double-storey block with more conventional en-suite hotel rooms. Profits go back to the diocese for its work in the local community. *Rfr15,000/20–25,000 sgl/dbl B&B; Rfr35,000 for a 2-bedroom apt; Rfr10,000/ tent camping.*

✖ **Jambo Beach** m 078 387 6961; ⏰ 06.00–22.00 daily. There's no accommodation at this resort, which lies a few hundred metres from Seeds of Peace along the road towards Kayonza (you can't miss the giraffe statues out front), but the restaurant is generally regarded to be superior, & it does serve beers & other alcoholic drinks along with coffee, snacks, & brochettes starting at Rfr1,000 & full meals around Rfr4,000.

NYAGATARE This scattered but rapidly growing town of around 16,000 souls is the administrative centre of the sizeable but thinly populated Nyagatare District, which extends over the northeast of Rwanda to the borders with Uganda and Tanzania. Prior to 2006, Nyagatare was also the capital of the now-defunct Umutara Province, much of which lay within the north of Akagera National Park and the adjacent

Mutara Wildlife Reserve before these areas were degazetted in 1997 to accommodate returned refugees. Set along the eastern bank of the forest-fringed Muvumba River, it lies at a relatively low altitude of 1,355m, making it hotter than most other parts of Rwanda, and it retains something of a dusty frontier feel, surrounded by rolling hills whose cover of scrubby acacias and cactus-like euphorbia trees is far more archetypically African than any other settled part of Rwanda.

It would be an act of febrile distortion to describe Nyagatare as any sort of travel magnet. All the same, if you are seeking a wholly untouristy experience, you could do worse than spend a night or two here. The surrounding area is great walking

---

KING OF THE ROCKS   *Janice Booth*

A NEW VERSION OF AN ANCIENT TALE The monarch Ruganzu II Ndori was so great and famous a king that the mountains, rocks and forests of Rwanda were proud when he passed among them. One day, one of the rocks boasted to an eagle flying overhead that the king and his entourage had walked across it that same morning.

'Krarrk!' croaked the eagle in mocking disbelief. 'With my keen eyes I can spot the smallest mouse as it slips into its hole or the thinnest snake coiled in the shadows. Yet I see no sign that the king has passed your way.'

The rock scratched its weather-beaten head and thought deeply. Then it devised a plan. The next time King Ruganzu approached, it softened itself slightly so that his footsteps left an impression on its surface. Now the eagles and the crows and the skimming bee-eaters could see clearly that the king had walked upon the rock.

Word got around, and other rocks soon adopted the same tactic. If you visit Rwanda today, you may still see various traces of Ruganzu's footprints. Then one of the more ambitious rocks thought: 'If I create a jug, and fill it with beer, the monarch can drink his fill when he passes and I will become the chief rock within his kingdom.'

Carefully it formed itself into a jug, and filled that jug with cool, refreshing banana beer, and the king and all his courtiers drank their fill. But then some other rocks nearby saw what was happening and were jealous; they quickly made bigger and better jugs, and filled some of them with sorghum beer too so that the monarch had a choice.

Today, if you visit the old district of Murambi, you can still see half-a-dozen of these jugs, and if you're very lucky you may even catch a fleeting, aromatic scent of ancient beer. The region is called Rubona rwa Nzoga (Rubona of the beer); and the local tradition is that whatever time a guest may arrive at a house, the hosts will always have a jug of beer ready and waiting to quench his thirst.

Of course rocks in several other parts of Rwanda eventually copied the idea and made their own jugs too ... but they never matched the quality or quantity of Murambi's beer, which remained the monarch's favourite throughout his reign.

Murambi was incorporated into Kayonza District in 2006. Nyagatare-bound vehicles pass through Kiramuruzi (between Murambi and Kiziguro on the Akagera National Park map on page 306), from where Rubona rwa Nzoga is about 30 minutes' walk. But don't expect exact replica jugs ...

country – ask for (and take note of) local permission and advice, fill up your water bottle and then just stroll off across fields, plains, hillsides… It's a wonderfully clear, open panorama (unlike in much of the rest of Rwanda with its jutting hills and intensive cultivation), fresh and gently green at moister times of year, parched and tinder dry just before the rainy season. For wildlife enthusiasts, local farmers claim that antelope and zebra often cross the border of Akagera to graze peacefully among their cattle (though this is considerably less likely since the western border of the park was fenced off in 2013), while the riparian woodland along the river as it passes the small town centre offers some potentially rewarding birdwatching. Also, in Nyagatare as in all of Rwanda, you can while time away pleasantly by people-watching and engaging in conversation – thanks to its proximity to Uganda and high population of returned refugees, this is one part of Rwanda where English is far more widely spoken than French.

With its relatively dry climate and infertile soil, this northeastern corner of Rwanda was very thinly settled prior to the gazetting of Akagera in 1935. It remains one of the few parts of the country dominated by pastoralism rather than agriculture: you won't travel far here without coming across herds of cattle – a mix of long-horned Ankole and hornless varieties said to produce more milk

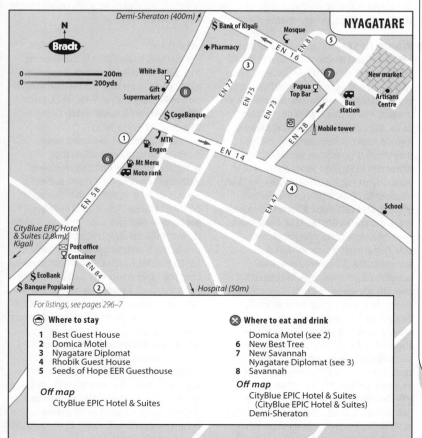

NYAGATARE

For listings, see pages 296–7

🛏 **Where to stay**
1 Best Guest House
2 Domica Motel
3 Nyagatare Diplomat
4 Rhobik Guest House
5 Seeds of Hope EER Guesthouse

Off map
  CityBlue EPIC Hotel & Suites

❌ **Where to eat and drink**
  Domica Motel (see 2)
6 New Best Tree
7 New Savannah
  Nyagatare Diplomat (see 3)
8 Savannah

Off map
  CityBlue EPIC Hotel & Suites
    (CityBlue EPIC Hotel & Suites)
  Demi-Sheraton

– plodding from clump to clump of bristly scrub. And as one might expect of an area so recently settled, there's a pioneering feel about the hamlets and villages, which were built (often with foreign funds) to provide for the returning refugees. Squatting defiantly on the empty plains, these are the houses of a child's pictures: plain and single-storied, with a small square window on either side of the front door. In fact they're dotted all over Rwanda, but the open landscapes here make them more visible.

Getting there and away Nyagatare lies about 155km from Kigali along a good surfaced road via Rwamagana and Kayonza. The drive should take under 3 hours in a private vehicle, and Nyagatare is 11km west of the main Kayonza–Uganda road, branching off at the junction village of Ryabega. There's talk of rerouting the road to Uganda so that it passes closer to or through Nyagatare itself, though this seems likely to be some years off. Both Yahoo Car Express (m *072 675 0202/6*) and Excel Tours (m *078 876 2860*) run midibuses to Nyagatare from Kigali, costing Rfr3,100 per person. These leave from the Nyabugogo bus station, but you can also pick up direct transport from the Remera taxi park on the east side of Kigali. Any Kigali-bound transport can also drop you in Kayonza, though northbound travellers to the Kagitumba border and Uganda will have better luck getting a lift on the main road at Ryabega, where there's plenty of passing traffic.

 Where to stay *Map, page 295, unless otherwise stated*

Best Guest House (6 rooms) m 078 390 6954/417 6535. On the 1st floor just above a shop on the main road into town, this reasonably spiffy place has a block of no-nonsense tiled rooms with mosquito nets on offer, & while there's no food on site, there are plenty of options within a few hundred metres. Unfortunately, the staff have been known to quote prices seemingly off the tops of their heads, so be sure to discuss rates in advance & get a receipt. *Rfr10,000 dbl using shared ablutions; Rfr15,000/20,000 en-suite dbl/exec.*

CityBlue EPIC Hotel & Suites [map, page 286] (76 rooms) m 078 760 3224; e reservations. rw@citybluehotels.com; w citybluehotels. com. Built at a cost of some Rfr16.4 billion, this unmissable (& admittedly somewhat unexplainable) 4-star hotel some 2km south of town officially opened in Dec 2017 & immediately became far & away the finest accommodation for km around. There are 5 categories of rooms & suites, many with balconies & all with safe, flatscreen TV & Wi-Fi. They've also got a large swimming pool, along with fitness centre & tennis court, & the restaurant does occasional barbecues on the terrace. *From US$100/130 sgl/dbl B&B.*

Domica Motel (4 rooms) m 078 888 3504/849 6455. About 250m from the post office at the entrance to town, this newish address has a handful of spic-&-span rooms with nets & en-suite cold ablutions. It's tiled & bright & good for the price, with receptive management & a popular restaurant-bar in the back with the usual dishes & footy on TV. Supposedly Wi-Fi too. *Rfr15,000 dbl.*

Nyagatare Diplomat Hotel (30 rooms) m 078 645 4916/850 3065; e nyagatarediplomatehotel@gmail.com/ reservations@kigalidiplomathotel.com; w kigalidiplomathotel.com. This prominent multi-storey hotel, formerly known as the Blue Sky, was for many years the smartest option in town until CityBlue showed up. Nonetheless, it's looking quite good after a 2017 remodel, & while the rooms still feel cheaply fitted, the facilities now include a swimming pool, fitness centre & free Wi-Fi. In the evenings the 1st-floor terrace bar (with pool table) is busy with local people & the restaurant serves a good-value buffet or à la carte menu. *Still a bit overpriced at US$40/60 sgl/dbl or twin; US$50/70 sgl/dbl deluxe; US$100/120 sgl/dbl suite; all rates B&B.*

Rhobik Guest House (9 rooms) m 078 835 3092; e rhobikguestho@gmail.com. In a small compound decorated with larger-than-life vegetables at the southeast edge of the city centre, this quiet place has clean & tiled en-suite rooms (with mozzie nets) that are nothing to shout about, but quite acceptable at the price. *Rfr10,000/12,000 small/large en-suite dbl.*

🏠 **Seeds of Hope EER Guesthouse** (20 rooms) 📱 078 900 1852. Situated in large grounds just around the corner from the Blue Sky, this friendly but rather rundown guesthouse, run by the Episcopal Church, offers the cheapest rooms in the town centre. *Rfr3,000/6,000 en-suite sgl/ twin; Rfr10,000 VIP room.*

🍴 **Where to eat and drink** The best option is probably the **Nyagatare Diplomat Hotel**, which serves heaped plates of meat or chicken with the starch of your choice for around Rfr3,500, and is open for breakfast, lunch and dinner. The restaurant at the **Domica Motel** also seems a popular spot for grills and beer, though for something more upmarket, the new restaurant at **CityBlue** is really your only choice. Otherwise, a good half-dozen eateries are scattered around town, serving the usual lunchtime mélanges of meat, rice and vegetables, including the **Demi-Sheraton**, **New Best Tree** and **New Savannah Restaurant** (📱 078 845 5318; ⏰ 06.00–midnight daily), which keeps long hours, charges Rfr1,000 for the buffet, and is not to be confused, of course, with the **Savannah Restaurant** a few blocks away.

THE RUSUMO ROAD

NGOMA (KIBUNGO) The largest town in the southeast of Rwanda (though this isn't saying much since the district is overwhelmingly rural), Ngoma (formerly Kibungo) sprawls westward from the main Rusumo road about 25km south of Kayonza. It is the eponymous capital of Ngoma District, a region suffering not only from the aftermath of the genocide, but also from several debilitating rainfall failures over recent years, so that it has often been dependent on outside food aid. It is a convenient enough base for the Akagera National Park if you don't fancy paying to stay at the upmarket game lodge or camping in the park itself, and it also forms a possible springboard for a half-day trip to the Rusumo Falls. Otherwise, Ngoma is no more distinguished than other towns in this part of Rwanda, with its main focal point being a small grid of scruffy roads lying 3km west of the altogether more dynamic junction suburb signposted as Cyasemakamba but more often referred to as Rompway (from the French 'rond-point' for roundabout, although there is no traffic circle, just a triangle!).

Getting there and away The town lies 100km from Kigali along a good surfaced road, branching southward at the main traffic circle in Kayonza after 75km. The drive should take no more than 2 hours. Matunda Express (📱 *078 822 8333*) and Stella (📱 *078 865 7070*) run scheduled midibuses between Kigali and Ngoma/ Kibungo throughout the day for Rfr2,000. There is also plenty of transport on to Rusumo on the Tanzanian border. The main taxi park is at Cyasemakamba, more-or-less opposite the Motel Umbrella Pine.

🏠 **Where to stay and eat** *Map, page 298*

🏠 **Centre de Formation de l'Eglise Anglicaine** (17 rooms plus dorm) 📱 078 425 8882/861 6797. Situated just off the feeder road to Kibungo & 250m from Cyasemakamba junction, the basic but clean rooms here are set around a maze of quiet grassy courtyards. Meals are provided to order; b/fast Rfr1,500–2,500 & mélange Rfr2,500 (or 4,000 for fish or chicken). *Rfr5,000/7,000 sgl/dbl with shared bathroom; from* Rfr8,000/10,000 en-suite sgl/dbl; Rfr3,000 bed in either of the cramped 32-bed single-sex dorms.

🏠 **Centre St Joseph** (59 rooms) 📱 078 834 4674/885 6156/830 3055; 📧 centresaintjosephkibungo@gmail.com; 🌐 centresaintjosephkibungo.com. Situated next to the eponymous church only 100m from the feeder road to Ngoma, this Catholic-run guesthouse has long been the best-value lodging in town. Rooms

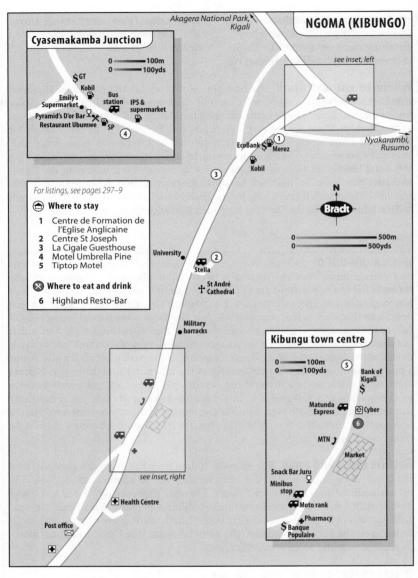

NGOMA (KIBUNGO)

Cyasemakamba Junction

0 — 100m
0 — 100yds

GT
Kobil
Emily's Supermarket
Bus station
IPS & supermarket
Pyramid's D'or Bar
Restaurant Ubumwe
SP
④

Akagera National Park, Kigali

see inset, left

Nyakarambi, Rusumo

EcoBank — Merez ①
Kobil
③

N

Bradt

0 — 500m
0 — 500yds

For listings, see pages 297–9

🛏 **Where to stay**

1 Centre de Formation de l'Eglise Anglicaine
2 Centre St Joseph
3 La Cigale Guesthouse
4 Motel Umbrella Pine
5 Tiptop Motel

✖ **Where to eat and drink**

6 Highland Resto-Bar

University ●
Stella
②
✝ St André Cathedral

Military barracks ●

see inset, right

✚ Health Centre

Post office ✉
✚

Kibungu town centre

0 — 100m
0 — 100yds
⑤

Bank of Kigali $

Matunda Express
Cyber
⑥

MTN

Market

Snack Bar Juru
Minibus stop
Moto rank
✚ Pharmacy
$ Banque Populaire

---

range from simple singles using shared toilets & showers to smarter, more recently built rooms & mini-suites with double bed & sitting area, all of which are reasonably clean & well maintained. The friendly restaurant has indoor & outdoor seating & it serves good, inexpensive local fare, as well as soft & alcoholic drinks – the bar stays open until 01.00 at w/ends. *Rfr5,000/7,500 sgl/ dbl using shared ablutions; Rfr15,000/25,000*

en-suite sgl/dbl; Rfr20,000/30,000 sgl/dbl suite; Rfr35,000/50,000 sgl/dbl in the new building.

🏠 **La Cigale Guesthouse** (8 rooms) m 072 250 5317/078 850 5317; e ruginajeandedieu@ yahoo.fr. This place alongside the road between the town centre & Cyasemakamba has meticulously clean but sparsely furnished rooms with en-suite cold shower. Unfortunately there is no restaurant. *Good value at Rfr11,000 dbl.*

Motel Umbrella Pine (8 rooms) m 078 252 5885/544 2322. Situated in Cyasemakamba 200m south of the main traffic circle, this simple lodge has been around for years now & is starting to look its age; aside from its convenient location on the main road, there isn't much going for it these days. Still, the restaurant is reliable enough, & can rustle up a picnic if you need it for visiting Akagera. The hotel can be hard to spot, tucked away behind a petrol station on the right coming from Kigali. *Rfr6,000/7,000/10,000 for a dingy en-suite sgl/dbl/twin.*

Tiptop Motel (5 rooms) 0252 566471; m 078 853 9604/289 8872. The most central lodge, situated almost opposite the market, this has adequate but rather dingy en-suite rooms with double bed, net, writing desk & cold shower. A restaurant & bar is attached. *Middling value at Rfr10,000/14,000 sgl/dbl.*

Highland Resto-Bar m 078 882 5805; ⊕ lunch & dinner daily. On the lower level of the shopping arcade where you'll also find the internet café, this place does a daily lunch buffet for around Rfr1,000 & simple brochettes & the like at other times. It's neat, clean & a popular spot for a drink, with a whole gang of chatty regulars who'll be pleased to make your acquaintance.

Other practicalities Several banks are represented here with ATMs, including GT Bank and EcoBank near Cyasemakamba junction, plus Bank of Kigali and Banque Populaire in the town centre. There's also a post office on the main road, and the only internet café is in the double-storey mall between the Bank of Kigali and the central market.

NYAKARAMBI (KIREHE) If you are already heading to Rusumo, it's definitely worth stopping at this large village (also commonly known as Kirehe after the eponymous district), which straddles the road from Ngoma/Kibungo about 20km before the Rusumo border crossing. This part of Rwanda is noted for its distinctive *imigongo* (cow-dung) 'paintings' – earthy, geometric designs which are mostly used to decorate the interiors of houses. In Nyakarambi, however, the roadside planters and a couple of the houses have cow-dung paintings on their outer walls, and about 2km south of the town there's a long-running craft co-operative. This is where most of the geometric paintings and pottery you see in Kigali originate from, but it's more fun (and cheaper) to buy them at source, especially as the people who run the co-operative aren't at all pushy. The sign outside reads 'Cooperative Kakira – Art "*imigongo*"' (m *078 884 4779*) and shows geometric patterns. A small brochure, sometimes available in the workshop, explains (in more-or-less these words) the origin of the form in the early 19th century:

> In olden times, there was Kakira, son of Kimenyi, King of Gisaka in Ngoma province (southeastern Rwanda). Kakira invented the art of embellishing houses and making them more attractive. To decorate the inside walls, cow dung was used, in patterns with prominent ridges. Then the surfaces were painted, in red and white colours made from natural soil (white from kaolin, red from natural clay with ochre), or else in shining black made from the sap of the aloe plant – *ikakarubamba* – mixed with the ash of burned banana skins and fruits of the solanum aculeastrum plant. It was the art of mixing together the soil, fire, raw materials from the cow and medicinal art that is the source of this work.

Kakira's knowledge was disappearing, due to the increasing use of industrial materials (paint); and so a women's association was created to maintain Kakira's work. After the 1994 genocide, most of the women, now widows, restarted their work together. Since 2001, the association has benefited from better promotion. Previously the women made no more than 20 pieces a month; now it is much more as orders have increased. Today, the Kakira Association makes '*imigongo*'

10

ANKOLE CATTLE

From mountain gorillas to elephants, Rwanda is blessed with its fair share of impressive wild beasts. But it is also a major stronghold for what is unquestionably the most imposing of Africa's domestic creatures: the remarkable long-horned Ankole breed of cattle associated with the pastoralist peoples of the Uganda and Rwanda border areas.

Sometimes referred to as the Cattle of Kings thanks to their association with the royal lineages of Uganda and Rwanda, Ankole cattle come in a variety of different colours, ranging from uniform rusty-yellow to blotched black-and-white, but always have a long head, short neck, deep dewlap and narrow chest; the male often sports a large thoracic hump. What most distinguishes Ankole cattle from any familiar breed, however, is their preposterous, monstrous horns, which grow out from either side of the head like inverted elephant tusks, and in exceptional instances can reach a length up to 2.5m – dimensions unseen on any Rwandan or Ugandan tusker since the commercial ivory poaching outbreak of the 1980s.

The ancestry of Ankole cattle has been traced back to Eurasia as early as 15000BC, but the precursors of the modern long-horned variety originate in Ethiopia, where the humpless Egyptian longhorn (as depicted on ancient Egyptian pictographs) and humped Asian zebu were crossed about 4,000 years ago to form a long-horned, humped breed known as the Ethiopian sanga. A number of credible oral traditions indicate that the sanga was introduced to northwest Uganda in medieval times, probably as part of the same wave of southward migration from Ethiopia associated with the foundation of the legendary Bacwezi Kingdom in Uganda circa AD1350.

Hardy, and capable of subsisting on limited water and poor grazing, these introduced cattle were ideally suited to local conditions, except that they had no immunity to tsetse-borne diseases, which forced the pastoralists who tended them to keep drifting southward. The outsized horns of the modern cattle are probably a result of selective breeding subsequent to their ancestors' arrival in southern Uganda about 500 years ago, at around the time the Ankole Kingdom was founded near modern-day Mbarara. Although the long horns were bred primarily for aesthetic reasons, the artificial process of breeding might have involved an element of natural selection. When threatened by large predators such as hyena or lion, it is customary for Ankole cattle to form a tight circle with horns facing outward, and it has also been noted how the calf often walks closely in front of its mother, protected by her horns.

Both in Uganda and Rwanda, pastoralists traditionally value cows less for their individual productivity than as status symbols: the wealth of a man would

art: modelled and painted tiles, panels, tables and other objects. There's a fantastic traditional house done up completely in *imigongo* patterns here now as well, though they'll charge you a small fee to take photos.

Working hours are 07.00–12.30 and 14.00–17.00 Monday–Saturday. Kakira products can be ordered from the workshop here or at a number of craft shops throughout the country.

There's a Bank of Kigali with ATM on the main road in the town centre, and if you're looking for a place to stay here, **Kirehe Guest House** (m *078 847 0070/970 3199/358 2383*) has simple rooms and a resto-bar about 400m off the main road at the north end of town.

be measured by the size and quality of his herd, and the worth of an individual cow by its horn size and, to a lesser extent, its coloration. In Rwanda, the noblest cow is the inyambo, which has an even deep blackish- or brownish-red hide, large lyre-shaped horns, and long hooves. Other long-horned cows of any coloration are called *ibigarama*, while stockier short-horned cows are referred to as *inkuku* – which may or may not be a pejorative derived from the widespread Bantu word for chicken!

Traditionally, the closely related pastoralist cultures of Rwanda and Uganda were as deeply bound up with a quasi-mystical relationship to cattle as the Maasai are today. Like Inuit and their physical landscape, this abiding mental preoccupation is reflected in the 30 variations in hide coloration that are recognised linguistically by the Bahima of Ankole, along with at least a dozen peculiarities of horn shape and size. The Bahima day is traditionally divided up into 20 periods, of which all but one of the daylight phases is named after an associated cattle-related activity. And, like the Maasai, Rwandan and Ugandan pastoralists traditionally looked down on any lifestyle based around fishing or agriculture – and they also declined to hunt game for meat, with the exception of buffalo and eland, which were sufficiently bovine in appearance to make for acceptable eating.

In times past, the diet of the pastoralists of Uganda and Rwanda did not, as might be expected, centre on meat, but rather on blood tapped from the vein of a living cow, combined with the relatively meagre yield of milk from the small udders that characterise the Ankole breed. Slaughtering a fertile cow for meat was regarded as akin to cannibalism, but it was customary for infertile cows and surplus bullocks to be killed for meat on special occasions, while the flesh of any cow that died of natural causes would be eaten, or bartered for millet beer and other fresh produce. No part of the cow would go to waste: the hide would be used to make clothing, mats and drums, the dung to plaster huts and dried to light fires, while the horns could be customised as musical instruments.

Today, neither Rwanda nor Ankole is as defiantly traditionalist as, say, Ethiopia's Omo Valley or Maasailand, and most rural Bahima today supplement their herds of livestock by practising mixed agriculture of subsistence and cash crops. But the Ankole cattle and their extraordinary horns, particularly common in eastern Rwanda, pay living tribute to the region's ancestral bovine preoccupations. Meanwhile, on a more prosaic note, this hardy breed – first farmed in the USA in the 1960s, where they are most often called Watusi cattle, a name no longer used in Rwanda – is of growing interest to international stock farmers because its meat has the lowest cholesterol levels of any commercial breed.

RUSUMO FALLS The Rusumo border with Tanzania, 60km southeast of Ngoma/ Kibungo (✪ S 02°22.798, E 030°46.999, 1,320m), is also the site of Rwanda's most impressive waterfall. Rusumo Falls isn't particularly tall, and can't compete with the Victoria or Blue Nile Falls, but it is a voluminous rush of white (or muddy, depending on the season!) water nevertheless, as the Akagera River surges below the bridge between the two border posts.

A huge new fenced-off border facility and bridge opened here in 2014, making the smaller bridge closest to the falls redundant to road traffic. To get to the falls, keep right as you enter the village (so as to stay out of the border facility) and follow the road for just over 1km until it dead-ends. When we visited, the gate here was

A NEW VERSION OF AN ANCIENT TALE The great King Gihanga ruled a part of Rwanda in the early 12th century – or perhaps the late tenth. Some historians say that he was the first of the royal dynasty, others claim that many kings preceded him. That's the trouble with oral history – the facts are elusive, and who knows whether or not any of this story is true! Anyway, it's certain that Gihanga had many wives and many children.

One day, his favourite daughter Nyirarucyaba lost her temper with a wife who was not her mother, scratching at the woman's face and tearing her hair until she screamed in pain. To lose control was considered very shameful and all the courtiers had seen what happened, so the king had no choice. He banished Nyirarucyaba into the deep forest where only wild beasts live. She wept pitifully but he would not yield, although his heart was torn.

After many days alone, the girl heard a rustling in the leaves and a snapping of branches – and crouched to the ground in fear. But it was a young man who had, like her, been cast into exile. Now, together, they began to contact the animals around them. There was one that seemed friendly, despite its great size and ugly voice. By day it munched the forest grasses and by night they kept warm against its soft hide.

In time it gave birth to a young one, with wet matted skin and shaky legs, which nuzzled under its mother and sucked at her teats. They saw that it drank a white liquid and learnt that it was milk. Now they had food indeed! They shared the milk with the calf and grew strong and healthy. In time they bore children of their own and the cow had many more calves.

Meanwhile the king had fallen sick with an illness that robbed him of all strength and joy. Doctors could find no cure. Finally three of the court's wisest men, so old that their hair was white and thin upon their heads, recognised it as grief, and took it upon themselves to speak. They told him Nyirarucyaba was still alive – and at once he sprang from his couch and dispatched hunters to the forest to search for her. They found her beside a stream, her children at her side and many cattle grazing nearby. Her return to her delighted father was a time of great celebration at the court.

The cattle came too, with their rich supply of milk. The courtiers gained a taste for it, and grew fat and strong. There was great competition to own the calves, which the king presented to courtiers who had served him particularly well. Needless to say, the families of his three old advisers were given the pick of the herd. As the years and the generations passed, the people could no longer remember a time when the kingdom had been empty of cattle. And that is how it still is, in Rwanda today …

open and you could wander right out on to the new bridge – check in with the Rwandan officials you'll see sitting at its base and they'll let you walk over to the old bridge to goggle at the falls, though they'll likely ask to see a passport first. If this gate is closed, you'd have to head back and go through the border facility, but (should this be the case) make it clear you're only here to see the falls and return to Rwanda. At present you can photograph the falls from the bridge, but nothing else in the immediate vicinity. It's best to ask permission anyway.

It's here at Rusumo that the German Count von Götzen, later to become Governor of German East Africa, entered Rwanda in 1894. He then travelled across the country to Lake Kivu, visiting the mwami on the way. Later, in 1916, when the Belgians were preparing to wrest the territory from the Germans, Belgian troops dug a trench and mounted artillery at the spot where one can see the falls today, in order to dislodge the German troops ensconced on the other bank who were guarding the only negotiable crossing. In 1994, Rusumo Bridge served as the funnel through which an estimated 500,000 Rwandans – half of them within one 24-hour period – fled from their home country to refugee camps around Ngala and elsewhere in northwest Tanzania. Journalists reporting on the exodus described standing on the bridge and counting the bloated bodies of genocide victims tumbling over the waterfall at a rate of one or two per minute.

Practicalities So far as travel practicalities go, the surfaced road between Ngoma/Kibungo and Rusumo is in good condition, and can be covered in under an hour. Regular minibus-taxis service the route, and there are also direct scheduled midibuses to/from Kigali with Matunda Express (m *078 822 8333*) and Select Express (m *078 216 6851*) for around Rfr3,200. The bus station sits at the entrance to the new border post, and about 300m further on heading into the village, the surprisingly pleasant **Falls Guest House** (m *078 513 6286;* e *birasa.joseph@yahoo. fr*) has a total of five very clean rooms with hot water, a kitchen open to guests, and secure parking at Rfr10,000/18,000 single/twin. The affiliated **Mount Fuji Garden Bar** sits on a green rise just behind the hotel with lovely views over the border post and surrounding hills and serves up the usual variety of hot food and cold drinks. Bank of Kigali has an ATM inside the border facility, but otherwise your closest option to draw cash is 20km back up the road in Nyakarambi (Kirehe).

11

Akagera National Park

Named after the river that runs along its eastern boundary, Akagera National Park is Rwanda's counterpart to the famous savannah reserves of Kenya, Tanzania and the like. In contrast to the rest of the country, it is located in a relatively warm and low-lying area of undulating plains supporting a cover of dense, broad-leafed woodland interspersed with lighter acacia woodland and patches of rolling grassland studded evocatively with stands of the superficially cactus-like *Euphorbia candelabra* shrub. To the west of the plains lies a chain of low mountains, reaching elevations of between 1,600m and 1,800m. The eastern part of the park supports an extensive wetland: a complex of a dozen lakes linked by extensive papyrus swamps and winding water channels fed by the meandering Akagera (sometimes called Kagera) River.

In terms of game-viewing, it would be misleading to compare Akagera to East Africa's finest savannah reserves. The northern and western portions of the original 2,500km² park were degazetted in 1997 (along with the adjoining 300km² Mutara Wildlife Reserve) to accommodate returned refugees, reducing the protected area to 1,085km². Though largely under control now, poaching has also impacted negatively on wildlife populations, and those lakes that remain within the national park were until not so long ago often used to water domestic cattle – indeed, in the early 2000s, long-horned Ankole cows were the most commonly seen large mammal in Akagera.

However, since the 2010 formation of the Akagera Management Company (AMC) under the joint management of the RDB and the non-profit African Parks Network (APN), the park has seen a dramatic resurgence. Since then, a number of new roads have been constructed in the park, a fabulous upmarket tented camp opened at the end of 2012, and the 120km western boundary fence was completed in 2013. Most excitingly of all, perhaps, is the ongoing programme of reintroductions, which has now seen both lions and rhinos once again taking up residence in Akagera for the first time in more than a decade.

More so than it has been at any time in recent decades, Akagera today is emphatically worth visiting. For one thing, it ranks among the most scenic of Africa's savannah reserves, with its sumptuous forest-fringed lakes, tall mountains and constantly changing vegetation. On top of that, the birdlife is quite phenomenal – for specialist birders, the checklist of almost 500 species includes several good rarities, while for first-time African visitors, it's a great place to see eagles and other large raptors along with some truly impressive concentrations of water-associated birds.

Akagera also still retains a genuinely off-the-beaten-track character: this is one African game reserve where you can still drive for hours without passing another vehicle, never knowing what wildlife encounter might lie around the next corner.

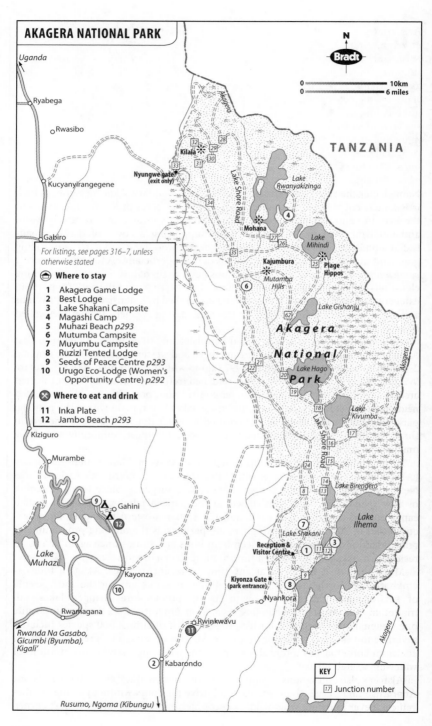

AKAGERA NATIONAL PARK

Uganda

○ Ryabega

○ Rwasibo

TANZANIA

Kilala ☀

Nyungwe gate
(exit only)

Lake Akagera

○ Kucyanyirangegene

○ Gabiro

Lake Shore Road

Mohana ☀

④

Lake Rwanyakizinga

②⑧ ②⑨
③② ③⓪
③①

③③

③④

③⑤

②⑦ ②⑥

Kajumbura ☀

Mutamba Hills

⑥

Lake Mihindi

②⑤

Plage Hippos

Lake Gishanju

Akagera

For listings, see pages 316–7, unless
otherwise stated

🛏 **Where to stay**

1   Akagera Game Lodge
2   Best Lodge
3   Lake Shakani Campsite
4   Magashi Camp
5   Muhazi Beach *p293*
6   Mutumba Campsite
7   Muyumbu Campsite
8   Ruzizi Tented Lodge
9   Seeds of Peace Centre *p293*
10   Urugo Eco-Lodge (Women's
      Opportunity Centre) *p292*

✖ **Where to eat and drink**

11   Inka Plate
12   Jambo Beach *p293*

⑥②

National

Lake Hago

②① ②②

②⓪

Park

①⑨

①⑧

Lake Kivumba

①⑦

①⑥

Akagera

Lake Shore Road

① ⑤

② ④

○ Kiziguro

○ Murambe

①④   Lake Birengero

⑧ ①③

⑨ ▲ ○ Gahini
  ▲ ⑫

⑤

Lake Muhazi

⑦ Lake Shakani

Reception &
Visitor Centre

① ⑪ ⑫

③

⑨

Lake Ilhema

○ Kayonza

⑩

Kiyonza Gate
(park entrance)

⑧

○ Rwamagana

○ Nyankora

*Rwanda Na Gasabo,
Gicumbi (Byumba),
Kigali'*

⑪ ○ Rwinkwavu

② ○ Kabarondo

Akagera

Rusumo, Ngoma (Kibungu) ↓

KEY

⑰ Junction number

N ☒ Bradt

0 ———— 10km
0 ———— 6 miles

And contrary to some reports, there *is* plenty of wildlife around, with the likes of zebra, giraffe, hippo, baboon, warthog and half-a-dozen antelope species all reasonably visible, and less skittish than one might expect. In addition, the lakes support some of the highest concentrations of hippo you'll find anywhere in Africa, as well as numerous large crocodiles.

As for the coveted Big Five, buffalo are plentiful and easily seen, elephants are quite common but more difficult to track down, and leopards are present but secretive as ever. For the best part of two decades, lion sightings here had been little more than the stuff of rumour, but with the June 2015 reintroduction of seven lions (two males and five females) flown in from reserves in South Africa, Akagera is once again home to the most charismatic member of the quintet. Two more males were brought in in 2017, and signs indicate that they're all settling in nicely –nearly a dozen cubs have been born here since the reintroductions began. The last black rhino was seen in 2007, but in May 2017 two planeloads of rhinos – 18 in all – arrived in the park and they've since had a calf here as well. All in all, it's been a magnificent few years for Akagera National Park, and all signs point to more exciting times ahead.

NATURAL HISTORY

Akagera is notable for protecting an unusually wide diversity of habitats within a relatively small area. Prior to the civil war, it was regarded as one of the few African savannah reserves to form a self-sustaining ecological unit, meaning that its resident large mammals had no need to migrate seasonally outside of the park boundaries. Whether that is still the case today is an open question: roughly two-thirds of the original park was degazetted in 1997, and, while some of this discarded territory is still virgin bush, it is probably only a matter of time before it will all be settled, putting further pressure on Akagera's diminished wildlife populations.

The modern boundaries of the park protect an area of 1,120km², stretching along the Tanzanian border for approximately 60km from north to south, and nowhere wider than 30km. The eastern third of the park consists of an extensive network of wetlands, fed by the Akagera River, and dominated by a series of small-to-medium-sized lakes. Lake Ihema, the most southerly of the lakes to lie within the revised park boundaries, is also the largest body of open water, covering about 100km². The lakes are connected by narrow channels of flowing water and large expanses of seasonal and perennial papyrus swamps. The eastern wetlands are undoubtedly the most important of the habitats protected within the park: not only do they provide a permanent source of drinking water for the large mammals, they also form an important waterbird sanctuary while harbouring a number of localised swamp-dwellers.

Akagera's dominant terrestrial habitat is dense broad-leafed woodland, though pockets of acacia woodland also exist within the park, while some of the lake fringes support a thin belt of lush riparian woodland. Ecologically, the savannah is in several respects unique, a product of its isolation from similar habitats by the wetlands to the east and mountainous highlands of central Rwanda to the west. The flora shows strong affinities with the semi-arid zones of northern Uganda and Kenya, but the fauna is more typical of the Mara–Serengeti ecosystem east of Lake Victoria. Akagera's geographical isolation from similar habitats is emphasised by the natural absence of widespread plains animals such as rhino and giraffe, both of which have been introduced, and are now thriving in their adopted home. Much of the bush in Akagera is very dense, but there are also areas of light acacia woodland and open grassland, notably on the Mutumba Hills and to the northeast of Lake Rwanyakizinga.

MAMMALS While Akagera's considerable scenic qualities and superb birdlife are largely unaffected by many years of turmoil, the large mammal populations have suffered badly at the hands of poachers. Having said that, on every visit over the course of researching seven editions of this book we've been pleasantly surprised at how much wildlife still remains, and since the 2010 AMC takeover, the longstanding decline of animal populations has finally been reversed, with the 2017 census counting more than 12,000 individuals. Though the populations of all large mammals remain depleted in comparison with their pre-1994 levels, trends are moving reliably in the right direction, and most large mammal species are still sufficiently numerous to form a viable breeding population.

Extirpated species include the **African wild dog**, probably a victim not of poaching but, in common with many other African reserves, of a canine plague which would have been introduced into the population through contact with domestic dogs. Of the larger predators, **spotted hyena** and **leopard** are still around, but infrequently observed (though you might well come across hyena spoor, particularly the characteristic white dung, and one female leopard was regularly seen in the vicinity of Akagera Game Lodge in 2011).

Prior to 1994, the park supported an estimated 250 **lion**, including a couple of prides that were uniquely adapted to foraging in the swamps, and others specialised in climbing trees. During the civil war, large numbers of lion were hunted out by the army to protect the presidential cattle herds; more recently they were poisoned by cattle herders living outside the park. Until 2015, the last confirmed sighting was of a female with three cubs in the north of the park in the year 2000. Published estimates later in the decade placed the population at anywhere from 15 to 60 individuals, but local sources considered it highly unlikely that any fully resident lions remained. Fortunately, the 2010 takeover by AMC and the 2013 fencing of the

AKAGERA'S HISTORY

From 1920 onwards, the Belgian colonisers put conservation measures into practice through various legislative and administrative decrees. It was the decree of 26 November 1934 that created the Parc National de la Kagera, on about 250,000ha. The park included – which was extremely rare before 1960 – a Strict Natural Reserve and an adjoining area where certain human activities were tolerated. It came under the jurisdiction of the Institut des Parcs Nationaux du Congo Belge et du Ruanda-Urundi, which was also responsible for the three parks (Albert, Garamba and Upemba) in the Belgian Congo. (In fact 8% of the Albert Park was also in Rwanda; now representing the Volcanoes Park in the northwest.) Kagera was renamed Akagera after independence, when the new Republic's leaders announced their intention of maintaining the park (and the Volcanoes Park) despite population pressure. Akagera's borders were altered – a few thousand hectares were retroceded to local communities while almost 20,000ha of the lacustrine zone to the south were incorporated. In 1975, 26 elephants were transported, first by helicopter and then by truck, from Bugesera, which was to be developed for agriculture. In November 1984, Rwanda held an official celebration of the park's 50th anniversary.

park cleared the way for this regal feline to return to Akagera, and in June 2015 it did just that when an airlift of two males and five females arrived in the park. One of the new arrivals has since died, but otherwise they have been remarkably successful in settling in to their new home. A further two males arrived from South Africa in May 2017, and 11 cubs have now been born in the park, bringing Akagera's lion population to 19 and growing as of early 2018.

Smaller predators are well represented. Most likely to be encountered by day are dwarf, banded and black-tailed **mongoose**, while at night there is a chance of coming across viverrids such as the lithe, heavily spotted and somewhat cat-like **genet**, and the bulkier black-masked **civet**. Also present, but rarely seen, are the handsome spotted **serval cat** and the dog-like **side-striped jackal**.

One of the most common terrestrial mammals is the **buffalo** and, while the population is nowhere near the estimated 8,000 that roamed the park in the 1980s, it's still thought to stand close to 3,000 individuals today. **Hippo**, too, are present in impressive numbers: on some of the lakes there must be at least a dozen pods of up to 50 animals, and the total population exceeds 1,600. Small herds of **Burchell's zebra** are regularly encountered in open areas, and these are thought to number almost 2,000 in the park. The handsome **impala** is probably the most common and habitat-tolerant large mammal at Akagera, and of the park's 11 antelope species (see box, pages 310–11), only the aquatic **sitatunga** is unlikely to be seen by visitors.

Also very common are three savannah primates: the dark, heavily built **olive baboon** (boldly resident around the game lodge), the smaller and more agile **vervet monkey**, and the tiny wide-eyed **bushbaby** (the last a nocturnal species likely to be seen only after dusk). The forest-dwelling **blue monkey** is probably now quite rare, due to habitat loss, but sightings are quite regular in the vicinity of lakes Ihema and Birengero. It is unlikely that Africa's largest swine, the **giant forest hog**, still occurs in Akagera. The smaller **bushpig**, a secretive nocturnal species, is present but rarely encountered, while the diurnal **warthog** is very common and often seen trotting off in family parties, stiff tail held high.

Two large mammal species that don't occur naturally were introduced to the park prior to the civil war. The first of these is the **Maasai giraffe**, which was introduced from the Magadi region of southern Kenya in January 1986. The original herd of two males and four females produced its first offspring in 1988 and has since multiplied to a population of around 90, which tends to stick to patches of acacia woodland close to the park headquarters and game lodge.

In 1957, Akagera became the recipient of Africa's first **black rhino** translocation, when a herd comprising five females and one male was flown across from the bordering Karagwe region of Tanzania, to be supplemented by another male a year later. The rhino prospered in the dense bush and by the early 1970s had colonised most of the park – one individual is known to have strayed south almost as far as the Rusumo Falls – and by the end of that decade the population comfortably exceeded 50. Then came the wholesale rhino poaching of the 1980s: by the end of that decade no more than a dozen individuals survived, and it was long thought that the remainder were shot in the civil war. An 11-year-old female nicknamed Patricia, who died of natural causes in July 2006, was then thought to be the last of her kind in Akagera, though aerial footage of another rhino taken from a helicopter in 2007 provided scant hope of another straggler remaining. Either way, the rhino population is happily no longer the stuff of hazy glimpses and speculation, as 18 critically endangered eastern black rhinos – eight males and ten females – were translocated from South Africa to Akagera in May 2017, symbolically crowning

The 11 antelope species in Akagera range from the eland, the world's largest antelope, through to the diminutive common duiker. The most common, however, is the **impala** (*Aepeceros melampus*), a slim handsome antelope which bears a superficial similarity to the gazelles, but belongs to a separate family. Chestnut in colour, the impala has diagnostic black and white stripes running down its rump and tail, and the male has large lyre-shaped horns. It is one of the most widespread antelope species in East and southern Africa, normally seen in large herds in woodland habitats, and common in the woodland around and between the lakes of Akagera.

The **Defassa waterbuck** (*Kobus ellipsiprymnus defassa*) is a large, shaggy brown antelope with a distinctive white rump. The male has large lyre-shaped horns, thicker than those of the impala. The waterbuck inhabits practically any type of woodland or grassland provided that it is close to water, and it is probably the most common large antelope after impala in the far south of Akagera.

Very common in the north of the park and in the Mutumba Hills, the **topi** or **tsessebe** (*Damaliscus lunatus*) is a large, slender dark-brown antelope with striking yellow lower legs. It has a rather ungainly appearance, reminiscent of the hartebeest and wildebeest, to which it is closely related, and is often seen using an anthill as a sentry point. Oddly, the herds of topi in northern Akagera seem to be far larger than those found in the Serengeti ecosystem.

Similar in size to a topi, but far more handsome, the **roan antelope** (*Hippotragus equinus*) has, as the Latin name suggests, a horse-like bearing. The uniform fawn-grey coat is offset by a pale belly, and it has short decurved horns and a light mane. After the civil war in the early 1990s, roan were very rare in Akagera: a 1998 estimate put their number at below 20, and the population today stands at around 100.

Much larger still is the **common** or **Cape eland** (*Taurotragus oryx*), which attains a height of up to 1.75m and can weigh as much as 900kg. The common eland is light-brown in colour, with faint white vertical stripes, and a somewhat bovine appearance accentuated by the relatively short horns and large dewlap. In Akagera, small herds are most likely to be seen on the open grassland of the Mutumba Hills, where the population is thought to exceed 200.

A trio of smaller antelope are also mainly confined to the Mutumba Hills. The largest of these is the **Bohor reedbuck** (*Redunca redunca*), a light-fawn animal

Akagera's extraordinary journey from blighted reserve to a 'Big Five' park once again. The first rhino calf born in Rwanda in more than a decade arrived just four months later. Thanks to the astronomical value of their horns, rhinos require extraordinary security and monitoring measures, but all signs indicate that Rwanda and African Parks are more than up to the challenge. In a tragic turn of events, Hungarian conservationist Krisztián Gyöngyi was killed by a rhino while tracking the new arrivals in June 2017.

Although the **African elephant** used to occur naturally in Akagera, the last recorded sighting of the original population was on the shores of Lake Mihindi in 1961. The present-day herd is descended from a group of 26 youngsters that was translocated to Akagera in 1975, part of an operation to clear all the elephants from the increasingly densely populated Bugesera Plains to the south of Kigali. Up to 100 adult elephants were shot in the process, while the young American filmmaker Lee Lyon was killed by one of the survivors upon its release into Akagera. By the late 1980s an estimated 45 individuals roamed Akagera and,

with moderately sized rounded horns; reedbucks are almost always seen in pairs, and in Akagera are rather skittish.

The smaller **oribi** (*Ourebia ourebi*) is a tan grassland antelope with short straight horns and a small but clearly visible circular black glandular patch below its ear. It is the commonest antelope on the Mutumba Hills, typically seen in parties of two or three, and has a distinctive sneezing alarm call.

The **klipspringer** (*Oreotragus oreotragus*) is a goat-like antelope, normally seen in pairs, and easily identified by its dark, bristly grey-yellow coat, slightly speckled appearance and unique habitat preference. Klipspringer means 'rock jumper' in Afrikaans and it is an apt name for an antelope which occurs exclusively in mountainous areas and rocky outcrops. It is often seen from the road between the entrance gate and Lake Ihema.

The only small antelope found in thicker bush is the **common duiker** (*Sylvicapra grimmia*), an anomalous savannah representative of a family of 20-plus small hunchbacked antelopes associated with true forests. Generally grey in colour, the common duiker has a distinctive black tuft of hair sticking up between its small straight horns. It is common in all bush areas, though it tends to be very skittish.

A widespread resident of thick woodland and forest, the pretty **bushbuck** (*Tragelaphus scriptus*) is a medium-sized, rather deer-like antelope. The male is dark brown or chestnut, while the much smaller female is generally pale red-brown. The male has relatively small, straight horns, while both sexes have pale throat patches, white spots and sometimes stripes. The bushbuck tends to be secretive, but might be seen anywhere in Akagera except for open grassland.

Similar in appearance to the bushbuck, and a close relation, the semi-aquatic **sitatunga** (*Tragelaphus spekei*) is a widespread but infrequently observed inhabitant of West and Central African swamps. The male, with a shoulder height of up to 125cm (much taller than a bushbuck) and a shaggy fawn coat, is unmistakable, while the smaller female might be mistaken for a bushbuck except for its more clearly defined stripes. The status of the sitatunga within Akagera is uncertain, but the 2017 census counted around 55, largely restricted to inaccessible swampy areas.

although population growth was stunted by poaching during the civil war, the current population of around 100 is the largest the park has supported in more than half a century.

BIRDS Akagera is the country's second most important ornithological site after Nyungwe, and these two bird-rich national parks complement each other to such an extent that very few species recorded in Rwanda aren't found in one or the other. Before Akagera's area was reduced in 1997, the park checklist stood at around 550 species, but today it is thought to be around 480, of which as many as 100 are unrecorded in no other protected area in Rwanda. In addition to being the best place in Rwanda to see a good selection of savannah birds and raptors, Akagera is as rich in waterbirds as anywhere in East Africa, and one of the few places where papyrus endemics can be observed.

Among the more colourful and common of the savannah birds are the gorgeous lilac-breasted roller, black-headed gonolek (easily picked up by its jarring duets), little bee-eater, Heuglin's robin-chat, Meyer's parrot, spot-flanked barbet and double-toothed barbet. Less colourful, but very impressive, are the comical grey hornbill and noisy bare-faced go-away bird. The riparian woodland around the lakes hosts a number of specialised species, of which Ross's turaco, a bright-purple, jay-sized bird with a distinctive yellow mask, is the most striking.

A notable feature of Akagera's avifauna is the presence of species such as the crested barbet, white-headed black chat and Souza's shrike, all of which are associated with the *brachystegia* woodland of southern Tanzania and further south, but have colonised the mixed woodland of Akagera at the northernmost extent of their range. More noteworthy still is the red-faced barbet, a localised endemic of savannahs between Lake Victoria and the Albertine Rift. It is quite often seen in the car park and gardens of Akagera Game Lodge. A localised species associated with broken grassland in Akagera is the long-tailed cisticola.

Finally, the savannah of Akagera is one of the last places in Rwanda where a wide range of large raptors is resident: white-backed and Rüppell's griffon vultures soar high on the thermals, the beautiful bateleur eagle can be recognised by its wavering flight pattern and red wing markings, while brown snake eagles and hooded vultures are often seen perching on bare branches.

Most of the savannah birds are primarily of interest to the dedicated birder, but it is difficult to imagine that anybody would be unmoved by the immense concentrations of water-associated birds that can be found on the lakes. Pelicans are common, as is the garishly decorated crowned crane, the odd little open-bill stork and the much larger and singularly grotesque marabou stork. Herons and egrets are particularly visible and well represented, ranging from the immense goliath heron to the secretive black-capped night heron, reed-dwelling purple heron and very localised rufous-bellied heron. The lakes also support a variety of smaller kingfishers and shorebirds, and a prodigious number of fish eagles, whose shrill duet ranks as one of the most evocative sounds of Africa.

On a more esoteric note, the papyrus swamps are an excellent place to look for a handful of birds restricted to this specific habitat: the stunning and highly vocal papyrus gonolek, as well as the more secretive and nondescript Carruthers's cisticola and white-winged warbler. Akagera is also one of the best places in Africa to see the shoebill, an enormous and unmistakable slate-grey swamp-dweller whose outsized bill is fixed in a permanent Cheshire-cat smirk (see box, pages 314–15). A useful birding report on Akagera can be sourced online at w worldtwitch.com/rwanda_uganda_des.htm.

REPTILES The **Nile crocodile**, the world's largest reptile and a survivor from the age of the dinosaurs, is abundant in the lakes, with 500 counted in the 2017 census. Some of the largest wild specimens you'll encounter anywhere are to be found sunning themselves on the mud-banks of Akagera, their impressive mouths wide open until they slither menacingly into the water at the approach of human intruders. Not unlike a miniature crocodile in appearance, the **water monitor** is a type of lizard which often grows to be more than a metre long and is common around the lakes, tending to crash noisily into the bush or water when disturbed. Smaller lizards are to be seen all over, notably the colourful rock agama, and a variety of snakes are present but, as ever, very secretive.

DANGEROUS ANIMALS Although it is technically forbidden to leave your vehicle except at designated lookout points, the guides in Akagera seem to enforce this rule somewhat whimsically, so it is worth emphasising the folly of disembarking from your vehicle in the presence of elephant, buffalo or lion.

Hippo and crocodile are potentially dangerous, and claim far more human lives than any terrestrial African animal. For this reason, you should be reasonably cautious when you leave the car next to a lake, particularly at dusk or dawn or in overcast conditions, when hippos are most likely to come out of the water to graze. The danger with hippos is getting *between* them and the water; you have nothing to worry about when they are actually in the water. Special caution should be exercised if you camp next to a lake – don't wander too far from your site after dark, and take a good look around should you need to leave your tent during the night (if there are hippo close by, you'll almost certainly hear them chomping at the grass). Crocs are a real threat only if you are daft enough to wade into one of the lakes.

The most dangerous animal in Akagera is the malaria-carrying *Anopheles* mosquito. Cover up after dark – long trousers and thick socks – and smear any exposed parts of your body with insect repellent. Many tents come with built-in mosquito netting. This will protect you when you sleep, provided that you don't hang a light at the entrance to your tent, which will ensure that a swarm of insects enter it with you. Incidentally, never leave any food in your tent: fruit might attract the attention of monkeys and elephants, while meat could arouse the interest of large predators.

Not so much a danger as a nuisance are tsetse flies, which are quite common in dense bush and can give a painful bite. Fortunately, the pain isn't enduring (though people who tend to react badly to insect bites might want to douse any tsetse bite in antihistamine cream) and there is no risk of contracting sleeping sickness during a short stay in Akagera. Insect repellents have little effect on these robust little creatures, but it's worth noting that they are attracted to dark clothing (especially blue). Thus, given the tsetses' chromatic proclivities, the park authorities have put up more than 600 blue and black 'tsetse flags' that attract and attack (or trap) the tsetses when they get near, which greatly reduces the potential nuisance for visitors.

FURTHER INFORMATION The AMC produces a fold-out map for Akagera, available at the reception for Rfr1,000, but the 16-page full-colour guidebook for Rfr2,500 is far more enriching and very much worth the asking price. Inside is an up-to-date fold-out centrefold map of the park showing all new roads and junction numbers, along with descriptions of several recommended self-drive routes, a history of the park, tracking tips, bird checklist, and further details on commonly spotted plants and animals.

The popular coffee-table book *Akagera: Land of Water, Grass and Fire* by Jean-Pierre Vande Weghe was first published in 1990 and has subsequently gone out of print, but there's now talk of producing an updated edition to chronicle Akagera's remarkable resurrection. Also by Jean-Pierre Vande Weghe, in collaboration with his son Gaël, the 336-page *Birds in Rwanda*, published by RDB in 2011, is a striking full-colour guide full of detailed maps and fine photographs. It's usually available at the park reception for Rfr18,000.

GETTING THERE AND AWAY

The reception centre (where you'll find interpretive materials and a small café serving Question Coffee) lies in the south of the park about 1km from Akagera Game Lodge, and 3km past the Kiyonza Entrance Gate. It is reached via a 27km

Perhaps the most eagerly sought of all African birds, the shoebill is also one of the few that is likely to make an impression on those travellers who regard pursuing rare birds to be about as diverting as hanging about in windswept railway stations scribbling down train numbers. Three factors combine to give the shoebill its bizarre and somewhat prehistoric appearance. The first is its enormous proportions: an adult might stand more than 150cm (5ft) tall and typically weighs around 6kg. The second is its unique uniform slatey-grey coloration. Last but emphatically not least is its clog-shaped, hook-tipped bill – at 20cm long, and almost as wide, the largest among all living bird species. The bill is fixed in a permanent Cheshire-cat smirk that contrives to look at once sinister and somewhat inane, and when agitated the bird loudly claps together its upper and lower bill, rather like outsized castanets.

The first known allusions to the shoebill came from early European explorers to the Sudan, who wrote of a camel-sized flying creature known by the local Arabs as Abu Markub – Father of the Shoe. These reports were dismissed as pure fancy by Western biologists until 1851, when Gould came across a bizarre specimen among an avian collection shot on the Upper White Nile. Describing it as 'the most extraordinary bird I have seen', Gould placed his discovery in a monotypic family and named it *Balaeniceps Rex* – King Whale Head! Gould believed the strange bird to be most closely allied to pelicans, but it also shares some anatomic and behavioural characters with herons, and until recently it was widely thought to be an evolutionary offshoot of the stork family. Recent DNA studies support Gould's original theory, however, and the shoebill is now placed in a monotypic subfamily of the Pelecanidae.

The life cycle of the shoebill is no less remarkable than its appearance. One of the few birds with an age span of up to 50 years, it is generally monogamous, with pairs coming together during the breeding season (April to June) to construct a grassy nest of up to 3m wide on a mound of floating vegetation or a small island. Two eggs are laid, and the parents rotate incubation duties, in hot weather filling their bills with water to spray over the eggs to keep them cool. The chicks hatch after about a month, and will need to be fed by the parents for at least another two months until their beaks are fully developed. Usually only one nestling survives, probably as a result of sibling rivalry.

The shoebill is a true swamp specialist, but it avoids dense stands of papyrus and tall grass, which obstruct its take-off, preferring instead to forage from patches of low floating vegetation or along the edge of channels. It consumes up to half its weight in food daily, preying on whatever moderately sized aquatic creature might come its way, ranging from toads to baby crocodiles, though lungfish are especially favoured. Its method of hunting is exceptionally sedentary: the bird may stand semi-frozen for several hours before it lunges down with remarkable speed and power, heavy wings stretched backward, to grab an item of prey in its large, inescapable bill. Although it is generally a solitary hunter, the shoebill has

dirt road that branches east from the main surfaced road between Kigali and Rusumo at Kabarondo, about 15km north of Ngoma/Kibungo, and an equal distance south of Kayonza. This dirt road is in fair condition and regularly graded, so it should be passable in any vehicle except perhaps after heavy rain, when a 4x4 may be necessary. (In any case, a 4x4 is advisable for roads within the park, though any vehicle with good clearance should be OK in the dry season.)

occasionally been observed hunting co-operatively in small flocks, which splash about flapping their wings to drive a school of fish into a confined area.

Although the shoebill is elusive, this is less a function of scarcity than of the inaccessibility of its swampy haunts. Nevertheless, today it's IUCN-listed as 'Vulnerable', and it is classed as CITES Appendix 2, which means that trade in shoebills, or their capture for any harmful activity, is banned by international law. Estimates of the global population vary wildly. In the 1970s, only 1,500 were thought to persist in the wild, but this estimate has subsequently been revised to 5,000–8,000 individuals concentrated in five countries – South Sudan, Uganda, Tanzania, Congo and Zambia. Small breeding populations also occur in Rwanda and Ethiopia, and vagrants have been recorded in Malawi and Kenya.

The most important shoebill stronghold is the Sudd Floodplain on the South Sudanese Nile, where 6,400 individuals were counted during an aerial survey undertaken over 1979–82, followed by the inaccessible Moyowosi-Kigosi Swamp in western Tanzania, whose population was thought to amount to a few hundred prior to a 1990 survey that estimated it to be greater than 2,000. Ironically, although Uganda is the easiest place to see the shoebill in the wild, the national population probably amounts to no more than a few hundred birds.

Outside of Uganda, Akagera National Park is potentially one of the most accessible shoebill haunts anywhere in Africa. In the 1980s, the local shoebill population was estimated at around 15–20 pairs, and there is no particular reason to think this has changed greatly in the interim – shoebills are not hunted as food, they pose no threat to cattle herders, and the inaccessible swamps they inhabit were largely unaffected by the 1997 reduction in Akagera's area. Certainly, at least one pair is resident in the papyrus beds fringing the eastern shore of Lake Birengero, and they are regularly seen by visitors, though lack of road access means you need decent binoculars to pick them out from the distant western shore. We have also had unverified reports of sightings on Lake Ihema. Three shoebills were spotted in the 2017 census, but little effort has been made to make the bird's habitat accessible to tourists by boat.

The major threat to the survival of the shoebill is habitat destruction. The construction of several dams along the lower Nile means that the water levels of the Sudd are open to artificial manipulation. Elsewhere, swamp clearance and rice farming pose a localised threat to suitable wetland habitats. Lake Opeta, an important shoebill stronghold in eastern Uganda, has been earmarked as a source of irrigation for a new agricultural scheme. A lesser concern in some areas is that shoebills are hunted for food or illegal trade, while in others local fishermen often kill the shoebills in the belief that seeing one before a fishing expedition is a bad omen. As is so often the case, tourism can play a major role in preserving the shoebill and its habitat: a classic example being Uganda's Mabamba Swamp, where the local community has already seen financial benefits from ornithological visits from nearby Entebbe.

In a private vehicle, the main gate is about 2½ hours' drive from Kigali, or 1 hour from Ngoma/Kibungo or Rwamagana.

In the north of the park, Nyungwe Gate (⊕ S 1°26.779, E 30°32.779) (not to be confused with the eponymous national park on the other side of the country), is an exit only – visitors *cannot* enter the park here. Thus, entering the park at Kiyonza Gate and exiting via Nyungwe Gate is a great way to explore a large part of the park from south to north in one go, but unless you wake up at one of the lodges (which we wholly recommend), it can make for a long day in the car as you'll need to allow the best part of a day (*at least 5–6hrs*) between the two gates, plus whatever time it takes to get to/from your lodging before and after. Departing via Nyungwe Gate, you're spit out on to a rough dirt road that rejoins the Kigali–Nyagatare road after 22km at the village of Kucyanyirangegene (sometimes referred to as Kizarakome) about 60km north of Kayonza. This route requires high clearance as a minimum, but preferably a 4x4, and it may be challenging after rain.

Reaching Akagera on public transport is problematic. Any minibus-taxi travelling between Kayonza and Ngoma can drop you at the junction in Kaborondo, from where there are theoretically a couple of minibuses or bush taxis that trundle down the road to Rwinkwavu (where there's a large hospital and the worthwhile **Inka Plate restaurant** [map, page 306] (m *078 602 5105;* f), serving an unexpectedly ambitious menu of chapatti pizzas, burgers, pastas, and Mexican-style tacos and quesadillas for Rfr2,000–4,000, and Nyankora (the last village before the park), but even from Nyankora you're still some 5km from the entrance gate and nearly 9km from reception. Thus, the only realistic option is a moto-taxi, and you should be able to get one to take you from Kaborondo to the park for around Rfr3,500. Inside the park, except within the grounds of the hotels, no walking is permitted with or without a guide. Half- or full-day game drives using their safari vehicle are available, but you have to book the entire car, so, unless you can find a group, it might be prohibitively expensive for solo travellers. Night drives, on the other hand, can be booked by the seat and represent a better deal for the unaccompanied (page 322).

PARK FEES

Under the simplified 2019 fee structure, entrance costs US$50 per person per night for international visitors, US$35 per person for foreign residents of Rwanda and other states in the East African Community (EAC), and Rfr7,500 for nationals of Rwanda and other EAC states, with a roughly 40% reduction for under 12s in all cases. Unlike in some neighbouring countries, the fee is not calculated per 24-hour period but per night – were you to arrive at 07.00 on one day and exit at 17.00 the next day, you are still charged for only one night. However, day visitors will pay the same entrance fee as people spending one night in the park. The only other fees applicable to self-drive visitors are a vehicle fee of Rfr10,000 (US$40 if it's registered outside the EAC) and an optional guide fee of US$25/40 per party per half/full day.

WHERE TO STAY AND EAT   *Map, page 306*

Set to open in 2019, Wilderness Safaris' top-end **Magashi Camp** (w *wilderness-safaris.com*) will soon be the first accommodation in the north of the park, boasting six luxury standing tents set on the shores of Lake Rwanyakizinga.

UPMARKET

Karenge Bush Camp (6 tents) m 078 711 3300/426 7501; e karenge@african-parks.org; w akagera.org. The newest accommodation option in Akagera, this intriguing seasonal camp had its first guests in Aug 2015, & is open biannually every Jul–Sep & mid-Dec–Feb. Uniquely, it has no permanent location at all – the camp is designed & built to leave no trace behind & rotates sites based on the ideal location for the season, making for an enthralling & authentic bush experience that's never the same twice. The tents themselves are spacious & set on raised platforms with private viewing terraces, & comfortably equipped with solar lights & reed-mat flooring. Ablutions are outdoors, with eco-loos & (hot) bucket showers. Guests are accommodated on a full-board basis & meals are taken outdoors, with commanding views over the surrounding bush. Contact them in advance to make a booking & find out this season's location. *US$245/350 sgl/dbl foreign visitors; US$210/300 residents; all rates FB.*

🏠 **Ruzizi Tented Lodge** (9 rooms)
✪ S 1°54.384, E 30°43.022; 📱 078 711 3300; e ruzizi@african-parks.org; w ruzizilodge.com/african-parks.org. Opened at the end of 2012, this delightful tented camp sits in a patch of lush riparian woodland on the shores of Lake Ihema about 15mins' drive from the entrance gate. Accommodation is in handsomely equipped lakeshore standing tents, elevated & widely spaced along a boardwalk to the central restaurant & lounge. Each room comes with en-suite hot showers & a private terrace, & it's not uncommon for hippos to come out of the water & graze around the (once again, elevated!) tents at night. The treetop tent is even more luxurious, & well named given its perch in the canopy atop 4m stilts. With a clawfoot bathtub inside, open-air shower on the balcony, & even a pair of hammocks, it's a wonderfully indulgent spot. Meals are taken on a stilted wooden terrace at the water's edge (the views at b/fast are fabulous), & there are nightly campfires here as well. It's a genuine bush alternative to the more conventional Akagera Game Lodge, & a most welcome sign that Akagera has once again come into its own as a national park. *US$325/470 sgl/dbl foreign visitors; US$330/460 sgl/dbl residents; US$335/470 treetop foreign; US$350/500 sgl/dbl treetop residents; all rates FB.* All rates high season. See ad, 4th colour section.

MODERATE
🏠 **Akagera Game Lodge** (36 rooms)
✪ S 01°52.314, E 030°42.911, 1,610m; 📱 078 520 1206/253 5717; e reservations@mantiscollection.com; w mantiscollection.com. Built in the 1970s,

this motel-style lodge reopened in 2003 & has switched hands several times since, most recently becoming part of the luxury Mantis Collection in late 2017. Major renovations were underway as this book went to print, & the once-outmoded rooms will be thoroughly fashionable by early 2019 – expect an increase in price to match. The lodge has a wonderful setting in wooded hilltop grounds that host a rich birdlife & offer superb views over Lake Ihema into the hills of Tanzania. Facilities include a good à la carte restaurant (expect gastronomic upgrades here as well), a swimming pool, Wi-Fi, conference facilities & tennis courts, & the overall level of service is impressive. Be aware that the baboons that loiter around the lodge grounds occasionally enter & raid rooms, so avoid leaving your door open, especially if you have any food inside. *Email for rates.*

BUDGET
Camping aside, there is no budget accommodation in the park itself, but it can easily be visited as a day trip from Kayonza or Ngoma/Kibungo. The closest budget accommodation is in the junction town of Kabarondo (where you'll also find 2 ATMs), only 27km from the entrance gate.

🏠 **Best Lodge** (12 rooms) 📱 078 700 5614. Situated about 100m from the bus station in Kabarondo, & on the opposite side of the main road, this is a very basic place offering en-suite rooms with ¾ bed & cold shower. *Rfr7,000 sgl.*

🏕 **Camping** For the self-sufficient, this is allowed at 3 locations in the park: **Muyumbu** & **Lake Shakani** in the south, & **Mutumba** further north. It costs US$25pp/night including firewood & water, irrespective of residence status. Tents sleeping 6 are available for hire at US$20/night. Also note that there are rain-fed water pumps at Muyumbu & Mutumba campsites (not at Lake Shakani), but these may run out during the dry season, so remember to fill up your containers at reception. Also note that the campsites at Muyumbu & Mutumba are both fenced to keep out large animals, while Lake Shakani is not.

ACTIVITIES

BOAT TRIPS Boat trips are available on Lake Ihema, and are worthwhile. Close encounters with outsized crocodiles and hippo are all but guaranteed, and you might also pass substantial seasonal breeding colonies of African darter, various cormorants, and open-bill stork. Other waterbirds are abundant: the delicate and colourful African jacana can be seen trotting on floating vegetation, fish eagles are posted in the trees at regular intervals, jewel-like malachite kingfishers hawk from the reeds, while pied kingfishers hover high above the water to swoop down on their fishy prey. Of greater interest to enthusiasts will be the possibility of marsh and papyrus specialists such as papyrus gonolek, white-winged warbler, blue-headed coucal and marsh flycatcher. Dedicated birders might also want to book a private tour, in order to visit a fantastic heronry where the likes of squacco heron, purple heron, striated heron, rufous-bellied heron and both types of night heron breed seasonally. Trips last 1 hour, and there are two morning

WEAVERS

Placed by some authorities in the same family as the closely related sparrows, the weavers of the family Ploceidae are a quintessential part of Africa's natural landscape, common and highly visible in virtually every habitat from rainforest to desert. The name of the family derives from the intricate and elaborate nests – typically but not always a roughly oval ball of dried grass, reeds and twigs – that are built by the dextrous males of most species.

It can be fascinating to watch a male weaver at work. First, a nest site is chosen, usually at the end of a thin hanging branch or frond, which is immediately stripped of leaves to protect against snakes. The weaver then flies back and forth to the site, carrying the building material blade by blade in its heavy beak, first using a few thick strands to hang a skeletal nest from the end of a branch, then gradually completing the structure by interweaving numerous thinner blades of grass into the main frame. Once completed, the nest is subjected to the attention of his chosen partner, who will tear it apart if the result is less than satisfactory, and so the process starts all over again.

All but 12 of the 113 described weaver species are resident on the African mainland or associated islands, with some 21 represented within Rwanda alone. All but five of the Rwandan species are placed in the genus *Ploceus* (true weavers), which is among the most characteristic of all African bird genera. Most of the *Ploceus* weavers are slightly larger than a sparrow, and display a strong sexual dimorphism. Females are with few exceptions drab buff or olive-brown birds, with some streaking on the back, and perhaps a hint of yellow on the belly.

Most male *Ploceus* weavers conform to the basic colour pattern of the 'masked weaver' – predominantly yellow, with streaky back and wings, and a distinct black facial mask, often bordered orange. Five Rwandan weaver species fit this masked weaver prototype more-or-less absolutely, and a similar number approximate it rather less exactly, for instance by having a chestnut-brown mask, or a full black head, or a black back, or being more chestnut than yellow on the belly. Identification of the masked weavers can be tricky without experience – useful clues are the exact shape of the mask, the presence and extent of the fringing orange, and the colour of the eye and the back.

The golden weavers, of which only one species is present in Rwanda, are also brilliant yellow and/or light orange with some light streaking on the back, but they lack a mask or any other strong distinguishing features. The handful of forest-associated *Ploceus* weavers, by contrast, tend to have quite different and very striking colour patterns; and, although sexually dimorphic, the female is often

(*07.30–08.30* & *09.00–10.00*) and two afternoon (*15.00–16.00* & *16.30–17.30*) outings for US$35 per person, but the 16.30 sunset trips cost US$45 per person. (Alternatively, hiring out the whole boat for an hour is US$180.) Trips are organised and paid for at the reception centre (m *078 618 2871*) when you enter the park, and may sell out at weekends.

GAME DRIVES Between the normal opening hours of 06.00 and 18.00, visitors can do their own game drives in whatever vehicle they used to get to the park. A vehicle with high clearance is mandatory (though a 4x4 is ideal), and guides are optionally available at US$25/40 per party per half/full day. In addition, daytime game drives in the southern part of the park can be organised in the park's game-viewing

as boldly marked as the male. The most aberrant among these is Vieillot's black weaver, the males of which are totally black except for their eyes, while the black-billed weaver reverses the prototype by being all black with a yellow facemask.

Among the more conspicuous *Ploceus* species in Rwanda are the black-headed, Baglafecht, slender-billed, yellow-backed and Vieillot's black weavers – for the most part gregarious breeders forming single- or mixed-species colonies of hundreds, sometimes thousands, of pairs. The most extensive weaver colonies are often found in reed beds and waterside vegetation, such as can be seen around the lakes of Akagera. Few weavers have a distinctive song, but they compensate with a rowdy jumble of harsh swizzles, rattles and nasal notes that can reach deafening proportions near large colonies. One more cohesive song you will often hear seasonally around weaver colonies is a cyclic 'dee-dee-dee-Diederik', often accelerating to a hysterical crescendo when several birds call at once. This is the call of the Diederik cuckoo, a handsome green-and-white cuckoo that lays its eggs in weaver nests.

Oddly, while most East African *Ploceus* weavers are common, even abundant, in suitable habitats, seven highly localised species are listed as range-restricted, and four of these – one Kenyan, one Ugandan and two Tanzanian endemics – are regarded to be of global conservation concern. Of the other three, the strange weaver *Ploceus alienus* – black head, plain olive back, yellow belly with chestnut bib – is an Albertine Rift Endemic restricted to a handful of sites in Rwanda and Uganda, notably Nyungwe National Park.

Most of the colonial weavers, perhaps relying on safety in numbers, build relatively plain nests with a roughly oval shape and an unadorned entrance hole. The nests of more solitary weavers are often more elaborate. Several weavers, for instance, protect their nests from egg-eating invaders by attaching tubular entrance tunnels to the base – in the case of the spectacled weaver, which inhabits riverine woodland in Akagera, this tunnel is sometimes twice as long as the nest itself. The Grosbeak weaver (a peculiar larger-than-average brown-and-white weaver of reed beds, distinguished by its outsized bill and placed in the monospecific genus *Amblyospiza*) constructs a large and distinctive domed nest, which is supported by a pair of reeds, and woven as precisely as the finest basketwork, with a neat raised entrance hole at the front. By contrast, the scruffiest nests are built by the various species of sparrow- and buffalo-weaver, relatively drab but highly gregarious dry-country birds which are poorly represented in Rwanda.

Akagera National Park   ACTIVITIES

11

vehicle, but they only have two, so these should be booked in advance (m *078 618 2871*) to avoid disappointment. The drives are booked by vehicle, not seat, so costs are US$180/280 for a half-/full-day game drive (*max 7 people*), and include vehicle, driver and a guide. (Solo travellers would be better off taking a night drive, which can be booked individually – page 322.) Pickup is from the park reception, either hotel, or any campsite except Mutumba.

Simplistically, the road network comprises two roughly parallel main roads that run northward from the main entrance gate. These are an eastern lowland route, which follows the lakes' western shores to the Kilala Plains in the far north, and a western highland route that passes through the Mutumba Hills *en route* to the northern Nyungwe Gate. The two main roads are connected by several shorter roads (mostly running east–west) that create a number of road loops of varying length running north from the main entrance gate, Akagera Game Lodge or Ruzizi Tented Lodge.

All these loops are quite lengthy, however, so those with only an hour or two might prefer to stick to one of two short drives: the Giraffe Area west of the main entrance gate; or the network of roads running along the eastern shores of lakes Ihema and Shakani. Another option is a full-day drive to the Mutumba Hills and far north, but be aware it's a 10–12-hour round trip from the south of the park. Alternatively, you could break the journey by camping at Mutumba, or simply do the 5–6-hour one-way trip up to Nyungwe Gate and exit there when you're done.

Giraffe Area This area of dense woodland can be explored along a 13km figure-of-eight loop road running west from the park reception. As the name suggests, giraffe are frequently seen in the area, but the relatively open plains between junctions 5, 6 and 40 are also often good for zebra, buffalo and various open-country antelope. A dam and series of seasonal pools here can also be worthwhile for plovers, ducks and other water-associated birds. Birders might also want to divert to the **Muyumbu Campsite**, shaded by fruiting trees that often host various barbets along with green wood-hoopoe, Meyer's parrot and many smaller acacia-associated species. Note that the Giraffe Area isn't advisable after heavy rain, since it is in a valley that often gets waterlogged so it's easy to get stuck!

Lakes Ihema and Shakani Starting from the entrance gate, a hilly 5km road through very thick scrub (where oribi, klipspringer and buffalo are often seen) leads to **Lake Ihema**. Today, Defassa waterbuck are common residents around Ihema, as are impala, olive baboon, vervet monkey and buffalo (the last with a reputation for aggression). You can get out of the car at the fishing camp and boat jetty, where you may see hippos and crocodiles, and are bound to encounter the ghoulish-looking marabou stork, various waterbirds, and the localised white-winged black chat that is resident.

Lake Ihema is a site of minor historical interest. It was here, on a humid and mosquito-plagued island near the eastern shore, that Henry Stanley, the first European to enter what is now Rwanda, set up camp on the night of 11 March 1876, only to turn back into what is now Tanzania the next day after being repulsed by the locals from the lake's western shore.

About 4km north of the main junction towards Lake Ihema or Ruzizi Tented Lodge, a road forks through more thick scrub to the small **Lake Shakani**, a scenic camping spot and home to large numbers of hippo. The bush here is rattling with birdlife (listen out for the jarring duet of the black-headed gonolek, a type of bush-shrike with a brilliant scarlet chest), and the rough track along the marshy western lakeshore is a good place to pick up the likes of African jacana, long-toed lapwing, open-billed stork, squacco heron and common moorhen. Mammals are less numerous, but you might well see impala, bushbuck and other grazers on the floodplains.

Rwisirabo Loop This 35km loop is the shortest to connect the eastern lakeshore road to the western highland road, and it makes for an excellent morning game drive, taking around 3 hours, depending on how often you stop. Starting at **Lake Ihema**, and diverting to Lake Shakani (see opposite), you then continue for another 8km north to **Lake Birengero,** a shallow, muddy body of palm-fringed water that supports huge numbers of waterbirds, notably pelicans and storks. It is also known for semi-regular shoebill sightings; try your luck by parking at one of the open areas on the western shore and scanning the papyrus beds opposite with binoculars.

At Junction 13, turn left on to a road that climbs northeast towards the Rwisirabo Ranger Post, where it's worth stopping to look for white-winged black chat and long-tailed cisticola. Then turn left again at Junction 23 to connect with the main highland road running back south to the park reception. Here you'll pass through lightly vegetated slopes that offer lovely views to the lakes below, and are often good for grassland antelope such as topi and oribi, as well as giraffe and buffalo.

Kitabili Loop This is a longer variation of the Rwisirabo Loop, about 70km in total, or 5 hours, and probably as far as you'd want to go on a day drive out of Akagera Game Lodge or Ruzizi Tented Lodge during the wet season. (With an early enough start in the dry season, you should be able to get up to the Mohana Plain – see below) It follows the same route as far as Lake Birengero, but instead of turning left at Junction 13, you continue straight ahead. From here it's about 15km to **Lake Hago**, passing turn-offs to the right for the **Kageyo** (34km) and **Nyampiki** (25km) peninsulas, both of which loop back to the main road and would make a diverting side trip with sufficient time. The Nyampiki Peninsula track follows Lake Hago's eastern shore, and is a fine spot to see elephant, as well as small herds of buffalo and zebra, and the lake must support several hundred hippo. Away from the lakeshore, the vegetation is mostly very dense, and animals are difficult to spot, though you can be reasonably confident of seeing baboons, vervet monkeys and impala. From here you continue north a short way to Junction 20, where you need to turn left along the road to Junction 21 at Kitabili, and keep bearing left at Junction 22. From here, you will follow the highland route back south to Rwisirabo and the park reception, mostly through open or lightly wooded grassland where topi, zebra and oribi are quite common.

The far north Game-drive options north of Kitabili are restricted by the area's remoteness from the cluster of accommodation near the main entrance gate. This is a shame, because the game viewing is generally far better than in the south. However, you could realistically travel from the lodge as far north as the Mohana Plain and back in a day. If you want to head further north than Mohana, save it for your last day in the park, and plan on exiting through the Nyungwe Gate west of Lake Rwanyakizinga. The tracks up here are now marked and are generally in decent shape, so while it's no longer critical to bring a guide along to avoid getting lost, if you want to bring one anyway, they can be dropped off in Kayonza after you exit (or at the road junction if you're headed north). Note that if you take a guide from south to north, it is automatically charged as a full day, even if you do the trip in half a day.

The **Mutumba Hills** are one of the most rewarding parts of the park. From Kitabili, you first ascend through an area of park-like woodland whose large acacias are favoured by giraffe. Eventually the woodland gives way to open grassland where you can be certain of seeing the delicate oribi and reedbuck, as well as the larger topi. With luck, you'll also encounter eland, zebra, roan antelope, and (in the wet season) large herds of buffalo.

North of the Mutumba Hills, the vegetation is again very thick, and animals can be difficult to spot, though impala, buffalo and zebra all seem to be present in significant numbers. The papyrus beds around **lakes Gishanju** and **Mihindi** form the most accessible marshy areas in the park, and are worth taking slowly by anybody who hopes to see papyrus-dwellers. Hippo Beach (or Plage Hippos) on Lake Mihindi is a pretty spot with appropriately reliable hippo sightings, and is one of three dedicated viewpoints/picnic spots (all marked on the map) where visitors are allowed to get out of their vehicles. (Note that the Mihindi picnic area has long-drop toilets and shaded benches, while the other two are unimproved; none is fenced.)

Heading further north, **Lake Rwanyakizinga** is another favoured spot with elephants, and the Mohanda Plains to the south of the lake are excellent for plains animals such as warthog, zebra and herds of 50-plus topi. The **Kilala Plains** northwest of the lake are equally good for plains animals and may even offer a wider panorama. Both Lake Rwanyakizinga and the Kilala Plains have viewpoint spots where you can get out of your car as well.

NIGHT DRIVES Organised night drives in an open-topped game-viewing vehicle are the only way to explore the park after 18.00, offering the best chance of seeing some of the most sought-after species. Leopard and hyena generally top the wish list, and are sometimes observed; more common nocturnals include the agile bushbaby and oddball elephant-shrew, along with small predators such as genet, civet and various mongooses as well as owls and nightjars. Night drives last about 2½ hours and start from 17.30: US$40 per person, with a minimum of two people.

OTHER ACTIVITIES All activities are bookable through the park's reception centre.

Behind-the-scenes tour (*US$25pp, min 4 guests*) Since the formation of Akagera Management Company a significant amount of work has been done in Akagera National Park, much of it not visible to the tourist's eye. This illuminating tour includes a presentation on the park and recent conservation efforts, as well as a visit to the park headquarters and an opportunity to meet the rangers and other staff integral to park management. Along the way, you'll also meet the park's canine rangers – five Belgian malinois, one Dutch shepherd, and two mixed breeds from just outside the park – who are being trained up to sniff out poachers in the park, along with some 100 endangered grey-crowned cranes, who have been given refuge in two fenced areas – one near the park headquarters and the other near the boat launch – after being surrendered by illegal pet owners as part of an ongoing amnesty. (More information can be found at ◼ *cranesrwanda*.)

Walk the line (*US$30/20 adult/child, min 3 participants*) Since Akagera's 120km western boundary was fenced in 2013, a team of rangers have been deployed every day to walk the entirety of the fence line and check for damage (intentional or otherwise). Though the walking path follows the outside of the fence, it's nonetheless a unique opportunity to see the park on foot, and animal sightings are not uncommon. The 7km morning walks begin at the entrance gate and finish atop a ridge with views to Lake Ihema.

Community cultural experiences (*US$30/20 adult/child, min 3 participants*) Led by the community freelance guides (**f** *ACOFREGCO*) who have all been recruited from the area and trained in the park, these half-day tours take you to surrounding villages – possibly even your guide's home – and offer a personal insight into a variety of local traditions and occupations. Depending on your interest, tours can explore local pastoralism (where you'll try your hand at milking a cow), traditional brewing and apiculture, *imigongo* art (where you'll have a chance to make your own artwork), as well as Rwandan cuisine, music and dance.

UPDATES WEBSITE

Go to **w** bradtupdates.com/rwanda for the latest on-the-ground travel news, trip reports and factual updates. Keep up to date with the latest posts by following Philip on Twitter (**y** *@philipbriggs*) and via Facebook (**f** *pb.travel. updates*). And, if you have any comments, queries, grumbles, insights, news or other feedback, you're invited to post them directly on the website, or to email them to Philip (**e** *philip.briggs@bradtguides.com*) for inclusion.

11

Experience the adventure of Virunga National Park

Virunga National Park is one of the jewels of Africa, home to some of the last of the world's critically endangered mountain gorillas and playing host to wide savannahs, lush forests and bubbling volcanoes. Experience the majesty of this stunning UNESCO World Heritage Site for yourself.

The park has a range of different accommodation options, including the newly constructed Kibumba Tented Camp, the perfect base for visiting Virunga's two most popular attractions – the mountain gorillas and Nyiragongo Volcano.

Tchegera Island also offers a peaceful lakeside retreat. Enjoy activities such as kayaking, or simply take in the breathtaking views of the surrounding landscape.

A visit to Virunga is truly a once-in-a lifetime experience; find out more at
www.visitvirunga.org

12

Virunga National Park and Eastern DRC

Sean Connolly and Philip Briggs

The second-largest country in Africa, the Democratic Republic of the Congo (DRC) extends over an area of 2,344,858km² running west from the Albertine Rift (where its long eastward border runs from northern Uganda via Rwanda and Burundi to southwest Tanzania) to the distant Atlantic coastline. Scarred by long years of poor governance and debilitating civil war, it is one of the continent's least-visited countries, yet also one of its most intriguing.

The DRC is arguably the most biodiverse country in Africa, best known for the green swathes of rainforest associated with the vast Congo River Basin, but also home to the western slopes of the immense Ruwenzori and Virunga mountains, both of which are protected in Virunga National Park. And while political instability has left much of the DRC off-limits to visitors, Virunga National Park formally reopened in 2009, following the signature of a management agreement between the Institut Congolais pour la Conservation de la Nature (ICCN) and the Africa Conservation Fund (ACF) (today known as the Virunga Foundation), a dynamic British-based organisation funded mainly by the EU.

Of the 3,000-odd adventurers who visited Virunga National Park over the course of 2015, more than 80% did so as an excursion from Rwanda or Uganda. Partly this is because Virunga National Park offers much cheaper gorilla tracking than either of its neighbours (not to mention a far better chance of obtaining a permit at short notice), as well as the opportunity to hike to the rim of Nyiragongo, an active volcano whose immense crater contains the world's largest lava lake. Partly it is simply because travel from elsewhere in the DRC is so logistically challenging. As a result, Virunga National Park seems likely to function as an extension of the travel circuit through Rwanda and Uganda for the foreseeable future.

THE DRC IN BRIEF

Capital Kinshasa, more than 1,500km west of Goma as the crow flies
Population 80 million
International dialling code +243
Time zone GMT+2 in the east (the same as Rwanda)
Currency The Congolese franc was trading at around Cfr1,600 to the US dollar in early 2018 (which means that Rfr1 equals roughly Cfr1.9). In practice, most items and services likely to be bought by tourists are priced and can be paid for in US dollars, although small change is often given in local currency.
Language The official language is French. Other officially recognised national languages are KiSwahili, Lingala, Kikongo and Tshiluba.

Mirroring Goma and Virunga, at the southern end of the lake (and also most easily accessed from Rwanda) the city of Bukavu and nearby Kahuzi-Biega National Park sit adjacent to the Rwandan border at Rusizi/Cyangugu. Kahuzi-Biega is the only place in the world to track the eastern lowland or Grauer's gorilla, and would make a compelling addition to any Virunga itinerary, or an eminently worthwhile standalone excursion. Even further off the beaten track, the remarkably isolated Idjwi – the tenth-largest lake island in the world – is accessible by daily boats from Goma and Bukavu. It's now entirely feasible to enter the DRC at either Goma or Bukavu, visit one or both of the national parks, and exit back to Rwanda from the other side of the lake after a fast ferry ride between the aforementioned cities.

Note it is customary to refer to the DRC by its full name, or the acronym, in order to distinguish it from the similarly named Congo Republic. Having clarified that, in the rest of this chapter we refer to it simply as the Congo.

ENTRANCE AND BORDER FORMALITIES

All visitors require a valid passport, visa, and yellow-fever certificate to enter the Congo. With the exception of visas arranged along with a booking at Virunga National Park as detailed below (or through Kahuzi-Biega – page 342), Congolese visas **must** be arranged in advance at (and only at) the Congolese embassy *in your home country and/or country of residence* (or a neighbouring country if these don't have an embassy), and this can be quite a complicated and costly process (the embassy in the UK, for instance (w *ambardc.london*) will require you to produce a letter of invitation certified by the Ministry of Foreign Affairs in Kinshasa. Embassies differ, however, and at others (we've had success in Berlin) a confirmed booking at Virunga may be enough.

Thus, unless you have a valid Rwandan residence permit, you will **not** be able to purchase a Congolese visa at the embassy in Kigali. And if you *do* have a valid Rwandan residence permit, rather than applying to the Congo, it's cheaper and easier to apply through Rwandan immigration for a Communauté Économique des Pays des Grands Lacs (CEPGL) visa, which gets you three months of multiple-entry access to both the Congo and Burundi for an unbelievable US$10. (More information on the CEPGL visa is available at w migration.gov.rw/index.php?id=66 and w livinginkigali. com/information/new-arrivals/applying-for-your-cepgl-burundi-drc-congo.)

For tourists, a better option, assuming you are not exploring deeper into the Congo (Bukavu is fine), is to buy a 14-day single-entry visa in advance through Virunga National Park's website (w *visitvirunga.org/visa*) or an affiliated tour operator. This can be arranged only in conjunction with the purchase of a permit to track gorillas in Virunga National Park, to climb Nyiragongo, or with a booking

PRICES IN THE DRC

Many things in DRC are a lot more expensive than on the other side of the border. Here's a rough idea of the kind of prices you can expect:

1.5l bottle of water Cfr1,500
1GB mobile data US$10
Large local beer Cfr2,500
Local buffet meal Cfr4,000–8,000
Sit-down restaurant meal US$10–20
En-suite hotel room US$40–60

at Mikeno Lodge. The visa currently costs US$105 (payable with a credit card or PayPal), requires two weeks to process, and will be delivered to you by email. All you need to do then is print it and present it at either the Grande Barrière (corniche), Goma airport, or Bunagana border crossings, and you should be able to enter the Congo in 15–30 minutes. Note that the letter won't be accepted at other borders. If you plan to enter the Congo at Bukavu, see page 342.

If you plan to visit the Congo as a return trip out of Rwanda, be sure to have US$30 ready to purchase another Rwandan visa upon your return.

SECURITY

The Congo as a whole remains volatile. Rebel activity forced Virunga National Park to close to tourism in May 2012 and, while a peace agreement was reached at the end of 2013, tourist facilities in the south only resumed full operation in late 2014, and the northern and central areas remain unambiguously unstable. As of late 2017, Goma, Bukavu, Idjwi, Kahuzi-Biega National Park and the southern sector of Virunga National Park (where nearly all tourism activity takes place) were considered to be reasonably safe, and visited by the updater of this book. It would, however, be misleading to make glib reassurances about future security, especially in the light of two subsequent ambushes that took place in Virunga National Park. In April 2018, the park suffered its deadliest attack yet when five rangers and a driver were ambushed and murdered in central Virunga. And in May 2018, a vehicle carrying tourists was ambushed about 10km north of Goma; one ranger was killed in the incident, and two British tourists and their driver were kidnapped, to be released unharmed two days later. In the wake of this second incident, park management announced the suspension of tourism at least until the end of 2018. The park is nevertheless likely to reopen during the lifetime of this edition, so check our updates website for the latest news (w *bradtupdates.com/rwanda*).

Most government travel advisories explicitly warn against visiting the Congo. As of May 2018, for instance, the British FCO website warns 'against all travel' to North and South Kivu (among numerous other provinces). The only exceptions to this are the towns of Bukavu and Goma, to which the FCO advise against 'all but essential travel'. Even if you choose to disregard such advice as overly conservative, be aware that a government warning of this sort will negate most travel insurance policies. And even given the current relative stability, it would be incautious to venture beyond Goma, Bukavu, Idjwi and those parts of Virunga and Kahuzi-Biega national parks that are formally open to tourism.

GOMA

Capital of the volatile province of Nord-Kivu, Goma lies on the north shore of Lake Kivu bordering the practically contiguous Rwandan port of Rubavu/Gisenyi. With a population currently estimated at anything from 400,000 to one million, Goma is much larger than Rubavu (or, for that matter, any Rwandan centre other than Kigali) and it has always enjoyed a reputation as a livelier and more colourful town, particularly when it comes to bar culture and nightlife. Goma is also the urban gateway for travellers heading to the nearby southern sector of Virunga National Park, home to the Congolese population of mountain gorillas and site of the spectacular volcano Nyiragongo, which dominates the town's northern skyline in clear weather.

Over the past 25 years, Goma has been blighted by a succession of natural and political crises. In July 1994, Nord-Kivu Province received an influx of around one million refugees from Rwanda; this led to an acute food and water shortage, and a cholera outbreak that claimed thousands of lives. Natural disaster struck in January 2002, when Nyiragongo erupted, and a 1km-wide river of lava steamrolled the city centre, destroying more than 4,500 buildings and forcing most of the human population into temporary exile in and around Rubavu.

GOMA

For listings, see pages 331–3

🛏 Where to stay
1	Centre d'Accueil Bienheureux Isidore Bakanja	A1
2	Centre d'Accueil Caritas	B7
3	Eclipse	C5
4	Hotel Bassin du Congo	D5
5	Hotel des Grands Lacs	B3
6	Hotel la Versailles	C1
7	Ihusi	C7
8	Linda	A5
9	Planet	C7
10	Shu-Shu Guest House	D5
11	Tony Guest House	C3

Off map
	Lac Kivu Lodge	B1

❌ Where to eat and drink
12	Au Bon Pain	B1
13	Deo's Café	D3
14	Lapa	B4
15	Petit Brussels	C3
16	Salt & Pepper	B2, C2

Off map
	Chez Leontine (Maghali Fan Club)	A1
	Le Chalet	B1
	Nyumbani Lounge & Café	B1

Goma has frequently been a focal point of the protracted Congolese civil war, which was initiated by a coup in 1997 and has since reputedly claimed some five million civilian lives, more than any other conflict since World War II. Since then, the town has witnessed a series of conflagrations, including clashes between the UN-backed Congolese army and the Congrès National pour la Défense du Peuple (CNDP) rebel movement led by the Tutsi general Laurent Nkunda in October 2008, which saw unknown thousands of casualties, and some 250,000 civilians forced to flee their homes. Despite several calls for ceasefires, the fighting continued intermittently until 22 January 2009 when Nkunda was arrested after crossing into Rwanda, where he remains under lock and key to this day.

Most recently, the rebel Mouvement du 23-Mars (M23) was formed in April 2012 when former CNDP solders, who had been integrated into the Congolese army after the 23 March 2009 peace accords (from which M23 took its name), mutinied under the leadership of Bosco Ntaganda. The rest of the year saw sporadic attacks throughout North Kivu Province, culminating in the seizure of Goma by M23 forces on 20 November 2012. They withdrew from the city some days later on 1 December, and intense military and political pressure saw Ntaganda turn himself in to the US embassy in Kigali on 20 November 2012, from where he was subsequently transferred to the International Criminal Court (ICC) in The Hague. M23's fortunes continued to decline, and it ceased to exist as a movement with the surrender of Ntaganda's replacement, Sultani Makenga and his remaining troops in November 2013. Ntaganda's ICC trial, on charges of war crimes and crimes against humanity, began in September 2015.

Considering its turbulent recent past, Goma today has a surprisingly agreeable and vibrant atmosphere. Solidified flows of craggy black lava rock still lie beside some of the roads, but most of the town has been cleared and rebuilt (though one

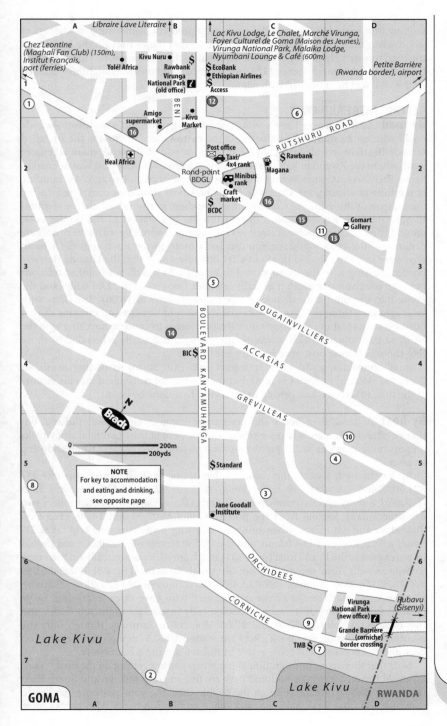

GOMA

Lake Kivu

Lake Kivu

RWANDA

A — Libraire Lave Literaire ↑ **B**

Lac Kivu Lodge, Le Chalet, Marché Virunga,
Foyer Culturel de Goma (Maison des Jeunes),
Virunga National Park, Malaika Lodge,
Nyumbani Lounge & Café (600m)

Chez Leontine
(Maghali Fan Club) (150m),
Institut Français,
port (ferries)

Petite Barrière
(Rwanda border), airport

Kivu Nuru ●

Yolé! Africa ●

Rawbank $

● EcoBank
● Ethiopian Airlines
$ Access

Virunga
National Park
(old office)

Amigo
supermarket

Kivu
Market

Heal Africa

Post office
✉ ≡ Taxi/
      4x4 rank

Rawbank $

Magana

Rond-point
BDGL

Minibus
rank

Craft
market

$ Rawbank

BCDC $

Gomart
Gallery

BOULEVARD KANYAMUHANGA

BOUGAINVILLIERS

ACCASIAS

BIC $

GREVILLEAS

Bradt

N

0   200m
0   200yds

$ Standard

NOTE
For key to accommodation
and eating and drinking,
see opposite page

Jane Goodall
Institute

ORCHIDEES

CORNICHE

Virunga
National Park
(new office)

Rubavu
(Gisenyi)

Grande Barrière
(corniche)
border crossing

TMB $

RUTSHURU ROAD

BENI

striking informal monument to the eruption, a group of planes trapped where they stood when the lava flowed through, can be seen at the airport on the left side of the road towards Nyiragongo and the national park). Furthermore, Goma has also been reasonably peaceful since M23's withdrawal – and the lively nightlife curtailed by the civil war has resumed with vigour.

GETTING THERE AND AWAY

By road Assuming you have a visa (page 326), getting to Goma from Rwanda could scarcely be more straightforward. The easiest place to cross is the so-called Grande Barrière (corniche) [329 D7] at the west end of Rubavu's main lakeshore road, where the Rwandan half of a shiny new integrated border post was opened in September 2017. (Congo immigration was still operating out of an older building at the time of writing, but their side of the new post should be completed during the lifespan of this edition.) Coming from elsewhere in Rwanda, there are plentiful minibus-taxis to Rubavu, and a moto from the bus station to the border costs around Rfr400. Once you've crossed to Goma, several hotels lie within easy walking distance of the border post, or you can get a moto to the town centre. (A moto anywhere in Goma should be about Cfr1,000.) Be aware that the Grande Barrière border crossing is in theory supposed to be open 24 hours, but political tensions between the countries mean it actually operates from 06.00 to 22.00 daily (and the Petite Barrière on the north side of town always closes at 18.00). Travellers with visas arranged through Virunga National Park would be better off crossing during business hours just in case Congo immigration needs to confirm anything with the Virunga park office (which, conveniently enough, is actually scheduled to move into the new border post once it's complete).

Road connections and some transport does exist to towns further north, ie: Butembo (310km) or Beni (365km), but these were not considered safe for visitors at the time of writing, and getting to Bukavu is best done by boat.

By boat A handful of boats and companies connect Goma and Bukavu, but they're often in dangerously poor repair – there were at least two fatal shipwrecks on government ferries in 2014 alone – so it pays to be circumspect when choosing a vessel.

By far the best, fastest, and most reliable option is **Ihusi Express** (m *099 481 3235/097 464 5680/081 838 2590 (Goma), 099 423 4071/882 1195, 081 398 2333 (Bukavu);* e *ihusiexpress@gmail.com;* w *iexpress.ihusigroup.com*), which offers two departures daily, leaving from the port in Goma at 07.30 and 14.30, except on Thursdays and Saturdays, when only the morning boats run. The trip takes 2½ hours with a stop on Idjwi Island, and the US$50 tickets often sell out and should be purchased at the Ihusi Hotel (page 331) in advance (or theoretically on their new website as well). Your second-best option is with **Emmanuel** (m *081 170 2600, 099 440 7879/776 4897 (Goma), 099 052 4957/081 170 0993/082 272 2513 (Bukavu);* e *bateauxsil@gmail.com;* w *silimu-system.com*), who have three multi-deck boats (at least one of which features a chronologically insouciant nightclub deck), and two departures daily at 07.00 and 17.00 Monday to Saturday, though only the evening boat runs on Fridays. Tickets are around US$25 (though this depends on deck and ticket class), and boats arrive in Bukavu around 6 hours later.

Note that there is an immigration check when you are getting on the boat – visas arranged through Virunga National Park are fine to go to Bukavu and South Kivu (assuming they're in date), though the people checking your passport may try to convince you otherwise; have the park office number on hand. Also know where you're planning to stay in Bukavu and relevant details of your itinerary, as you may be asked for them.

By air It's now possible to fly directly into Goma from Addis Ababa with **Ethiopian Airlines** [329 B1](w *flyethiopian.com*) four-times weekly, which opens up the possibility of an open-jaw itinerary for visitors to Rwanda and Goma/Virunga, eliminating the need to backtrack to Kigali for a return flight.

For travel further into the Congo, you've now got a few options. Congo's new national carrier, **Congo Airways** (*Av Vanny Bisheweka 20 at Bd Kanyamuhanga*; m *082 978 1924*; e *contact@congoairways.com*; w *congoairways.com*), was launched in 2015 and now connects Goma to Kinshasa, Bunia, Kisangani, Kindu, Kalemie and Lubumbashi. The longer-serving, but perhaps less-reliable, **Compagnie Africaine d'Aviation (CAA)** (*35/2, Bd Kanyamuhanga*; m *082 000 2776/099 590 3831*; e *goma.escale@caacongo.com*; w *caacongo.com*) runs regular flights from Goma to Kinshasa, Beni and Bunia, though do be aware that they have a chequered safety record. Finally, the smaller **Busy Bee Congo** (*8 Av des Grevellias, Quartier les Volcans*; m *081 170 0117/446 8300, 099 772 3259/862 4267*; e *contact@busybeecongo.com*; w *busybeecongo.com*) runs scheduled services to Butembo, Beni, and Bunia, with customisable charters available throughout the east of the country.

There's a US$10 departure tax for domestic flights and US$50 for international; these may or may not be incorporated into the cost of your ticket – ask when booking.

WHERE TO STAY There is no shortage of accommodation in Goma, though prices are higher than you'll be used to coming from Rwanda. A few reliable options are listed below, but there are plenty more to choose from, and further recommendations can be obtained from the Virunga National Park office or the thoroughly informative Living in Goma website (w *livingingoma.com*), whose founder, Timo Mueller, was an indispensable resource in putting together this chapter.

Upmarket

Ihusi Hotel [329 C7] (75 rooms) m 081 312 9560/353 2300, 099 377 3396; e ihusihotel@ yahoo.fr/ihusihotel@ihusigroup.com; w hotels. ihusigroup.com. Boasting a pretty lakeshore location on Bd Kanyamuhanga only 100m or so from the border post, this is about the smartest hotel in Goma, & a popular rendezvous for NGO workers & other foreigners. The large grounds offer great views over the lake, there is a good restaurant, & facilities include a swimming pool, tennis courts, gym, Wi-Fi, & satellite TV in all rooms. *US$81–93 sgl room; US$104/116 standard sgl/dbl; US$128/139 sgl/dbl VIP; apts & suites from US$174; all rates B&B.*

Lac Kivu Lodge [329 B1] (26 rooms) m 097 183 9028/186 8749, 081 151 0760; e booking@congo-lodge.com; w lackivulodge. com. About 5km northwest of central Goma on Av de la Paix, this tranquil lakeside retreat is almost certainly the most scenic accommodation in town, & an excellent choice if you want to put some distance between yourself & the hubbub of the city centre. The grounds are overflowing with greenery, & the standard rooms come with private terrace, canopy bed, flatscreen TV, espresso machine, & a view over the garden or lake. There's a swimming pool, lakefront restaurant & bar, & a good feel about the place overall. The pool is for guests only, but non-guests can swim in the lake here for the price of a drink at the bar. *US$70/84 economy sgl/ dbl; US$137/163 standard sgl/dbl; US$158/188 newly renovated standard sgl/dbl; US$215 deluxe dbl; US$265 suite; all rates B&B.*

Moderate

✳ Centre d'Accueil Caritas [329 B7] (35 rooms) m 081 067 9199/099 539 5303; e guesthousecaritas@yahoo.fr; w guesthousecaritas.org. A few hundred metres west of the Ihusi Hotel, this reliable waterfront option is associated with the Catholic Church & its positively charitable room rates may not quite be the cheapest, but probably represent the best value for money in town. The en-suite rooms, many of which come with private terraces, are simple & well kept, & the carefully manicured grounds are a fine spot for a meal or a drink. Wi-Fi. *US$40/50/60 sgl depending on size; US$50/75/90 dbl depending on size; all rates B&B.*

🏠 **Hotel des Grands Lacs** [329 B3] (18 rooms) m 099 760 3103/084 057 3717. This faded colonial relict, on Bd Kanyamuhanga just south of the main roundabout, is stronger on character than facilities or cleanliness, though recent renovations mean it's looking sharper than it has for a long time. Decent value. From *US$50 dbl B&B.*

🏠 **Linda Hotel** [329 A5] (65 rooms) m 099 548 7783/081 247 6084; e lindahotel@ yahoo.fr; w lindahotelgoma.com. Set along the lakeshore about 1km west of the border, this is another reliable & seemingly well-managed mid-range option with en-suite rooms in a variety of configurations from single rooms to apartments. There's a swimming pool, restaurant, & garden seating overlooking the lake. *US$60–120 dbl B&B.*

🏠 **Planet Hotel** [329 C7] (39 rooms) m 099 986 9903/070 1284/346 4644; e planethotelg18@yahoo.fr. Though it's not on the level of the Ihusi across the street, it's modern enough & the prices are considerably lower as well. All rooms come with hot water & Wi-Fi, & some have balconies as well. There's a resto-bar in front serving the usual variety of meals for around US$10. *US$60/80 sgl/dbl.*

Budget

🏠 **Centre d'Accueil Bienheureux Isidore Bakanja** [329 A1] (11 rooms) m 097 160 3918; w cabakanja.e-monsite.com. Centrally located about 400m from the Rond-Point BDGL, this Diocese of Goma-affiliated guesthouse is a find for the indecisive, offering clean tiled rooms with Wi-Fi, TV, hot water & canopy beds with mosquito nets. The resto-bar at the back sits in a green & geometrically hedgerowed garden, serving

Congolese meals at around Cfr8,000–16,000. *US$40–50 en-suite dbl.*

🏠 **Eclipse** [329 C5] (3 rooms) m 097 595 4442. A couple of blocks off Bd Kanyamuhanga, this is essentially a converted residence with a handful of large, cosy rooms, all of which have TV, mosquito nets, en-suite bath & tiled floors. The gardens out front are a comfortable spot to sit with a drink, & the friendly manager can arrange meals on request. *US$40 dbl.*

🏠 **Hotel Bassin du Congo** [329 D5] (31 rooms) m 099 786 0671/082 942 0746. The compound here feels a bit hodgepodge & institutional (wonky animal statuary & all), but the rates are good by Goma standards & the unremarkable en-suite rooms seem reasonably cared for. *US$35 budget dbl; US$45 standard dbl.*

🏠 **Hotel la Versailles** [329 C1] (12 rooms) m 099 701 5808/085 924 9901. Situated on Av Idjwi about 200m northeast of Rond-Point BDGL, this is a decent budget hotel with clean en-suite rooms, Wi-Fi, & a fair restaurant attached. *US$30/50 sgl/dbl.*

🏠 **Shu-Shu Guest House** [329 D5] (8 rooms) m 099 914 9766. In a simple compound on Av des Grevilleas, directly opposite the Hotel Bassin du Congo, the rooms here come in a long block using shared ablutions & are just about the cheapest in town. They're reasonably clean, come with mozzie nets, & are quite acceptable for the price (in Goma, that is). *US$20 dbl.*

🏠 **Tony Guest House** [329 C3] (40 rooms) m 097 440 4525/081 806 8093; e tonyguesthouse@yahoo.com. In a bright green compound clearly signposted about 100m east of Petit Brussels, the no-nonsense rooms here are centrally located & budget-friendly, & as such are often booked up long-term by traders & other folks with business in Goma. All come with fans & nets, & they've recently opened a restaurant with simple grills & other meals from US$3–7. Wi-Fi is available. *US$25 dbl using shared ablutions; US$30–35 en-suite dbl; US$50 deluxe en-suite dbl; all rates B&B & negotiable.*

✖️ **WHERE TO EAT AND DRINK** Goma is known for its lively nightlife, which has resumed in full force since the civil war ended. Most of the hotels listed previously all serve adequate to good food, but there are also plenty of standalone restaurants, bars and nightclubs worth exploring. A few recommendations:

✖️ **Au Bon Pain** [329 B1] m 082 371 7625/097 062 3824; ⏰ 07.00–19.00 Mon–Sat,

10.00–15.00 Sun. Not many restaurants can claim to have made the international press when they opened, but it's not every day that an upscale *boulangerie-patisserie* opens in eastern Congo, either. On the 1st floor with a balcony overlooking Bd Kanyamuhanga, this new café has the best perch in town for watching Goma whizz by, & the excellent pastries, croissants, coffee, & Wi-Fi seal the already-impressive deal. The menu also covers soups, salads & sandwiches for US$5–10, along with meat & pasta mains from US$10–15.

✖ **Chez Leontine (Maghali Fan Club)** [329 A1] m 097 366 6302; ◷ noon–20.00 Mon–Sat. The heaping & hugely popular buffet here has a new location, but is still piled just as high with a mouthwatering variety of Congolese cuisine, including meat, fish & chicken, as well as sauces with veggies, peas & greens, & all served alongside rice, potatoes, cassava, or matoke (bananas). A vegetarian helping will cost you under US$3, & meat will bring you up to around US$5.

✖ **Deo's Café** [329 D3] m 099 445 2437; ◷ 07.00–late daily. Feel the vibes at this chilled-out coffee shop & gallery, where you can get a good cup of coffee & check your email during the day & get loose to the reggae sound system or live music by night. They also do a good menu of salads, sandwiches & pizzas for US$5–10.

✖ **Lapa** [329 B4] m 084 709 7970/089 717 3367/099 786 8000/082 222 7246; ☐ Goma Lapa; ◷ 11.00–late Tue–Sun. Known among Gomatraciens as quite possibly the most beautiful restaurant in town, this breezy & stylish address is known for its long list of signature cocktails (*US$7*) & themed nights throughout the month (including jazz fusion, Brazilian dance, pub quiz, & more – check their Facebook for the latest). There's indoor/outdoor seating on a wide wooden terrace & a menu of pizzas, grills, pasta, & a rotating *plat du jour* for US$7–15.

✖ **Le Chalet** [329 B1] m 081 945 0284/315 0000; ☐ Le Petit Chalet. Set in pretty lakeshore

gardens about 5km west of the town centre, this popular upmarket eatery is known for its Wed evening buffets & excellent pizzas, but it also serves a good daily selection of continental meat & fish dishes. There's Wi-Fi & a well-attended Sun brunch, & it's also home to Kayak Kivu, should you fancy getting out on the water. Their new café, Le Petit Chalet, opened here in 2017 & serves a healthy variety of salads & fresh juices. *Mains from US$10.*

✖ **Nyumbani Lounge & Café** [329 B1] m 084 119 3478; ◷ 08.00–midnight daily. Set in a new location on Av Mont Goma about 500m west of Rond-Point Chukudu, the creative menu here covers a range of continental dishes, pizzas & more (foie gras with caramelised mango, anyone?) from around US$15, & it's a reliable bet for coffee, pastries, sandwiches, & Wi-Fi as well. There's also a long menu of cocktails & shisha pipes to keep you entertained in the evenings. It's probably the slickest address in town, & is reliably packed with Gomatraciens & expats alike, seeing & being seen.

✖ **Petit Brussels** [329 C3] m 099 757 2666/085 087 1614; ◷ 10.00–23.30 Mon–Sat. This lively restaurant near the main rond-point specialises in Belgian & continental cuisine, & there's a rotating menu of specials chalked up out front that included *fondue bourguignonne*, *ossobuco* & *saucisson fraîche* when we checked in. They also do very good pizzas & host both live music & karaoke on Thu nights. *Mains in the US$12–17 range.*

✖ **Salt & Pepper** [329 C2] m 097 863 8240/099 709 7316; ◷ 10.00–midnight daily. Situated almost next door to Petit Brussels, this long-serving favourite produces perhaps the best Chinese & Indian food in town, & they've got a good range of vegetarian options as well. There's a buffet from 12.30 to 15.00 every Mon, Wed & Fri. Rather confusingly, there's now a second location just a few blocks away on the other side of the roundabout [329 B1]. *Mains US$4–10.*

OTHER PRACTICALITIES

Tourist information The booking office for Virunga National Park [329 B1] (m *099 171 5401*; e *visit@virunga.org*; w *visitvirunga.org*; ◷ *08.30–17.00 Mon–Fri, 08.00–noon Sat*), on Boulevard Kanyamuhanga, north of the Rond-Point BDGL and right next to a large Airtel office, is the place for independent travellers to arrange or collect pre-booked gorilla-tracking and other park permits. The efficient staff here can also arrange transport to the park's various attractions at fixed rates, advise on accommodation, and offer assistance with most other queries relating to tourism in and around Goma. Note that this office is scheduled to move into the Congolese side of the new Grande Barrière (corniche) border post before the end of 2018 [329 D7].

Tour operators There are quite a few in Goma, all specialising in tourism to Virunga National Park, but the following are specifically recommended:

Amani Safaris m 099 066 1474 (DRC), 078 468 5285 (Rwanda); e info@amanisafaris-congo.com; w amanisafaris-congo.com
Go Congo m 081 183 7010/099 816 2331; e info@gocongo.com; w gocongo.com
Kasitu Eco-Tours m 099 772 8103/885 8405; e ecotourskasitu@yahoo.com; w kasituecotours.com

Kivu Travel m 081 313 5608; e info@kivutravel. com; w kivutravel.com
Okapi Tours m 082 556 6810 (DRC), 078 358 9405 (Rwanda); e okapitoursandtravelcompany@ gmail.com/emmanuelrufubya@yahoo.fr; w okapitoursandtravel.org. See ad, page 190.

Shopping For those climbing Nyiragongo Volcano or visiting other attractions in Virunga National Park on a self-catering basis, the best supermarket is **Amigo** (formerly Shoppers) [329 B2] near Rond-Point BDGL, which has a good selection of packaged goods, along with meats, cheeses and alcoholic drinks. The bookshop **Librairie Lave Littéraire** [329 B1] (m *099 413 3614;* e *librairie.lave.litteraire@ gmail.com*) on Avenue Beni has a useful stock of books (including Bradt guides!), newspapers, magazines, cards, maps, etc. It's under the same ownership as the Ikirezi in Kigali (w *ikirezi.biz*).

If you're a fan of markets, **Marché Virunga** [329 B1] is just over 2km north of the Rond-Point BDGL, near the recently rebuilt Cathédrale Saint-Joseph. The market is by far the biggest in town: expect non-stop, multi-sensory stimuli, and thousands of people wheeling and dealing on everything from potatoes to padlocks. Keep a close eye on your valuables here – better yet, don't bring any.

At the other end of the shopping spectrum and one of the best spots in town for soigné souvenirs, the **Kivu Nuru** [329 B1] boutique (m *099 550 2550/081 261 7401;* e *kivunuru@gmail.com;* w *kivunuru.com*) near Librairie Lave Littéraire on Avenue Beni does a super-stylish range of African-inspired clothing, jewellery and accessories.

Masks and other carvings can be purchased at the surprisingly good **craft market** [329 C2] facing the taxi rank at Rond-Point BDGL or in front of the Ihusi Hotel [329 C7] (usually at inflated prices).

Banks and foreign exchange The economy in Goma is almost entirely dollarised – international Visa and Mastercard can be used to withdraw US dollars from numerous ATMs dotted around Goma, including one at the Ihusi Hotel (Trust Merchant Bank) [329 C7], Standard Bank further up Boulevard Kanyamuhanga, and the Rawbank, Access Bank, FiBank, and EcoBank branches found within a block or two of the Rond-Point BDGL [329 B2]. Note that ATMs generally, but not always, dispense large bills (ie: US$100 or US$50), so getting change can be a problem if you want to buy something small, though Amigo Supermarket is used to accepting big notes, and some of the hotels can also change them. Rawbank ATMs can also dispense Congolese francs, should you want them. We've had reports of ATMs denying a withdrawal but debiting the account regardless – check your accounts after the fact should you have a transaction rejected.

Moneychangers on the street will exchange US dollars for Congolese francs at current rates; they can usually be located in front of the old Virunga National Park office [329 B1] or near the Grande Barrière border crossing. As in Rwanda, the Congolese are very strict about what bills they accept: anything printed before the year 2009 will be rejected, as will notes with any rips or tears on them.

Cultural centres No matter what calamity befalls Goma, the indefatigable cultural scene seems to be among the first things to bounce back. Today there are several admirable cultural centres and festivals in the city and, given the hardships the city has suffered, the cultural calendar puts a number of cities around the continent to shame.

A good place to start is **Yolé! Africa** [329 A1] (*Av Pelican 8;* m *099 712 3055/082 020 7799;* w *yoleafrica.org;* f), which puts on weekly film screenings on Saturday afternoons at 16.00, along with dance competitions on the last Saturday of the month and a variety of other cultural programming in between – check their website for the latest. They're also involved with presenting the week-long Salaam Kivu International Film Festival every July. The **Foyer Culturel de Goma (Maison des Jeunes)** [329 B1] (*2 Av du Collège;* m *099 392 0998;* f) is another nucleus of *Gomatracien* culture, and offers lessons in music, art and theatre, in addition to regular concerts and poetry events. They also organised the first Amani Festival (w *amanifestival.com*) in 2014, which featured African superstars like Tiken Jah Fakoly as well as Congolese acts including the Goma-based Will'Stone and Bill Clinton Kalonji; the fifth edition took place in February 2018.

The biggest hub for contemporary art in the city is the new **Gomart Gallery** [329 D3] (m *097 072 1121;* e *gomartgallery@gmail.com;* f), based at Deo's Café (page 333), where a rotating schedule of exhibitions, concerts and stand-up comedy means that there's inevitably something to drop in and see. Another new address of note is the **Institut Français** [329 A1] (*171 Av des Ronds-Points, Quartier les Volcans;* m *084 119 3478/097 089 2960;* w *institutfrancaisgoma.org*), which opened here in April 2017 and is worth a look for their active calendar of cultural events and courses.

Sport Go to w *livingingoma.com/sports* for a full breakdown of the Goma sporting scene. The website covers everything from salsa to saunas, but for the casual visitor it's worth mentioning a few possibilities to get active without having to go too far outside the city.

Based at Le Chalet restaurant, **Kayak Kivu** [329 B1] (m *099 062 2714/433 9147, 081 365 1131;* e *flyboymikey@gmail.com;* f) rents out kayaks on the lake for US$15/20 per hour for a single/double kayak, or US$55/68 for the whole day; they can arrange overnight trips around the lake as well. To **swim**, the pier at Lac Kivu Lodge is a good bet, where you can splash in the lake all you like if you're drinking at the bar. Otherwise, the Ihusi Hotel has a swimming pool non-guests can use for a rather steep US$10. **Tennis** is also available at the Ihusi for a similar fee.

Perhaps the most unexpected offering in the area is the dramatically located **Malaika Lodge** [329 B1] (m *085 862 4594/099 778 0694/ 097 106 4311/081 2139121;* f *Malaika Lodge Mushaki*), where **horseriding** is available at US$20 per hour, as well as fine accommodation at US$50 per person B&B. It's set in Mushaki Village, 40km from town in the hills west of Sake.

One of Africa's most biodiverse conservation areas, the 7,900km² Virunga National Park runs for more than 300km along the border with Rwanda and Uganda. It protects the entire Congolese portion of the Virunga Volcanoes, Ruwenzori Mountains and Lake Edward, and habitat range encompassing glacial peaks, Afromontane moorland, high-altitude forest, lowland rainforest, and open savannah. It is Africa's richest protected area in terms of avian diversity, with an astonishing 706 bird species recorded (more than in the whole of Rwanda), including several Congolese or Albertine Rift Endemics. A checklist of 208 mammal species contains 23 primates (including mountain gorilla, eastern lowland gorilla, and common chimpanzee) along with Congolese endemics such as the okapi (a rather bizarre striped, horse-sized relative of the giraffe) and typical savannah-dwellers such as lion, elephant and buffalo.

Virunga National Park was established in 1925, and inscribed as an IUCN World Heritage Site in 1979. In its original incarnation as the Albert National Park, it extended over just 200km², centred on the Virunga Mountains, but a series of boundary extensions over the next ten years meant it had more-or-less taken its modern shape by 1935. Since then, it has alternated between periods of conservation priority and high tourist volumes (notably during the late colonial era and over the 1970s and early 1980s) and periods of almost total neglect and abandonment. In 2010, after decades of being near-ungovernable, the park enjoyed an upsurge in fortune, one that saw the resumption of formal volcano climbs, and of gorilla and chimp tracking, as well as the opening of a new upmarket lodge and tented camp in 2011. Sadly, hostilities in the region meant tourism at the park once again ground to a halt in 2012, but calm returned to the area with a peace agreement signed at the end of 2013, and 2014 saw visitors once again returning to the park in numbers, and all park lodges and activities are once again up and running, including new camps near Kibumba Village and on Tchegera Island in Lake Kivu. Visitor numbers have rebounded impressively and, as peace hopefully takes root in the region once and for all, Virunga saw more than 6,000 visitors in 2017.

The award-winning 2014 film *Virunga* raised the profile of the park considerably and brought to light some of the threats facing its future, including the utterly distasteful but frighteningly realistic prospect of oil drilling within the park. Along with the publicity generated by the film, pressure from local NGOs and civil society groups seems to have forced a moratorium on further exploration – the main investor pulled out in 2015 – but proposals to redraw the park's boundaries and place the drilling sites outside the park still retain support among members of the Congolese government. Equally alarmingly, drilling licences for the Ugandan side of Lake Edward were mooted in 2016. There was no tinkering with the park's boundaries or drilling in Ugandan waters when this book went to print in early 2018, but it's clear that the fight to preserve Virunga is anything but over.

GETTING THERE AND AWAY Several local operators offer organised tours to Virunga National Park. These include the operators listed on page 334, as well as the Rwandan operator **Green Hill Eco-tours** in Rubavu/Gisenyi (page 217). Alternatively, all accommodation, activities and transport within the park can be booked through the website w visitvirunga.org or the park's booking office in Goma (page 333).

Self-drive is possible, but the police have a reputation for hassling drivers of non-Congolese cars, so it is only recommended with an escort (this can be arranged with the park for free). People can use their own transport to reach park activities, but they need to inform the park when they make their booking so an escort can be arranged. The park advises against people driving themselves in non-park areas.

WHERE TO STAY AND EAT *Map, right*

🏠 **Bukima Tented Camp** (6 tents) ✤ S
1°22.784, E 29°26.004; m 099 171 5401; e visit@virunga.org; w visitvirunga.org. Set at an altitude of 2,130m among the cultivated fields immediately bordering the national park, this upmarket rustic tented camp, fully renovated in 2014, is the ideal place to spend the night before gorilla tracking, as it is also the starting point for visits to the gorilla groups living around Bukima. It has a magnificent setting, with Mounts Karisimbi & Mikeno – the two tallest Virunga volcanoes – providing a dramatic backdrop & panoramic views over the plains below Nyiragongo, which smoulders on the horizon after dark. The en-suite standing tents are large & widely spaced along lava-rock paths, & each one is set on a shaded platform, with solar-heated running showers, private terrace, sitting area & wardrobe. Good meals & drinks are available. Bring warm clothes, as it can get cold at night (though the nightly campfires & hot-water bottles in your bed go a long way towards staving off the chill). *US$316/450 sgl/dbl FB.*

🏠 **Kibumba Tented Camp** (18 tents) m 099 171 5401; e visit@virunga.org; w visitvirunga.org. Opened in Oct 2017, this is the newest accommodation in Virunga National Park & sits way up on a hilltop with dramatic views to Nyiragongo Volcano from the open-sided fireplace lounge & bar. The comfortably equipped standing tents are set into a ridgeline leading back from the dining area & each has a private terrace overlooking the surrounding forest. All come with solar-heated hot showers – quite welcome given the nearly 2,200m elevation! It's the most budget-friendly accommodation in the park & represents excellent value for money, with a level of service & meals that would fit right in at any of its more expensive counterparts. *US$140/200/280 sgl/dbl/trpl FB.*

🏠 **Lulimbi Tented Camp** (10 tents) m 099 171 5401; e visit@virunga.org; w visitvirunga.org. This new tented camp consists of 10 standing tents

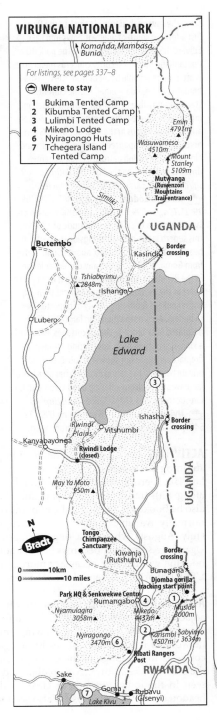

VIRUNGA NATIONAL PARK

Komanda, Mambasa, Bunia

For listings, see pages 337–8

🏠 **Where to stay**
1 Bukima Tented Camp
2 Kibumba Tented Camp
3 Lulimbi Tented Camp
4 Mikeno Lodge
6 Nyiragongo Huts
7 Tchegera Island Tented Camp

Emin 4791m
Wasuwameso 4510m
Mount Stanley 5109m
Mutwanga (Ruwenzori Mountains Trail entrance)
Simliki
UGANDA
Butembo
Kasindi ○ Border crossing
Tshiaberimu ▲2848m
Ishango ○
Lubero ○
Lake Edward
③
Ishasha ○ Border crossing
Rwindi Plains Vitshumbi
Kanyabayonga
Rwindi Lodge (closed)
May Ya Moto 950m ▲
N
Bradt
Tongo Chimpanzee Sanctuary
Kiwanja (Rutshuru)
Border crossing
Bunagana ○
Djomba gorilla tracking start point
0 — 10km
0 — 10 miles
Park HQ & Senkwekwe Centre
Rumangabo ④
Nyamulagira 3058m ▲
Mikeno 4437m ▲ ①
Muside 3000m
Nyiragongo 3470m ⑥
② Karisimbi 4507m ▲ Sabyinyo 3634m
Bibati Rangers Post
Sake ○
⑦ Goma ○ Rubavu (Gisenyi)
Lake Kivu
RWANDA
UGANDA

set in the savannah alongside the Ishasha River, just a few km south of where it flows into Lake Edward. It's about a 4hr drive from the park HQ at Rumangabo, though security concerns mean access is often more reliable by air or from the Ishasha border with Uganda – email for the current status. It's possible to spot waterbucks, elephant, buffalo & lion here (among other things), & there are plenty of hippos in the river out front. Guests here can join chimpanzee habituation walks and elephant monitoring patrols, as well as game drives & boat trips on the lake. *US$340/475/760 sgl/dbl/trpl FB, plus a US$40 local permit fee.*

🏠 **Mikeno Lodge** (12 rooms) ✪ S 1°20.309, E 29°21.794; m 099 171 5401; e visit@virunga.org; w visitvirunga.org. Set at an altitude of 1,550m, this superb lodge opened alongside the park headquarters at Rumangabo, about 90mins' drive from Goma, in 2011. Unlike any upmarket lodge in the Rwandan side of the Virungas, it is set in the heart of the rainforest, an environment teeming with monkeys & offering plenty of opportunities to birders. Accommodation is in large & stylishly decorated lava-block-&-thatch cottages, each with a king-size or twin beds, cosy sitting area with fireplace, en-suite hot shower & tub, & secluded private balcony. The raised dining & bar area has a large wooden balcony offering good views into the forest canopy. *US$330/475/705 sgl/dbl/trpl FB.*

🏠 **Nyiragongo Huts** (8 rooms) m 099 171 5401; e visit@virunga.org; w visitvirunga.org.

Perched at an altitude of 3,400m immediately outside the rim of Nyiragongo Crater, these basic huts each contain 2 beds with waterproof mattresses but no bedding. A common drop toilet lies about 50m from the huts. There are no cooking facilities & no food is provided, unless you arrange a packed meal with the park in advance. Use of the huts is included in the price of the permit to visit Nyiragongo Volcano (*US$300*).

🏠 **Tchegera Island Tented Camp** (8 tents) ✪ S 1°38.922, E 29°07.087; m 099 171 5401; e visit@virunga.org; w visitvirunga.org. Set on a startlingly green, crescent-shaped sliver of land some dozen-odd kilometres from Goma, this upmarket camp sits in an exclave of parkland on a diminutive crater island in Lake Kivu, just off the northeastern tip of the Bulenga Peninsula. Accommodation is in comfortably equipped standing tents situated steps from the lakeshore, all of which come with solar-heated showers. There are magnificent views from practically every corner of the island, including across the water to the Nyiragongo & Nyamulagira volcanoes & their night-time blush. It's a great place to put your feet up after hiking in the park, & birders will have no trouble keeping themselves busy, but if you'd still like to get in a bit of a workout, there are paddleboards & kayaks available as well. *US$218/276/400 sgl/dbl/trpl FB, plus US$100pp permit & round-trip boat transfer.*

ACTIVITIES Gorilla and chimp tracking are both available in the park, as is a stunning but tough hike to the top of Nyiragongo Volcano, with its spectacular live lava lake. Permits for all activities can be booked online at w visitvirunga.org/shop, along with transport from Goma and Congolese visas. Permits and transport can also be booked in person at the booking office in Goma (page 333). Permits are still normally available at short notice, except during the peak gorilla-tracking season (July–August), when the Congolese gorillas attract an overspill from Rwanda and Uganda. As the park becomes better known, however, it seems likely that advance booking will become necessary more often, especially with the now-stratospheric US$1,100 price differential between here and Rwanda.

Around Rumangabo Visitors to Mikeno Lodge (see above), which stands adjacent to the park headquarters, will find the surrounding forest offers plenty of opportunity for free primate viewing and birdwatching, whether from the small network of roads that encircles Rumangabo, or from the short walking trail that connects to the lodge to the entrance gate. The most common primates here are the blue monkey, Ruwenzori colobus and olive baboon, all of which are frequently seen in the lodge grounds or close to the main administration building in the headquarters. Wild chimps are also seen in the forest from time to time.

Birdlife is varied, and includes a wide range of forest specialists, most conspicuously perhaps Sladen's Barbet (a Congo endemic), white-headed wood-hoopoe, cinnamon-chested bee-eater, yellow-whiskered greenbul and grey-green bush-shrike. Other attractive forest residents that often draw attention through their calls include black-billed turaco, Ross's turaco, black-and-white casqued hornbill, double-toothed barbet, yellow-billed barbet, narrow-tailed starling and Sharpe's starling.

Set in a jungle clearing 5 minutes' walk from the lodge, the **Senkwekwe Centre** is the only facility in the world for orphaned mountain gorillas. It is named after the silverback Senkwekwe, who was killed by gunmen, along with six other members of his group, on 22 July 2007. The 1ha enclosure is currently home to Senkwekwe's daughter Ndeze, an 11-year-old female survivor of this massacre, and another female of the same age called Ndakasi. It also shelters the youngest member of the family, Matabishi, who was found alone outside the park boundaries near Bikenge Village as a baby in 2013. The orphans can be watched from several viewing platforms, but tourists are forbidden to enter the enclosure.

The **Congohounds** programme is also based at the park HQ in Rumangabo, where specially trained bloodhounds and springer spaniels are used to patrol the park, tracking the scents of both poachers and contraband. Ask for a demonstration if you're staying at Mikeno Lodge – watching the bloodhounds track a ranger hundreds of metres based solely on a piece of ivory the ranger held is a truly impressive feat, and even more so when you consider that the tracking done in the park will usually extend for kilometres, not metres!

Nyiragongo Volcano

The most popular activity in Virunga National Park is the hike up the live volcano Nyiragongo, whose perfect cone rises above Goma and the Lake Kivu shore to an altitude of 3,470m. One of Africa's most active volcanoes, Nyiragongo was responsible for massive killer lava flows that devastated Goma in 2002, and the hike to the top passes the subsidiary cone formed by this most recent eruption. At the top, sheer windswept cliffs plummet into the nested main crater, which is at least 600m deep and has an average diameter of 1.2km. At the heart of this immense natural cauldron, a circular lake of live lava bubbles away like a massive casserole, its surface pattern ceaselessly mutating as blackened crusts of magma collide, crumble and melt, spewing bright red flumes of molten rock tens of metres into the air. It is a thrilling, mesmerising spectacle, especially towards dusk, when the glowing lava eerily illuminates a swirling red mist – no less so because the violent heat of the lake contrasts so strikingly with the chilly windy conditions experienced by observers on the crater rim, and with the more sedate view south over the nightlights of Goma on the Kivu shore.

The standard trip runs overnight, sleeping in one of the huts on the rim, which is highly recommended as the view of the lava lake is most spectacular at dusk and after dark. However, it is possible to hike there and back in a day, and a one-day trip can usually be organised upon request. Hikers should bring all the food and liquid they will need; there are no cooking facilities at the top, and you should bank on at least 3–4 litres of water per person. It can be very cold and windy at the top, so a sleeping bag is also necessary, as is a good rain jacket or windbreaker, hiking boots or sturdy walking shoes, plenty of warm clothes (ideally including gloves), and a change of clothes in case of rain. A torch and spare batteries are also essential. And once there, do step cautiously on the edge of the crater: in July 2007, a tourist died after falling into the crater while taking photographs. Packed meals and water are available for an additional US$75 per person (known as a 'half backpack'), or meals, water and cold-weather gear (sleeping bag, jacket, etc) for US$100 per person (known as 'full backpack').

The hike starts at Kibati Ranger Camp (✪ S 1°34.140, E 29°16.707), about 15km from Goma on the west side of the main road to Rumangabo. It is only 6.3km from here to the rim, but it is a steep climb, starting at an altitude of 2,000m and gaining more than 1,400m, and the ascent takes around 4–6 hours, depending less on your individual fitness than on the overall fitness of the party (all hikers on any given day are expected to stick together for security reasons), as well as how acclimatised they are to high altitudes, and the duration of the customary breaks at each of the four 'posts' along the route.

The first 2.5km, from Kibati to Post One, follows a flattish trail that is generally easy underfoot through an area of montane forest, and takes around 40 minutes. The second stage to Post Two (2,533m) is steeper: a 1.1km, 20–30-minute ascent of the scree-strewn southeastern slope of the dormant subsidiary cone created by the 2002 eruption. From here, it is slightly less than 1km to Post Three (2,762m), a 20–30-minute ascent along an old lava flow to the base of the main cone, which rises a daunting near-45° angle ahead. The toughest leg follows, gaining almost 500m over 1.3km, a 60–90-minute hike that brings you to Post Four (3,235m), site of a ruinous old mountain hut. *En route*, the trail passes some active steam vents (emanating from what is presumably a subterranean magma flow connecting the main crater to the subsidiary cone), as well as running through some stunning fields of giant lobelia, and offering views over the 2002 crater to Lake Kivu. From Post Four, the breathlessly steep scramble up the final 400m of loose rocks leading to the crater rim and cabaña site should take 20–30 minutes.

Up to 16 overnight volcano permits are issued daily, corresponding to the number of beds in the eight double huts at the rim (it's possible that some new huts will be built during the lifespan of this edition, which would bump the number of daily permits up to 24), and these cost US$300 for foreign adults, US$175 for foreign children, US$90 for Congolese adults or US$25 for Congolese children. Porters can be hired for US$12 a day (US$24 for the overnight trip) to carry up to 15kg of luggage each. In addition, you will need to pay for transport to/from Kibati, which can be arranged through the park website or booking office in Goma. This costs US$28 per person one-way from Goma or US$56 from Mikeno Lodge in a Hilux or Land Cruiser (carrying up to six people). Backpackers staying in Goma and looking to save some francs should ask the park office to arrange a moto transfer instead. Transport can also be arranged through any tour operator in Goma. Check-in at the Kibati post starts at 09.00 and the hike departs at 09.30 sharp (which means you need to leave Goma or Mikeno Lodge about an hour earlier), and most hikers are back at the base by around 10.00 the next day. Note that even the most experienced hikers tend to suffer some leg stiffness after the steep ascent, so it is best saved for after other activities such as gorilla or chimpanzee tracking (which will also give you additional time to adjust to the altitude).

Gorilla tracking Virunga National Park offers a mountain-gorilla-tracking experience comparable in quality and in most other respects to that of neighbouring Rwanda. Seven gorilla groups are habituated to tourist visits, with six permits being issued daily for larger groups, and four for smaller groups, creating a total availability of 36 permits daily. Ten of these permits apply to two gorilla groups based in the area around Djomba, which lies close to the Ugandan border and is most normally visited as a day trip from the Ugandan town of Kisoro (so it falls outside the scope of a guidebook to Rwanda). Another 20 permits apply to four groups that are normally tracked from Bukima, which lies on the slopes of Mount Mikeno about 90 minutes' drive from Mikeno Lodge and twice that distance from Goma. There is now also one recently habituated group that can be tracked from near Kibumba Tented Camp (page 337).

Gorilla-tracking permits for Virunga National Park cost US$400 (or US$150 for Congolese citizens), a fair bit cheaper than the US$600 charged in Uganda, and categorically more affordable than the US$1,500 asked in Rwanda. An even better deal is to be had from 15 March to 15 May and 15 October to 15 December, when low-season permits are available for only US$200. The experience is broadly similar to tracking in Rwanda, with the same 1-hour limit imposed on tourist visits, but the setting is a lot more remote and underutilised – indeed, there are still days when nobody goes tracking at Bukima. In addition, there is the option of overnighting at the magnificently located Bukima Tented Camp before you track, which really sets the tone for the adventure. For independent travellers, the logistics of reaching Bukima are more complicated than getting to Kinigi (the base for tracking in Rwanda) and transport costs are higher, but the increased price of permits in Rwanda means Virunga is now an unambiguously better choice for the budget-minded. Transfers arranged through the park website or booking office cost US$94 per person one-way from Goma, US$50 from Kibumba Tented Camp or US$38 from Mikeno Lodge in a Hilux or Land Cruiser (carrying up to six people). Transfers can also be arranged through any tour operator in Goma.

Chimp tracking Set a few-dozen kilometres to the northwest of Rumangabo, Tongo is a 10km² block of medium-altitude forest isolated from other similar habitats by lava flows. Traversed by an 80km network of walking trails, Tongo is home to a community of around 35 chimpanzees first habituated by the Frankfurt Zoological Society (FZS) and opened to tourism in the late 1980s, only to close again in 1993 because of instability. The FZS relaunched the Tongo habituation programme in 2010, but it was once again shuttered because of fighting in the area in 2012. The habituation team at Tongo is once again working with the chimps on a daily basis, but it remained closed to visitors as this book went to print in 2018. It's hoped that Tongo can reopen to tourists at some point soon – see our updates website (w *bradtupdates. com/rwanda*) for the latest.

Thus, today the only chimpanzee tracking currently available at Virunga is with a habituated group resident near the park HQ at Rumangabo. Habituation at Rumangabo is still ongoing – the FZS teams only started working here in February 2014 – but for the most part the chimps are now very accustomed to visitors, so, while the quality and ease of sightings varies from one day to the next, the experience is comparable to tracking chimps at Nyungwe. Tracking starts at 06.00 from Mikeno Lodge and, given the distances involved from any other accommodation, this means that participants are restricted to guests staying at the lodge. Hikers set out in groups of four or fewer, and time with the chimps is limited to 1 hour. Note that the chimps at Rumangabo will occasionally migrate in and out of tracking range, so visits are sometimes cancelled because of the chimps' movements; the Virunga website indicates whether they're currently in the area or not. Permits cost US$100 per person for foreigners and US$25 for Congolese citizens.

Further afield The activities described previously all take place in the far south of the national park, but there are many undeveloped attractions further afield, their potential unrealised at the moment largely as a result of ongoing insecurity and/or lack of funding. However, several other attractions are likely to be developed if the region continues to stabilise, and eventually new tented camps or lodges may be constructed. The closest such site to Mikeno Lodge is the Tongo Hippo Pools (near the eponymous forest), where around 100 hippos live in water so clear you can see them under the surface. Further north, the Rwindi Plains protect a lush savannah

12

habitat similar to that of the Ishasha sector of Uganda's Queen Elizabeth National Park, while the Semliki Forest protects a lowland forest habitat hosting numerous bird species endemic to the Congo Basin, and habituated eastern lowland gorillas are present in the Tshiaberimu Forest west of Lake Edward. As of 2017 there's accommodation nearby at the new Lulimbi Tented Camp (page 337), set along the Ishasha River on the east side of Lake Edward.

In the far north of the park, the Congolese portion of the **Ruwenzori Mountains** is technically open to tourists, though far less accessible than the Uganda side. From the Congo, road travel between Goma and the north of the park was considered unsafe at the time of writing, so the Ruwenzoris are usually accessed via flights to the town of Beni or via the Ugandan border crossing at Kasindi. Circuits from five to nine days (potentially including a summit of Margherita Peak from the Congolese side) can be arranged here, but hikers and climbers must be fully self-sufficient in terms of all food and gear. Permits cost US$200 for foreign visitors or US$25 for Congolese, and there are mountain huts along the trails accessible for an additional US$325–425. Email the park well in advance to make the relevant arrangements.

For the latest on new tourist developments, check w visitvirunga.org or visit our update website w bradtupdates.com/rwanda.

BUKAVU

With an almost comically scenic location along the hills at the south end of Lake Kivu, the five aggressively green and densely populated peninsulas of Bukavu (known in colonial times by the decidedly less catchy appellation of Costermansville) bend and stretch northwards into the lake at odd angles, revealing a surfeit of panoramic views around nearly every corner. Its tropical abundance stands in a sharp contrast to Goma's harsh, elemental feel, and indeed the city, thought to have some 800,000 residents, has seen considerably less trauma (both natural and manmade) than its hard-luck cousin at the north end of the lake.

The town's situation vis-à-vis its neighbours, however, mirrors the north end of the lake with uncanny repetition. Just as with Goma, Bukavu also sits directly on the Rwandan border, here facing the much smaller Rwandan town of Rusizi, and again like Goma, Bukavu also enjoys access to a national park known for its gorilla treks, Kahuzi-Biega, just a short drive outside of town.

It's not unusual to hear residents declare Bukavu as the most attractive city in the Congo and, while it would take a whole lot of exploring to double-check that claim properly, on the face of it the city's stunning location and surprisingly easy charm make it quite difficult to take issue with the idea. So while it's often overshadowed by the notoriety and singularity of the northern lakeshore and its attractions, if you've got the time, a visit to Bukavu would still be a highlight of any eastern Congo itinerary – it might just end up as one of your favourite towns too.

GETTING THERE AND AWAY Note well that if you arranged your visa through the Visit Virunga website, you *must* enter the Congo at Goma, as the email printout is not accepted in Bukavu. Kahuzi-Biega National Park now has a similar scheme for visitors to the park arriving in Bukavu, which can be arranged in conjunction with the purchase of a Kahuzi-Biega gorilla-tracking permit. The 14-day visa currently costs US$100 (payable in US dollars at the border crossing) and requires two weeks to process, after which you will receive an email confirmation that must be printed out and presented at the lakeshore border crossing (Rusizi I) between Rusizi and

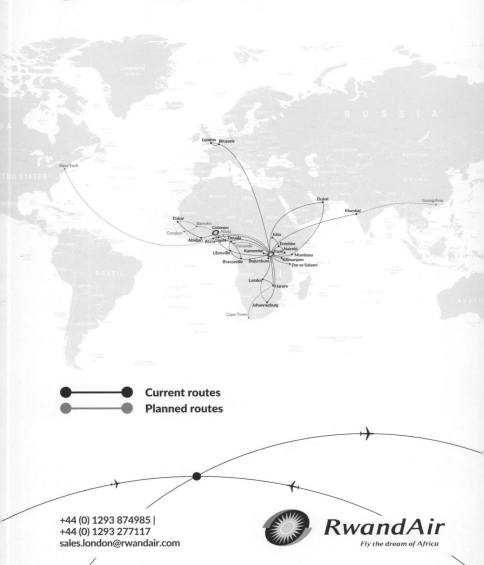

Rwiza Village is a resort by the shore of Lake Kivu in Kibuye (West Province of Rwanda) built with local materials and the contribution of local artisans and operating since 2013.

ACCOMMODATION

Beautiful Rwandan-style rooms with stunning views of the green gardens and Lake Kivu. The sound of birdsong and waves lapping the nearby shore soothe you to sleep in a peaceful environment. Our rooms perfectly combine tradition and luxury and are equipped with toilets and hot-water showers.

RESTAURANT

Our menu offers an excellent selection of Rwandan, African and international dishes to suit all tastes.

Email: info@rwizavillage.org   Web: rwizavillage.org
Tel: + 250 (0) 789 714 551   f rwiza.lodge

Discover our Rwanda...

www.journeysdiscoveringafrica.com

NATIONAL PARK
RWANDA

ruzizi@african-parks.org · +250 (0) 787 113 300

www.ruzizilodge.com · www.akagera.org

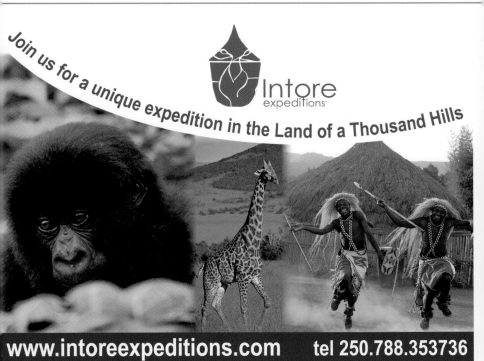

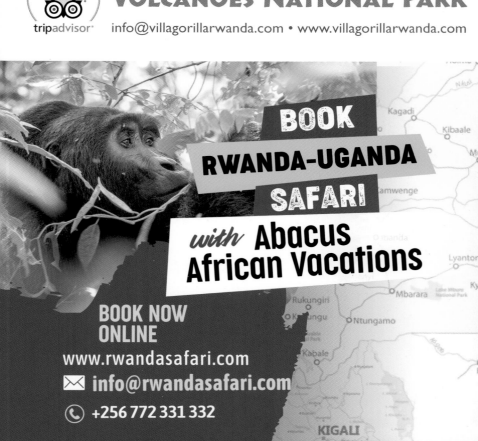

WHERE YOUR JOURNEY INTO NATURE BEGINS...

- Guided tours across East Africa
- Primate safaris in Rwanda, Uganda & the DR Congo
- Cultural safaris
- Mountain climbing
- Birdwatching
- City tours

- Tailor-made luxury & budget tour packages upon request including: group safaris, family trips & trips for honeymoon travellers

BOOK YOUR TRIP TODAY

+250788838109 / +250728838109 (office)
info@astepintonature.com
janvier647@gmail.com

A Step into NATURE Tours

facebook.com/AStepIntoNatureTours
www.astepintonature.com

INDIVIDUAL TOURS
Your personal introduction to Rwanda

Experience Africa from A to Z in the "Land of a Thousand Hills"
Gorilla trekking and the Big Five
The excitement of the rainforest and the savannah
All in easy travelling distances
Individually planned tours for small groups or individuals
www.individual-tours.com

RWANDA'S TOP RESTAURANT AND BOUTIQUE HOTEL

Boutique Hotel: +250 737886307
boutiquehotel@heavenrwanda.com
Restaurant: +250 788486581
restaurant@heavenrwanda.com
www.heavenrwanda.com

- Modern African cuisine and artisanal goods
- Conference rooms and services
- Open-air state-of-the-art fitness centre with weekly fitness & yoga classes
- Heated saltwater pool
- Spa services
- Travel & tourism services
- Colorful rooms with air conditioning, television & fiber-optic internet
- Azizi Life's onsite fair-trade crafts boutique
- Art gallery
- Multiple lounge & work spaces
- Kids' playground

THE RETREAT BY HEAVEN

KIGALI'S FIRST LUXURY ECO-FRIENDLY RESORT

The Retreat: +250 782000001
theretreat@heavenrwanda.com
www.theretreatrwanda.com

- Fusion restaurant & bar featuring farm-to-table cuisine
- Solar powered by Rwanda's largest private solar facility
- Private outdoor terraces built in sustainable teak & with outdoor rain showers
- Saltwater heated pool with diving rocks, hot tub & sauna
- Open-air state-of-the-art fitness centre with weekly fitness & yoga classes
- Yoga & meditation room
- Kids' playground

Bukavu, where the visa itself is issued. See w kahuzi-biega.org or email e contact@ kahuzi-biega.org for further details on how to apply, and page 326 for further details on entering the Congo.

By road Travellers in Rwanda should first aim for Rusizi, from where it's a short moto ride from the bus station and an easy walk across the bridge spanning the border. Another moto ride (*Cfr500*) will take you to central Bukavu.

If you're headed south to Bujumbura or Uvira, **La Colombe** [344 C4] (m *099 096 9090/487 2822 (Bukavu), 099 766 9788/751 9707 (Uvira), +257 799 24 363 (Bujumbura)*) runs three minibuses daily, charging US$10 to Bujumbura and US$7 to Uvira. Depending on conditions on the Congolese road to Uvira (unsafe at the time of writing in early 2018), vehicles will generally transit via Rwanda, so be aware of the security situation and any consequences this could have for your visas.

By boat Here, your best option is with **Ihusi Express** (m *099 481 3235/097 464 5680/081 838 2590 (Goma), 099 423 4071/882 1195, 081 398 2333 (Bukavu); e ihusiexpress@gmail.com; w iexpress.ihusigroup.com*), which offers two departures daily, leaving from the port at the west end of town at 07.30 and either 11.00 or 14.00, except on Thursdays and Saturdays, when only the 11.00 boats run. The trip to Goma takes a speedy 2½ hours with a stop on Idjwi Island, and the US$50 tickets often sell out and should be purchased in advance, possibly on their new website, but most reliably at either of the Ihusi petrol stations – one facing the Place de l'Indépendance [344 A3] and the other at the port itself [344 A2]. Other boat options to/from Goma are detailed on pages 330–1.

By air As of early 2018, no airlines were flying to Bukavu. Should flights start back up with **Congo Airways** (w *congoairways.com*) or **Compagnie Africaine d'Aviation (CAA)** (w *caacongo.com*), be aware that the airport is in Kavumu, some 35km north – the Rusizi/Kamembe airport in Rwanda is actually closer! If your budget allows, the Goma-based **Busy Bee Congo** (w *busybeecongo.com*) can arrange charters.

WHERE TO STAY
Upmarket

Hotel Begonias [344 G2] (25 rooms) m 084 701 6035; e hotelbegoniasbukavu@ gmail.com; w begonias-bukavu.com. The closest accommodation to the border, this brand-new hotel has large & comfortable tiled rooms with balconies, some of which have fabulous views over the lake. It's aimed largely at the business market, but the swimming pool (*US$5 for non-guests*) & sauna should keep leisure visitors pleased as well. *US$120– 150 dbl, depending on size & view; all rates B&B.*

Hotel Elizabeth [344 D4] (35 rooms) m 099 323 3553/081 010 2744/084 215 2300; e direction@ elizabethhotelbukavu.com; w elizabethhotelbukavu. com. Though it only opened in 2017, the reliance on wood panelling gives this new business hotel a vaguely dated air, but the rooms are decent enough, if overpriced. The real winner here, however, is the rooftop restaurant-bar, with fabulous views over the

city & a good menu of continental & African meals at surprisingly reasonable prices – worth stopping in for a drink even if you're staying elsewhere. *US$100/180 small/large dbl.*

Lodge CoCo [344 E3] (8 rooms) m 099 385 5752/861 0946/870 7344; e carlosschuler@ outlook.com; w lodgecoco.com. With something approaching the feel of a safari lodge, the characterful en-suite rooms here are trimmed out in wood & all are comfortably appointed with big beds, writing desk, flatscreen TV & mozzie nets. The resto-bar is a popular hangout & does a range of meat, fish & Indian-inspired dishes starting around US$15, & there's a live band every Fri. The lodge can also arrange vehicles for trips into Kahuzi-Biega. *US$120/150 sgl/dbl B&B.*

Orchids Safari Club [344 E3] (30 rooms) m 081 312 6467/078 444 4137 (Rwanda); e info@ orchids-hotel.com; w orchids-hotel.com. In a

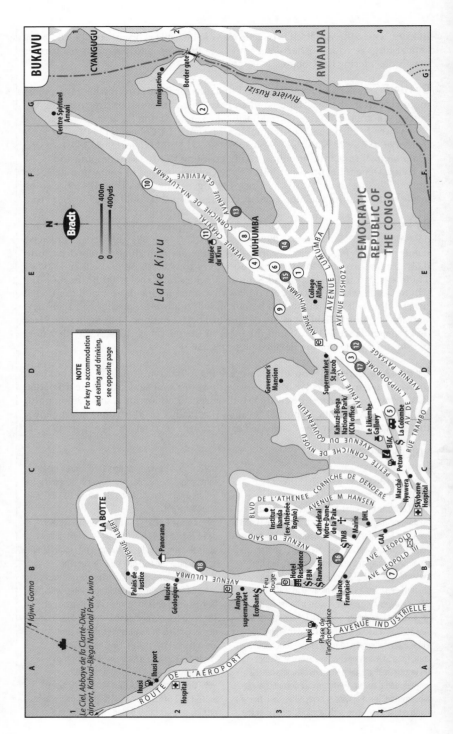

BUKAVU *Overview*
For listings, see pages 343–6

🛏 **Where to stay**
1 Agence Espérance..............E3
2 Hotel Begonias....................G2
3 Hotel Belvedere.................D4
4 Hotel Elila...........................E3
5 Hotel Elizabeth..................D4
6 Hotel Horizon......................E3
7 Hotel Lac Tanganyika.......B4
8 Lodge CoCo.........................E3
9 Orchids Safari Club............E3
10 Prokamu Guesthouse.......F2
11 Xaverian Mission.................E2

😋 **Where to eat and drink**
12 Chez Maman Kindja..........D4
13 Chez Wendy........................F3
14 Cosmo-Koweit.....................E3
15 Karibu Café.........................E3
16 La Lutte Contre La Soif.....B4
17 Le Meridien........................D4
18 Salt & Pepper.....................B2

Off map
   Le Ciel...................................A1

beautifully manicured hillside compound just above the water, rooms at this owner-managed lodge are impressively up to date & the most luxurious in town. The décor & furnishings are modish & minimalist, with parquet flooring, flatscreen TV, glass-door showers, & full-length mirrors. There's lake access for swimming or using their kayaks, & a sophisticated restaurant with indoor & outdoor seating & mains starting around US$20. *US$145– 190 sgl; US$180–225 dbl; US$245 suite; all rates B&B.*

Moderate

❋ 🏠 **Agence Espérance** [344 E3] (3 rooms) m 099 822 5588/994 1197; e luc.henkinbrant@ gmail.com; w agenceesperance.net. Opposite the Karibu Café (page 346), this charming family home makes for an eminently comfortable base in Bukavu, & is an ideal place to get further information about the city & region from Luc & Espérance, who have deep roots in Bukavu. Rooms are bright, simple & homely, with net, desk & reading lamps, & there's a comfortable living room as well. There's a tranquil garden out back & excellent meals (courtesy of Espérance) are available at request. Wi-Fi. *US$40 dbl B&B, with discounts for stays over a week.*

🏠 **Hotel Elila** [344 E3] (32 rooms) 21 Av Kabare; m 099 576 2566/097 002 1132/082 313 2376; e elilahotel@yahoo.fr; w hotelelila.com. Equidistant between the more expensive Orchids & Lodge CoCo, the en-suite rooms at this newish place are small but well maintained, with hot water, mozzie nets, TV, &

Wi-Fi, & some with private balcony. It's well regarded as a sensible mid-range option without the bells & whistles of its more expensive neighbours, though they've recently added a swimming pool. Meals & drinks on site. *US$80–120 dbl, depending on category.*

🏠 **Hotel Horizon** [344 E3] (35 rooms) m 099 440 6270/085 305 4302/081 788 5994; e hotelhorizonbkv@yahoo.fr; w hotelhorizonbukavu. com. In a big meandering complex that seems to be quite popular for conferences, the rooms here are nothing to shout about, but are reliably well kept & all come with TV, Wi-Fi, & en-suite ablutions with hot water. The more expensive rooms have balconies with lake view. There's also 2 restaurants. *US$50–100 dbl depending on size; US$140 suite.*

Budget

🏠 **Hotel Belvedere** [344 D4] (30 rooms) m 099 867 2367/085 315 0622. The en-suite rooms here don't have much in the way of views (walls, mostly), but they're very tidy, with tiled floors, decent furnishings, TV, mozzie net, cold shower & Wi-Fi. There are officially 3 price categories, but the differences between them hardly justify the cost, so just go for the cheapest. Meals & drinks can be arranged. *US$30–50 dbl B&B.*

🏠 **Prokamu Guesthouse** [344 F2] (12 rooms) m 081 636 3585/085 288 5728; e hmukungilwa@ gmail.com. Run by the Diocese of Kasongo, this pleasant guesthouse is hidden away behind an unmarked red gate (No 7) near the German consul's residence & has simple, clean rooms in a quiet, grassy garden right on the lake. They weren't providing meals when we checked in, so note that the nearest eateries are some 800m–1km away. *Very good value at US$20–30 dbl.*

🏠 **Xaverian Mission** [344 E2] (31 rooms) m 099 508 4501. Set in a charming, multi-tiered lakefront compound with a creative assortment of garden furniture made from recycled pallets & an old satellite dish-turned-umbrella, the simple en-suite rooms here all come with hot water & are justifiably popular for the price. Better still, it's in the same compound as the fantastic Musée du Kivu (page 347). The building here is unmarked – knock on the gate at 25 Rue Kabare. *US$35 dbl.*

Shoestring

🏠 **Hotel Lac Tanganyika** [344 B4] (26 rooms) Av Leopold; m 099 047 2091/085 379 4812. This has been the go-to cheapie in Bukavu for some

Virunga National Park and Eastern DRC   **BUKAVU**

12

years now, & though far from salubrious, it's not quite as grim as it looks from the exterior. There's a resto-bar doing the basics inside, & a whole new floor of rooms going in on top. The en-suite rooms all have mozzie nets. *US$15 dbl using shared bathroom; US$20 en-suite dbl.*

✕ **WHERE TO EAT AND DRINK** The hotels listed on pages 343–6 also serve food, and there's no shortage of standalone eateries, but these are a few favourites:

✕ **Chez Maman Kindja** [344 D4] m 099 861 1536. Recommended for Congolese traditional fare; grab a seat at one of the secluded tables here for goat, grills, *ugali*, matoke & more. *US$5–10.*

✕ **Le Ciel** [344 A1] m 085 075 6841; ⏱ 07.30–19.00 daily. Just over 7km outside town on the road to the national park, this waterfront hangout is a favourite for families & friends to while away the afternoon under a gazebo & over some brochettes (*US$8*), frites & beer. Bukaviens swear they do the best chicken in town.

✕ **Cosmo-Koweit** [344 E3] m 081 075 0735/099 728 9537; 🏧 cosmo.koweit.restaurant; ⏱ noon–21.00 daily. This popular buffet restaurant is Bukavu's answer to the Maghali Fan Club in Goma (page 333), serving a heaping buffet of beans, greens, bananas, meat, fish, cassava, & more for US$2–5.

✕ **Le Meridien** [344 D4] m 099 717 6255/082 135 6158/085 943 9364. Directly next to the Belvedere Hotel, this well-loved eatery seems a bit cramped once you clamber up the wooden staircase to the 1st-floor dining room, but a 2018 remodel may change that. It's consistently popular for meals or drinks, & is especially renowned for its rabbit. *US$5–10.*

✕ **Salt & Pepper** [344 B2] m 097 004 8060/089 923 9072; ⏱ 10.00–midnight daily. Under the same ownership as the branch in Goma (page 333), this 1st-floor place does a good menu of Indian & Chinese dishes, with plenty of vegetarian fare as well. *Mains US$4–10.*

♀ **Chez Wendy** [344 F3] m 099 161 6901; 🏧 wendysbarbukavu; ⏱ evenings daily. Little more than a house built from planks of wood with some tables in the yard, this rootsy local bar has become an unlikely hub for foreigners based in Bukavu, & is a sure bet to get you started on the w/ends.

♀ **Karibu Café** [344 E3] m 099 309 7044; 🏧 Popular with Congolese & foreigners alike, this is a relaxed bar with plenty of garden seating, DJ nights & occasional theme parties at the w/end, plus a reliably meaty offering of barbecue meals & brochettes.

♀ **La Lutte Contre La Soif** [344 B4] With a cheeky, NGO-inspired name that translates to 'the fight against thirst', this laid-back bar on the main drag is one of several drinking holes in the area good for cold beers, plastic tables & Congolese tunes. It was closed for remodelling at the time of writing.

OTHER PRACTICALITIES
Tourist information
The **Kahuzi-Biega National Park/Institut Congolais pour la Conservation de la Nature (ICCN) office** [344 C4] (m 081 343 1239/097 130 0881/082 288 1012; e info@kahuzi-biega.org; w kahuzi-biega.org; ⏱ 07.00–16.00 Mon–Fri) on Avenue Lumumba can arrange transport, permits and other practicalities for visits to the park and its surrounding attractions, including the Centre de Rehabilitation des Primates de Lwiro (page 351) and the Centre de Recherche en Sciences Naturelles (page 351).

Tour operators
All the larger hotels can arrange trips to Kahuzi-Biega and surrounds, and the Goma-based operators on page 334 can arrange trips to Bukavu and Kahuzi-Biega as well. The following agencies are based in Bukavu and can arrange trips anywhere in the region, including Idjwi Island.

Agence Espérance m 099 822 5588/994 1197; e info@agenceesperance.net; w agenceesperance.net. Ardent promoters of sustainable tourism throughout the Kivu region, they also recently set

up Idjwi Island's first ecolodge (page 354) & have very pleasant rooms in Bukavu as well (page 345). **Pole Pole Foundation** m 099 899 9598; e popof_drc@polepolefoundation.org;

w polepolefoundation.org. Community-based conservation group active in the region since 1992 & winner of the 2016 Prince William Award for Conservation in Africa.

Shopping The perpetually busy central market, known as **Marché Nyawera** [344 C4], carries everything from machetes to makeup, and is a sure way to get a feel for what really makes Bukavu tick. For art and souvenirs, **Le Likembe** [344 C4] (m *099 776 2707;* ⊕ *08.00–16.00 Mon–Fri, 10.00–15.00 Sat*) has a dusty but interesting selection of carvings, bags, paintings, masks, wire-frame children's toys and the like; prices here are marked but a bit of negotiation probably wouldn't hurt. There's also a good selection of carvings and masks at the front of the Orchids Safari Club (page 343).

Banks and foreign exchange BIAC [344 C4], Rawbank [344 B3], Trust Merchant Bank (TMB) [344 B4] and EcoBank [344 B3] are all represented with ATMs along the main road dispensing US dollars. Rawbank's ATMs also dispense Congolese francs if you want them. The best place to find moneychangers is near the Rwandan border, but keep your wits about you.

Swimming The Orchids Safari Club has lake access and a little grassy patch for sunbathing at the bottom of their compound, and they're pretty relaxed about people heading down there to use it, even if they're not staying at the hotel.

KAHUZI-BIEGA NATIONAL PARK (See ad, page 355)

About 30km northwest of Bukavu lies the 6,000km² Kahuzi-Biega National Park, a UNESCO World Heritage Site named for the two extinct volcanoes that dominate its skyline, Mounts Kahuzi (3,300m) and Biega (2,900m), which constitute the two highest peaks of the Mitumba range. Divided into two unequal sections linked by a narrow strip of forest, the park's eastern portion covers a habitat of largely montane primary forest between 1,800m and 3,300m in elevation, while the much larger western section of the park sees elevations drop to between 600m and 1,500m (except for Mount Kamami at 1,700m) and a habitat of low, forested mountains punctuated by deep river valleys leading west towards the Lualaba River.

On the list of World Heritage Sites in danger since 1997, the last two decades have not been kind to Kahuzi-Biega. Starting in 1994, refugees from the Rwandan genocide took up residence in the park, and three years later it became a hideout for rebel militias when the Congolese civil war kicked off in 1997. At the start of this century, a spike in global mineral prices, particularly for coltan, saw more than 10,000 miners move into park territory which had long since fallen out of government control, and within a couple of years the elephant population had disappeared entirely and gorillas were reduced by as much as 90%.

From these inauspicious beginnings, however, a small renaissance is taking place in Kahuzi-Biega, and, as in its more famous cousin Virunga, recent years have witnessed impressive strides in terms of both management and conservation. Despite the years of turmoil, Kahuzi-Biega today remains the only place in the world where you can track the critically endangered eastern lowland, or Grauer's gorilla (*Gorilla beringei graueri*). Their worldwide population is estimated at under 4,000, but Kahuzi-Biega is the only place where these numbers are increasing – some 200–300 individuals are now thought to be resident in the park according to the most recent census in 2015. Even if you don't go gorilla tracking, keen hikers can trek out to the Tshibati Waterfalls or even summit Mount Kahuzi, and ornithologists can make light work of their eastern Congo checklists here, as the park has been recognised as an Important Bird Area since 2001.

Activities at Kahuzi-Biega have been unaffected by the 2018 suspension of tourism at Virunga.

GETTING THERE AND AWAY There's no public transport to the park HQ, so visitors to Kahuzi-Biega will require a private vehicle. It's possible to organise one (along with the necessary permits) at the Kahuzi-Biega National Park/Institut Congolais pour la Conservation de la Nature (ICCN) office [344 C4] (m *081 343 1239/097 130 0881/082 288 1012;* e *info@kahuzi-biega.org;* w *kahuzi-biega.org;* ⏲ *07.00–16.00 Mon–Fri*) on Avenue Lumumba in Bukavu. It's US$150 per day for a 4x4 arranged through the park office, with a maximum five passengers and pickup/drop-off in Bukavu. If that sounds a bit steep, it's also possible to hire a private taxi in town for closer to US$50. If you'd rather not try and negotiate this yourself, Agence Espérance (page 346) can recommend a driver. All tour agents and nicer hotels can also arrange vehicles.

All park activities (except visits to the Lwiro science centre and primate sanctuary) start at the Tshivanga visitors' centre/park HQ (✪ *S 2°18.901, E 28°45.513*), plus another drive to the trailheads once you've picked up the necessary rangers and guides. Tshivanga is 7km north of the left-hand turn-off at Miti Village (✪ *S 2°21.324, E 28°47.596*) and 30km from Bukavu. To reach Lwiro, bear right at Miti and continue north for 14km, passing the airport at Kavumu. The Lwiro turn-off is signposted to the left at ✪ S 2°14.836, E 28°49.622, and the centre is just under 3km beyond at ✪ S 2°14.376, E 28°48.740. There's a US$2.50/5 road tax for saloon cars/4x4s levied between Miti and Kavumu, on the road to Lwiro and the airport.

WHERE TO STAY The first accommodation in Kahuzi-Biega itself is scheduled to open during the lifespan of this edition; ten upmarket stone chalets with fireplace and private terrace, along with four standing tent sites, were under construction next to the park HQ at Tshivanga in 2018. They were still building and seeking an operator when this book went to print, so check with the park office (see above) for the latest updates.

Aside from this, there's no other accommodation in the park but, with your own equipment, overnight camping can be arranged in the park on the slopes of Mount Bugulumiza, though at US$50/35/25 foreign adult/student/child; US$35/25/15 adult/student/child CEPGL/EAC/SADC resident; and US$15/7/3 Congolese adult/student/child, it's hardly a bargain.

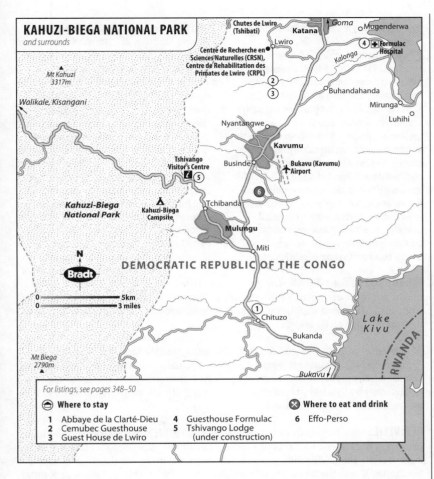

KAHUZI-BIEGA NATIONAL PARK
and surrounds

Mt Kahuzi
3317m

Walikale, Kisangani

Chutes de Lwiro
(Tshibati)
Katana
Goma
Mugenderwa
Lwiro
Centre de Recherche en
Sciences Naturelles (CRSN),
Centre de Rehabilitation des
Primates de Lwiro (CRPL)
②
③
Buhandahanda
Mirunga
Luhihi

Kalonga
④ ✚ Formulac
Hospital

Nyantangwe
Kavumu
Tshivango
Visitor's Centre
Businde
Bukavu (Kavumu)
Airport
⑥

Kahuzi-Biega
National Park
Kahuzi-Biega
Campsite
Tchibanda
Mulungu
Miti

N
Bradt

0 ———— 5km
0 ———— 3 miles

Mt Biega
2790m

DEMOCRATIC REPUBLIC OF THE CONGO

Chituzo
Bukanda
Bukavu

Lake
Kivu

RWANDA

For listings, see pages 348–50

⊖ **Where to stay**
1 Abbaye de la Clarté-Dieu
2 Cemubec Guesthouse
3 Guest House de Lwiro
4 Guesthouse Formulac
5 Tshivango Lodge
   (under construction)

⊗ **Where to eat and drink**
6 Effo-Perso

Otherwise, the nearest accommodation to the park is as follows, though most visitors overnight in Bukavu:

🏠 Abbaye de la Clarté-Dieu (9 rooms) Murhesa; ⊕ S 2°22.625, E 28°47.716; m 099 059 9372/084 037 7392/085 935 6578; e clartedieumurhesaa@yahoo.fr; w ocso.org. In Murhesa Village, 2.5km south of the turn-off at Miti & 21km north of Bukavu, this brick-built abbey of Trappistine nuns sits in expansive, lovingly tended & pine-studded grounds just east of the main road from Bukavu. As is the Trappist tradition, the nuns make a variety of excellent food & other goods, including yoghurt, ice cream, honey, jams, candles, cookies & more. There are a handful of equally well-kept guestrooms, though they are often booked on church business. The

nuns keep busy, so ring the bell if you don't see anyone around. *US$15pp FB*.

🏠 Cemubec Guesthouse (4 rooms) Lwiro; m 099 071 5630; e info@lwiroprimates.org. Set in a delightfully time-warped Belgian villa just opposite the Centre de Rehabilitation des Primates de Lwiro (CRPL), this is nothing if not a memorable place to stay, with a formal, colonial feel – think massive old furnishings, multiple fireplaces & heavy wooden doors with carved accents. The rooms are simply furnished; all come with mosquito nets & most are en suite. Meals are available with advance notice at US$4 for b/fast & US$8 for lunch or dinner. It's not officially run by

12

349

the CRPL, but they're the most reliable contact for making a reservation. *US$20 dbl.*

🏠 **Guesthouse Formulac** (14 rooms) Ciranga; m 085 283 7575/089 955 1648; e cabwinejc@ yahoo.fr/cabwinejc@gmail.com. Set about 4km from the main road along the shores of Lake Kivu in Ciranga Village, this is another enjoyably anachronistic auberge, built in the 1930s alongside the Formulac Hospital, & now administered by the Archdiocese of Bukavu. The dated, high-ceilinged rooms (with mozzie nets) are in a fetching old porticoed stone-&-brick building on a little bluff overlooking the lake, & many come with private terraces as well. Meals are available at US$7pp, along with cold beers & sodas. If they're full (unlikely), there are further rooms available at the neighbouring nursing college. They can also arrange boat transfers from here to Kashofu on

Idjwi Island for about US$100. To get here, take the right-hand turn-off 1.2km north of the turning for Lwiro. *US$15/30 sgl/dbl using shared ablutions; US$30/40 en-suite sgl/dbl; all rates B&B.*

🏠 **Guest House de Lwiro** (8 rooms) Lwiro; m 085 095 3286/317 5055. In a stately manor in the grounds of the Centre de Recherche en Sciences Naturelles, the ground floor here is pure colonial splendour, with formal sitting & dining rooms centred on an enormous fireplace & covered in dark wood wainscoting & still-life paintings, all of which looks to have changed precious little in at least 50 years, save for the occasional Primus-branded tablecloth. The cobbled-together 1st-floor rooms are certainly a let-down, but the beds are clean & kitted out with mozzie nets & rates are cheap. Camping is theoretically allowed, but it's the same price as a room. *US$15/20 sgl/dbl.*

✖ **WHERE TO EAT AND DRINK** The guesthouses listed on pages 349–50 can all arrange meals, but there are no supplies available in the park so campers must be fully self-sufficient. Meals and supplies will likely become available with the opening of the upmarket lodge at Tshivanga.

✖ **Effo-Perso** m 099 031 9000/085 573 1000; ◐ supposedly 24hrs. This large bar, restaurant, nightclub & swimming pool complex is rather inexplicably set in a farm field 1km east of the main road, about 2km south of Kavumu, but it's

well signposted & hard to miss. There are loads of garden tables for noshing on brochettes & swilling Primus beer outside, plus a dance club inside that goes at all hours, sometimes with live music.

ACTIVITIES The biggest draw for visitors to Kahuzi-Biega is also the world's biggest primate – the eastern lowland, or Grauer's gorilla (*Gorilla beringei graueri*). It's the largest of all the gorilla subspecies (even bigger than its cousins in Virunga and Volcanoes!), and the average male weighs in at a hefty 160kg. Living in Kahuzi-Biega's forests between 2,100m and 2,400m above sea level, the few hundred gorillas thought to live in the park can be visited on treks from the park HQ/Tshivanga visitors' centre, and the practicalities of **gorilla tracking** here are broadly similar to those in Virunga or Volcanoes – trackers set out at 08.00, visits last 1 hour, and the mountainous hike to find the gorillas can take anywhere from 30 minutes to a couple of hours depending on their movements. As of 2018, there were three habituated families in the park: Chimanuka with 19 members, Bonne Année with eight, and Pungwe with 22, plus a solitary male called Mugaruka. Like at Virunga, it's still possible to get permits here without advance notice; these can be arranged at the park office in Bukavu and cost US$400/200/150 foreign adult/student/child; US$200/100/80 adult/student/child CEPGL/EAC/SADC resident; and US$20/10/5 Congolese adult/student/child.

Other activities on offer at the park include an ascent of the 3,300m **Mount Kahuzi**, which is done in a thigh-burning full-day round-trip hike setting out from the Tshivanga visitors' centre no later than 09.00. It's about 4 hours up and 3 hours to get back down, through lush montane forest which opens up to a stunning panorama of the park, Lake Kivu, and even Bukavu from the summit. For fans of the arcane,

Mount Kahuzi is also the only earthly habitat of the critically endangered Mount Kahuzi climbing mouse (*Dendromus kahuziensis*), of which only two have ever been found – 100m away from each other on Mount Kahuzi. Permits cost US$100/70/50 foreign adult/student/child; US$60/50/25 adult/student/child CEPGL/EAC/SADC resident; and US$15/7/3 Congolese adult/student/child, and can be arranged at the office in town, or even same-day at the visitors' centre if you show up early enough. Much easier are any of the four new 3–4km **trails** – designated as marsh, cultural, birding or forest – recently cut near Tshivanga, or the 6km trail to **Mount Bugulumiza**, which takes about 3 hours return and offers fabulous views over Mounts Kahuzi and Biega. This is also where you'll find the park's campsite. There aren't any functional trails up **Mount Biega** at the moment, but there are plans to open up a route in the future. Another highlight is the hike out to the **Tshibati Falls** (also known as Les Chutes de Lwiro). If you've already arranged your permit for this in Bukavu, you can head straight to Lwiro, otherwise you'll need to pick up a ranger and guide at Tshivanga then get back in the car to reach the trailhead. The hike starts with a short trip through farms and fields before crossing into the park for another bushwhacking hour or so until you reach the roaring falls at the end of a long valley. There's not really any good place to swim, but you'll be so covered in mist you'll hardly notice. Permits for the waterfall or any of the trails cost US$35/25/15 foreign adult/student/child; US$25/15/10 adult/student/child CEPGL/EAC/SADC resident; and US$5/4/2 Congolese adult/student/child. For all of the above, note that the CEPGL/EAC/SADC discount category may be phased out during the lifespan of this edition; foreign residents of the Congo will remain eligible for the discount.

If you've had enough hiking and trekking for the time being, there are two compelling and physically undemanding sights located just outside the park boundaries in Lwiro. Taking the prize for otherworldliness, the **Centre de Recherche en Sciences Naturelles (CRSN)** (m *099 777 0616/085 254 8241*; w *crsn-lwiro.blogspot. com*) is, apropos of absolutely nothing, an enormous and majestic educational campus, replete with impressive ponds, fountains, archways, porticoes and spiral staircases, built here by the Belgians in the mid 20th century to serve as the nucleus of scientific research in the region. Miraculously, it still just about functions and is home both to students and to several slightly wacky but nonetheless compelling museum exhibits – see box, page 352, for further details. The admission fee of US$60/15/4 foreigners/residents/Congolese is exorbitant unless you can manage to get the resident rate, but everything is expensive in the Congo anyway, and it's almost worth it for the singular atmosphere alone. Redeemingly, half of the admission fee goes to support the neighbouring **Centre de Rehabilitation des Primates de Lwiro (CRPL)** (m *099 071 5630*; e *info@lwiroprimates.org*; w *lwiroprimates.org*; ▪ *lwiro*), which cares for primates that have been orphaned by illegal hunting and the bush meat trade. Founded in 2002, they now have 77 chimpanzees and 95 monkeys (from 11 different species, including the inimitable owl-faced guenon (*Cercopithecus hamlyni*)) in their care – with more arriving all the time – and the large, well-kept enclosures (some as large as 3ha) and visibly dedicated staff of 46 would be praiseworthy in any location – such an operation here is an almost-miraculous feat. Visitors are welcomed with a tour of the grounds (in English, Spanish or French) and a first-name introduction to whichever of the chimpanzees stops by to check out the new arrival.

IDJWI ISLAND

Magnificently green and unrelentingly hilly (Idjwi means 'voice' in the island's Kihavu language, for calling across the many valleys), the 285km² Idjwi Island sits

About an hour's drive from Bukavu, past the airport and skirting Kahuzi-Biega National Park, is the small town of Lwiro. I might have even called it a village, with its dirt road and mud-straw houses … except that it has more (potential) tourist attractions than any one village could have.

From my base in Bukavu, we spent two weekends in a row in lovely Lwiro recently.

First, we paid a visit to Lwiro's very own Research Center for Natural Sciences. Built in the 1940s, the fact that the research centre is still maintained and running is an inspiring example of tenacity in a country where, in the past few decades, the norm leans more towards pillage and decay.

Thanks to recent funding donations and the hard work of the dedicated Lwiro scientists, this giant compound is still home to a diverse array of educational exhibits and natural science laboratories.

We visited first a museum of local cultural artefacts – kitchen tools, hunting tools, musical instruments, and, my favourite part, a showcase of chief hats.

We were told that the hat covered in buttons was indicative of the chief with the most power. Personally though, I think the woven, feathered fedora is much more hip by today's standards.

Another tour highlight was the Biodiversity Center – a taxidermy tribute to the many unique animals that call the Congo home, including a giant pangolin, which looked like the love-child of a pinecone and an anteater. From snout to tip of the tail, it was at least 6ft long.

We also visited the ophiology lab, which sounds innocuous, but was actually full of snakes – both dead and alive. On one side of the lab, the walls were lined with glass jars filled with thousands of dead snakes. On the other side, in glass cages, two huge vipers cuddled in a peaceful yin-yang, and a small but agitated cobra, hood taut, struck in the direction of anything that moved.

But forget high fashion, stuffed animals and feisty cobras. For me, the most stunning part of our tour was the library.

The research centre maintained a gorgeous wood-panelled, spiral-staircased, double-decker library, complete with a card catalogue system, brass chandeliers and a massive fireplace. It reminded me of the library that Belle loved so much in the castle in *Beauty and the Beast*.

The library is home to an eclectic mix of scientific and historical volumes, not all of which were particularly politically correct by today's standards, including 'My Pygmy and Negro Host' and 'My Dark Companions and their Strange Stories'. One jewel of a find was 'How I Found Livingstone in Central Africa', the 1911 publication of a travel book written by Henry Morton Stanley, one of the first European explorers to venture through the Congo.

The following weekend found us back in Lwiro, for a hike to Les Chutes de Lwiro – the Lwiro Waterfalls in Kahuzi-Biega National Park. The hike wasn't too long, but it took us through fields and forests, ending at two big beautiful waterfalls. The mist from the crashing water made the whole area lush and muddy, and the water was surprisingly freezing cold when we dipped our feet in.

On the way back to Bukavu, we stopped for lunch at a little restaurant on the lake called Le Ciel. It's supposed to have the best chicken in town, but it was the giant brochettes that actually stole the show.

at the centre of Lake Kivu, 40km long and nearly 12km wide at its largest, making it the biggest island in the lake by an exponential margin and the tenth-largest lake island in the world. Chronically underdeveloped, even by Congolese standards, Idjwi's estimated 250,000 people, including a sizeable Bambuti pygmy population, have long been isolated from events taking place on the mainland, both for better and for worse. The horrors of the Congolese civil war and its ongoing aftershocks have largely passed the island by, but so has any of the peacetime development seen on the mainland; the dozens of agricultural and fishing villages (Idjwi is known for its pineapple) on the island are as authentic a rural African scene as you could hope to get anywhere, and entirely bereft of tourists – be prepared to cause a big commotion wherever you go.

Indeed, the people of Idjwi have long been isolated from events on the mainland – sometimes quite intentionally so. Local oral history says the island was used as a place of exile in pre-colonial times, specifically for women who became pregnant before marriage or were otherwise condemned as adulterous. Banished by the kingdoms on the mainland, the growing community of unattached women on the island unsurprisingly began to attract the attention of local fishermen. Either unable or unwilling to pay the dowries required to marry in their communities back on the mainland, the frisky fishermen would pitch up to the island from time to time and try their luck with the women there, until a number of them eventually settled down with partners and moved to the island themselves.

Given Idjwi's isolation from the war, security concerns here are minimal compared with the mainland, and you could easily spend a couple of days happily exploring the island's dozens of coves and cow paths, hills and valleys, and fishing and farming villages. There's even a few ruins: the island is home to a derelict mansion originally built by Eugène, 11th Prince of Ligne and later used by Mobutu on his visits to the island. The islands are perhaps best explored by hiring a moto, and, as getting around can be quite the challenge, you may find it useful to have a guide; any Goma- or Bukavu-based tour agency can arrange trips to Idjwi, but Agence Espérance in Bukavu (page 346) and Okapi Tours in Goma (page 334) both have strong links to the island and are particularly recommended.

Administratively, the island is divided into Idjwi-Nord and Idjwi-Sud, and any of the daily boats heading between Goma and Bukavu will call here. A visit to Idjwi-Nord can be done as a return trip out of Goma, or Idjwi-Sud from Bukavu, but it makes an especially compelling stopover if you're headed between the two towns. There are no banking facilities of any kind on the island.

GETTING THERE AND AWAY As with other destinations on the lake, the **Ihusi Express** (m *099 481 3235/097 464 5680/081 838 2590 (Goma), 099 423 4071/882 1195, 081 398 2333 (Bukavu);* e *ihusiexpress@gmail.com;* w *iexpress.ihusigroup.com*) remains the best bet, though they unfortunately charge the same US$50 for a one-way ticket to Idjwi as they do for a ticket all the way through to Goma or Bukavu (page 330), so you're looking at US$100 to get on and off the island with them. The boat always stops at Bugarula and will also stop at Momvu, but *only* if there's a passenger there to be picked up or dropped off, so you must confirm this when buying your tickets, and reconfirming by phone the day before would be a wise move as well.

If you'd like to head directly to Lwiro and Kahuzi-Biega from here without going to Bukavu first, the **Lake Kivu Express** boat runs from Goma to Katana (*US$20*) via Bugarula (*US$10*) on Mondays and Wednesdays, returning on Tuesdays and Thursdays, and departing at 07.30 in either direction, though we are unable to attest to the comfort or quality of the vessel.

On the island itself, there are no roads worthy of the name and only perhaps a dozen cars, so motos are king; any guesthouse will be able to connect you with a driver.

⌂ **WHERE TO STAY** There are a handful of guesthouses on the island, most of which are quite basic, though there are now a few more comfortable options as well. Most are concentrated within a few kilometres of Bugarula on the northern half of the island.

⌂ **Auberge Mon Village** (5 rooms) Bushonga; m 099 722 4557/819 8497. Set in grassy grounds in the village of Bushonga, this is some of the only accommodation in the centre of the island. By most measures it's rather rundown, but by Idjwi standards it's in pretty decent nick. It's cheap, the beds have nets, & meals & drinks can be arranged with enough notice. Generator power only if you pay fuel. Same-sex travellers must get separate rooms. *US$10 dbl.*

⌂ **Centre de Promotion Rurale (CPR) Guesthouse** (5 rooms) Bugarula centre; m 099 877 0848/671 8520/429 9505, 085 946 6820. This very basic NGO-affiliated guesthouse sits in central Bugarula, about 800m up from the docks. Rooms use shared baths & there are 2 dorms. They can arrange 4x4 transfers (US$150 from Bugarula to the south of the island). *US$5–10 dorm bed; US$15 dbl.*

⌂ **Congomani Guesthouse** (14 rooms) Kashofu; m 099 175 8814/084 092 9727/085 372 9045; e fredkahmad2@gmail.com/mbakarobert@yahoo.fr. The only proper guesthouse on the southern half of the island, this neat & green compound sits along the shore just outside Kashofu Village & offers somewhat basic rooms in the main house, plus a few smarter standalone chalets in the gardens. Also known locally as the *maison blanche* after its white walls, they do generously portioned meals (*US$5 b/fast, US$10 other meals*), drinks (nothing cold, however), & pirogue excursions on request. A moto from here to the southern boat dock at Momvu should be roughly Cfr7,000. *US$25–30 dbl using shared ablutions; US$40 en-suite dbl.*

⌂ **Guesthouse Balamage** (6 rooms) Bugarula port; m 097 731 3389/085 041 0554. It's dingy compared with the Hope Land (see below), but also a fair bit cheaper & the lakeshore compound is trim & appealing. *US$25 dbl.*

✳ ⌂ **Hope Land Guesthouse** (15 rooms) Bugarula port; m 099 494 3307/423 0238; e hopelandidjwi@gmail.com; w hopelandidjwi.com. Not even 100m from the boat dock in Bugarula, this unexpectedly lovely guesthouse run by a pair of ophthalmologists consists of 2 sets of rooms – 1 upper & 1 lower – built into a lush hillside facing the coast, plus a thatched resto-bar perched right on the water. The spotless rooms all have solar hot water, mosquito nets & Wi-Fi, & some have balconies. Camping in the gardens should also be possible & there are plans to start taking credit card payments. *US$25/50/60 sgl/dbl/twin B&B.*

✳ ⌂ **Idjwi Ecolodge** (11 rooms) Between Bugarula port & Kishenyi; m 099 822 5588/994 1197; e idjwi.ecolodge@gmail.com/luc.henkinbrant@gmail.com; w idjwi-ecolodge.org/agenceesperance.net. Just opening at the time of research, this new lodge is connected to the estimable Agence Espérance in Bukavu (page 346) & represents the first accommodation built on Idjwi specifically with tourists in mind. Set 4.5km north of Bugarula port on a big parcel of forested land with their own sand beach, the rooms here come in large duplex or triplex thatched bungalows right on the water, with either flush or compost toilets & some with a lofted sleeping area. The central resto-bar serves some of the finest meals on the island, using ingredients from their own permaculture garden, & all manner of aquatic & terrestrial activities are planned, including kayaking, mountain-bike & hiking excursions, badminton, archery, & trips to the diminutive Shu Shu Island offshore for a rustic barbecue on the beach. *US$30–90 dbl, depending on the room.*

⌂ **Iko Idjwi Resort** (4 rooms) Ile Mohembe; m 099 971 1062/785 7300; e iko.idjwi@gmail.com; w ikoidjwi.com. Set on an emerald flyspeck of an island just off Idjwi's southwestern coast, there's only room for 8 guests at this sleepy resort, with en-suite rooms in a main house & 2 outlying bungalows connected by flower-lined paths. There's a basketball court, barbecue facilities, & aquatic activities can be arranged. Advance reservations are essential. *US$100/150 sgl/dbl; US$300 2-bedroom villa; US$500 whole resort; all rates FB.*

⌂ **Maison Planches Hewa Bora** (5 rooms) Bugarula port; m 097 064 4696/108 4531, 085

384 8302. More bar than guesthouse, the gardens here are pleasant but expect the tiny rooms built from planks of wood with external ablutions to be noisy. *US$15 dbl.*

New Ntabona Guesthouse (Chez Paon) (4 rooms, 5 under construction) Between Bugarula port & Kishenyi; m 099 867 6799/887 9639. On the way to Kishenyi, 4km north of Bugarula port (about Cfr2,000 on a moto), this new guesthouse has several smart standalone chalets on a grassy promontory jutting into the lake, each with private terraces, TV, terracotta tiled floors & solar hot water. Meals are available at US$5pp. Good value. *US$35 en-suite dbl or twin B&B.*

Paroisse de Kashofu (6 rooms) Kashofu; m 099 762 2222/773 8572, 085 844 1967. The scenic brick-built church buildings in Kashofu date to 1936 & have a handful of very basic single & twin rooms available for visitors. The older rooms are set around a central courtyard & use shared ablutions, while a new block in the back has en-suite facilities. All have mosquito nets & solar power. Meals are taken communally with the priests at 07.30, 12.30, & 19.30. *US$20pp FB.*

Virunga National Park and Eastern DRC   IDJWI ISLAND

12

Appendix 1

LANGUAGE *Jake Freyer*

In general, you may pronounce Kinyarwanda consonants as though they are English consonants, with the following exceptions: the letter *c* always makes the sound of *ch* in *chat*; *j* always makes the sound of *s* in *treasure*; and *r* is tapped as in Spanish *pero*. (Several other consonants and consonant combinations also have quite different pronunciations – for instance, *bw* is pronounced more like *bg* – but not enough to seriously impede comprehension.)

Vowels are pronounced approximately as in Spanish: *a, e, i, o* and *u* are similar to the vowels in *father, bait, beet, boat* and *boot*, respectively. They are never silent, and are pronounced the same everywhere. Vowels can be lengthened, which means that they are pronounced exactly the same but for a longer period of time. In this appendix, long vowels are notated by doubling the letter (eg: *muraaho*). Vowels with an accent mark (eg: *á*) have a high tone, which means to raise the pitch of your voice. Note that tones and long vowels are not included in standard spellings, but are included here for clarity.

English	French	Kinyarwanda
COURTESIES		
good day/hello	*bonjour*	*muraaho*
good morning	*bonjour*	*mwaáramutse*
good afternoon	*bonjour*	*mwiíriwe*
good evening	*bonsoir*	*mwiíriwe*
sir	*monsieur*	*bwáana*
madam	*madame*	*madaámu*
how are you?	*ça va?*	*amakúru?*
I'm fine, thank you	*ça va bien, merci*	*ni méézá*
please	*s'il vous plaît*	*mubishoboye*
thank you	*merci*	*murakóze*
excuse me	*excusez-moi*	*imbabázi*
I'm sorry	*je suis désolé*	*muumbabárire*
no problem	*pas de problème*	*ntaa kibázo*
goodbye (before evening)	*au revoir*	*mwiírírwe*
good night	*bonne nuit*	*muramúke*
goodbye (for ever)	*au revoir/adieu*	*murabého*
BASIC WORDS		
yes	*oui*	*yeego*
no	*non*	*oya*
that's right	*c'est ça*	*ní byo*
maybe	*peut-être*	*wéenda*
good	*bon*	*ni byíízá*

English	French	Kinyarwanda
hot	*chaud*	*ubushyuúhe*
cold	*froid*	*ubukoónje*
and	*et*	*ná*

QUESTIONS

how?	*comment?*	*gute?*
how much?	*combien?*	*angááhé?*
what's your name?	*quel est votre nom?*	*Mwiitwa ndé?*
when?	*quand?*	*ryáárí?*
where?	*où?*	*hééhé?*
who?	*qui?*	*ndé? (s)/báándé? (pl)*

FOOD/DRINK

beans (kidney)	*haricots*	*ibishyíimbo*
beer	*bière*	*inzogá*
bread	*pain*	*umugati*
butter	*beurre*	*amavúta y'íinká*
coffee	*café*	*ikááwá*
drinks	*boissons*	*ibinyoóbwa*
eggs	*œufs*	*amagí*
fish	*poisson*	*amafí*
meat	*viande*	*inyama*
milk	*lait*	*amatá*
potatoes	*pommes de terre*	*ibiraayi*
rice	*riz*	*umuceri*
salad	*salade*	*saladi*
soup	*potage*	*isupú*
sugar	*sucre*	*isúkáári*
tea	*thé*	*icyáayi*
tomatoes	*tomates*	*inyáanya*
water	*eau*	*amáazi*

SHOPPING

bank	*banque*	*baánki*
bookshop	*librairie*	*isomero*
chemist	*pharmacie*	*farumasi*
shop	*magasin*	*idúúká*
market	*marché*	*isóko*
battery	*pile/batterie*	*bateri*
film	*filme*	*filími*
map	*carte*	*ikaríta*
money	*argent*	*amafaraanga*
soap	*savon*	*isábúné*
toothpaste	*dentifrice*	*umutí w'ááméenyo*

POST

post office	*poste (PTT)*	*iposita*
envelope	*enveloppe*	*ibáháshá*
letter	*lettre*	*urwaandiko*
paper	*papier*	*urupapuro*

English	French	Kinyarwanda
postcard	*carte postale*	*ifoto*
stamp	*timbre*	*teémburi*

GETTING AROUND

bus	*bus*	*biísi*
bus station	*gare routière*	*gaári*
taxi	*taxi*	*váátííri*
car	*voiture*	*imódóká*
petrol station	*station d'essence*	*steésheni*
plane	*avion*	*indeége*
far	*loin*	*kure*
near	*près*	*haáfi*
to the right	*à droite*	*iburyó*
to the left	*à gauche*	*ibumosó*
straight ahead	*tout droit*	*imbere*
bridge	*pont*	*ikiraro*
hill	*colline*	*umusózi*
lake	*lac*	*ikiyága*
mountain	*montagne*	*igisózi*
river	*fleuve*	*urúuzi*
road	*route*	*umuhaánda*
street	*rue*	*inzira*
town	*ville*	*umujyi*
valley	*vallée*	*umubáándé*
village	*village*	*umudugúdu*
waterfall	*chute*	*isuumo*

HOTEL

bed	*lit*	*igitaánda*
room	*chambre*	*icyuúmba*
key	*clef/clé*	*urufuunguuzo*
shower	*douche*	*dushe/urwíiyuhagiriro*
bath	*baignoire*	*urwóogero*
toilet/WC	*toilette*	*umusárááni*
hot water	*l'eau chaude*	*amáazi ashyúushye*
cold water	*l'eau froide*	*amáazi akóonje*

MISCELLANEOUS

dentist	*dentiste*	*umugaanga w'ááméenyo*
doctor	*médecin*	*umugaanga*
embassy	*ambassade*	*ambasaáde*
tourist office	*bureau de tourisme*	*ibiro by'úbukeerarugeendo*

TIME

minute	*minute*	*umunoóta*
hour	*heure*	*isááhá*
day	*jour*	*umuúnsi*
week	*semaine*	*icyúúmwéeru*
month	*mois*	*ukwéezi*
year	*an/année*	*umwáaka*

English	French	Kinyarwanda
now	*maintenant*	*ubu/nóonaha*
soon	*bientôt*	*mu kaánya*
today	*aujourd'hui*	*uyu muúnsi*
yesterday	*hier*	*ejo hashizé*
tomorrow	*demain*	*ejo hazáázá*
this week	*cette semaine*	*iki cyúúmwéeru*
next week	*semaine prochaine*	*icyúúmwéeru gitahá*
morning	*matin*	*igitóondo*
afternoon	*après-midi*	*amanywá*
evening	*soir*	*umugórooba*
night	*nuit*	*ijoro*
Monday	*lundi*	*ku waa mbere*
Tuesday	*mardi*	*ku wa kábiri*
Wednesday	*mercredi*	*ku wa gátatu*
Thursday	*jeudi*	*ku wa káne*
Friday	*vendredi*	*ku wa gátaanu*
Saturday	*samedi*	*ku wa gátáándátu*
Sunday	*dimanche*	*ku cyúúmwéeru*
January	*janvier*	*ukwaa mbere*
February	*février*	*ukwaa kábiri*
March	*mars*	*ukwaa gátatu*
April	*avril*	*ukwaa káne*
May	*mai*	*ukwaa gátaanu*
June	*juin*	*ukwaa gátaandátu*
July	*juillet*	*ukwaa káriindwi*
August	*août*	*ukwaa múnááni*
September	*septembre*	*ukwaa cyéenda*
October	*octobre*	*ukwaa cúmi*
November	*novembre*	*ukwaa cúmi ná rimwé*
December	*décembre*	*ukwaa cúmi ná kabiri*

NUMBERS

1	*un/une*	*rimwé*
2	*deux*	*kabiri*
3	*trois*	*gatatu*
4	*quatre*	*kané*
5	*cinq*	*gataanu*
6	*six*	*gatáándátu*
7	*sept*	*kariindwi*
8	*huit*	*umunaáni*
9	*neuf*	*icyeénda*
10	*dix*	*icúmi*
100	*cent*	*ijana*
1,000	*mille*	*igihuumbi*
2,000	*deux mille*	*ibihuumbi bibiri*
3,000	*trois mille*	*ibihuumbi bitatu*
4,000	*quatre mille*	*ibihuumbi biné*
5,000	*cinq mille*	*ibihuumbi bitaanu*

6,000	*six mille*	*ibihuumbi bitáándátu*
7,000	*sept mille*	*ibihuumbi biriindwi*
8,000	*huit mille*	*ibihuumbi umunaáni*
9,000	*neuf mille*	*ibihuumbi icyeénda*

AFRICAN ENGLISH *Philip Briggs*

Although a high proportion of Rwandans were raised in Kenya, Uganda or Tanzania and so speak English as a second language, not all get the opportunity to use it regularly, and as a result they will not be as fluent as they could be. Furthermore, as is often the case in Africa and elsewhere, an individual's pronunciation of a second language often tends to retain the vocal inflections of their first language, or it falls somewhere between that and a more standard pronunciation. It is also the case that many people tend to structure sentences in a second language similar to how they would in their home tongue. As a result, most Rwandans, to a greater or lesser extent, speak English with Bantu inflections and grammar.

The above considerations aside, I would venture that African English – like American or Australian English – is overdue recognition as a distinct linguistic entity, possessed of a unique rhythm and pronunciation, as well as an idiomatic quality quite distinct from any form of English spoken elsewhere. And learning to communicate in this idiom is perhaps the most important linguistic skill that the visitor to any African country where English is spoken can acquire. If this sounds patronising, so be it. There are regional accents in the UK and US that I find far more difficult to follow than the English spoken in Africa, simply because I am more familiar with the latter. And precisely the same adjustment might be required were, for instance, an Australian to travel in the American south, a Geordie to wash up in my home town of Johannesburg, or vice versa.

The following points should prove useful when you speak English to Africans:

- Greet simply, using phrases likely to be understood locally: the ubiquitous sing-song 'How-are-you! – I am fine', or if that draws a blank try the pidgin Swahili 'Jambo!' It is important always to greet a stranger before you plough ahead and ask directions or any other question. Firstly, it is rude to do otherwise; secondly, most Westerners feel uncomfortable asking a stranger a straight question. If you have already greeted the person, you'll feel less need to preface a question with phrases like 'I'm terribly sorry' or 'Would you mind telling me' which will confuse someone who speaks limited English.
- Speak slowly and clearly. There is no need, as some travellers do, to take this too far, as if you are talking to a three-year-old. Speak naturally, but try not to rush or clip phrases.
- Phrase questions simply, with an ear towards Bantu inflections. 'This bus goes to Huye?' might be more easily understood than 'Could you tell me whether this bus is going to Huye?' and 'You have a room?' is better than 'Is there a vacant room?' If you are not understood, don't keep repeating the same question more loudly. Try a different and ideally simpler phrasing, giving consideration to whether any specific word(s) – in the last case, most likely 'vacant' – might particularly obstruct easy understanding.
- Listen to how people talk to you, and learn from it. Vowel sounds are often pronounced as in the local language (see Kinyarwanda pronunciation above), so that 'bin', for instance, might sound more like 'been'. Many words, too, will be pronounced with the customary Bantu stress on the second-last syllable.
- African languages generally contain few words with compound consonant sounds or ending in consonants. This can result in the clipping of soft consonant sounds such as 'r' (important as eem-POT-ant) or the insertion of a random vowel sound

between running consonants (so that pen-pal becomes pen-I-pal and sounds almost indistinguishable from pineapple). It is commonplace, as well, to append a random vowel to the end of a word, in the process shifting the stress to what would ordinarily be the last syllable eg: pen-i-PAL-i.

- The 'l' and 'r' sounds are sometimes used interchangeably (hence Lake Burera/Bulera and Mt Karisimbi/Kalisimbi), which can sometimes cause confusion, in particular when your guide points out a lilac-breasted roller! The same is to a lesser extent true of 'b' and 'v' (Virunga versus Birunga), 'k' and 'ch' (the Rwandan capital, spelt Kigali, is more often pronounced 'Chigari') and, very occasionally, 'f' and 'p'.
- Some English words are in wide use. Other similar words are not. Some examples: a request for a 'lodging' or 'guesthouse', is more likely to be understood than one for 'accommodation', as is a request for a 'taxi' (or better 'special hire') over a 'taxi-cab' or 'cab', or for 'the balance' rather than 'change'.
- Avoid the use of dialect-specific expressions, slang and jargon! Few Africans will be familiar with terms such as 'feeling crook', 'pear-shaped' or 'user-friendly'.
- Avoid meaningless interjections. If somebody is struggling to follow you, appending a word such as 'mate' to every other phrase is only likely to further confuse them.
- We've all embarrassed ourselves at some point by mutilating the pronunciation of a word we've read but not heard. Likewise, guides working in national parks and other reserves often come up with innovative pronunciations for bird and mammal names they come across in field guides, and any word with an idiosyncratic spelling (eg: yacht, lamb, knot).
- Make sure the person you are talking to understands you. Try to avoid asking questions that can be answered with a yes or no. People may well agree with you simply to be polite or to avoid embarrassment.
- Keep calm. No-one is at their best when they arrive at a crowded bus station after an all-day bus ride. It is easy to be short tempered when someone cannot understand you. Be patient and polite; it's you who doesn't speak the language.
- Last but not least, do gauge the extent to which the above rules might apply to any given individual. It would be patently ridiculous to address a university lecturer or an experienced tour guide in broken English, equally inappropriate to babble away without making any allowances when talking to a villager who clearly has a limited English vocabulary. Generally, I start off talking normally to anybody I meet, and only start to refine my usage as and when it becomes clear it will aid communication.

SEND US YOUR SNAPS!

We'd love to follow your adventures using our *Rwanda* guide – why not send us your photos and stories via Twitter (@*BradtGuides*) and Instagram (@*bradtguides*) using the hashtag #rwanda? Alternatively, you can upload your photos directly to the gallery on the Rwanda destination page via our website (w *bradtguides.com/rwanda*).

Appendix 2

BOOKS
Historical background

Fegley, Randall (compiler) *Rwanda – World Bibliographical Series volume 154* Clio Press, 1993. This selective, annotated bibliography contains over 500 entries covering a wide range of subjects including Rwanda's history, geography, politics, literature, travellers' accounts, flora and fauna. Its preface and introduction give a condensed but useful (although somewhat dated) overview of Rwanda from early times until just before the genocide.

Kagame, Alexis *Un abrégé de l'ethno-histoire du Rwanda* and *Un abrégé de l'histoire du Rwanda de 1853 à 1972* Editions Universitaires du Rwanda, Huye, 1972 and 1975. These works are now out of print (and there are no English translations) but the seriously interested should try to track down secondhand copies. Drawing on oral tradition, Kagame describes the country and its people from several centuries before the arrival of the Europeans (in the first book) through to the first decade of colonisation (in the second).

Reader, John *Africa: A Biography of the Continent* Hamish Hamilton, 1997. This award-winning book, available as a Penguin paperback, provides a compulsively readable introduction to Africa's past, from the formation of the continent to post-independence politics – the ideal starting point for anybody seeking to place their Rwandan experience in a broader African context.

Natural history

Briggs, Philip *East African Wildlife* Bradt, 2nd edition; 2015. This is a handy and lavishly illustrated one-stop handbook to the fauna of East Africa, with detailed sections on the region's main habitats, varied mammals, birds, reptiles and insects. It's the ideal companion for first-time visitors whose interest in wildlife extends beyond the Big Five but who don't want to carry a library of reference books.

Field guides (mammals)

Dorst, J and Dandelot, P *Field Guide to the Larger Mammals of Africa* Collins, 1983 and Haltenorth, T and Diller, H *Field Guide to the Mammals of Africa including Madagascar* Collins, 1984. Formerly the standard field guides to the region, these books are still recommended in many travel guides. In my opinion, they have largely been superseded by subsequent publications, and now come across as very dated and badly structured – with mediocre illustrations to boot.

Estes, Richard *The Safari Companion* Green Books (UK), Russell Friedman Books (SA), Chelsea Green (USA). This unconventional book might succinctly be described as a field guide to mammal behaviour. It's probably a bit esoteric for most one-off visitors to Africa, but a must for anybody with a serious interest in wildlife.

Kingdon, Jonathan *The Kingdon Field Guide to African Mammals* Academic Press, 2nd edition, 1997. This is my first choice: the most detailed, thorough and up to date of several field guides covering the mammals of the region. The author, a highly respected biologist, supplements detailed descriptions and good illustrations of all the continent's large mammals with an ecological overview of each species. Essential for anybody with a serious interest in mammal identification.

Stuart, Chris and Tilde *Southern, Central and East African Mammals* Struik, 1995. This excellent mini-guide, compact enough to slip into a pocket, is remarkably thorough within its inherent space restrictions. Highly recommended for one-off safari-goers, but not so good on forest primates, which limits its usefulness in Rwanda.

Stuart, Chris and Tilde *The Larger Mammals of Africa,* Penguin, revised and expanded edition, 2017. This useful field guide doesn't quite match up to Kingdon's, but it's the best of the rest, and arguably more appropriate to readers with a relatively casual interest in African wildlife. It's also a lot cheaper and lighter!

Field guides and atlases (birds)

Stevenson, Terry and Fanshawe, John *Field Guide to the Birds of East Africa* T & A D Poyser, 2002. The best bird field guide, with useful field descriptions and accurate plates and distribution maps. It covers every species found in Rwanda as well as in Uganda, Kenya, Tanzania and Burundi. For serious birdwatchers, this is *the* book to take.

Vande Weghe, J P and G R *Birds of Rwanda: An Atlas and Handbook* Rwanda Development Board, 2011. Available from the RDB office in Kigali, this is a must for anybody with a serious interest in Rwanda's birds, containing detailed modern and historical distribution details and maps for all 701 species recorded in the country. Other features include an overview of the country's natural history, and detailed descriptions and checklists for several key birding sites. Though not a field guide, it would be the perfect country-specific companion to the one listed above.

Van Perlo, Ber *Illustrated Checklist to the Birds of Eastern Africa* Princetown, updated edition, 2009. This is the next best thing to the above (and is cheaper and lighter), since it illustrates and provides a brief description of every species recorded in Uganda and Tanzania, along with a distribution map. I don't know of any bird found in Rwanda but not in Tanzania or Uganda, and I found that distribution details can normally be extrapolated from the maps of neighbouring countries. Be aware that the descriptive detail is succinct and many of the illustrations are misleading

Williams, J and Arlott, N *Field Guide to the Birds of East Africa* Collins, 1980. As with the older Collins mammal field guides, Williams's was for years the standard field guide to the region, and is still widely mentioned in travel literature. Unfortunately, it feels rather dated today: less than half the birds in the region are illustrated, several are not even described, and the bias is strongly towards common Kenyan birds.

Zimmerman et al *Birds of Kenya and Northern Tanzania* Russell Friedman Books, 1996. This monumentally handsome hardback tome is arguably the finest field guide to any African territory. The geographical limitations with regard to Rwanda are obvious, but its wealth of descriptive and ecological detail and superb illustrations make it an excellent secondary source. A lighter and cheaper but less detailed paperback version was published in 1999.

Others

Behrens, Boix and Barnes *Wild Rwanda: Where to Watch Birds, Primates and Other Wildlife* Lynx, 2015. A welcome addition to the limited literature about Rwanda's wildlife, this refreshingly up-to-date 256-page gazetteer includes detailed site accounts to wildlife-viewing destinations both famous and obscure, based on the authors' first-hand experience. Essential for anyone with more than a passing interest in birds and other wildlife.

Eckhart, Gene and Lanjouw, Annette *Mountain Gorillas: Biology, Conservation, and Coexistence* Johns Hopkins University Press, 2008. Lovely pictures and authoritative but accessible text make this the perfect layperson's introduction to every aspect of the natural history and conservation of mountain gorilla.

Fossey, Dian *Gorillas in the Mist* Hodder & Stoughton, 1983. Enjoyable and massively informative, Fossey's landmark book is recommended without reservation to anybody going gorilla tracking in the Parc des Volcans.

Goodall, Jane *Through A Window* Houghton Mifflin, 1991. Subtitled *My Thirty Years with the Chimpanzees of Gombe*, this is one of several highly readable books by Jane Goodall about the longest ongoing study of wild primates in the world. Set in Tanzania, but obvious pre-trip reading for anybody intending to track chimps in Nyungwe.

Kingdon, Jonathan *Island Africa* Collins, 1990. This highly readable and award-winning tome about evolution in ecological 'islands' such as deserts and montane forests is recommended to anybody who wants to place the natural history of Nyungwe and the Virungas in a continental context.

Mowat, Farley *Woman in the Mists* Futura, 1987. An excellent biography of Dian Fossey, one which leans so heavily on her own journals that parts are almost autobiography.

Rouse, Andy (in partnership with World Primate Safaris) *Gorillas: Living on the Edge* Electric Squirrel Publishing, 2011. Over 100 beautiful, powerful and appealing images of Rwanda's gorillas by award-winning photographer Rouse, with a personal commentary adding depth and insight. A quarter of profits go towards supporting conservation projects in Rwanda.

Stuart, Chris and Tilde *Africa's Vanishing Wildlife* Southern Books, 1996. An informative and pictorially strong introduction to the endangered and vulnerable mammals of Africa, this book combines coffee-table production with impassioned and erudite text.

Weber, Bill and Vedder, Amy *In the Kingdom of Gorillas* Simon & Schuster, 2002. This superb and immensely readable account of the authors' pioneering conservation work in Volcanoes and Nyungwe national parks featured as one of *BBC Wildlife*'s 'most influential books from the past 40 years of wildlife publishing' in 2003.

Background to the genocide

Barnett, Michael *Eyewitness to a Genocide: The United Nations and Rwanda* Cornell University, 2002. Tracing the history of the UN's involvement with Rwanda, Barnett argues that it did bear some moral responsibility for the genocide. A clear and factual study, also covering the warnings raised by the genocide and the question of whether it is possible to build wholly moral institutions.

Dallaire, Lt Gen Roméo *Shake Hands with the Devil: the failure of humanity in Rwanda* Arrow Books, 2004. Dallaire was force commander of the UN Assistance Mission for Rwanda at the time of the genocide. This angry, moving and deeply human book describes the impossible situation he faced, caught up in a nightmare of killing and terror and yet denied the men and the operational freedom he needed in order to quell it. We see the unfolding of the genocide, in all its aspects, from the perspective of probably the one man who, had he been better heeded and supported, could have lessened its effects.

Gourevitch, Philip *We wish to inform you that tomorrow we will be killed with our families* Picador, 1998. Subtitled 'Stories from Rwanda', this winner of the *Guardian* First Book Award is war reporting of the highest order. Blending starkly factual narrative with human anecdotes and observations, Gourevitch paints on a broad canvas and the picture he creates is unforgettable. He shows us 'little people' caught up in unstoppable horrors – and reaching great heights of heroism.

Keane, Fergal *Season of Blood – a Rwandan Journey* Penguin, 1995. Keane's prose is always impeccable. Here he blends factual narrative and analysis with spontaneous emotion in such a way that the reader is both moved and informed in a single phrase. As a BBC correspondent, he was travelling around Rwanda – among the killers and among the victims – as the genocide spread countrywide. His reports at the time brought home the extent of the human tragedy and their essence is preserved in this book, which won the 1995 Orwell Prize.

Kinzer, Stephen *A Thousand Hills: Rwanda's Rebirth and the Man Who Dreamed It* John Wiley & Sons, 2008. This is one of the few books to deal with post-genocide Rwanda, focusing primarily on and quoting heavily from President Paul Kagame (who granted the author several exclusive interviews), and while the bias is slightly pro-Kagame, it nonetheless provides a worthwhile and insightful overview of Rwanda's post-millennial recovery.

Leave None to Tell the Story African Rights Watch, 1999. Another painfully comprehensive account, full of personal testimonies based on Rwandan government records, showing how ordinary administrative structures and practices were used as mechanisms of murder. It describes the opposition to and termination of the killing and how it was crushed, while survivors relate how they resisted and escaped. Using diplomatic and court documents, the survey shows what might have been the result had the international reaction been swifter and more determined.

Mamdani, Mahmood *When Victims Become Killers* Princeton University Press, 2002. Commonly used in university courses on the Rwandan genocide, this text, written by the highly regarded Ugandan political scientist Mahmood Mamdani, explores the complex ethnic identities and competing interests that ultimately culminated in genocide, starting in pre-colonial times and continuing through the post-genocide era, including the political and ethnic ripple effects felt throughout the region long after the killing had ended.

Melvern, L R *A People Betrayed – the Role of the West in Rwanda's Genocide* Zed Books, 2000, revised 2nd edition 2009. Linda Melvern's investigative study of the international background to Rwanda's genocide contains a full account of how the tragedy unfolded. Documents held in Kigali, and previously unpublished accounts of secret UN Security Council deliberations in New York, reveal a shocking sequence of events, and the failure of governments, organisations and individuals who could – had they opted to do so – have prevented the genocide. Described by Lt General Roméo Dallaire (see opposite) as 'the best overall account of the background to the genocide, and the failure to prevent it … She discovered so much that we did not know'.

Melvern, L R *Conspiracy to Murder: the Rwandan Genocide* Verso, 2004; extended paperback edition 2006. This powerful sequel to *A People Betrayed* (above) continues the investigation, drawing on a vast amount of new material including documents abandoned by the *génocidaires* when they fled Rwanda. It also features a confession by the interim prime minister, Jean Kambanda, who pled guilty in the International Criminal Tribunal for Rwanda to the crime of genocide, describing how Rwanda's full state apparatus was mobilised to carry out the killing.

Prunier, Gérard *The Rwanda Crisis – History of a Genocide* Hurst & Company, 1998. This painstakingly researched history of the Rwandan genocide, full of personal anecdotes and individual stories, describes with icy clarity the composition of the time bomb that began ticking long before its explosion in 1994. Prunier presents the genocide as part of a deadly logic, a plan hatched for political and economic motives, rather than the result of ancient hatred. He helps the reader to understand not only Rwanda's genocide but also the complexities of modern conflict in general.

Rusesabagina, Paul *An Ordinary Man: The True Story Behind Hotel Rwanda* Bloomsbury, 2007. This is a powerful and readable, but very controversial, autobiographic account of the genocide, written by the former manager of Hotel des Mille Collines, who claims to have sheltered more than a thousand refuges at the height of the killing.

Rwanda – Death, Despair and Defiance African Rights, London, 1995. This 1,200-page compilation by the UK-based organisation African Rights is a painfully thorough and detailed account of the genocide and its effect on Rwanda's people – the careful preparations, the identities of the killers and their accomplices, the massacres, the attacks on churches, schools and hospitals, and the aftermath. Victims tell their own stories and those of their families, and the horror and immensity of the slaughter are highlighted by the simplicity of their narratives. The impact is powerful, sometimes overwhelming. The index enables the reader to discover easily what happened in any particular area or village.

Sibomana, André *Hope for Rwanda* Pluto Press, 1999. In this very personal account, subtitled *Conversations with Laure Guilbert and Hervé Deguine*, the speaker describes the unfolding of the genocide, and his own experiences, with impressive fairness, clarity and lack of accusation. A touching and informative book by a remarkable man.

Miscellaneous

Crisafulli, Patricia and Redmond, Andrea *Rwanda, Inc.* Palgrave MacMillan, 2012. Subtitled 'How a Devastated Nation Became an Economic Model for the Developing World', this is an intriguing – and unusually upbeat – account of post-genocide Rwanda's achievements.

Halsey Carr, R and Howard Halsey, A *Land of a Thousand Hills* Viking, 1999. Rosamond Halsey Carr moved to Rwanda as a young bride in 1949 and stayed until her death in 2006. She watched the decline of colonialism, the problems of independence and the growing violence. When the genocide started she was evacuated by the American embassy but returned four months later, and began turning an old pyrethrum drying-house on her flower plantation into a home for genocide orphans. This very readable and moving book chronicles the extraordinary life of an extraordinary woman, in the country she loved and made her home.

Hunt, Swanee *Rwandan Women Rising* Duke, 2017. This new book talks to some 70 Rwandan women about their critical role in Rwanda's post-genocide peace-building efforts, and examines the ways in which their strong and organised responses were critical in rebuilding a shattered society and paved the way for the successes of Rwanda today, including the extraordinary and rightfully vaunted 64% rate of women in parliament.

Lewis, Jerome and Knight, Judy *The Twa of Rwanda* World Rainforest Movement (UK), 1996. The Twa are the smallest 'ethnic' group in Rwanda. This report, published by the World Rainforest Movement in co-operation with the International Work Group for Indigenous Affairs (Denmark) and Survival International (France), traces their history, highlights their impoverished situation, quotes their opinions about their past and future, and allows them to express their fears and aspirations. It also shows the dilemma faced by African governments as they try to build national unity while respecting cultural diversity.

Mukasonga, Scholastique *Cockroaches* Archipelago, 2016. Published in French in 2006 and in English for the first time in 2016, this short autobiography recounts the experiences of a Tutsi child growing up in pre-genocide Rwanda, and of the steadily increasing persecution in the decades leading up to the genocide that would first make her a refugee in Burundi and ultimately an exile in France, while dozens of her family perished at home in 1994.

Mukasonga, Scholastique *Our Lady of the Nile: A Novel* Archipelago, 2014. Set in an all-girls' high school overlooking the Nile, this novel by a France-based Rwandan author explores both the school-age and political tensions bubbling beneath the surface in 1970s' Rwanda over the course of a rainy season spent at boarding school.

Parkin, Gaile *Baking Cakes in Kigali* Atlantic Books, 2009. This bestselling novel tells the story of Angel Tungaraza, a philosophical baker from Tanzania who settles in Rwanda with her husband and five orphans after the genocide. It has drawn several comparisons to the popular Botswana-set *No.1 Ladies Detective Agency* series.

Stassen, Jean-Philippe *Déogratias* Aire Libre, Dupuis (Belgium) 2000. If you can read at least some French, this 80-page *bande dessinée* (graphic novel) tells the story of a young Hutu who killed during the genocide and how this, together with drink, destroyed him. With skill and humanity, the creator succeeds in 'telling the untellable' and producing a powerful document.

Other Africa guides For a full list of Bradt's Africa guides, see **w** bradtguides.com/shop

Briggs, Philip *Ethiopia* Bradt, 2015.
Briggs, Philip *Tanzania* Bradt, 2017.
Briggs, Philip *Uganda* Bradt, 2016.
Lovell-Hoare, Max and Sophie *South Sudan* Bradt, 2013.
Rorison, Sean; Scafidi, Oscar and Stead, Mike *Angola* Bradt, 2013.

Bradt travel literature

Jackman, Brian *Savannah Diaries* Bradt, 2014. A celebration of Africa's wild places and creatures, seen through the eyes of one of Africa's most distinguished observers.
Jackman, Brian; Scott, Jonathan and Angela *The Marsh Lions: The Story of an African Pride* Bradt, 2012. A wildlife classic, this is a compelling and fascinating account of the daily drama of life and death in Kenya's finest big-game country.
Kent, Princess Michael of *A Cheetah's Tale* Bradt, 2017. A wonderful story of a vanished Africa, of a girl growing up and of the incredible bond that can exist between humans and animals.
Scott, Jonathan and Angela *The Leopard's Tale* Bradt, 2013. A unique and moving portrait of Africa, and the most intimate record ever written about the secretive lives of leopards.

MAPS The best **map** available outside Rwanda is currently *Rwanda and Burundi*, scale 1:300,000, published in Canada by ITM (**w** *itmb.com*). There is also *Tanzania, Rwanda and Burundi*, scale 1:1,500,000, published by Nelles Guides & Maps (**w** *nelles-verlag.de*).

WEBSITES For up-to-the-minute news reports from Rwanda and elsewhere in Africa, the most comprehensive site is probably **w** allafrica.com. Follow links to Rwanda. The website of the Rwandan newspaper *The New Times* has a range of local news items not picked up elsewhere: **w** newtimes.co.rw. For regular updates and reader feedback covering all aspects of travel to Rwanda, visit **w** bradtupdates.com/rwanda, overseen by Philip Briggs as an interactive update service for travellers, volunteers and service providers in Rwanda.

A good site for checking the latest currency exchange rate (not all include the Rwandan franc) is **w** xe.com. Conditions in Rwanda – as elsewhere in Africa – may change, so as a precaution, before travelling, always check the Foreign Office website **w** fco.gov.uk/travel, or that of the US State Department: **w** travel.state.gov. For changes in visa requirements (and online application), visit **w** migration.gov.rw.

Four further websites on Rwanda are **w** rwandaembassy.org (set up by the Rwandan embassy in Washington, DC); that of the Rwandan high commission in London, **w** rwandahc.org; and that of RDB (Rwanda Development Board), **w** rdb.rw and **w** rwandatourism.com. All have numerous links and between them cover a wide range of topics, including Rwanda's history, geography, economy, business potential and tourism. On the whole the essentials are up to date although some sections haven't been touched for a while at the time of writing.

The University of Rwanda Science and Technology website reports interestingly on small-scale development and appropriate technology: **w** cst.ur.ac.rw. The site of the UN International Criminal Tribunal for Rwanda, **w** unictr.org, has archival information on genocide criminals and trials. Human Rights Watch on **w** hrw.org carries news of Rwanda, as does Amnesty International: **w** amnesty.org. For news relating to the genocide and its commemorations, visit the Aegis Trust's website **w** aegistrust.org.

For specific out-of-print books on Rwanda (and any other subject under the sun), try the unmatchable **w** abebooks.co.uk. Other good sources of books, new and used, are **w** amazon.co.uk and **w** amazon.com.

Index

Page numbers in **bold** refer to major entries; those in *italics* indicate maps.

INDEX OF ADVERTISERS